P9-CDK-274

NEW PERSPECTIVES ON
Microsoft® Project 2010

INTRODUCTORY

NEW PERSPECTIVES ON

Microsoft® Project 2010

INTRODUCTORY

Rachel Biheller Bunin

COURSE TECHNOLOGY
CENGAGE Learning™

Australia • Brazil • Japan • Korea • Mexico • Singapore • Spain • United Kingdom • United States

COURSE TECHNOLOGY
CENGAGE Learning™

New Perspectives on Microsoft Project 2010, Introductory

Vice President, Publisher: Nicole Jones Pinard

Executive Editor: Marie L. Lee

Associate Acquisitions Editor: Amanda Lyons

Senior Product Manager: Kathy Finnegan

Product Manager: Leigh Hefferon

Associate Product Manager: Julia Leroux-Lindsey

Editorial Assistant: Jacqueline Lacaire

Director of Marketing: Elisa Roberts

Senior Marketing Manager: Ryan DeGrote

Developmental Editor: Pam Conrad

Content Project Manager: Matthew Hutchinson

Composition: GEX Publishing Services

Art Director: Marissa Falco

Text Designer: Althea Chen

Cover Designer: Roycroft Design

Cover Art: © Cavan Images/Photodisc/Getty Images

Copyeditor: Michael Beckett

Proofreader: Foxxe Editorial

Indexer: Alexandra Nickerson

© 2012 Course Technology, Cengage Learning

ALL RIGHTS RESERVED. No part of this work covered by the copyright herein may be reproduced, transmitted, stored or used in any form or by any means graphic, electronic, or mechanical, including but not limited to photocopying, recording, scanning, digitizing, taping, Web distribution, information networks, or information storage and retrieval systems, except as permitted under Section 107 or 108 of the 1976 United States Copyright Act, without the prior written permission of the publisher.

For product information and technology assistance, contact us at
Cengage Learning Customer & Sales Support, 1-800-354-9706
For permission to use material from this text or product, submit all requests online at **www.cengage.com/permissions**
Further permissions questions can be emailed to
permissionrequest@cengage.com

Some of the product names and company names used in this book have been used for identification purposes only and may be trademarks or registered trademarks of their respective manufacturers and sellers.

Microsoft and the Office logo are either registered trademarks or trademarks of Microsoft Corporation in the United States and/or other countries. Course Technology, Cengage Learning is an independent entity from the Microsoft Corporation, and not affiliated with Microsoft in any manner.

Disclaimer: Any fictional data related to persons or companies or URLs used throughout this book is intended for instructional purposes only. At the time this book was printed, any such data was fictional and not belonging to any real persons or companies.

Library of Congress Control Number: 2011925576

ISBN-13: 978-0-538-74676-2

ISBN-10: 0-538-74676-9

Course Technology
20 Channel Center Street
Boston, MA 02210
USA

Cengage Learning is a leading provider of customized learning solutions with office locations around the globe, including Singapore, the United Kingdom, Australia, Mexico, Brazil, and Japan. Locate your local office at:
international.cengage.com/global

Cengage Learning products are represented in Canada by Nelson Education, Ltd.

To learn more about Course Technology, visit **www.cengage.com/course technology**

To learn more about Cengage Learning, visit **www.cengage.com**

Purchase any of our products at your local college store or at our preferred online store **www.cengagebrain.com**

Printed in China
5 6 7 8 9 15 14

Preface

The New Perspectives Series' critical-thinking, problem-solving approach is the ideal way to prepare students to transcend point-and-click skills and take advantage of all that Microsoft Project 2010 has to offer.

In developing the New Perspectives Series, our goal was to create books that give students the software concepts and practical skills they need to succeed beyond the classroom. We've updated our proven case-based pedagogy with more practical content to make learning skills more meaningful to students.

With the New Perspectives Series, students understand *why* they are learning *what* they are learning, and are fully prepared to apply their skills to real-life situations.

About This Book

This book provides thorough coverage of Microsoft Project 2010, and includes the following:
- Detailed, hands-on instruction of Project 2010 skills, including entering tasks and durations, establishing dependencies, creating calendars, assigning resources and costs, and updating progress
- In-depth coverage of important project management concepts, including understanding task relationships, analyzing the critical path, and leveling overallocations
- Presentation of the exciting new features of Project 2010, including the Ribbon interface, Backstage view, enhanced copy and paste, the Timeline, and the Team Planner

New for this edition!
- Each session begins with a Visual Overview, a new two-page spread that includes colorful, enlarged figures with numerous callouts and key term definitions, giving students a comprehensive preview of the topics covered in the session, as well as a handy study guide.
- New ProSkills boxes provide guidance for how to use the software in real-world, professional situations, and related ProSkills exercises integrate the technology skills students learn with one or more of the following soft skills: decision making, problem solving, teamwork, verbal communication, and written communication.
- Important steps are highlighted in yellow with attached margin notes to help students pay close attention to completing the steps correctly and avoid time-consuming rework.

System Requirements

This book assumes a complete installation of Microsoft Project 2010 Standard or higher and Microsoft Windows 7 Ultimate using an Aero theme. You can also complete the material in this text using another version of Windows 7, such as Home Premium, or earlier versions of the Windows operating system. You will see only minor differences in how some windows look compared to the figures in the book. To complete portions of Tutorial 6, you must also have Microsoft Office 2010 installed with Word 2010, Excel 2010, PowerPoint 2010, and Outlook 2010 running on the computer. You should also have an Internet connection. The browser used for any steps that require a browser is Internet Explorer 8.

www.cengage.com/ct/newperspectives

"This text is filled with excellent explanations and activities. My students vary in their abilities, and this text covers exactly what they need in a logical, incremental fashion. It's a great reference book that students will find useful for years."

—Sandra Hume
Chippewa Valley Technical College

The New Perspectives Approach

"The clear step-by-step instructions, real-world data files, and helpful figures make New Perspectives texts excellent for courses taught in the classroom, the hybrid/blended format, or entirely online."
—Sylvia Amito'elau
Coastline Community College

Context

Each tutorial begins with a problem presented in a "real-world" case that is meaningful to students. The case sets the scene to help students understand what they will do in the tutorial.

Hands-on Approach

Each tutorial is divided into manageable sessions that combine reading and hands-on, step-by-step work. Colorful screenshots help guide students through the steps. **Trouble?** tips anticipate common mistakes or problems to help students stay on track and continue with the tutorial.

VISUAL OVERVIEW

Visual Overviews

New for this edition! Each session begins with a Visual Overview, a new two-page spread that includes colorful, enlarged figures with numerous callouts and key term definitions, giving students a comprehensive preview of the topics covered in the session, as well as a handy study guide.

PROSKILLS

ProSkills Boxes and Exercises

New for this edition! ProSkills boxes provide guidance for how to use the software in real-world, professional situations, and related ProSkills exercises integrate the technology skills students learn with one or more of the following soft skills: decision making, problem solving, teamwork, verbal communication, and written communication.

KEY STEP

Key Steps

New for this edition! Important steps are highlighted in yellow with attached margin notes to help students pay close attention to completing the steps correctly and avoid time-consuming rework.

INSIGHT

InSight Boxes

InSight boxes offer expert advice and best practices to help students achieve a deeper understanding of the concepts behind the software features and skills.

Margin Tips

Margin Tips provide helpful hints and shortcuts for more efficient use of the software. The Tips appear in the margin at key points throughout each tutorial, giving students extra information when and where they need it.

REVIEW

APPLY

Assessment

Retention is a key component to learning. At the end of each session, a series of Quick Check questions helps students test their understanding of the material before moving on. Engaging end-of-tutorial Review Assignments and Case Problems have always been a hallmark feature of the New Perspectives Series. Colorful bars and brief descriptions accompany the exercises, making it easy to understand both the goal and level of challenge a particular assignment holds.

REFERENCE

TASK REFERENCE

GLOSSARY/INDEX

Reference

Within each tutorial, Reference boxes appear before a set of steps to provide a succinct summary and preview of how to perform a task. In addition, a complete Task Reference at the back of the book provides quick access to information on how to carry out common tasks. Finally, each book includes a combination Glossary/Index to promote easy reference of material.

Our Complete System of Instruction

BRIEF

INTRODUCTORY

COMPREHENSIVE

Coverage To Meet Your Needs

Whether you're looking for just a small amount of coverage or enough to fill a semester-long class, we can provide you with a textbook that meets your needs.

- Brief books typically cover the essential skills in just 2 to 4 tutorials.
- Introductory books build and expand on those skills and contain an average of 5 to 8 tutorials.
- Comprehensive books are great for a full-semester class, and contain 9 to 12+ tutorials.

So if the book you're holding does not provide the right amount of coverage for you, there's probably another offering available. Visit our Web site or contact your Course Technology sales representative to find out what else we offer.

COURSECASTS

CourseCasts – Learning on the Go. Always available…always relevant.

Want to keep up with the latest technology trends relevant to you? Visit our site to find a library of podcasts, CourseCasts, featuring a "CourseCast of the Week," and download them to your mp3 player at http://coursecasts.course.com.

Our fast-paced world is driven by technology. You know because you're an active participant— always on the go, always keeping up with technological trends, and always learning new ways to embrace technology to power your life.

Ken Baldauf, host of CourseCasts, is a faculty member of the Florida State University Computer Science Department where he is responsible for teaching technology classes to thousands of FSU students each year. Ken is an expert in the latest technology trends; he gathers and sorts through the most pertinent news and information for CourseCasts so your students can spend their time enjoying technology, rather than trying to figure it out. Open or close your lecture with a discussion based on the latest CourseCast.

Visit us at http://coursecasts.course.com to learn on the go!

Instructor Resources

We offer more than just a book. We have all the tools you need to enhance your lectures, check students' work, and generate exams in a new, easier-to-use and completely revised package. This book's Instructor's Manual, ExamView testbank, PowerPoint presentations, data files, solution files, figure files, and a sample syllabus are all available on a single CD-ROM or for downloading at http://www.cengage.com/coursetechnology.

WebTUTOR

Content for Online Learning

Course Technology has partnered with the leading distance learning solution providers and class-management platforms today. To access this material, visit www.cengage.com/webtutor and search for your title. Instructor resources include the following: additional case projects, sample syllabi, PowerPoint presentations, and more. For students to access this material, they must have purchased a WebTutor PIN-code specific to this title and your campus platform. The resources for students might include (based on instructor preferences): topic reviews, review questions, practice tests, and more. For additional information, please contact your sales representative.

SAM: Skills Assessment Manager

SAM is designed to help bring students from the classroom to the real world. It allows students to train and test on important computer skills in an active, hands-on environment.

SAM's easy-to-use system includes powerful interactive exams, training, and projects on the most commonly used Microsoft Office applications. SAM simulates the Office application environment, allowing students to demonstrate their knowledge and think through the skills by performing real-world tasks, such as bolding text or setting up slide transitions. Add in live-in-the-application projects, and students are on their way to truly learning and applying skills to business-centric documents.

Designed to be used with the New Perspectives Series, SAM includes handy page references, so students can print helpful study guides that match the New Perspectives textbooks used in class. For instructors, SAM also includes robust scheduling and reporting features.

Acknowledgments

This book, now in its fifth edition and in living color, would not be possible without the support and guidance of the New Perspectives team. I would like to thank Kathleen Finnegan for her vision, leadership, and expertise; she is the driving force behind the series and this book. Thanks also to Marie Lee for all you do. My deepest gratitude goes to Pamela Conrad—my colleague and friend for over 20 years. It is Pam's dedication to excellence, professionalism in her work, attention to detail, drive to perfection, and good humor that makes it all worthwhile and brought this book in on time with the high standards worthy of a text in the New Perspectives Series. In addition, many thanks to the quality assurance team of testers: Susan Pedicini, Susan Whalen, John Freitas, Danielle Shaw, and Christian Kunciw, who worked tirelessly to ensure the quality of this book. Thanks also to Louise Capulli and Matthew Hutchinson and the Production team for their efforts to meet a rigorous production schedule and create this excellent book. My sincere thanks to our superb team of academic reviewers: Debi Griggs at Bellevue College, Sandra Hume at Chippewa Valley Technical College, and Lou Piermatteo at Dover Business College, for their outstanding feedback and suggestions on the manuscript. Finally, a special thank you and shout-out to David, Jennifer, Emily, and Michael for making this all worthwhile. –Rachel Biheller Bunin

BRIEF CONTENTS

PROJECT

TABLE OF CONTENTS

Planning a Project

Planning the Installation of AV Presentation Rooms

OBJECTIVES

Session 1.1
- Learn project management terminology
- Understand the benefits of project management
- Explore the Project 2010 window
- Check and change default settings
- Enter tasks and save a project

Session 1.2
- Open and explore an existing project
- Examine different project views
- Compare the Gantt chart and Network Diagram views
- Use the project time scale and calendar
- Use Backstage view and the Page Setup dialog box

Case | *ViewPoint Partners*

ViewPoint Partners, an opinion research firm, is moving into a larger space in Princeton, New Jersey. The building previously housed a small private school, so there is a lot of work to be done before ViewPoint Partners can set up shop in the new space. Emily Michaels is the technology specialist who maintains the company conference rooms, communication tools, media systems, computer networks, and video conferencing systems. As project coordinator, you often work with Emily in this small and growing business. The owner of ViewPoint Partners, Sidney Simone, recently asked you to manage a new and exciting project: overseeing the installation of the five audiovisual (AV) presentation rooms. ViewPoint Partners needs to be able to conduct five focus groups simultaneously. Presentation rooms provide large screen displays, computers, DVRs, DVD players, and ports for laptop computers as well as other audiovisual devices. ViewPoint Partners currently employs several employees, including Emily and you. The budget for this project is $100,000. Sidney is eager to move to the larger space and she wants the AV presentation rooms fully functional in three months.

STARTING DATA FILES

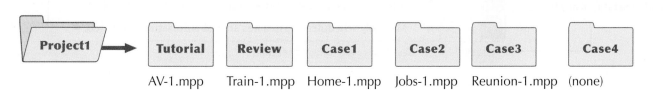

Project1 →	Tutorial	Review	Case1	Case2	Case3	Case4
	AV-1.mpp	Train-1.mpp	Home-1.mpp	Jobs-1.mpp	Reunion-1.mpp	(none)

SESSION 1.1 VISUAL OVERVIEW

The **Ribbon** provides commands grouped on tabs to perform tasks necessary to set up and manage a project.

Gantt Chart Tools

Project1 - Microsoft Pr

| File | Task | Resource | Project | View | Format |

Subproject | Project Information | Custom Fields | Links Between Projects | WBS | Change Working Time | Calculate Project | Set Baseline | Move Project

Insert | Properties | Schedule

The **Timeline** shows an overview of the entire project schedule.

Timeline

Start
Mon 6/2/14

| ⓘ | Task Mode | Task Name | Duration | Start | 5, '14 |
| | | | | | T | W |

The **column headings** identify the contents of each column for each task entered in a project.

The **active cell** is where information you are currently typing will appear in the project.

The **Gantt Chart**, one of several available views, shows task information in columns and rows on the left side of the window, with corresponding bars to the right of the window.

Gantt Chart

Tasks can be manually or automatically scheduled; you set the default for each new task and change the mode for any specific task.

The **status bar** displays important information such as whether tasks are manually or automatically scheduled, the cell mode, and the status of any filters.

New Tasks

Auto Scheduled - Task dates are calculated by Microsoft Project.

Manually Scheduled - Task dates are not automatically updated.

Ready   New Tasks : Manually Scheduled

PROJECT WINDOW IN GANTT CHART VIEW

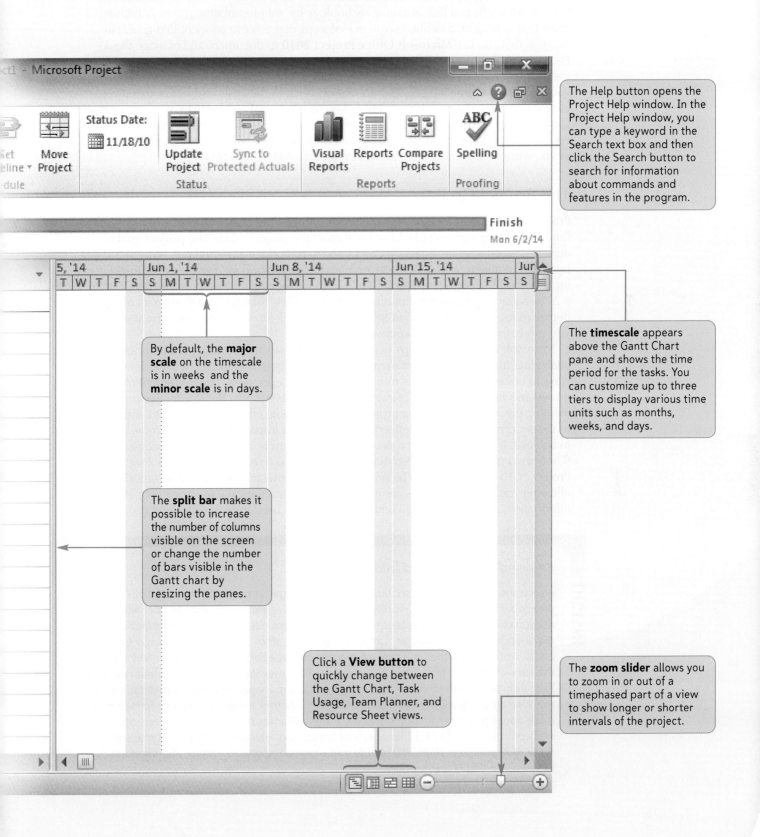

The Help button opens the Project Help window. In the Project Help window, you can type a keyword in the Search text box and then click the Search button to search for information about commands and features in the program.

The **timescale** appears above the Gantt Chart pane and shows the time period for the tasks. You can customize up to three tiers to display various time units such as months, weeks, and days.

By default, the **major scale** on the timescale is in weeks and the **minor scale** is in days.

The **split bar** makes it possible to increase the number of columns visible on the screen or change the number of bars visible in the Gantt chart by resizing the panes.

Click a **View button** to quickly change between the Gantt Chart, Task Usage, Team Planner, and Resource Sheet views.

The **zoom slider** allows you to zoom in or out of a timephased part of a view to show longer or shorter intervals of the project.

Introduction to Project Management

Having never managed a facility installation, you seek the advice of your friend, Alex Salazar. Alex tells you that installing technology for AV presentation rooms is nothing more than a **project**, a defined sequence of steps that achieve an identified goal. He suggests that you use **Microsoft Office Project 2010** to document and manage the AV Presentation Rooms Installation project because of its ability to help you calculate dates, assign responsibilities, and estimate costs. Alex explains that Project 2010 will also help you clearly communicate project information, such as the costs and status, to Sidney. He explains that all projects can benefit from professional project management but that technical and computer projects are especially good candidates due to their increased complexity, cost, and management expectations. You will learn how to use Project 2010 as you work on the ViewPoint Partners project.

The Project Goal

Project management includes the processes of initiating, planning, executing, controlling, and closing various tasks in order to meet the project's goal. The **project goal** is achieved when a series of tasks is completed that produce a desired outcome, at a specified level of quality, and within a given time frame and budget. Examples of project goals include: install a new computer system within six months for less than $100,000; build a 2500-square-foot house within three months for less than $350,000; earn a college degree in four years for less than $80,000; and find a job within two months at which you can earn at least $40,000 per year.

Microsoft Project 2010 helps you meet project goals by providing a tool for entering, analyzing, tracking, and summarizing information about the project. It also identifies ways to complete project tasks more efficiently and effectively. Being **efficient** means doing tasks faster, with fewer resources, and with lower costs. Being **effective** means meeting the actual goals of the project. Although being efficient is important and leads to greater productivity, being effective is much more important, as well as more difficult to achieve. It doesn't matter if a new computer system is installed in the specified time frame and under budget if the system doesn't work as intended. Using a tool such as Project 2010 will help you to be both efficient *and* effective by organizing task details, by allowing you to see how tasks are interrelated, by automatically updating date and cost information, and by providing communication tools used to make informed decisions.

Knowing Where to Find Information

INSIGHT

As a project manager, you should know where to get information that can help you in your job. Having resources readily available will give you an advantage as challenges and new phases of a project present themselves. One excellent source for information is an experienced project manager. Large corporations often employ several project managers all working together in a project management department to manage and support the various projects across the organization. The Internet is another excellent resource. Research the wealth of information about project management and related topics on the Web by using your favorite search engine. Another excellent resource for learning more about project management is the Project Management Institute's Web site at *www.pmi.org*. The Project Management Institute publishes the *Project Management Body of Knowledge (PMBOK®) Guide* and provides access to Project Management Professional (PMP) certification.

The first step in formally managing a project of any size is to define the project goal. The project goal should be as short and simple as possible, yet detailed enough to clearly communicate the specific scope, time frame, and budget expectations of the project. **Scope** refers to all the work involved in creating the project products and the processes used to create them. Time frame refers to the length of time it will take to complete the project — from start to finish. Budget refers to the actual cost of the project. The **project manager** is the central person to whom all of the details of the project converge for entry into the project plan and the primary source of information regarding project status. The project manager along with management determines when a project is finished. A project is finished when all agree that the project goal has been met.

In your case, the project goal is to *install five AV presentation rooms to display media resources, to complete the installation within a time frame of three months, and to stay within a budget of $100,000.* This broad goal assumes that you will describe additional project details, such as steps to define resources that need to be shared. Obtaining agreement from management on a project goal that addresses the issues of scope, time frame, and budget is essential if both the project manager and management are to stay synchronized with project expectations. Figure 1-1 compares vague project goals with improved project goals.

Figure 1-1	Setting project goals

Vague Project Goals	Improved Project Goals
Find a job	Secure a local job within the next six months working for a local college or high school that pays at least $35,000 annually
Organize the company retreat	Plan the annual company retreat during the month of January in a convention center in a warm climate and within a budget of $100,000
Build a house	Build a four-bedroom house in Dumont within a $500,000 budget by July 1
Run a fund-raiser	Hold a fund-raising event to finance the new band uniforms by September 1

TIP

Project management skills can be applied to any project. You can apply project management skills to a small project, such as redecorating a room, or to a large project, such as building a bridge.

Often, during the course of a project, you will need to revise the project goal as unexpected issues alter the original plan. For example, you might have initially underestimated the cost or time required to complete the project. Project 2010 helps both the project manager and management predict and understand project progress and issues in order to minimize negative effects on the scope, time frame, or budget of the project.

Project Management Process Groups

A **process group** is a set of processes, or series of steps, that need to be completed in order to move on to the next phase of the project. The duration of a project is divided into five process groups: initiating, planning, executing, controlling, and closing. Each process group requires appropriate communication to management if you hope to stay synchronized with its needs and desires. Figure 1-2 describes some of the typical tasks and responsibilities that occur within each process group. Project 2010 supports each of these process groups by providing an integrated database into which you enter the individual pieces of project information. It uses the project information to create the screens and reports necessary to communicate project status throughout each process group.

Figure 1-2	Project management process groups

Process Group	Typical Responsibilities
Initiating	Setting the project goal
	Identifying the necessary project start or finish date limitations
	Identifying the project manager
	Identifying project budget and quality considerations
Planning	Entering project tasks, durations, and relationships
	Identifying project subdivisions and milestones
	Documenting available resources as well as their associated costs
	Entering applicable resource or task restrictions such as intermediate due dates or not-to-exceed costs
	Assigning resources to tasks
Executing	Producing work results, including the products or services required to meet project goals
	Requesting changes to the project
	Recommending quality and performance improvements
	Creating project records, reports, and presentations
Controlling	Updating project start, finish, and resource usage to completed or partially completed tasks
	Managing resource and task conflicts
	Working with the project to meet management timing, resource, and cost objectives
	Changing the project to meet new or unexpected demands
Closing	Entering the final status of the finished project, including task date, resource, and cost information
	Printing the final reports used to analyze the performance of the project

INSIGHT

Using Forms as Part of the Initiating Process

Many companies use forms, either electronic or paper, for collecting and organizing information to start the project planning and management process. Completing and approving forms can be a required part of the initiating phase or process group. For some companies, forms are regimented with strict guidelines. For others, forms are loosely organized and more flexible. Forms can identify the key players, general contact information, chain of command, and even scope and goals of a project. These forms often must be completed and approved through the management structure before a project can begin.

Project Management Terminology

Understanding key project terminology is fundamental to your success as a project manager. This section defines a few key terms that will help you when using Project 2010.

Task

A **task** is a specific action that needs to be completed in order to achieve the project goal. Because tasks are actions, task names generally start with a verb. Examples of tasks within the AV Presentation Rooms Installation project include "detail current status," "purchase new equipment," "wire the office," and "train the users." The specificity of the task depends on its complexity as well as on the needs of the users of the project information. If the task "train the users" involves learning multiple software applications, such as spreadsheets, word processing, and new accounting software, a single training task is probably too broad. If the task is to train the new users on how to create a new password for anything related to the AV presentation rooms, however, a single task describing this effort is probably sufficient.

Duration

Each task has a **duration**, which is how long it takes to complete the task. Some task durations are not flexible; they do not change regardless of the amount of resources applied. Meetings, for example, fall into this category because it generally doesn't matter if five or six employees attend the orientation meeting—the scheduled duration of the meeting is still two hours. Most tasks, however, have a flexible duration, meaning that if two people of equal qualifications are assigned to a task, the task could be completed in less time. Wiring the office and taking the new equipment out of the boxes are examples of tasks with flexible durations.

   In Project 2010, durations can be estimated or firm. An estimated duration appears with a question mark (?) after the duration unit of measure (such as day). So, for example, if you do not enter a duration for a new task, it will appear with an estimated default duration of one day, which appears as "1 day?." By providing for both estimated and firm durations, Project 2010 gives you the ability to quickly find and filter tasks with durations that are not firm.

Start and Finish Dates

The **Start date** is the date that the project will begin. The **Finish date** is the date that Project 2010 calculates for completion of the project. By default, if you enter a Start date, Project 2010 will calculate the Finish date based on the task durations and relationships within the project. However, if you enter a Finish date, Project 2010 will calculate the Start date based on the task durations and relationships within the project.

Predecessors and Successors

A **predecessor** is a task that must be completed before a different task can be started, and a **successor** is a task that cannot be started until another task is completed. For example, if you are building a house, you cannot frame the roof until the walls are framed. Putting up the walls is the predecessor task for putting on the roof, and the roof task is a successor to the walls task. You can, however, start picking out flooring materials for the inside of the house without waiting for the walls or roof to be put up, so the task of choosing flooring materials does not have a predecessor.

Resources

Resources are the people, equipment, or facilities (such as a conference room) that must be assigned to a task in order to complete it. Some resources have defined hourly costs that will be applied as the task is completed (for example, the software trainer charges $100 per hour). Some resources have per-use costs (for example, the conference room charge is $200 per use). Some resource costs are not applied to a particular task but rather to the entire project (for example, a temporary receptionist is hired for the duration of the training task while existing employees are being trained). The degree to which you track task and project costs is defined by what management wants. If management is mainly concerned about when a project will be finished and if the project is well within budget, it might be unnecessary to spend extra time and energy tracking detailed costs and instead it might be acceptable to simply maintain a general accounting of costs. If management needs to track detailed project costs, then resource assignments and their associated costs must be entered and managed as part of the project.

Project Manager

As explained earlier in this tutorial, the project manager is the central person to whom all of the details of the project converge for entry into the project plan. The project manager also supervises the project's execution and is the main source of project status information for management. The project manager is expected to balance conflicting business needs, such as to not only finish a project by July 1 but also to finish it under budget. As such, the project manager must have excellent leadership, organizational, and communication skills.

Scope

As mentioned previously, scope is all the work involved in creating the products of the project and the processes used to create them. A clear project goal will help communicate the scope of the project. The more precise the project objectives and deliverables, the more clear the scope becomes. Projects that are not well defined, or those that do not have appropriate management involvement and support, can suffer from scope creep. **Scope creep** is the condition whereby projects grow and change in unanticipated ways that increase costs, extend deadlines, or otherwise negatively affect the project goal. For example, if a contractor is building a home with the help of an interior designer, scope creep can occur if the designer adds features and embellishments that were not part of the original plan.

Quality

Quality is the degree to which something meets an objective standard. Almost every project and task has implied quality standards. Without effective communication, however, they can be interpreted much differently by the project manager and by the employee or contractor completing the task. The more clearly those standards are defined, the more likely the task will be completed at a quality level acceptable to the project manager. Both the project manager and the person completing the task must agree on key quality measurements. For example, the task "install computer cabling" involves other issues that determine whether the task will be completed in a high-quality manner.

Quality concerns for the AV Presentation Rooms Installation project you are responsible for include the following:

- Will the installation be completed in a manner that doesn't interrupt the regular workday?
- How will the office furniture be moved and returned to its original location?
- What testing will be conducted?
- What type of documentation will be provided?
- When will payment be due?

Risk

Risk is the probability that a task, resource, or cost is miscalculated in a way that creates a negative impact on the project. Obviously, all risk cannot be eliminated. People get sick, accidents happen, and Murphy's Law is alive and well. Later in this book, you will learn how to use Project 2010 to minimize project risk.

INSIGHT

Maintaining Control of a Project

Just as all projects are unique, so too are the ways that project managers approach each project. Different project managers and businesses develop various methods for initiating and running a project. For example, some businesses set parameters and guidelines for their projects that do not exist in other businesses. Although approaches may differ, the project manager must always maintain control of the assignment of tasks, durations, and resources as well as watch for scope creep, monitor quality, and adjust for risk. If the project manager maintains this control, the project will be well managed.

Benefits of Project Management Software

As you have learned, the major benefit of formal project management is allowing you to complete a project goal at a specified level of quality within a given time frame and budget. On an organizational or enterprise level, providing consistent project delivery capability provides many advantages. As you review these advantages, shown in Figure 1-3, you begin to understand the benefits of project management as they relate to your project at ViewPoint Partners and your decision to use Project 2010.

| Figure 1-3 | Why would you use project management software? |

Benefits of Using Project Management Software
Better understanding of overall project goals and alignment with business objectives
Better understanding of project tasks, durations, schedule dates, and costs
More organized and streamlined way to manage the many details of a project
More accurate and reliable project status information
More efficient use of project resources
Better communication among management, the project manager, project participants, and other stakeholders
Faster response to conflicting project goals
Greater awareness of project progress
Faster project completion
Lower project costs
Fewer project failures

How Project 2010 Supports Successful Project Management

You use project management software, such as Project 2010, to manage and store all project information using one program. Project 2010 allows you to enter project information into one database so the information is centralized. By using one program, you are able to see how the various factors are interrelated and how changes to some of the information can impact the rest of the project. Project 2010 offers an organized, secure, and easy way to manage the many project details. In so doing, Project 2010 combines the functions of several types of application software, as explained in Figure 1-4. You could use all these different applications to assist in managing projects; however, Project 2010 allows you to use *one* software application to manage the entire project.

| Figure 1-4 | Project 2010 compared to other software applications |

Application Software	**Project 2010 Similarities**
Database	Manages lists of tasks, durations, dates, resources, costs, constraints, and notes
Spreadsheet	Automatically recalculates durations and costs, task start and finish dates, and project start or finish dates
Chart	Provides several graphical views of project information, including the Gantt chart, Network Diagram, and Calendar views, to offer a visual overview of important data
Report Writer	Includes several predefined reports that provide varying degrees of detail in all areas of the project; allows the user to customize existing reports to show exactly the amount of detail needed
Enterprise Management	Allows integration with other enterprise applications when using Microsoft Project Server 2010

TIP

Software cannot tell if
your tasks make sense
in a real-world situation,
and it will process the
information based on what
is entered in the program.
So, be sure to input only
valid and reasonable
information.

With Project 2010, you start a project by entering a few tasks, often in sequential order. The integrated approach of Project 2010 allows you to expand the project as needed. As your project information requirements evolve, you can always enter and evaluate more information, such as planned, scheduled, and actual time frames, costs, and resource allocations.

Project 2010 includes several specialized tools to help you manage your projects. It also provides project planning assistance in the form of a guide.

Chart and Diagram Tools

The Gantt chart and the network diagram are two important project management tools you can create using Project 2010.

Gantt Chart

The Gantt chart provides a graphical visualization of the project, with each task shown as a horizontal bar. The length of each bar in the Gantt chart corresponds to the duration of the task. Named for Henry Gantt (a pioneer of project management techniques), the Gantt chart graphically displays project schedule information by listing project tasks and their corresponding Start and Finish dates in a calendar format. The Gantt chart also depicts the dependencies between tasks by illustrating whether one task must be completed before another task begins. An example of a Gantt chart is shown in Figure 1-5. Project 2010 creates Gantt charts that you can view on the screen or print.

| Figure 1-5 | Example of a Gantt chart |

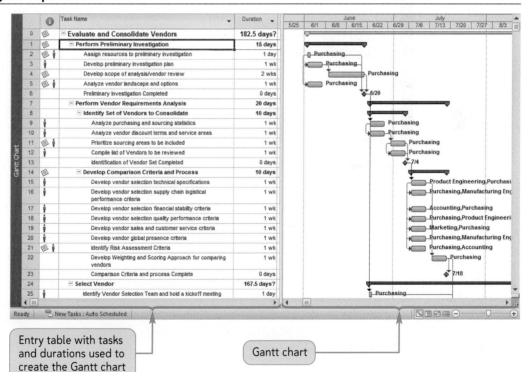

Entry table with tasks and durations used to create the Gantt chart

Gantt chart

Network Diagram

Although a Gantt chart illustrates whether one task is dependent on another, a **network diagram**, which displays each task as a box or **node**, more clearly illustrates the inter-dependencies of tasks. See Figure 1-6. Dependent tasks are linked together through link lines, thus creating a clear picture of how the tasks are sequenced. The primary purpose of the network diagram is to display the critical path. The **critical path** is the series of tasks (or even a single task) that dictates the calculated Finish date of the project. In other words, the critical path determines the earliest the project can be completed. Used together, the network diagram and the Gantt chart form a solid foundation for effective and efficient project management. You will create a simple Gantt chart and network diagram in this first tutorial and learn to create more complex ones in later tutorials.

| Figure 1-6 | Example of a network diagram |

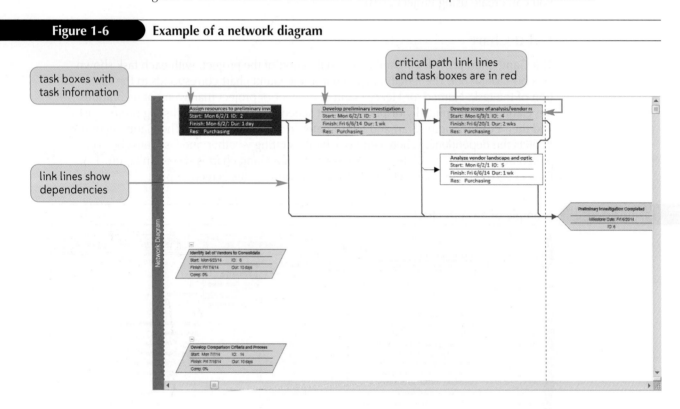

PROSKILLS

Decision Making: Choosing the Best Version of Project 2010 to Meet Your Needs

Because there are three versions of Microsoft Office Project 2010, it is useful to understand the differences among them so you can choose the version that best meets your needs. Fundamentally, you need to determine if a single-user version for individual contributors is appropriate, or if you need a server version that permits multiple users to work together using common data.

If you plan to manage projects independently from your desktop computer, you should choose **Project Standard 2010**, which provides the core tools that project managers, business managers, and planners need to manage schedules and resources independently. With Project Standard 2010, you can efficiently organize and track tasks and resources to keep your projects on time and within budget. You can integrate any Project 2010 project file with any Microsoft Office 2010 software, such as Microsoft PowerPoint and Microsoft Excel.

If you think that your needs will grow and you will eventually want to collaborate with others, then you should select **Project Professional 2010**, which can integrate with Project Server 2010, the enterprise management version. Project Professional 2010 provides all the capabilities in Project Standard 2010, however, Project Professional 2010 also includes the **Team Planner**, which shows resources and work over time. It also provides enterprise project management (EPM) capabilities, such as providing up-to-date information on resource availability as well as skills and project status across stakeholders. **Project Server 2010** is built on Microsoft SharePoint Server 2010, bringing together powerful business collaboration platform services with structured execution capabilities to provide flexible work management solutions. When a team publishes project information to the Microsoft Project Server, team members can view the information and report progress for their assigned tasks.

If you need to do any or all of the following:

* Communicate and collaborate with project team members and other stakeholders or partners over the Web, an intranet, or an extranet,
* Standardize project management processes across the organization,
* Understand resource workload and availability across projects, whether managed by you or others in the organization,
* Report across projects in the organization,

then you should choose the **Microsoft Project Server** solution. All versions of Microsoft Project integrate with the other Microsoft Office 2010 programs.

Project 2010 supports many features that help you to perform as an effective project manager. You will learn how to take advantage of these tools as you work through this book. Now that you know the benefits of project management and the basic terminology, you can start Project 2010 and begin to plan the AV Presentation Rooms Installation project for ViewPoint Partners.

Starting Microsoft Project 2010

Before you can create a project, you need to start Project 2010, set up your screen to match the figures in this book, and then learn about the organization of the Project 2010 window.

TIP

You can also start Project by clicking the Project button if it has been pinned to the taskbar.

To start Project 2010:

▶ 1. On the taskbar, click the **Start** button to display the Start menu, click **All Programs** to display the programs installed on your computer, and then click Microsoft Office. The Microsoft Office folder opens displaying the list of Microsoft Office programs installed on your computer.

2. Click **Microsoft Project 2010**. The Microsoft Project window opens. Refer back to the Session 1.1 Visual Overview shown earlier.

Trouble? If you don't see Microsoft Project 2010 after you click Microsoft Office, try typing "Project 2010" in the Search programs and files box on the Start menu. If you still don't see Microsoft Office Project 2010 on the menu, ask your instructor or technical support person for help.

Trouble? Project 2010 will prompt you to register or activate the product the first time it is used. If you are working with your own copy of Project 2010, it's a good idea to register the product with Microsoft in order to receive support and future product information.

The View Bar, when open, provides quick access to the many project views. Each view is represented as an icon. You click the icons to switch views. (If the View Bar is open by default, skip Step 1.)

To open the View Bar:

1. Right-click the **Gantt Chart** text on the left side of the window, and then click **View Bar**. The View Bar opens on the left side of the window.

   Trouble? If the Gantt Chart button is not selected in the View Bar (it should have an orange background), click it to select it.

2. If the Project program window is not maximized, click the **Maximize** button in the upper-right corner of the program window. Compare your screen to Figure 1-7.

Figure 1-7	Project window with View Bar open

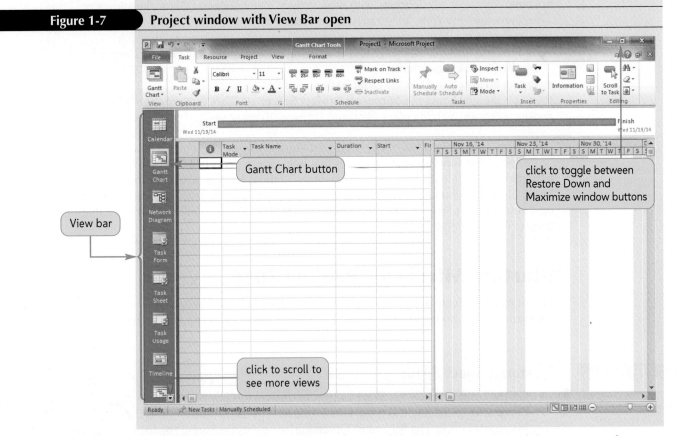

Project 2010 is now running, and you can start entering tasks and durations. But first, you will take a closer look at the Project 2010 window.

Viewing the Project 2010 Window

The Project 2010 window consists of a number of elements that are common to Windows applications, such as the title bar, which identifies both the project name and the application name, the Ribbon for all the commands, and the status bar. Additional elements in the window are specific to Project 2010.

View Bar

The **View Bar**, which appears to the left of the project window, contains View buttons that you use to switch from one project **view** to another. Views, such as Calendar, Gantt Chart, and Network Diagram, are different ways you can display your project. Each view displays task, resource, and cost information with varying levels of detail. If the bottom of the View Bar includes a small black triangle that points down, it indicates that more View buttons are available. Refer back to Figure 1-7. If your Window doesn't fill the screen, or your screen is set to a lower resolution, you might see fewer than the nine View buttons. To switch views, you click a button on the View Bar.

Depending on your personal preferences for the way the screen is set up, you may or may not want to open the View Bar. If you prefer to use the Ribbon interface, you click the View tab on the Ribbon, and then click the desired View button in the Task Views or Resource Views group.

To review the View tab and close the View Bar:

▶ **1.** Click the **View** tab on the Ribbon. See Figure 1-8.

Figure 1-8	View Bar and View tab on the Ribbon

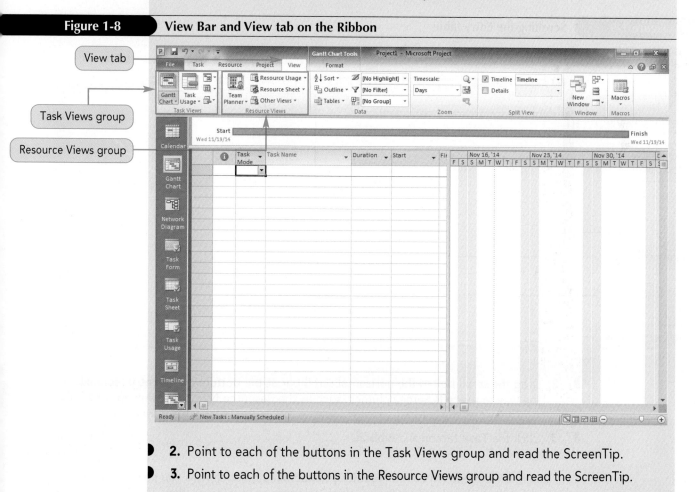

▶ **2.** Point to each of the buttons in the Task Views group and read the ScreenTip.

▶ **3.** Point to each of the buttons in the Resource Views group and read the ScreenTip.

> **4.** Right-click the **View Bar**, and then click **View Bar**. The View Bar closes and the Entry table expands to fill the space.

You will learn about changing views in the next session.

Entry Table

The default view is Gantt Chart view. In this view, the pane on the left lists the tasks and associated information about each task. The pane on the right displays the Gantt chart. The list of tasks on the left is the **Entry table**, a spreadsheet-like display of project information organized in rows and columns. Each task entered becomes a new row, and the columns contain the individual pieces of information related to each task. The two most important pieces of information about a task are provided in the Task Name and Duration columns.

The Entry table consists of many more columns of information than are shown in Figure 1-8. To see these other columns, you can use the horizontal scroll bar at the bottom of the Entry table.

To scroll the Entry table:

> **1.** Click the right scroll arrow in the horizontal scroll bar at the bottom of the Entry table pane as many times as necessary to scroll the table so that you can see the Resource Names column and the *Add New Column* column. Refer to Figure 1-9.

| Figure 1-9 | Scrolling the Entry table |

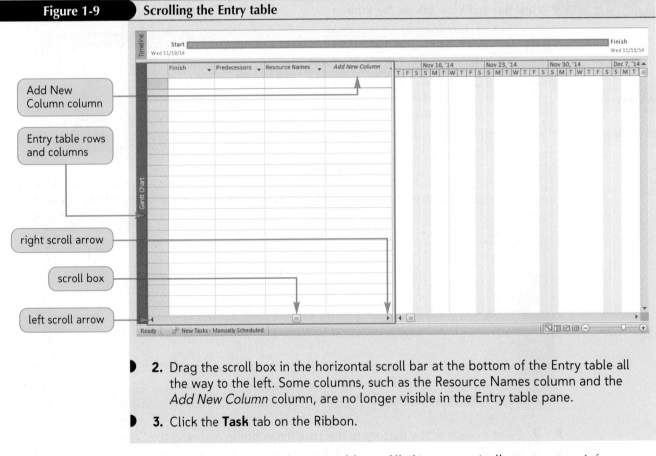

> **2.** Drag the scroll box in the horizontal scroll bar at the bottom of the Entry table all the way to the left. Some columns, such as the Resource Names column and the *Add New Column* column, are no longer visible in the Entry table pane.

> **3.** Click the **Task** tab on the Ribbon.

Often, the columns in the Entry table are filled in automatically as you enter information about the task in another view, such as Calendar or Task Usage view. The Start date, for example, is the current date, unless you specify something else. If you are using the Automatically Scheduled task mode, the Finish date is automatically calculated as the Start date plus the duration. The Predecessors and Resource Names columns will be filled in automatically as you specify task relationships and assign resources. You may type directly into the Entry table, but generally the Task Name and Duration columns are the only pieces of information that you enter manually. You will learn more about task modes when you enter tasks later in this Tutorial.

Gantt Chart

You have already learned that the Gantt chart is a primary tool used by project managers to graphically communicate information about a project. Each task is identified as a horizontal bar, the length of which corresponds to the duration of the task as measured by the timescale at the top of the Gantt chart. The Gantt chart can be formatted to show many other attributes of the project, including relationships between tasks, resource assignments, and dates. As you enter more information into the project, the Gantt chart changes to display the information.

In the project window, the Entry table and the Gantt chart are in separate panes with a vertical split bar dividing them. You can drag this split bar to resize the panes.

To drag the split bar:

1. Place the mouse pointer on the **split bar** between the Entry table and the Gantt chart. The pointer changes to ◀‖▶.

2. Press and hold the left mouse button, drag the ◀‖▶ pointer to the right, and then release the mouse button. The bar becomes a solid dark bar when you click and drag it.

3. Use the ◀‖▶ pointer to continue to drag the split bar as needed until you can see the Resource Names column in the Entry table, as shown in Figure 1-10.

| Figure 1-10 | Dragging the split bar |

Trouble? You might see more or less information in the Gantt chart depending on your screen resolution.

4. Use the ◄║► pointer to drag the split bar to the left until it is positioned at the right edge of the Finish column in the Entry table.

Timeline

The Timeline, displayed above the Entry table pane and the Gantt chart pane and below the Ribbon, provides a visual overview of the project from the Start date to the Finish date. You can elect whether or not to display the Timeline in the Gantt Chart view by right-clicking the Timeline and clicking Show Timeline, or by clicking the View tab and clicking the Timeline check box in the Split View group. When the Timeline is active, the Timeline Tools Format tab is available, providing access to commands you can use to enhance the Timeline. The Timeline has orange highlights when active. See Figure 1-11.

| Figure 1-11 | The Timeline |

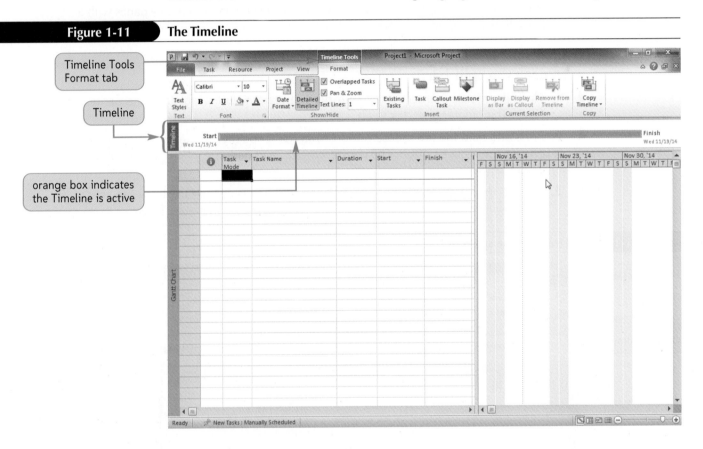

Timescale

The timescale, displayed along the top edge of the Gantt chart pane, displays the unit of measure that determines the length of each bar. See Figure 1-12. The timescale normally has two rows: a major scale (the upper scale) and a minor scale (the lower scale). By default, the major scale is measured in weeks and displays the date for the Sunday of that week, and the minor scale is measured in days and displays the first letter of the days of the week.

Figure 1-12   **The timescale**

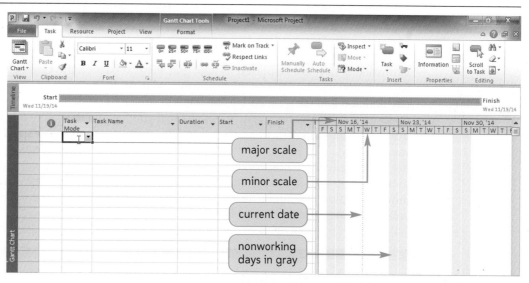

Both the major and minor scales can be modified to display a different unit of measure (minutes, hours, days, weeks, months, quarters, and years) as well as different labels. For example, week labels can be displayed in different ways, such as January 30, 2014; Jan 30, '14; 1/30/14; and Tue 1/30/14. You can also add a third level to the timescale, which is used to further distinguish the time.

As with the Entry table pane, you can scroll the Gantt chart to see parts of the chart not currently in view. When you scroll the Gantt chart, you are essentially moving the timescale. Nonworking days are shaded in gray, by default. For new Project files, the current date is identified by default as a gold vertical line.

To scroll the Gantt chart:

1. Drag the **horizontal scroll** box in the Gantt chart pane to the far right of the scroll bar. As you drag the scroll box, a date ScreenTip appears to indicate how far you are moving the timescale.

   Often, you'll want to return to the first bar in the Gantt chart.

2. Press and hold the **Alt** key, and then press the **Home** key. The Alt+Home keystroke combination moves the Gantt chart to the project's Start date so that the first bar is visible. The Alt+End keystroke combination moves the Gantt chart to the project's Finish date.

3. Click anywhere on the **Timeline**. Notice how the gray bar now has an orange outline. Colors, specifically orange highlighting, are used throughout Project 2010 as an indicator for active panes, columns, and buttons. If you place your pointer over a column in the Entry table, it too will take on an orange glow.

Current Date

By default, the **current date** is today's date, as determined by your computer's clock. It is represented in the Gantt chart by a gold vertical line. The Start date is represented by a dotted line. Unless specified differently, all tasks are scheduled and all progress is measured from the current date. You can, however, easily change the current date. Some project managers find it useful to change the current date when planning future projects. As you work on projects, you will develop your own preferences for working with the current date settings. Note that the dotted line is not clearly visible if the current date is Saturday or Sunday or Monday because it appears in or next to the nonworking day line.

Working Days and Nonworking Days

Nonworking days are displayed as light gray vertical bars on the Gantt chart. By default, Saturday and Sunday are considered nonworking days. Therefore, if a task has a three-day duration and starts on Friday, the bar will stretch through Saturday and Sunday, and finish on the third working day, Tuesday. Or, if you happen to specify that a task starts on a Sunday, Project 2010 will move that task to begin on Monday. For specific holidays or vacation days in which no work should be scheduled, you can open the project's calendar and specify more nonworking days. Similarly, you can change Saturday or Sunday to be working days if you need to schedule work on those days. Later, you'll learn that individual resources can be assigned individual calendars to accommodate individual work schedules, vacations, and holidays.

PROSKILLS

Teamwork: Considering Working Days in a Global Economy

In order for teams to work together, the team members need to know when everyone is available to work. In many countries, working days are typically Monday through Friday, and Saturdays and Sundays are nonworking days. In some countries, however, work weeks are six rather than five days, and in still other countries, work weeks are a four-day week. Holidays also differ from country to country and from one group of people to another. All of this needs to be taken into consideration when planning a project so that team members are not being asked to work on a nonwork day or a holiday particular to them. Project 2010 allows you to specify any date as a working or a nonworking day. For example, if you work for a company in the United States that allows its employees to take the Friday after Thanksgiving off, you can set that day as nonworking. In Canada, the Canadian Thanksgiving is celebrated in October. For those projects that require different nonworking days for different project participants, you can specify the different working and nonworking days in the calendar so that all project participants are aware of the days that team members are and are not working. You will learn later how to apply different calendars to the different resources to accommodate those differences.

Understanding Start and Finish Dates and Manual or Automatic Scheduling

When you create a new project, the program assigns a Start and Finish date. The Start date is assumed to be the current date, unless specified otherwise. If you enter a Start date, Project 2010 will calculate the Finish date based on the task durations and relationships within the project. You can change this so that you can enter a Finish date, and Project 2010 will calculate a Start date, again based on task durations and relationships within the project. Specifying a Finish date is appropriate and necessary for projects such as conventions that must occur on a specific date. You can only set the Start date *or* the Finish date of the project. Project 2010 will calculate the other one. When there are no tasks in the project, the Start date and Finish date are the same date.

In addition to setting the Start or Finish date, you can set how tasks are scheduled. If tasks are set to be Automatically Scheduled by Project 2010, then task dates are automatically calculated and updated by Project. If tasks are set to be Manually Scheduled (which is the default setting), you enter Start and Finish date and these dates are not calculated by Project, regardless of changes. Manually scheduled tasks give project managers greater control over tasks, durations, Start, and Finish dates because project managers can assign durations that are not changed by dependencies or delays in other tasks.

To set the automatic scheduling:

1. In the Tasks group on the Task tab, click the **Mode** button. The two options for determining how new tasks are scheduled are displayed on the menu that opens. See Figure 1-13.

Figure 1-13	Setting the scheduling mode

TIP

You can quickly switch between automatic and manual scheduling by clicking New Tasks: Manually Scheduled or New Tasks: Auto Scheduled on the status bar and selecting the option (manual or automatic) on the menu that opens to toggle between the two modes.

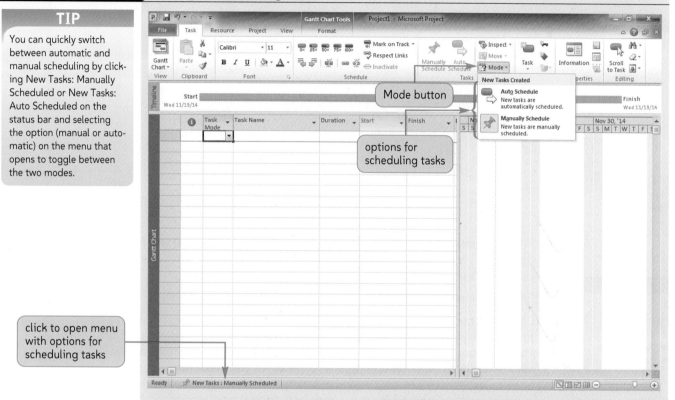

Mode button

options for scheduling tasks

click to open menu with options for scheduling tasks

2. Click **Auto Schedule**. All new tasks for this project file will be scheduled automatically.

Now, Emily wants you to review the current project information which will change automatically as you enter new tasks, dependencies, calendars and constraints.

To set the project Start and Finish dates:

1. Click the **Project** tab on the Ribbon, and then, in the Properties group, click **Project Information** to open the Project Information dialog box. See Figure 1-14. The current date is listed as both the Start and Finish dates, and the Schedule from option indicates that the schedule will be calculated based on the Start date. When there are no tasks in the project, the Start date and Finish date are the same date. As you add tasks, the Finish date is recalculated based on the durations and relationships of the tasks entered. Notice that the Finish date option is in light gray, or dimmed. This means you cannot change it unless you change the Schedule from option to Project Finish Date.

Figure 1-14   **Project Information dialog box for a new project**

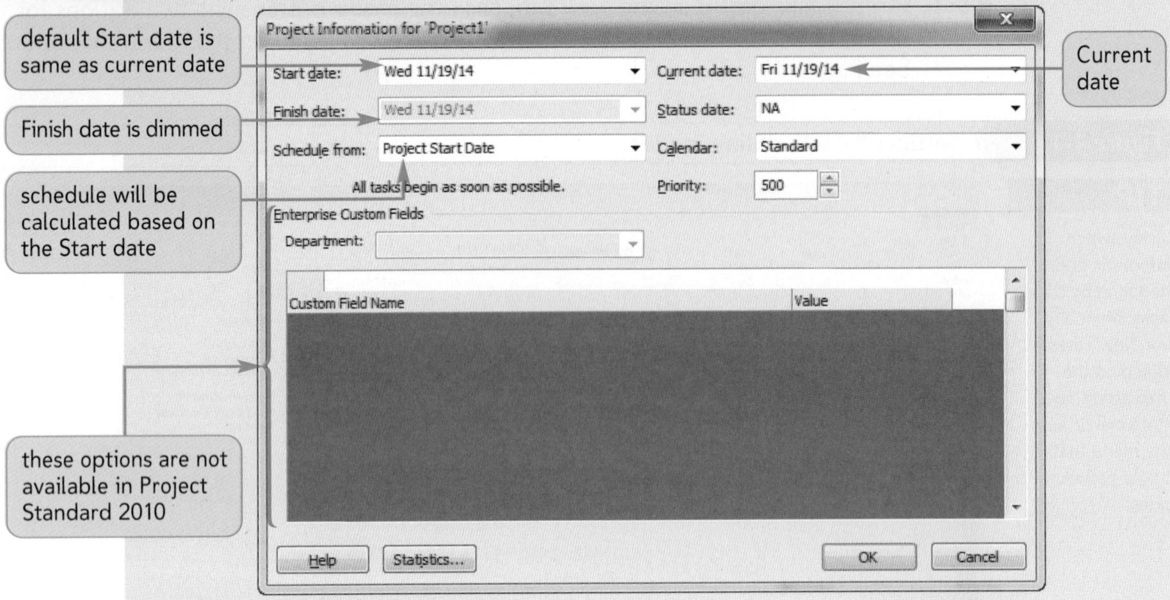

default Start date is
same as current date

Finish date is dimmed

schedule will be
calculated based on
the Start date

these options are not
available in Project
Standard 2010

Current
date

2. Click the **Schedule from** arrow, and then click **Project Finish Date**. Now the Start
date option is dimmed. Next, you'll change the schedule option back to its default
setting and set the Start date.

3. Click the **Schedule from** arrow, and then click **Project Start Date**.

4. Click the **Start date** arrow, click the **right** or **left arrow** on the calendar to scroll
to September, 2014, and then click the **1** on the calendar, as shown in Figure 1-15.
The Start date is now set to Monday, September 1, 2014. The Finish date will
automatically change to September 1, 2014 when you close the dialog box.

TIP

You can also type the date
using any format such as
mm/dd/yy or mmm/dd
in the Start date or Finish
date text boxes.

Figure 1-15   **Changing the current date**

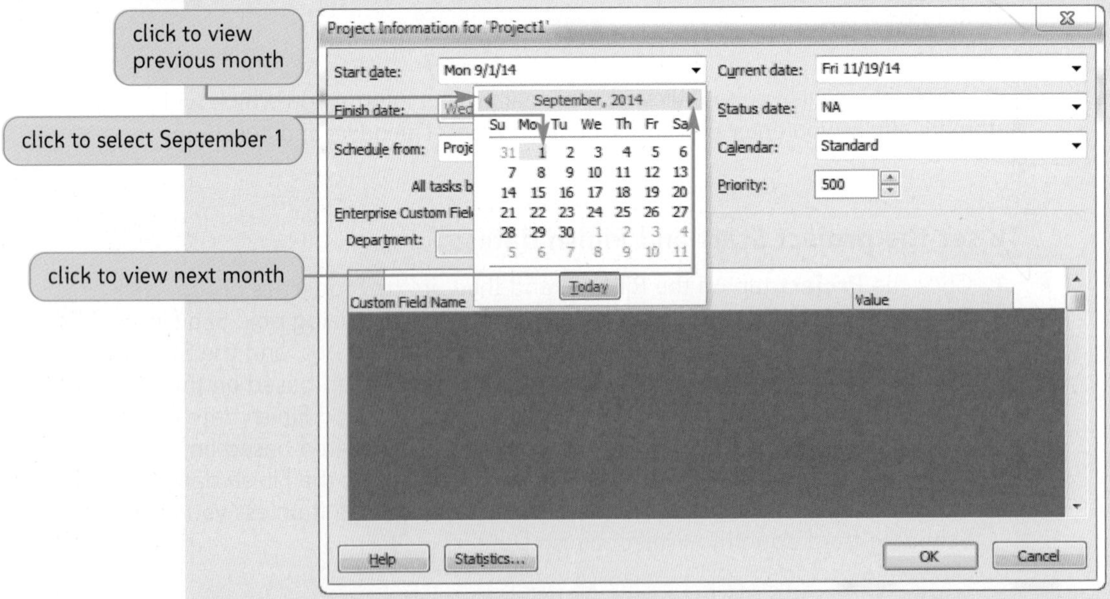

click to view
previous month

click to select September 1

click to view next month

5. Click **OK** in the Project Information dialog box to apply your changes. Notice that the Gantt chart has scrolled to display the week in which September 1, 2014 appears, and the Timeline shows the updated Start and Finish dates as 9/1/2014.

Entering Your First Tasks

Every project contains tasks. Sidney and Emily met, and they gave you have a list of a few tasks necessary for the installation project. You will enter those tasks next. When you enter a task, Project 2010 enters a default estimated duration of one day. You can change this to any amount of time. The default unit of measurement is days, so to enter a duration of five days, you can enter "5," "5d," or "5days."

TIP

Task names should be as short as possible, and yet long enough to clearly identify the task.

To enter tasks and durations:

1. Click the **Task** tab on the Ribbon, verify that **New Tasks: Auto Scheduled** appears on the status bar, click the **Task Name** cell in row 1, type **Document hardware**, and then press the **Tab** key. See Figure 1-16.

| Figure 1-16 | Adding a task |

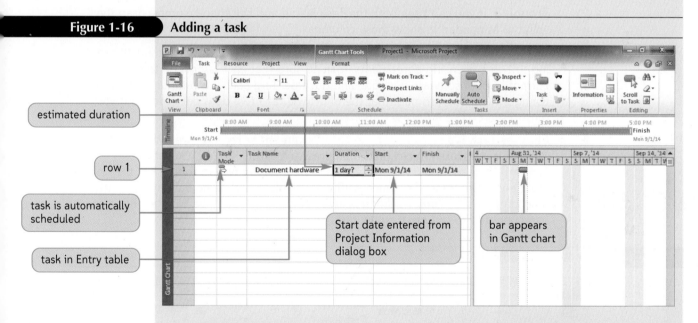

The Duration cell for the first row is now the active cell. The default entry is 1 day?. The question mark indicates that the duration is an estimate. The default duration for a task is estimated at 1 day, but the unit of measure, such as hours, days, weeks, or months, for the duration can be changed at any time. The Task Mode column has the icon that identifies this task as an automatically scheduled task. Note that the row now contains a row number in the first column.

2. Type **5**, and then press the **Enter** key. You have made the duration for this task five days because it will involve researching, inspecting, and documenting each existing piece of equipment. ViewPoint Partners will be installing five AV presentation rooms and you think that this task will take one day per room. Because this project is scheduled from a Start date and not from a Finish date, tasks begin on the Start date. If the Start date you set is a nonworking day, the project starts on the next working day. Notice that the Timeline spans the five days of the project and a blue bar stretching five days has been added to the Gantt chart. Your screen should look like Figure 1-17.

Figure 1-17 First task entered

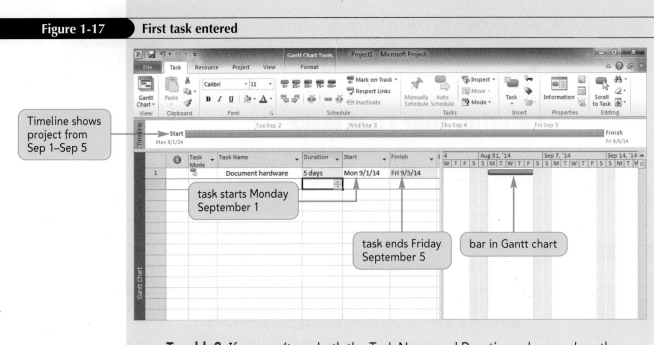

Timeline shows project from Sep 1–Sep 5

task starts Monday September 1

task ends Friday September 5

bar in Gantt chart

Trouble? If you can't see both the Task Name and Duration columns, drag the split bar as needed to show those columns.

The second task that you will enter, Document software, involves finding all existing software licensing agreements, making sure that each user is on the most current level of software possible, and documenting each workstation's software configuration. You estimate that the effort will take two days per room, and you must research five AV presentation rooms.

3. Click the **Task Name** cell in row 2, type **Document software**, press the **Tab** key, type **10** in the Duration cell, and then press the **Enter** key. As you can see in Figure 1-18, the Finish date is 9/12. The bar corresponding to this task in the Gantt chart ends September 12, which is 10 working days, but 12 actual days from the Start date. It spans one weekend or two nonworking days. The Timeline has also been updated to include the new task.

Figure 1-18 Two tasks entered

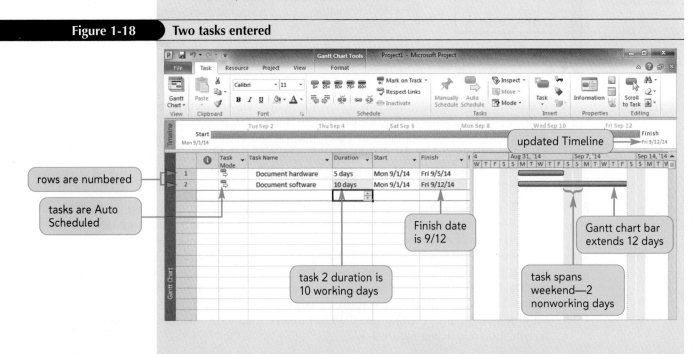

updated Timeline

rows are numbered

tasks are Auto Scheduled

Finish date is 9/12

Gantt chart bar extends 12 days

task 2 duration is 10 working days

task spans weekend—2 nonworking days

Trouble? The bars on the Gantt chart might or might not be visible, depending on the time period displayed on the timescale. You will learn more about the timescale later.

You can use the horizontal scroll bars at the bottom of each pane to scroll each pane. For example, you can scroll the pane on the left to see additional columns, or you can scroll the pane on the right to see more of the Gantt chart. When working on a project you will find you need more or less space in each pane. When this happens, you can close the Timeline or you can open or close the View Bar to organize your window panes to best meet your needs.

Saving a Project

Saving a project file is very similar to saving a word processing document or a spreadsheet. You specify a filename as well as a location for the file. The rules for filenames in Project 2010 follow Windows filenaming conventions. The location consists of the specified drive and folder or subfolders.

REFERENCE

Saving a Project for the First Time

- Click the Save button on the Quick Access toolbar *or* click the File tab on the Ribbon and then click Save.
- Change the folder and drive information to the location where you want to save your file.
- In the File name box, type the filename.
- Click the Save button (or press the Enter key).

Project 2010 automatically appends the .mpp filename extension to identify the file as a Project 2010 file. Depending on how Windows is set up on your computer, however, you might not see the .mpp extension. These tutorials assume that filename extensions are displayed.

To save the project:

1. Click the **File** tab on the Ribbon. Project 2010 Backstage view opens. See Figure 1-19.

Figure 1-19   **Backstage view**

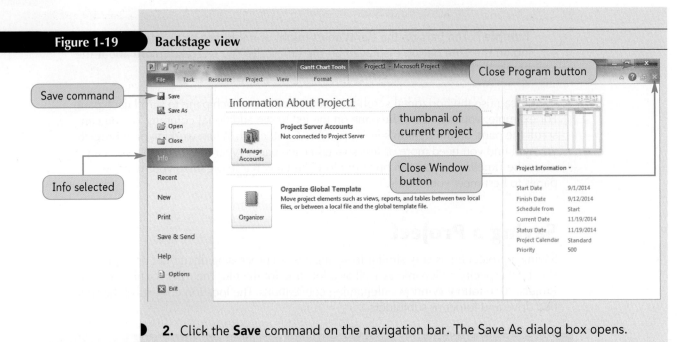

2. Click the **Save** command on the navigation bar. The Save As dialog box opens.

3. Type **Rooms** in the File name box.

4. Navigate to the **Project1\Tutorial** folder included with your Data Files.

   Trouble? If you don't have the starting Data Files, you need to get them before you can proceed. Your instructor will either give you the Data Files or ask you to obtain them from a specified location (such as a network drive). In either case, make a backup copy of the Data Files before you start so that you will have the original files available in case you need to start over. If you have any questions about the Data Files, see your instructor or technical support person for assistance.

5. Click the **Save** button in the Save As dialog box. The dialog box closes and the file is saved in the location you specified with the filename you specified.

TIP

If you choose not to display filename extensions, the file extensions will not appear in the Open or Save As dialog boxes.

    The name of your file, Rooms.mpp, now appears in the title bar, and the file is saved. If you have your system set up not to display filename extensions, you will see Rooms in the title bar.

Closing a Project File

As with other Windows applications, you may have more than one file open (in this case, a project file). You can switch between the open files by using commands in the Window group on the View tab or by hovering over the Project button on the taskbar and then clicking the thumbnail of the project you want as the active project. If, however, you are finished working with the current project, you have saved it, and you want to work on another project, you should close the current project to free computer resources for other tasks.

REFERENCE

Closing a Project File

- Click the Close Window button for the Project 2010 file *or* click the File tab on the Ribbon to open Backstage view, and then click the Close command on the navigation bar.
- If you're prompted to save changes to the project, click the Yes button to save the project with the existing filename.

You want to close the AV Presentation Rooms Installation project file to take a quick break before continuing to add tasks.

TIP

You can click the Close Window button under the Close Program button in the upper-right corner of the Project window to close a project but not exit the program.

To close the project file:

1. Click the **File** tab on the Ribbon.
2. Click the **Close** command on the navigation bar. If you have made any changes to the project file since you last saved the file, you will be prompted to save the file before closing it.

REVIEW

Session 1.1 Quick Check

1. When is the project goal achieved?
2. Differentiate "efficient" from "effective."
3. Define "scope creep."
4. What is a project manager?
5. What are the five process groups of project management?
6. Describe what a Gantt chart looks like, and identify its primary purpose.
7. Describe what a network diagram looks like, and identify its primary purpose.
8. Define the following project management terms:
   - task
   - duration
   - resources
   - quality
9. When entering a new task in Gantt Chart view, two pieces of information are generally entered first. What are they?
10. What does it mean if you see a question mark after a number in the Duration column?
11. Describe the default timescale in Gantt Chart view.

SESSION 1.2 VISUAL OVERVIEW

The **Task tab** for the Gantt Chart provides buttons for changing the formatting, scheduling, and properties of selected tasks as well as for inserting new tasks.

The **Finish column** displays the date the task is scheduled to finish or be completed.

The **Task Name column** contains all the tasks for the project. Subsequent columns display the information for each task.

The **row number**, entered automatically as you insert tasks, helps identify the sequential order of the tasks.

The **Indicators** column is an information column that displays relevant icons as needed to help with the project.

The **active task** has a border around the task name. Task information is available for this task in the Task Information dialog box.

The **Duration column** displays the time allocated for a task.

The **Start column** displays the date the task starts.

The **Entry table** is used to enter and contains task information, such as task name, duration, Start date, and Finish date.

P						Gantt Chart Tools	NewAV-1.mpp - Microsoft
File	Task	Resource	Project	View		Format	

Arial   8   0% 25% 50% 75% 100%   Mark on Track
B I U   Respect Links
Inactivate

View   Clipboard   Font   Schedule

Gantt Chart
Paste

	ⓘ	Task Name	Duration	Start	Finish
1		Detail current status	5 days		Fri 6/6/14
2		Conduct needs analysis	ys	Mon 6/9/14	Fri 6/27/14
3		Build RFP	3 days	Mon 6/30/14	Wed 7/2/14
4		Gather bids	15 days	Thu 7/3/14	Wed 7/23/14
5		Install hardware	3 days	Thu 7/24/14	Mon 7/28/14
6		Install software	3 days	Tue 7/29/14	Thu 7/31/14
7		Conduct training	5 days	Fri 8/1/14	Thu 8/7/14

Gantt Chart

Ready   New Tasks : Auto Scheduled

TASK INFORMATION IN PROJECT

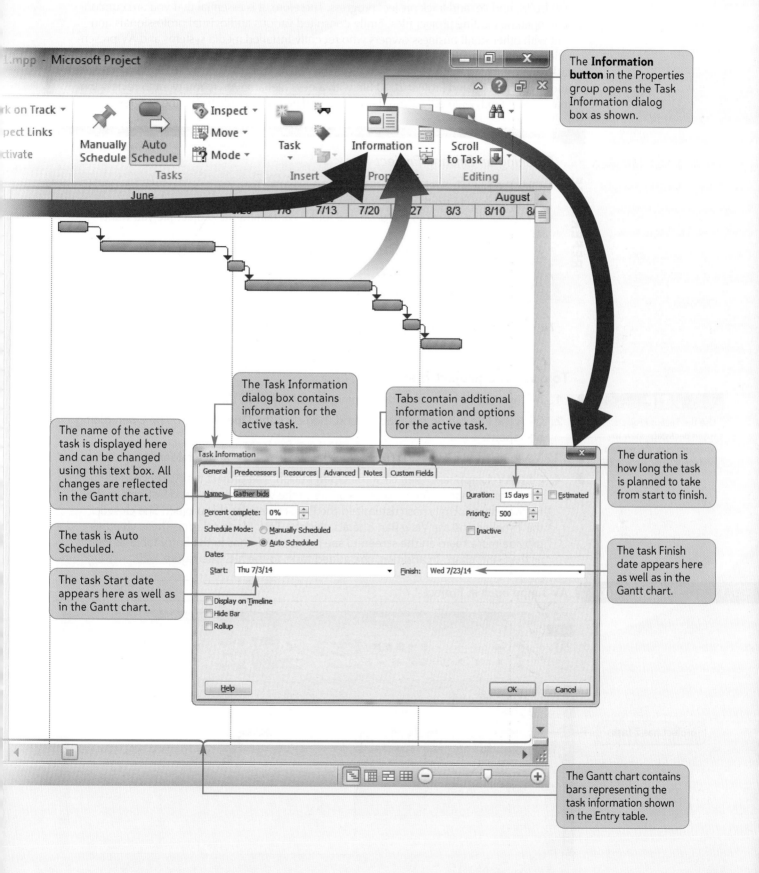

The **Information button** in the Properties group opens the Task Information dialog box as shown.

The Task Information dialog box contains information for the active task.

Tabs contain additional information and options for the active task.

The name of the active task is displayed here and can be changed using this text box. All changes are reflected in the Gantt chart.

The task is Auto Scheduled.

The task Start date appears here as well as in the Gantt chart.

The duration is how long the task is planned to take from start to finish.

The task Finish date appears here as well as in the Gantt chart.

The Gantt chart contains bars representing the task information shown in the Entry table.

Using Existing Projects

Often, you'll use the same project file over a period of several days, weeks, or months as you build, update, and track project progress. Therefore, it is essential that you are comfortable opening existing project files. Emily consulted various audiovisual professionals and met with other small business owners who recently installed media systems and AV presentation rooms for their company. Based on those meetings, she determined seven essential tasks and estimated durations for each task. She entered this information in the project file and saved her updated Project 2010 file with a new filename AV-1. You want to review the information Emily entered, so you'll open the updated project file to see the progress.

REFERENCE

Opening an Existing Project

- Click the File tab on the Ribbon, and then click the Open command on the navigation bar or click a file from the Recent files list.
- If necessary, navigate to the drive and folder containing the project file you want to open.
- In the list of files, click the filename of the project that you wish to open.
- Click the Open button (or press the Enter key or double-click the file that you wish to open).

Next, you'll open the updated Project file, which is named AV-1.mpp.

To open the project file:

TIP

Use the Recent Projects list in Backstage view to open projects you worked on recently.

1. If Project 2010 is not already running, start Project 2010.

2. Click the **File** tab on the Ribbon, and then click the **Open** button. The Open dialog box opens.

3. Navigate to the **Project1\Tutorial** folder if it is not the active folder.

4. Click **AV-1.mpp**, and then click the **Open** button. The project file AV-1 opens in the Project window. The project file opens in the view that was used last before the file was closed. Emily has customized the Project view for this project. She closed the Timeline and the View Bar. She also hid the Task Mode column. These changes provide more room on the screen to see relevant columns in the Entry table as well as the Gantt chart. In addition, she added tasks to the file. See Figure 1-20.

Figure 1-20   AV-1.mpp open in Project

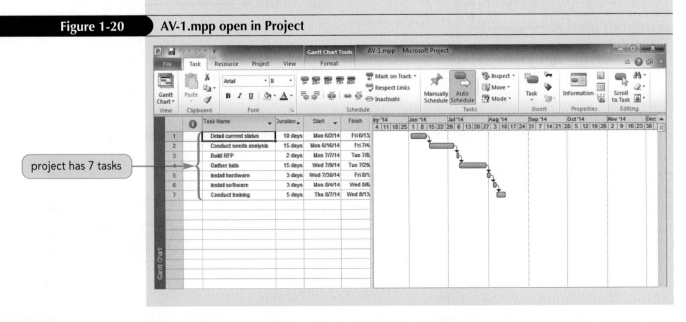

project has 7 tasks

Examine the tasks that Emily added to the project. Notice that she changed the two tasks you created, Document hardware and Document software, to the single task, Detail current status, and the Start date is June 2, 2014, instead of September 1. The most significant addition to the file is that now the tasks are linked. Notice that the Start date for each task is the next working day after the Finish date of the previous task.

You will learn about linking tasks, customizing views, and displaying and hiding columns as you work with Project 2010.

Saving a Project with a New Name

When changes are made to a project, you need to determine whether you want to save the updates to the existing project file or if you want to create a new project file with a new project name. Usually, updates to an existing project file are saved to the existing project name by clicking the Save button on the Quick Access toolbar. Throughout this book, however, you'll be asked to open a partially completed project file and then to save the changes that you made to the project with a new name. This keeps your Data Files in their original state in case you want to repeat a tutorial.

REFERENCE

Saving a Project with a New Name

- Click the File tab on the Ribbon, and then click Save As on the navigation bar.
- Navigate to the drive and folder where you want to save the file.
- In the File name box, type the filename.
- Click the Save button (or press the Enter key).

You'll save the AV-1 project file with the name NewAV-1.

TIP

Always check with your instructor regarding how to name files and how to submit files.

To save the project file with a new name:

1. Click the **File** tab on the Ribbon, and then click **Save As** on the navigation bar. The Save As dialog box opens.

2. Navigate to the **Project1\Tutorial** folder included with your Data Files, and then, in the File name box, type **NewAV-1**.

3. Click the **Save** button in the Save As dialog box. The dialog box closes and the file is saved with the new filename, as indicated in the title bar.

INSIGHT

Creating New Projects from Existing Projects

Many projects have similar characteristics. If you work in a business where others are using Project 2010, you might find that many of the tasks and resources are similar. Rather than always starting from scratch, you can use an existing file as the basis for your new project, and then save the project with a new name. In addition, you can use an existing template. Templates are project files that have been designed for a specific purpose, such as planning a trade show, that you can customize for your needs. Many Project templates are created by professionals for sale or distribution. Project template files have .mpt filename extensions. To access a template, click the File tab on the Ribbon, then click New on the navigation bar. The Available Templates pane offers many options. You can click New from existing project, New from Excel workbook, or New from SharePoint task list. You can also create a project based on a template from Microsoft Office Online, a Web site that provides templates for Microsoft Office products. To access these online templates, click one of the options in the Office.com Templates section. Templates are divided into Plans, Planners, Schedules, and More categories. After clicking a selection, a browser window opens, displaying the Available Templates page on Office.com. Type "project" in the Search box to the right of Office.com Templates, then click the Start searching button. A list of templates related to the word "project" appears. The list of results includes templates for other Microsoft Office applications in addition to Project 2010, but several for Project 2010 appear near the top of the list.

Working in Different Views

Project 2010 provides many different views of a project that support the informational needs of different users and purposes. Some views (such as the chart views) present a broad look at the entire project, others (such as the sheet views) present information in a grid of columns and rows, and still others (such as the form views) focus on specific pieces of information about each task. Three major categories of views are available.

- **Chart or Graphic**—A chart or graphical representation of data using bars, boxes, lines, and images.
- **Sheet or Table**—A spreadsheet-like representation of data in which each task is displayed as a new row and each piece of information (field) about the task is represented by a column. Various tables are applied to a sheet to display different fields.
- **Form**—A specific view of many pieces of information (fields) of *one task*. Forms are used to focus on the details of one task.

Views are further differentiated according to the type of data that they analyze (task or resource information). Because tasks and their corresponding durations are the first pieces of data entered into a project, you will focus on the task views now. Later, when resources and their corresponding costs are entered, you will explore resource views.

Figure 1-21 describes some of the views within each category that Project 2010 provides to help you display the task information that you need.

Figure 1-21	Common project views (views for tasks)

Category	View	Purpose
Chart or Graphic	Gantt Chart	Shows each task as a horizontal bar, the length and position of which correspond to a timescale at the top of the chart
	Network Diagram	Shows each task as a box, with linking lines drawn between related tasks to emphasize task sequence as well as the critical path
	Calendar	Shows the tasks as bars on a typical desk calendar in a month-at-a-time format
Task Sheet or Table	Entry Table	Columns are Task Mode, Task Name, Duration, Start (date), Finish (date), Predecessors, and Resource Names; the default Gantt Chart view displays the Task Sheet with the Entry Table on the left
	Cost Table	Contains task cost information, much of which is calculated when resources are assigned
	Schedule Table	Presents dates and whether the task is on the critical path
	Summary Table	Presents what percentage of the task's duration, costs, and assigned hours have been completed
	Tracking Table	Presents actual and remaining durations and costs
	Variance Table	Compares actual Start and Finish baseline dates to the dates that the tasks would be completed had the project been executed according to the original plan
	Work Table	Compares actual and remaining work to be completed to baseline measurements; baseline work is the amount of work (number of hours) required to finish a task if the task is executed according to the original plan
Form	Task Details Form	Provides all of the information about a single task in one window
	Task Name Form	Provides limited information about a single task: task name, resources, and predecessors
Combination	Gantt Chart (top) Task Name Form (bottom)	Provides an overview of many tasks of the project at the top of the screen, and displays the details of the current task at the bottom; usually a table or chart view on the top and a form view on the bottom of the screen; a common combination view places the Gantt Chart view on the top and the Task Name Form on the bottom

As you work with Project 2010, you will find that you need to see the information using different views. Don't become overwhelmed by trying to learn all of the project views now. As you build your project and your information needs grow, studying these views will be more natural and meaningful. Two key points to remember are that several views are available, and changes made in one view of the project are automatically updated and displayed in all other views. You can easily access common views by clicking their respective buttons in the View Bar or in the Task Views group on the View tab on the Ribbon.

To change the view and update task information:

▶ 1. Click the **View** tab on the Ribbon, and then, in the Task Views group, click the **Calendar** button ▦. The project is now displayed as a desk calendar in a month-at-a-time format. See Figure 1-22.

Each task is displayed on the calendar as a horizontal bar. The length of each bar represents the duration of the task, placed at the appropriate Start and Finish dates. The task name and duration appear within the bar. The Calendar Tools Format tab is available on the Ribbon. When you need to make changes to tasks in Calendar view, you open the Task Information dialog box for that task. Double-clicking the task to display the Task Information dialog box is one way to edit a task in almost any view.

Figure 1-22   Calendar view

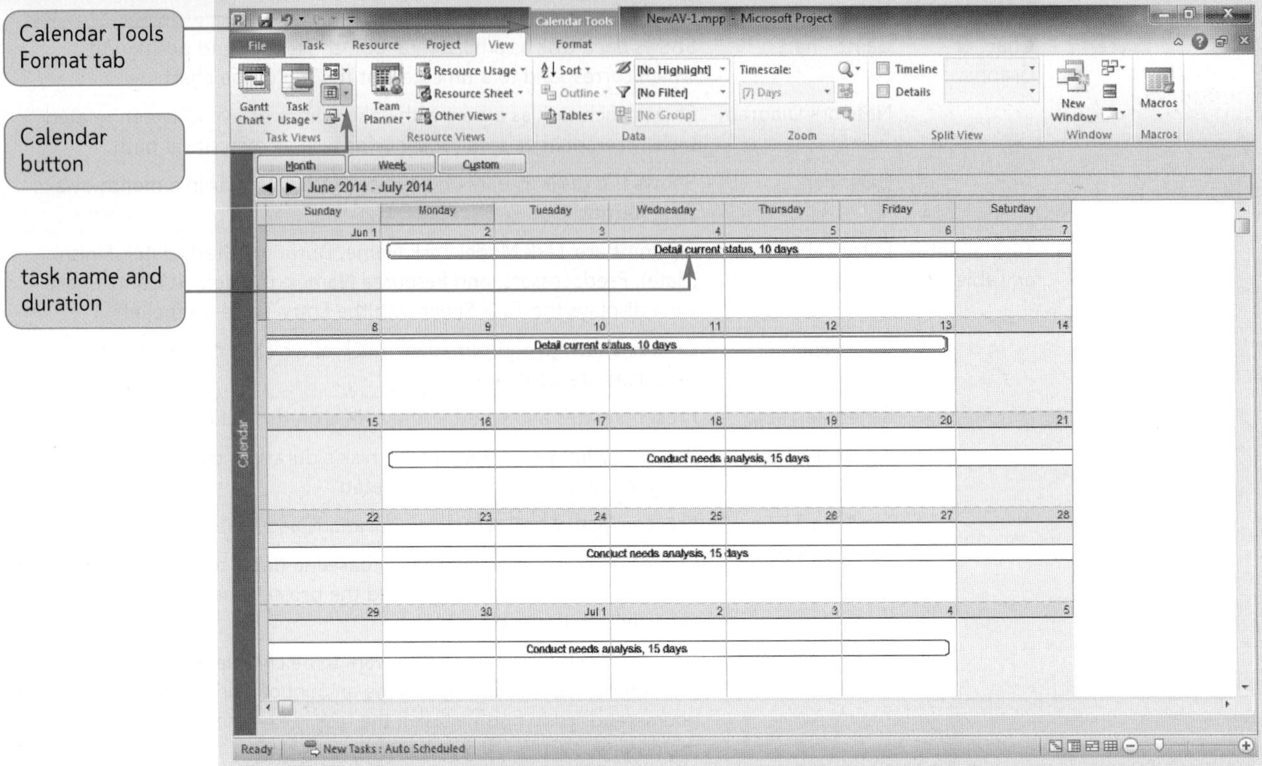

Calendar Tools Format tab

Calendar button

task name and duration

2. Double-click the **Detail current status, 10 days** bar in either week to open the Task Information dialog box, and then click the **General tab** if it is not already selected. See Figure 1-23.

Figure 1-23   Task Information dialog box

General tab

task name

Duration box

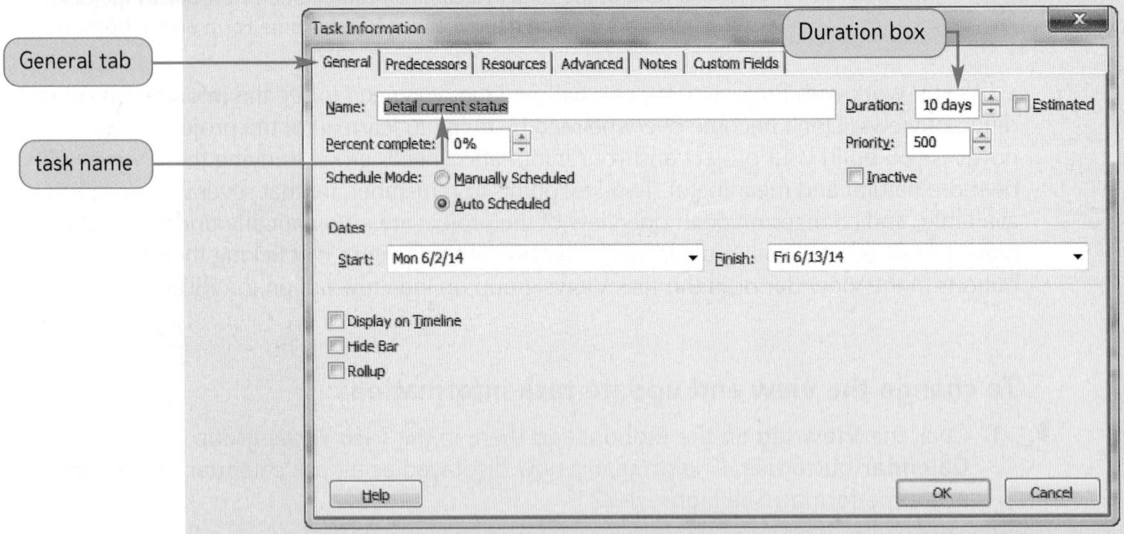

3. In the Duration box, double-click **10**, type **5**, and then click the **OK** button. The change in duration from 10 days to 5 days is immediately updated in Calendar view (the current view) and in all other views.

4. In the Task Views group on the View tab, click the **Network Diagram** button 🔲. The project is now displayed as a series of boxes connected by lines, as shown in Figure 1-24.

| Figure 1-24 | Network Diagram view |

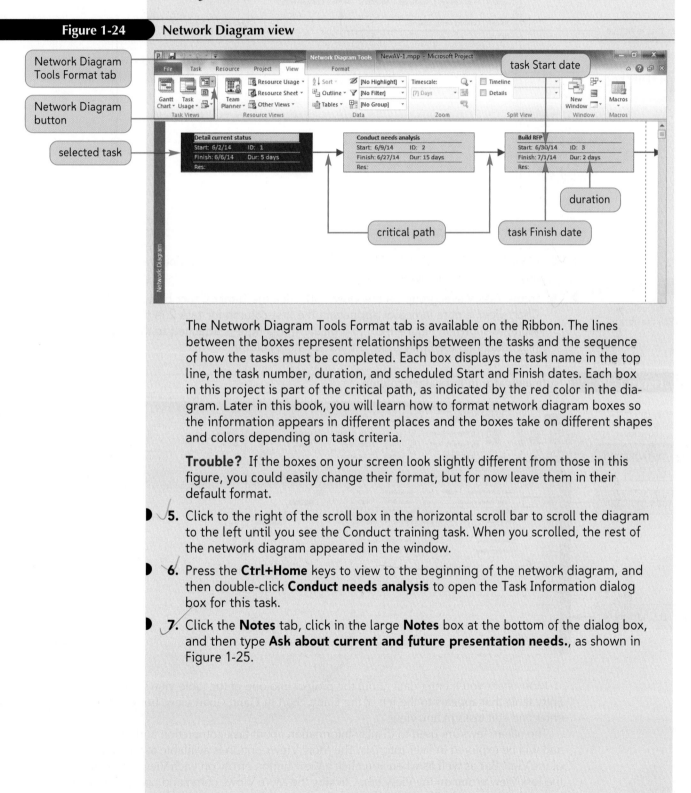

The Network Diagram Tools Format tab is available on the Ribbon. The lines between the boxes represent relationships between the tasks and the sequence of how the tasks must be completed. Each box displays the task name in the top line, the task number, duration, and scheduled Start and Finish dates. Each box in this project is part of the critical path, as indicated by the red color in the diagram. Later in this book, you will learn how to format network diagram boxes so the information appears in different places and the boxes take on different shapes and colors depending on task criteria.

Trouble? If the boxes on your screen look slightly different from those in this figure, you could easily change their format, but for now leave them in their default format.

5. Click to the right of the scroll box in the horizontal scroll bar to scroll the diagram to the left until you see the Conduct training task. When you scrolled, the rest of the network diagram appeared in the window.

6. Press the **Ctrl+Home** keys to view to the beginning of the network diagram, and then double-click **Conduct needs analysis** to open the Task Information dialog box for this task.

7. Click the **Notes** tab, click in the large **Notes** box at the bottom of the dialog box, and then type **Ask about current and future presentation needs.**, as shown in Figure 1-25.

Figure 1-25   Notes tab in Task Information dialog box

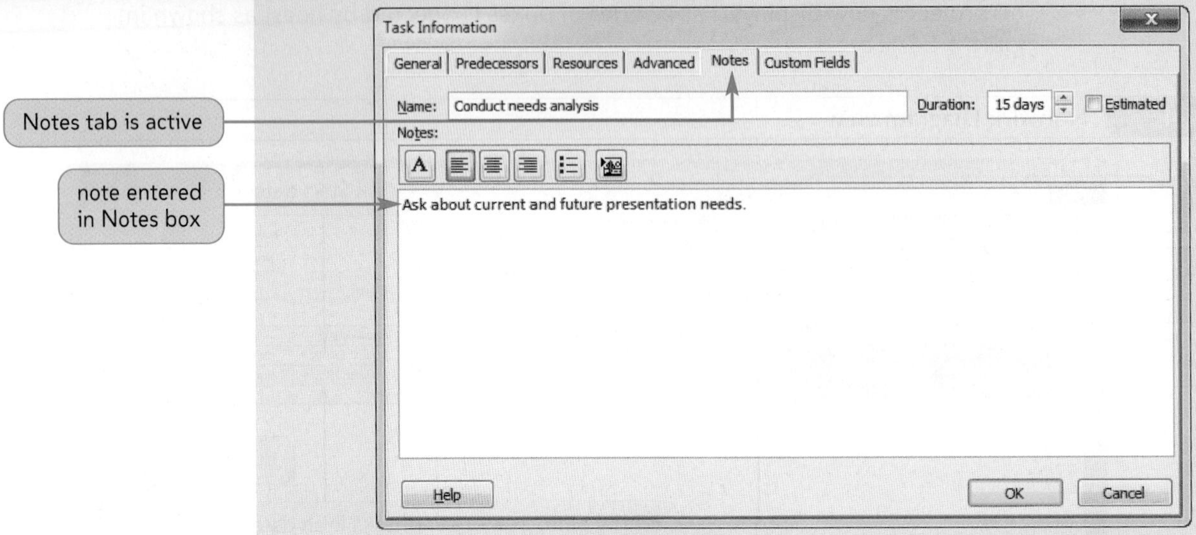

Notes tab is active

note entered
in Notes box

▶ ✓**8.** Click the **OK** button. The dialog box closes. The box for task 2 does not appear any different in the network diagram.

▶ ✓**9.** In the Task Views group on the Views tab, click the **Gantt Chart** button. In Gantt Chart view, a note indicator appears in the first column for task 2 in the Entry table, as shown in Figure 1-26, to indicate that a note is attached to this task. The first column in the Entry table is the Indicators column.

TIP

To display the note, you double-click the note indicator.

Figure 1-26   Note indicator in Indicators column

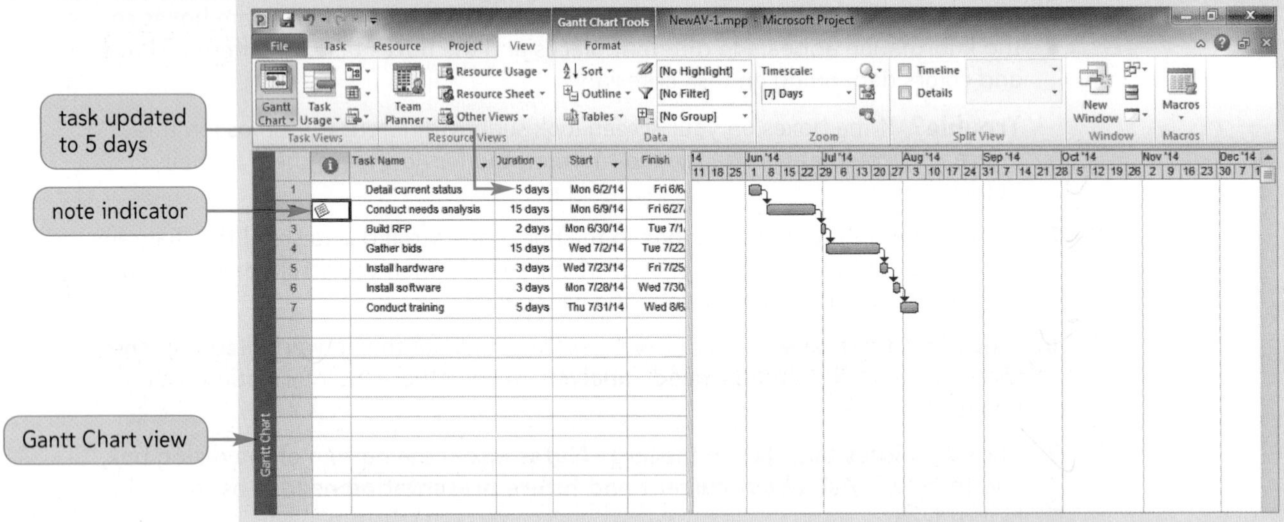

task updated
to 5 days

note indicator

Gantt Chart view

Most often, you'll enter data about the project into one of the table views, such as the Entry table that appears to the left of the Gantt chart in Gantt Chart view, but you can enter and edit tasks in any view.

The other views are used to display information about task completion and resources and will be explored in later tutorials. The More Views option is available at the bottom of the View Bar as well as when you click a View button arrow on each View button in the Task View group on the View tab. Clicking the More Views command opens the More Views dialog box that lists all the views—the commonly used views with a corresponding button in the Task Views group on the View tab and on the View Bar as well as the less commonly used views. The current view is highlighted in the More Views dialog box.

To see additional views:

1. In the Entry table, click anywhere in **row 4** (the Gather bids task), and then, in the Task Views group on the View tab, click the **Gantt Chart** button arrow. When you click a task row, you make that task the current task. Clicking the Gantt Chart button arrow displays a menu of options.

2. Click **More Views** on the menu. The More Views dialog box opens, listing all of the available views, with Gantt Chart selected because that is the current view.

3. Scroll the list, and then double-click **Relationship Diagram**. The project appears in Relationship Diagram view. You use this view when you want to focus on the relationships between tasks. **Relationship Diagram** view shows the predecessor and successor for the selected task. Notice task 4 is selected and appears in the middle of the window. See Figure 1-27.

| Figure 1-27 | Relationship Diagram view |

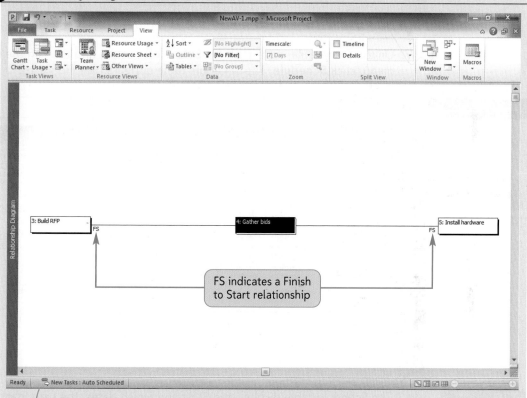

4. Click to the left of the scroll box in the horizontal scroll bar. The diagram scrolls to the previous task and task 3 is now selected in the center of the window.

5. Click to the right of the scroll box in the horizontal scroll bar to position the Relationship Diagram on the fourth task again, and then, in the Task Views group, click the **Gantt Chart** button. The project appears in Gantt Chart view with task 4 selected.

   The default table in Gantt Chart view is the Entry table. You can change this to display additional columns.

6. Drag the **split bar** to the right until you can see all of the columns through Resource Names in the Entry Table and including the *Add New Column* column, as shown in Figure 1-28. The square at the top left of the table (above the row numbers and to the left of the column names) is the Select All button.

Figure 1-28   Entry table

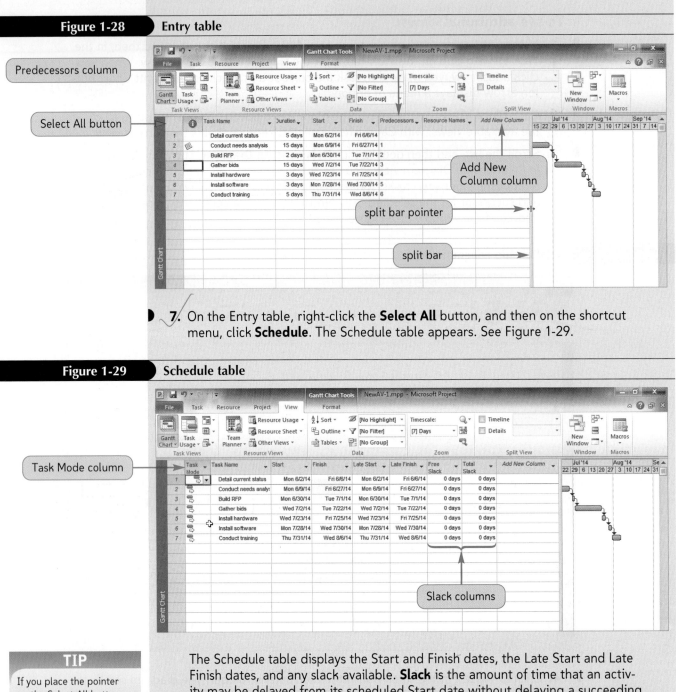

Predecessors column

Select All button

Add New Column column

split bar pointer

split bar

▶ **7.** On the Entry table, right-click the **Select All** button, and then on the shortcut menu, click **Schedule**. The Schedule table appears. See Figure 1-29.

Figure 1-29   Schedule table

Task Mode column

Slack columns

TIP

If you place the pointer on the Select All button, a ScreenTip appears that tells you the table name and the current view.

The Schedule table displays the Start and Finish dates, the Late Start and Late Finish dates, and any slack available. **Slack** is the amount of time that an activity may be delayed from its scheduled Start date without delaying a succeeding activity or the entire project. All of the tasks in this file are part of the critical path and are completed in sequence, so there is no slack. If there were slack, alternate dates would appear in the Late Start and Late Finish columns, indicating the latest that the task could start or finish if you used all of the slack. The Schedule table also includes the Task Mode column, showing if a task is automatically or manually scheduled. The Schedule table is important because it helps you see the relationship that exists between tasks, and how changing one date can impact all the other components in the project. It also provides you with information regarding what slack is available if a project task does slip.

▶ **8.** On the Schedule table, right-click the **Select All** button, and then on the shortcut menu, click **Entry**. The Entry table appears again.

As you complete a project plan, assign resources, and start tracking an actual project, the rest of the tables will become more useful.

Splitting the Window

TIP

To change the view displayed in either half of the split window, click in the part of the window you want to change and then click the appropriate button in the Task Views group on the View tab.

Sometimes it is helpful to use more than one view at a time so that you can see information about many tasks in one area and details about the current task in another. This type of arrangement is called a **split window**. When you split the window, the default is to display the tasks in the current view in the top part of a split window, and the Task Form view in the bottom part. **Task Form view** is intended to display detailed information about one task at a time. You can add, delete, or edit information within the form just as you can in the Entry table or the Task Information dialog box. The Task Form consists of rows and columns where information, such as Task Resources and Task Predecessors, is displayed. In addition to the task form, many types of forms are available, each focusing on different details of the project. Changes made in the Task Form view, or any view, are simultaneously updated in all of the other views. When changes are made to a project, all affected task and resource fields are highlighted. This way, you can see how your change affects the dates of successor tasks.

To work with split views and Task Form view:

1. Drag the **split bar** so that Predecessors is the last visible column in the Entry table.

2. Make sure **task 4** is the current task, and then, in the Split View group on the View tab, click the **Details** check box. Your screen should look like Figure 1-30. The tasks are displayed in the Gantt Chart view on top, and the information for task 4 is displayed in Task Form view on the bottom. The form currently displays the resource information for the selected task on the left and the predecessor information for the selected task on the right.

Figure 1-30   Split view

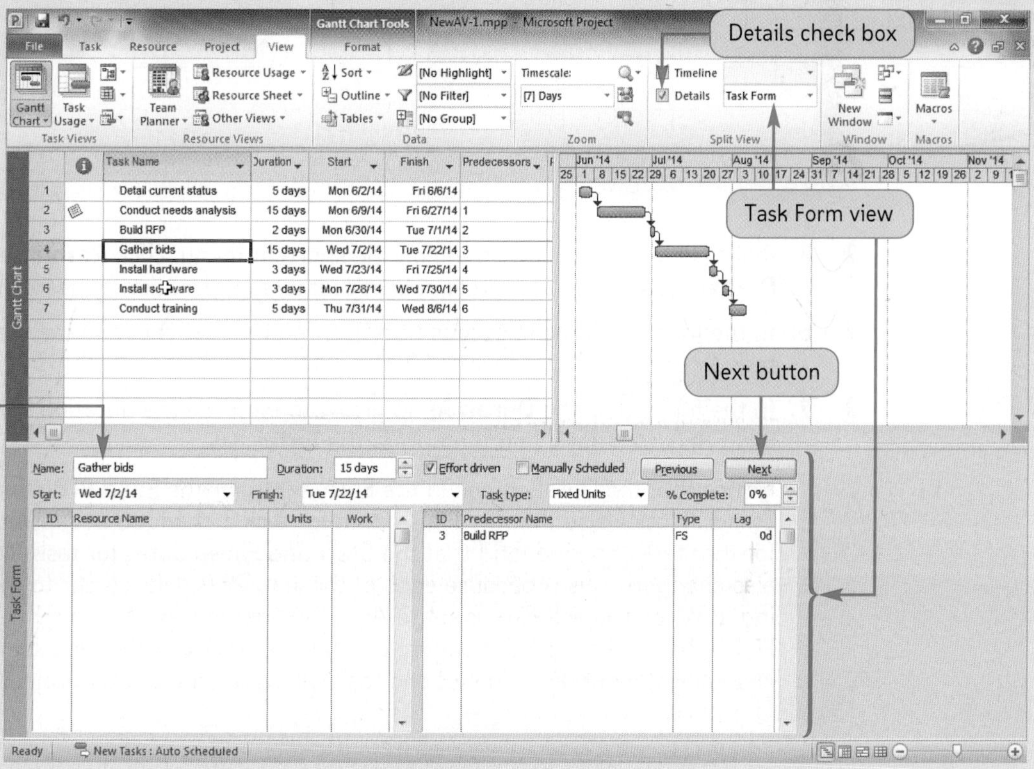

3. In the form, click the **Next** button to move to the task form for task 5, and then click the **Next** button again to display task 6 in the form.

Notice that as you move from task to task in the form, the same task is selected in the Entry table and you are able to view the details for the selected task in the form.

4. Right-click anywhere on the form, and then on the shortcut menu, click **Predecessors & Successors**. Now the form displays the task that comes before the sixth task on the left and task that follows the sixth task on the right, as shown in Figure 1-31.

Figure 1-31 **Task form displaying predecessor and successor information**

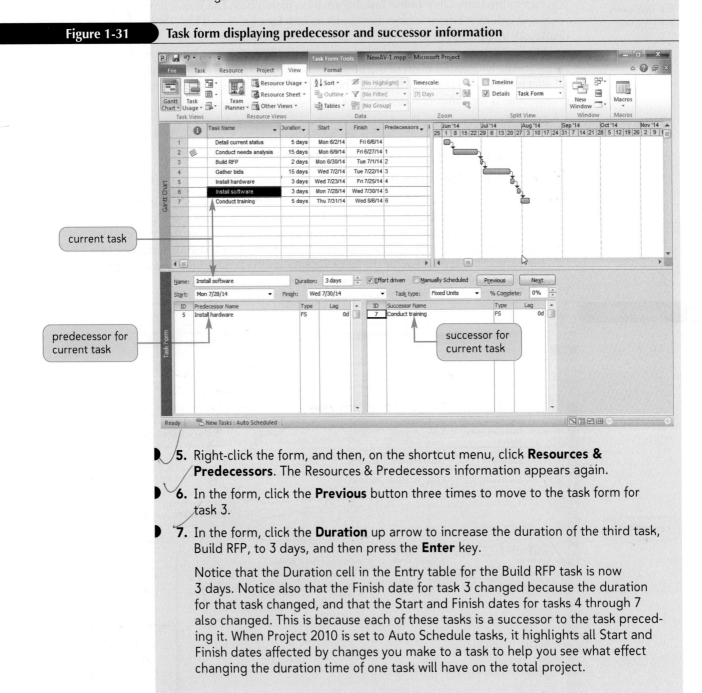

5. Right-click the form, and then, on the shortcut menu, click **Resources & Predecessors**. The Resources & Predecessors information appears again.

6. In the form, click the **Previous** button three times to move to the task form for task 3.

7. In the form, click the **Duration** up arrow to increase the duration of the third task, Build RFP, to 3 days, and then press the **Enter** key.

Notice that the Duration cell in the Entry table for the Build RFP task is now 3 days. Notice also that the Finish date for task 3 changed because the duration for that task changed, and that the Start and Finish dates for tasks 4 through 7 also changed. This is because each of these tasks is a successor to the task preceding it. When Project 2010 is set to Auto Schedule tasks, it highlights all Start and Finish dates affected by changes you make to a task to help you see what effect changing the duration time of one task will have on the total project.

TIP

You can also remove the split window by placing the pointer on the horizontal split bar, and then double-clicking.

8. In the Split View group on the View tab, click the **Details** check box to remove the check mark. The form closes, and you return to Gantt Chart view.

9. Click the **Save** button 🔲 on the Quick Access toolbar to save your work.

Being able to move quickly from one view to the next is a critical Project 2010 skill. Over time, you'll learn many other views. For now, however, you need to know only that many views exist and how to move among them. The default Gantt Chart view with the Entry table on the left is the primary view in which you enter project information, so that's the one that you need to focus on as you begin to build a project.

Zooming the Timescale

As your project grows, it gets difficult to see all tasks in the chart views. You'll need to know how to change the timescale to magnify and reduce the size of the project on the screen. In Gantt Chart view, the timescale determines the length of the bar. Therefore, if the timescale is measured in hours, then the bar for a task that lasts 8 hours will be very long. If the timescale is measured in days, however, then the bar will be quite short.

Zooming In and Zooming Out

Changing the magnification of a project is called **zooming in** and **zooming out**. The easiest way to adjust the Gantt chart timescale to see more or less of the project at one time is to use the Zoom In and Zoom Out buttons in the Zoom group on the View tab. Clicking the Zoom In button displays smaller units of measure on the Gantt chart timescale (such as days instead of weeks), which in turn expands the size of each bar. You can also use the Zoom Slider to dynamically change the zoom level, or you can click the Zoom Out and Zoom In buttons on the status bar.

To zoom in on the Gantt chart:

1. Drag the **split bar** to the left to position it to the right of the Duration column in the Entry table. Notice that the major timescale shows months and the minor timescale shows the first day of each week.

2. In the Zoom group on the View tab, click the **Zoom** button 🔍▾, and then click **Zoom In**. The Gantt chart zooms in so the bars in the chart are bigger, and the minor timescale changes to display many more days in the month. Notice also that the Timescale list box in the Zoom group changed from [7] days to [3] days.

3. On the status bar, click the **Zoom In** button ⊕ as many times as necessary until the scale does not change anymore, observing how the major and minor timescales change as you click. Each time you click the Zoom In button, the timescale shows smaller and smaller units of measure until it cannot zoom any more.

4. In the Zoom group on the View tab, click the **Timescale arrow**, and then click **Quarter Days**. The timescale displays days as the major scale and 6-hour intervals as the minor scale.

5. In the Zoom group, click the **Zoom Selected Tasks** button 🔍. You see the bar for Build RFP, task 4. The timescale displays days as the major scale and 2-hour intervals as the minor scale. Depending on the resolution of your screen, these values may be different. See Figure 1-32.

Figure 1-32   Zooming in on the Gantt chart view

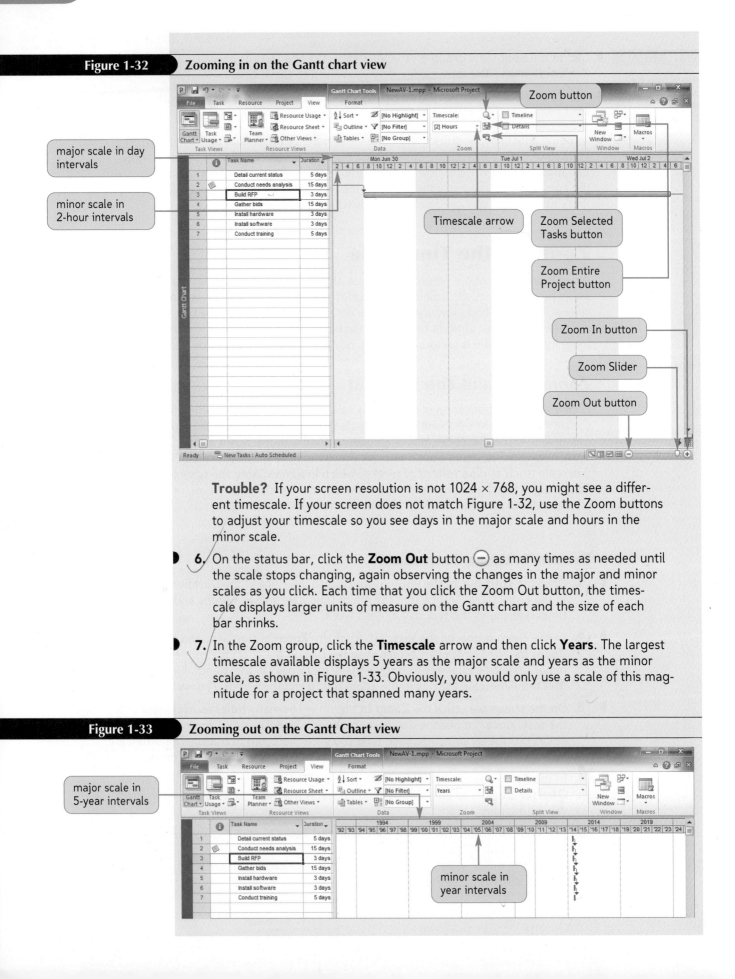

major scale in day intervals

minor scale in 2-hour intervals

Zoom button

Timescale arrow

Zoom Selected Tasks button

Zoom Entire Project button

Zoom In button

Zoom Slider

Zoom Out button

Trouble? If your screen resolution is not 1024 × 768, you might see a different timescale. If your screen does not match Figure 1-32, use the Zoom buttons to adjust your timescale so you see days in the major scale and hours in the minor scale.

6. On the status bar, click the **Zoom Out** button ⊖ as many times as needed until the scale stops changing, again observing the changes in the major and minor scales as you click. Each time that you click the Zoom Out button, the timescale displays larger units of measure on the Gantt chart and the size of each bar shrinks.

7. In the Zoom group, click the **Timescale** arrow and then click **Years**. The largest timescale available displays 5 years as the major scale and years as the minor scale, as shown in Figure 1-33. Obviously, you would only use a scale of this magnitude for a project that spanned many years.

Figure 1-33   Zooming out on the Gantt Chart view

major scale in 5-year intervals

minor scale in year intervals

You can also zoom in and out of the Network Diagram and Calendar views. While neither of these views displays a timescale, the overall effect of zooming is the same. Zooming in shows fewer tasks or days, allowing you to see the details for what *is* displayed more clearly, and zooming out shows more tasks or days with fewer details.

To zoom in and out of the Network Diagram and Calendar views:

1. In the Task Views group on the View tab, click the **Network Diagram** button, and then, on the status bar, click the **Zoom In** button ⊕ three times. Zooming in on the Network Diagram view increases the size of the boxes, thereby making the text in each box easier to read.

2. On the status bar, click the **Zoom Out** button ⊖ as many times as needed to show dotted lines intersecting on the screen. The dotted lines indicate where page breaks will occur if the network diagram is printed.

   Your screen should look similar to Figure 1-34. Zooming out in Network Diagram view decreases the size of the boxes, thereby allowing more boxes to appear on the screen at one time.

Figure 1-34	Zooming out on the Network Diagram view

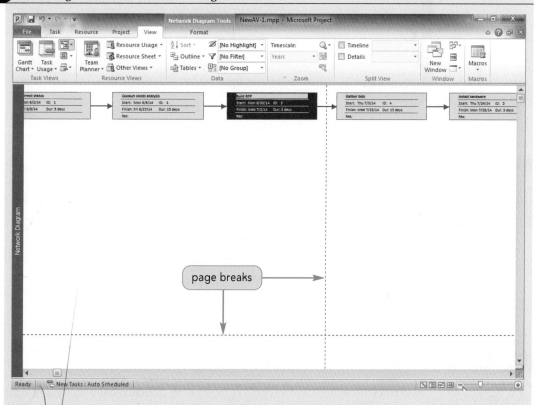

3. In the Task Views group on the View tab, click the **Calendar** button. You can see six weeks on the screen. (You might only see the top half of the last week.)

4. On the status bar, click the **Zoom In** button ⊕ as many times as necessary so your screen displays only three weeks, as shown in Figure 1-35. Zooming in on the Calendar view increases the size of the daily squares, thereby allowing you to see more information in each day.

| Figure 1-35 | Zooming in on the Calendar view |

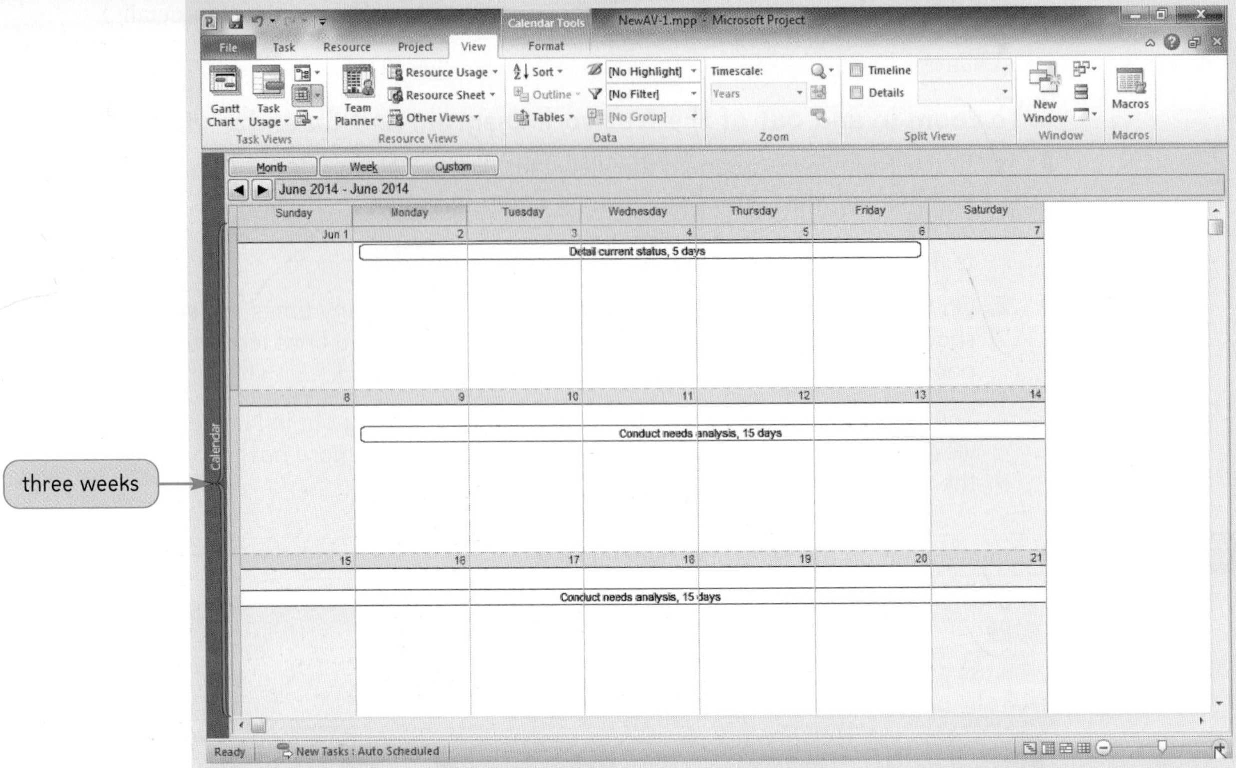

three weeks

5. In the Zoom group on the View tab, click the **Zoom** button arrow, and then click **Zoom**. The Zoom dialog box opens.

6. Select **3** in the Number of weeks box, type **6**, and then click **OK**. Zooming out on the calendar decreases the size of the boxes, thereby allowing more days to be displayed on the screen at one time. You should see six weeks on your screen again.

7. In the Task Views group on the View tab, click the **Gantt Chart** button to return to Gantt Chart view.

8. Zoom in as necessary to display spelled-out months as the major scale and date numbers as the minor scale.

> **TIP**
>
> Select the number in the number of weeks box if it differs from 3, and type 6.

Working in the Timescale Dialog Box

> **TIP**
>
> The Timescale dialog box also offers options to change the alignment, tick lines, and nonworking times. You will explore these later in the book.

If the existing timescale does not meet your needs, you can modify it to represent a custom unit of time and custom label. For example, you might want one timescale to display a two-week increment and a second timescale to display a daily increment with the format 1/30/14, 1/31/14, 2/1/14, and so on. Or you might want to display a third time-scale. The Timescale dialog box allows you to customize the timescale in any timephased view. **Timephased** views are the Calendar, Gantt, or any view that shows information distributed over time. The ViewPoint Partners project will span several months. Emily wants to modify the timescale so that she can show Sidney tasks as they span the entire project, and then she wants to be able to show others working on the project tasks during specific weeks.

To modify the timescale:

TIP

To quickly see a task in the Gantt chart, click the task you want to scroll to in the Entry table, click the Task tab on the Ribbon, and then, in the Editing group, click the Scroll to Task button.

1. Click **Detail current status** (task 1), press **Alt+Home** to return to the beginning of the project, and then, on the status bar, drag the **Zoom slider** to show Weeks (May 25, '14; June 8, '14 and so forth) on the major scale of the timescale.

2. Double-click anywhere on the timescale to open the Timescale dialog box with the Middle Tier tab selected, as shown in Figure 1-36.

Units specify the time units, such as days, weeks, or months. Label specifies the display format to show the time unit. Count specifies the frequency of unit labels for the given units on the timescale tier. The default is to display only two timescales, or tiers. The Middle Tier tab corresponds to the top scale currently displayed in Gantt Chart view. You can also add a third tier, the Top Tier, if desired, but most users find that two tiers meet their needs.

Figure 1-36 | Timescale dialog box – Middle Tier

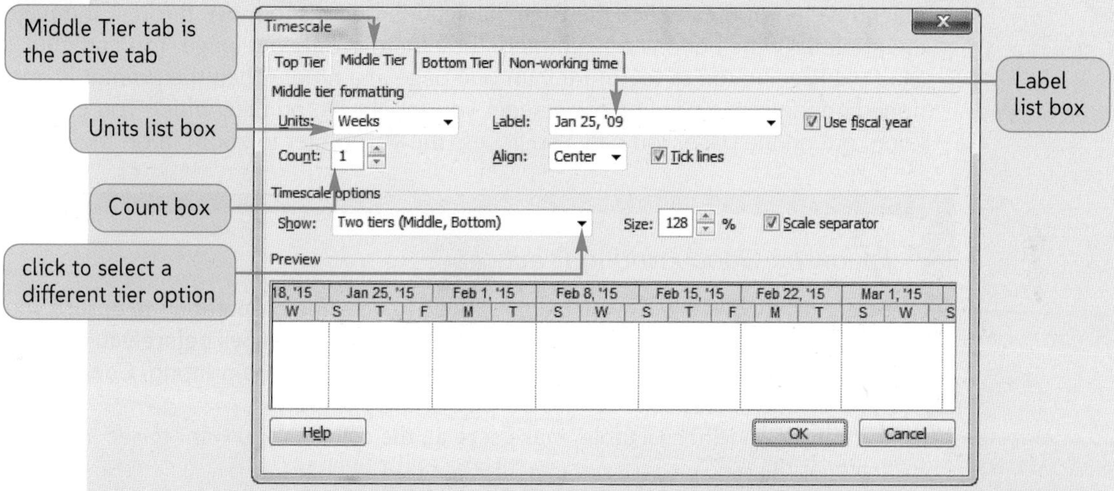

3. Click the **Count** up arrow to change it to **7**, click the **Units** arrow, click **Days**, click the **Label** arrow, and then click **Wed Jan 28** if it is not already displayed. The changes are reflected in the Preview box at the bottom of the dialog box.

4. Click the **Bottom Tier** tab, click the **Count** down arrow as needed to change it to **1**, click the **Label** arrow, and then click **Su, Mo, Tu.** The change is shown in the Preview box. See Figure 1-37.

Figure 1-37 | Changing the timescale – Bottom Tier

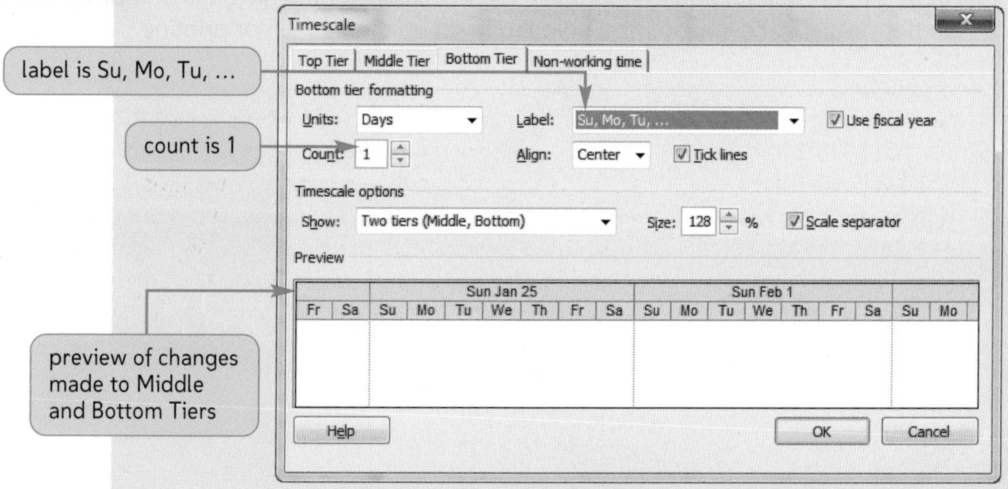

5. Click the **OK** button. You see the timescale changes in the Gantt chart.

Printing a View

TIP

You will see the Gantt chart, or any view in the Backstage Preview pane, in color, even if your computer is attached to a black and white printer.

Almost every view of a project can be printed. The chart views of a project can be quite large, so printing involves several extra considerations, the most important of which is to make sure that you preview the printout on the screen before you print it in order to check the magnification and total number of pages.

Printing is managed through Backstage view. When you view a Gantt chart in the Preview pane, you will notice a few elements. The **legend** appears in the bottom portion of each page to provide information about the bars. By default, the project title and today's date appear to the left of the legend. The default footer appears with the word "Page" and the current page number centered at the bottom of the page. The status bar indicates the number of pages that will print with the Gantt chart at the current level of magnification. You can click the Page Navigation buttons to move through the pages of the printout. If the buttons are dimmed, then there is only one page. You can click the Multiple Page button to see more than one page at a time. When the pointer is positioned on top of the page on the screen, you see the ⊖ pointer, which you can use to zoom out on the page. You can also access the ⊕ pointer to zoom in on the page.

INSIGHT

Following Good Printing Practices

Before printing in any view, it's a good idea to do some preparation to ensure your printed copy meets your expectations. Follow these guidelines before you click Print:

- Set an appropriate magnification level in the view you are printing. Consider zooming out on the timescale to reduce the size of the printout.
- If the view includes a table, make sure all the columns you want to see in the printout are visible.
- Use the Backstage view Preview feature to view each page layout and to check the total number of pages.
- Open the Page Setup dialog box to make changes to the orientation, margins, header, footer, legend, and other printing options.

Emily knows that meetings take place out of the office and Sidney may want to show an overview of the project to contractors hired to work on the installation. Sidney does not travel with a laptop computer, therefore, in some meetings, it will be easier for Sidney to present printouts rather than to carry a copy of the file on a USB drive and ask to borrow a local computer. You help Emily set up the project for printing.

To print the project in Gantt Chart view:

▶ 1. Click the **File** tab, and then click **Print** on the navigation bar. The project appears in the Preview pane, as shown in Figure 1-38.

Figure 1-38   **Gantt chart in Preview pane**

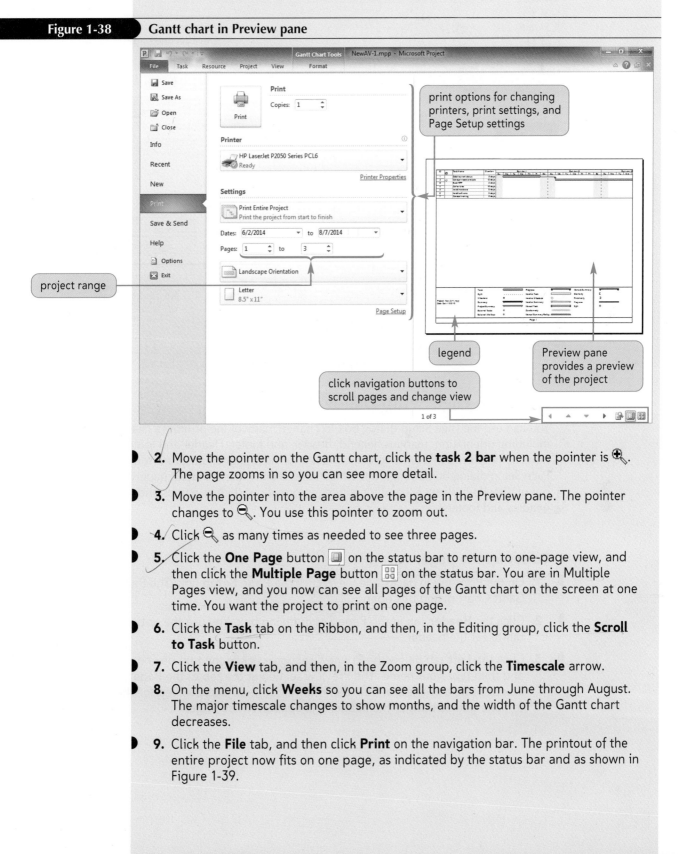

project range

print options for changing printers, print settings, and Page Setup settings

legend

Preview pane provides a preview of the project

click navigation buttons to scroll pages and change view

1 of 3

▶ 2. Move the pointer on the Gantt chart, click the **task 2 bar** when the pointer is 🔍. The page zooms in so you can see more detail.

▶ 3. Move the pointer into the area above the page in the Preview pane. The pointer changes to 🔍. You use this pointer to zoom out.

▶ 4. Click 🔍 as many times as needed to see three pages.

▶ 5. Click the **One Page** button 🔲 on the status bar to return to one-page view, and then click the **Multiple Page** button 🔳 on the status bar. You are in Multiple Pages view, and you now can see all pages of the Gantt chart on the screen at one time. You want the project to print on one page.

▶ 6. Click the **Task** tab on the Ribbon, and then, in the Editing group, click the **Scroll to Task** button.

▶ 7. Click the **View** tab, and then, in the Zoom group, click the **Timescale** arrow.

▶ 8. On the menu, click **Weeks** so you can see all the bars from June through August. The major timescale changes to show months, and the width of the Gantt chart decreases.

▶ 9. Click the **File** tab, and then click **Print** on the navigation bar. The printout of the entire project now fits on one page, as indicated by the status bar and as shown in Figure 1-39.

Figure 1-39 **Gantt chart zoomed to print on one page**

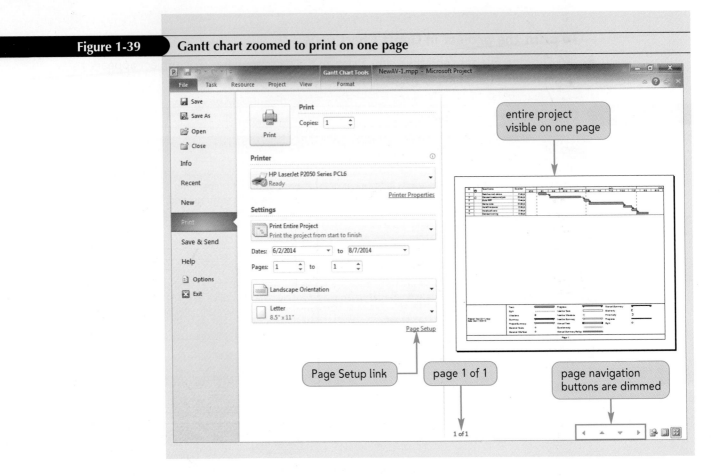

Using the Page Setup Dialog Box

You can use the Page Setup dialog box to change many of the printout's characteristics, including orientation, margins, legend, header, and footer. Header and footer information can be placed in a left-aligned, centered, or right-aligned position. You access the Page Setup dialog box through Backstage view. Sidney insists that all paperwork coming out of ViewPoint Partners carry identifying information, such as names and dates in the headers and footers.

To set up the page:

1. On the Print tab in Backstage view, click the **Page Setup** link. The Page Setup – Gantt Chart dialog box opens.

2. Click the **Header** tab in the Page Setup dialog box. You use the options on this tab to set the header.

3. Click the **Left** tab below the Preview section, click in the text box on the Left tab, and then type your name. The Preview section at the top of the Page Setup dialog box displays a preview of how the information that you specified for the left, center, or right portions of the header will appear on the page.

4. Click the **Legend** tab in the Page Setup dialog box, and then, under the Preview section, click the **Left** tab. The Legend tab allows you to set the information that will appear to the left of the legend. The ampersand (&) indicates that the text that follows is a code. The &[File] code represents the actual filename as shown in the preview section of the Page Setup dialog box. If you change the filename, this code will automatically change the filename on the printout. The &[Date] code will display the current date. You can also click one of the buttons below the box where the text appears to insert a code automatically.

5. Double-click the word **Project** to select it, and then type **Name of File**. Your dialog box should look like Figure 1-40.

Figure 1-40   Page Setup – Gantt Chart dialog box

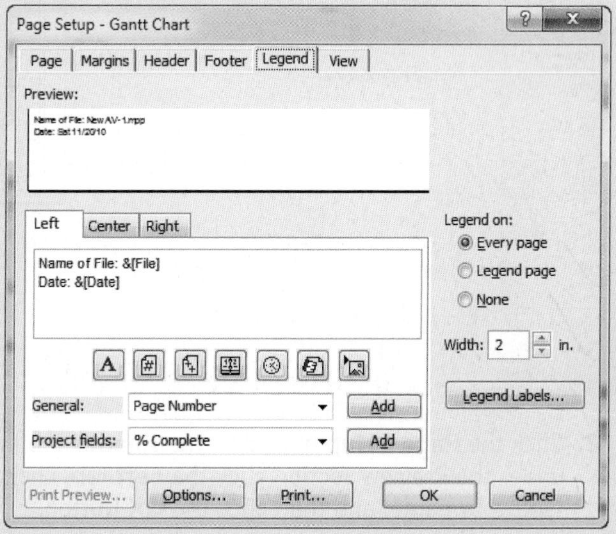

---

6. Click the **OK** button to accept the changes and close the dialog box. Notice your name appears left-aligned in the Header and the label Name of File appears to the left of the filename in the legend.

7. Save your file.

8. Submit the finished project to your instructor, either in printed or electronic form, as requested.

Next, you need to review how to print a page in Calendar and Network Diagram views. You have to set up the header, margins, footer, and legends for each view that you print.

To print a page in Calendar and Network Diagram views:

1. Click the **View** tab, click the **Calendar** button in the Task Views group, click the **File** tab, and then click **Print** on the navigation bar. The Calendar view of the project appears in the Preview pane of Backstage view. See Figure 1-41.

| Figure 1-41 | Printing the Calendar view |

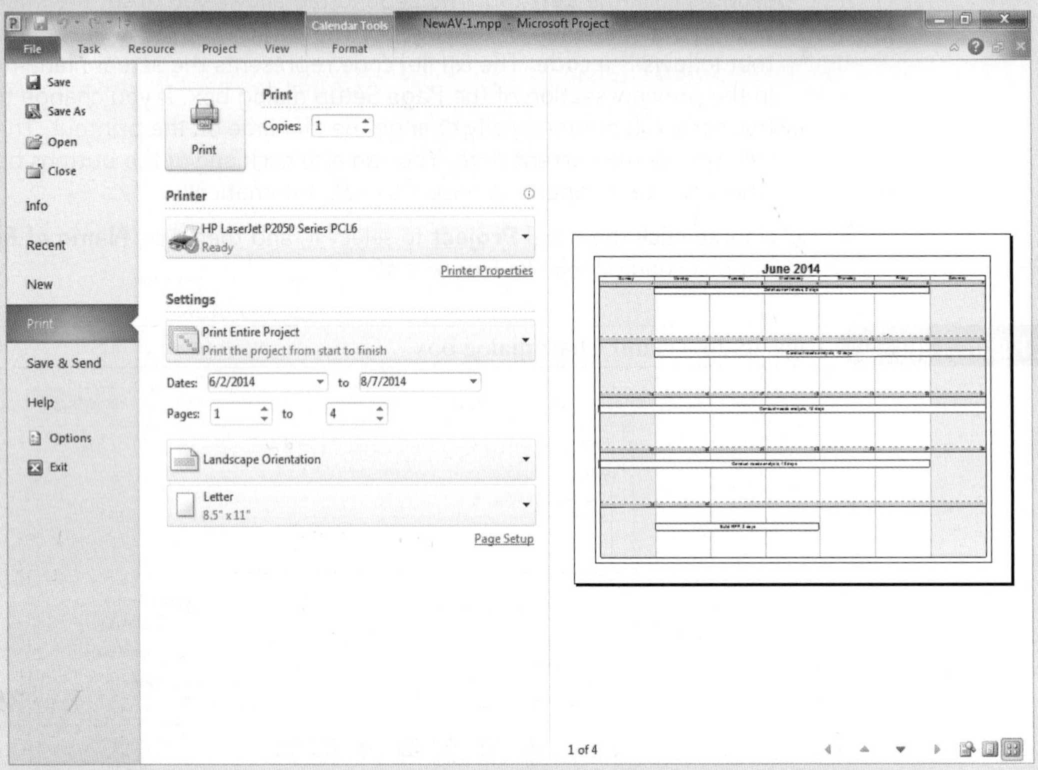

2. Click the **Page Setup** link, click the **Header** tab in the Page Setup dialog box, under the Preview section click the **Left** tab, click in the **text box** on the Left tab, type your name, and then click the **OK** button.

3. In the Page Navigation buttons group under the preview, click the **Page Down** button ▼ four times. The calendar scrolls from June through August, and then to the fifth page titled "Overflow Tasks." In Calendar view, tasks that are successors to preceding tasks print a little lower in the block than their predecessors. To get these tasks to print properly, you need to adjust the row height in Calendar view by dragging the bottom border of the affected week down until the task appears in the block. For now, you'll leave the Calendar alone.

4. Click the **View** tab, and then, in the Task Views group, click the **Network Diagram** button 📇. You can see the page breaks identified by the dashed lines. You will learn how to arrange the Network diagram boxes for optimal printing later in this book.

5. Click the **File** tab, and then click **Print** in the navigation bar. You see there are several pages currently ready for printing.

6. Click the **Page Setup** link, click the **Header** tab in the Page Setup dialog box, under the Preview section click the **Left** tab, click in the text box on the Left tab, type your name, and then click the **OK** button.

You can insert other codes into the header, footer, and legend by using the ampersand with specific words, or you can click the buttons in the Page Setup dialog box to insert the codes. Refer to Figure 1-42 for an explanation of each code.

Figure 1-42   **Description of print code buttons**

Button Name	Button	Code	Description
Format Text Font	[A]	(no code)	Allows you to format selected text by changing the font, font size, bold, italic, underline, and text color
Insert Page Number	[#]	& [Page]	Inserts the current page number
Insert Total Page Count	[⊡]	& [Pages]	Inserts the total number of pages for the entire printout
Insert Current Date	[▦]	& [Date]	Inserts the current date as established by the computer's clock or network server
Insert Current Time	[⊗]	& [Time]	Inserts the current time as established by the computer's clock or network server
Insert File Name	[▨]	& [File]	Inserts the project's filename
Insert Picture	[▨]	(no code)	Inserts a picture (for example, clip art, scanned photo, or logo)

Page Setup options vary slightly when printing a Calendar, Network Diagram, or Table view. The key aspects of successful printing (zooming to an acceptable magnification level, previewing your work, and using the Page Setup dialog box to make changes) remain the same regardless of the view you are printing.

INSIGHT

Protecting Confidential Information

Often you share files with other people. What you may not know is that files created in Microsoft Office programs carry information about the people who created the file and work on the file in a Properties dialog box. Sometimes you do not want this information to travel with a shared file. To access and change these properties in Microsoft Project, open Backstage view, click Info on the navigation pane, and then click the Project Information arrow in the right pane. On the Project Information menu, click Advanced Properties. Review the information on the General and Summary tabs. You can make changes to the Summary tab as needed.

Exiting Microsoft Office Project 2010

After exploring many of the features and capabilities of this powerful program, you are now ready to **exit**, or quit, Project 2010. When you exit Project 2010, it is no longer running on your computer. To work on another Project 2010 file, you must start the program again.

To save the existing project with the same filename and exit Project 2010:

▶ 1. Click the **File** tab, and then click **Save** on the navigation bar. The changes to the project are saved. You should always save your work before exiting the program.

▶ 2. Click the **File** tab, and then click **Exit**. The project and the program close.

The next time you open this file, it will display the most recent view, in this case, the Network Diagram view.

PROSKILLS

Problem Solving: Getting Help

The Project 2010 Help system provides quick access to information about commands, features, and screen elements to help you find information and solve problems. In order to get the most benefit from the Help system, your computer must be connected to the Internet. To open the Help window, click the Help button. Project Help includes a Table of Contents that you can use to identify specific content. You can also type a keyword in the Search box and then click the Search button to find articles as well as videos. You can use Help to learn more about Project 2010 features and about how to perform specific tasks. Updates and documents are accessed by Project 2010 through the Microsoft Web site to provide you with the most accurate and up-to-date information as you request it. When working with a project team, you will find your colleagues often need information about how to use the program. You can always refer them to the Help system for immediate action.

Now that you have learned the vocabulary of project management, as well as how to view, navigate, and enter a task in Project 2010, you are ready to build the project for ViewPoint Partners. You will do this in the next tutorial. You report your progress to Emily. She is pleased that you have learned so much about Project 2010 in such a short time. She's confident that you are ready to tackle the AV Presentation Rooms Installation project for ViewPoint Partners.

REVIEW

Session 1.2 Quick Check

1. What categories of task views are available in Project 2010?
2. Name three types of tables listing tasks that are available in Project 2010.
3. What is the purpose of Form views?
4. What is one way to open the Task Information dialog box?
5. What is the purpose of the Task Information dialog box?
6. How does zooming out change the timescale on a Gantt chart?
7. How does zooming in change the bars on the Gantt chart?
8. How do you open the Timescale dialog box in Gantt Chart view?

Practice the skills you learned in the tutorial using the same case scenario.

PRACTICE

Review Assignments

Data File needed for the Review Assignments: Train-1.mpp

A very important component of the AV Presentation Rooms Installation project at ViewPoint Partners involves training the users. It will be your job to coordinate this effort. In this assignment, you will open a partially completed project file that documents training tasks. You will explore the project, add tasks, and print several views.

1. Start Project 2010, open the **Train-1** file located in the **Project1\Review** folder included with your Data Files, and then save the project file as **VPTrain-1** to the same folder.
2. Drag the **split bar** so that you can see the Finish column in the Entry table.
3. Open the Project Information dialog box. Change the Start date to 9/1/2014.
4. In row 8, add the task **Schedule classes**, and set the duration as 1 day.
5. In row 9, add the task **Conduct training**, and set the duration to 3 days.
6. Change the duration for the task 1, Identify existing skills, from 3 days to 2 days.
7. Add a note to task 4, Develop contract, that reads **Call legal team to confirm requirements.**
8. In Gantt Chart view, open the Print tab in Backstage view, and then open the Page Setup dialog box. Change the left section of the legend to display your name instead of the word Project in the first line. (*Note*: Your name will be followed by the filename when the project is printed.)
9. Verify that the Gantt chart fits on one page. Submit the finished Gantt chart to your instructor, either in printed or electronic form, as requested.
10. Switch to Network Diagram view.
11. Zoom out until you can see all of the tasks on the screen. (There are nine total tasks.)
12. Open the Print tab to preview the Network Diagram view of this project, view it in Multiple Page view, and then open the Page Setup dialog box and change the left section of the header to display your name.
13. Submit the finished network diagram to your instructor, either in printed or electronic form, as requested.
14. Switch to Calendar view.
15. Open the Print tab to preview the Calendar view of this project, and then open the Page Setup dialog box and change the left section of the footer to display your name.
16. Submit the finished Calendar view to your instructor, either in printed or electronic form, as requested.
17. Use the Help system to search for the keyword phrase "Start date."
18. Click the topic: "Create and schedule a new project". Write a brief paragraph describing why you would use a Start date and why you would use a Finish date to schedule a project. (*Note*: Check with your instructor regarding the format you should use for creating and submitting written responses.)
19. Close the Help window, and then save your changes to the project.

Apply your skills to complete a project for building a new home.

APPLY

Case Problem 1

Data File needed for this Case Problem: Home-1.mpp

River Dell Development, Inc. You work for a general contractor, River Dell Development, Inc., which manages residential construction projects for group homes. The manager, Karen Reynolds, has asked you to use Project 2010 to enter and update some of the general tasks involved in building a new home. She wants to use this project file as a basis for future projects. *Note:* Throughout this assignment you will be asked to make notes and write short responses. Check with your instructor regarding the format you should use for creating and submitting written responses. Complete the following:

1. Start Project 2010, open the **Home-1** file located in the **Project1\Case1** folder included with your Data Files, and then save the project file as **NewHome-1** in the same folder.

2. Resize the Entry table pane so that you can see the Finish column.

3. Open the Project Information dialog box, and then write down the date that is displayed in the Finish date box. Close the Project Information dialog box without making any changes. Tue 11/4/14

4. Enter the following tasks and corresponding durations in rows 12, 13, and 14: **Paint interior**, **3 days**; **Lay carpet**, **3 days**; **Install wood trim**, **16 days**. Notice that all tasks start on the project Start date. You will learn in later tutorials how to change this.

5. Open the task form below the Gantt chart. View the Predecessors & Successors for tasks 6, 7, and 8. Close the Details view.

6. Change the duration for the first two tasks—Secure financing and Purchase lot—to 4 days each.

7. Display the Timescale dialog box. Change the Units, Label, and Count for the Middle tier to options of your choice. Close the dialog box.

8. Open the Print tab to preview the Gantt Chart view of this project, and then use the Page Setup dialog box to enter your name in the left portion of the header.

⊕ **EXPLORE** 9. Use the Page Setup dialog box to change the Fit to settings so that the printout fits on one page, and then submit the finished Gantt chart to your instructor, either in printed or electronic form, as requested.

10. Switch to Calendar view of this project.

⊕ **EXPLORE** 11. Do you notice anything different about this view from previous work in the Tutorial? Write down an explanation as to why you think this is useful. Open the Timescale dialog box for Calendar view and notice the check mark next to the Display month pane check box.

12. Open the Print tab to preview the Calendar view of this project, and then use the Page Setup dialog box to enter your name in the left portion of the header. Submit the finished calendar to your instructor, either in printed or electronic form, as requested.

13. Switch to the Network Diagram view, open the Print tab, and then use the Page Setup dialog box to print your name in the left portion of the header. Submit the finished network diagram to your instructor, either in printed or electronic form, as requested.

14. Use the Help system to search for the phrase "critical path," and then read relevant articles. Write down at least two reasons why the critical path is so important to project managers.

15. Return to Gantt Chart view, save the project **NewHome-1**, and then close the project file.

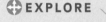

Apply your skills to organize a job search.

APPLY

Case Problem 2

Data File needed for this Case Problem: Jobs-1.mpp

Community Works   You work for Community Works, a growing grassroots organization that helps recent college graduates find employment, has hired you to work as a jobs counselor. You are assigned to help people who have technical degrees. You decide to use Project 2010 to help these recent graduates organize their job search efforts. *Note:* Throughout this assignment you will be asked to make notes and write short responses. Check with your instructor regarding the format you should use for creating and submitting written responses. Complete the following:

1. Start Project 2010, and then open the **Jobs-1** file in the **Project1\Case2** folder included with your Data Files.
2. Save the file as **MyJobs-1** in the same folder.
3. Open the Project Information dialog box. Change the Start date to 7/30/2014.
4. Enter the following new tasks and corresponding durations in rows 9 and 10: **Write cover letter**, **1 day**; **Buy interview suit**, **2 days**.
5. Display the Finish date column in the Gantt chart Entry table.
6. Change the duration of the second task, Edit resume, from 1 day to 3 days.
7. Change the timescale so that the Middle Tier scale is Thirds of Months with the label set to January Beginning 2009. Set the Bottom Tier scale as Days with the label set to Sun, Mon, Tue. Make sure the Count is at 1 for both tiers. View the Gantt chart after you make these changes.
8. Open the Print tab to preview the Gantt Chart view of this project. Add your name under the current date in the legend, and then submit the finished Gantt chart to your instructor, either in printed or electronic form, as requested.
9. Switch to Calendar view, and then zoom in so that you see only two weeks on the screen and all tasks are visible on the calendar. (*Hint:* You can use Ctrl + Home to move to the beginning of the project.)

EXPLORE 10. Open the Print tab to preview the Calendar view of this project, and then add the text **Filename:** and the filename code in the left section of the header. Enter your name on the right side of the header, and then submit the first page of the Calendar view to your instructor, either in printed or electronic form, as requested.

11. Switch to Network Diagram view, and then open the Print tab to preview the Network Diagram view of this project.
12. Add the text **Filename:** and the filename code in the left side of the header, enter your name on the right side of the header, and then submit the first page of the network diagram to your instructor, either in printed or electronic form, as requested.
13. Return to Gantt Chart view, with the Duration column as the last visible column, and then save your changes to the project.
14. Submit the finished project file to your instructor, either in printed or electronic form, as requested.

How long it will take to complete the project
what are the critical tasks that must be
completed before starting other dependent tasks.

The Diagram makes it easier to visualize the
important tasks of a project, which will

Expand your skills to work on the project file for planning a college reunion weekend.

CHALLENGE

Case Problem 3

Data File needed for this Case Problem: Reunion-1.mpp

Western College Reunion   As a proud graduate of Western College, you have been asked to help organize the 20th reunion for the graduating class of 1994. The college looks to graduates to keep the endowment fund growing and enhance school pride for current and future students. In 2014, the reunion takes place on March 7, 8, and 9. You'll use Project 2010 to enter and track the many tasks that must be completed for a successful reunion to occur. (*Note*: Check with your instructor regarding the format you should use for creating and submitting written responses.) Complete the following:

1. Start Project, and then open **Reunion-1** located in the **Project1\Case3** folder included with your Data Files.

2. Save the file as **WReunion-1** to the same folder.

3. Set the project so the schedule is created based on the Finish date, and then change the Finish date to March 7, 2014.

4. Enter the following new tasks and corresponding durations in rows 9 and 10: **Create gift baskets**, **5 days**; **Make college visit**, **2 days**.

⊕ **EXPLORE** 5. Open the Task Information dialog box for task 1, click the Advanced tab, and then write down the option for the Constraint type. Close the Task Information dialog box without making any changes.

6. Change the timescale so that the Middle Tier scale is weeks, the Count is 2, and the Label displays 1/25, 2/1, and then change the Bottom Tier scale to days, the Count to 1, and the Label displays to Sun, Mon, Tue.

7. Switch to Network Diagram view, and then zoom out to see all the tasks.

8. Open the Print tab to preview the Network Diagram view of this project, and then add your name as the first line of the left section of the header and the current date as the second line of the left section of the header. Submit the finished network diagram to your instructor, either in printed or electronic form, as requested.

⊕ **EXPLORE** 9. View the Gantt chart, open the Task Form, view the Predecessors and Successors, and starting with the first task, click the Next button to view all the tasks. Write down why you don't see any predecessors or successors for this project. Close the Task Form.

10. Add a note to the Set budget task that says, **Meet with college president.**

11. Switch to Calendar view, open the Print tab to preview the Calendar view of this project, and then add your name as the first line of the left section of the header and the current date as the second line of the left section of the header. Submit the Calendar view to your instructor, either in printed or electronic form, as requested.

⊕ **EXPLORE** 12. Return to Calendar view, and then right-click any bar to view the menu. Click Bar Styles and explore to see how this dialog box can work to change the appearance of the calendar. Use the Pattern arrow and Color arrow to change the bars on the calendar so they are filled with dark blue vertical stripes.

13. Make all tasks visible in Calendar view. (*Hint*: Experiment with zooming and dragging the edges of the lines that separate the weeks.)

14. Open the Print tab to preview the Calendar view of this project again.

⊕ **EXPLORE** 15. Open the Page Setup dialog box, and then click the View tab. Click the Week height as on screen option button, and then click OK. Preview the calendar. Compare the results to the view you saw in Step 11. What are the differences?

16. Return to Gantt Chart view, with the Finish column as the last visible column, save your changes, and then close the project file.

Use your skills to create a new project for managing a fund-raising project for a park.

CREATE

Case Problem 4

There are no Data Files needed for this Case Problem.

NatureSpace   NatureSpace is a company that specializes in creating play structures for communities. They can also help in securing grants for the project. You are the project manager assigned to manage the fund-raising and building of the new play structure at a local neighborhood park. NatureSpace products and services are in high demand, and it is critical that they complete projects on time. Also, most towns do not have extra funds available and cannot afford any cost overruns. All of the equipment must be ready by September 6, 2014, before the end of the fiscal year. You need to create the project shown in Figure 1-43.

Figure 1-43   **Tasks and durations for the NatureSpace project**

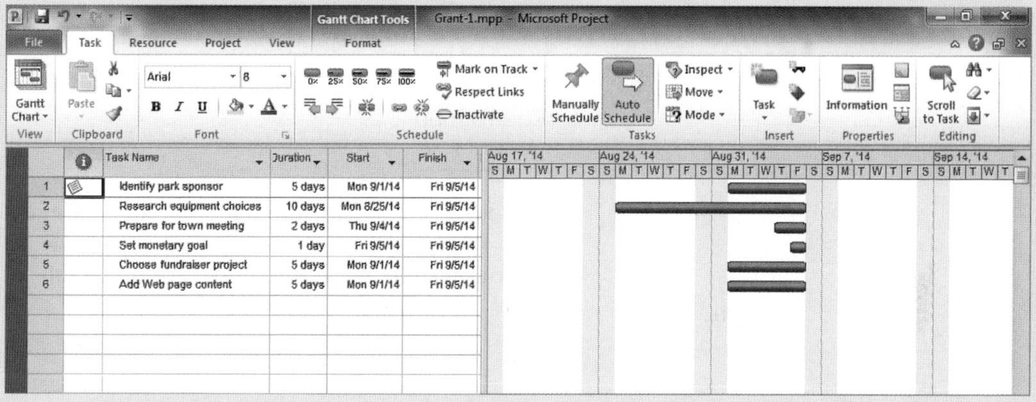

Complete the following:

1. Start Project 2010, and then save the new project as **Grant-1** to the **Project1\Case4** folder included with your Data Files.

2. Set the project so the schedule is created based on the Finish date, and change the Finish date to September 6, 2014.

3. Make sure that the tasks are set to be Automatically Scheduled. Enter the following tasks and corresponding durations:

    - **Identify park sponsor**, **5 days**
    - **Research equipment choices**, **10 days**
    - **Prepare for town meeting**, **2 days**
    - **Set monetary goal**, **1 day**
    - **Choose fundraiser project**, **5 days**
    - **Update Web page content**, **5 days**

4. Add the following note to task 1, "Identify park sponsor": **Start with Mayor Brian Griffin.**

5. Open the Print tab to preview the Gantt Chart view of this project. Add the text **File Name:** followed by the filename code to the left portion of the header, and then add the text **Name:** followed by your name in the right portion of the header. Print the project in Gantt Chart view.

6. Switch to Calendar view, and then resize the rows of the calendar if necessary so that all of the tasks are visible for the weeks of August 25 and September 1.

7. Open the Print tab to preview the Calendar view of this project. Add the text **File Name:** followed by the filename code to the left portion of the header, and then add the text **Name:** followed by your name in the right portion of the header. Submit the Calendar view to your instructor, either in printed or electronic form as directed.

8. Switch to the Network Diagram view of this project, then open the Print tab.

9. Add the text **File Name:** followed by the filename code to the left portion of the header. Enter the text **Name:** followed by your name in the right portion of the header.

10. On the Legend tab in the Page Setup dialog box for the Network Diagram view, specify that the legend is to print on every page instead of the legend page, and then submit the first page of the Network Diagram view to your instructor, either in printed or electronic form as directed.

11. Return to Gantt Chart view, with the Finish column as the last visible column.

12. Save your changes, and then close the project file.

ENDING DATA FILES

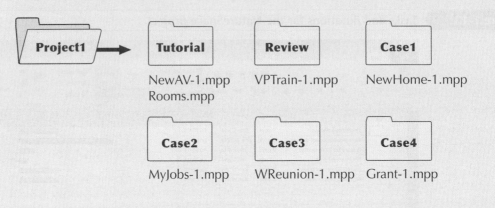

Project1 → Tutorial
NewAV-1.mpp
Rooms.mpp

Review
VPTrain-1.mpp

Case1
NewHome-1.mpp

Case2
MyJobs-1.mpp

Case3
WReunion-1.mpp

Case4
Grant-1.mpp

Creating a Project Schedule

Creating Calendars and Scheduling Tasks and Durations for the Project

OBJECTIVES

Session 2.1
- Start a new project
- Examine scheduling defaults
- Change a project calendar
- Create a task calendar
- Enter and edit tasks and durations
- Enter and edit recurring tasks and milestones
- Enter lag and lead times

Session 2.2
- Enter and edit task dependencies
- View project statistics
- Show the project summary
- Review project statistics
- Manipulate summary tasks
- Develop a work breakdown structure

Case | *ViewPoint Partners*

Tutorial 1 introduced you to project management terminology and the Project 2010 user interface. In addition, you established the project goal, which is to install the equipment and software for the company's five AV presentation rooms within a time frame of three months and within a budget of $100,000. Meeting the project goal will determine the success of the project. Now you are ready to use your knowledge about Project 2010 as the project manager at ViewPoint Partners. You have to define the specific tasks, durations, milestones, constraints, and dependencies that are appropriate for the installation of AV presentation rooms at ViewPoint Partners. Although you will continue to work closely with Emily, the technology specialist, Sidney wants you to start creating the project file and manage the installation. You start by entering the details of this project into Project 2010.

STARTING DATA FILES

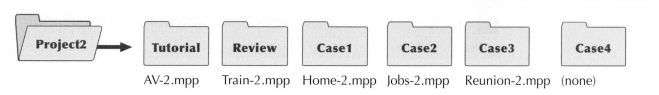

| Project2 → | Tutorial | Review | Case1 | Case2 | Case3 | Case4 |
| | AV-2.mpp | Train-2.mpp | Home-2.mpp | Jobs-2.mpp | Reunion-2.mpp | (none) |

SESSION 2.1 VISUAL OVERVIEW

You use the Change Working Time dialog box to change the project calendar.

Any changes will be based on the Standard (Project Calendar). The **Standard (Project Calendar)** is the default calendar used to schedule tasks within a project that specifies Monday through Friday as working days with eight hours of work completed each day, and Saturday and Sunday as nonworking days.

You use the **row selector** to select all columns for a task.

You set exceptions using this tab.

You change hours for work weeks using this tab.

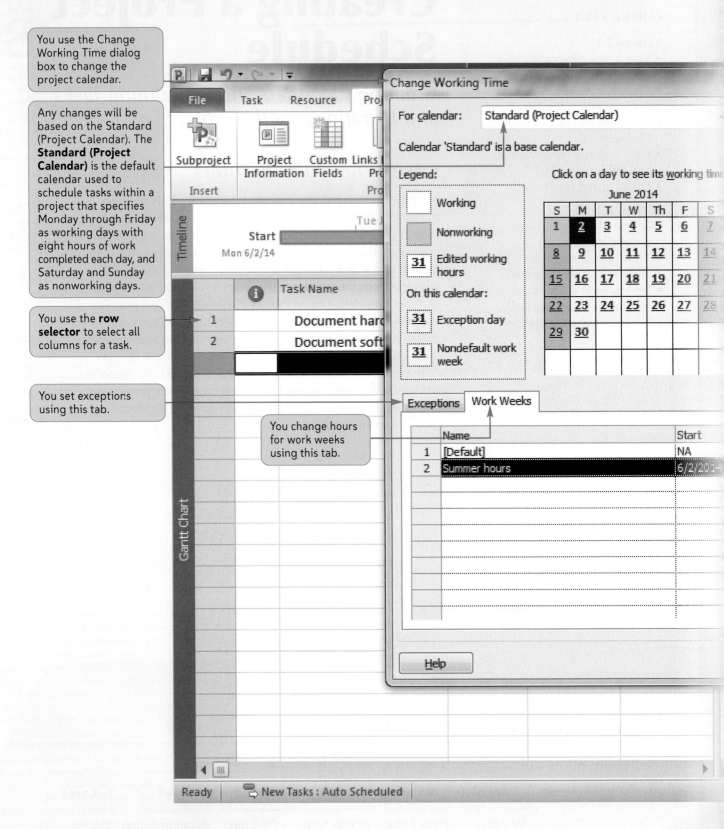

CHANGING PROJECT CALENDARS

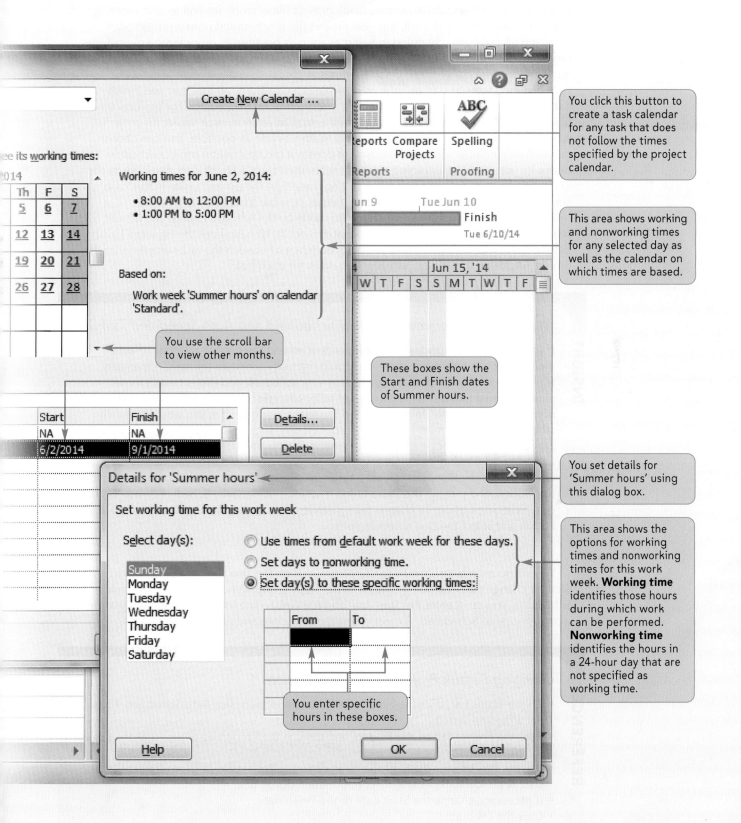

Create New Calendar ...

You click this button to create a task calendar for any task that does not follow the times specified by the project calendar.

Reports Compare Spelling
Projects
Reports Proofing

ee its working times:

2014

	Th	F	S
	5	6	7
	12	13	14
	19	20	21
	26	27	28

Working times for June 2, 2014:

- 8:00 AM to 12:00 PM
- 1:00 PM to 5:00 PM

Based on:

Work week 'Summer hours' on calendar 'Standard'.

You use the scroll bar to view other months.

Jun 9   Tue Jun 10
                 Finish
                 Tue 6/10/14

This area shows working and nonworking times for any selected day as well as the calendar on which times are based.

Jun 15, '14
W T F S S M T W T F

These boxes show the Start and Finish dates of Summer hours.

Start	Finish
NA	NA
6/2/2014	9/1/2014

Details...

Delete

You set details for 'Summer hours' using this dialog box.

Details for 'Summer hours'

Set working time for this work week

Select day(s):

- Use times from default work week for these days.
- Set days to nonworking time.
- ● Set day(s) to these specific working times:

Sunday
Monday
Tuesday
Wednesday
Thursday
Friday
Saturday

From	To

You enter specific hours in these boxes.

This area shows the options for working times and nonworking times for this work week. **Working time** identifies those hours during which work can be performed. **Nonworking time** identifies the hours in a 24-hour day that are not specified as working time.

Help   OK   Cancel

Starting a New Project and Examining Scheduling Defaults

When you start Project 2010, a new, blank project file is ready for you to start entering tasks and durations. By default, the new project file is scheduled from a project Start date, and all tasks are scheduled to begin as soon as possible in order for the overall project to be finished as quickly as possible. You can open the Project Information dialog box to review or change these default settings.

Scheduling tasks to start as soon as possible is a constraint on the Start and Finish dates for tasks in a project. A **constraint** is a restriction on the project. For projects scheduled from a Start date, the default constraint is to start as soon as possible; for projects scheduled from a Finish date, the default is to start as late as possible. You can choose a different constraint if the default constraint does not create a useful project schedule. For example, you might be planning a project scheduled from a Finish date that is far in the future, but there is no reason to delay getting started on the project tasks. In this case, you would change the constraint from *as late as possible* to *as soon as possible*.

Tasks are also set to Manually Scheduled mode by default. You change the default scheduling to Automatic Scheduling so that Project 2010 calculates the project's Finish date based on the tasks, durations, and dependencies between the tasks entered into the project file, using as soon as possible Start dates for each task.

INSIGHT

The Difference Between Manually Scheduled and Auto Scheduled Tasks

If you do not want changes to task dependencies and the project calendar to automatically adjust task dates, then you should manually schedule the task. A manually scheduled task can be placed anywhere in your schedule, and Project won't move dates assigned to that task regardless of other changes. Manually scheduled tasks have user-defined Start and Finish Dates and Durations. For example, you would manually schedule a task that must happen on a specific day, such as an event that must occur on January 1. As a project manager, you might prefer to take advantage of the Project 2010 automatic scheduling feature and turn on the manually scheduled feature only for specific tasks. At any time, you can set a task scheduling option by clicking the Task tab on the Ribbon, and then, in the Tasks group, clicking the Manually Schedule button or the Auto Schedule button. To change the schedule mode for any new tasks, click the Mode button and select the task schedule option.

When you enter a task, you can use commands on the Task tab on the Ribbon to view or change the scheduling options in the Tasks group. When a project is Manually Scheduled, you must enter the Start date and the Finish date for the task manually. When a project is Auto Scheduled, Project enters the Start date and the Finish date.

REFERENCE

Changing Default Project Scheduling Options

- On the status bar, click the New Tasks button, and then click Auto Scheduled if it is not already selected.
- Click the Project tab on the Ribbon, and then, in the Properties group, click the Project Information button.
- If necessary, change the Schedule from option to Project Finish Date (Project Start Date is the default) in the Project Information dialog box.
- If necessary, change the Start date or the Finish date.
- Click the OK button.

You want to examine default project scheduling options and how they affect the scheduling of individual tasks. You met with several consultants and determined that your initial time estimates for some of the tasks were not quite right. After reviewing your file from the last tutorial, you realize you don't need as many days to complete the Document hardware and Document software tasks. You have new estimates and will use these new durations to examine the scheduling options.

To examine the scheduled from a Start date project scheduling options:

1. Start Project 2010, and then, on the status bar, click the **New Tasks** button and set the new tasks in this project to **Auto Scheduled**. By default, a new project file is scheduled from today's date as the Start date.

2. Right-click the **Task Mode** column, and then click **Hide Column**. Because you are using Auto Scheduled tasks for this project, you do not need to see the task mode column, which identifies if a task is manually or automatically scheduled.

3. Click the **Task Name cell** in the first row, type **Document hardware**, press the **Tab** key, type **3**, and then press the **Enter** key.

4. On the Ribbon, click the **Project** tab, and then, in the Properties group, click **Project Information**. As shown in Figure 2-1, the default options in the Project Information dialog box confirm the way that the first task was scheduled—that is, to begin as soon as possible based on the project's Start date. The Schedule from option is Project Start Date. As a result, the Start date of the project and of the first task is today's date and the project Finish date is calculated based on three working days, including today's date.

Figure 2-1	Project Information dialog box

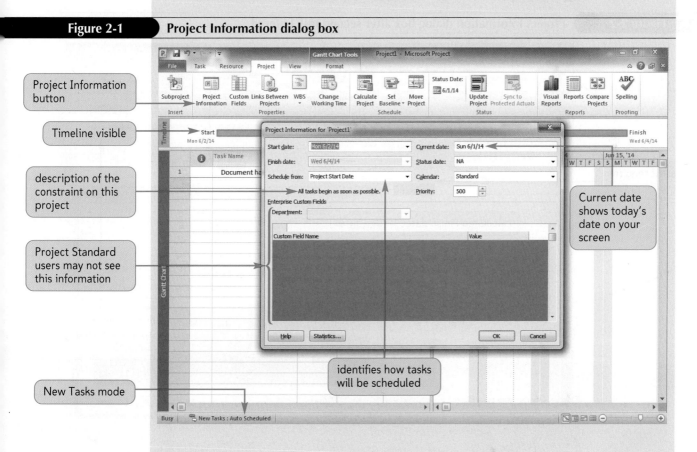

Project Information button

Timeline visible

description of the constraint on this project

Project Standard users may not see this information

Current date shows today's date on your screen

identifies how tasks will be scheduled

New Tasks mode

TIP

You can also type the date in the date text box.

You need to change the Start date of the project to June 2, 2014.

5. Click the **Start date** arrow, click the **month arrows** to scroll right or left to **June, 2014**, and then click **2**. The Start date is changed to Monday 6/2/14. The text box formats the day of the week as Mon.

6. Click the **OK** button. The dialog box closes.

Changes made in the Project Information dialog box are reflected in all views, such as the Gantt Chart view and Network Diagram view, and can affect the way the project is scheduled after one or more tasks have been entered. Notice as you start typing the second task, which begins with the same text as the first, that the AutoComplete feature displays the complete word to help you with entering the task.

To further examine default project scheduling options:

1. Click the **Task Name** cell in the second row, type **Document software**, press the **Tab** key, type **6** in the Duration column, and then press the **Enter** key. The second task has a longer duration than the first, so the project's calculated Finish date changes to accommodate the duration of this task.

2. In the Properties group on the Project tab, click the **Project Information** button. The Finish date is now calculated as six working days after the project Start date. See Figure 2-2. The Start date is included as a working day. Because the second task spans two nonworking days, the Finish date for that task is more than six days after the Start date.

Figure 2-2   **Project Information dialog box after second task entered**

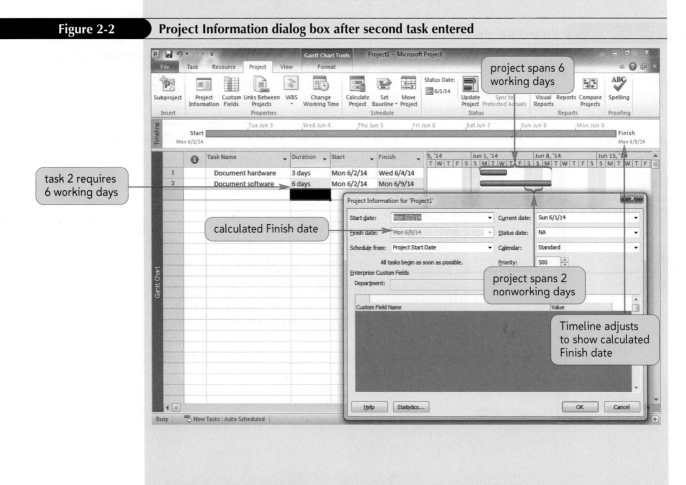

3. Click the **OK** button to close the Project Information dialog box.

4. In the Project window, click the **Close Window** button (but do not exit Project 2010), and then click the **No** button to close the sample project without saving changes.

Trouble? If you are returned to the desktop and Project 2010 is no longer running, you exited Project 2010 by clicking the Close button in the program window title bar rather than closing the file by clicking the project file Close Window button. Restart Project 2010 to continue with the tutorial.

If your project should be scheduled from a Finish date (such as an event that is planned for a specific date), you must change the Schedule from option in the Project Information dialog box. When you schedule a project from the Finish date, and you use Automatic scheduling, Project 2010 calculates the project's Start date based on the tasks, durations, and dependencies between the tasks using dates that start as late as possible. When a project is scheduled from a Finish date, the default is for all tasks to be scheduled to begin as late as possible in order for the overall project to be started as late as possible and yet still meet the required Finish date. It is often more efficient to wait to start a project until you really need to do work on it instead of starting too early and wasting resources for each task. If a project is to be scheduled from a Finish date, you should apply this setting as soon as the project is created.

You'll set up a new project for the AV Presentation Rooms Installation project that is scheduled from a Finish date.

To examine the scheduled from a Finish date project scheduling options:

1. Click the **File** tab on the Ribbon, click **New** on the navigation bar, and then, in the Available Templates section, click **Blank project**.

2. Click **Create** to open a new project file.

3. On the status bar, click the **New Tasks** button and set the new tasks in this project to **Auto Scheduled**, right-click the **Task Mode** column, and then click **Hide Column**.

4. Click the **Project** tab on the Ribbon if it is not the active tab, and then, in the Properties group, click the **Project Information** button.

5. In the Project Information dialog box, click the **Schedule from** arrow, click **Project Finish Date**, click the **Finish date** arrow, click the **month arrows** on the calendar to scroll to **July, 2014**, click **1**, and then click the **OK** button.

6. Click the **Task Name** cell in the first row, type **Document hardware**, press the **Tab** key, type **3**, and then press the **Enter** key.

7. Click the **Task Name** cell in the second row, type **Document software**, press the **Tab** key, type **6**, and then press the **Enter** key. See Figure 2-3. Because the project Finish date was entered as 7/1/14 in the Project Information dialog box, the second task, Document software, is scheduled to finish on 7/1/14 and to start six working days earlier, based on the as late as possible scheduling constraint.

TIP

You can also type a date directly into the project Start and Finish date boxes if you do not want to select a date using the calendar.

Figure 2-3 Gantt Chart view for a project scheduled from a Finish date

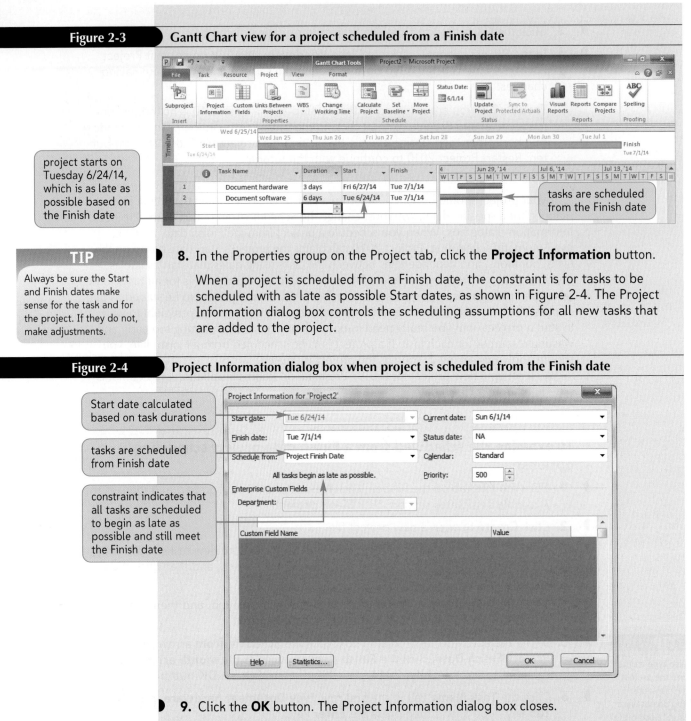

project starts on Tuesday 6/24/14, which is as late as possible based on the Finish date

tasks are scheduled from the Finish date

TIP

Always be sure the Start and Finish dates make sense for the task and for the project. If they do not, make adjustments.

8. In the Properties group on the Project tab, click the **Project Information** button.

When a project is scheduled from a Finish date, the constraint is for tasks to be scheduled with as late as possible Start dates, as shown in Figure 2-4. The Project Information dialog box controls the scheduling assumptions for all new tasks that are added to the project.

Figure 2-4 Project Information dialog box when project is scheduled from the Finish date

Start date calculated based on task durations

tasks are scheduled from Finish date

constraint indicates that all tasks are scheduled to begin as late as possible and still meet the Finish date

9. Click the **OK** button. The Project Information dialog box closes.

You notice that task 2 starts before task 1. This is not appropriate. You will change the constraint for task 1 so that it begins on the same day as task 2.

Reviewing Task Information

Each task in a project has unique and specific information that defines that task. Most of this information is entered when the task is created, and some of the information is generated by Project as a result of parameters such as whether the task is a Fixed Duration or Fixed Work task and whether or not the task is effort driven. You will learn about these parameters later in the book. Task information changes as the project progresses. All task information for any task at any time can be found by reviewing the Task Information dialog box.

The Task Information Dialog Box

The Task Information dialog box is a comprehensive collection of all information associated with each task. The information is organized into six categories, represented by these tabs: General, Predecessors, Resources, Advanced, Notes, and Custom Fields. The Task Information dialog box is another view by which you can examine and enter data about a task. For example, you can change the constraint for an individual task by using the Task Information dialog box. You can also change the scheduling mode from Auto Scheduled to Manually Scheduled.

TIP

You can also double-click a task to open its Task Information dialog box.

To change the scheduling constraint using the Task Information dialog box:

1. Click **Document hardware** (task 1) in the Entry table, click the **Task** tab on the Ribbon, and then, in the Properties group, click the **Task Information** button.

2. Click the **Advanced** tab if it is not the active tab. See Figure 2-5.

| Figure 2-5 | Advanced tab in the Task Information dialog box |

3. Click the **Constraint type** arrow. You can see that many options are available for Constraint types. You will learn how each of these constraint types affects the project schedule in later tutorials.

4. Click **As Soon As Possible**, and then click the **OK** button. The Document hardware bar on the Gantt chart moved to the left. You changed the constraint from "as late as possible" to "as soon as possible." Task 1 and task 2 now start on the same date. The project will still finish on the specified Finish date, but the first task is now scheduled to start as soon as possible.

From this example, you can see that careful attention to how the project is originally scheduled (from a Start date or from a Finish date) is extremely important. This choice determines the initial Constraint type (as soon as possible or as late as possible) for each task, and the Constraint type impacts the calculated Start and Finish dates for each task entered into the project.

Now that you've examined the Project Information dialog box and the Task Information dialog box as well as the type of information each dialog box contains, you are ready to examine the project calendar.

Examining Project Calendars

The **Standard (Project Calendar)** is the base calendar used by Project 2010 to schedule new tasks within the project. It specifies **working time**, the hours during which work can occur. It also specifies **nonworking time**, the hours of a 24-hour day that are not specified as working time, as well as any other global working time issues (such as a scheduled holiday) that affect the entire project.

Changing the Project Calendar

By default, the entire project, each task, and each resource is scheduled according to the **Standard calendar**, which specifies that Monday through Friday are working days with eight hours of work completed each day (8:00 AM to 12:00 PM and 1:00 PM to 5:00 PM). Saturday and Sunday are designated as nonworking days. You can modify the Standard calendar to identify holidays or other nonworking days or times in which work should not be scheduled. You can also create unique calendars for tasks and resources that do not follow the working and nonworking times specified by the Standard calendar.

REFERENCE

Creating an Exception to the Project Calendar

- Click the Project tab on the Ribbon, and then, in the Properties group, click the Change Working Time button to open the Change Working Time dialog box.
- Click the date on the calendar.
- In the lower section of the dialog box, click the Exceptions tab, click the next empty cell in the Name column, enter a Name to describe the exception, and then press the Tab key to select the Start cell.
- Click the Details button to open the Details for 'exception name' dialog box.
- Select the Nonworking or Working times option button.
- Edit the From and To times in the table at the top of the Details dialog box.
- Click OK in both dialog boxes to apply the changes.

ViewPoint Partners closes the office on certain days, so you need to examine the project calendar and mark those days as nonworking days. Project 2010 does not assume that any holidays (whether traditional, such as July 4th, or nontraditional, such as a company-designated holiday) will be observed. As a result, you need to mark any holiday that ViewPoint Partner offices will be closed as a nonworking day. ViewPoint Partners closes on July 4th of every year to celebrate Independence Day. Since the current project spans the month of July, you will add this to the calendar.

To change a project calendar:

▶ **1.** Click the **Project** tab on the Ribbon, and then, in the Properties group, click the **Project Information** button. Notice that the default Calendar type is the Standard calendar.

▶ **2.** Click the **Schedule from** arrow, click **Project Start Date**, change the Start date to **6/2/14**, and then click the **OK** button to close the Project Information dialog box. This project is now scheduled using the Standard calendar from a Project Start Date.

▶ **3.** In the Properties group on the Project tab, click the **Change Working Time** button to open the Change Working Time dialog box, as seen in the Session 2.1 Visual Overview. You can modify all project, task, and resource calendars in this dialog box. Currently, the Standard (Project Calendar) is selected. It serves as the base calendar for the entire project.

▶ **4.** On the calendar, drag the **scroll box** or click the **scroll arrows** until the calendar displays **July 2014**.

▶ **5.** On the calendar, click the box for **Friday July 4**, click the **Exceptions** tab if it is not already selected, click the first row in the Name column, type **Independence Day**, press the **Tab** key, click the **Independence Day Start date** cell, and then click the **Details** button. The Details for 'Independence Day' dialog box opens. Notice that the Nonworking time option button is selected.

▶ **6.** In the Recurrence pattern section, click the **Yearly** option button because ViewPoint Partners takes July 4th off every year. Even though the project is likely to end before next year, you never know if a project will extend or if you will use the file for a new project, so you have set the date to repeat. Notice how the pattern shows "On July 4."

▶ **7.** Click the **End after** option button if it is not already selected, and then, in the occurrences text box, double-click the **1**, type **5**, and click the **OK** button. The number "4" on the July 2014 calendar is now highlighted and underlined on the calendar to indicate that the date was edited and is an exception.

Some holidays, such as Thanksgiving, span more than one day. Thanksgiving, however, does not occur on the same date each year so you would have to specify the days off for each year. For now, just set this year's exception. You can change more than one day at the same time.

TIP

To select noncontiguous days, click the first day, and then press and hold the Ctrl key while clicking the other days to select them as a group.

▶ **8.** Click the **down scroll arrow** on the calendar until you reach the month of November 2014, drag through the boxes for **Thursday November 27** and **Friday November 28**, and then, on the Exceptions tab, click the **second row** in the Name column.

▶ **9.** Type **Thanksgiving**, and then press the **Tab** key. The dates you selected are entered in the Start and Finish columns.

▶ **10.** Click the **Thanksgiving Start date** cell, and then click the **Details** button.

▶ **11.** Click the **End by option** button and notice that the Finish date (Fri 11/28/14) appears in that list box.

▶ **12.** Click the **OK** button. Your Change Working Time dialog box should look similar to Figure 2-6.

If a day of the week such as Monday or Tuesday is edited, the day's abbreviation is underlined. If an individual day is edited, the day's number is underlined. The Legend in the Change Working Time dialog box provides the key to the shading on the calendar. Working days appear as white, nonworking days as light gray, and edited working hours white with underlined dates. If you create an exception, it appears in a bluish-green shaded box. Dates that have been designated as non-default work weeks using the Work Weeks tab appear in yellow boxes.

| Figure 2-6 | Change Working Time dialog box |

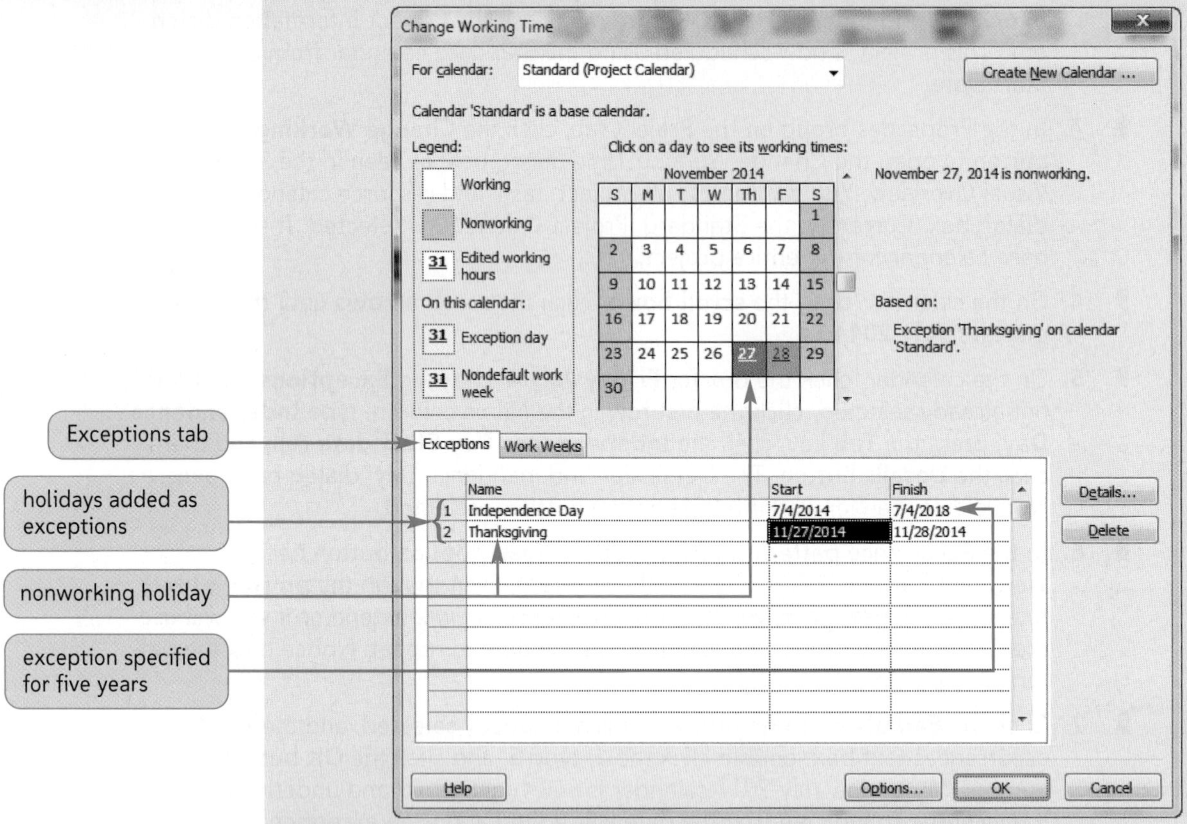

13. Click the **OK** button to close the Change Working Time dialog box.

Decision Making: Understanding Holidays in Project 2010

It may seem odd that you need to enter all the holidays for your project in a calendar when standard holidays do exist that are often considered nonworking days. Although many businesses observe standard holidays, such as January 1, all businesses do not offer the same holidays as nonworking days for their employees. As a project manager, you may be working on a project for a company that offers nonstandard holidays as well as standard holidays. For example, some employers close during the week before New Years Day. As project manager, you need to communicate with the Human Resources department and be sure you know the days which will be nonworking for the employees or staff. Project 2010 does not recognize holidays you observe as nonworking days until you enter them manually. It is important to enter all holidays as nonworking days at the beginning of a project so that those days can be factored into scheduling tasks. Having nonworking holidays figured into your project calendar will help you when you have to make scheduling decisions about ways to adjust the critical path.

PROSKILLS

In addition to making adjustments to the calendar at the day level, you can modify the number of hours worked during any day of the week. For example, a company might want to specify summer hours for June, July, and August. ViewPoint Partners ends their workday at 3:00 PM on Fridays, starting with the first Friday in June and ending with the Friday before Labor Day. In 2014, Labor Day is September 1.

To modify the project working times during any day of the week:

▶ **1.** In the Properties group on the Project tab, click the **Change Working Time** button to open the Change Working Time dialog box.

▶ **2.** In the Change Working Time dialog box, scroll to **June 2014**, click **2** on the calendar to select June 2nd, click the **Work Weeks** tab, and then click the **Name cell** in the second row.

▶ **3.** Type **Summer hours**, and then press the **Tab** key. The selected date is inserted in the Start and Finish cells.

▶ **4.** Click the **Summer hours Start** cell, verify that it is 6/2/2014, click the **Summer hours Finish** cell, click the **date** arrow, scroll the calendar to **August, 2014**, and then click **29** on the calendar to select August 29th.

▶ **5.** Click the **Details** button to open the Details for 'Summer hours' dialog box, and then, in the Select day(s) section, click **Friday** and click the **Set day(s) to these specific working times** option button.

▶ **6.** In the 5:00 PM cell, select **5**, and then type **3** to set the To time to 3:00 PM. See Figure 2-7. Summer hours will end before Labor Day on the last Friday in August, which is 8/29/2014. Summer hours means that work will end at 3:00 PM on Fridays from June 2, 2014 through August 29, 2014.

Figure 2-7   **Details for 'Summer hours' dialog box**

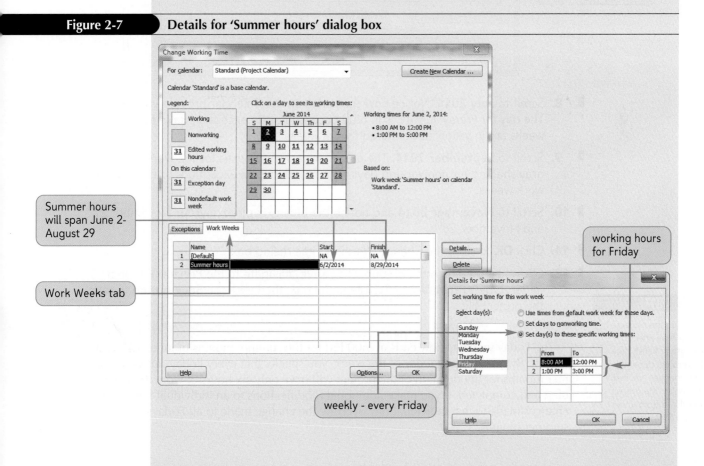

7. Click **OK** to close the Details for 'Summer hours' dialog box, click any **Monday** and look at the working times to the right of the calendar, and then click **Friday June 27**. See Figure 2-8.

Figure 2-8 ▶ Summer work hours

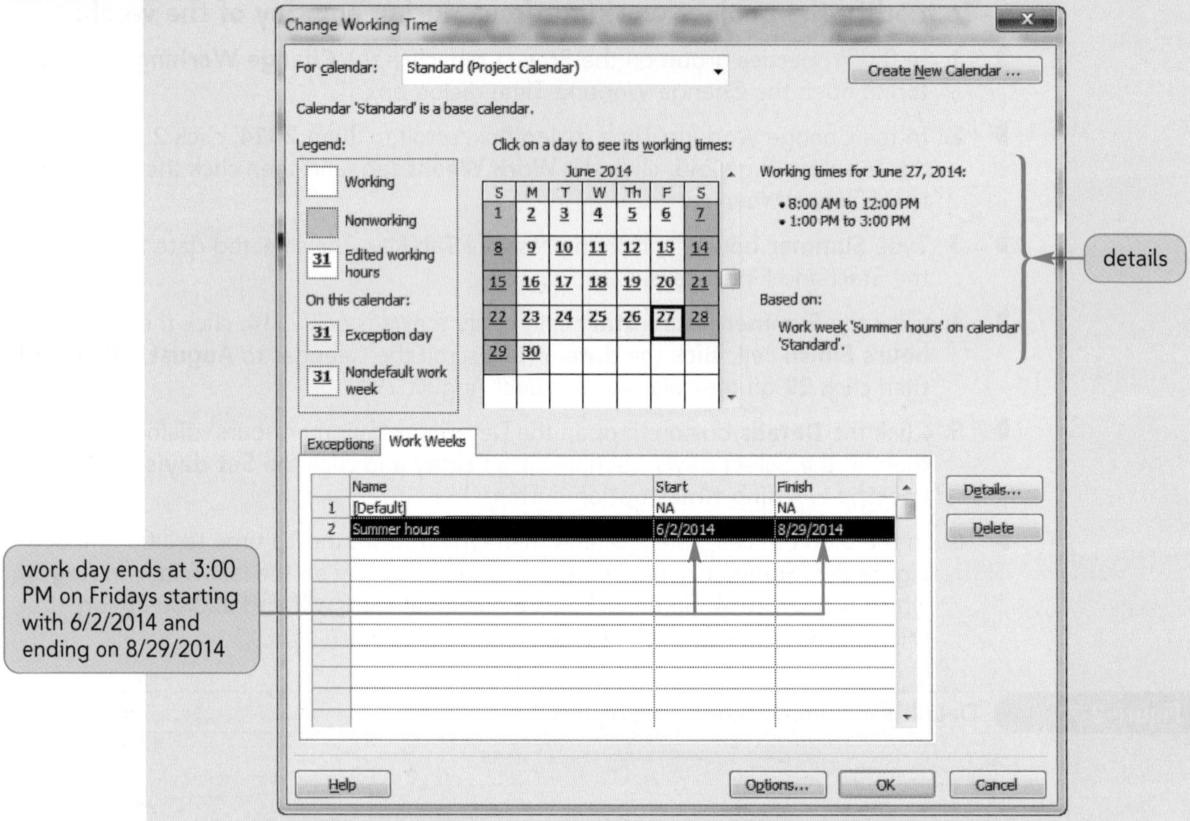

callout: details

callout: work day ends at 3:00 PM on Fridays starting with 6/2/2014 and ending on 8/29/2014

8. Scroll to **July 2014**. Notice how the colors on the Calendar provide information. The day for Friday July 4th is in blue because it is an exception day; the other weeks are in yellow as nondefault work weeks.

9. Scroll to **September 2014**. The calendar has white boxes for the work days and gray shading for nonworking days. This month has no exceptions or nondefault work weeks.

10. Scroll to **November 2014** and notice the blue exception days for November 27th and November 28th.

11. Click **OK** to close the Change Working Time dialog box.

12. Click the **File** tab on the Ribbon, click **Save**, navigate to the Project2\Tutorial folder, type **VPInstall-2** in the File name box, then click the **Save** button to save the project file.

TIP

Changes to the project calendar may affect the Start date or Finish date of the project depending on the changes you make and whether the project is scheduled from a Start date or a Finish date.

The Friday workday now ends at 3:00 PM for the summer months of June, July, and August. By modifying that day of the week, you specify that every Friday during the summer months for the duration of the project will have only six hours of work to be scheduled and completed. If you make additional modifications to an individual Friday, the changes made to that individual day override the change made to all Fridays during the summer months.

Changes to the project calendar can be made at any time during the development of the project. Now that you've examined the project calendar and made changes that affect the entire project, you will create an individual task calendar.

Creating Task Calendars

You can create an individual **task calendar** for any task that does not follow the working and nonworking times specified by the project calendar. For example, your company might have a policy that training tasks may occur only from 8:00 AM to 12:00 PM. To accommodate this, you could create a task calendar called Training calendar and apply it to the training tasks, which would prevent Project 2010 from scheduling any training activities in the afternoon. A task requiring 40 hours of training would take 5 days using the Standard calendar (8-hour workdays), however that same task would take 10 days using the Training calendar.

Likewise, you can create an individual **resource calendar** for a resource that does not follow the working and nonworking times specified by the project calendar. For example, contracted electricians might want to work from 7:00 AM to 11:30 AM and 12:30 PM to 4:00 PM. By assigning a resource to a resource calendar, you allow the resource to be scheduled on the days and times specified by the resource calendar rather than the project calendar. By default, all tasks and resource assignments inherit the project calendar unless you specify something else. How resource calendars affect task scheduling is discussed in more detail in a later tutorial.

REFERENCE

Creating a Task Calendar

- Click the Project tab on the Ribbon, and then, in the Properties group, click the Change Working Time button to open the Change Working Time dialog box.
- Click the Create New Calendar button, enter a name for the task calendar, click the appropriate option to determine whether the calendar should be created from scratch (a new Standard calendar without any holidays or other working time changes) or based on a copy of another calendar you created, and then click the OK button.
- Scroll to the date on the calendar that you want to select, and then click the date.
- Click the Work Weeks tab, click the next empty cell in the Name column, enter a Name to describe the changed work week, and then press the Tab key to select the Start cell. *Or,* if there is overlap in the work weeks, then you cannot create different working hours for the same span of time: click the Exceptions tab, click the next empty cell in the Name column, enter a Name to describe the changed work week, and then press the Tab key to select the Start cell.
- Click the Details button to open the Details dialog box.
- Select the Nonworking or Working times option button.
- Edit the From and To times in the table at the top of the Details dialog box.
- Click OK in both dialog boxes to apply the changes.

Sidney, the owner of ViewPoint Partners, has requested that the training on how to use the presentation rooms be scheduled at a time that does not disrupt the daily activities of ViewPoint Partners. Because most interviews and presentations occur Monday through Thursday in the afternoons at ViewPoint Partners, you create a calendar that allows training tasks to be scheduled only between the hours of 8:00 AM and 12:00 PM Monday through Thursday. Friday is a regular day so it is not affected by the Training calendar. Any tasks that are assigned the Training calendar will be affected for working hours Monday through Thursday. If the task is during the summer months, the summer hours that have been applied to the Standard calendar will apply on that Friday. You name the new calendar "Training," using a meaningful name to help you remember the tasks associated with the calendar.

To create a task calendar:

1. In the Properties group on the Project tab, click the **Change Working Time** button. The Change Working Time dialog box opens.

2. Scroll to **June 2014**, and then click **2**.

3. Click the **Create New Calendar** button. The Create New Base Calendar dialog box opens. You want to create a Training calendar based on the Standard calendar, which is a 40-hour work week (8:00 AM to 12:00 PM and 1:00 PM to 5:00 PM), Monday through Friday, with Saturday and Sunday designated as nonworking days.

4. In the Name box, type **Training**, and then click the **Make a copy of Standard calendar** option button if it is not already selected. See Figure 2-9.

TIP

You can make a copy of the Standard calendar so all of the holidays and working time changes that you already made to the Standard calendar will apply to this task calendar.

| Figure 2-9 | Creating a new calendar |

creating a new calendar named "Training" based on the Standard calendar

Click to select a different calendar on which to base the new calendar

5. Click the **OK** button to close the dialog box. "Training" appears in the For calendar: box at the top of the Change Working Time dialog box. Next, you will create an exception and change the working time for Monday through Thursday on the Training calendar to 8:00 AM to 12:00 PM. You select exception for the work times associated with the Training calendar because the Training hours for the days Monday, Tuesday, Wednesday, and Thursday will be different than the hours for other tasks not assigned to this calendar on that date.

6. In the Change Working Time dialog box, click the **Exceptions** tab if it is not already selected, click the first empty **Name** cell in in the Name column, type **Monday-Thursday**, and then press the **Tab** key. The selected date appears in the Start and Finish columns.

7. Click in the **Monday-Thursday Finish date** cell in the third row.

8. Click the **Details** button to open the Details for 'Monday-Thursday' dialog box, click the **Working times** option button, and then, in the Recurrence pattern section, click **Weekly** and click the check boxes for **Monday**, **Tuesday**, **Wednesday**, and **Thursday**.

9. In the Range of recurrence section, click the **End by** option button, click the calendar arrow, click the **Month** right arrow as many times as needed to display June 2015, and then click **2** to select **June 2, 2015**. This is one year from the Start date of the project.

10. In the Working times table, click the **2** row label to select the entire row, and then press the **Delete** key. The hour times in the second row are deleted. The training now will take place only from 8:00 AM to 12:00 PM, Monday through Thursday. See Figure 2-10.

Figure 2-10   **Working hours for Monday-Thursday on the Training calendar**

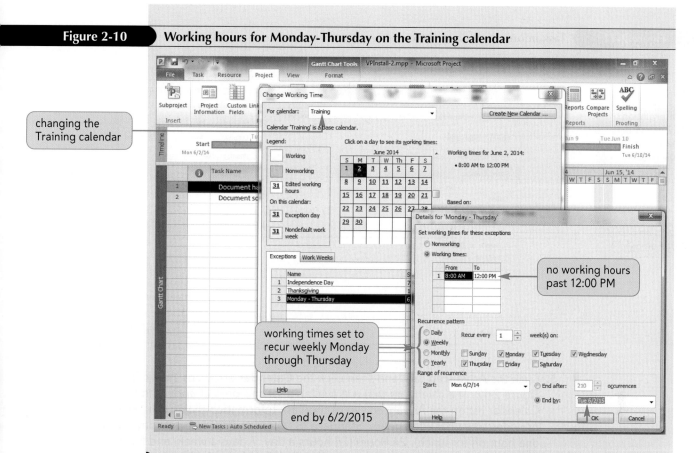

changing the Training calendar

working times set to recur weekly Monday through Thursday

no working hours past 12:00 PM

end by 6/2/2015

11. In the Details for 'Monday-Thursday' dialog box, click the **OK** button, and then click the **OK** button to close the Change Working Time dialog box. The Standard (Project Calendar) and Training calendars are now set up in the project file.

By default, all new tasks follow the project calendar, but you can apply a different calendar to a task by using the Task Information dialog box. Emily has asked you to assign the Training calendar to a task. Next, you assign the new calendar to a task and you observe how information associated with the task is affected by the calendars.

To apply a task calendar to a task:

1. Click the **Task Name** cell for the third row, type **Train users**, press the **Tab** key, type **2** for the duration, and then press the **Enter** key. The new task will take 16 hours, which is two days in the Standard calendar. You need to open the Task Information dialog box to change the calendar to the Training calendar for this task.

2. Click **Train users,** click the **Task** tab on the Ribbon, and then, in the Properties group, click the **Information** button to open the Task Information dialog box for that task. See Figure 2-11.

Figure 2-11   **Task information dialog box**

task duration is 2 days

Task Information dialog box contains information for the Train users task

task starts on 6/2/14 and ends on 6/3/14

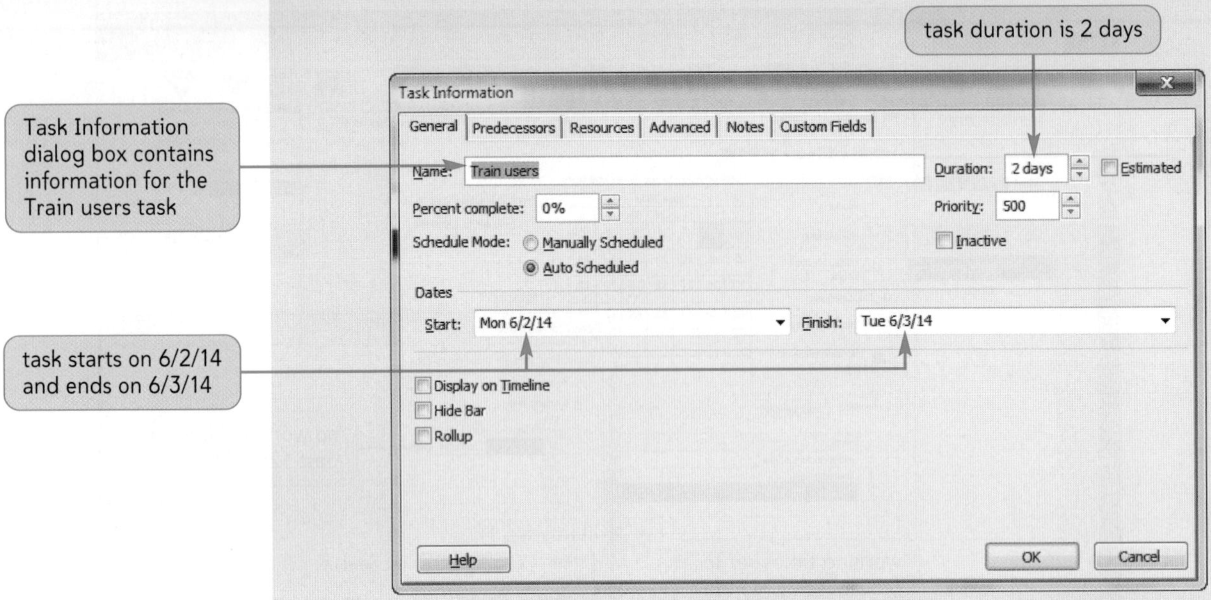

▸ **3.** Click the **Advanced** tab, and then click the **Calendar** arrow, as shown in Figure 2-12. The calendars that are available for this project appear in the Calendar list on the Advanced tab of the Task Information dialog box. Project provides three base calendars: Standard (8:00 AM to 5:00 PM weekdays, with one hour off for lunch), 24 Hours (24 hours a day, 7 days a week) and Night Shift (11 PM – 8 AM with a one-hour break between 3 AM and 4 AM).

Figure 2-12   **Changing the calendar for a task**

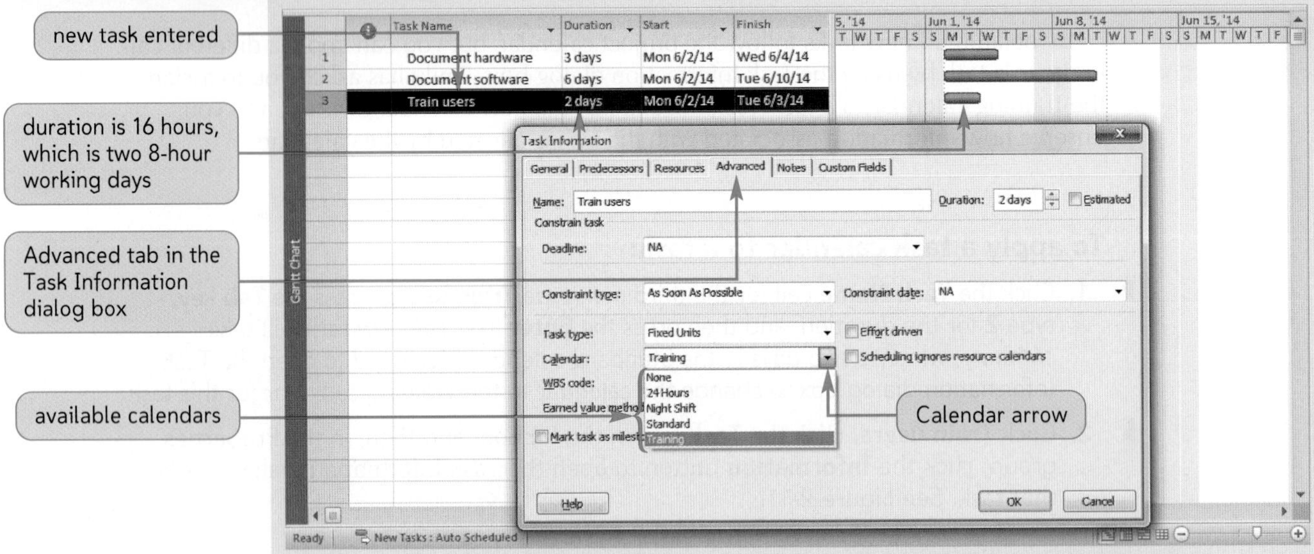

new task entered

duration is 16 hours, which is two 8-hour working days

Advanced tab in the Task Information dialog box

available calendars

Calendar arrow

▸ **4.** Click **Training**.

▸ **5.** Click the **OK** button, and then click the empty **Task Name** cell below Train users. Your screen should look like Figure 2-13. Although the duration did not change (a two-day duration still equals 16 hours of work), the task bar on the Gantt chart extended to four days to reflect the fact that this task can be completed only according to the working hours on the Training calendar, that is, 8:00 AM to 12:00 PM Monday through Thursday.

Figure 2-13   **Training calendar applied to the task**

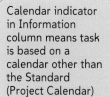

Calendar indicator in Information column means task is based on a calendar other than the Standard (Project Calendar)

length of bar extends 4 days because each day is only 4 working hours for this task

		Task Name	Duration	Start	Finish
1		Document hardware	3 days	Mon 6/2/14	Wed 6/4/14
2		Document software	6 days	Mon 6/2/14	Tue 6/10/14
3		Train users	2 days	Mon 6/2/14	Thu 6/5/14

duration still a standard 2 days or 16 hours of work

6. In the Train users task Indicators column for row 3, point to the **Calendar indicator**. The ScreenTip tells you that "The calendar 'Training' is assigned to the task." Many of the changes that you make in the Task Information dialog box, especially those that affect default settings, have corresponding indicators that appear in the Indicators column for that task.

7. On the Quick Access Toolbar, click the **Save** button 🔲 to save the project file.

Once you have finished the calendars, you are ready to enter additional tasks and durations for the project. Although you can alter the project calendar and create task calendars at any point during the project's creation, the more work that you put into developing realistic calendars up front, the more accurately Project 2010 will schedule task Start and Finish dates.

INSIGHT

Understanding the Hierarchy of Calendar Assignments

As you work with a project, occasionally you may wonder how Project calculated certain Start and Finish dates. Simple changes may generate dates that do not seem logical. Therefore, it's helpful to understand the hierarchy of calendar assignments. Project calculates when a resource and task are scheduled by using the calendars in the following order: project calendar, resource calendar, and task calendar. If a task has no resources and no task calendar, it is scheduled according to the project calendar. If a task has resources assigned and no task calendar, and the resources have resource calendars assigned, it is scheduled according to the related resource calendar. If the resource does not have a resource calendar, the project calendar is used. Then Project checks to see if any task calendars have been applied, and if so, calculates the dates in the same manner as if a resource calendar had been applied.

Entering Tasks and Durations in the Entry Table

After you have gathered all of the preliminary information required to plan your project and created your calendars, you are ready to enter tasks and durations into Project 2010. It is critical to be as comprehensive as possible in order to develop a useful project file. If tasks are omitted or durations underestimated, the value of the project's scheduling and cost information is compromised and the success of the project might be jeopardized. To gather the task and duration information, ask whether similar projects have been completed within your company and interview the staff members who have been involved so that you can document their experiences. If the project is a first-time endeavor, work with vendors and research the project on the Internet. The more sample task lists, checklists, and real-world experiences that you can bring to your project, the more likely that your project will represent realistic dates and costs.

Task names and durations are usually entered via the Entry table. Entering data in the table portion of the project file is similar to entering data in a spreadsheet such as Microsoft Excel. Before entering or editing the contents of a cell in the table, you must select the cell to make it active. As you may recall from Tutorial 1, the active cell is the cell that you are editing; a dark border surrounds it. Pressing the Enter key moves the active cell down one row in the same column. Refer to Figure 2-14 for more information on ways to navigate within a table, such as the Entry table.

| Figure 2-14 | Methods to navigate within a table |

Keys to Press	Result
[↑][↓][→][←]	Moves the active cell up, down, left, or right one cell
[Tab], [Shift]+[Tab]	Moves the active cell right or left one cell
[Pg Up], [Pg Dn]	Moves the active cell one screen up or down
[Home], [End]	Moves the active cell to the first or last column in that row
[Ctrl]+[Home], [Ctrl]+[End]	Moves the active cell to the first column of the first row or the last column of the last row (that contains a task name)
Left click	Makes the cell you click the active cell

You continue to enter the tasks for the ViewPoint Partners project. Project 2010 makes entering tasks easy with enhanced features such as AutoComplete, which displays a list of previously used values that can be selected to enter information. If you have already typed part of a task, such as "Create a diagram," and if another task is "Create a budget," then the text "Create a" will appear in the cell. For task names that exceed the column width, automatic text wrap eliminates extra formatting steps by adjusting row height to display the full task name.

To enter tasks and durations:

TIP

Because days is the default duration and the durations for these tasks are specified in days, you need to enter only the number portion of the duration.

1. Click the **Task Name** cell for the fourth row, type **Document current environment**, press the **Tab** key, type **5**, and then press the **Enter** key. Notice how the task name wrapped in the cell so you can see the entire task name within the current column width.

2. Click the **Task Name** cell for the fifth row, and then enter the following seven tasks and durations in the Entry table: **Conduct needs analysis**, **15 days**; **Build RFP**, **2 days**; **Gather bids**, **15 days**; **Choose vendors**, **2 days**; **Install hardware**, **3 days**; **Install software**, **3 days**; **Conduct training**, **5 days**.

   Trouble? The Entry table has many columns of information, some of which are currently hidden by the Gantt chart. If the active cell moves under the Gantt chart, press the Home key to position the active cell in the first column of that row or drag the split bar right to show more columns in the Entry table.

3. Click the **View** tab on the Ribbon, and then, in the **Zoom** group, click the **Zoom** button 🔍▾.

4. Click **Zoom** on the menu, click the **Entire project** option button, click the **OK** button, and then save your work.

Based on the duration of the eleven tasks, this project, VPInstall-2, starts on June 2, 2014 and ends on Monday June 23, 2014, as shown in Figure 2-15.

Figure 2-15   **Project after tasks and durations are entered**

Timeline shows overview of project

text wraps so entire task is visible in column

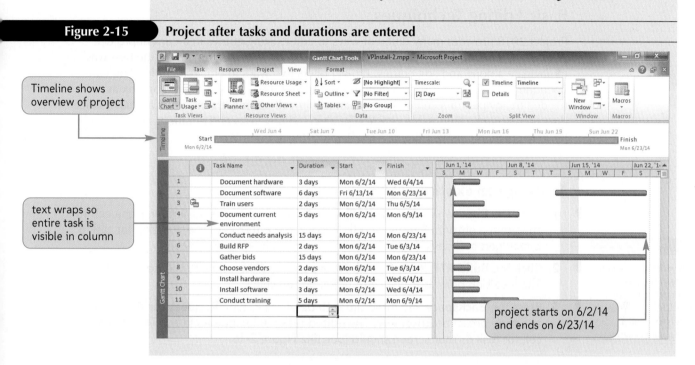

project starts on 6/2/14 and ends on 6/23/14

The tasks all start on the same date, which is not how projects work in the real world. In the second session, you learn how to link tasks by creating dependencies. **Dependencies** determine which tasks have to wait for other tasks to finish in order to begin. Dependencies change start and finish dates for tasks and for the project.

INSIGHT

Using AutoComplete

As you entered the task Install software, you probably noticed that AutoComplete entered "Install hardware" highlighted in the cell as soon as you typed "Ins". If you wanted to reenter that task or expand the phrase by using "Install hardware" as the first part of a new task, such as "Install hardware center," you could press the right arrow key or the Enter key to accept the AutoComplete suggestion. AutoComplete is a feature that exists in many Office programs such as Project, Word, Excel, Access, PowerPoint, and Outlook. You use AutoComplete to facilitate entering repeated phrases and words. AutoComplete is helpful if you have a field that has several repeated entries. For example, you might create a custom field called "Color" which can include limited entries such as red, blue, yellow, and green. When entering task information, you simply have to type the first letter of each color and then press the Enter key to enter the information.

When you are building a new project, your goal is to enter all of the task names and durations correctly. If you are creating a file based on chronological tasks, you also want to enter tasks in the order in which they are to be completed. Often, however, as you build the project, you will need to insert a new task or you will need to delete or move an existing task.

Editing Tasks and Durations in the Entry Table

Project 2010 makes it very easy to edit an existing project. Editing tasks includes changing the information associated with a specific task as well as inserting or deleting tasks. Over the span of a project, you will have many opportunities to edit project components.

Basic Editing Techniques

Project 2010 provides many different ways to edit existing entries in a current project. As you work with the program, you will develop your own preferences for the best way to navigate among and edit entries. Project offers two ways to edit cell entries: You can open the task's Task Information dialog box and edit the entries in the dialog box as needed to any part of a cell entry. You can use **in-cell editing**, that is, you can make edits directly within the Entry table cell. You practice editing tasks and durations as you continue to create the project file for ViewPoint Partners.

To change an existing entry:

TIP

You can widen the column to see the entire task name in the one row by double-clicking between the Task Name and Duration column headings.

1. Click the **Choose vendors (task 8) Duration** cell, click the **up arrow** in the cell to change the entry to **3 days**, and then press the **Enter** key. The duration for task 8 is changed to 3 days, and the task 9 Duration cell is the active cell.

2. Click the **Build RFP (task 6) Task Name** cell, and then click to the right of "P". The insertion point is to the right of RFP in the cell.

3. Press the **Backspace** key three times to delete RFP, type **Request for Proposal**, and then press the **Enter** key. The edited task name appears in the Task Name cell for task 6. Your screen should look like Figure 2-16.

Figure 2-16   Editing tasks and durations

task name changed

duration changed

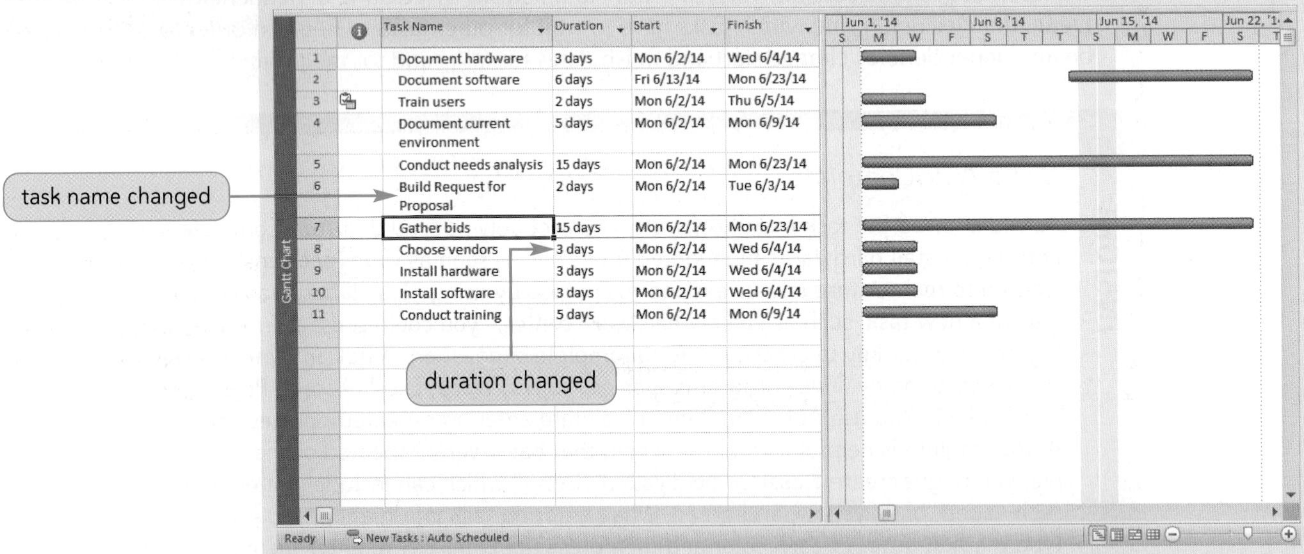

4. Double-click the **Gather bids (task 7) Task Name** cell. The Task Information dialog box for task 7, Gather bids, opens. The Name text box is selected.

5. In the name text box, click to the right of "r" in Gather, press the **Spacebar**, type **vendor**, and then press the **Enter** key. You can see the change in the Entry table.

In addition to editing information associated with individual tasks, other common editing activities include inserting and deleting tasks. As you continue to plan the project by conducting research and meeting with management, you might find that new tasks are required. There are many ways to insert a new task: You can use the shortcut menu, the Ribbon, or the keyboard. Each method inserts a new task. The method you choose will depend on your personal computing preferences.

REFERENCE

Inserting a Task

- In the Entry table, click any cell in the row below where you want to insert the new task.
- Click the Task tab on the Ribbon, and then, in the Insert group, click the Task button. (*Or Click the Task tab on the Ribbon, and then, in the Insert group, click the Task button arrow and click one of the options for a new task.*)

or

- In the Entry table, click any cell in the row below where you want to insert the new task, right-click, and then click Insert Task on the shortcut menu. (*Note*: You can also press the Insert key to insert a new task above the selected row.)
- Enter the Task Name and Duration information.

To insert a task:

▶ **1.** Click the **Install hardware (task 9) Task Name** cell, click the **Task** tab on the Ribbon, and then, in the Insert group, click the **Task** button. A new row 9 appears in the Entry table with a <New Task> placeholder, ready for you to enter the new task name. The task that formerly occupied row 9 has been moved down to row 10; all subsequent tasks have moved down one row and have been renumbered as well.

▶ **2.** Type **Install cabling**, press the **Tab** key, type **1**, and then press the **Enter** key. The new task is inserted as task 9 in the project.

TIP

You can also press the Insert key to insert a new task.

Sometimes during project planning, you will determine that all or part of a task is no longer required and you want to delete it. Deleting and editing tasks in Project 2010 is similar to performing those operations in spreadsheet software. As with many editing tasks, you will find there are several ways to perform the same tasks. In addition, Smart Tags appear in certain situations when you have a choice as to how you want to proceed with a task. If you press the Delete key when you have a task selected, a Smart Tag will appear in the Indicators column offering you the choice of either clearing the contents of that cell or deleting the entire task. Which method you choose to use when deleting tasks or contents of cells is just a matter of personal preference.

REFERENCE

Deleting a Task or the Contents of a Cell in the Entry table

To delete an entire task:
- Click any cell for the task that you want to delete, click the Task tab on the Ribbon, and then, in the Editing group, click the Clear button to open the menu. Click Entire Row to delete the entire task.

or
- Click the row number, and then press the Delete key.

or
- Click the row number, right-click the task, and then click Delete Task on the shortcut menu.

To delete the contents of a task cell:
- Click the cell that you want to delete, click the Task tab on the Ribbon, and then, in the Editing group, click the Clear button, and then click Clear All on the menu that opens. (*Note:* Other Clear options include Clear Hyperlinks, Notes, Entire Row, and Formatting.)

or
- Right-click the task cell, and then, on the shortcut menu, click Clear Contents.

or
- Click in the Task Name cell, and then press the Delete key.

TIP

You can also click the row number to select the entire row, and then press the Delete key. Or you can right click the task name, and then click Delete Task.

To delete a task:

1. Click the **Document current environment (task 4) Task Name** cell, and then press the **Delete** key. The task name is deleted and a Smart Tag ⊠ appears in the Indicators column for task 4. The Smart Tag allows you to specify exactly what you want to delete if you press the Delete key with only one cell selected.

2. Click the **Smart Tag** ⊠ to reveal the two menu choices, as shown in Figure 2-17. The default is to clear only the contents of the Task Name cell.

Figure 2-17   **Smart Tag selection for deleting all or part of a task**

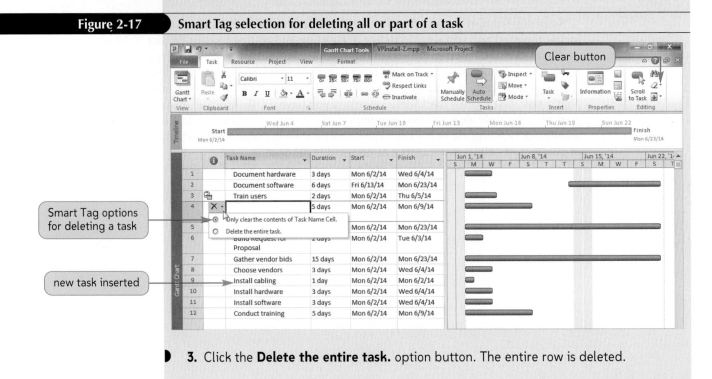

3. Click the **Delete the entire task.** option button. The entire row is deleted.

Correcting Mistakes by Using Undo and Redo

In the business community, you will find that the process for creating a viable Project file, or to any completed document or spreadsheet for that matter, is not always a straight one. To create the best project file, you can test different names, durations, and ideas. When changes to a project file are necessary, Project 2010 makes it easy to test these changes with the Multiple Level Undo feature. As a project manager, you may want to try different task names and durations. If you make a mistake while making edits or if you decide you prefer the previous version of the tasks, you can click Edit on the menu bar, and then click Undo. The Multiple Level Undo and Redo feature gives you an easy way to experiment with different scenarios, and enables you to undo and redo changes to views, data, and options.

You can undo and redo multiple changes you made before or after the last change. The default setting is 20. If you find that you need more levels of Undo, you can increase the setting by changing the option in the Project Options dialog box. To open the Project Options dialog box, click the File tab on the Ribbon, click Options, click the Advanced tab, and then change the number in the Undo levels box as needed. It is important to note that once you save your Project file, the Undo actions are deleted and you can no longer undo the actions made prior to saving the file.

You decide you want to keep the Document current environment task after all. You also want to change the name of the Conduct training task.

TIP

Click the Undo or Redo button arrow to see the list of actions that you can undo and redo.

To undo an action and edit a task name:

▶ 1. On the Quick Access toolbar, click the **Undo** button ↻ twice. You clicked once to undo the Delete command and again to undo the Clear command. The Document current environment task appears in the Entry table again.

▶ 2. Right-click the **Conduct training (task 12) Task Name** cell, click **Clear Contents** on the shortcut menu, type **Promote new services**, and then press the **Enter** key. Using the shortcut menu is often more efficient than pressing either the Backspace key or the Delete key to change a cell's contents.

Cutting, Copying, Pasting, and Moving Tasks

Cutting, copying, pasting, and moving tasks are important task editing skills. When you cut a task, you remove it from its current location and place it on the clipboard. When you copy a task, you leave the task in its current location and place a copy on the clipboard. When you paste a task, you insert it from the clipboard to a new location. Project 2010 offers a variety of techniques that you can use to accomplish these common tasks, including Ribbon commands, mouse actions, quick keystrokes, and right-click shortcut menus. Moving tasks is even easier than copying and pasting them. You could use the Cut, Copy, and Paste buttons on the Ribbon, or the Cut Cell, Copy Cell, Cut, and Paste commands on the shortcut menus. If you are familiar with the Paste Special commands in Office programs such as Word, Access, PowerPoint, and Excel, these features will be similar in Project.

The Paste Special dialog box gives you the option to Paste the contents of the clipboard or to Paste a link. The Paste a link option will be discussed later in this book when you learn about integrating Project with other programs. Paste Special options include Microsoft Word Document, Project Data, HTML, Picture, or Text Data.

REFERENCE

Cutting or Copying and Moving Tasks

To cut and move tasks:
- Right-click the row selector for the task that you want to cut and move, and then, on the shortcut menu, click Cut; or, click the task row selector, click the Task tab on the Ribbon, and then click the Cut button in the Clipboard group.
- Right-click the row selector of the row in which you want the cut task to appear, and then, on the shortcut menu, click Paste or Paste Special; or, click the row selector of the row in which you want the cut task to appear, and then, on the Task tab on the Ribbon, click the Paste button; or, click the Paste button arrow and select the desired option.

To copy and move tasks:
- Right-click the row selector for the task that you want to copy and move, and then, on the shortcut menu, click Copy; or, click the task row selector, click the Task tab on the Ribbon, and then click the Copy button in the Clipboard group.
- Right-click the row selector of the row in which you want the copied task to appear, and then, on the shortcut menu, click Paste or Paste Special; or, click the row selector of the row in which you want the cut task to appear, and then, on the Task tab on the Ribbon, click the Paste button; or, click the Paste button arrow and select the desired option.

To copy and paste a task:

1. Right-click the **Train users (task 3) row selector**, and then, on the shortcut menu, click **Copy**. The row selector, which is the box containing the row number, is selected, and the task is copied to the Clipboard.

   Trouble? If you right-click a cell instead of the row selector to the left of the task row, the command Copy Cell appears on the shortcut menu instead of Copy. Press the Esc key to close the shortcut menu, and then repeat Step 1.

2. Right-click the **task 13 row selector** (the blank row selector below row 12), and then, on the shortcut menu, click **Paste**. The task is copied to the new row, as shown in Figure 2-18. You can edit the copied task to create a new task.

Figure 2-18	Copying and pasting a task

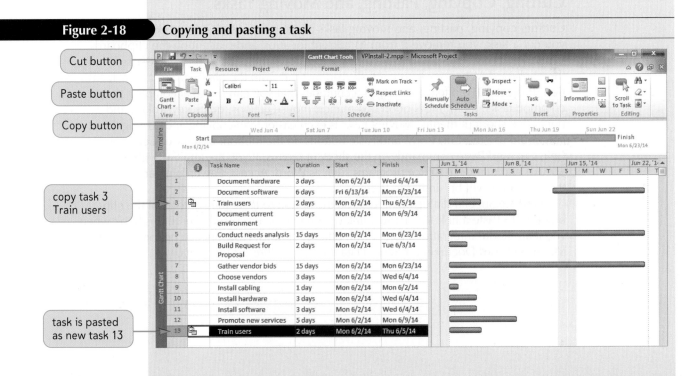

Cut button

Paste button

Copy button

copy task 3
Train users

task is pasted
as new task 13

3. Double-click the **Train users (task 13) Task Name** cell to open the Task Information dialog box, double-click **users** in the Name text box, type **management**, and then press the **Enter** key.

4. Click the **Choose vendors (task 8) Task Name** cell, and then, in the cell, drag to select **vendor** (do not select the ending "s").

5. Right-click the selected cell, and then, on the shortcut menu, click **Copy**. The word "vendor" is copied to the Clipboard. This method can be helpful if long or hard-to-spell words are part of task names.

6. Click the **Build Request for Proposal (task 6) Task Name** cell, click to the right of "d" in "Build" in the active cell, press the **Spacebar**, right-click, and then click **Paste** on the shortcut menu. The word "vendor" is pasted into the task name. The task name for task 6 is now Build vendor Request for Proposal.

7. Press the **Enter** key, and then save your work.

Another easy way to move a task is to drag its **row selector**. When copying and pasting tasks, it doesn't matter what method you choose. What does matter is that you first click the row selector before initiating the Copy command if you want to copy all of the information for that particular task and not copy only the active cell's contents.

To move a task:

1. Click the **Train management (task 13) row selector**, press and hold the mouse button, and then drag the row selector up between tasks 11 and 12, as shown in Figure 2-19. A horizontal bar indicates the position of the task as you drag.

Figure 2-19   Moving a task

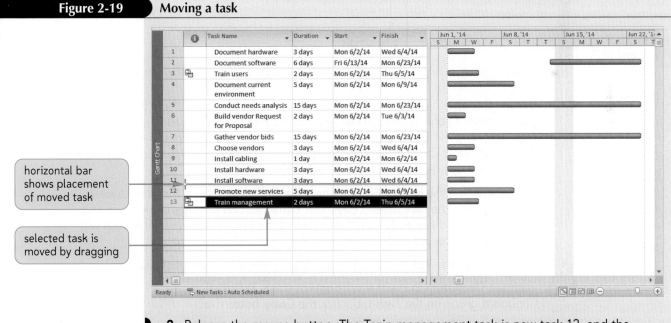

horizontal bar shows placement of moved task

selected task is moved by dragging

2. Release the mouse button. The Train management task is now task 12, and the Promote new services task is renumbered as task 13.

3. Right-click the **Train users (task 3) row selector**, and then click **Cut** on the shortcut menu. The task is removed from the Entry table and placed on the Clipboard.

Make sure you right-click the row selector to cut and then paste the entire task, not just selected cell data.

> **4.** Right-click the **Promote new services (task 12) row selector**, click **Paste Special** on the shortcut menu, be sure the **Paste** option button is selected, be sure **Project Data** is selected in the As: box, and then click the **OK** button. Train users is inserted as task 12, and Promote new services moves down to task 13.

If several task names or durations are the same, you can either use the copy and paste features to quickly enter the task names or durations or use the fill handle to populate cells. If you have used the fill handle in Excel or another spreadsheet program, you will find it a very similar process in Project 2010. The **fill handle** is a small square, which appears in the lower-right corner of the selected cell, that you can drag to copy the contents of the active cell to the cells below it.

To use the fill handle and Copy and Paste buttons to copy and paste information in a cell:

TIP

The fill handle cannot be used when cells are not contiguous.

> **1.** Click the **Install software (task 10) Duration** cell, point to the small square in the lower-right corner of the active cell so that the pointer changes to ✛, press and hold the left mouse button, and then drag down two rows so that the outline surrounds the Duration cells for tasks 11 and 12, as shown in Figure 2-20.

| Figure 2-20 | Using the fill handle |

Training calendar still in effect for these two tasks

dragging to select rows 10, 11, and 12

fill handle

> **2.** Release the left mouse button. The 3-day duration from task 10 fills in the duration cells for tasks 11 and 12. As you can see, the Train management and Train users tasks are using the Training calendar—so even though you changed the duration to 3 days, the Gantt Chart shows the task spanning 6 working days because they work 4 hours each day rather than 8 hours each day.

Notice also that the bar for Promote new services extends into Monday, June 9. This is because the task takes 5 days, but Friday follows summer work hours and so work ends at three on Friday. Two hours of the Promote new services task will need to be completed on Monday, June 9.

You think that the Install cabling task will take five days instead of one day.

> **3.** Click the **Document current environment (task 3) Duration** cell, and then, in the Clipboard group on the Task tab, click the **Copy** button.

> **4.** Click the **Install cabling (task 8) Duration** cell, and then, in the Clipboard group on the Task tab, click the **Paste** button. The duration 5 days for task 3 is copied and pasted as the duration for task 8.

▶ **5.** Click the **Paste Options** button 📋 ▾, review the Paste Options menu, then click the **Install cabling (task 8) Task Name** cell. When you copy and paste, you have the option of keeping the source formatting or matching the destination formatting. When you format the Entry table in the next tutorial, this will be more valuable. Emily, technology specialist for ViewPoint partners, says that task 8 will really take only one day, so you need to undo the change.

TIP

You can also press [Ctrl]+[Z] to undo the last action.

▶ **6.** On the Quick Access toolbar, click the **Undo** button 🔄. The Undo button undoes your last action in the current project, whether it was to paste a cell entry, delete a task, or modify some other aspect of the current project.

▶ **7.** On the Quick Access toolbar, click the **Save** button 💾 to save your project file.

Working with Duration Units of Measure

Entering and editing durations involves understanding the units of measure available for them. The default unit of measure is "day", and therefore "day" does not need to be entered. Most project tasks take days or hours. However, some projects require greater or lesser levels of detail so you might need to use weeks or months for some tasks, or minutes for others. To use any other unit, you must type it. You can type the whole word or use its abbreviation, as shown in Figure 2-21.

Figure 2-21	Units of measure abbreviations

Type This Abbreviation	To Get This Unit of Measurement	Type This Abbreviation	To Get This Unit of Measurement
m	minute	em	elapsed minute
h	hour	eh	elapsed hour
d (default)	day	ed	elapsed day
w	week	ew	elapsed week
mon	month	emon	elapsed month

Elapsed time refers to clock time rather than working time. Some tasks are completed over an elapsed period of time regardless of whether the time is working or nonworking. An example is the task "Allow paint to dry." The paint will dry in exactly the same amount of time regardless of whether it dries on a workday, a weekend, or a holiday. If it takes one day to dry, the duration is one elapsed day and should be entered as "1ed."

If you are not sure how long to enter for a task's duration and want to be reminded to study it later, enter a question mark (?) after the duration entry to indicate that it is estimated. Later, you will learn how to quickly find and filter tasks based on estimated durations. Recall that if you do not enter a duration for a task, Project 2010 displays "1d?" to indicate a default estimated duration of one day.

You want to change the durations for tasks 4 and 6 from 15 days to three weeks. Fifteen days of work is equal to three weeks of work in a standard five-workday week, but you prefer to show the duration in the week unit of measure.

To edit durations:

▶ 1. Click the **Conduct needs analysis (task 4) Duration** cell, type **3w**, and then press the **Enter** key. The duration for task 4 is changed from 15 days to three weeks. Next, you adjust the duration for Gather vendor bids (task 6). You think you know how long the task will take, but you want to remember to revisit the task 6 duration at a later date. So, in addition to changing the unit of measure for the duration from days to weeks, you'll change the duration to an estimated duration. The question mark indicates that you are not really quite sure how long this task will take and want a reminder that this is your best guess at this time.

▶ 2. Click the **Gather vendor bids (task 6) Duration** cell, type **3w?**, and then press the **Enter** key. Your screen should look like Figure 2-22.

| Figure 2-22 | Changing task durations |

duration in weeks

duration in estimated weeks

		Task Name	Duration	Start	Finish	Jun 1, '14	Jun 8, '14	Jun 15, '14	Jun 22, '1
1		Document hardware	3 days	Mon 6/2/14	Wed 6/4/14				
2		Document software	6 days	Fri 6/13/14	Mon 6/23/14				
3		Document current environment	5 days	Mon 6/2/14	Mon 6/9/14				
4		Conduct needs analysis	3 wks	Mon 6/2/14	Mon 6/23/14				
5		Build vendor Request for Proposal	2 days	Mon 6/2/14	Tue 6/3/14				
6		Gather vendor bids	3 wks?	Mon 6/2/14	Mon 6/23/14				
7		Choose vendors	3 days	Mon 6/2/14	Wed 6/4/14				
8		Install cabling	1 day	Mon 6/2/14	Mon 6/2/14				
9		Install hardware	3 days	Mon 6/2/14	Wed 6/4/14				
10		Install software	3 days	Mon 6/2/14	Wed 6/4/14				
11		Train management	3 days	Mon 6/2/14	Mon 6/9/14				
12		Train users	3 days	Mon 6/2/14	Mon 6/9/14				
13		Promote new services	5 days	Mon 6/2/14	Mon 6/9/14				

Ready   New Tasks : Auto Scheduled

▶ 3. On the Quick Access toolbar, click the **Save** button to save the project.

While most of your task and duration entry and editing will be done in the Entry table displayed to the left of the Gantt chart, tasks and durations can be entered and edited in any view.

Editing Tasks and Durations in Other Views

Anything changed in one view will be reflected in all of the other views. You can use the View Bar or the View tab on the Ribbon to quickly switch between views. As you learned in Tutorial 1, the way the data is displayed differs by view, and each view satisfies different communication and reporting needs.

To edit durations in the Gantt chart:

▶ 1. In the Gantt chart, click the **Choose vendors (task 7) bar,** and then place the ⊕ on the bar. A ScreenTip appears that gives information about the task's name, duration, and Start and Finish dates.

2. Verify that the zoom of the Gantt chart is set so the top tier is in weeks and the bottom tier is days or every other day (depending on your screen resolution) to give you a better view of the days.

3. In the Gantt chart, point to the right edge of the **Choose vendors (task 7)** bar. The pointer changes to ⊩ and appears on the right edge of the bar, indicating that you can drag the length of the bar to the right to increase the duration for that task. Notice that durations can be fractions of days.

4. Using the ⊩ pointer, drag the **Choose vendors (task 7) bar** to the right until the ScreenTip displays a duration of 5.25d, as shown in Figure 2-23. You had to drag over the nonworking weekend days to reach your goal.

Figure 2-23   Changing a task duration by dragging the Gantt chart bar

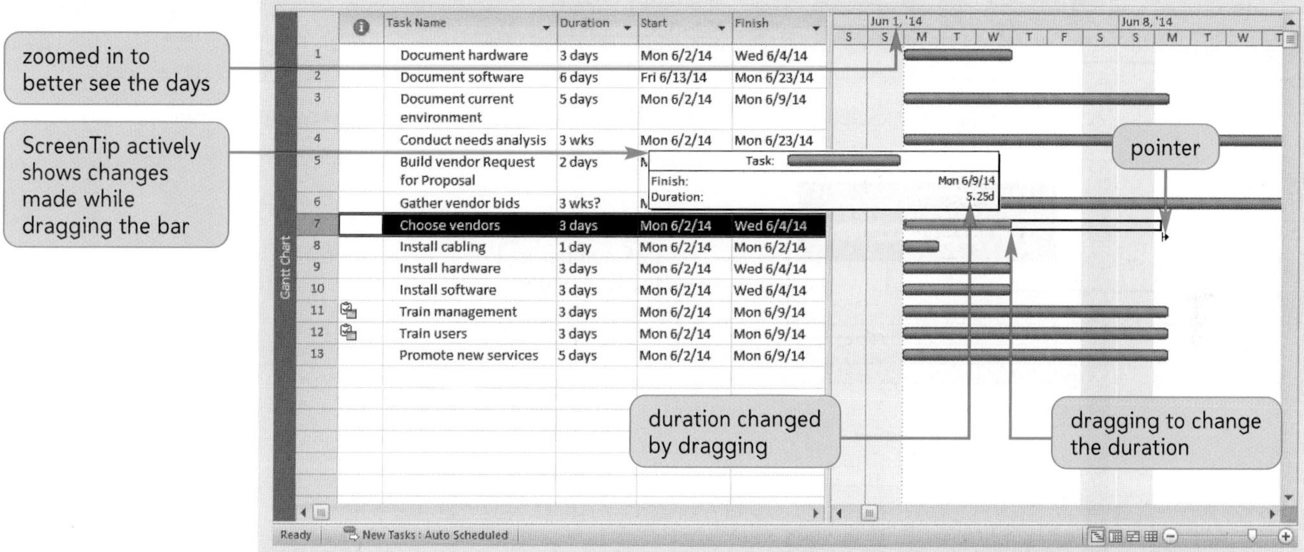

5. Release the mouse button. Notice that when you stop dragging the pointer, the duration in the Choose vendors (task 7) Duration cell in the Entry table also changed to 5.25 days.

The Gantt Chart, Network Diagram, and Calendar views are usually not used for extensive data entry; they are useful for viewing patterns and relationships. However, if you are viewing your project in one of these views and need to edit a task, Project 2010 provides a way. For example, in addition to changing the duration of a task by dragging a bar in Gantt Chart view, you can increase or decrease the length of the bars in Calendar view to increase or decrease the duration of a task. Regardless of the current view, you can edit any task by double-clicking it to open its Task Information dialog box.

Changing Durations in the Network Diagram

You need to change the durations for several tasks. You'll do the first task in Network Diagram view.

To enter and edit durations in Network Diagram view:

▶ **1.** Click the **View** tab on the Ribbon, and then, in the Task Views group, click the **Network Diagram** button. The view changes to the Network Diagram view. The Network Diagram Tools Format tab is available on the Ribbon, and the View tab is still the active tab.

▶ **2.** In the Network Diagram, scroll to the top of the page to view the **Document hardware (task 1) box**, click **Dur: 3 days** (the duration for task 1), type **4**, and then press the **Enter** key. The duration for task 1 is changed to four days. See Figure 2-24.

Figure 2-24	Duration changed in Network Diagram

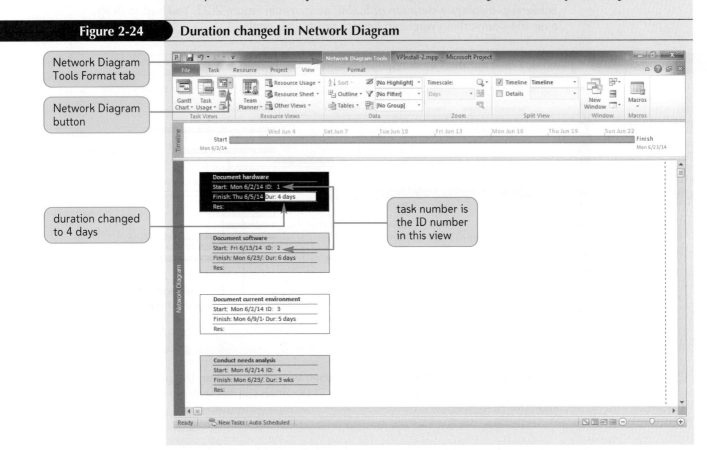

Now you want to edit the duration of Install cabling (task 8) in Calendar view. Calendar view shows bars similar to the bars in the Gantt chart.

To enter and edit durations in the Calendar view:

▶ **1.** In the Task Views group on the View tab, click the **Calendar** button. The view changes to Calendar view. The Calendar Tools Format tab is available on the Ribbon. The Month pane is open on the left side of the Calendar.

▶ **2.** Right-click the space next to the Custom button above the Calendar, click **Timescale** on the shortcut menu to open the Timescale dialog box, click the **Display month pane** check box to remove the check mark, and then click the **OK** button. You cannot see all the tasks in the first week. Black arrows in the date boxes indicate that there are more tasks to be seen.

▶ **3.** Click the **black down arrow** ↓ to the left of the "3" for June 3rd to open the tasks list for that date. The task list has a scroll bar so you can scroll to see all the tasks, and a black box surrounds the tasks in the first week for June 3.

4. Click **Tuesday** to close the tasks list, point to the bottom of the black box that encloses the first week tasks until the pointer changes ✛, and then use the ✛ to drag the bottom border of the first week down approximately two inches so that all of the tasks that start in the first week are visible and the black arrows no longer appear. See Figure 2-25.

Figure 2-25   **Expanding the size of the weeks on the Calendar**

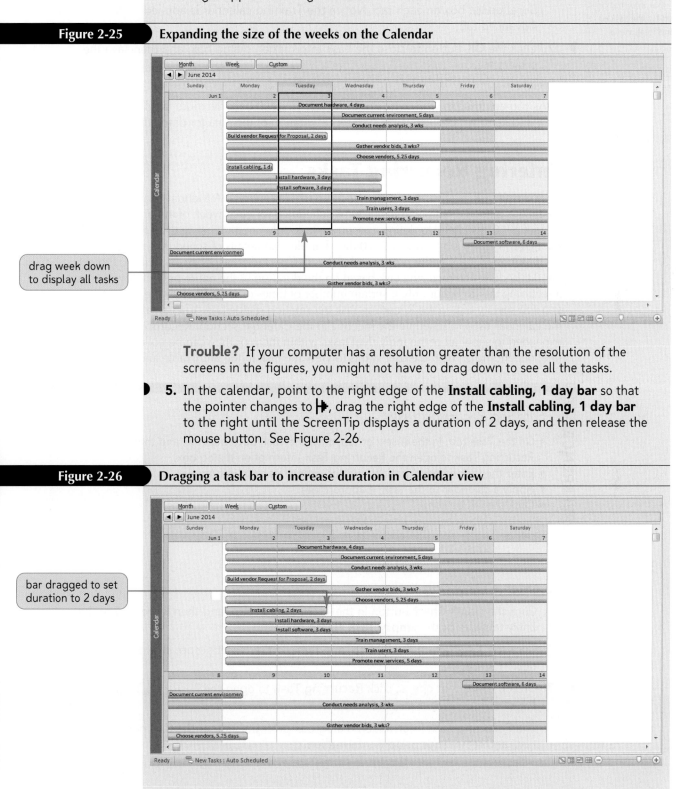

drag week down to display all tasks

Trouble? If your computer has a resolution greater than the resolution of the screens in the figures, you might not have to drag down to see all the tasks.

5. In the calendar, point to the right edge of the **Install cabling, 1 day bar** so that the pointer changes to ↔, drag the right edge of the **Install cabling, 1 day bar** to the right until the ScreenTip displays a duration of 2 days, and then release the mouse button. See Figure 2-26.

Figure 2-26   **Dragging a task bar to increase duration in Calendar view**

bar dragged to set duration to 2 days

TIP

Regardless of which tab in the Task Information dialog box you use to change the task name or duration, that information is changed for the task on all tabs and in all views.

6. In the first week, double-click the **Train management task** to open the Task Information dialog box, and then click each tab in the Task Information dialog box (General, Predecessors, Resources, Advanced, Notes, and Custom Fields) to observe the types of task information that can be modified on each tab. Notice that the task name appears in the Name box and the duration appears in the Duration list box on each tab. Notice the Training calendar is applied on the Advanced tab.

7. Click the **OK** button to close the Task Information dialog box, and then save the project file.

As you continue to work with Project 2010, you will become more familiar with each view and learn which view is the best representation of the data for different purposes.

Entering Recurring Tasks

A **recurring task** is a task that is repeated at a regular interval. A Monday morning status meeting is a good example; it needs to be scheduled for each week of the project. In Project 2010, you need to define a recurring task only one time using the Recurring Task Information dialog box. Project 2010 then handles the details of scheduling the task on each Monday for the entire project or for the time period you specify. By default, Project 2010 schedules the recurring task based on the duration of the entire project. If you want a recurring task to occur only a certain number of times or to end before the project ends, you can specify that in the Recurring Task Information dialog box. You can also change the calendar used to schedule the meeting in the Calendar section. Recurring tasks can be expanded to show all of the individual tasks within them or they can be collapsed to one line, depending on how the user wants to view the task in the Entry table and Gantt chart.

REFERENCE

Entering Recurring Tasks

- On the Task tab, in the Insert group, click the Task button arrow, and then click Recurring Task to open the Recurring Task Information dialog box.
- Enter the task name, duration, and recurrence pattern information.
- Apply a calendar to the task, if appropriate.
- Click the OK button.

To enter a recurring task:

1. Click the **Gantt Chart** button in the Task Views group, and then, in row 14 of the Entry table, click the **empty Task Name** cell.

2. Click the **Task** tab on the Ribbon, and then, in the Insert group, click the **Task** button arrow.

3. On the menu that opens, click **Recurring Task** to open the Recurring Task Information dialog box.

The Recurring Task Information dialog box prompts you for the task name, duration, and recurrence pattern information.

4. In the Task Name box, type **Weekly status meeting**, select **1d** in the Duration box, type **2h**, and then click the **Monday** check box. The Recurring Task Information dialog box should look like Figure 2-27, showing that you scheduled a two-hour status meeting for every Monday. The Start and End by dates in the dialog box reflect the current Start date and Finish date for the project and will change as the project is developed. If you enter specific dates or a number of occurrences for the recurring task, those choices will override the default assumption that the recurring task is to be scheduled for each Monday throughout the life of the project.

Figure 2-27	Recurring Task Information dialog box

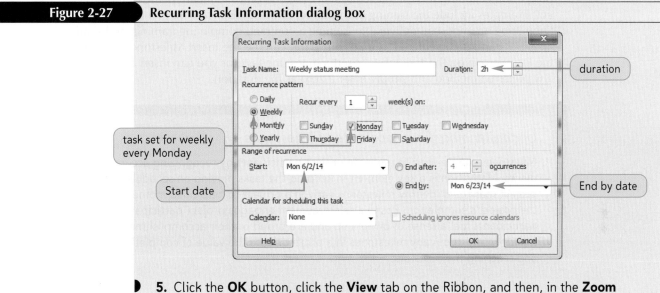

5. Click the **OK** button, click the **View** tab on the Ribbon, and then, in the **Zoom** group, click the **Zoom** button.

6. On the menu that opens, click **Zoom**, click the **Entire project** option button, and then click the **OK** button. The dialog box closes and the Gantt chart shows the recurring task 14 for each Monday. See Figure 2-28. A Recurring Task indicator appears in the Indicators column for this task; if you place the pointer on it, a ScreenTip appears providing information about the task.

Figure 2-28	Recurring task in Entry table

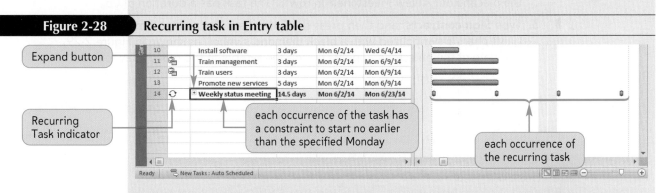

7. In the Entry table, click the **Weekly status meeting (task 14) Expand** button to the left of the task name to see the details of a recurring task. The task expands and the Expand button changes to the Collapse button.

▶ **8.** Click the **Weekly status meeting (task 14) Collapse** button ⊟. The details of
the recurring task collapse into one row in the Entry table.

▶ **9.** Save the project.

Entering Milestones

A **milestone** is a task with zero duration that marks a significant point in time or a
progress checkpoint. It is often used to mark the end of a significant phase of the project. Examples include the signing of a contract or the announcement of a new product.
Submitting an important deliverable, signing a contract, completing training, and similar
activities can also be entered as milestones. You can use the Insert Milestone button in
the Insert group on the Task tab to insert a milestone task, or you can insert a task using
any preferred method and simply enter a zero as the duration.

INSIGHT

Understanding the Importance of Milestones

Milestones can be used to motivate project participants by recognizing accomplishments. Motivation is a key element in keeping the tasks moving on schedule. Many
project managers identify milestones early in a project to help build momentum toward
the project's completion. Positive reinforcement engages project participants. Engaged
participants feel a sense of ownership and are proud of their accomplishments. Use milestones wisely; too many milestones in a project dilute the value of completing the task
and reaching the milestone.

To enter a milestone:

▶ **1.** Click the **Task** tab on the Ribbon, and then click the **Install cabling (task 8) Task
Name** cell.

▶ **2.** In the Insert group, click the **Insert Milestone** button ⬇ to insert a new task with
the placeholder <New Milestone> in row 8. The task has a duration of 0d.

▶ **3.** Type **Sign contracts**, and then press the **Enter** key. Notice that a milestone in the
Gantt chart is symbolized with a black diamond symbol, as shown in Figure 2-29.
The date of the milestone appears beside the symbol in the month/day format.

Figure 2-29   **Entering a milestone**

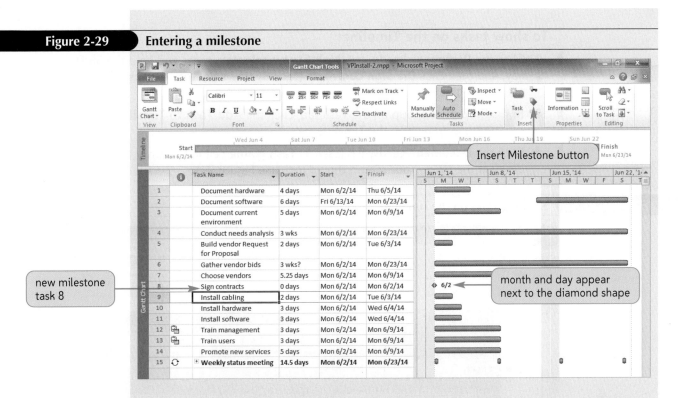

4. Save the project.

Trouble? If the Duration column displays a series of pound signs (##), the information is too wide to display within the width of the column. Double-click the line that separates the Duration column heading and the Start column heading.

Because milestones have no duration, they are scheduled without regard to working and nonworking time. Therefore, if you enter a milestone task that falls on a weekend, your milestone might be scheduled during the nonworking weekend before the task that the milestone marks. Obviously, the milestone you've entered for Sidney cannot occur until tasks 1 through 7 are finished. The next session introduces you to task dependencies, which help determine the sequencing and scheduling for each task in the project, including milestones.

Moving Tasks to the Timeline

Your project is taking shape, and although you can see the scope of the project through the Gantt chart, you want to see how it looks on the Timeline. You select the tasks that are listed before the milestone.

To show tasks on the Timeline:

To add tasks to the
Timeline, you can also
right-click the selected
row selectors area, and
then click Add to Timeline
on the shortcut menu.

TIP

1. Click the **Document hardware (task 1) row selector**, press and hold the **Shift** key, and then click the **Sign contracts (task 8) row selector**. The first eight tasks are selected.

2. In the Properties group on the Task tab, click the **Add Task to Timeline** button 🔳. The tasks appear on the Timeline.

3. Click the **Document hardware (task 1) Task Name** cell in the Entry table to deselect the tasks. Your screen should look like Figure 2-30.

Figure 2-30   Showing tasks on the Timeline

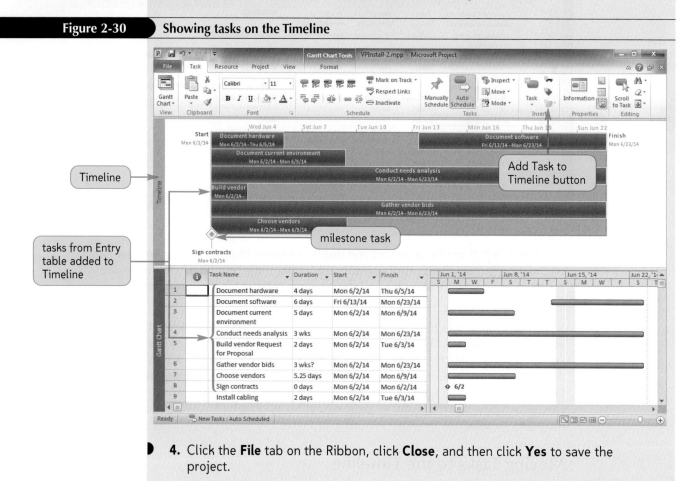

4. Click the **File** tab on the Ribbon, click **Close**, and then click **Yes** to save the project.

Now that you have finished entering tasks (including recurring tasks and milestones) and their associated durations, you are ready to establish task dependencies.

REVIEW

Session 2.1 Quick Check

1. In the Project Information dialog box, if the Schedule from option is set to Project Finish Date, how are the project Start and Finish dates scheduled?

2. In the Project Information dialog box, if the Schedule from option is set to Project Start Date, what constraint is used to assign individual Start dates to tasks?

3. What is the default calendar used to schedule the entire project?

4. If you click the row selector for a task and then press the Delete key, what will you erase?

5. How do you enter an estimated duration for three weeks?

6. How do you change the duration of a task in Calendar view?

7. What is the duration of a milestone?

SESSION 2.2 VISUAL OVERVIEW

You use the WBS button to open the WBS Code Definition dialog box or to renumber existing WBS codes.

The WBS column shows the WBS code. The **WBS (work breakdown structure) code** is an alphanumeric code used to represent each task's position within the hierarchical structure of the project.

This summary task is expanded. A **summary task** identifies a group of tasks that logically belong together.

The Subtasks for the Design summary task are indented. **Subtasks** are tasks that are grouped under a summary task.

Gantt Chart Tools   NewAV-2.mpp - Microsof

File	Task	Resource	Project	View	Format

Subproject | Project Information | Custom Fields | Links Between Projects | WBS | Change Working Time | Calculate Project | Set Baseline | Move Project

Insert   Properties   Schedule

Gantt Chart

	WBS	Task Name	Duration	Start	Finish	Pred
0		⊟ **Your Name**	**60.88 days**	**Mon 8/4/14**	**Wed 10/29/14**	
1	A	⊟ **Analysis**	**15 days**	**Mon 8/4/14**	**Mon 8/25/14**	
2	A.1	Detail current status	5 days	Mon 8/4/14	Mon 8/11/14	
3	A.2	Conduct needs analysis	3 wks	Mon 8/4/14	Mon 8/25/14	
4	B	⊟ **Design**	**18 days**	**Thu 8/21/14**	**Wed 9/17/14**	
5	B.1	Build Request for Propos	4 days	Thu 8/21/14	Wed 8/27/14	3FS-
6	B.2	Gather vendor bids	2 wks	Wed 8/27/14	Thu 9/11/14	5
7	B.3	Choose vendors	4 days	Thu 9/11/14	Wed 9/17/14	6
8	B.99	Sign contracts	0 days	Wed 9/17/14	Wed 9/17/14	7
9	C	⊟ **Installation**	**7.5 days**	**Wed 9/24/14**	**Fri 10/3/14**	
10	C.1	Install cabling	2 days	Wed 9/24/14	Fri 9/26/14	8FS
11	C.2	Install hardware	3 days	Thu 9/25/14	Tue 9/30/14	10S
12	C.3	Install software	3 days	Fri 9/26/14	Wed 10/1/14	11F
13	C.4	Test system	2 days	Wed 10/1/14	Fri 10/3/14	12
14	D	⊟ **Training**	**14.13 days**	**Thu 10/2/14**	**Wed 10/22/14**	
15	D.1	Train management	3 days	Thu 10/2/14	Mon 10/13/14	12
16	D.2	Train users	3 days	Mon 10/13/14	Wed 10/22/14	12,1
17	E	⊟ **Marketing**	**5 days**	**Wed 10/22/14**	**Wed 10/29/14**	14
18	E.1	Promote new services	5 days	Wed 10/22/14	Wed 10/29/14	

◄ |⫴|

Ready   New Tasks : Auto Scheduled

TASK DEPENDENCIES

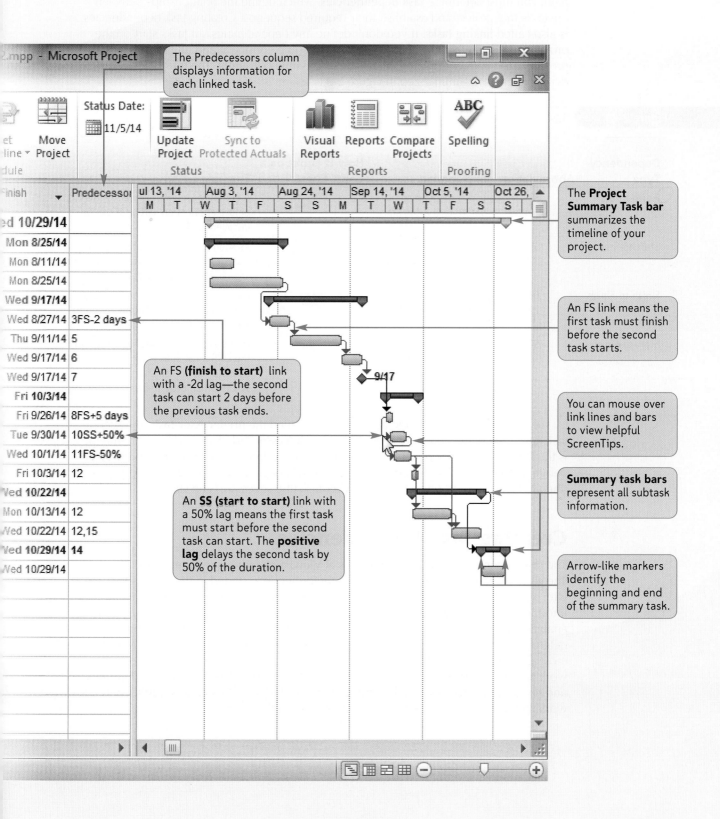

Understanding Task Dependencies

In order to use important project management techniques, such as analysis of the critical path, you must determine **task dependencies**, which define the relationships between the tasks in a project and establish their required sequence. Creating task dependencies is also called **linking tasks**. If you don't define any dependencies, all tasks start on the project Start date when using the as soon as possible constraint and all tasks finish on the project Finish date when using the as late as possible constraint. The four types of task dependencies are summarized in Figure 2-31.

Figure 2-31	Task dependencies

Dependency Type	Abbreviation	Explanation	How It Looks on a Gantt Chart	Example
Finish-to-Start	FS	Task 1 must finish before task 2 can start.		A computer must be installed (task 1) before application software can be installed (task 2).
Start-to-Start	SS	Task 1 must start before task 2 can start.		As soon as you start installing hardware (task 1), you can start documenting serial numbers (task 2).
Finish-to-Finish	FF	Task 1 must finish before task 2 can finish.		A computer backup (task 1) must be finished before the shutdown of the system is completed (task 2).
Start-to-Finish	SF	Task 1 must start before task 2 can finish.		In the event of a power interruption, the UPS must start (task 1) before the operator can finish shutting down the system in an orderly fashion (task 2).

The first task described in the dependency is called the **predecessor task**. The second task described in the dependency is called the **successor task**. By far the most common is the Finish-to-Start (FS) dependency, which indicates that the first task must be finished before the second task can start. Finish-to-Start (FS) dependency means that a certain task (the predecessor) must finish before another task (the successor) can start.

Creating Task Dependencies

The installation of the presentation rooms at ViewPoint Partners requires linked tasks. The partners had a meeting and reviewed the project you started in the last session. As with all projects, situations change and Sidney Simone, the owner of ViewPoint Partners, informed the team that work on the project cannot begin until August. The partners then analyzed the tasks and durations you proposed in the last session. In the meeting, they determined that Finish-to-Start (FS) dependencies between the tasks of the project are the most appropriate. Emily, the technology specialist at ViewPoint Partners, has done some work on your original project file. She changed the Project Start date, several durations, and several tasks. She also made some changes to the project calendars. You'll continue working on that file and create task dependencies in the project.

REFERENCE

Linking Tasks with an FS Dependency in Gantt Chart View

- In the Entry table, drag to select the tasks to link, and then, on the Task tab in the Schedule group, click the Link Tasks button ⬚.

or

- Press Ctrl + F2.
- In the Gantt chart, drag the pointer from the middle of the Start task to the middle of the Finish task for an FS dependency.

To create a Finish-to-Start dependency between tasks using the Entry table:

1. Open the project file **AV-2** located in the **Project2\Tutorial** folder included with your Data Files.

2. Save the project as **NewAV-2** in the same location.

3. Open the Project Information dialog box, make a note of the current Finish date, and then close the Project Information dialog box. Adding dependencies will move the Project Finish date as well as the Start dates of linked tasks.

4. In the Entry table, drag the pointer ✛ from **Detail current status** (task 1) down through **Conduct needs analysis** (task 2) to select both tasks. When you select multiple cells in the Entry table, the first cell in the selection is surrounded by a black border and all subsequent selected cells appear in reverse image, with a black background and white text. You want to indicate that task 1 must be completed before task 2 is started.

5. Click the **Task** tab, and then, in the Schedule group on the Task tab, click the **Link Tasks** button ⬚. A Finish-to-Start link line is added between the tasks in the Gantt chart, as shown in Figure 2-32.

| Figure 2-32 | Creating a Finish-to-Start relationship using the Entry table |

Link Tasks button

two tasks selected

task Start and Finish dates have moved out

6. In the Entry table, drag the **split bar** to the right until you can see the Predecessors column. Notice that task 2 has a 1 in the Predecessors column, indicating that task 1 is now a predecessor of task 2.

In much the same way that you can enter a task in the graphical views (Gantt Chart view, Network Diagram view, and Calendar view), you can also establish task dependencies in these views.

To create a Finish-to-Start dependency between tasks using the Gantt Chart view:

▶ 1. Drag the **split bar** to the left so the Finish column is the last visible column in the Entry table.

▶ 2. In the Gantt chart, point to the middle of the **Conduct needs analysis (task 2) bar**. The pointer changes to ✛.

Be sure that you point to the middle of the bar to create an FS relationship between two tasks in the Gantt chart. The pointer will change to the linking pointer as you drag.

Trouble? If you point to the end of a bar in the Gantt chart, you will change the duration instead of creating a link.

▶ 3. Drag down from the middle of the **Conduct needs analysis (task 2) bar** to the middle of the **Build Request for Proposal (task 3) bar**, making sure you see the linking pointer ⌐ and the linking ScreenTip, as shown in Figure 2-33.

Because of the new dependency, Build Request for Proposal (task 3) moves to a new position after Conduct needs analysis (task 2) in the Gantt chart.

TIP

The pointer changes to the linking pointer when you are creating a link between tasks in any of the graphical views (Gantt Chart, Network Diagram, and Calendar).

| Figure 2-33 | Creating a Finish-to-Start relationship using the Gantt chart |

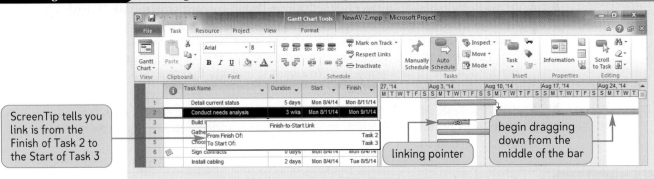

ScreenTip tells you link is from the Finish of Task 2 to the Start of Task 3

As you would expect, creating task dependencies affects the Start and Finish dates of the linked tasks. Changing and linking tasks also affects the critical path. Recall that the critical path consists of the tasks that must be completed with the given schedule dates in order for the overall project to be completed in the shortest amount of time. Project 2010 defines the **critical path** as consisting of those tasks that have zero slack. Remember that slack is the amount of time by which an activity may be delayed from its scheduled Start date without the delay setting back the entire project, and **free slack** is the amount of time by which an activity may be delayed without delaying the early start of any task that immediately follows the task with free slack.

The graphical views in Project 2010 visually represent information about the project. So, in Network Diagram view, for example, the **critical tasks**—tasks that are on the critical path—are displayed in a red box within a red border. A task that is not on the critical path is a **noncritical task**, that is, it doesn't necessarily have to start on its currently scheduled Start date in order for the overall project to be completed on time. Next, you'll create an FS dependency in Network Diagram view.

To create an FS dependency between tasks using Network Diagram view:

1. Click the **View** tab on the Ribbon, and then, in the Task Views group, click the **Network Diagram** button. Tasks 1, 2, and 3 and their FS dependencies represent the shortest amount of time required to complete the project; they are the current critical path. The boxes and lines are red, which is the default formatting for critical path tasks in Network Diagram view. Gather vendor bids (ID 4) and Choose vendors (ID 5) are displayed as noncritical tasks and are in blue rectangular boxes. The milestone task, Sign contracts (ID 6), is also currently a noncritical task. It is a blue hexagon shape to indicate it is a milestone task. Gather vendor bids (ID 4) and Choose vendors (ID 5), should be linked together in an FS relationship.

2. Point to inside the **Gather vendor bids (ID 4) box**, and then drag to inside the **Choose vendors (ID 5) box**, as shown in Figure 2-34.

| Figure 2-34 | Creating a Finish-to-Start relationship using the network diagram |

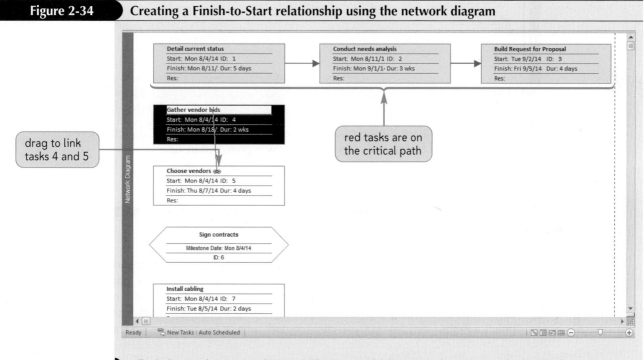

3. Release the mouse button. The network diagram changes to display Gather vendor bids (ID 4) and Choose vendors (ID 5) on the same row with a linking line between them. Because these tasks are not on the critical path, they are still displayed in rectangular boxes with a blue border and a black linking line.

4. Drag from inside the **Build Request for Proposal (ID 3) box** to inside the **Gather vendor bids (ID 4) box**. Now that task 3 is related to task 4 with an FS relationship, both Gather vendor bids (ID 4) and Choose vendors (ID 5) are now on the same row as tasks 1, 2, and 3 and are part of the critical path. All critical tasks are formatted in red.

5. Click the **Detail current status (ID 1) box**, click the **View** tab on the Ribbon, and then click the **Zoom** button in the Zoom group.

6. On the menu that opens, click **Zoom**, click the **Entire project** option button, and then click the **OK** button so that your screen looks like Figure 2-35.

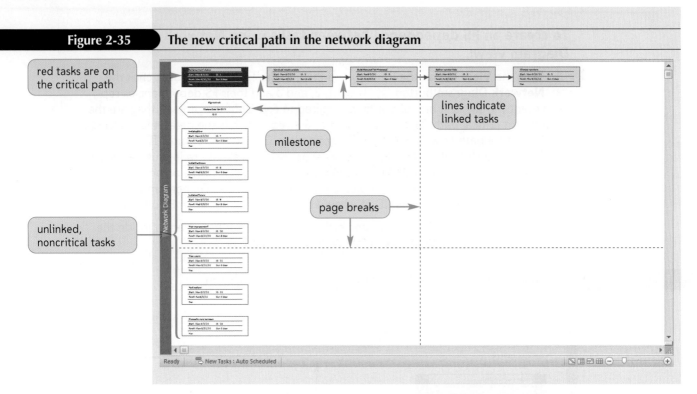

Figure 2-35

Figure 2-35   The new critical path in the network diagram

red tasks are on the critical path

lines indicate linked tasks

milestone

page breaks

unlinked, noncritical tasks

Ready   New Tasks : Auto Scheduled

The network diagram is used mainly to view and analyze the critical path. More information on how to change and manage this view is provided in Tutorial 3.

Next, you need to create a Finish-to-Start dependency between the Install hardware and Install software tasks. You'll do this in Calendar view.

INSIGHT

Getting an Overview of the Project

You might want to view and print the Calendar view because it most clearly indicates the tasks that are occurring, in a weekly and monthly format. The network diagram gives a clear picture of the relationships and critical path. The calendar does not make the critical path clear. Learning how to manage views and which view is most appropriate for a task is a Project skill that you will develop over time as you work with the software.

To create an FS dependency between tasks using the Calendar:

1. In the Task Views group on the View tab, click the **Calendar** button ▦. The project appears in Calendar view. The first day of the first task in the project is visible on your screen. Notice that the Install hardware task is above the Install software task and that they have the same Start date. Black down arrows to the left of the date on the calendar let you know that more tasks can be viewed if you expand the week.

   Trouble? If the first task of the first day is not visible on your screen, use the scroll bar to scroll to the first task, or press and hold the Alt key and then press the Home key.

2. Point to the middle of the **Install hardware bar**, and then drag down to the middle of the **Install software bar** using the linking pointer ☞. The Install software bar moves so it starts after the Install hardware task bar, as shown in Figure 2-36. Notice that link lines are not displayed in Calendar view and you cannot visually distinguish critical tasks.

Figure 2-36   Creating a Finish-to-Start relationship in Calendar view

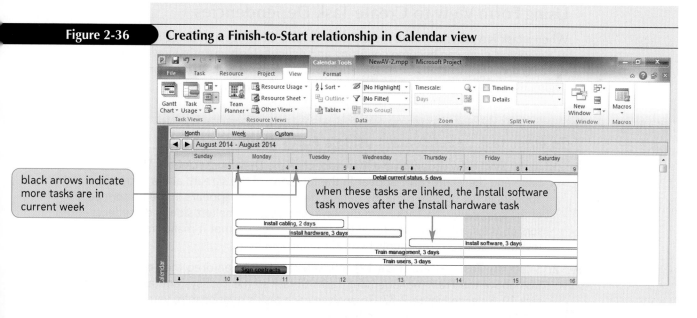

black arrows indicate more tasks are in current week

when these tasks are linked, the Install software task moves after the Install hardware task

Deleting Task Dependencies

You can enter and edit task relationships in any view. As project planning continues, you might discover that certain tasks should no longer be linked together. In such cases, you must delete the task relationships. Detail current status (task 1) and Conduct needs analysis (task 2) can be done concurrently, so you need to remove the task dependency between them.

To delete a task dependency:

Be sure to read the ScreenTips to ensure you click the correct button and to avoid splitting the task.

1. On the status bar, click the **Gantt Chart** button to switch to Gantt Chart view, and then, in the Entry table, click **Detail current status (task 1)**.

2. Click the **Task** tab on the Ribbon, and then, in the Editing group, click the **Scroll to Task** button. The Gantt chart is repositioned to display the first task in the project.

3. In the Entry table, click and drag ✛ to select **Detail current status (task 1)** and **Conduct needs analysis** (task 2), and then, in the Schedule group on the Task tab, click the **Unlink Tasks** button. The Finish-to-Start link line between the tasks is deleted.

    Conduct needs analysis (task 2) is now scheduled to start on the project Start date of 8/4/14 because it no longer has a predecessor task. All dates affected by the change to task 2 are highlighted in blue in the Entry table. These dates are affected because task 2 is linked to the tasks associated with these highlighted tasks.

4. Click the **View** tab, and then, in the Task Views group, click the **Network Diagram** button. Notice that Detail current status (task 1) is no longer on the critical path because it is no longer linked to the other tasks on the critical path.

5. Click the **Gantt Chart** button in the Task Views group to return to the Gantt chart view, and then, on the Quick Access toolbar, click the **Save** button to save your changes to the project.

Using Form View to Create Task Dependencies

When a task is a predecessor to more than one task, the process of dragging link lines in a graphical view can become confusing and difficult. Using a Form view can make it easier to enter many details for a single task. For example, if tasks 10, 11, and 12 cannot begin until task 9 finishes, you can create this dependency in Form view.

To enter task dependencies using a Form view:

▶ 1. In the Split View group on the View tab, click the **Details** check box. The Entry table and the Gantt chart appear in the top pane of the screen, and a Form view appears in the bottom pane. By default, the Task Form appears in the bottom pane of the split view. The Task Form displays resources on the left side and predecessors on the right side. Looking at the tasks, you realize that it makes more sense to test the installed components before training can begin.

▶ 2. Select the **Test system (task 12) row selector**, and then drag the **Test system** task above the Train management (task 10) task so the Test system task becomes task 10. Refer to Figure 2-37. To analyze each task's relationship, you can display predecessors and successors in the form.

Figure 2-37	Split view showing Gantt chart view and Form view

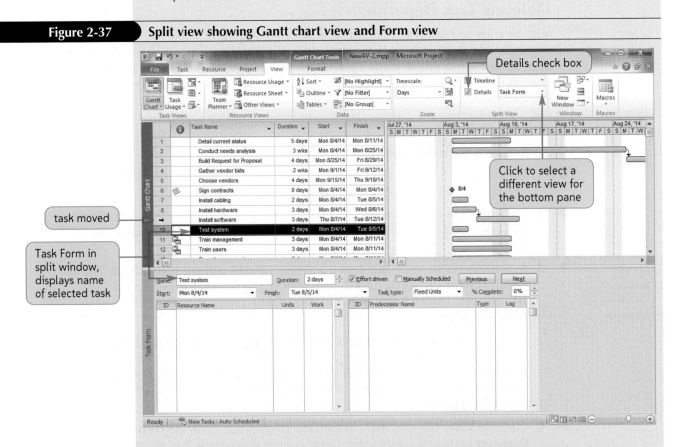

▶ 3. Right-click the form, and then click **Predecessors & Successors** on the shortcut menu. The form changes to display the predecessors on the left side of the form and successors on the right side. You can enter as many predecessor and successor task IDs in the form as needed.

4. In the Entry table, click the **Install software (task 9) Task Name** cell. Corresponding information for the selected task is displayed in the form. You want to specify Test system (task 10), Train management (task 11), and Train users (task 12) all as successors to Install software (task 9). The columns in the form contain cells. When a cell is selected, it appears with a border.

5. On the right side of the form, click the **first cell under ID**, type **10**, press the **Enter** key, type **11**, press the **Enter** key, type **12**, and then click the **OK** button. See Figure 2-38. Project 2010 adds the task names for tasks 10, 11, and 12 to the Successor Name column in the form and adds the appropriate link lines to the Gantt chart.

| Figure 2-38 | Creating a Finish-to-Start relationship using Form view |

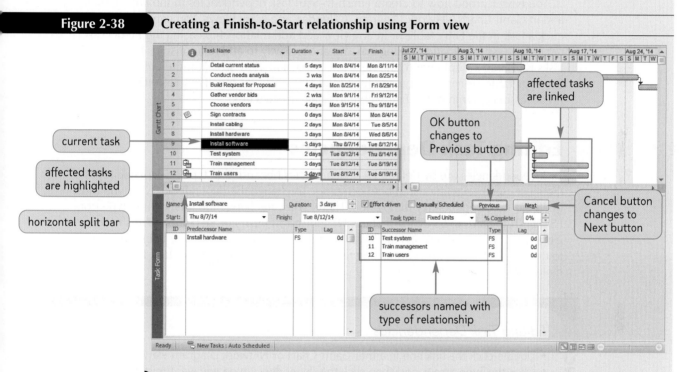

6. In the form, click the **Next** button. Test system (task 10) is selected in the Entry table, and Install software (task 9) appears in the Predecessor Name column in the form.

7. In the form, click the **Next** button. Train management (task 11) is selected in the Entry table, and Install software (task 9) appears in the Predecessor Name column in the form. Notice the link line that appears in the Gantt chart.

8. In the form, click the **Previous** button three times to select Install hardware (task 8), point to the **horizontal split bar** so the pointer changes to ⇼, and then double-click the **split bar** between Gantt Chart view and Form view to remove the split. As you continue to work with Project 2010 you will learn different ways to perform similar tasks.

After carefully assessing the tasks required for the ViewPoint Partners AV Presentation Rooms Installation project, you determine the rest of the required task relationships and enter them into the project file. As you continue to work with Project 2010, you will develop preferences for your working style. You know that you can quickly create links between consecutive tasks in the Entry table—the most common way to create task dependencies.

To create task dependencies using the Entry table:

▶ **1.** In the Entry table, click and drag to select the task names **Choose vendors** (task 5) through **Install hardware** (task 8).

▶ **2.** Click the **Task** tab on the Ribbon, and then, in the Schedule group, click the **Link Tasks** button 🔗. The bars on the Gantt chart are no longer visible in the window because linking these tasks in an FS relationship moved the dates further away from the Start date.

▶ **3.** Save your changes.

You have learned how to create Finish-to-Start task dependencies in the Entry table and in Gantt Chart, Network Diagram, Calendar, and Form views. You can also double-click a task in the Entry table or in any view and add relationships using the Predecessors tab of the Task Information dialog box. Yet another way to add relationships between tasks is to drag the split bar to the right in Gantt Chart view so that more columns of the Entry table are visible. You can then relate two tasks by specifying task IDs in the Predecessors column of the Entry table to relate the two tasks.

Editing Task Dependencies

Task dependencies are by default FS dependencies because that type of dependency is the most common relationship between tasks. To change the dependency type, you must open the Task Dependency dialog box. There, you can change the relationship type from FS (Finish-to-Start) to SS (Start-to-Start), FF (Finish-to-Finish), or SF (Start-to-Finish). You usually edit task relationships in Gantt Chart or Network Diagram view because it is easy to double-click a link line connecting tasks in these views to open the Task Dependency dialog box.

REFERENCE

Editing Task Dependencies

• Double-click the link line in either Gantt Chart or Network Diagram view.
• Click the Type arrow, and then click the dependency type you want to switch to.
• Click the OK button.

Emily reviewed your work and she mentioned that the Install cabling and Install hardware tasks can begin on the same day. You need to change the dependency between Install cabling (task 7) and Install hardware (task 8) to a Start-to-Start dependency.

To edit a task dependency:

▶ **1.** In the Entry table, click the **Install cabling (task 7) Task Name** cell, and then, in the Editing group on the Task tab, click the **Scroll to Task button**. Now you can see the link between Install cabling (task 7) and Install hardware (task 8) in the Gantt chart.

▶ **2.** In the Gantt chart, point to the **link line** connecting Install cabling (task 7) to Install hardware (task 8). A ScreenTip identifies the Finish-to-Start (FS) link from ID 7 to ID 8 to confirm that you have located the correct link line.

Trouble? If the ScreenTip doesn't confirm the correct link, point to another link line until you are sure that you have identified the correct link line.

▶ **3.** Double-click the **link line** connecting Install cabling (task 7) to Install hardware (task 8). The Task Dependency dialog box opens, describing the current dependency type.

▶ **4.** Click the **Type** arrow, and then click **Start-to-Start (SS)**. See Figure 2-39. Because the hardware installation can start at the same time the cabling installation starts, the SS dependency more clearly indicates the relationship between these two tasks.

Figure 2-39   Task Dependency dialog box

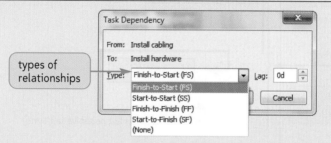

types of relationships

▶ **5.** Click the **OK** button. The Gantt chart link line changes so that it points from the left edge (the start) of the Install cabling (task 7) bar to the left edge (the start) of the Install hardware (task 8) bar to indicate that an SS relationship exists between the two tasks.

You can also edit the relationships between tasks in the Task Information dialog box by using the Predecessors column of the Entry table. Alternatively, you can use a Form view that displays predecessor and successor information. To remove a task dependency, double-click the link line to open the Task Dependency dialog box, and then click the Delete button in the Task Dependency dialog box.

Entering Lead and Lag Times

When a project is scheduled from a Start date, lead and lag times refer to an amount of time that the second task of a relationship is moved backward (lead) or forward (lag) in time. **Lead time** moves the second task *backward* in time so that the two tasks overlap. For example, suppose that two tasks have an FS relationship, such as Installing hardware and Installing software, and yet the second task (Installing software) can be started *before* the Finish date of the first. You can create an FS relationship between the two tasks with a lead time of 50% so that the successor task (Installing software) starts when the predecessor task (Installing hardware) is 50% completed.

Lag time is the opposite of lead time. It moves the second task *forward* in time so that Start dates between the tasks are further apart. Consider the tasks Sign contracts and Install cabling, which have an FS relationship. While in theory the second task Install cabling could be started immediately upon completion of the first task Sign contracts, you might want to allow for some lag time (a gap of time between the finish of the first task and the start of the second task) to wait until the contract is finalized. Figure 2-40 illustrates lead and lag times for a project that is scheduled from a Start date. An experienced manager may build lag time into a project to prepare for unknown factors such as inclement weather, but adding lag time will most likely increase the project duration.

Figure 2-40   Positive and negative lag times for the same task for a project scheduled from a Start date

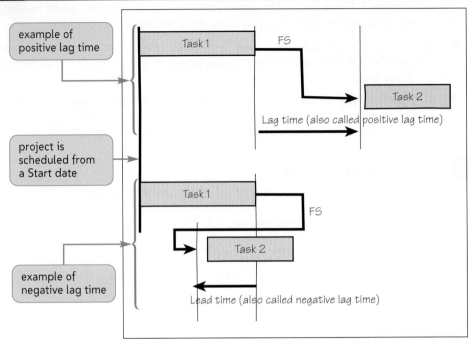

Project 2010 combines the concepts of lead and lag times into one term, lag time. When a project is scheduled from a Start date, **positive lag time** moves the second task forward in time. Positive lag time is the traditional definition of lag time in general project management discussions. **Negative lag time** moves the second task backward in time so that the tasks overlap. Negative lag time is called lead time in general project management discussions. The rest of this text refers to lag time using Project 2010 terminology, that is, as either positive lag time or negative lag time. In Figure 2-40, the first example shows how positive lag time affects the second task. The second example shows how negative lag time affects the second task.

REFERENCE

Entering Lag Time

- Double-click the link line in either Gantt Chart or Network Diagram view.
- Enter either a positive number or percentage in the Lag text box to move the second task forward in time or a negative number or percentage to move the second task backward in time.
- Click the OK button.

Lag durations use the same duration units (d for days, h for hours, and so forth) used for task durations. You also can enter a positive or a negative percentage that will calculate the lag as a percentage of the duration of the first task. In a Finish-to-Start relationship, +25% lag time pushes the second task forward in time. The second task will not start until after the first task is completed plus an additional 25% of the duration of the first task. A –25% lag time pulls the second task backward in time. In this case, the second task will start when the first task is 75% completed.

Emily has indicated that the lag time for several tasks in the project need to be adjusted. Based on the information Emily has given you, you will adjust the lag time for several of the tasks in the project.

To enter lag time for tasks that are assigned relationships:

TIP

Zoom in and use the ScreenTips on the link lines to locate the correct line, and then double-click the correct line.

▸ **1.** In the Gantt chart, scroll to view the link line between Conduct needs analysis (task 2) and Build Request for Proposal (task 3), and then double-click the **link line**. The Task Dependency dialog box opens for the two tasks. It identifies the link as From: Conduct needs analysis To: Build Request for Proposal. You can change lag time by using the arrows in the Lag box or typing a value directly into the Lag box.

▸ **2.** Click the **Lag** down arrow twice to set the lag to **–2d**, and then click the **OK** button. Your screen should look like Figure 2-41. Negative lag has moved the Start date of Build Request for Proposal (task 3) backward in time.

Figure 2-41 Negative lag time associated with an FS link

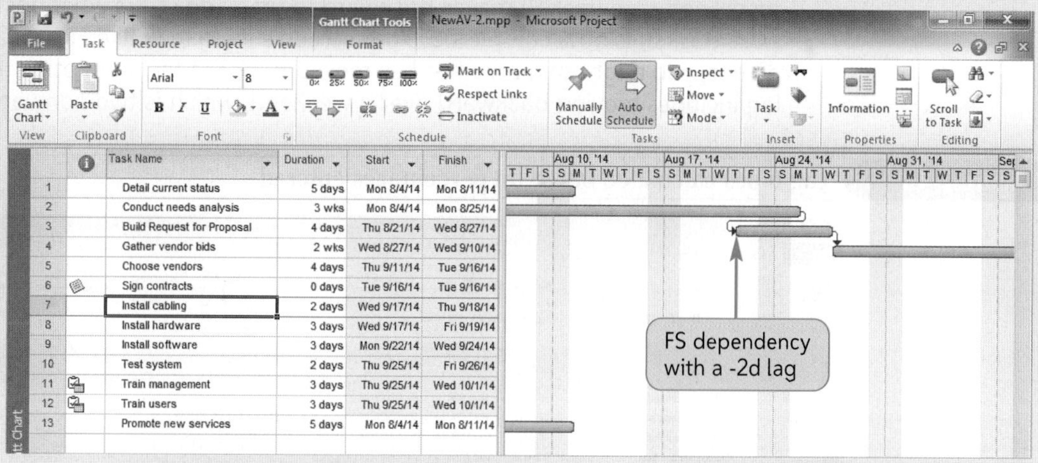

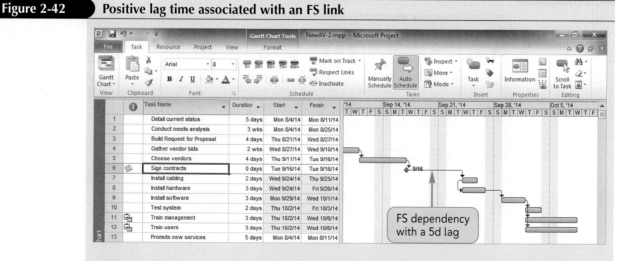

▸ **3.** In the Entry table, click **Sign contracts** (task 6), and then, in the Editing group on the Task tab, click the **Scroll To Task** button to view the link line between Sign contracts (task 6) and Install cabling (task 7).

▸ **4.** In the Gantt chart, double-click the **link line** between Sign contracts (task 6) and Install cabling (task 7). The Task Dependency dialog box opens for From: Sign contracts To: Install cabling.

▸ **5.** Click the **Lag** up arrow five times to set the lag to **5d**, and then click the **OK** button. Your screen should look like Figure 2-42. Positive lag has moved the Start date of the second task in the dependency, Install cabling (task 7), forward in time.

Figure 2-42 Positive lag time associated with an FS link

6. Double-click the **link line** between Install cabling (task 7) and Install hardware (task 8).

7. In the Lag box, double-click **0d**, type **50%**, and then click the **OK** button. Install hardware (task 8) moves forward in time and starts when Installing cabling (task 7) is 50% completed. Lag can be applied to any type of dependency. In this case, it is applied to an SS dependency. Regardless of the dependency type, when projects are scheduled from a Start date, lag always moves the Start date of the second task in the dependency.

8. Double-click the **link line** between Install hardware (task 8) and Install software (task 9).

9. In the Lag box, double-click **0d**, type **–50%**, and then click the **OK** button. Install software (task 9) moves backward in time and starts when Install hardware (task 8) is 50% completed. Your screen should look like Figure 2-43. At first glance, you might think the bar has moved back too far, but notice that the -50% lag includes moving backward over a weekend, which is two nonworking days.

| Figure 2-43 | Lag times calculated based on percentages entered |

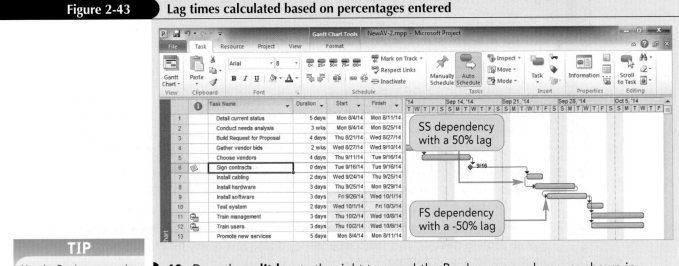

TIP

Use the Predecessors column to verify positive and negative lag times.

10. Drag the **split bar** to the right to reveal the Predecessors column, as shown in Figure 2-44. The entries in the Predecessors column show the dependencies you've created.

| Figure 2-44 | The Predecessors column shows predecessors and lag times |

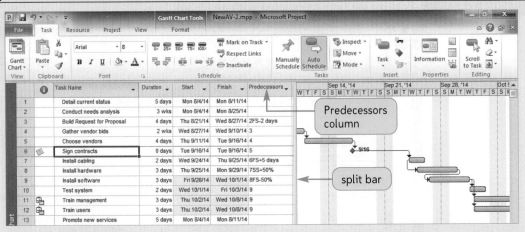

Upon review of the project, you see that you haven't linked Promote new services (task 13). This task can also start when the Install software (task 9) is completed.

▶ **11.** Click the **Promote new services (task 13) Predecessors cell**, type **9**, and then press the **Enter** key.

▶ **12.** Drag the **split bar** to the left so that the Duration column is the last column, press the **Alt+Home** keys, and then click the **View** tab on the Ribbon.

▶ **13.** In the Zoom group, click the **Zoom** button 🔍▾, click **Zoom**, click the **Entire project** option button, and then click the **OK** button to get a view of the whole project.

Once the tasks, durations, and relationships are entered, you should check the Project Information dialog box to verify the project's calculated Finish date if the project is scheduled from a Start date, or the calculated Start date if the project is scheduled from a Finish date. Emily has asked you to check the project Finish date and to see what effect entering lag times has had on it. You check the project Finish date and analyze the effect of the lag times.

To check for lag time effects on the finish date:

▶ **1.** Click the **Project** tab on the Ribbon, and then, in the Properties group, click the **Project Information** button. The Finish date of 10/8/14 was calculated based on the Start date of 8/4/14. Prior to your entering task dependencies and lag times, the project had a calculated Finish date of 8/25/14 because the longest task duration was three weeks and each task started on day 1. As you can see, entering task dependencies greatly affects project scheduling.

▶ **2.** Click the **Cancel** button, and then save your changes to the project file.

When a project is scheduled from a Start date, applying negative lag time to task dependencies that are on the critical path is a common way to shorten the critical path because it allows tasks to overlap. When a project is scheduled from a Finish date, all tasks are scheduled using the as late as possible schedules and lag time affects the *first* task rather than the second task. So, when a project is scheduled from a Finish date, positive lag moves the Start date of the first task further away from the Start date of the second task, and Negative lag moves the Start date of the first task closer to the Start date of the second task, which can create overlap of the two tasks. Figure 2-45 shows how positive and negative lag times affect the first task of a project scheduled from a Finish date.

Figure 2-45   **Positive and negative lag times for the same task for a project scheduled from a Finish date**

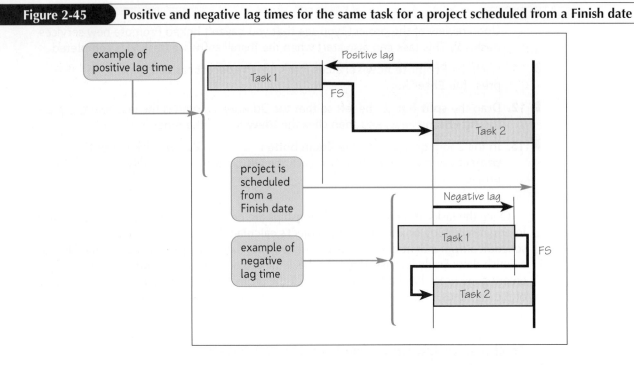

It is easy to confuse positive and negative lag times. Remember, positive lag time always increases the amount of time between tasks, and negative lag time always causes the tasks to overlap. This rule holds true regardless of whether the project is scheduled from the Start date or the Finish date.

Creating a Work Breakdown Structure with Summary Tasks

A very important strategy for managing projects well is to organize the work that needs to be done in a logical manner. A **work breakdown structure (WBS)** is an outcome-oriented analysis of the work involved in a project that defines the total scope of the project. A WBS is a foundation document in project management because it provides the basis for planning and managing project schedules, costs, and changes. The WBS provides a hierarchy, similar to the hierarchy used in an outline, for listing project tasks.

In order to use a WBS in Project 2010, you must organize tasks into summary tasks, which are groups of tasks that logically belong together. The duration associated with a summary task is calculated based on the task information and constraints for all the tasks that make up the summary task. The Start and Finish dates for a summary task reflect the earliest Start date and the latest Finish date associated with that same group of tasks. In later tutorials, when you enter cost information, the cost information for a summary task is also the sum of the costs of the subtasks.

Deciding on the structure of a WBS for a particular project can be difficult, but once you have decided, it is easy to enter the WBS in Project 2010 by outdenting and indenting tasks. Project 2010 also supports top-down summary tasks.

TIP

Remember that a summary task is not a task to be completed (like individual tasks in the project) but rather it identifies, or summarizes, a group of tasks that belong together.

PROSKILLS

Decision Making: Top-Down Versus Bottom-Up Project Planning

Sometimes summary tasks are developed based on the five project management process groups (Initiating, Planning, Executing, Controlling, Closing); other times it makes sense to organize summary tasks by products produced. When developing a new, large project, some project managers prefer to start with broad groupings of summary tasks and then break them down into smaller tasks. Planning a project by starting with broad categories of tasks is called the **top-down method** of creating a WBS. Top-down project managers start with the "Big Picture." Other project managers prefer to list all of the individual tasks, and then collect them into logical groupings using the **bottom-up method**.

If you decide to use the top-down method, which is a new feature with Project 2010, you have to identify the summary tasks (or major phases) of the project first, and then break the summary tasks down into subtasks (or individual tasks). For each summary task that you enter, you must enter a duration, Start date, or Finish date, or you will not be able to create a top-down phase. However, if you create a summary task without a duration, Start date, or Finish date, you can add this information later to make the task a summary task. If you decide to create top-down summary tasks in Project 2010, summary tasks are manually scheduled, so they do not automatically roll up durations from the individual tasks. If you want a summary task to roll up the durations automatically, then you must use the bottom-up method and create the individual tasks before creating the summary tasks. Whether you use the top-down method or the bottom-up method depends on your working style.

Outdenting and Indenting Tasks

Once you have identified your summary tasks and are ready to enter them for the project, the actual technique for creating a summary task is simple. To create summary tasks, you need to outdent and indent tasks. **Outdenting** moves a task to the left (a higher level in the WBS), and **indenting** moves a task to the right (a lower level in the WBS). You use the Outdent button and the Indent button in the Schedule group on the Task tab to create your WBS. You can also create a new summary task that includes the selected tasks automatically by clicking the Insert Summary Task button in the Insert group on the Task tab. All selected tasks are grouped under the newly created summary task. Summary tasks will reflect the Start and Finish dates as well as durations based on their subtasks. If you are using the bottom-up method, this information is added automatically to the summary tasks, if you are using the top-down method, you need to add this information manually unless you change the schedule mode for the summary tasks to Auto Scheduled.

Because the project for Sidney, the owner of ViewPoint Partners, is fairly small, you will need only two levels for the WBS. You will create summary tasks and identify their associated subtasks.

TIP

A WBS uses the same organization as an outline, with summary tasks at the highest level and subtasks at a lower level. For large projects, summary tasks can be nested to create more levels.

REFERENCE

Creating a Summary Task

- In Gantt Chart view, enter a task name for each summary task in the Entry table above its subtasks.
- Select all the subtasks under a summary task.
- In the Schedule group on the Task tab, click the Indent button.
- If you enter a summary task beneath a subtask for another summary task, click the Outdent button on the Task tab in the Schedule group while the summary task is selected.

or

- Select the tasks you want as subtasks in the new summary task.
- In the Insert group on the Task tab, click the Insert Summary Task button.
- Type the name of the new summary task.

To create a summary task:

> **1.** In the Entry table, click **Train management (task 11) Task Name** cell, press the **Insert** key to insert a new row, type **Training**, and then press the **Enter** key. You have inserted a new task that will become a summary task. Train management (task 12) is selected. The summary task Training will consist of the two subtasks, Train management and Train users. Because you are creating this WBS from the bottom up, you do not specify a duration for the summary task. Instead, it is calculated based on the durations and relationships of the individual tasks within that summary task.

> **2.** Press and hold the **Shift** key, and then click **Train users** (task 13) to select both Train management (task 12) and Train users (task 13).

> **3.** Click the **Task** tab, and then, in the Schedule group, click the **Indent Task** button ![indent icon]. Training (task 11) is now a summary task, and the duration of the Training task is calculated as 4.5 days. The Training calendar, which is assigned to these subtasks, and the dependencies between the subtasks were factored in to the total number of days required for this Training summary task.

> **4.** Click **Training** (task 11), and then zoom as needed so your screen looks similar to Figure 2-46. Notice that in the Gantt chart, a **summary task bar** is a solid black line with arrow-like markers that indicate where the summary task starts and stops.

TIP

To insert a new task, you can right-click a task ID number and then click Insert Task, or you can click the Task button in the Insert group.

| Figure 2-46 | Training summary task created |

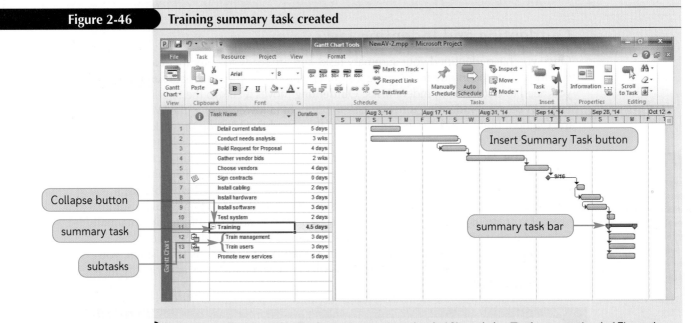

> **5.** Drag to select the **Train management** (task 12) and the **Train users** (task 13), and then, in the Schedule group on the Task tab, click the **Link Tasks** button ![link icon]. These tasks are now linked in an FS relationship, and the duration of the Training summary task is changed from 4.5 to 9.5 days. Remember that the Training calendar is applied to these tasks for Monday through Thursday as well as summer hours ending at 3:00 PM on Friday, which affects the Start and Finish dates for the tasks.

Summary tasks are listed in bold text in the Entry table and display a Collapse/Expand toggle button to the left of the task so that you can easily show or hide the subtasks within that summary task. The duration cell of a summary task cannot be edited directly when creating a WBS from the bottom up; it is calculated from the durations and relationships of the individual summary tasks it contains. In Project 2010, you can change the duration of a summary task without changing the durations of the subtasks that make up that summary task. If the duration of the summary task does not equal the sum of the durations of the subtasks, the Gantt Chart view will display a red line highlighting the difference.

Now you will create additional summary tasks.

To create additional linked summary tasks:

1. In the Entry table, click **Install cabling** (task 7), and then drag ✛ to select **Install cabling** (task 7) through **Test system** (task 10). These four tasks will be subtasks for a new Installation summary task.

2. In the Insert group on the Task tab, click the **Insert Summary Task** button ⟨🖼⟩. A <New Summary Task> placeholder appears in row 7. The Duration column already displays the 7.5 days that are needed for the four subtasks.

3. Type **Installation**, and then press the **Enter** key. You created a summary task named Installation that consists of the next four subtasks. The Installation summary task's duration is calculated based on the dependencies of the subtasks. Your screen should look like Figure 2-47.

| Figure 2-47 | Creating the Installation summary task |

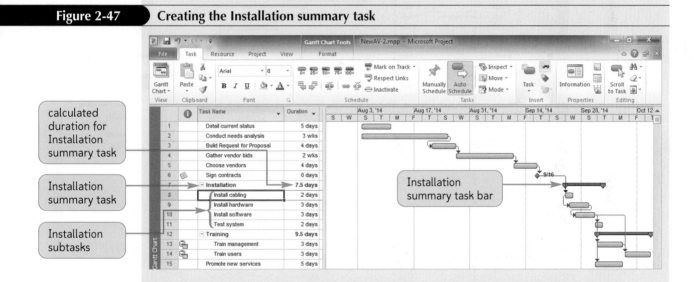

calculated duration for Installation summary task

Installation summary task

Installation subtasks

Installation summary task bar

4. In the Entry table, drag the pointer ✛ to select **Detail current status** (task 1) and **Conduct needs analysis** (task 2), click the **Insert Summary Task** button ⟨🖼⟩, type **Analysis** to replace the **<New Summary Task>** placeholder, and then press the **Enter** key. The new task Analysis is a summary task with two subtasks and a calculated duration of 15 days.

You need to enter two more summary tasks for this project's WBS, named Design and Marketing. The Design summary task will include the tasks for the Design phase of the project, and the Marketing summary task will include one subtask, Promote new services.

5. In the Entry table, click **Build Request for Proposal** (task 4), drag the pointer ✛ to select **Build Request for Proposal** (task 4) through **Sign contracts** (task 7), and then click the **Insert Summary Task** button ⟨🖼⟩.

6. In the <New Summary Task> placeholder, type **Design**, and then press the **Enter** key. Design is now a summary task that has four subtasks and a calculated duration of 18 days.

TIP

Click the Outdent Task button in the Schedule group on the Task tab to promote a task to a higher level if you no longer want it to be a subtask under a summary task. Click the Indent Task button to create a new subtask beneath a summary task.

7. Click **Promote new services** (task 17), click the **Insert Summary Task** button ▣, type **Marketing** to replace the <New Summary Task> placeholder, and then press the **Enter** key. Marketing is now a summary task that has one subtask and a calculated duration of 5 days, the same as its subtask.

8. Scroll to move to the beginning of the Gantt chart, drag the **split bar** so Duration is the last column in the Entry table, and then click **Analysis** (task 1).

9. On the status bar, click the **Zoom Out** button as needed to see the entire project in the Gantt chart. Your screen should look similar to Figure 2-48.

Figure 2-48   **AV Presentation Rooms Installation project with five major phases in the WBS**

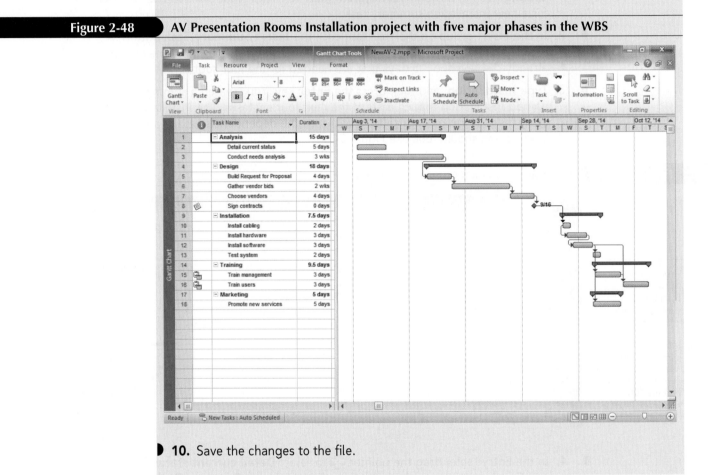

10. Save the changes to the file.

Displaying Outline Numbers

The tasks and subtasks have been organized in an outline, with tasks in a hierarchy. Each task has a task number, and the built-in outline is based on these task numbers. In addition to the outline structure you specify with summary tasks and subtasks, you will learn how to create your own outline using WBS codes. However, if you want to view the built-in outline numbers, you can do so by clicking the Gantt Chart Tools Format tab, and then clicking the Outline Number check box. The outline numbers will display in the Task Name cells for all tasks.

To show outline numbers:

1. Click the **Gantt Chart Tools Format tab**, and then, in the Show/Hide group, click the **Outline Number** check box. See Figure 2-49.

Figure 2-49   **Viewing the built-in outline numbers**

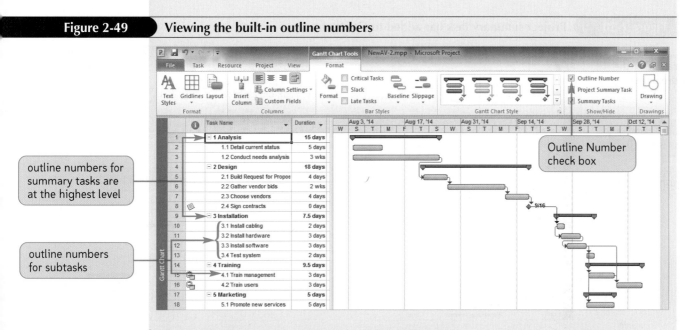

outline numbers for summary tasks are at the highest level

outline numbers for subtasks

Outline Number check box

2. In the Show/Hide group, click the **Outline Number** check box. The outline numbers are no longer visible in the Entry table.

Many project managers like to see the Start and Finish dates for their projects on the Gantt chart and how those dates change as they enter and edit tasks, durations, and dependencies. You can create a summary task bar for the entire project; this project summary task bar appears at the top of the Gantt chart.

To create a project summary task bar:

1. In the Show/Hide group, click the **Project Summary Task** check box. The project summary task bar appears at the top of the Gantt chart, and the project summary is named Project 2010 in the Entry table. This is the information that was previously entered as the Title of this project in the Properties dialog box. You will learn about the Properties dialog box and how to control and change its contents later in this book. The project summary name can be changed directly in the Entry table.

Trouble? If hash signs (###) fill the Duration column, it means you have to double-click the column divider to widen the duration column to fit the number.

2. Click the **Project 2010 Task Name** cell, type your name, and then press the **Enter** key. Your screen should look like Figure 2-50.

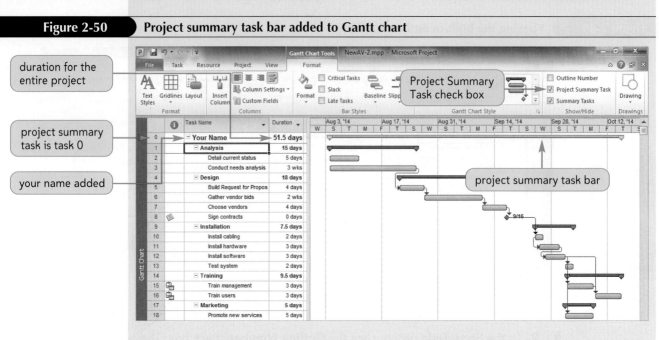

Figure 2-50   Project summary task bar added to Gantt chart

duration for the entire project

project summary task is task 0

your name added

Project Summary Task check box

project summary task bar

3. In the Gantt chart, point to the **project summary** task bar. The duration, 51.5 days, is calculated based on the Start and Finish dates of all tasks entered for the entire project.

4. Save your work.

Summary tasks help to improve the clarity of the project by organizing tasks into major groups or phases and by calculating the total duration for each phase. They also can identify areas that are not yet fully developed. In this project, for instance, the addition of summary tasks clearly identifies major phases. Testing is a task that is currently part of the Installation phase. However, Testing should have its own summary task and include tasks for testing the final installation. Testing is an important phase in any project, so the project team will add testing tasks to the WBS for this project in the next tutorial.

INSIGHT

Nesting Summary Tasks

For larger projects, summary tasks can be nested to create more levels in the WBS to help define and manage all the work required to successfully complete your project. For example, after you complete this project, ViewPoint Partners might ask you to manage a project to install several installations in different buildings. You could create a Project 2010 file to manage all of these installations, grouping them by location and then by phases.

Expanding and Collapsing Tasks

Once your project has been organized into summary tasks, you can easily expand (show) and collapse (hide) the individual tasks within each phase. As your project for ViewPoint Partners develops, you will find that you need to view different phases in various levels of detail. You may not want to share some information with all vendors or members of the project team. To display and hide individual tasks, you use the Show Subtasks and Hide Subtasks commands, which are accessed using the Outline button in the Data group on the View tab. You can also click the Expand and Collapse buttons next to summary tasks in the Entry table. When you click a summary task Collapse button, the subtasks are hidden and the Collapse button changes to the Expand button. When you click the summary task Expand button, the subtasks are displayed. To expand and collapse more than one summary task at a time, you click the Outline button in the Data group to open a menu and select the level that you want to display.

When working on a project, you might want to get an overview of the entire project by looking only at the summary tasks, or you might want to look at specific tasks in detail without being distracted by other tasks.

To expand and collapse tasks:

1. In the Entry table, click the **Analysis (task 1) Collapse** button $\boxed{-}$, and then click the **Design (task 4) Collapse** button $\boxed{-}$. Your screen should look like Figure 2-51. When summary tasks are collapsed, the subtask names do not appear in the Entry table and the subtask bars no longer appear in the Gantt chart. You want to see an overview of the entire project, so you decide to look at only the summary tasks.

| Figure 2-51 | Two summary tasks are collapsed |

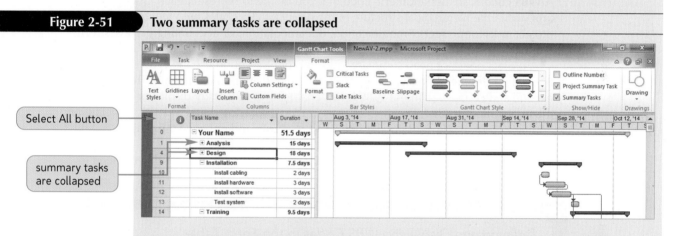

Select All button

summary tasks are collapsed

2. In the Entry table, click the **Select All** button to select the entire Entry table.

3. Click the **View** tab on the Ribbon.

4. In the Data group on the View tab, click the **Outline** button, and then click **Hide Subtasks** on the menu. All of the summary tasks are collapsed at the same time. Because you have a project summary task bar, all the tasks, including the summary tasks, are collapsed.

5. With all of the tasks still selected, click the **Outline** button in the Data group, and then click **Show Subtasks**. The summary tasks, which are the subtasks for the project summary (task 0), are displayed in both the Entry table and in the Gantt chart.

6. Click the **Outline** button in the Data group, and then click **All Subtasks**. All the summary tasks are expanded to show their subtasks in both the Entry table and the Gantt chart. When multiple levels of summary tasks exist, every subtask is displayed. You can also use the Outline Level options to display tasks through a specific level.

7. Click the **Outline** button in the Data group, and then click **Outline Level 1**. Only the summary tasks, which are Level 1, are displayed in both the Entry table and the Gantt chart.

▶ **8.** Click the **Outline** button in the Data group, and then click **Outline Level 2**. All the summary tasks subtasks, which are Level 2, are displayed in both the Entry table and the Gantt chart. This project has only two levels of tasks, so clicking Outline Level 2 displays all the tasks for each summary task. If you had created multiple levels of summary tasks, you could use options on the Outline button menu to choose exactly the level of detail you needed.

▶ **9.** Click **Analysis** (task 1) to deselect the table.

As you continue to work on developing your project, you will find that viewing various levels of detail provides different information.

Using WBS Codes

Many people like to number tasks in their WBS to show the logical groupings of work. A **WBS code** is an alphanumeric code that you define to represent each task's position within the hierarchical structure of the project. WBS codes help identify and group project tasks for project communication, documentation, or accounting purposes. WBS codes are an outline numbering system that you define.

A project does not need summary tasks in order for you to use the WBS column, but the outline structure helps visually clarify the organization of the project. The ability to expand and collapse different WBS levels enables you to quickly display or print only the information needed. Creating summary tasks, displaying different levels of detail, and adding a column with WBS codes helps you to clarify and enhance the project, but it does not change any of the scheduled Start and Finish dates.

By default, WBS codes are not visible in the Entry table. To view them, you need to display the WBS column in the Entry table.

REFERENCE

Defining and Displaying WBS Codes in the Entry Table

- On the Ribbon, click the Project tab, in the Properties group, click the WBS button, and then click Define Code to open the WBS Code Definition dialog box.
- Click the Sequence cell arrow for the first level, define the sequence for the first level, press the Enter key, and then define any subsequent levels.
- Click the OK button.
- In the Entry table, right-click the Task Name column heading, click Insert Column to insert a new column, type WBS to scroll to the WBS column headings, and then press the Enter key to insert the WBS column.

or

- In the Entry table, drag the split bar to reveal the Add New Column column, click the Add New Column arrow, scroll the list, click WBS, and then click the OK button to insert the WBS column.

Project 2010 lets you create and modify a WBS code by using predefined outline numbers. The default WBS code is the task's outline number. The predefined outline numbering system works well when you want to numerically code each task and do not need a different coding scheme for representing the WBS. You can, however, develop your own coding system. To develop your own coding system, you first must define the WBS codes.

To create WBS codes:

▶ 1. Click the **Project** tab on the Ribbon.

▶ 2. In the Properties group on the Project tab, click the **WBS** button to open a menu, and then click **Define Code** on the menu. The WBS Code Definition dialog box opens, where you can determine how each level of tasks should be coded.

▶ 3. In the WBS Code Definition dialog box, click the **arrow** next to the empty cell in the Sequence column, and then click **Uppercase Letters (ordered)**. This option creates a sequence for the first level that follows an A, B, C pattern.

▶ 4. Click the **cell** under Uppercase Letters (ordered) in the Sequence column, click the **arrow** next to the empty cell in the Sequence column, click **Numbers (ordered)**, and then click the next empty cell in the Sequence column. The Code preview box near the top of the dialog box shows you a sample of how the WBS code will appear for a Level 2 task. Your screen should look like Figure 2-52. If you had more than two levels, you would continue defining each level's code using the WBS Code Definition dialog box.

| Figure 2-52 | WBS Code Definition dialog box |

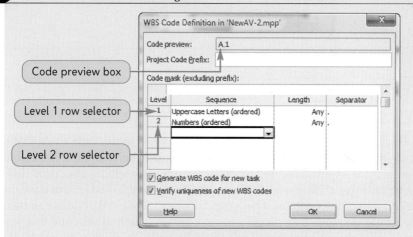

▶ 5. Click the **OK** button. In order to see the codes you created, you need to display the WBS column in the Entry table.

▶ 6. Right-click the **Task Name** column heading, and then click **Insert Column**. The new column, which includes a list of possible column types, is inserted to the left of the Task Name column. When you type a column name in the [Type Column Name] placeholder, the list collapses to show only the choices associated with the word or phrase you typed.

▶ 7. Type **WBS** to highlight the WBS column type options in the list, and then press the **Enter** key to insert the WBS column. The WBS column is inserted to the left of the Task Name column, which is the column you right-clicked. This WBS column contains the WBS coding scheme that you defined in the WBS Code Definition dialog box.

▶ 8. Double-click the right **WBS** column divider to resize the column to best fit, and then drag the **split bar** to display the Task Name column. Your screen should look like Figure 2-53.

Figure 2-53   **Entry table with new WBS column**

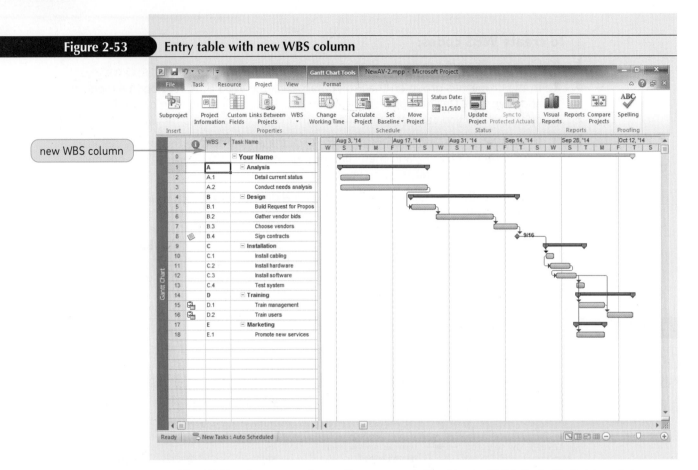

new WBS column

The WBS column uses the coding system defined in the WBS Code Definition dialog box to make a default entry for each field. Because the WBS field is user-created, however, you can override the default entry and enter something else, provided that it follows the hierarchical coding rules that you previously established (in this case, for example, the first part of the code must be a capital letter). Since WBS codes can be used to correlate tasks and their associated costs to a cost accounting structure that was created previously, you must be able to edit the WBS codes manually. You might also want to be able to edit WBS codes so you can find, filter, and report on them.

To override a WBS code with a manual entry:

1. Click the **Sign contracts (task 8) WBS** cell.

2. Type **B.99**, and then press the **Enter** key. The WBS code for Sign contracts (task 8) changes to B.99. It still follows the coding system you defined in the WBS Code Definition dialog box. If another task is added after Sign contracts, it will be assigned the WBS code B.4, unless you manually assign it a different task.

3. Drag the **split bar** to display the Duration column, click **Your Name** (task 0), click the **View** tab on the Ribbon, and then, in the **Zoom** group, click the **Zoom** button 🔍▾.

4. On the menu, click **Zoom**, click the **Entire project** option button, and then click the **OK** button. Refer to Figure 2-54.

Figure 2-54	Final project

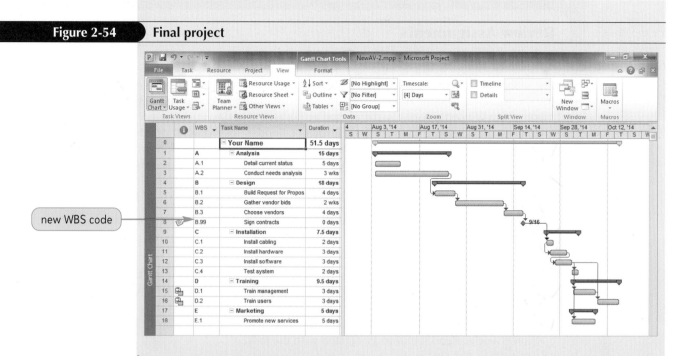

new WBS code

▶ **5.** Save the changes to your file.

▶ **6.** Submit the final NewAV.mpp file to your instructor in printed or electronic form as requested, and then close the file.

Now that you have worked with Emily and Sidney at ViewPoint Partners to establish the task dependencies and lag times, you're able to provide realistic Start and Finish dates for each task and to predict the overall Finish date for the project.

Session 2.2 Quick Check

REVIEW

1. What are the four types of task dependencies?
2. When a project is scheduled from a Start date, how does positive lag time affect two tasks in a finish-to-start relationship?
3. When a project is scheduled from a Start date, how can you use lag time to shorten the critical path?
4. When a project is scheduled from a Finish date, how does positive lag time affect two tasks in a Finish-to-Start relationship?
5. What are summary tasks?
6. What is the method of project planning that starts with broad groupings of summary tasks, and then breaks them down into smaller tasks?
7. What is the method of project planning that lists all of the individual tasks, and then collects them into logical groupings?
8. How does a WBS help you manage your project?
9. What is the purpose of the WBS codes?

Practice the skills you learned in the tutorial using the same case scenario.

PRACTICE

Review Assignments

Data File needed for the Review Assignments: Train-2.mpp

Part of the AV Presentation Rooms Installation project involves training people who will use the facilities. Training has to begin after the installation is complete. In this assignment, you will open a partially completed project file that documents training tasks. You have to make some changes to the project calendar. You will explore the project, add tasks, create summary tasks to reflect the WBS, change the durations of tasks, create relationships between tasks, create a summary task bar, show outline numbers and WBS codes, and print the Gantt Chart view to show the new project schedule. Complete the following:

1. Open the **Train-2** file located in the **Project2\Review** folder included with your Data Files.
2. Save the project file as **VPTrain-2** to the same folder.
3. Open the Project Information dialog box. This project was scheduled from a Start date of 11/3/14. On a separate piece of paper, record the project Finish date, and then close the Project Information dialog box.
4. Change the duration for Develop training documentation (task 3) from 15 days to three weeks. Read the note associated with the task.
5. Delete Interview trainers (task 5).
6. Use the fill handle to copy the duration of two days from Hire trainers (task 5) to Secure lab space (task 6).
7. The company holiday party is Friday, December 19, 2014. Change that day to non-working time on the project calendar, and name the exception **VP Family Party**.
8. Create a new calendar named **Staffing** by making a copy of the Standard calendar. On the Work Weeks tab, change the working time for the Staffing calendar to Monday through Friday from 8:00 AM to 12:00 PM. The calendar should extend for one year from 11/3/14 to 11/3/15.
9. Apply the Staffing calendar to the Hire trainers task (task 5).
10. In Calendar view, link Identify existing skills (task 1) and Identify needed skills (task 2) in an FS relationship.
11. In Network Diagram view, link Identify needed skills (task 2) and Develop training documentation (task 3) in an FS relationship.
12. In Gantt Chart view, edit the relationship between Identify needed skills (task 2) and Develop training documentation (task 3) so that there is a –50% lag time. View the Predecessors column and note the predecessor for task 3.
13. In Gantt Chart view, link tasks 3, 4, 5, and 6 with FS relationships. (*Hint*: Select all the tasks, and then click the Link Tasks button in the Schedule group on the Task tab.)
14. Edit the relationship between Hire trainers (task 5) and Secure lab space (task 6) so that it is an SS relationship with a lag time of one day.
15. Insert a new task 1 with the task name **Documentation**. Make tasks 2, 3, and 4 subtasks to task 1.
16. Insert a new task 5 with the task name **Trainers**. Make task 5 a level 1 summary task for tasks 6 and 7.
17. Insert a new task 8 with the task name **Lab**. Make task 8 a level 1 summary task for task 9.
18. Insert a new milestone task 10 with the task name **Sign lab contract** and at the same level as task 9. Link tasks 9 and 10 with an FS relationship.
19. Insert the task **Distribute progress report** as a recurring task in row 11. The duration is two hours, and the task needs to be scheduled for every Monday throughout the duration of the project. Use the Outdent button to make this a top-level task.

20. Create a project summary task bar, and then rename the project summary task bar using your name.

21. Using the Project Information dialog box, note the new Project Finish date and compare it to the Finish date you recorded in Step 1.

22. Create WBS codes for this project using uppercase letters for the first level and numbers for the second level. Display the WBS column to the left of the Task Name column in the Entry table.

23. Change the WBS code for the Distribute progress report task to **X**.

24. Show all the tasks and subtasks in the project, and then collapse the Distribute progress report task.

25. Show the Outline numbers.

26. Zoom out so that all of the task bars are visible on the Gantt chart. Be sure that Entry table columns display the Indicators column through the Duration column.

27. In Page Setup, add your name to the left side of the Header in the Gantt Chart.

28. Save your changes, submit the project, file in electronic or printed form as requested, and then close the project file.

Apply your skills to complete a project for building a new home.

Case Problem 1

Data File needed for this Case Problem: Home-2.mpp

River Dell Development, Inc.   You work for a general contractor, River Dell Development, Inc., which manages residential construction projects for group homes. The manager, Karen Reynolds, has asked you to use Project 2010 to enter and update some of the general tasks and durations involved in building a new home. She wants to use this project file as a basis for future projects. She has already created and entered some of the tasks. Now you must continue to develop the project file and show WBS codes and Outline numbers. Complete the following:

1. Open the **Home-2** file located in the **Project2\Case1** folder included with your Data Files.

2. Save the project file as **NewHome-2** in the same folder.

3. Create a new summary task 1 named **Planning**, and then make Secure financing (task 2) and Purchase lot (task 3) subtasks of the summary task Planning.

4. Delete Install flooring (task 10).

5. Insert a new task 4 with the task name **Exterior**, and then make task 4 a level 1 summary task for subtasks tasks 5 through 10.

6. Insert a new summary task 11 with the task name **Interior** and with tasks 12 through 14 as subtasks.

7. Select tasks 1 through 14, and create FS relationships among tasks 1 through 14. (*Note*: Select all the tasks, then click the Link Tasks button in the Schedule group on the Task tab.)

8. Edit the task relationship between Secure financing (task 2) and Purchase lot (task 3) to reflect a negative two-day lag time.

9. Switch to the network diagram, noticing the tasks on the critical path. Click Exterior (summary task 4), press and hold the Ctrl key, click Interior (summary task 11), and then unlink the selected tasks. View the Gantt chart and then view the network diagram again, and explain the changes to the critical path.

10. Link the tasks Brick exterior (task 10) and Install plumbing (task 12) in an FS relationship.

11. Switch to Gantt Chart view, and then insert **Paint** (task 15) as a new subtask of summary task Interior (task 12) and with a duration of 4 days. Create an FS link to Install drywall (task 14) with a 1 day lag.

12. Insert a level 1 recurring task as the last task in the Entry table named **Meet building inspector**, that is a weekly two-hour meeting every Tuesday for the duration of the project.

13. Add a milestone after the task Purchase lot and name it **Sign all contracts**. Link the milestone in an FS relationship to Purchase lot (task 3).

14. Create a project summary task bar, and then rename the project summary task bar using your name.

15. Create WBS codes for this project using uppercase letters for the first level and numbers for the second level, and display the WBS column after the Indicators column in the Entry table.

16. Change the WBS code for the Sign all contracts task to **A.99**.

17. Display the Outline numbers. Drag the split bar so Duration is the last visible column.

18. Zoom out as needed to see the entire Gantt chart, and then enter your name as a header on the Gantt chart.

19. Save your changes, submit your project in electronic or printed form as requested, and then close the file.

Apply your skills to organize a job search.

APPLY

Case Problem 2

Data File needed for this Case Problem: Jobs-2.mpp

CommunityWorks CommunityWorks is a growing grassroots organization that helps recent college graduates find employment, has hired you to work as a jobs counselor. You are assigned to support people who have technical degrees. You decide to use Project 2010 to help these recent graduates organize their job search efforts. Based on your experience, you identify several tasks that will help your clients to organize their job search efforts. You organize the tasks into summary tasks and link the tasks to give them a better assessment of the work at hand. Complete the following:

1. Open the **Jobs-2** file located in the **Project\Case2** folder included with your Data Files.

2. Save the file as **MyJobs-2** in the same folder.

3. Add a note to the Get a cell phone task that states: **Consider a Smartphone or Blackberry for email access**.

4. Insert a new summary task 1 with the task name **Resume**, and then make Create a resume (task 2) and Edit a resume (task 3) subtasks of the summary task Resume.

5. Insert a new summary task 4 with the task name **Research**, with the following subtasks: Set appointment with recruiter (task 5), Develop contact database (task 6), and Research newspaper ads (task 7).

6. Insert a new summary task 8 with the task name **Phone Calls**, and make Get a cell phone (task 9), Call references (task 10), and Call business contacts (task 11) subtasks of the summary task Phone Calls.

7. Insert a new task 10 with the task name **Existing Contacts**, and then make task 11 Call references and task 12 Call business contacts subtasks of the summary task Existing Contacts.

⊕EXPLORE

8. Insert a new task 13 with the task name **New Contacts**. Use the Indent Task and Outdent Task buttons in the Schedule group on the Task tab to make "New Contacts" a level 2 task.

EXPLORE

9. Copy and paste the tasks in rows 11 and 12 to rows 14 and 15. In doing so, you retain the tasks in rows 11 and 12 and you replace the existing tasks, "Write cover letter" and "Buy interview suits," in rows 14 and 15. (*Hint*: Be sure to select the entire row for each task you want to copy, and then select the entire row in the location where you want to paste the task.)

EXPLORE

10. Indent tasks 14 and 15 so that New Contacts (task 13) becomes a second-level summary task at the same level as Existing Contacts (task 10).

11. Drag the Gantt chart bar for Set appointment with recruiter (task 5) to change the duration to 2 days.

12. Select all 15 tasks, and then click the Link Tasks button to link all tasks in FS relationships.

13. Add a –50% lag time between Research (task 4) and Phone Calls (task 8). View the Predecessors column and note the predecessor for task 8.

14. Change the dependency between Existing Contacts (task 10) and New Contacts (task 13) from Finish-to-Start to Start-to-Start.

EXPLORE

15. In the Tasks group on the Task tab, click the Inspect button to open the Task Inspector pane, and then click each task in the project and review the information presented.

16. Close the Task Inspector pane when you are finished.

17. Create a project summary task bar, and then rename the bar using your name.

18. Zoom out so that all of the task bars are visible on the Gantt chart, drag the split bar so the Duration column is the last column showing, and then resize the Task Name and Duration columns, if needed, to view all the content.

19. Display the Outline numbers.

20. Add your name to the left header of the Gantt Chart.

21. Save the changes to the file, submit the project in electronic or printed form as requested, and then close the file.

Expand your skills to work on a project for the reunion.

CHALLENGE

Case Problem 3

Data File needed for this Case Problem: Reunion-2.mpp

Western College Reunion   As a proud graduate of Western College, you have been asked to help organize the 20th reunion for the graduating class of 1994. The college looks to graduates to keep the endowment fund growing and enhance school pride for current and future students. In 2014, the reunion takes place on March 7, 8, and 9. You scheduled the project from a Finish date and let Project 2010 determine the project Start date. Now you must continue to work on the project by creating summary tasks to reflect the WBS, establishing dependencies between tasks, and adding lag times. You will keep a watchful eye on the critical path as you work on this file. Complete the following:

1. Open the **Reunion-2** file located in the **Project2\Case3** folder included with your Data Files.

2. Save the file as **WReunion-2** to the same folder.

3. Switch to Network Diagram view. Record which tasks are on the critical path and explain why they are on the path.

4. In Network Diagram view, link tasks 1 and 2 with an FS relationship. Note which tasks are on the critical path, and then record this information.

5. In Network Diagram view, link tasks 2 and 3 with an FS relationship. Note which tasks are on the critical path, and then record this information.

6. In Network Diagram view, link task 3 to 4, 4 to 5, 5 to 6, 6 to 7, and 7 to 8 in FS relationships. Zoom out in Network Diagram view in order to expand the number of task boxes that you can see on the screen.

7. In the Entry table in Gantt Chart view, drag Determine number of attendees (task 3) to position it between tasks 1 and 2 so that it becomes task 2 and Determine reunion goals becomes task 3.

8. Add a project summary task bar. Verify the project summary task bar is named Western College Reunion.

9. Use the Insert Summary Task button to add three summary tasks, as follows:
   - Task 1, **Research**, which contains subtasks Survey alumni, Determine number of attendees, and Determine reunion goals
   - Task 5, **Financial Planning**, which contains subtasks Set budget and Set agenda
   - Task 8, **Activity Planning**, which contains subtasks Book entertainment, Determine menu, and Develop promotional brochure

⊕ EXPLORE 10. Edit the relationship between Set budget (task 6) and Set agenda (task 7) so that the tasks overlap by two working days. View the Predecessors column and note the predecessors for task 7.

11. Substitute an SS relationship between Book entertainment (task 9) and Determine menu (task 10).

12. Edit the relationship between Determine menu (task 10) and Develop promotional brochure (task 11) so that it is an SS relationship with a one-day lag.

13. Create WBS codes for this project using uppercase letters for the first level and numbers for the second level. Display the WBS column after the Indicators column in the Entry table.

⊕ EXPLORE 14. You hired Dumont Printers to develop the brochure. Monday through Thursday the workday for this company is 7 AM to 2 PM. Friday is a regular work day as specified by the Standard calendar so you do not need to make any changes to Friday hours when you create the new calendar. Create a new calendar named **Dumont Printers** based on the Standard calendar, and then use the Work Weeks tab to specify that their work week follows these hours for Monday through Thursday. Start the calendar on 1/1/14 and have it extend to 12/31/14. Assign the Dumont Printers calendar to Develop promotional brochure (task 11).

⊕ EXPLORE 15. Increase the duration for Develop promotional brochure (task 11) to 5 days, click the warning tag, read the message window that appears in the upper-left corner of the cell, accept the default option, and then click Research (task 1) to close the message window.

16. Zoom out so that all of the task bars are visible on the Gantt chart, and be sure that all of the Entry table columns through the Duration column are visible.

17. Display the Outline numbers.

18. Add your name to the left side of the header on the Gantt Chart.

19. Save your changes, submit the file in electronic or printed form as requested, and then close the project file.

Use your skills to create a new project for a play structure at your neighborhood park.

CREATE

Case Problem 4

There are no Data Files needed for this Case Problem.

NatureSpace   NatureSpace is a company that specializes in creating play structures for communities. They can also help in securing the money and grants for the project. You are the project manager assigned to manage the fundraising and construction of the new play structure at a local neighborhood park. The products and services of NatureSpace are in high demand, and completing projects on time is critical. Also, most towns do not have any extra funds and cannot afford cost overruns. All of the equipment must be ready by September 6, 2014. You must establish the task relationships and create summary tasks to reflect the WBS, as shown in Figure 2-55.

Complete the following:

1. Create a new project, and then save the project as **Grant-2** in the **Project2\Case4** folder included with your Data Files.
2. Schedule the project from the Finish date, and then change the Finish date to September 6, 2014 and set the tasks to Auto Scheduled.

EXPLORE

3. Enter the task names and durations for the project. Use Figure 2-55 for the task names, task levels, and durations. Notice that "Planning," "Fund-Raising," and "Building" are summary tasks containing subtasks. Be sure to let Project determine the summary task durations. Notice that three "Building" subtasks have subtasks.

Figure 2-55 **Tasks and durations for the NatureSpace project**

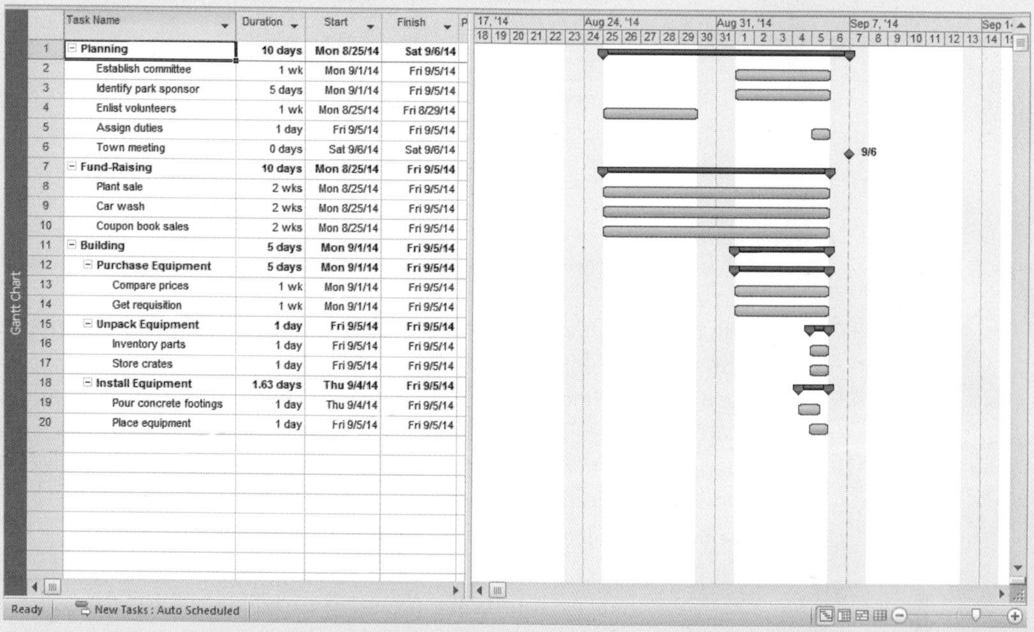

	Task Name	Duration	Start	Finish
1	Planning	10 days	Mon 8/25/14	Sat 9/6/14
2	Establish committee	1 wk	Mon 9/1/14	Fri 9/5/14
3	Identify park sponsor	5 days	Mon 9/1/14	Fri 9/5/14
4	Enlist volunteers	1 wk	Mon 8/25/14	Fri 8/29/14
5	Assign duties	1 day	Fri 9/5/14	Fri 9/5/14
6	Town meeting	0 days	Sat 9/6/14	Sat 9/6/14
7	Fund-Raising	10 days	Mon 8/25/14	Fri 9/5/14
8	Plant sale	2 wks	Mon 8/25/14	Fri 9/5/14
9	Car wash	2 wks	Mon 8/25/14	Fri 9/5/14
10	Coupon book sales	2 wks	Mon 8/25/14	Fri 9/5/14
11	Building	5 days	Mon 9/1/14	Fri 9/5/14
12	Purchase Equipment	5 days	Mon 9/1/14	Fri 9/5/14
13	Compare prices	1 wk	Mon 9/1/14	Fri 9/5/14
14	Get requisition	1 wk	Mon 9/1/14	Fri 9/5/14
15	Unpack Equipment	1 day	Fri 9/5/14	Fri 9/5/14
16	Inventory parts	1 day	Fri 9/5/14	Fri 9/5/14
17	Store crates	1 day	Fri 9/5/14	Fri 9/5/14
18	Install Equipment	1.63 days	Thu 9/4/14	Fri 9/5/14
19	Pour concrete footings	1 day	Thu 9/4/14	Fri 9/5/14
20	Place equipment	1 day	Fri 9/5/14	Fri 9/5/14

4. Edit Fund-Raising (task 7) so it is **Fundraising**. Edit the summary task names in rows 12, 15, and 18 to **Purchase play equipment**, **Unpack play equipment**, and **Install play equipment**. Resize the column to fit all task names on one row.
5. Create an FS relationship between the three summary tasks called "Planning," "Fundraising," and "Building."
6. Switch to Network Diagram view and create an FS relationship between the three summary tasks Purchase play equipment, Unpack play equipment, and Install play equipment.
7. Create a new calendar based on the Standard calendar named **Builders** with non-standard working hours of Monday-Friday 8:00 AM to 12 PM and 1:00 PM to 2:30 PM, and assign it to Pour concrete footings (task 19). The calendar should start on August 4, 2014 and end 2 years later.

EXPLORE

8. Create a different calendar with an exception nonworking day that recurs annually for 10 years and assign it to one of the tasks.
9. Switch back to Gantt Chart view. Add durations and dependencies between the su tasks, using Figure 2-56 as a guide. Figure 2-56 shows the final project.
10. Define the WBS code, as shown in Figure 2-56, for the three levels in th and then display the WBS column as shown.

Figure 2-56	Final NatureSpace project file

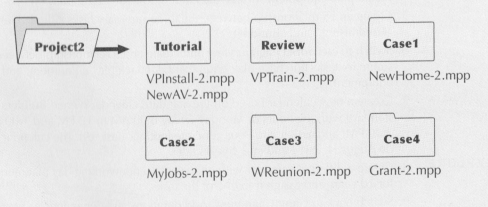

	ⓘ	WBS	Task Name	Duration	Start	Finish	Predecessors
0			⊟ **Your Name**	**60.63 days**	**Fri 6/13/14**	**Fri 9/5/14**	
1		A	⊟ Planning	17 days	Fri 6/13/14	Tue 7/8/14	
2		A.1	Establish committee	1 wk	Fri 6/13/14	Fri 6/20/14	
3		A.4	Identify park sponsor	5 days	Fri 6/20/14	Fri 6/27/14	2
4		A.3	Enlist volunteers	1 wk	Mon 6/30/14	Mon 7/7/14	3FS+1 day
5		A.2	Assign duties	1 day	Mon 7/7/14	Tue 7/8/14	4
6		A.5	Town meeting	0 days	Tue 7/8/14	Tue 7/8/14	
7		B	⊟ Fundraising	30 days	Tue 7/8/14	Tue 8/19/14	1
8		B.1	Plant sale	2 wks	Tue 7/8/14	Tue 7/22/14	
9		B.2	Car wash	2 wks	Tue 7/22/14	Tue 8/5/14	8
10		B.3	Coupon book sales	2 wks	Tue 8/5/14	Tue 8/19/14	9
11		C	⊟ Building	13.63 days	Tue 8/19/14	Fri 9/5/14	7
12		C.1	⊟ Purchase play equipme	10 days	Tue 8/19/14	Tue 9/2/14	
13		C.1.1	Compare prices	1 wk	Tue 8/19/14	Tue 8/26/14	
14		C.1.2	Get requisition	1 wk	Tue 8/26/14	Tue 9/2/14	13
15		C.2	⊟ Unpack play equipment	2 days	Tue 9/2/14	Thu 9/4/14	12
16		C.2.1	Inventory parts	1 day	Tue 9/2/14	Wed 9/3/14	
17		C.2.2	Store crates	1 day	Wed 9/3/14	Thu 9/4/14	16
18		C.3	⊟ Install play equipment	1.63 days	Thu 9/4/14	Fri 9/5/14	15
19		C.3.1	Pour concrete footings	1 day	Thu 9/4/14	Fri 9/5/14	
20		C.3.2	Place equipment	1 day	Fri 9/5/14	Fri 9/5/14	19FS-1 day

⊕ **EXPLORE**   11. Switch to Calendar view and note how the summary tasks do not appear in this view. Explain why you think this is so.

⊕ **EXPLORE**   12. Open the Task Information dialog box for one of the tasks. Where is the WBS code located?

⊕ **EXPLORE**   13. Open the Task Information dialog box for one of the summary tasks. Where is the predecessor information located?

14. Display the Project Summary Task bar and change the Task Name for task 0 to your name.

15. Save your changes, submit the file in electronic or printed form as requested, and then close the file.

ENDING DATA FILES

Project2 →

Tutorial
VPInstall-2.mpp
NewAV-2.mpp

Review
VPTrain-2.mpp

Case1
NewHome-2.mpp

Case2
MyJobs-2.mpp

Case3
WReunion-2.mpp

Case4
Grant-2.mpp

TUTORIAL 3

OBJECTIVES

Session 3.1
- Review reports in Project 2010
- Examine the critical path
- Filter tasks
- Format a Gantt chart

Session 3.2
- Enter and edit tasks and dependencies in a network diagram
- Expand, collapse, move, and filter tasks in a network diagram
- Format a network diagram
- Shorten the critical path by changing task durations, dependencies, and lag time
- Analyze task constraints

Communicating Project Information

Improving the AV Project

Case | *ViewPoint Partners*

Sidney Simone, the owner of ViewPoint Partners, reviewed the Project 2010 file that you have been developing. She examined the tasks, durations, and dependencies that you determined are necessary to install the five AV presentation rooms for ViewPoint Partners. Sidney deleted the Training calendar because she prefers to have the training be part of the Standard calendar, and she asked Emily, the technology specialist at ViewPoint Partners, to make a few other changes to the project file. As a result of these changes, the Finish date calculated by Project 2010 is two weeks later than Emily had anticipated, so she has asked you to use the features of Project 2010, such as reports, filters, and custom formats, to emphasize certain tasks. Emily also wants to analyze the project and shorten the critical path so the project Finish date is pulled back to an earlier date.

PROJECT

STARTING DATA FILES

 Project3 → Tutorial   Review   Case1   Case2   Case3 Case4

AV-3.mpp
AVPath-3.mpp

Train-3.mpp Home-3.mpp Jobs-3.mpp Reunion-3.mpp Grant-3.mpp

SESSION 3.1 VISUAL OVERVIEW

The Gantt Chart Tools Format tab provides many options for formatting a Gantt chart.

You click the Format Bar button to open a menu; you select Bar to open the Format Bar dialog box or Bar Styles to open the Bar Styles dialog box.

You use the Text Styles dialog box to format types of text, such as critical tasks in red and bold.

You use the Layout dialog box to specify the way the Gantt chart summary bars are formatted when summary tasks are collapsed.

Gantt Chart Tools   NewAV-3.mpp - Microsoft Pro

File   Task   Resource   Project   View   Format

Text Styles   Gridlines   Layout   Insert Column   Column Settings   Custom Fields   Format

☑ Critical Tasks
☑ Slack
☐ Late Tasks

Baseline   Slippage

Format   Columns   Styles

🖎 Bar
🖎 Bar Styles

Gantt Chart

	Task Name	Duration	Qtr 3, 2014 August
			7/27	8/3	8/10	8/17	8/24
1	⊞ Analysis	20 days					
5	⊟ Design	18 days					
6	Build Request for Proposal	4 days					
7	Gather vendor bids	2 wks					
8	Choose vendors	4 days					
9	Sign contracts	0 days					
10	⊟ Installation	5.5 days					
11	Install cabling	2 days					
12	Install hardware	3 days					
13	Install software	3 days					
14	Installation completed	0 days					
15	⊟ Security	2 days					
16	Create user IDs and passwords	1 day					
17	Create access hierarchy	2 days					
18	Create touch panel images	2 days					
19	Security completed	0 days					
20	⊟ Testing	2 days					
21	Test hardware	1 day					
22	Test software	2 days					
23	Test security	1 day					
24	Testing completed	0 days					
25	⊟ Training	6 days					
26	Train management	3 days					
27	Train users	3 days					
28	Training completed	0 days					

Ready   New Tasks : Auto Scheduled

CUSTOMIZED GANTT CHART

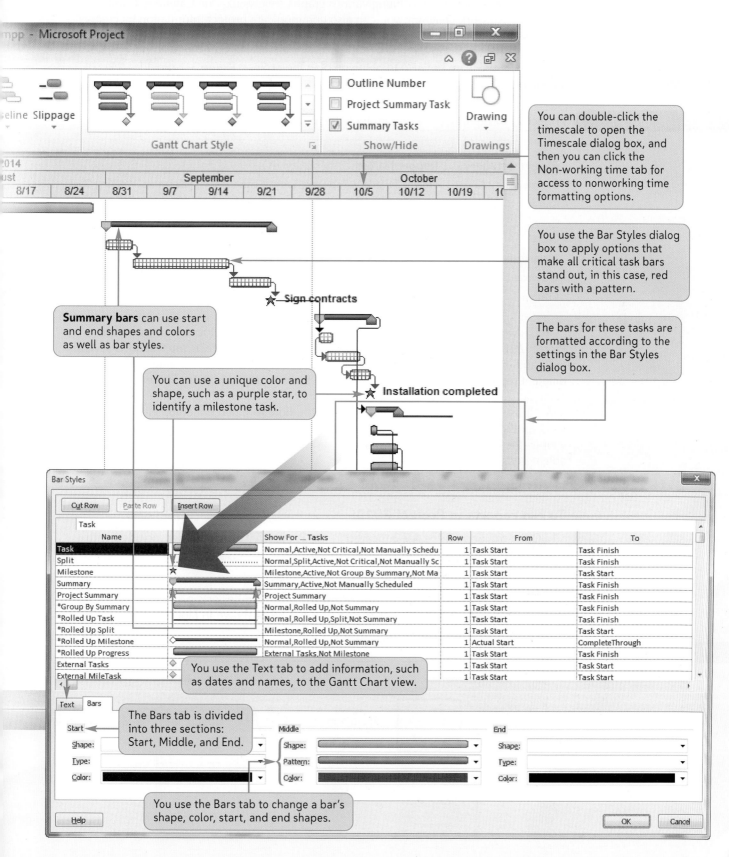

You can double-click the timescale to open the Timescale dialog box, and then you can click the Non-working time tab for access to nonworking time formatting options.

You use the Bar Styles dialog box to apply options that make all critical task bars stand out, in this case, red bars with a pattern.

Summary bars can use start and end shapes and colors as well as bar styles.

The bars for these tasks are formatted according to the settings in the Bar Styles dialog box.

You can use a unique color and shape, such as a purple star, to identify a milestone task.

You use the Text tab to add information, such as dates and names, to the Gantt Chart view.

The Bars tab is divided into three sections: Start, Middle, and End.

You use the Bars tab to change a bar's shape, color, start, and end shapes.

Creating Reports Using Project 2010

In addition to displaying or printing various graphics views like the Calendar, Gantt Chart, and Network Diagram, you can also communicate project information by creating several types of reports. **Reports** are used to disseminate information. You can use a report not only to inform members of the team about project status and to collect information from the team but also to help you plan the project. Figure 3-1 provides a list of the main types of reports available in Project 2010.

| Figure 3-1 | Project 2010 reports that assist project planning |

Report Category	Report Names
Overview	Project Summary, Top-Level Tasks, Critical Tasks, Milestones, Working Days
Current	Unstarted Tasks, Tasks Starting Soon, Tasks In Progress, Completed Tasks, Should Have Started Tasks, Slipping Tasks
Costs	Cash Flow, Budget, Overbudget Tasks, Overbudget Resources, Earned Value
Assignments	Who Does What, Who Does What When, To-Do List, Overallocated Resources
Workload	Task Usage, Resource Usage
Custom	Users can customize report templates or create other customized reports

You have worked with tech specialist Emily Michaels to develop a more complete Project 2010 file for the AV Presentation Rooms Installation project. You've added several tasks and milestones, entered task durations, and determined task dependencies. Viewing different reports will help you to analyze your current project plan in different ways. For example, a Top-Level Tasks report lists the highest-level tasks, which often are summary tasks. It lists the scheduled Start and Finish dates, duration, percent complete, cost, and work for those top-level tasks. You can use this information to determine if you need to shorten the overall schedule or make other adjustments. You'll view some of the available reports now.

To run reports in Project 2010:

1. Open the project file **AV-3** located in the **Project3\Tutorial** folder included with your Data Files.

2. Save the project as **NewAV-3** to the same location.

3. Click the **Project** tab on the Ribbon, and then in the Reports group, click the **Reports** button. The Reports dialog box opens, as shown in Figure 3-2.

| Figure 3-2 | Reports dialog box |

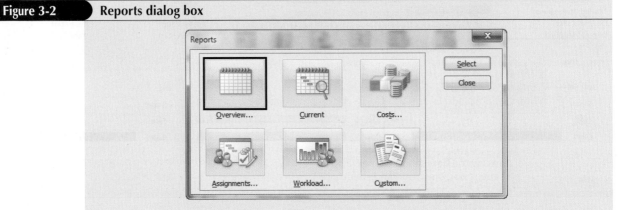

4. Double-click the **Overview** icon to open the Overview Reports dialog box, and then double-click the **Top-Level Tasks** icon. The Top-Level Tasks report appears on the screen in Backstage view. Your screen should look similar to Figure 3-3.

Figure 3-3 ▶ **Top-Level Tasks report**

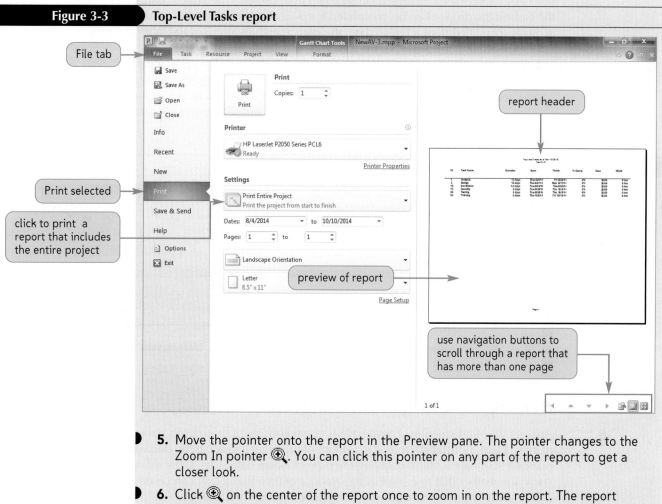

5. Move the pointer onto the report in the Preview pane. The pointer changes to the Zoom In pointer 🔍. You can click this pointer on any part of the report to get a closer look.

6. Click 🔍 on the center of the report once to zoom in on the report. The report view expands so you can see the text more clearly, and the pointer changes to the Zoom Out pointer 🔍. The first top-level task, Analysis, is currently scheduled to begin on 8/4/14, and the last top-level task, Training, is scheduled to end on 10/10/14. This information is useful for planning the project.

7. Click the **Project** tab on the Ribbon, and then, in the Reports group, click the **Reports** button.

8. In the Reports dialog box, double-click the **Overview** icon, and then double-click the **Critical Tasks** icon. The Critical Tasks report opens, and you see thumbnails of all four pages on the screen. Although this report might look overwhelming, it can help you identify which tasks are critical in the project.

9. Click 🔍 on the thumbnail in the second row, second column to zoom in on the report. On the status bar, click the **Previous Page** navigation button ◀ and then click the **Multiple Pages** navigation button 🔡. As you can see, there is no information on pages 3 and 4. If you were to print this report, you would reformat it to reduce the number of pages that print.

10. Click the **Task** tab on the Ribbon to return to Gantt Chart view.

Understanding the Critical Path

Recall that a critical task is one that must be completed as scheduled in order for the project to finish by the Finish date; any delay in a critical task could delay the project completion date. The critical path is the series of critical tasks (or even a single critical task) that dictates the calculated Finish date of the project. The critical path determines the earliest the project can be completed for projects scheduled from a Start date. For projects scheduled from a Finish date, the critical path determines the latest the project can be started. Project 2010 offers several techniques to view the critical path. For example, you can format the critical path in the Gantt chart. The critical path changes if tasks on the critical path are completed ahead of or behind schedule. A simple example of a project with one critical path is shown in Gantt Chart view in Figure 3-4. This Gantt chart has been formatted so tasks on the critical path are shown as red bars. Tasks 1, 3, and 4 are critical tasks.

Figure 3-4   Gantt chart showing the critical path

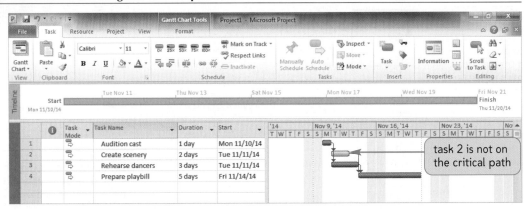

Defining the Critical Path Using Slack

Another way to define the critical path is that it consists of those tasks having a float of zero. **Float**, or **total slack**, is the amount of time that a task can be delayed from its planned Start date without delaying the project Finish date. Total slack differs from free slack. Remember that free slack is the amount of time that a task can be delayed without delaying any successor tasks; it is examined further in a later tutorial. If any tasks on the critical path take longer than planned, the project completion date will slip unless corrective action is taken. Tasks without any free slack cannot be delayed; if they are, the critical path will be affected.

Network diagram view makes it easy to see the critical path because critical tasks are displayed in red by default. Figure 3-5 shows the current network diagram for this simple project. Notice that task 2 is on the same linear path as tasks 1 and 4, but it is not a critical task.

Network diagram showing the critical path

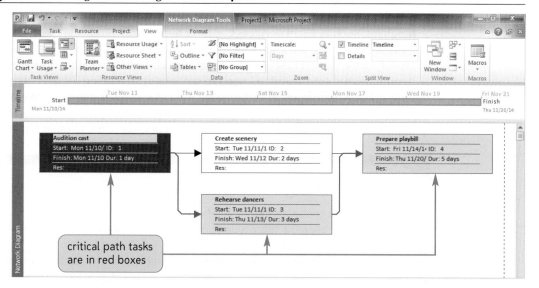

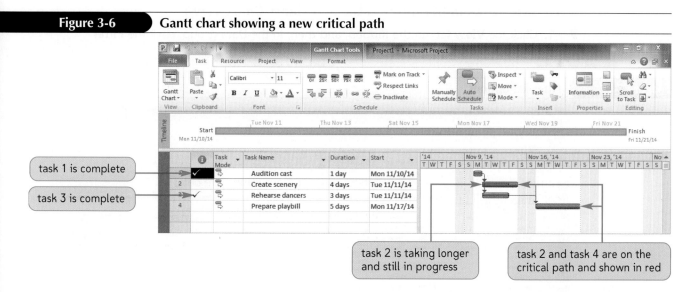

How would the critical path change, however, if tasks 1 and 3 were completed as planned, but task 2 was only partially complete and will take four days? Figure 3-6 shows the new formatted Gantt chart with progress bars displaying the current status of each task. The indicators column shows that tasks 1 and 3 are 100 percent complete. The duration for task 2 has been changed to four days. Notice that task 2 is now on the critical path. Because task 2 has an FS dependency to task 4, and task 2 has a longer duration, the project completion date has been pushed out.

Figure 3-6   **Gantt chart showing a new critical path**

Even in this small example, it is easy to see how the critical path can change quickly as the project is progressing. It is very important for a project manager to find, analyze, and communicate information about the critical path throughout the life of the project. Filters, formats, and customizing the network diagram help the manager accomplish this.

Filtering Tasks for Information

Filtering features within Project 2010 are similar to filtering features used in other software programs, such as Excel or Access. A **filter** temporarily hides some of the tasks so that only those tasks that you are interested in are displayed. This helps you to focus on specific aspects of the project based on different criteria. Note that a filter does not delete tasks; it just hides the ones you don't need to see for the time being. Project 2010 offers many built-in filters, which are available using the Filter arrow in the Data group on the View tab. The Critical filter is used frequently and filters out all tasks not currently on the critical path. This option makes it easy to see the critical tasks in the familiar Gantt Chart view.

REFERENCE

Filtering Tasks

- In the Data group on the View tab, click the Filter arrow.
- On the list, click the filter type you want to use (for example, Critical, Summary Tasks, or Unstarted Tasks).
- To remove the filter, click the Filter arrow, and then choose the No Filter option.

You decide to use the Project 2010 filtering capabilities to review the tasks in the ViewPoint Partners project file that are on the critical path. You want to stay in Gantt Chart view but see only the critical tasks.

To filter tasks in the Entry table and Gantt Chart view:

1. Click the **View** tab on the Ribbon, and then, in the Data group, click the **Filter arrow**. An alphabetical list of filters opens, as shown in Figure 3-7.

Figure 3-7   Filter list options

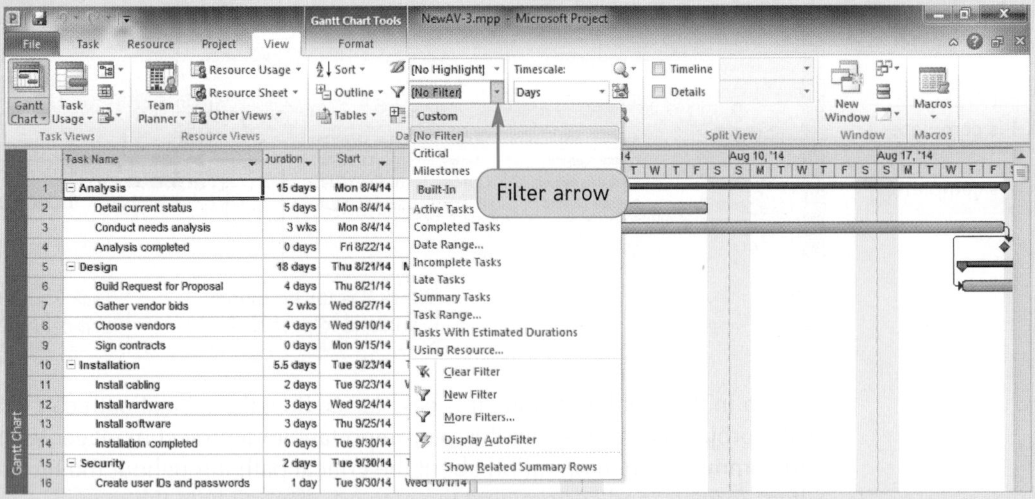

2. In the filter list, click **Critical**. The Entry table and Gantt chart display only those tasks on the critical path (the summary tasks and critical tasks), as shown in Figure 3-8. Tasks not on the critical path (tasks 2, 4, 15, 16, 17, 18, 19, 21, and 23) are hidden. Nothing has changed in the project file; the only difference is the way that you view the data. The status bar displays Filter Applied to help you know when a filter is applied to a view.

Figure 3-8 **Gantt Chart view filtered for critical tasks**

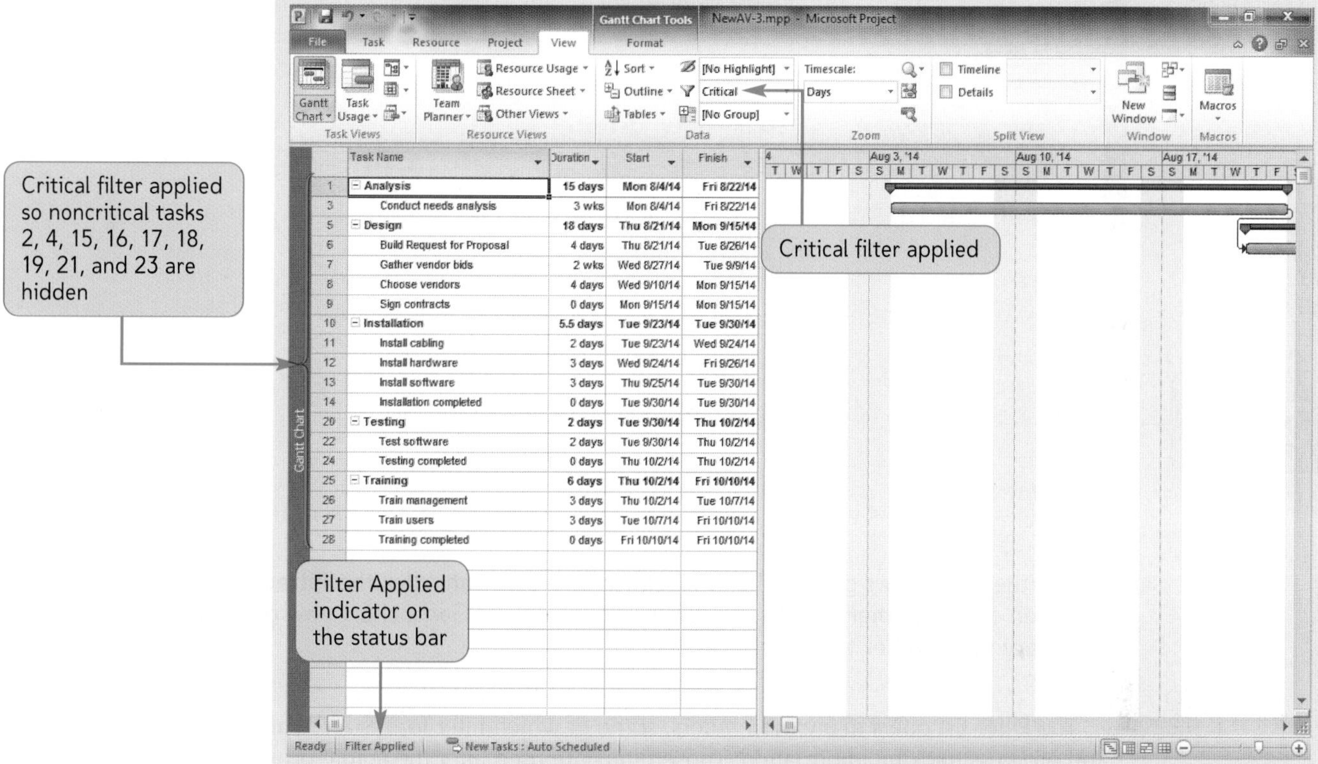

Critical filter applied so noncritical tasks 2, 4, 15, 16, 17, 18, 19, 21, and 23 are hidden

Critical filter applied

Filter Applied indicator on the status bar

Filters can be applied in any view, but each view is filtered independently of the others. For example, the Critical filter that you applied to Gantt Chart view is not applied to any other views, such as Network Diagram view.

3. In the Task Views group, click the **Network Diagram** button. The Filter box in the Data group displays No Filter; there are no filters applied and you can see all the tasks in this view.

4. In the Data group, click the **Filter** arrow, click **Summary Tasks**, and then zoom out as needed to see the six summary tasks. The network diagram displays only the summary tasks, as shown in Figure 3-9. Notice that not all summary tasks are on the critical path.

Figure 3-9   Filtering for summary tasks in Network Diagram view

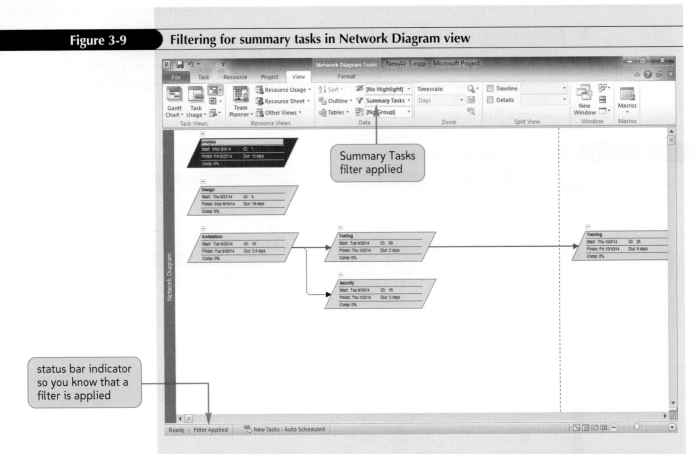

Summary Tasks filter applied

status bar indicator so you know that a filter is applied

5. In the Task Views group, click the **Gantt Chart** button, click the **Filter** arrow, and then click **Summary Tasks**. The Entry table and the Gantt chart now display summary tasks rather than critical tasks.

The Filter list offers many more filters, some of which filter for resource allocations and progress tracking information. Those filters are used after the actual project is under-way. Other filters, such as Milestones, Task Range, and Date Range, can be used at any time. Filters, such as the Date Range filter, require that you enter parameters to specify the exact details of the filter. For the Date Range, you must enter two parameters: one to specify criteria for the Start or Finish after date and another to specify criteria for the before date. Sidney is concerned about the schedule, and she wants to know which tasks in the project currently are scheduled to start or finish between August 1 and September 1. You apply a filter to find this information.

To filter for a date range:

TIP

You can click the arrow in each Date Range dialog box to open a calendar and scroll to the date you want to set as the criterion for that parameter of the date range.

1. In the Data group, click the **Filter** arrow, and then click **Date Range**. The Date Range dialog box opens. You want to find all tasks that are scheduled to start or scheduled to end between 8/1/2014 and 9/1/2014. Tasks will be included as long as they meet either criterion.

2. Click in the **Show tasks that start or finish after** box, type **8/1/2014**, and then click the **OK** button. The Date Range dialog box changes to display the And before box.

3. Click in the **And before** box, type **9/1/2014**, and then click the **OK** button. The dialog box closes.

4. Click **Analysis** (task 1) if it is not already selected, click the **Task** tab, zoom out as needed to see all the bars in the Gantt chart, and then click the **Scroll to Task** button in the Editing group. Your screen should look like Figure 3-10, with tasks displayed that match the criteria you set in the Date Range filter.

Figure 3-10 | Filtering for a date range

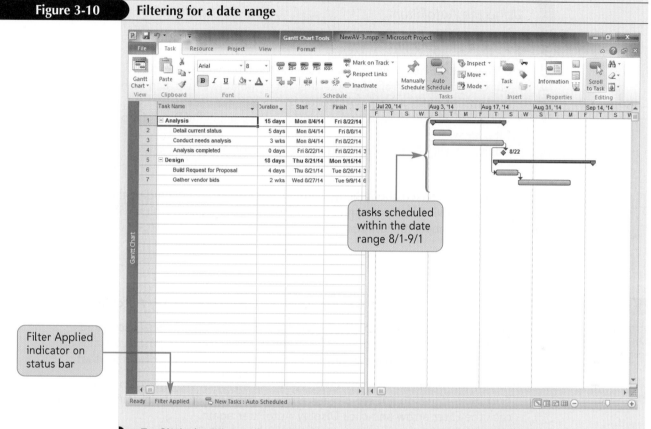

tasks scheduled within the date range 8/1-9/1

Filter Applied indicator on status bar

5. Click the **View** tab, and then, in the Data group, click the **Filter** arrow.

6. On the list, click **[No Filter]**. All tasks are again displayed.

The filters in each view are independently applied and removed, so each view of the project can have a different filter applied at the same time. It is also important to note that filters are only correct as of the moment they are applied. They do not dynamically update the current view of the project as the project is modified. In other words, if you make a change to a filtered project, you must reapply the filter to make sure that tasks meeting the filter's criteria are currently displayed. For example, if you have the Critical filter applied and make a change to a task (such as shortening its duration) that causes it to be a noncritical task, it will still be displayed as a critical task until you reapply the Critical filter.

Using the AutoFilter

Another type of filter, the **AutoFilter**, allows you to determine the filter criteria by selecting from a list associated specifically with each column in the Entry table. When you turn on the AutoFilter feature, an arrow is displayed to the right of each column name in the Entry table. You choose filter criteria for a column by clicking the arrow in the column heading.

REFERENCE

Using the AutoFilter

- Click the View tab, and then, in the Data group, click the Filter arrow.
- On the list, click Display AutoFilter.
- Click the AutoFilter arrow for the column in the table you wish to filter.
- Click a criteria entry from the AutoFilter list, or point to Filters, and then click Custom... to create a custom AutoFilter.
- To remove an AutoFilter, click the View tab, and then, in the Data group, click the Filter arrow.
- On the list, click Display AutoFilter to toggle off the AutoFilter feature.

Emily has often talked about the powerful features in Project, including the AutoFilter feature. You decide to become familiar with the AutoFilter feature, which will help you find information about the tasks quickly.

TIP

The AutoFilter feature in Project 2010 is similar to AutoFilters in Excel.

To use an AutoFilter:

1. In the Data group, click the **Filter** arrow, and then click **Display AutoFilter**.

   Black AutoFilter arrows appear to the right of the column names (also called the field names) at the top of each column in the Entry table. When you click an AutoFilter arrow, the list that appears contains possible filter criteria for that column.

   Trouble? If you do not see a black arrow to the right of each column name, then click the Filter arrow and click Display AutoFilter again.

2. In the Entry table, click the **Start AutoFilter** arrow to display the list of available filter criteria for the Start column, then point to **Filters** on the filter criteria list. You can see the possible filter options available for the Start date in Project.

3. Click the **August** check box to clear the August 2014 dates, click the **October** check box to clear the October 2014 dates, and then click **OK**. Only the tasks that start in September 2014 are displayed.

Notice that the summary task Design, which has a Start date of 8/21/14, is included in the list. This is because the summary task has subtasks that meet the criteria. Notice that only the subtasks that meet the criteria are shown in the Entry table and the Gantt chart. Notice, too, that the column heading Start has a filter icon ▼, as shown in Figure 3-11. This indicates that a filter has been applied to this column in the Entry table. The status bar also provides a way for you to know when an AutoFilter is applied to a view. In the next step you will see how Filter and AutoFilter can be used together.

Figure 3-11   Entry table with Start AutoFilter

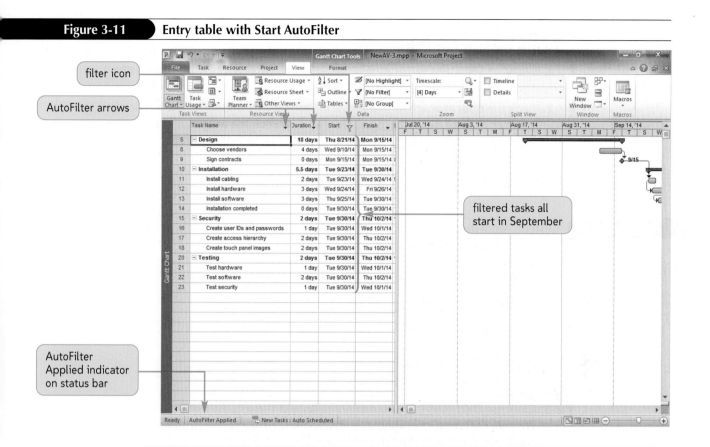

To use the Filter and AutoFilter features together to find information:

▶ **1.** In the Data group, click the **Filter** arrow, and then click **Critical**. Three summary tasks and seven tasks meet both filter criteria—that is, the task starts in September and it is on the critical path.

▶ **2.** In the Data group, click the **Filter** arrow, and then click **[No Filter]** so that all tasks are visible. The AutoFilter is still available, as you can see from the arrows in the column headings.

Custom filters are useful when you want to filter using two criteria or when you want to compare criteria. Comparison operators such as greater than >, less than <, less than or equal to <=, and greater than or equal to >= can be combined with the logical operators AND and OR to create conditions to display very specific information that you might need in the project. The Custom AutoFilter dialog box makes creating these criteria very simple. You can apply custom filters using the AutoFilter arrows.

To use custom AutoFilters:

▶ **1.** Click the **Duration AutoFilter** arrow, point to **Filters**, and then click **Custom...**. The Custom AutoFilter dialog box opens.

▶ **2.** Click the **operator** arrow (the arrow in the first box under Duration), click **is greater than or equal to**, press the **Tab** key, click the **arrow**, and then click **5 days** to specify that you want to display the tasks with a duration greater than or equal to five days, as shown in Figure 3-12. To create a filter using two criteria, in the Custom AutoFilter dialog box, click either the And or the Or option button, and then add the second criterion using the second row.

Figure 3-12	Custom AutoFilter dialog box

▶ **3.** Click the **OK** button. Four summary tasks and three tasks meet the custom criteria. Each has a duration of five or more days. Note that a summary task is displayed if it meets the filter criteria, even if none of its subtasks meet the filter criteria.

▶ **4.** In the Data group, click the **Filter** arrow, and then click **[No Filter]**. The selection No Filter clears an AutoFilter.

▶ **5.** On the Quick Access toolbar, click the **Save** button 🔲 to save the project file.

INSIGHT

Specifying Filter Details On Printouts

Gantt Chart view of a filtered project is an excellent way to communicate information about the project with your staff. You can print any filtered view of a project, but it is important to identify on the printed copy what is being represented. For example, you already know how to use headers and footers to enter information such as your name, the date, a time, and a filename to help identify the project file on the printout. You can also enter information about what filter has been applied to create the view on the printout.

Formatting a Project

Sometimes you need to highlight information in a project in order to view or communicate important information. You can change the appearance of the default view. For example, you might change the color of certain types of task bars within the Gantt chart or change the text font size within a table. Project 2010 provides many ways to format the colors, shapes, and text within each project view to help you communicate your message clearly. You can change the format of individual tasks, or you can change the format of all tasks that meet a specific criteria or category, such as a summary task, critical summary task, or a milestone. You use different dialog boxes depending on what you want to format. When you want to format specific individual tasks not based on the type of task or any criteria, you select the task or tasks you want to format and then select options in the Font dialog box to make formatting changes to the font or the Format Bar dialog box to make formatting changes to the bar associated with the selected task. When you want to format all tasks associated with a category, such as critical milestone, milestone, or critical summary task, you open the Text Styles dialog box to make font formatting changes or the Bar Styles dialog box to make bar formatting changes to all tasks associated with the selected category.

INSIGHT

Formatting Your Projects for Better Visual Communication

Sometimes it is helpful to have a wizard guide you through steps to create a formatted view in Project. You always have access to the Format commands through the Gantt Chart Tools Format tab, but if you want some guided help to format a Gantt chart, you can use the Gantt Chart Wizard. To do so, you first have to add the Gantt Chart Wizard to a new group on the Ribbon. You should do this only if you have permission to modify the installation of Project on your computer. Click the File tab, then click Options to open the Options dialog box. Click the Customize Ribbon option, and then complete the steps to add the Gantt Chart Wizard command from the Commands Not in the Ribbon list to a new Group on the Gantt Chart Tools tab. Give the new Group a meaningful name, such as Wizards. Once on the Ribbon, click the Gantt Chart Wizard button and follow the steps to work through the wizard to format the Gantt chart. The Gantt Chart Wizard is a very powerful and easy-to-use tool that you can access as many times as you want to format the Gantt chart.

Formatting a Gantt Chart

Project 2010 applies default formatting choices, such as solid blue for automatically scheduled task bars and black for summary bars. By default, manually scheduled tasks have light blue shaded bars and critical tasks have red bars. You can change start and end shapes on the bars to highlight the Start date and End date for each task. You can change the default options individually or by using Gantt Chart styles. Enhancing the appearance of certain task bars of a Gantt Chart customizes the project to make it easier for you to work with and helps you communicate the information to management.

REFERENCE

Applying Format Changes to Bars for a Task Category in a Gantt Chart

- To format all the bars associated with a specific task category, such as milestone or critical, in Gantt Chart view, click the Gantt Chart Tools Format tab, click the Format button in the Bar Styles group, and then click Bar Styles to open the Bar Styles dialog box or click the Dialog Box Launcher in the Gantt Chart Style group to open the Bar Styles dialog box.
- Click the category (type) of task that you want to modify in the Name column, and then choose the formatting changes using the options in the lower section of the dialog box.
- When you are finished making formatting choices, click the OK button.

or

- In the Gantt Chart Style group on the Gantt Chart Tools Format tab, click a Gantt Chart style in the Gantt Chart Style gallery.

or

- In the Gantt Chart Style group on the Gantt Chart Tools Format tab, click the More button to open the Gantt Chart Style gallery, and then click a style.

Sidney and Emily will review the project file using computers. When they show the file to prospective contractors, it needs to look professional. Because color and patterns enhance any presentation, you format bars in the Gantt chart to convey information based on color and style. The formatted Gantt chart bars will help Sidney, Emily, and any other people involved in the installation project understand aspects of the project more quickly.

To format the Gantt chart using the Gantt Chart Style gallery:

1. Click the Gantt Chart Tools Format tab, and then, in the Gantt Chart Style group, click the More button ⬇ to open the Gantt Chart Style gallery.

2. In the Scheduling Styles section, point to the style shown in Figure 3-13, then click the style in the gallery.

| Figure 3-13 | Gantt Chart Style gallery |

3. View the changes to your Gantt chart bars.

4. In the Bar Styles group on the Gantt Chart Tools Format tab, click the **Critical Tasks** check box, and then click the **Slack** check box. Critical tasks are shown in red and slack bars are added to the Gantt Chart view. **Slack bars** help show how many days a noncritical task can be delayed and not affect the project Finish date.

5. In the Gantt Chart Style group, click the More button ⊽ to open the Gantt Chart Style gallery.

6. In the Presentation Styles section in the Gantt Chart Style gallery, click the style icon near the end of the list that has green bars.

7. Drag the **split bar** to the left so the Duration column is the last column showing, and then scroll the Gantt chart so that your screen looks similar to Figure 3-14.

Figure 3-14	Formatted Gantt chart

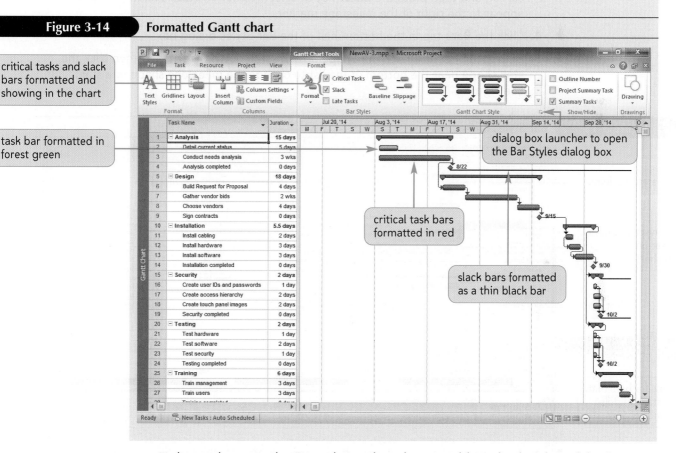

critical tasks and slack bars formatted and showing in the chart

task bar formatted in forest green

dialog box launcher to open the Bar Styles dialog box

critical task bars formatted in red

slack bars formatted as a thin black bar

Tasks are shown on the Gantt chart as bars that extend from the date the task begins to the date it ends. Bars will appear longer on the screen as you zoom in on the Gantt chart and shorter as you zoom out. The most common task categories include Normal, Critical, Noncritical, Milestone, and Summary. By selecting the Critical Tasks check box, you highlight the critical task bars in red. The slack bars appear on the chart when you click the Slack check box. If the Critical Tasks check box is not selected, bars will not be seen as critical in Gantt view. If these check boxes are not checked, then neither Critical Tasks nor Slack Bars will be available for formatting in the Bar Styles dialog box. You can format slack bars using the Bar Styles dialog box to override the default formatting.

Formatting bars by category is one way to represent the Gantt chart bars in a unique way. Visual cues can help project mangers better understand the project plan. The bars in the Gantt chart also have start and end points on the days each task begins and ends. You can format the start and end points so each has a distinct appearance in Gantt Chart view.

To format the Gantt chart bars using the Bar Styles dialog box:

▶ **1.** In the Gantt Chart Style group on the Gantt Chart Tools Format tab, click the **Dialog Box Launcher** to open the Bar Styles dialog box. The Bar Styles dialog box opens displaying the current formatting choices for each type of task that appears in the Gantt chart. You use the Bar Styles dialog box when you want to make changes to all task bars associated with a task category, such as milestone or critical.

TIP

View task categories by clicking any Show For... Tasks cell, and then clicking the arrow.

▶ **2.** In the Name column, click the **Milestone** cell, click the **Text** tab in the bottom half of the Bar Styles dialog box, and then click the **Right** cell. A down arrow appears at the right end of the cell.

▶ **3.** Click the **down** arrow, press the **N** key to quickly scroll through the alphabetical list, and then press the **Enter** key to select Name. The task's name will now appear to the right of the milestone marker.

▶ **4.** Click the **Bars** tab in the bottom half of the Bar Styles dialog box.

▶ **5.** In the Start section, click the **Shape** arrow, scroll down the list, and then click the **star shape** near the bottom of the list to change the milestone shape to a star. See Figure 3-15.

| Figure 3-15 | Bar Styles dialog box |

▶ **6.** In the Name column, click the **Summary** cell. You want to change the start shape color as well as the end shape and color on the summary bars to help differentiate them on the chart.

TIP

Use the ScreenTips to identify the colors by name on the color palette.

▶ **7.** Click the **Bars** tab if it is not already selected, click the **Start Color** arrow, click the **Olive Green, Darker 25%** color box in the Theme Colors section, click the **End Shape** arrow, click the **upward pentagon** shape, click the **End Color** arrow, and then click the **Red, Darker 25%** color box in the Theme Colors section. Green for starting and Red for stopping will provide good visual cues in the chart for the summary tasks.

8. In the top section of the Bar Styles dialog box, scroll down to see the bottom of the Name column list, then click the **Slack** Name cell. You want to change the color of the slack bars to purple to help differentiate them from the black summary bars.

9. Click the **Color** arrow for the Middle section on the Bars tab, and then in the Standard Colors section, click **Purple**.

10. In top section of the Bar Styles dialog box, click the **Critical** Name cell.

11. In the bottom section of the Bar Styles dialog box, click the **Middle Pattern** arrow, and then click the **small grid** pattern (second from the last in the list).

   Trouble? If Slack or Critical does not appear in the Name column, be sure the Slack check box and the Critical check box in the Bar Styles group on the Gantt Chart Tools Format tab have check marks.

12. Click the **OK** button, click the **Task** tab on the Ribbon, and then scroll so that the August 3, 2014 date is near the Duration column. The Gantt chart should look like Figure 3-16.

| Figure 3-16 | Gantt chart with formatting |

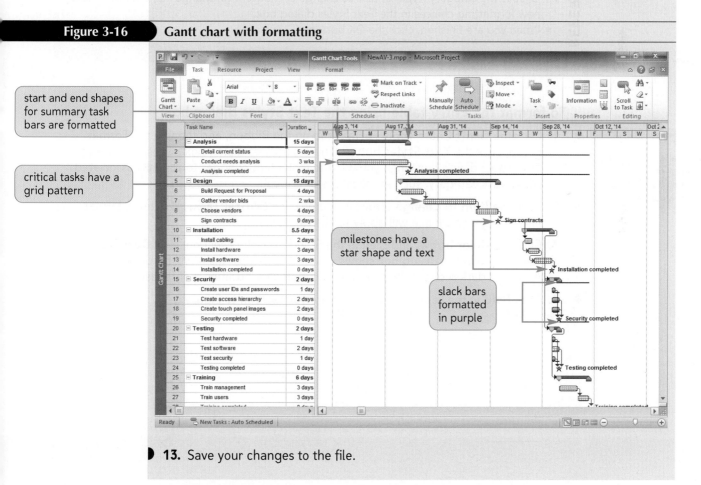

start and end shapes for summary task bars are formatted

critical tasks have a grid pattern

milestones have a star shape and text

slack bars formatted in purple

13. Save your changes to the file.

Project 2010 has many formatting options for the Gantt chart. For example, the Bar Styles dialog box also allows you to change the way that bars appear within different date parameters or summary tasks. The key to formatting the Gantt chart is that the final product should clearly and quickly communicate the information that is important to the project manager and management. As the project progresses, you can always reformat the Gantt chart to highlight important changes.

Formatting an Entry Table

Formatting an Entry table in Project 2010 is similar to formatting cells within an Excel spreadsheet or a Word table. You can click any cell within the Entry table and choose a new font, font size, font effect, or color from the Font group in the Task tab on the Ribbon. You can click the Font group Dialog Box Launcher to open the Font dialog box or you can use options on the Mini Toolbar that opens when you right-click a cell. Rather than making a change to a single task entry, however, you'll often want to apply formatting changes consistently to all tasks of one type. For example, you might want to change the text color of critical tasks to red or emphasize milestone tasks with a different font. By visually organizing the tasks, you help communicate what needs to be done in the project. To make changes to all tasks of one type, you use the Text Styles dialog box.

REFERENCE

Applying Formatting to Text for a Task Category in an Entry Table

- Click the Gantt Chart Tools Format tab on the Ribbon, and then click the Text Styles button.
- Choose the category (type) of task to change in the Item to Change list, and then make new formatting choices in the Text Styles dialog box.
- When you are finished, click the OK button.

To format the Entry table using the Text Styles dialog box:

TIP

You can also format individual task text using the buttons on the Task tab in the Font group.

▶ **1.** Click the **Gantt Chart Tools Format** tab on the Ribbon, and then, in the Format group, click the **Text Styles** button. The Text Styles dialog box opens. You use the Text Styles dialog box when you want to make font changes to all tasks associated with a task category, such as milestone or critical.

▶ **2.** Click the **Item to Change** arrow, and then click **Critical Tasks**. Whatever formatting changes you make will apply to all critical tasks.

▶ **3.** Click the **Color** arrow, and then in the Standard Colors section, click **Dark Red**. The sample in the dialog box shows you that all critical tasks will be displayed in Arial 8 pt dark red font. You can add attributes for additional emphasis.

▶ **4.** Click **Bold** in the Font style list. Compare your screen to Figure 3-17.

Figure 3-17   Text Styles dialog box

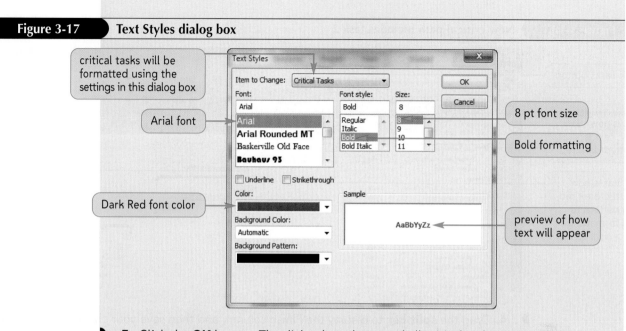

critical tasks will be formatted using the settings in this dialog box

Arial font

Dark Red font color

8 pt font size

Bold formatting

preview of how text will appear

> **5.** Click the **OK** button. The dialog box closes and all critical task names are displayed in dark red, bold text in the Entry table.

Because both the changes you made were made to a *category* of tasks (as compared to an individual bar or row), any task added to that category (such as when a noncritical task becomes a critical task) will automatically be formatted to match its new category. For example, Detail current status (task 2), which should be linked to Conduct needs analysis (task 3) in a Finish-to-Start (FS) dependency, currently is not linked. If you link task 2 to task 3, this new relationship will change the formatting for task 2 because it will become a critical task once it is linked to task 3.

To see how formatting changes are dynamic:

> **1.** In the Entry table, click **Detail current status** (task 2), and then drag ✚ down to select tasks 2 and 3.

> **2.** Click the **Task** tab, and then, in the Schedule group, click the **Link Tasks** button 🔗.

> **3.** In the Entry table, click **Analysis** (task 1). See Figure 3-18.

Figure 3-18 **New critical path includes task 2**

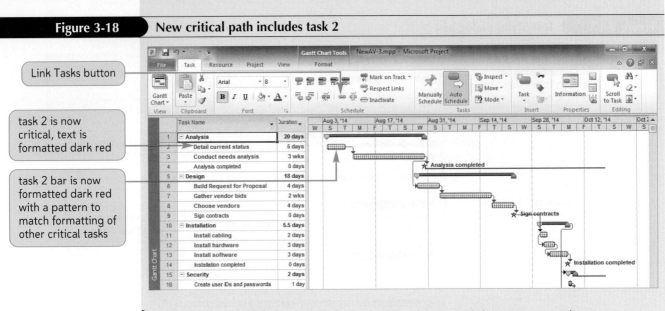

Link Tasks button

task 2 is now critical, text is formatted dark red

task 2 bar is now formatted dark red with a pattern to match formatting of other critical tasks

4. Drag the **split bar** to display the Finish column, and then save your changes.

After tasks 2 and 3 were linked, task 2 became critical, and so now both the task 2 text in the Entry table and the bar in the Gantt chart display the custom formatting for critical task text and bars. Notice also that most of the Start and Finish cells in the Entry table are now highlighted in pale blue. These cells are the Start and Finish dates that were affected by the change you just made.

Formatting tasks by category through the Text Styles and Bar Styles dialog boxes is a powerful tool because all tasks in the category will display the formatting specified for that category regardless of when the task is added to the category. Sometimes, however, you might want to make individual task formatting changes.

Formatting Individual Items in the Entry Table and Gantt Chart

Many options on the Task tab are used for formatting individual tasks; using these options overrides the options set for the task category. For example, you might want to format the tasks that you have assigned to an outside contractor with an italic font. Or, you might want to temporarily change the color of one Gantt chart bar to highlight it as a meeting.

REFERENCE

Formatting Individual Items in the Entry Table and Bars in the Gantt Chart

To format individual items in the Entry table:
- Select the task(s) that you want to change.
- Click the appropriate formatting option (font, font size, bold, italic, underline, or alignment) on the Task tab in the Font group (or, right click, and then, on the Mini Toolbar, click the appropriate formatting button).
  or
- Click the Dialog Box Launcher in the Font group on the Task tab to open the Font dialog box.
- In the Font dialog box, make the appropriate formatting choices for the selected task.
- When you are finished, click the OK button.

To format individual bars in the Gantt chart:
- To open the Format Bar dialog box, right-click a bar, and then click Format Bar; or, click Format in the Bar Styles group on the Gantt Chart Tools Format tab, and then, on the list, click Bar.
- In the Format Bar dialog box, make the appropriate formatting choices for the selected bar.
- When you are finished, click the OK button.

You have hired an outside contractor to install the cabling and hardware, and you want to format both the Entry table and Gantt Chart bars for these tasks differently than the other tasks. You can use the Font dialog box to make text formatting changes for the selected tasks, or you can click the Task tab and then click buttons in the Font group to apply formatting. You can enhance the text using any combination of formatting options including font color, font style, and size. You can apply bold or italic. You can also fill the cell by clicking the Background Color button. Use the Format Bar dialog box to change the formatting characteristics for the bars for selected tasks. To format an individual bar, you can also double-click the bar in Gantt Chart view to open the Format Bar dialog box for that individual task. Next, you format individual tasks associated with the outside vendor.

To format individual items in the Entry table and Gantt Chart:

Be sure to select both tasks to avoid having to format each bar one at a time.

1. In the Entry table, click **Install cabling** (task 11), and then drag ✛ down to select **Install cabling** (task 11) and **Install hardware** (task 12).

2. Click the **Task** tab if it is not already selected, and then, in the Font group, click the **Font Color** button arrow A▾.

3. In the Standard Colors section, click **Blue**.

4. With the two tasks still selected, click the **Gantt Chart Tools Format** tab on the Ribbon.

5. In the Bar Styles group, click the **Format** button, and then click **Bar**. The Format Bar dialog box opens with the Bar Shape tab active. Notice that you can change the color and pattern on the bar itself, and that you can add shapes to the start and end of the bars.

6. In the Middle section on the Bar Shape tab, click the **Color** arrow, and then, in the Standard Colors section, click **Blue**.

7. Click the **OK** button, click the **Task** tab on the Ribbon, and then, in the Editing group, click the **Scroll to Task** button. The bars for the selected tasks are formatted in blue.

8. Click **Analysis** (task 1). Your screen should look like Figure 3-19. Tasks 11 and 12 are still critical tasks and part of the critical path, but the individual formatting you applied to these two tasks overrode the formatting you applied earlier to all critical tasks. The font of these tasks in the Entry table and the bars in the Gantt chart are blue. Formatting does not change a task's status as a critical task.

Figure 3-19 **Formatting changes applied to individual tasks**

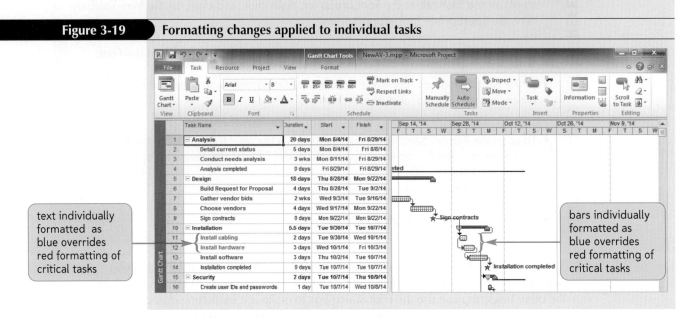

text individually formatted as blue overrides red formatting of critical tasks

bars individually formatted as blue overrides red formatting of critical tasks

Formatting the Timescale

You can make many other individual formatting changes in Gantt Chart view, such as changing the timescale, gridlines, and link lines. You use the Timescale dialog box to change the way that the Top Tier, Middle Tier, Bottom Tier, and Non-working timescales are measured, labeled, and aligned (beyond the default changes to the timescales when you zoom in and out). You have already learned how to change the timescales and labels. The Non-working time tab allows you to format bars representing nonworking time (such as Saturday and Sunday) in the Gantt chart. By default, these vertical bars appear 'behind' the Gantt bars so the Gantt bars cross over them on the chart. You can change this so that the nonworking time bars appear 'in front of' the Gantt bars so the Gantt bars appear behind the nonworking time bars. In addition, you can use the Timescale dialog box to display three tiers simultaneously on the timescale when you are working on a project that requires that level of detail on the timescale.

To format the timescale:

1. Click the **View** tab on the Ribbon, and then, in the Zoom group, click the **Timescale** arrow.

2. Click **Timescale**. The Timescale dialog box opens.

3. Click the **Non-working time** tab, click the **In front of task bars** option button, click the **Color** arrow, and then, in the Theme Colors section, click the **Tan, Darker 50%** color.

4. Click the **OK** button. The dialog box closes.

5. Drag the **split bar** so the last column you see is the Duration column, and then, on the status bar, click the **Zoom In** button ⊕.

▶ 6. Drag the scroll bars back and forth to view the Gantt Chart. The bars representing nonworking days appear as vertical bars, so you can quickly see the nonworking days. Your Gantt chart should be formatted similarly to Figure 3-20.

Figure 3-20   **Formatting the timescale**

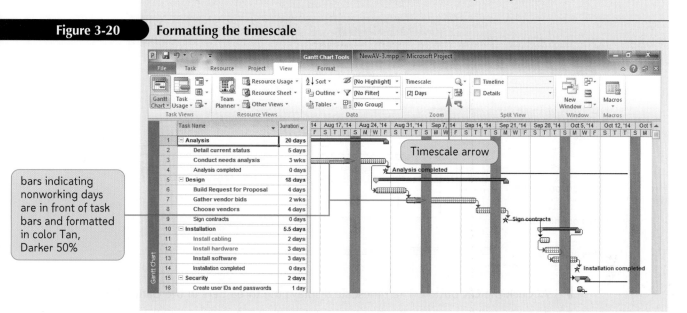

bars indicating nonworking days are in front of task bars and formatted in color Tan, Darker 50%

The timescale can display three tiers simultaneously. If you are working on a project that requires that level of detail on the timescale, you can set the timescale to show all three tiers and format each one. Some of the tasks in the ViewPoint Partners project require that you show this level of detail.

To display three tiers in the Gantt chart timescale:

▶ 1. Click the **View** tab, and then, in the Zoom group, click the **Timescale** arrow.

▶ 2. Click **Timescale**, and then click the **Top Tier** tab.

▶ 3. In the Timescale options section, click the **Show** arrow, and then click **Three tiers (Top, Middle, Bottom)**. The Preview window displays the current settings.

▶ 4. In the Top tier formatting section, click the **Units** arrow, and then click **Quarters**.

▶ 5. Click the **Middle Tier** tab, click the **Units** arrow, and then click **Months**.

▶ 6. Click the **Bottom Tier** tab, click the **Units** arrow, and then click **Weeks**. Your Timescale dialog box should look like Figure 3-21.

Figure 3-21 Timescale dialog box

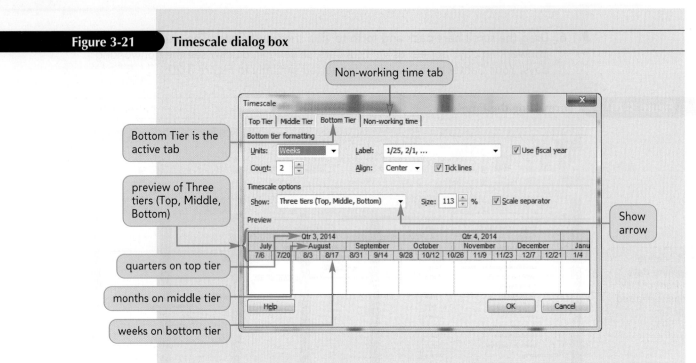

Non-working time tab

Bottom Tier is the active tab

preview of Three tiers (Top, Middle, Bottom)

Show arrow

quarters on top tier

months on middle tier

weeks on bottom tier

▶ **7.** Click the **OK** button. The timescale displays the three tiers in the Gantt chart.

▶ **8.** Click the **View** tab on the Ribbon, and then, in the Zoom group, click the **Zoom Entire Project** button 🔲 so you can see the entire project in the Gantt chart.

▶ **9.** Save your changes.

Formatting Gridlines

Gridlines are nonprinting lines that can improve the readability of a view by providing a visual guide to help you interpret the bars. Gridlines can help you locate the current date in a project or intervals on the timescale. You can turn the display of gridlines on or off by checking or unchecking the Gridlines check box in the Show group on the View tab to suit your working style. By default, gridlines are off. The Gantt Chart Tools Format tab provides access to the Gridlines dialog box. You use this dialog box to format gridlines in different ways.

To format gridlines:

▶ **1.** Click the **Gantt Chart Tools Format** tab, and then, in the Format group, click the **Gridlines** button.

TIP

Gantt Rows are helpful if you want help aligning the task name with its bar. You can set the interval so the vertical lines appear below each task, every two tasks, or whatever interval works best for you.

▶ **2.** On the list, click **Gridlines**. The Gridlines dialog box opens. The Line to change box provides a list of gridline types that can be changed, such as Gantt Rows, Page Breaks, and the Project Start line.

▶ **3.** In the Line to change box, click **Project Start**.

▶ **4.** In the Normal area, click the **Color** arrow, and then click the **Orange, Darker 25%** color on the color palette.

▶ **5.** In the Normal area, click the **Type** arrow, and then click the last dashed line. See Figure 3-22.

| Figure 3-22 | Gridlines dialog box |

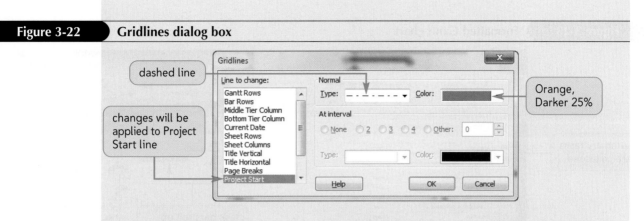

6. Click the **OK** button, and then press the **Alt+Home** keys to view the beginning of the project in the Gantt chart. A dark orange dashed line now marks the project Start date, Monday, August 4, 2014.

Link lines are the lines that show the connections between bars, such as a Finish to Start link line in Gantt Chart view. Like gridlines, link lines can be formatted to add visual impact to the view. You format link lines using the Gridlines dialog box. Unlike gridlines, link lines do print when you print the Gantt chart.

To format link lines:

1. Click the **Gantt Chart Tools Format** tab, and then, in the Format group, click the **Layout** button. The Layout dialog box opens and provides several formatting options for the link lines and bars. For example, using this dialog box, you can change bar height, change date format, and set the bar display to round to whole days.

2. Click the **Always roll up Gantt bars** check box, click the **Hide rollup bars when summary expanded** check box, and then click the **OK** button. These layout changes will change the way that the Gantt chart summary bars are formatted when summary tasks are collapsed.

3. In the Entry table, click the **Analysis (task 1) Collapse** button ⊟, click the **Task** tab, and then, in the Editing group, click the **Scroll to Task** button.

4. In the Entry table, click the **Design (task 5) Collapse** button ⊟.

5. Zoom out so you can see all the bars for the project. Your screen should look like Figure 3-23. The updated Gantt chart displays many formatting changes.

Figure 3-23   **Formatted Gantt chart**

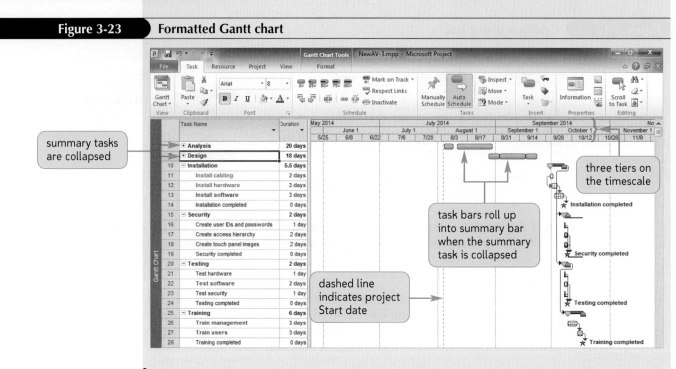

6. Add your name to the header in Network Diagram view, save your changes, submit the project in printed or electronic form, as requested, and then close the file.

PROSKILLS

Decision Making: Weighing the Benefits of Formatting

As you have seen, Project offers many formatting options. You should use these options wisely. Formatting can help you to communicate the project information visually and to present a pleasing picture of what is going on. However, you don't want to create a confusing array of lines, colors, and designs. As you are making formatting decisions, consider your audience as well as your presentation situation. If the information is to be printed, will the formatting and colors work together on the printed page? Will colors be easily distinguished on the printed page or are they too close in color, such as navy blue and black? Do you have to consider people who are unable to distinguish between red and green colors? If so, do not use these colors to distinguish content in a project. Are you presenting the information via a large screen to a large audience? If so, be sure to test your color palette using the computer system that will be used to display the information. Color presentation can vary from system to system. Also, consider using large contrasting fonts for the text in the Entry table and text in the Gantt chart. As you work with Project 2010, you will develop personal preferences for the types of formatting that best suit your communication needs.

Session 3.1 Quick Check

REVIEW

1. What are the main categories of reports that you can create using Project 2010?
2. Why is the critical path important to project managers?
3. Explain how a noncritical task could become a critical task as a project progresses. (Use the concept of float as part of your answer.)
4. What is the purpose of filtering? Name two common filters.
5. How can you format all of the bars of one task type within the Gantt chart?
6. How would you format the text in the Entry table for milestone tasks so that all milestone tasks appear with a different font and size?
7. Why must you first select a task or tasks before using the Font dialog box or the Format Bar dialog box, but not when using the Text Styles dialog box or Bar Styles dialog box?
8. Identify two types of gridlines that can be changed using the Gridlines dialog box.
9. Identify three items that can be modified using the Layout dialog box.

SESSION 3.2 VISUAL OVERVIEW

The Network Diagram Tools Format tab provides many options for formatting a network diagram.

You click the Box button to open the Format Box dialog box; you use the Format Box dialog box to override formatting options set using the Box Styles dialog box.

You click the Box Styles button to open the Box Styles dialog box.

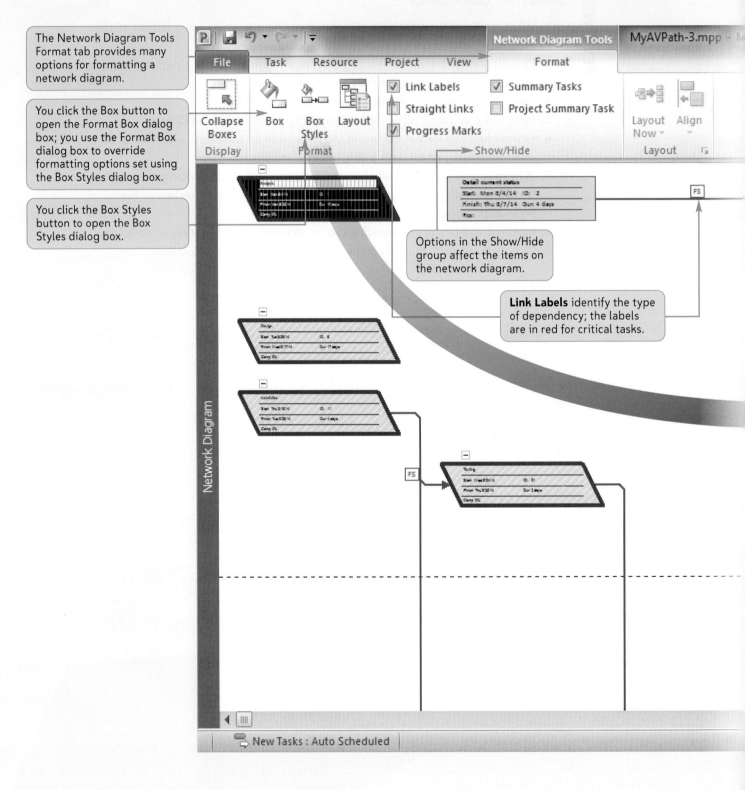

Options in the Show/Hide group affect the items on the network diagram.

Link Labels identify the type of dependency; the labels are in red for critical tasks.

CUSTOMIZED NETWORK DIAGRAM

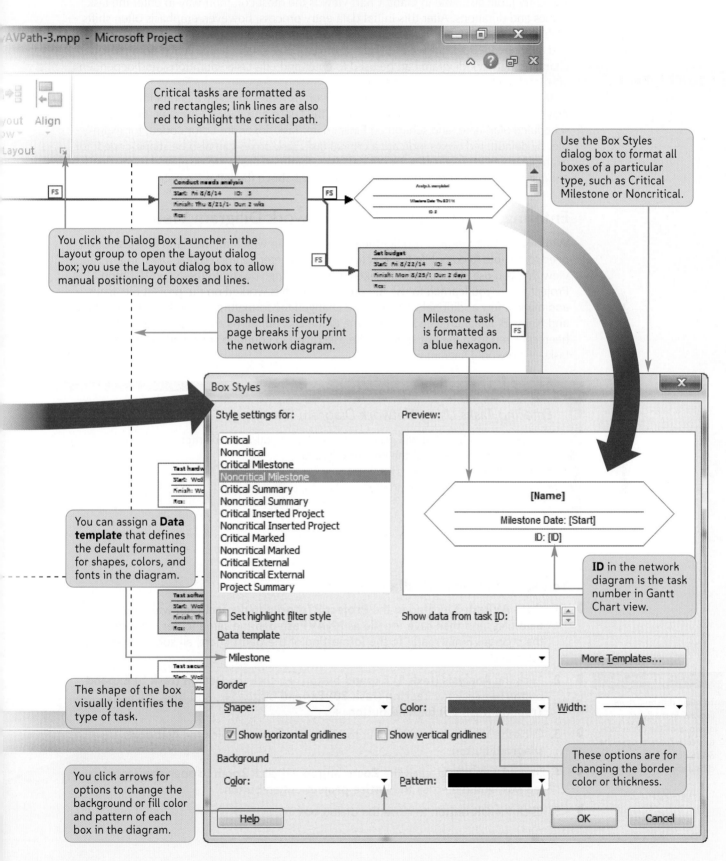

Critical tasks are formatted as red rectangles; link lines are also red to highlight the critical path.

Use the Box Styles dialog box to format all boxes of a particular type, such as Critical Milestone or Noncritical.

You click the Dialog Box Launcher in the Layout group to open the Layout dialog box; you use the Layout dialog box to allow manual positioning of boxes and lines.

Dashed lines identify page breaks if you print the network diagram.

Milestone task is formatted as a blue hexagon.

You can assign a **Data template** that defines the default formatting for shapes, colors, and fonts in the diagram.

ID in the network diagram is the task number in Gantt Chart view.

The shape of the box visually identifies the type of task.

These options are for changing the border color or thickness.

You click arrows for options to change the background or fill color and pattern of each box in the diagram.

Box Styles dialog box

Style settings for:
- Critical
- Noncritical
- Critical Milestone
- Noncritical Milestone
- Critical Summary
- Noncritical Summary
- Critical Inserted Project
- Noncritical Inserted Project
- Critical Marked
- Noncritical Marked
- Critical External
- Noncritical External
- Project Summary

Preview:

[Name]
Milestone Date: [Start]
ID: [ID]

Set highlight filter style   Show data from task ID:

Data template
Milestone   More Templates...

Border
Shape: Color: Width:
Show horizontal gridlines   Show vertical gridlines

Background
Color: Pattern:

Help   OK   Cancel

Working with the Network Diagram

The Entry table available in Gantt Chart view is the most common way to enter the task names and durations. After this initial data entry process, however, emphasis often shifts to the Network Diagram view because it most clearly identifies both the critical path and the dependencies (also called relationships) between the tasks. While both the Gantt chart and network diagram can be used to enter and edit tasks, durations, and dependencies, each technique has its strengths.

In Network Diagram view, each task category is represented by a geometrical shape that is further divided into cells that contain the task name, task ID number, duration, scheduled Start date, and scheduled Finish date. Task boxes are color-coded; for example, by default, red boxes indicate a critical task. Task boxes can also be shape-coded; for example, rounded rectangles for critical tasks. Summary tasks are displayed in the first column with a Collapse button (a minus sign) just above the left edge of the task box.

Entering and Editing Tasks in Network Diagram View

While Gantt Chart view is usually the primary view in which to enter and edit tasks, you need to be able to complete basic actions, such as entering and editing tasks, in any view that you use. Although Emily liked the formatting you did to the NewAV-3.mpp Project file as you learned to use the program, she has worked on the project file again and made a few additional changes. She changed the formatting for both the Gantt Chart and Network Diagram views. Also, some of the task durations and dependencies have been changed from the last session. She asked you to continue your work by entering tasks in Network Diagram view.

REFERENCE

Entering Tasks Using Network Diagram View

- Click the task box that will precede the task that you want to enter.
- Point to an open area of the network diagram.
- Drag a box using the mouse pointer.
- Type the task information in the appropriate cells.

To set up the network diagram:

1. Open **AVPath-3** located in the **Project3\Tutorial** folder included with your data files, and then save the file as **MyAVPath-3** in the same folder. You see the changes Emily made to the formatting of the Gantt chart; all subtasks are collapsed.

2. Click the **Analysis (task 1) Expand** button ⊞, click the **Design (task 5) Expand** button ⊞, click the **Testing (task 20) Expand** button ⊞, and then, click the **Training (task 25) Expand** button ⊞.

3. Click the **View** tab, and then, in the Task Views group, click the **Network Diagram** button.

4. In the Zoom group, click the **Zoom** button 🔲, click **Zoom** to open the Zoom dialog box, and then click the **Entire project** option button.

5. Click the **OK** button to close the dialog box.

TIP

To select different zoom options, in the Zoom group, click the Zoom button, click Zoom to open the Zoom dialog box, and then click a zoom option button.

6. On the status bar, click the **Zoom In** button ⊕ so you can see approximately six pages of the project. Depending on the size and resolution of your monitor, your screen should look similar to Figure 3-24.

Figure 3-24   **Tasks in the network diagram**

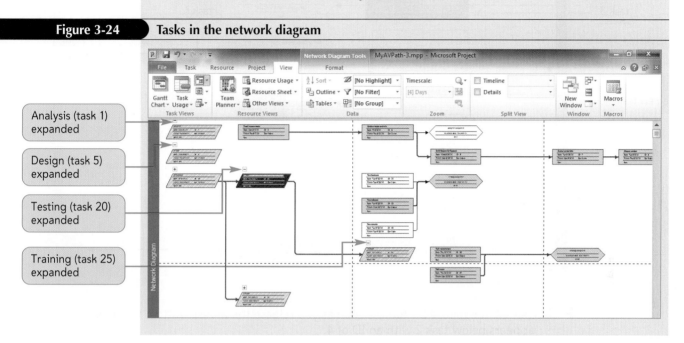

Analysis (task 1) expanded

Design (task 5) expanded

Testing (task 20) expanded

Training (task 25) expanded

The formatting displays the tasks for the project as a visual overview of the job at hand. Some of the boxes are blue, some are red, some are six-sided shapes, and some are trapezoidal (four sides, only two of which are parallel). Each shape or color conveys a meaning for the task. This formatting will be helpful when Emily and Sidney review the project file. Sidney wants to be sure there is time to set the budget and asks that you enter the task into the file.

To create a new task in Network Diagram view:

1. Place the pointer over several of the tasks, and notice how the box expands to better display the content.

2. Place the pointer over **Conduct needs analysis** (task 3), read the information, and then place the pointer over **Build Request for Proposal** (task 6). Both task boxes are centered in the window. You need to add a new task, Set budget, between these two tasks.

3. Click **Conduct needs analysis** (task 3) to make it the current task. The task is now filled with black.

4. Click the **Zoom In** button ⊕ on the status bar three times to get a better view of that center panel, place the pointer in the white space below task 3, press and hold the left mouse button, and then drag to draw a rectangle, as shown in Figure 3-25.

TIP

If you are unsure as to which box is a specific task and you know the ID or task number, press F5 to open the Go to dialog box, type the task ID number in the box, and then click OK.

Figure 3-25

Figure 3-25   **Creating a new task in the network diagram**

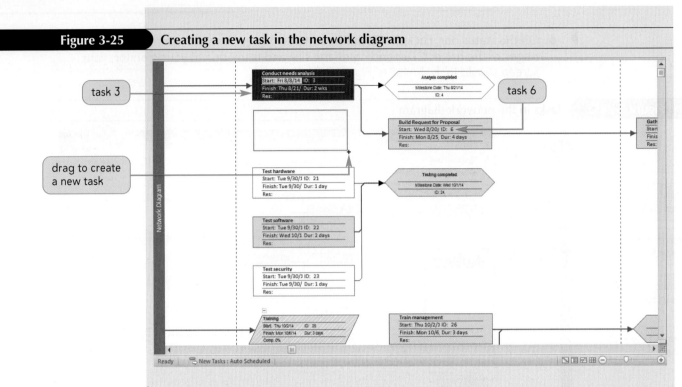

5. Release the mouse button. As soon as you release the mouse button, the new task appears below task 2 with an ID of 4.

TIP

If you are unsure whether the task you entered is correct, you can return to the Gantt Chart view to analyze the project, and then return to Network Diagram view.

The network diagram attempts to put task boxes in chronological order according to when they are scheduled. The project tasks are organized as if you had inserted the task using the Entry table. The previous task 4, Analysis completed, has been renumbered to become task 5, and so on. The new task appears below task 2 instead of task 3 because no dependency has been set for this task. It currently is scheduled to start on the project's scheduled Start date, which is the same time task 2 is scheduled to start. The task shape takes the default format for a noncritical task. The insertion point is in the Task Name cell of the new task rectangle, ready for you to name the new task.

To enter task information in the Network Diagram view:

1. On the status bar, click the **Zoom In** button ⊕ as many times as needed so you can read the text in the new box, and then scroll to center the box on the screen.

2. Type **Set budget**, click the **duration** cell, type **2**, and then press the **Enter** key. You have identified the new task and entered a duration of 2 days, as shown in Figure 3-26.

3. Save your work.

Figure 3-26   **Entering a task name and duration in the network diagram**

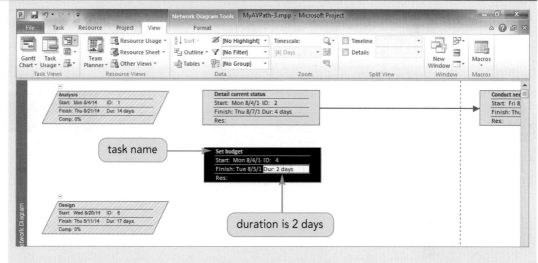

You can click any cell within a task box in the network diagram to enter or edit task information. If you double-click a task box, you will open its Task Information dialog box to gain access to all of the fields of information about that task (such as resources, predecessors, and so on), not just those that are displayed in the task box.

INSIGHT

A Familiar Interface: the Entry Bar

For users who are familiar with the Excel Entry bar, Project 2010 offers an Entry bar as well. If you open the Entry bar, it appears above the Gantt chart and if you switch to the Network Diagram view, it appears just above the network diagram. When you enter task information, it is displayed in the Entry bar. You can work directly in the task box, in the table, or in the Entry bar. To display the Entry bar, click the File tab, then click Options to open the Project Options dialog box. In the Project Options dialog box, click Display. In the Show these elements section, click the Entry bar check box.

Examining Dependencies and the Critical Path

The primary purpose of Network Diagram view is to clearly illustrate the sequential progression of tasks and the critical path. Project managers often use this view to enter and edit task dependencies.

To enter a dependency in Network Diagram view:

1. Click the **Right scroll arrow** ▶ on the Horizontal scroll bar until you can see task 3, and then click in the middle of **Conduct needs analysis** (task 3).

2. Drag the **linking pointer** from the middle of **Conduct needs analysis** (task 3) to the inside of the **Set budget** (task 4) box, as shown in Figure 3-27.

Be sure to link the tasks to avoid moving the tasks or creating a new task.

Figure 3-27 Creating task dependency in Network Diagram view

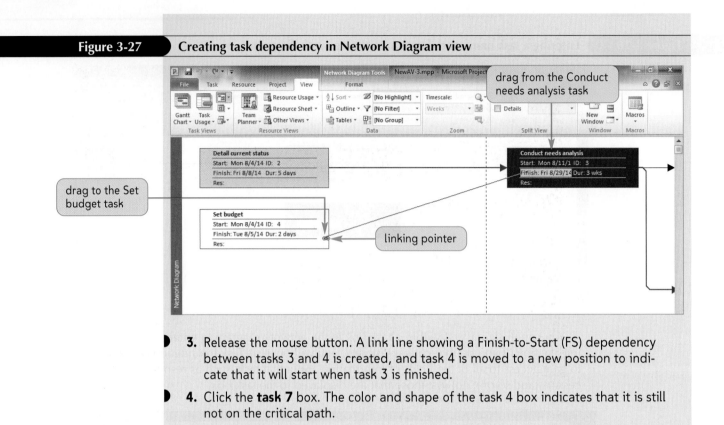

3. Release the mouse button. A link line showing a Finish-to-Start (FS) dependency between tasks 3 and 4 is created, and task 4 is moved to a new position to indicate that it will start when task 3 is finished.

4. Click the **task 7** box. The color and shape of the task 4 box indicates that it is still not on the critical path.

After further analyzing the network diagram, you realize that Build Request for Proposal (task 7) depends on Set budget (task 4) rather than Conduct needs analysis (task 3). You can change dependencies in the network diagram. To do this, you open the Task Dependency dialog box. It lists task names of the relationship that you are examining and allows you to change the dependency type (from FS to SS, FF, or SF), enter lag time, or delete the dependency.

To change a dependency in Network Diagram view:

1. Double-click the **link line** between Conduct needs analysis (task 3) and Build Request for Proposal (task 7) to open the Task Dependency dialog box, as shown in Figure 3-28.

Figure 3-28   **Changing a Task Dependency**

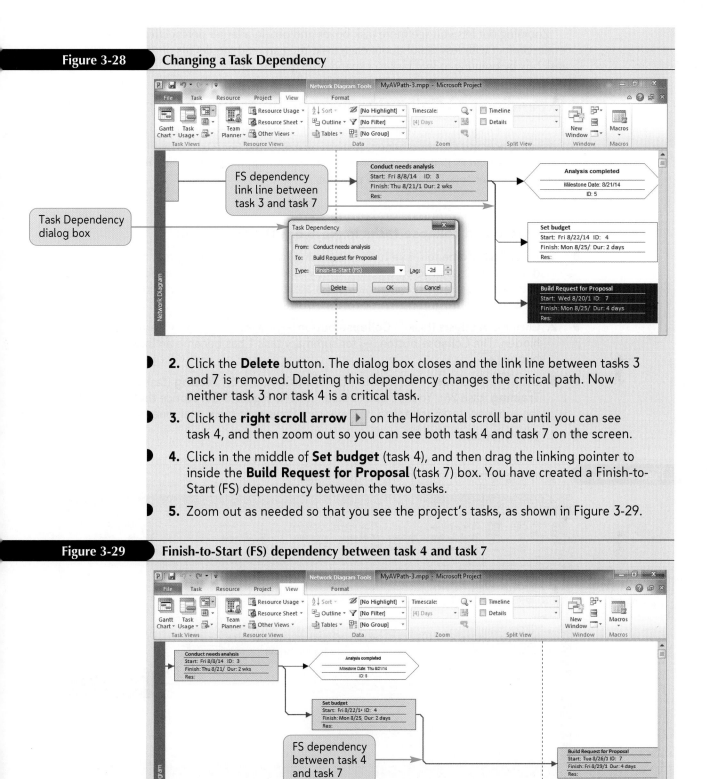

Task Dependency dialog box

2. Click the **Delete** button. The dialog box closes and the link line between tasks 3 and 7 is removed. Deleting this dependency changes the critical path. Now neither task 3 nor task 4 is a critical task.

3. Click the **right scroll arrow** ▶ on the Horizontal scroll bar until you can see task 4, and then zoom out so you can see both task 4 and task 7 on the screen.

4. Click in the middle of **Set budget** (task 4), and then drag the linking pointer to inside the **Build Request for Proposal** (task 7) box. You have created a Finish-to-Start (FS) dependency between the two tasks.

5. Zoom out as needed so that you see the project's tasks, as shown in Figure 3-29.

Figure 3-29   **Finish-to-Start (FS) dependency between task 4 and task 7**

6. Point to **Build Request for Proposal** (task 7) so that you can read the information more easily. Both task 4 and task 7 are now on the critical path.

7. Save your changes.

Zooming out lets you see more task boxes and obtain a larger perspective on the entire project with less detail about each task. You can read the details of a particular task box by pointing to that task to expand it on the screen.

Expanding and Collapsing Tasks in the Network Diagram

In Network Diagram view, you can expand and collapse summary tasks by clicking the Expand button and Collapse button, just as you can in the Entry table. By hiding the detail tasks for areas that you are not currently examining, you can greatly reduce the size of a Network Diagram view printout.

To expand and collapse tasks in Network Diagram view:

1. Press **Ctrl+Home** to move to the beginning of the network diagram, and then drag the horizontal scroll box all the way to left to view the beginning of the network diagram. Three summary tasks are in a column on the left side of the window.

2. Click the **Analysis** (task 1) **Collapse** button ⊟. Tasks 2, 3, 4, and 5 are now hidden. The Collapse button ⊟ for summary task 1 has become an Expand button ⊞.

3. Click ⊟ to collapse the following tasks: **Design** (task 6), **Testing** (task 21), and **Training** (task 26). Your screen should look like Figure 3-30. Notice that even with the summary tasks collapsed, the diagram flows over more than one page.

4. Save your work.

Figure 3-30	Collapsing summary tasks in the network diagram

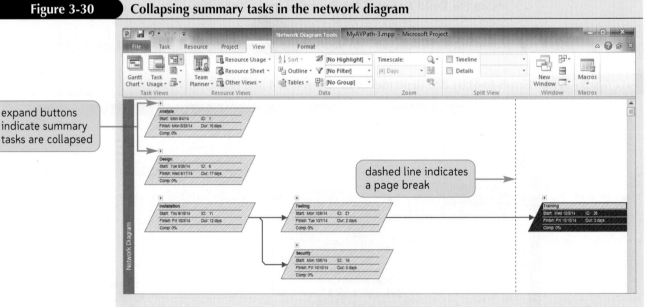

When possible, you should always try to reduce views to a single page, although you don't want to leave out important information or sacrifice legibility for the convenience of a single-page printout. Sidney often travels to meet with contractors. She likes to present them with professional-looking printouts. You set up the project to create these professional-looking printouts. As you know from Tutorial 1, you can use the Page Setup dialog box to fit a page, or you can move the tasks in Network Diagram view to create a one-page layout.

Manually Moving Tasks in Network Diagram View

Network Diagram views can be quite wide, so you might want to move tasks in order to better arrange them for printouts or viewing on a monitor. If you plan to show them to your colleagues or to management, they must be organized in a way that best communicates the information. To move tasks in Network Diagram view, you need to change the layout mode to allow you to manually position task boxes.

REFERENCE

Moving Tasks in Network Diagram View

- Click the Network Diagram Tools Format tab, and then, in the Format group, click the Layout button to open the Layout dialog box.
- Click the Allow manual box positioning option button, and then click OK.
- Point to the edge of a box, and then drag the task box to its new position.

To move tasks one at a time in Network Diagram view:

TIP

You can quickly look at the Gantt Chart view to make sure you have done this step properly.

1. Expand **task 1**, **task 6**, and **task 26**. Tasks 1, 6, and 26 should now be expanded (have minus signs above them), and tasks 11, 21, and 16 should now be collapsed (have plus signs above them).

2. Click the **Network Diagram Tools Format** tab, and then, in the Format group, click the **Layout** button. The Layout dialog box opens to display the different options available. You want to be able to move the boxes in the window.

3. Click the **Allow manual box positioning** option button in the Layout Mode section, and then click the **OK** button. Because tasks 7, 8, 9, and 10 are subtasks of summary task 6, you want to manually position those four tasks next to summary task 6.

TIP

Click the Network Diagram Tools Format tab and then click the Link Labels check box if you want to display the type of links on the link lines in the Network Diagram.

4. Zoom out and scroll as needed to see task 7, which is on the right side of the network diagram, and then click **Build Request for Proposal** (task 7). As you work with the diagram, you will have to zoom in and out and scroll to see the tasks you need on the screen.

5. Point to the edge of **Build Request for Proposal** (task 7) so that the pointer changes to the move pointer ⛶. You might not be able to see both task 6 and task 7 on the screen at the same time, so begin by displaying task 7.

   Trouble? Point to the rightmost edge or the ScreenTip will expand and you will not be able to see the pointer.

6. Drag the edge of **Build Request for Proposal** (task 7) to the right of the Design summary task (task 6). The diagram will scroll as you drag from right to left to display task 6, as shown in Figure 3-31.

Figure 3-31   Moving a task in Network Diagram view

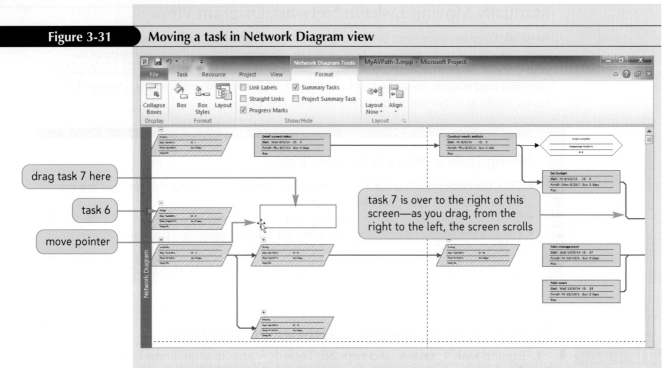

Trouble? If the task changed to task 8 and a black line connects it to task 7, you dragged using the linking pointer rather than the move pointer. On the Quick Access toolbar, click the Undo button, and then repeat Steps 5 and 6, making sure you drag the edge of task 7 and not its center.

Often you want to move more than one task at a time. You can use the pointer to draw a selection box to create a selection of tasks to move.

To move more than one task at a time in Network Diagram view:

1. Click the **Right scroll arrow** ▶ on the Horizontal scroll bar until you can view tasks 8, 9, and 10, and then press and hold the left mouse button in the white space above task box 8. The pointer changes to ✛.

2. Drag to draw a box around tasks 8, 9, and 10, as shown in Figure 3-32, then release the mouse button. All three tasks are selected.

TIP

Instead of drawing a box around multiple tasks to select them, you can click one task, press and hold the Ctrl key, and then select additional tasks.

Figure 3-32   Drawing a selection box

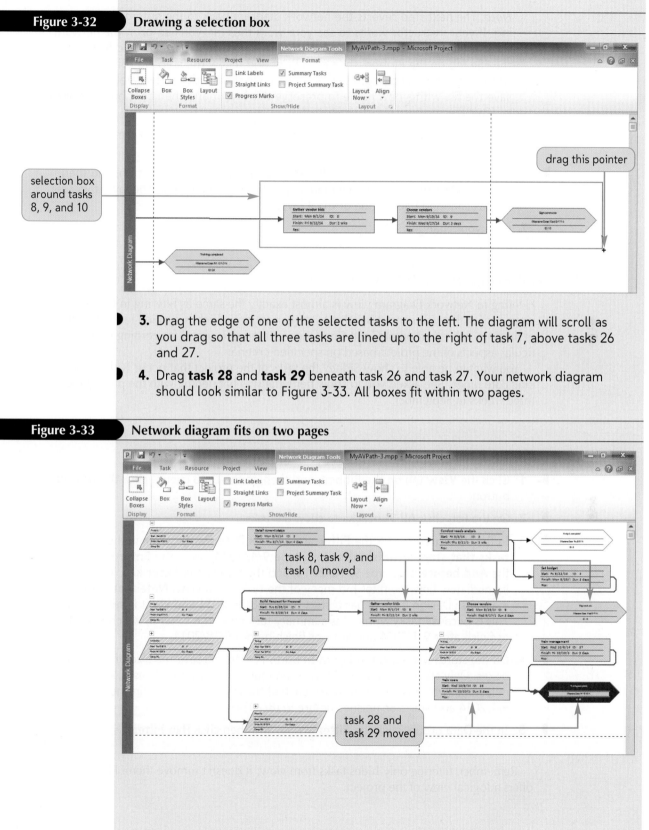

3. Drag the edge of one of the selected tasks to the left. The diagram will scroll as you drag so that all three tasks are lined up to the right of task 7, above tasks 26 and 27.

4. Drag **task 28** and **task 29** beneath task 26 and task 27. Your network diagram should look similar to Figure 3-33. All boxes fit within two pages.

Figure 3-33   Network diagram fits on two pages

Note: The next step reverts the network diagram back to the automatic positioning. If your instructor wants to see your work thus far, you can print the network diagram on two pages to show that you positioned your boxes correctly. Click the File tab on the Ribbon, then click Print and follow the steps to print the network diagram on two pages with your name in the header. Alternately, you can save the file with a new name to preserve this layout and then continue with your original file.

▶ **5.** Click the **Network Diagram Tools Format** tab, and then, in the Format group, click the **Layout** button.

▶ **6.** On the list, click the **Automatically position all boxes** option button, and then click the **OK** button to remove manual positioning. Notice that the layout you set up has changed back to the original layout.

▶ **7.** Save your changes.

Filtering in the Network Diagram

Filtering in Network Diagram view is almost exactly the same as filtering in Gantt Chart view, except that you cannot use the AutoFilter option (which is applied to the columns of the Entry table portion of Gantt Chart view). Filtering is useful for zeroing in on particular aspects of the project based on specified criteria.

You want to be able to show Sidney the tasks of the project that occur within a specific date range. She asked you to show her what was happening with the project the first three weeks in September.

To filter tasks in Network Diagram view:

▶ **1.** Click the **View** tab on the Ribbon, and then, in the Data group, click the **Outline** button.

▶ **2.** On the list, click **All Subtasks** to show all tasks.

▶ **3.** In the Data group, click the **Filter** arrow, click **Date Range**, click in the **Show tasks that start or finish after** box, type **9/1/2014**, press the **Enter** key, click in the **And before** box, type **9/18/2014**, and then press the **Enter** key. You can see immediately how the filter hid many of the tasks from view. Note that the summary task Design (task 6) has a start date of 8/26/2014 and yet it is still in view. This is because tasks within this summary task meet the criteria, which is to start or finish after 9/1/2014 and start or finish before 9/18/2014.

▶ **4.** On the status bar, click the **Zoom In** button ⊕ to increase the size of the task boxes. Only six boxes are visible: two summary tasks, three subtasks, and one milestone (which is also a subtask). Each of these tasks starts or finishes after 9/1/2014 and starts or finishes before 9/18/2014.

▶ **5.** In the Data group, click the **Filter** arrow, and then click **[No Filter]**.

Remember, filtering only hides tasks from view; it doesn't remove them. Filtering offers a logical view of the project.

PROSKILLS

Written Communications: Creating Visual Branding and Standards

Creating a common look for an organization's or corporation's printed material is a way to create professional-looking projects. If your company requires that a standard set of formatting choices be applied to each network diagram, you can save the choices as a template and apply it to other projects. By having a set of standards, project managers can look at the diagram and use visual cues to get an immediate understanding of the overall project. Critical paths, milestones, and other important factors will jump off the screen! You save a template using commands in Backstage view.

Formatting a Network Diagram

Formatting a network diagram is very similar to formatting a Gantt chart. You can make changes to all of the tasks in one category (for example, critical, noncritical, milestone) by changing settings in the Box Styles dialog box. To open the Box Styles dialog box, you click the Network Diagram Tools Format tab, and then, in the Format group, you click the Box Styles button. By changing settings in the Box Styles dialog box, you can differentiate some tasks from others—such as the critical summary task boxes from their individual tasks. In addition to changing the box shape, you can modify the border color, border width, background color, and background pattern.

You can also format an individual task box. Individual formatting changes override any changes made to the task category. To format an individual task box, you use the Format Box dialog box. To open the Format Box dialog box, you click the Network Diagram Tools Format tab, and then, in the Format group, you click Box to open the Format Box dialog box.

REFERENCE

Formatting All Tasks of One Type in Network Diagram View

- In the Format group on the Network Diagram Tools Format tab, click the Box Styles button to open the Box Styles dialog box.
- Make the desired formatting changes in the Box Styles dialog box.
- Click OK.

To format tasks within Network Diagram view:

1. Click the **Network Diagram Tools Format** tab, and then, in the Format group, click the **Box Styles** button. The Box Styles dialog box opens. It includes a preview pane for guidance as you design the view.

2. In the Style settings for section, click **Critical Summary** if it is not already selected, and then, in the Border section, click the **Shape** arrow.

3. In the list, click the **left-slanting parallelogram,** and then select these additional settings: click the **Border Color** arrow, and then, in the Theme Colors section, click **Purple, Darker 50%**; click the **Border Width** arrow, and then, in the list, click the **thickest line**; click the **Background Color** arrow, and then, in the Standard Colors section, click **Yellow**. You kept the default pattern. See Figure 3-34.

Be sure to select Critical Summary, do not select Critical to avoid applying the wrong style.

Figure 3-34   Box Styles dialog box

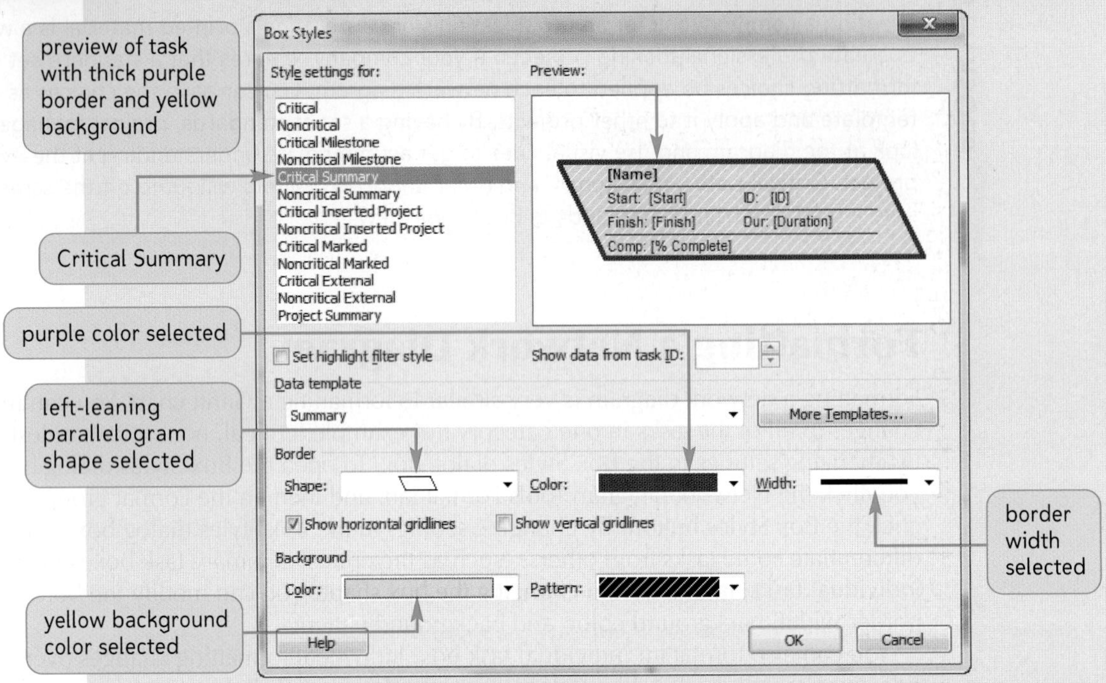

preview of task with thick purple border and yellow background

Critical Summary

purple color selected

left-leaning parallelogram shape selected

yellow background color selected

border width selected

▶ 4. Click the **OK** button, click the **View** tab on the Ribbon, and then, in the Zoom group, click the **Zoom** button.

▶ 5. In the Zoom dialog box, click the **Entire project** option button to view the entire project. Each critical summary task is modified with the new task shape and formatting colors.

Trouble? If your screen is not wide enough to zoom the entire project, drag the Zoom slide to view all the boxes in the network diagram.

In addition to formatting all of the tasks of one category, you might want to format an individual task box to bring attention to it. For example, if you are currently working within the first phase of the project, you might want to format the first critical summary task to be different from the rest. To format an individual task, you must select it before opening the Format Box dialog box.

REFERENCE

Formatting an Individual Task in Network Diagram View

- In Network Diagram view, click a task to select it.
- Click the Network Diagram Tools Format tab, and then, in the Format group, click the Box button.
- Make the desired formatting changes in the Format Box dialog box.
- Click OK.

To format tasks within Network Diagram view:

▶ **1.** Scroll and zoom the network diagram so you can see Analysis (task 1) at the top left of the screen and a page break near the right side of your screen, and then click **Analysis** (task 1).

▶ **2.** Click the **Network Diagram Tools Format** tab, and then, in the Format group, click the **Box** button. The Format Box dialog box opens with the currently selected task displayed in the Preview window with the current formatting.

▶ **3.** In the Background section, click the **Color** arrow, click **Orange, Lighter 40%**, click the **Pattern** arrow, and then click the **vertical bars** pattern. See Figure 3-35.

| **Figure 3-35** | Format Box dialog box |

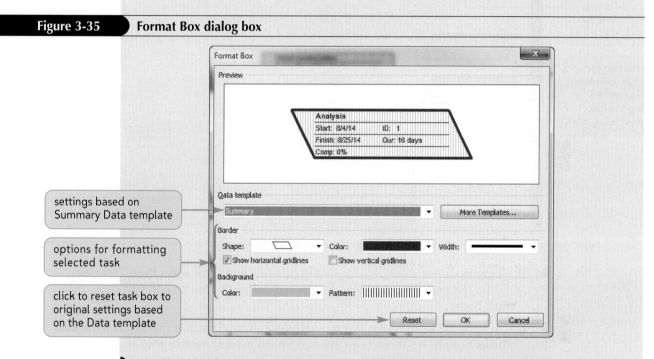

settings based on Summary Data template

options for formatting selected task

click to reset task box to original settings based on the Data template

▶ **4.** Click the **OK** button, and then click **task 2** so that you can observe the changes made to the background for Analysis (task 1). Your screen should look like Figure 3-36.

Figure 3-36 | **Formatted network diagram**

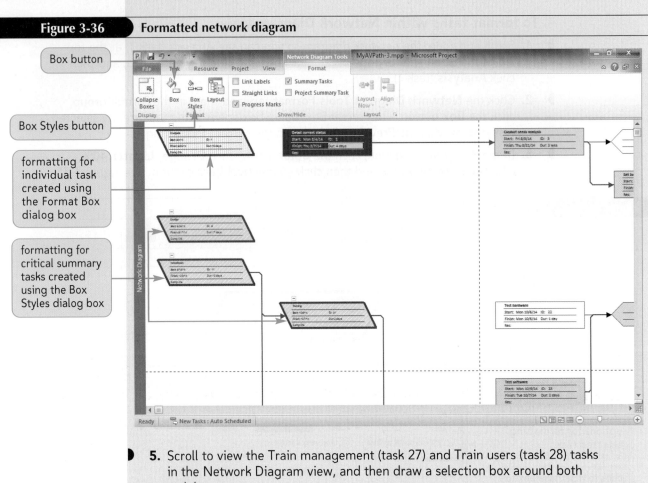

> **5.** Scroll to view the Train management (task 27) and Train users (task 28) tasks in the Network Diagram view, and then draw a selection box around both task boxes.

> **6.** Click the **Task** tab on the Ribbon, and then, in the Schedule group, click the **Link Tasks** button. These tasks are now linked in an FS relationship.

> **7.** Save your changes.

You can clearly see how using the formatting and filtering capabilities of Project 2010 can help you communicate the project information to Emily and the contractors working on the presentation rooms installation at ViewPoint Partners.

PROSKILLS

Written communication: Using Color and Shapes Effectively

Knowing your audience and having a good understanding of the technology is important as you prepare your project for others. If the project is to be viewed on the computer screen or from a color printout, color can be used effectively to emphasize and clarify information. If you will be distributing the network diagram through a printed black-and-white report, however, you probably want to use different shapes to highlight certain tasks, because solid colors often print as solid black boxes on a black-and-white printer or fax machine. Many programs have options for creating screen displays and printouts with unlimited choices for colors and patterns. As a user of software and creator of output, it is up to you to use the technology wisely. Do not overwhelm your audience with graphics and design; it will detract from the importance of the message. Use color and design to enhance your message and information, not to mask or confuse it.

Shortening the Critical Path by Changing Task Information

After developing the initial project, project managers often face the challenge of having to shorten the project without impacting its overall success or quality. You can shorten the path by changing task information—working directly with task durations, task dependencies, or task schedule dates—or by applying additional resources to tasks on the critical path.

Directly modifying the task information for a critical task is the easiest way to shorten the path. For example, if a critical task has an initial duration of three days and is modified to be completed in two days, the critical path will automatically be reduced by one day. However, a project manager must consider whether or not the quality of the work will be impacted in such a way as to harm the project. Reducing time also reduces cost. It is a delicate balance that must be reached by all seasoned project managers. Another way to shorten the critical path is to have tasks overlap. For example, you might have planned to finish all of the analysis work before starting design, but if you decide to start the design when the analysis is 75 percent complete, then the critical path will be shortened by 25 percent.

INSIGHT

Understanding Fast Tracking and Crashing

Another common term used in shortening project schedules is fast tracking. **Fast tracking** (or fast tracking the path, as it is sometimes called) is when you perform activities in parallel that you would normally do in sequence. Fast tracking is often the most effective way to shorten the duration of a project. Adding more resources to a project to shorten its duration is called **crashing**. Crashing the project isn't as simple as finding all the tasks on the critical path and assigning additional resources to them. Some tasks, such as tasks that use skilled labor, cost more to crash than others. So, when deciding which critical tasks to shorten by applying crashing, you must also take into account economic considerations for that course of action. You want to focus on shortening tasks with the least incremental cost.

An important factor to consider, however, is the assumption that any direct change to task information must be a true reflection of reality. To shorten the path only for the sake of shortening the project on paper serves no meaningful purpose—it only confuses and stresses out the project participants. Strive to find ways to shorten the critical path by using techniques that can realistically be accomplished once the project is started. There are various techniques to shorten the critical path by directly and realistically modifying task information, such as those listed next.

- Shorten task durations for critical tasks.
- Delete Finish-to-Start (FS) dependency between two critical tasks.
- Change Finish-to-Start (FS) dependency between two critical tasks to a Start-to-Start (SS) or a Finish-to-Finish (FF) dependency.
- Add negative lag time to a Finish-to-Start (FS) dependency between two critical tasks, thereby allowing the tasks to overlap.
- Modify the calendar on which a task is based to expand the available working time.
- Eliminate date constraints, especially those requiring that a task start on a particular date.

Changing Task Durations

Probably the quickest way to shorten the critical path is by directly shortening the durations of critical tasks. However, this method, while it works well on paper, must be examined to determine whether the tasks can really be accomplished in the shorter time frame.

To shorten the critical path by changing task durations:

▶ 1. Click the **View** tab, click the **Gantt Chart** button, click **Analysis (task 1),** and then scroll the Gantt chart to the start of the project.

▶ 2. Click the **Gantt Chart Tools Format** tab, and then, in the Bar Styles group, click the **Critical Tasks** check box. You see the critical tasks formatted as red bars.

▶ 3. Click the **Project** tab, and then, in the Properties group, click the **Project Information** button. Observe the current project Finish date of 10/15/14. Sidney has indicated that the presentation rooms must be up and running no later than October 1, 2014 to meet other business needs. You need to shorten the critical path to bring the current Finish date back to 10/1/14.

▶ 4. Click the **Cancel** button to close the dialog box, and then drag the **split bar** to display the Finish column. Since you want to monitor the Finish dates, it's a good idea to show the column in the Entry table.

▶ 5. Click the **View** tab, and then, in the Data group, click the **Filter** arrow.

▶ 6. On the list, click **Critical**. You have discussed Install hardware (task 13) and Install software (task 14) with your installation subcontractor, and you have renegotiated the duration for each task. All four tasks within the Installation summary task are still displayed, which indicates that they are all critical tasks.

▶ 7. In the Entry table, click the **Install hardware (task 13) Duration** cell, click the **down arrow** in the box to change the duration to 4 days, and then press the **Enter** key. Several cells are highlighted showing you the effect of the change to the duration.

▶ 8. Click the **Project** tab, and then, in the Properties group, click the **Project Information** button. The change to the Install hardware task has moved the Finish date up to Tuesday 10/14/14.

▶ 9. Click the **Cancel** button.

Be sure the Critical Tasks check box is selected or the Critical tasks will not be visually identified in Gantt Chart view.

Using the Task Inspector

Project 2010 includes a Task Inspector to help you identify factors that affect the Start date of tasks. The Task Inspector also displays any error messages for the tasks and offers suggestions for changing Start dates and dependencies. The Task Inspector can identify if a task begins before its predecessor ends. The Task Inspector can even be used to offer suggestions to "fix" tasks. The Task Inspector will offer options, and you can click Choose the Best Repair Option or click Identify Controlling Factors. Under Repair Options, you can choose the most appropriate repair option and review the effect on your schedule. Under Factors Affecting Task, you can analyze which predecessor or other factor, such as a task scheduled in Manually Scheduled task mode, is driving the start date.

Because you are working with Emily to change Start dates, you decide to take advantage of the Task Inspector feature to help you bring in the project Finish date.

To use the Task Inspector to help shorten the critical path by changing task durations:

▶ **1.** Click the **Task** tab, and then, in the Tasks group, click the **Inspect** button to open the Task Inspector task pane.

▶ **2.** In the Entry table, click **Install hardware** (task 13). Your screen should look like Figure 3-37.

| Figure 3-37 | Task Inspector task pane |

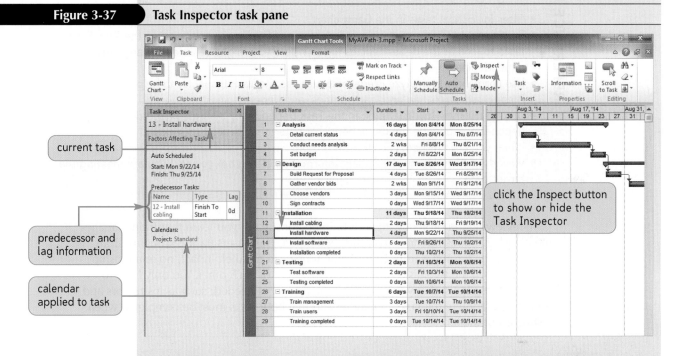

current task

predecessor and lag information

calendar applied to task

click the Inspect button to show or hide the Task Inspector

▶ **3.** In the Entry table, click the **Install software (task 14) Duration** cell, click the **down arrow** in the box twice to change the duration to three days, and then press the **Enter** key. The duration for both the current task and the Installation summary task change as you make the adjustments to reflect the shorter duration.

Next, you want to see how these changes affected the scheduled Finish date for the project. It is always good practice to view the Finish date in the Project Information dialog box to be sure you are meeting the target date.

▶ **4.** Click the **Project** tab, and then, in the Properties group click the **Project Information** button. Because three days were cut from the durations of critical tasks, the project Finish date was also cut by three working days, to Friday 10/10/14. (Because this is over a weekend, it's four calendar days sooner.)

▶ **5.** Click the **OK** button, and then save the project file. Notice when you click the Save button, the highlighting in the cells showing the effects of changing dates or durations no longer appears in the Entry table.

You have taken four calendar days off of the project's original Finish date, but you still need to find ways to cut more days from the schedule in order to meet the 10/1/14 deadline. You explore other ways to shorten the critical path.

Changing Task Dependencies

Another common way to shorten the critical path is to examine and modify task dependencies. Sometimes a Finish-to-Start (FS) dependency is created when it is not necessary, or when a dependency that requires less total time, such as a Start-to-Start (SS) or Finish-to-Finish (FF) dependency, would be appropriate.

REFERENCE

Changing Dependencies to Shorten the Critical Path

- Filter for critical tasks in the Gantt chart.
- Expand and collapse tasks as needed; view the Predecessors column in the Task Entry table to look at the dependencies to see where you might be able to change the dependencies.
- Use Form view to analyze Predecessors or use the Task Inspector to help identify Predecessor tasks, lag and lead settings, and dependencies.
- Double-click the link line to open the Task Dependency dialog box and delete the dependency, change the dependency, or enter a lag time.
- When you are finished, click the OK button.
- View the Finish date in the Project Information dialog box to see if you are meeting the target date.

In reviewing the project with your training consultant, you learn that Train management (task 27) does not have to be finished before Train users (task 28) begins. Both groups can be trained starting at the same time or in parallel. In fact, no relationship exists between the two tasks; they are independent of each other. You only have to consider these facts: that you must have the resources needed, such as instructors and rooms, to complete the tasks in parallel and that both tasks must be completed when testing is completed.

To shorten the critical path by changing task dependencies:

1. Click **Train management** (task 27), drag ✚ to select **Train management** (task 27) and **Train users** (task 28), click the **Task** tab, and then, in the Schedule group, click the **Unlink Tasks** button . The dependency between the two tasks is deleted. This results in task 28 being scheduled to begin on the same day as task 27. Deleting this dependency took three working days off the critical path; the Project Finish date is now Tuesday 10/7/14.

2. Drag the **split bar** to the right to display the Predecessors column. You can quickly see task dependencies in the Predecessors column as well as in the Task Inspector task pane. Notice the latest date in the Finish column, keeping in mind that the last task in the Entry table is not always the last task to be completed in a project. You can use this column to monitor the last Finish date as you work on changing dependencies. The project is now calculated to finish on 10/7/14. You are well on your way toward the target Finish date of October 1st.

3. Click the **View** tab, and then, in the Zoom group, click the **Zoom Entire Project** button to see all the bars in the Gantt chart.

4. Save your work, and then compare your screen to Figure 3-38.

Figure 3-38   **Shortening the schedule by deleting FS dependencies**

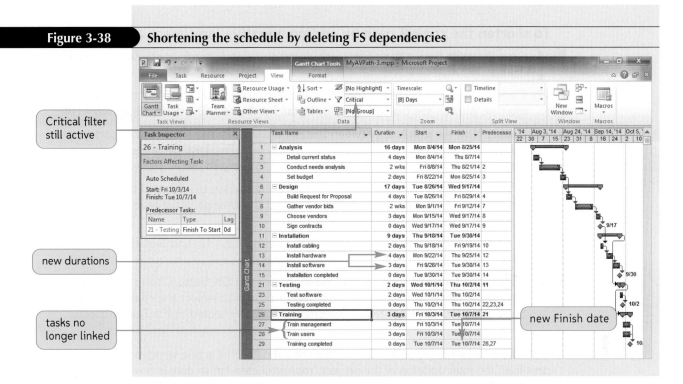

In addition to deleting unnecessary Finish-to-Start (FS) dependencies, you can also shorten the critical path by adding negative lag time to an existing Finish-to-Start (FS) dependency between two critical tasks. Negative lag time always allows the tasks to overlap, regardless of whether the project is scheduled from a given Start or Finish date. When a project is scheduled from a given Start date, negative lag time pulls the second task in the dependency backward in time. This in turn pulls the calculated Finish date backward. When a project is scheduled from a given Finish date, negative lag time pushes the first task in the dependency forward in time. This then pushes the calculated Start date closer to the specified Finish date.

After discussions with your installation team, you have learned that Install software (task 13) can start one day earlier than the finish date of Install hardware (task 12). The Installation phase currently has a duration of 9 days. You use negative lag to reflect this new information. You also learned that you can start installing hardware before all the cabling is installed for each room.

REFERENCE

Adding Negative Lag to Shorten the Critical Path

- Filter for critical tasks in the Gantt chart.
- Expand and collapse tasks as needed, and then view the Predecessors column in the Entry table to look at the dependencies to see where you might be able to change the dependencies. Or, use the Task Inspector to analyze dependencies.
- Double-click the link line to open the Task Dependency dialog box.
- Change the lag time to a negative number or a negative percent, or a larger negative number or a larger negative percent by clicking the down arrow in the Lag spin box.
- When you are finished, click the OK button.

To shorten the critical path by adding negative lag time:

▶ **1.** Drag the **split bar** so the rightmost column showing in the Entry table is the Finish column.

▶ **2.** Click the **Zoom In** button ⊕ on the status bar twice, and then scroll the Gantt chart so you can see the task bars for Install hardware (13) and Install software (14).

TIP

Remember to use the ScreenTips to locate the correct link line.

▶ **3.** Double-click the **link line** between Install hardware (task 13) and Install software (task 14) to open the Task Dependency dialog box. The Task Dependency dialog box identifies that the FS link is from Install hardware to Install software.

▶ **4.** Click the **down arrow** in the Lag box to change the lag to **–1d**, and then click the **OK** button. The Gantt chart updates to reflect the change in the Start date for Install software (task 14).

▶ **5.** Double-click the **link line** between Install cabling (task 12) and Install hardware (task 13) to open the Task Dependency dialog box.

▶ **6.** Click in the **Lag** box, type **–50%**, and then click the **OK** button. You changed the lag to a negative 50% lag. The Gantt chart updates to reflect the change in the Start dates for successor tasks. The change is also reflected in the Task Inspector.

Because tasks 12, 13, and 14 are on the critical path, this action removed four more days from the total duration of the project. Your projected Finish date is now 10/3/14.

Yet another way to use dependencies to shorten the critical path is to change the dependency type from Finish-to-Start (FS) to Finish-to-Finish (FF) or Start-to-Start (SS), in which the task durations automatically overlap. You have learned that Install hardware (task 13) and Install software (task 14) can be given a Start-to-Start (SS) dependency. The hardware technician plans to start one day after the software technician starts.

REFERENCE

Changing the Type of Dependency to Shorten the Critical Path

- Filter for critical tasks in the Gantt chart.
- Expand and collapse tasks as needed; view the Predecessors column in the Task Entry table to look at the dependencies to see where you might be able to change the dependencies. Also use the Task Inspector to identify dependencies.
- Double-click the link line to open the Task Dependency dialog box.
- Click the Type arrow, and then change the dependency type to Finish-to-Finish (FF) or Start-to-Start (SS).
- Add lag time if needed, for a realistic sequence of the tasks.
- When you are finished, click the OK button.

To shorten the critical path by changing the type of dependency:

▶ **1.** Double-click the **link line** between Install hardware (task 13) and Install software (task 14), click the **Type** arrow, click **Start-to-Start (SS)**, click the **Lag up** arrow to remove the lag time, and then click the **OK** button. Without lag time, the tasks start on the same day. You have gained two more days on the project Finish date. The Installation duration is now five days, and the calculated Finish date is now 10/1/14. The changes to the dependencies and lag times have shortened the project's overall duration.

2. Show all the subtasks and, in the Entry table, click each task and view the Task Inspector task pane and then, in the Entry table, click **Analysis** (task 1).

3. Click the **View** tab, and then remove the **Critical** filter by setting the Filter to **No Filter**.

4. In the Task Inspector task pane, click the **Close** button ✖.

5. Drag the **split bar** so the Finish column is the last column in the Entry table.

6. In the Zoom group, click the **Zoom Entire Project** button 🗓 so you can see all the bars. Your screen should look like Figure 3-39.

<table>
<tr><td>Figure 3-39</td><td>Project with changes to dependencies and lag times</td></tr>
</table>

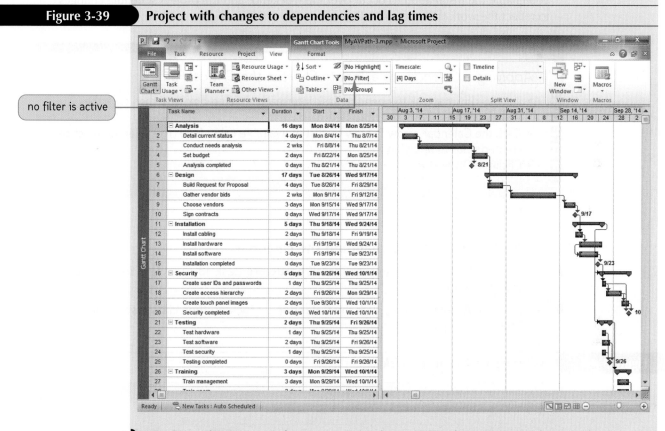

no filter is active

7. Open the Project Information dialog box, review the project Finish Date, then close the dialog box. You have met your target Finish date.

8. Save the project file.

Your efforts have cut several days from the total duration of the ViewPoint partners project. However, you should always consider all options to bring a project in sooner and to plan for any potential delays. Always check for all ways to shorten the critical path, even if you have met the desired Finish date.

Shortening the Critical Path by Changing Calendars and Task Constraints

Nonworking hours, such as weekends and scheduled holidays, extend the project's duration because work is performed only during working hours. If you know a task does not need to follow the Standard calendar, you should create a special calendar with the appropriate working and nonworking times, and then assign that calendar to the task.

You notice that Install hardware (task 13) spans a weekend (two nonworking days). The installation vendor is willing to work on Saturday and Sunday afternoons (1:00 PM to 5:00 PM) at no extra expense. Sidney approved the work, so Emily created a new calendar called Installation Team to apply to that task. By assigning this calendar to the task, you enable the installation to occur over the weekend, and the project schedule changes to reflect the work that occurs on those days.

REFERENCE

Applying a Calendar to a Task to Shorten the Critical Path

- Double-click the task to open the Task Information dialog box, and then click the Advanced tab.
- Click the Calendar arrow to view the list of available calendars. (The calendar must be created prior to applying it.)
- Click the OK button.

To shorten the path by changing the calendar:

1. In the Entry table, double-click **Install hardware** (task 13). The Task Information dialog box opens.

2. Click the **Advanced** tab, click the **Calendar** arrow, and then click **Installation Team**. See Figure 3-40.

Figure 3-40	**Assigning a calendar to a task**

Installation Team calendar

click the Calendar arrow to see a list of available calendars

3. Click the **OK** button. The Gantt chart adjusts the length of the bar for task 13 because four hours of work are being completed on Saturday and four hours on Sunday. You saved another day. The Finish date is now 9/30/14.

4. Right-click the **Task Name** column, click **Insert Column,** type **Ind** arrow, and then press the **Enter** key to select **Indicators**. The Indicators column appears to the left of the Task Name column in the Entry table, and a calendar indicator appears in the task 13 Indicators column to alert you to the fact that a special calendar applies to task 13.

5. Double-click the **Indicators** column divider to resize the column for best fit, and point to the **Calendar indicator** for more information. The ScreenTip confirms that the Installation Team calendar is assigned to the task.

Another way to shorten the critical path is to analyze and eliminate unnecessary date constraints that have been applied to the tasks within your project. Remember from Tutorial 2 that a constraint is a restriction that you put on a task's Start or Finish date. Constraints can be flexible or inflexible. **Flexible constraints** such as As Soon As Possible (ASAP) and As Late As Possible (ALAP) do not have specific dates associated with them. Setting these constraints allows you to start tasks as early as possible or as late as possible with the task ending before the project finishes. **Inflexible constraints** such as Must Start On (MSO) and Must Finish On (MFO) require that you specify a date, which determines the start or finish date of the task. These constraints are useful when you need to make decisions based on the availability of equipment or resources, deadlines, contract milestones, and start and finish dates. Constraints can extend the overall time to complete a project because they minimize or eliminate some of Project 2010's ability to freely move the scheduled Start and Finish dates of individual tasks. See Figure 3-41 for a list of constraint types.

Figure 3-41	Constraint types

Constraint	Description
As Soon As Possible (ASAP)	Schedules a task as soon as possible. This is the default constraint for tasks that are entered into a project with an assigned Start date.
As Late As Possible (ALAP)	Schedules a task as late as possible. This is the default constraint for tasks that are entered into a project with an assigned Finish date.
Finish No Earlier Than (FNET)	Schedules the Finish date of the task on or after the date that you specify. If the project is scheduled from a Start date and you enter a Finish date into the Entry table for a task, then Project 2010 will automatically apply this constraint type to that task.
Finish No Later Than (FNLT)	Schedules the Finish date of the task on or before the date that you specify. If the project is scheduled from a Finish date and you enter a Finish date into the Entry table for a task, then Project 2010 will automatically apply this constraint type to that task.
Start No Earlier Than (SNET)	Schedules the Start date of the task on or after the date that you specify. If the project is scheduled from a Start date and you enter a Start date into the Entry table for a task, then Project 2010 will automatically apply this constraint type to that task.
Start No Later Than (SNLT)	Schedules the Start date of the task on or before the date that you specify. If the project is scheduled from a Finish date and you enter a Start date into the Entry table for a task, then Project 2010 will automatically apply this constraint type to that task.
Must Finish On (MFO)	Schedules the Finish date of a task on the date that you specify.
Must Start On (MSO)	Schedules the Start date of a task on the date that you specify.

MFO and MSO constraints cannot be avoided or changed. For example, if your project contains a task in the middle of the project called Attend Multimedia Conference and that task is scheduled for September 6–9, no task that depends on this conference can be started until after September 9, regardless of how quickly the first half of the project is completed. Be very careful about entering date constraints because they remove flexibility in recalculating individual task Start and Finish dates. Fortunately, Project 2010 places an icon in the Indicators column for any constraint other than As Soon As Possible and As Late As Possible to alert you that a constraint has been placed on a task.

REFERENCE

Changing the Constraints to Shorten the Critical Path

- Double-click the task to open the Task Information dialog box.
- Click the Constraint type arrow.
- Select the desired constraint.
- If you select a constraint such as Must Start On or Must Finish On, specify a date in the Constraint date text box.
- Click the OK button.

The Start No Earlier Than constraint can be used to reflect a situation, such as a new employee Sidney hired who starts work at ViewPoint Partners on 9/19/14. Sidney thought it might be good training to have this new person watch the installation.

To change the critical path by changing constraints:

1. In the Entry table, double-click **Install cabling** (task 12) to open its Task Information dialog box. On the Advanced tab, click the **Constraint type** arrow, and then click **Start No Earlier Than**.

2. Press the **Tab** key, type **9/19/14** in the Constraint date text box, and then click the **OK** button. The Constraint added two days to the Project Finish date.

3. In the Entry table, click **Installation** (task 11), and then place the pointer on the **Constraint indicator** for task 12. The ScreenTip displays the 'Start No Earlier Than' constraint. See Figure 3-42.

| Figure 3-42 | Start No Earlier Than constraint applied to task 12 |

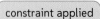

constraint applied

dates affected by constraint highlighted in blue

After adding this constraint, however, the project's completion date has been extended. Emily tells you that this person can start much earlier than previously assumed and that the constraint can be removed.

▶ **4.** In the Entry table, double-click **Install cabling** (task 12), click the **Constraint type** arrow, click **As Soon As Possible**, and then click the **OK** button. Your updated project is now predicting a 9/30/14 Finish date, beating the goal set by management.

Viewing the Entire Project Using the Timeline

Now you want to view the entire project. In Tutorial 2, you learned how to add individual tasks to the Timeline. Now, you decide to add the summary tasks to the Timeline to get an overview of how each summary task fits in across the time frame of the project. The Timeline is a helpful view of the tasks across the entire project. You show the Timeline by clicking the Timeline check box on the View tab. You can add tasks to the Timeline by right-clicking each task and then clicking Add to Timeline. You can also add tasks to the Timeline by clicking the Add Task to Timeline button, which is on the Task tab in the Properties group.

To add tasks to the Timeline:

▶ **1.** Click the **View** tab on the Ribbon, and then, in the Split View group, click the **Timeline** check box.

▶ **2.** Drag the **split bar** to the left to display the Duration column as the last column, and then double-click column heading dividers as necessary to display all the values in the columns.

▶ **3.** In the Entry table, click **Analysis** (task 1), and then, in the Zoom group, click the **Zoom Entire Project** button 🗓.

▶ **4.** In the Data group, click the **Outline** button, and then click **Outline Level 1** to collapse all subtasks.

▶ **5.** With **Analysis** (task 1) selected, press and hold **Shift**, and then click **Training** (task 26) to select all the Summary tasks.

▶ **6.** Click the **Task** tab on the Ribbon, and then, in the Properties group, click the **Add Task to Timeline** button 🗓. **Analysis** appears on the Timeline as a block from 8/4/14–8/25/14. All the summary tasks are added to the Timeline.

▶ **7.** Click the **View** tab on the Ribbon, in the Data group, click the **Outline** button, click **All Subtasks** to display all subtasks, and then, click **Analysis** (task 1). Your screen should look like Figure 3-43.

Figure 3-43 **Final project**

Outline button

Summary tasks on the Timeline

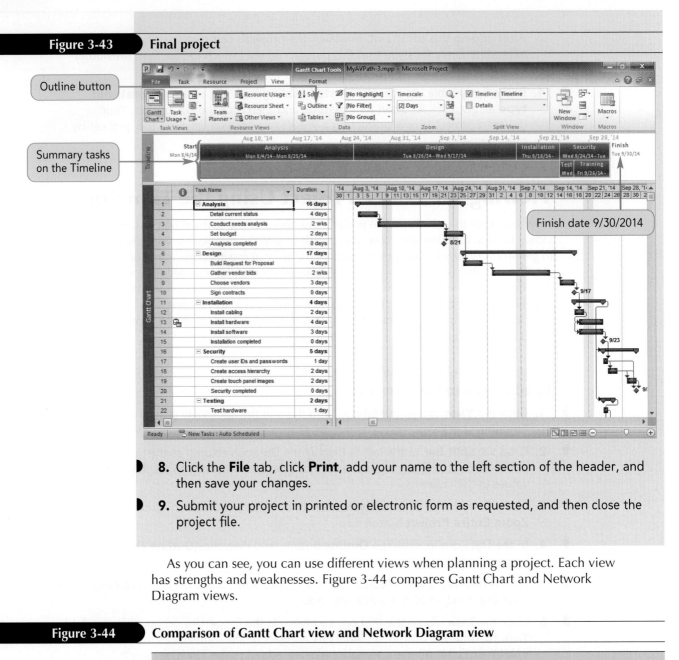

8. Click the **File** tab, click **Print**, add your name to the left section of the header, and then save your changes.

9. Submit your project in printed or electronic form as requested, and then close the project file.

As you can see, you can use different views when planning a project. Each view has strengths and weaknesses. Figure 3-44 compares Gantt Chart and Network Diagram views.

Figure 3-44 **Comparison of Gantt Chart view and Network Diagram view**

Project 2010 View	Other Common Name	Strengths	Actions Commonly Completed in This View
Gantt Chart	Bar Chart	Displays a sequential listing of task names (in the Entry table)	Entering tasks and durations
			Editing tasks and durations
		Graphically displays durations as bar lengths	Moving tasks
			Linking tasks
		Displays a timescale at the top of the chart that helps communicate task Start and Finish dates	Updating task completion progress
			Creating task dependencies
			Editing task dependencies
Network Diagram	Critical Path Diagram	Displays dependencies between tasks	Creating task dependencies
		Displays the critical path	Editing task dependencies

You have learned how to make changes to the critical tasks that determine the critical path, and you used different techniques to shorten the critical path. The final Finish date for the project meets the needs of Sidney and ViewPoint Partners. The project plan is coming along nicely.

REVIEW

Session 3.2 Quick Check

1. Explain what happens when you insert a task by drawing a box in the Network Diagram view.
2. What action must you take to manually rearrange task boxes in Network Diagram view?
3. What is the difference between formatting in Network Diagram view using the Box Styles dialog box and using the Format Box dialog box?
4. What do crashing and fast tracking mean?
5. Identify five ways to shorten the critical path.
6. How can using a different project calendar shorten a project schedule?
7. What is the purpose of the Indicators column? Give an example of an indicator you would want to monitor.
8. What is a constraint?
9. How do constraints relate to the critical path?
10. What are the default constraint types for projects scheduled from both a Start date and a Finish date?

Practice the skills you learned in the tutorial using the same case scenario.

PRACTICE

Review Assignments

Data File needed for the Review Assignments: Train-3.mpp

Part of the AV Presentation Rooms Installation project involves training the users. In this assignment, you will open a partially completed project file that documents the tasks that must be completed before the Training tasks in the AV Presentation Rooms Installation project can be completed. You will work on formatting the Gantt chart, work with filters to get a better understanding of the tasks in the project, take a close look at the critical path, and work with the Network Diagram view to enter new tasks. You will work with the formatting features and the Gantt Chart Wizard to create a Gantt chart that better communicates the information about the tasks. You will also format Network Diagram view. You then will use various techniques for shortening the critical path to move the Finish date earlier. Complete the following:

1. Start Project 2010, and then open the **Train-3** file located in the **Project3\Review** folder included with your Data Files.

2. Save the project as **VPTrain-3** in the same folder.

3. Open the Project Information dialog box. Record the project's scheduled Finish date on a notepad, and then close the Project Information dialog box. (Notice the project Finish date is not always the last date in the Finish column in the Entry table in Gantt Chart view.)

4. Apply the Staffing calendar to Hire trainers (task 7).

5. Filter for critical tasks in Gantt Chart view. Note how many tasks (not including summary tasks) are critical.

6. Turn off the critical tasks filter, and then turn on the AutoFilter.

7. Use the Duration AutoFilter button to set up a Custom AutoFilter, and then filter for those tasks greater than or equal to three days. Note which tasks meet that criteria. Remove the AutoFilter.

8. Apply a Gantt Chart style from the Gantt Chart Style gallery. Review how it changed the format of the chart.

9. Use the Bars tab in the Bar Styles dialog box to format the Gantt chart Summary tasks as follows: change the bar to dark red, change the starting shape to a green circle with an up arrow in it, and change the ending shape to a red circle with a down arrow. Change the Milestone shape to a purple circle with a diamond in it.

10. Use the Text tab in the Bar Styles dialog box to specify that the duration is to appear on the left side of the summary bars and the task name on the right side of the summary task bars. (*Note*: Select Name not Task Name from the list.)

11. Use the Format Bar dialog box to format the individual Gantt chart bar for Develop contract (task 6) so that the bar starts and ends with a solid yellow diamond shape. This will visually signal that the company attorney needs to be involved in this task.

12. Use the Text Styles dialog box to change the text styles for all Critical Tasks (but not Critical Summary tasks) to a purple italic style in the Entry table.

13. Remove any filters and use buttons on the Task tab in the Font group box to format the Sign lab contract (task 16) text so the task name is bold and red with a yellow fill to draw special attention to it.

14. Open the Timescale dialog box, and then change the label for the Bottom Tier to the 1/25/09, 2/1/09 style.

15. Preview the Gantt chart, add your name to the left section of the header, and then use the Fit to page, if necessary, so that the chart will print on only one page.

16. Switch to Network Diagram view, zoom out until you can see a portion of several pages on the screen, and then locate Develop training documentation (task 4).

17. Select task 4, then drag to draw a new task 5 below task 4. The task box will automatically appear below task 2 because it does not depend on any other tasks and can therefore start at the time that the project starts.

18. Use the Task Information dialog box for task 5 to enter **Distribute training manuals** as the task name and specify a duration of two hours. Add the note, **Sidney must approve manuals.** to the task.

19. Drag a link line between task 4 and the new task 5 to link them in a Finish-to-Start (FS) dependency.

20. Filter the network diagram for critical tasks and note which tasks are critical, and then remove the critical filter.

21. Allow manual box positioning for the layout. Draw a selection box to select tasks 7, 8, 16, and 17, and then drag the selected tasks to the left to position task 7 under task 2.

22. Change the shape of all Noncritical Summary tasks to an upside-down trapezoid (last shape in the list) with an Orange, Darker 25% thick border and an Olive Green, Darker 25% with the default pattern fill.

23. Format the Identify existing skills (task 2) box as a rounded rectangle (third in the list) with a Purple, Lighter 40% background, a small dotted pattern (the fourth pattern on the list), and a thick red border.

24. Preview the network diagram, and then add your name to the left section in the header. Change the layout so that the boxes are positioned automatically.

25. Return to Gantt Chart view, open the Project Information dialog box, and then make a note of the project Finish date.

26. Open the Task Inspector task pane.

27. Double-click the link line between Identify existing skills (task 2) and Identify needed skills (task 3), and then change the dependency type to Start-to-Start. How did changing the dependency change the Start and Finish dates for the tasks? Make a note as to how many days were saved or gained.

28. Change the duration for Develop training documentation (task 4) to four days.

29. Double-click the link line between Identify needed skills (task 3) and Develop training documentation (task 4), and specify a –50% lag time.

30. Close the Task Inspector task pane, open the Project Information dialog box, and then make a note of the project Finish date.

31. Open Reports, open Overview, view the Top-Level Tasks report, and then add your name to the left section of the header of the report. Print the report if requested.

32. Add the summary tasks to the Timeline.

33. Save the project, submit the project in electronic or printed form as requested, and then close the project file.

Apply your skills to format and make changes to the project file for building a new house.

APPLY

Case Problem 1

Data File needed for this Case Problem: Home-3.mpp

River Dell Development, Inc.   You work for a general contractor, River Dell Development, Inc., that manages residential construction projects for group homes. The manager, Karen Reynolds, has asked you to review the project file. She explains that it is important to present professional and attractive output to clients, and she wants you to format the Gantt chart and the network diagram to take advantage of the Project 2010 formatting features. She also asked you to shorten the critical path to bring the project in earlier than currently scheduled. Complete the following:

1. Open the **Home-3** file located in the **Project3\Case1** folder included with your Data Files.
2. Save the project file as **NewHome-3** in the same folder.
3. Open the Project Information dialog box, and note the project's scheduled Finish date.
4. Delete the Finish-to-Start (FS) dependency between Roof house (task 9) and Install insulation (task 10), and then add a Finish-to-Start (FS) dependency between Frame house (task 8) and Install insulation (task 10).
5. Change the duration for Install carpeting (task 16) to four days. Move the Install carpeting task below the Paint task so the Paint task is now task 16. Add a Finish to Start relationship with a 1-day lag between Paint (task 16) and Install carpeting (task 17).

⊕ **EXPLORE**

6. On the Gantt Chart Tools Format tab, click the Critical Tasks check box to display critical path information.
7. Refer to Figure 3-45 to format the Gantt chart.

Figure 3-45   **Formatted NewHome-3 project**

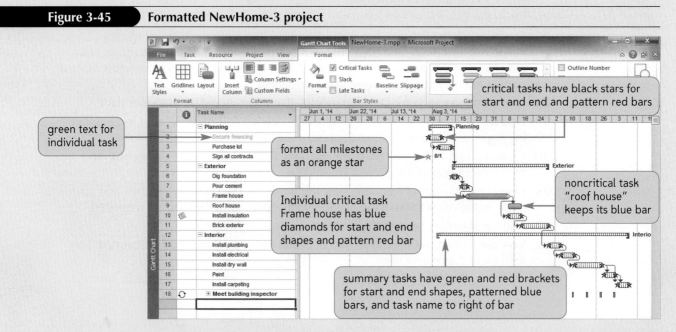

8. Double-click the Gantt chart timescale to open the Timescale dialog box, and then show three tiers, with the Top Tier showing months, the Middle Tier showing days, and the Bottom Tier showing hours. (*Hint*: You will need to change the Bottom Tier before you can change the Middle Tier.) Change the Bottom Tier count to 4.
9. Format the nonworking time bars to appear in front of the task bars with an Aqua, Lighter 80% color and a grid pattern. Zoom in to see the bars.

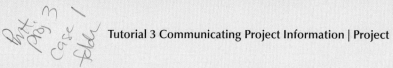

⊕ EXPLORE

10. Open the Gridlines dialog box and change the Gantt Rows to an Aqua, Lighter 80% color with an interval of 2.

11. Change the zoom to entire project, preview the Gantt chart, make it fit on one page, if necessary, and add your name to the left section of the header. Print this if requested.

12. Switch to Network Diagram view, and then collapse all summary tasks except Exterior (task 5).

13. Allow manual box positioning, and then move Install insulation (task 10) and Brick exterior (task 11) so that they are directly below Frame house (task 8) and Roof house (task 9), respectively.

14. Change the box styles of the noncritical tasks so the background is yellow and the border is blue.

15. Preview the network diagram, and then add your name so it is left-aligned in the header. Print this if requested.

16. Change the layout so that the boxes are automatically positioned.

17. Switch to Gantt Chart view, show all subtasks, collapse the recurring task Meet building inspector (task 18), and add a project summary task bar. Change Your Name to your name.

18. Change the duration for Frame house (task 8) to 14 days.

19. Apply the Electricians calendar to Install electrical (task 14).

20. Open the Task Inspector task pane to review all tasks, and then, in the Project Information dialog box, examine the new scheduled Finish date for the project.

⊕ EXPLORE

21. Click the Electricians link in the Task Inspector task pane to open the Electricians calendar. Review the calendar, and then close the Change Working Time dialog box.

22. Add a negative 1-day lag to the dependency between Install electrical (task 14) and Install dry wall (task 15).

23. Use the Project Information dialog box to note the new Finish date. Close the Task Inspector task pane. Resize the Duration column for the Project Summary task so all numbers are showing. Zoom so you can view the entire project in Gantt Chart view with Duration as the last column in the Entry table. Scroll as needed to review all components of the Gantt chart.

24. Save your changes, submit the project in electronic or printed form as requested, and then close the project file.

Apply your skills to format a project file that helps organize a job search.

APPLY

Case Problem 2

Data File needed for this Case Problem: Jobs-3.mpp

CommunityWorks As a counselor at CommunityWorks, a career counseling firm, you continue working on a project to help new college graduates with technical degrees find employment. You want to format the project so it is easy for your clients to read, and you want to shorten the critical path to help them attain their goal sooner. Complete the following:

1. Open the **Jobs-3** file in the **Project3\Case2** folder included with your Data Files.

2. Save the file as **MyJobs-3** in the same folder. Make a note of the Project Finish date.

3. Filter the Gantt chart for critical tasks. Note the tasks on the critical path. Clear the filter. Filter for the date range 5/1/14 to 5/7/14. Note the tasks that meet this criteria. Clear all filters.

4. Open the Task Inspector and review each task. What do you notice about Meet with counselor (task 3)? The team informed you that a counselor will be available. Review the current constraint assigned to the task, and then change it to As Soon As Possible.

5. Delete the link between Existing Contacts (task 11) and Establish new contacts (task 14). How is the Finish date impacted?

6. Customize the display of bars in the Gantt Chart view by specifying that the task name (Name) is displayed on the right side of the Gantt bars for tasks, that the Scheduled Start date is displayed on the left side of the summary Gantt bars, and that the Scheduled Finish date is displayed on the right side of the summary Gantt bars.

7. Open the Gridlines dialog box and format the Project Start line to a dashed red line.

8. Format the text for all Noncritical tasks to Broadway font, dark blue color, with an orange patterned background of your choice.

⊕ **EXPLORE**   9. Format the link lines by clicking the Layout button in the Format group to open the Layout dialog box. Select the middle link style to change the appearance of link lines in the Gantt chart.

10. Change the bar style for the Task bars. Use any colors and patterns you wish. Change the start and end shapes and colors.

11. Drag the split bar between the Entry table and the Gantt chart to the left so that no columns from the Entry table are visible.

12. Preview the Gantt chart, and then add your name to the left side of the header. Adjust the preview if necessary so it fits on one page, and then print this if requested. (*Note:* In the Preview, you see the Entry table Task ID column and the Task Name column because this information is needed to interpret the information in the Gantt chart.)

13. Save the project, and switch to Network Diagram view.

14. Draw a box directly below task 1 to add a new task 2. Working in the new box, add the task name **Design a business card** and specify a duration of four hours.

15. Link Design a business card (task 2) to Create resume (task 3) in a Finish-to-Start (FS) dependency.

16. Return to Gantt Chart view, drag the split bar to the right so that the Start and Finish columns of the Entry table are visible again, and then adjust the column widths as needed to display all the data.

17. Insert the Indicators column to the left of the Task Name column. Resize it to best fit.

⊕ **EXPLORE**   18. In the Entry table, change the Start date for Design a business card (task 2) to June 1, 2014. Read the explanation in the Planning Wizard dialog box that opens, and then choose the second option to make Sunday June 1, 2014 a working day. On a sheet of paper, write down what happened in the Indicators column. What happened in the Duration and Start columns?

19. Change the Start date for Create resume (task 3) to June 2, 2014. When the Planning Wizard opens, select the second option to move the task and keep the link.

20. Display the Timeline. Add the summary tasks Resume, Research, and Phone Calls to the Timeline.

21. Preview the project in Gantt Chart view.

22. Return to Gantt Chart view, with the Duration column as the last visible column. Zoom and scroll so you can see all the bars in the Gantt chart.

23. Save your changes, submit the project in electronic or printed form as requested, and then close the project file.

Expand your skills to enhance the file for the reunion planning project.

CHALLENGE

Case Problem 3

Data File needed for this Case Problem: Reunion-3.mpp

Western College Reunion   As a proud graduate of Western College, you continue to help organize the 20th reunion for the graduating class of 1994. Part of the job is encouraging donations, so you want the project to be presented in a professional way. In 2014, the reunion will take place on March 7, 8, and 9. You scheduled the project from a Finish date and let Project 2010 determine the project Start date. Now you need to review the critical path report, format Gantt Chart view and Network Diagram view, and then work to shorten the critical path. Complete the following:

1. Start Project, and then open **Reunion-3** located in the **Project3\Case3** folder included with your Data Files.
2. Save the file as **WReunion-3** in the same folder.
3. View the Critical Tasks report found in the Overview reports. Note the task numbers for the critical tasks.
4. Format the Gantt Chart view to do the following: display the critical path task bars and milestones using formatting of your choice, and create custom task information by displaying the duration on the left side of task and Summary Gantt bars, and displaying the Name to the left of milestone tasks. (*Note*: You will see this formatting applied after you enter a milestone task in the Entry table.)

⊕ **EXPLORE**   5. Insert **Sign contracts** as a new Milestone task using the Insert Milestone button as task 6. Notice the formatting you specified is applied to the new milestone task.

6. Enter a new task 10 with the name **Mail brochure** and a duration of three days. Enter a new task 11 with the name **Enroll attendees** and a duration of three months.
7. Create Finish-to-Start (FS) dependencies among tasks 9, 10, and 11.
8. Change the timescale so the middle tier scale is months and the bottom tier is weeks. Reposition Gantt Chart view to the beginning of the project, if it is not visible.
9. Open the Project Information dialog box and note the project's scheduled Start date.
10. Open the Task Inspector. Read the message and make a note of your findings. Then close the Task Inspector.
11. Add a –50% lag to the task dependency between Survey clients (task 1) and Determine reunion goals (task 2), and then add a –50% lag to the task dependency between Set budget (task 4) and Set agenda (task 5). On a sheet of paper, write down which task moves in the schedule when a negative lag is applied to a Finish-to-Start (FS) dependency in a project that is scheduled from a Finish date.
12. Format the Enroll attendees (task 11) bar in the Gantt chart so that the bar is an aqua color and the shape is a thin bar along the bottom (the fourth bar type in the Shape list). Format the text of Enroll attendees in the Entry table with a style and color of your choice.

⊕ **EXPLORE**   13. In Network Diagram view, format the link lines to be straight. To do this, open the Layout dialog box, and then choose the Straight option button in the Link style section. Also, change the noncritical link line color to black.

⊕ **EXPLORE**   14. In Network Diagram view, change the arrangement of the boxes so they are arranged with each week's tasks in a new column. To do this, open the Layout dialog box, click the Arrangement arrow, and then click Top Down by Week.

15. Allow manual positioning of the boxes and move the boxes so the diagram fits on two pages. Be sure to move the milestone task Sign contracts (task 6) so it is also on the two pages.

⊕ EXPLORE   16. Open the Box Styles dialog box, click Noncritical Milestone, then change the Data Template to Standard.

17. Preview the network diagram, and add your name so it is left-aligned in the header. Print this if requested.

18. Return to Gantt Chart view, and then add a new task 12 as a milestone task with the name **Start the party!**. Use the Format Painter in the Clipboard group to copy the formatting from task 11 to task 12.

19. Drag the split bar so Duration is the last column visible.

20. Preview the Gantt chart, and add your name so it is left-aligned in the header.

21. Open the Project Information dialog box, and note the new Start date.

22. Save your changes, submit the project in electronic or printed form as requested, and then close the project file.

With the figure provided as a guide, continue to format the file for a playground.

CREATE

Case Problem 4

Data File needed for this Case Problem: Grant-3.mpp

NatureSpace   As a project manager at NatureSpace, a company that specializes in creating play structures for communities, you continue to work on a project to fund and build a new neighborhood park. All of the equipment must be ready by September 6, 2014 before the end of the fiscal year, so you scheduled the project from a Finish date and let Project 2010 establish the project Start date. The project currently requires too much time prior to September 6, so you need to find ways to shorten the critical path. Also, because you will be working with the mayor and town council, you want to present attractive reports and printouts to explain the project plans. Complete the following:

1. Open the file **Grant-3** located in the **Project3\Case4** folder included with your Data Files.

2. Save the file as **MyGrant-3** in the same folder.

3. Open the Project Information dialog box, and note the project's scheduled Start date.

4. The mayor, Brian Griffin, has already found a park sponsor, so you can shave time off of Identify park sponsor (task 3). Also, you have equipment pricing research done on another project for a similar-sized playground installation, so the duration of Compare prices (task 13) can be shortened. Lower the duration for both by two days each.

5. Change the dependency between Identify park sponsor (task 3) and Enlist volunteers (task 4) to a Start-to-Start (SS) dependency.

⊕ EXPLORE   6. Create a new calendar named **Volunteers** based on the Standard calendar. The volunteers that will build the playground are willing to work on the weekend, so create an exception in this calendar by changing both Saturday and Sunday to nondefault working time. The calendar can run the full year.

7. Change the relationships between the three Fundraising tasks so they are SS dependencies.

8. Switch to Network Diagram view and make a note of the critical tasks.

9. Switch to Gantt Chart view, and specify the Volunteers calendar for tasks 8, 9, 10, 17, 18, and 21. What happened to the critical tasks?

10. Insert a new Milestone task, **Opening day**, as task 22, and then use the Outdent Task button to make this a top-level task.

11. Make sure the Indicators, Task Name, and Duration columns are visible, zoom so you can see the entire project on one screen, preview the Gantt chart, and add your name so it is left-aligned in the header.

12. Create the Critical Tasks report. Add your name left-aligned in the header, and then print it, if requested.

13. Create the Top-Level Tasks report. Review the report on the screen. Add your name left-aligned in the header, and then print it, if requested.

⊕ EXPLORE 14. Create the Working Days report. Change the page orientation to landscape. Add your name left-aligned in the header. View the report in Multi-Page view, and then print the report, if requested.

⊕ EXPLORE 15. Switch to the Network Diagram view. Format the diagram using colors and borders in a way that appears professional to you. Use text styles and distinct formatting for different types of tasks. Format the box for Opening day using a special formatting style.

16. Return to Gantt Chart view and format the Entry table and Gantt Chart according to Figure 3-46.

| Figure 3-46 | Final MyGrant-3 project |

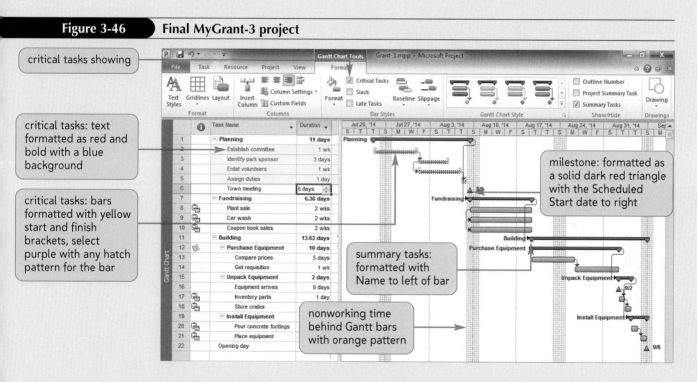

critical tasks showing

critical tasks: text formatted as red and bold with a blue background

critical tasks: bars formatted with yellow start and finish brackets, select purple with any hatch pattern for the bar

milestone: formatted as a solid dark red triangle with the Scheduled Start date to right

summary tasks: formatted with Name to left of bar

nonworking time behind Gantt bars with orange pattern

17. Save your changes, and submit the reports in printed form, if requested. Submit the project in electronic or printed form as requested, and then close the project.

ENDING DATA FILES

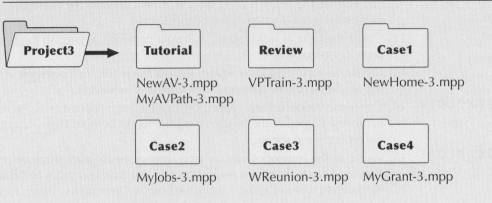

OBJECTIVES

Session 4.1
- Use resource and cost views
- Enter and edit resource and cost data
- Organize resources into logical groups
- Assign resources and costs to tasks

Session 4.2
- Edit task information based on the relationship among work, duration, and units
- Create fixed-work and fixed-duration tasks
- Sort, filter, and group tasks for resource information

Session 4.3
- Correct for overallocations
- Analyze resource usage and entered project costs
- Examine the critical path and slack
- Use cost reports
- Use the Team Planner

Assigning Resources and Costs

Determining Resources and Costs for the Installation of AV Presentation Rooms

Case | *ViewPoint Partners*

Emily has created a Project 2010 file that contains the tasks, durations, and dependencies necessary to manage the installation of the five AV presentation rooms for the opinion research firm, ViewPoint Partners. To complete the project, Emily needs to hire contractors, purchase equipment, and commit resources and costs to accomplish the tasks. A complete project file must include resources, the names and cost information for the people who actually do the work, and the costs for any materials used during the project. These resources and costs have to be assigned to the tasks. Sidney Simone, the owner of ViewPoint Partners, has asked you to use Emily's file to enter, schedule, and analyze resource information and project cost data in the project file.

STARTING DATA FILES

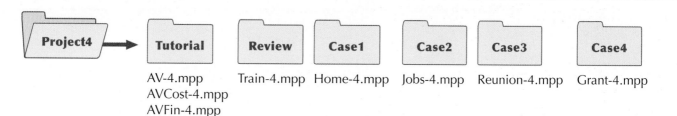

| Project4 → Tutorial | Review | Case1 | Case2 | Case3 | Case4 |

AV-4.mpp
AVCost-4.mpp
AVFin-4.mpp
AVLvl-4.mpp

Train-4.mpp   Home-4.mpp   Jobs-4.mpp   Reunion-4.mpp   Grant-4.mpp

SESSION 4.1 VISUAL OVERVIEW

You use the Task Usage button to display the Task Usage sheet.

The Task Usage sheet shows tasks and assigned resources as well as hours assigned to each day.

The overallocated resources indicator tells you this resource has too much work assigned and leveling must occur to redistribute the work.

Resources for each task appear below the task.

Two resources are assigned to work this task.

Task Form Tools   NewAV-4.mpp - Microsoft Project

| File | Task | Resource | Project | View | Format |

Gantt Chart ▾ | Task Usage ▾

Team Planner ▾

Resource Usage ▾
Resource Sheet ▾
Other Views ▾

Sort ▾
Outline ▾
Tables ▾

Timescale:

Task Views | Resource Views | Data | Zoom

	ℹ	Task Mode	Task Name	Work	Duration	Start	Details		T	W
2	👤	⇨	⊟ Detail current status	40 hrs	5 days	Mon 8/4/14	Work			
			Your Name	40 hrs		Mon 8/4/14	Work			
3	👤	⇨	⊟ Conduct needs analysis	120 hrs	3 wks	Mon 8/4/14	Work		8h	8h
			Your Name	120 hrs		Mon 8/4/14	Work		8h	8h
4		⇨	Analysis completed	0 hrs	0 days	Fri 8/22/14	Work			
5		⇨	⊟ Design	176 hrs	16 days	Thu 8/21/14	Work			
6	👤	⇨	⊟ Build Request for Proposal	64 hrs	4 days	Thu 8/21/14	Work			
			Emily Michaels	32 hrs		Thu 8/21/14	Work			
			Your Name	32 hrs		Thu 8/21/14	Work			
7		⇨	⊟ Gather vendor bids	80 hrs	2 wks	Wed 8/27/14	Work			
			Your Name	80 hrs		Wed 8/27/14	Work			
8		⇨	⊟ Choose vendors	32 hrs	2 days	Wed 9/10/14	Work			
			Emily Michaels	16 hrs		Wed 9/10/14	Work			

Task Usage

Name: Build Request for Proposal   Duration: 4 days   ☑ Effort driven   ☐ Manually Scheduled   Pr

Start: Thu 8/21/14   Finish: Tue 8/26/14

ID	Resource Name	Units	Work	Ovt. Work	Baseline Work	Act. W
1	Emily Michaels	100%	32h	0h	0h	0h
2	Your Name	100%	32h	0h	0h	0h

Task Form

This is the duration for the task used to calculate work; using a Standard Calendar with 8 hour work days then 4 days = 32 hours.

The Work column shows the total work for the task divided among assigned resources.

At this point, no overtime has been assigned. No progress has been made on this task, so baseline and actual work are zero.

Ready   New Tasks : Auto Scheduled

ASSIGNING RESOURCES

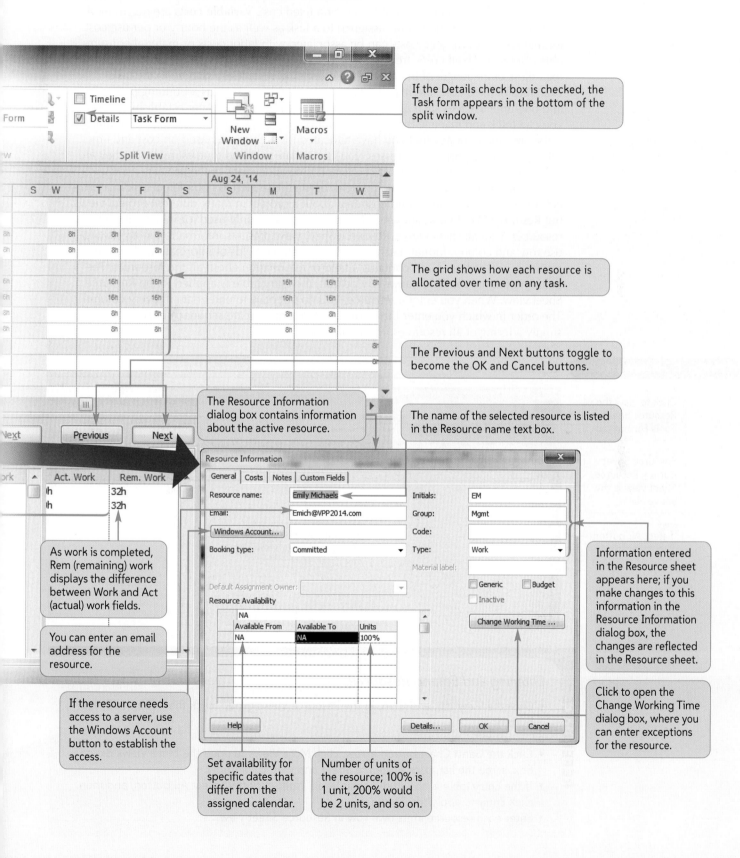

If the Details check box is checked, the Task form appears in the bottom of the split window.

The grid shows how each resource is allocated over time on any task.

The Previous and Next buttons toggle to become the OK and Cancel buttons.

The Resource Information dialog box contains information about the active resource.

The name of the selected resource is listed in the Resource name text box.

As work is completed, Rem (remaining) work displays the difference between Work and Act (actual) work fields.

You can enter an email address for the resource.

Information entered in the Resource sheet appears here; if you make changes to this information in the Resource Information dialog box, the changes are reflected in the Resource sheet.

If the resource needs access to a server, use the Windows Account button to establish the access.

Click to open the Change Working Time dialog box, where you can enter exceptions for the resource.

Set availability for specific dates that differ from the assigned calendar.

Number of units of the resource; 100% is 1 unit, 200% would be 2 units, and so on.

Entering Cost and Resource Data

A significant component of planning and managing your project is accurately controlling and tracking cost and resource data. **Cost** is an expenditure made to accomplish a task. A cost can be either a variable cost or a fixed cost. **Variable costs** are determined by the number of resource units assigned to a task as well as the hourly or per-use cost for that resource. Variable costs can be associated with labor costs or material consumable resources. **Fixed costs** are expenses that are associated with a task but do not vary regardless of the length of the task or the number of resources assigned to the task. Examples of fixed costs are insurance, one-time legal fees such as a building permit fee and one-time use fees such as renting a booth at a convention. After establishing costs, you can track and manage them so that your project stays within the budget. The **budget** is the amount of money that you have allocated for the project based on cost and time estimates. As the project progresses, you can update cost and time estimates so they are in better alignment with the actual costs and time allocations of the project.

A **resource** is the person(s), equipment, or materials used to complete a task in a project. You can enter resource and cost data about a project in many different project views, but **Resource Sheet view**, shown in Figure 4-1, is commonly used for initial data entry of resources. Like all sheet views, Resource Sheet view presents information in an easy-to-use row and column format. Each row contains all the fields of information about one resource, and each column contains a field of information about all the resources. The column titles are the field names. By default, the Entry table is applied to the Resource Sheet view. When you enter a resource, you do not have to enter data in every column. The order in which you enter the resources does not indicate sequence or priority; it is simply a listing of all resources for the project.

Figure 4-1	Resource Sheet view

Click to view the Resource Sheet Tools Format tab

Resource Sheet button; Resource Sheet view is the active view

Select All button

default columns in Resource Sheet view

REFERENCE

Entering and Editing Resources

- Click the View tab, and then, in the Resource Views group, click the Resource Sheet button.

or

- Click the Gantt Chart button arrow, click More Views to open the More Views dialog box, scroll the list, click Resource Sheet and then click Apply.
- If the Entry table is not already displayed, right-click the Select All button, and then click Entry to apply the Entry table.
- Enter each resource in its own row in Resource Sheet view.

TIP

The column titles displayed in a sheet are determined by the active table.

Figure 4-2 provides a description of each default field (column title) available in the Entry table.

Figure 4-2	Fields in Resource Sheet view

Field	Description
Indicators	A field that automatically displays small icons to represent various conditions about the resource. For example, a note icon indicates that a note is stored about the resource.
Resource Name	A field that stores the resource name entered by the user.
Type	A field that specifies whether a resource is a Work (hourly) resource, Material (consumable) resource, or Cost resource. Work resources have associated hourly costs and include people, rooms, and equipment. Material resources include building materials or supplies. Cost resources include multiple arbitrary costs (not based on work time); you use custom fields to specify a resource as a cost type. Identifying a resource as a Cost type allows you to more accurately monitor project finances. You can assign a financial code to a Cost resource that allows you to keep your project in sync with data in accounting systems. This field is used to filter and find Work, Material, and Cost resources.
Material	A field that stores a material label, which can be displayed and printed on various views and reports.
Initials	A field that stores an initials entry that can be used to identify resources instead of the longer entry in the Resource Name field, such as YN for Your Name.
Group	A field that stores an entry used to define groups of resources. You create the designation. For example, you can assign a Group, such as Mgmt, to each resource associated with management, or Temp for all temporary workers. You can use the field to filter, find, and report all resources in a group.
Max.	This field determines the maximum number of units or portion of a unit of the resource that is available for the project. By default, the Max. Units field is 100%. If a resource is available on, for example, a half-time basis, the entry will be 50%. If the resource entry contains multiple units, such as the General Labor resource that might include more than one laborer, then the entry will reflect the number of units, such as 200% for two people or 500% for five people assigned to the same resource.
Std. Rate	This field identifies the standard hourly rate for a single resource of that type. By default, the Std. Rate and Ovt. Rate entries are costs per hour. You can override this assumption by entering the value and a new unit of measure as follows: /m (per minute), /d (per day), /w (per week), /mon (per month), or /y (per year).
Ovt. Rate	This field identifies the overtime hourly rate for a single resource of that type. Project does not calculate the cost of additional work hours by using the overtime rates that you entered until you specify those hours as overtime work.
Cost/Use	This field identifies the one-time cost per use for a single resource of that type. This cost may be used with or instead of hourly charges. For example, some resources might charge a flat fee for a service regardless of the number of hours of service that are rendered. An initial consultation with an attorney might fit into this category. Other resources, such as a rental car, might charge a minimum fee plus a daily or hourly rate.
Accrue	This field determines when the costs associated with that resource will be applied to any task to which it has been assigned. Three choices are available for this field: Start, Prorated, and End. Prorated is the default entry. If a resource has costs that must be paid at the start or end of the project, you would change the default to either Start or End for the resource to more accurately reflect the costs that have been committed for that task.
Base	This field determines which base calendar the resource calendar uses to determine working and nonworking time. By default, Project 2010 provides three base calendars: Standard, Night Shift, and 24 Hours. Standard is the default choice for the Base field.
Code	This field contains any code, number, or abbreviation that you want to enter to help identify that resource. This field is often used to identify the resource's cost center.

Emily has made a list of resources that will be used for the AV presentation rooms installation project. You'll use the list to enter and edit resources in Resource Sheet view. You will assign these resources to tasks later in this tutorial.

To enter resources in Resource Sheet view:

▶ **1.** Open the **AV-4** project file located in the **Project4\Tutorial** folder included with your Data Files, and then save the file as **NewAV-4** in the same folder. The project file opens in Gantt Chart view and includes 28 linked tasks in six phases.

▶ **2.** Scroll through the tasks to view the project, and then, in the Entry table, click **Analysis (task 1)**.

▶ **3.** Click the **View** tab, and then, in the Resource Views group, click the **Resource Sheet** button. Resource Sheet view is the preferred way of entering new resources because it provides so many more columns in which to enter information about a new resource.

▶ **4.** Point to the **Select All** button. The ScreenTip tells you that the Entry table is applied, that this is Resource Sheet view, and that you right-click to select and change tables by choosing a different table (such as Cost, Hyperlink, Summary, Usage, or Work) from the shortcut menu.

▶ **5.** Right-click the **Indicators** column heading, and then click **Hide Column**. You hid the Indicators column at this time so the screen will be less cluttered as you enter the resources. Refer back to Figure 4-2 for an explanation of each field (column) as you enter information in the resource sheet.

▶ **6.** Click the **Resource Name** cell in row 1, type **Emily Michaels**, and then press the **Tab** key. Values are automatically entered in many of the columns.

▶ **7.** Press the **Tab** key twice, type **EM**, press the **Tab** key, type **Mgmt**, press the **Tab** key twice, type **100**, and then press the **Enter** key. Emily is added as resource 1. Enter the next two work resources, as shown in Figure 4-3. Make sure to enter your name and your initials in row 2.

| Figure 4-3 | Three resources entered into the resource sheet |

enter your name and your initials in the second row

resources are Work Resource types

the General Labor resource consists of many people; greater than 100% means that a resource has more than one unit assigned to a task. In the example, five people (500%) have been assigned to the General Labor resource.

enter standard and overtime rates for the third row

You edit entries in Resource Sheet view by clicking the cell that you want to edit and then typing the change, or by choosing an option from the drop-down list associated with the selected cell. Sidney asks you to edit the group field for the General Labor resource. You will do this by typing the new group name directly in the field. You also will enter an additional resource.

To edit resources in Resource Sheet view:

▶ **1.** Click **Labor** in the Group column in row 3 for the General Labor resource, type **Temp**, and then press the **Enter** key. This replaces the group "Labor" with a group named "Temp" that will be used to track and report all temporary resources (people) that are hired for this project.

▶ **2.** Enter the Coordinator resource information in row 4, as shown in Figure 4-4.

Figure 4-4   Entering and editing resources in the resource sheet

Group changed to Temp

new resource entered in row 4

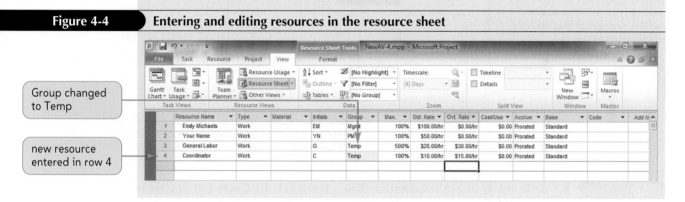

The resource sheet for ViewPoint Partners has four resources entered, and corrections have been made to one of the entries.

Exploring Resource Information

You can view Resource Information in a variety of ways, including the Resource Information dialog box, the Resource Sheet view, and the Resource Task Form.

Exploring the Resource Information Dialog Box

The Resource Information dialog box is a comprehensive collection of all of the data stored for a single resource. The data is organized on four tabs: General, Costs, Notes, and Custom Fields. It is analogous to the Task Information dialog box for a task. Some fields, such as Email and Resource Availability (on the General tab), Cost rate tables (on the Costs tab), and Notes (on the Notes tab), are available only in the Resource Information dialog box.

You take a quick look at the Resource Information dialog box before you continue to enter and edit the resources for ViewPoint Partners' installation project.

To enter information using the Resource Information dialog box:

▶ **1.** Double-click **Coordinator** (resource 4). The Resource Information dialog box opens.

▶ **2.** Click the **General** tab if it is not already selected, as shown in Figure 4-5.

Figure 4-5 **Resource Information dialog box**

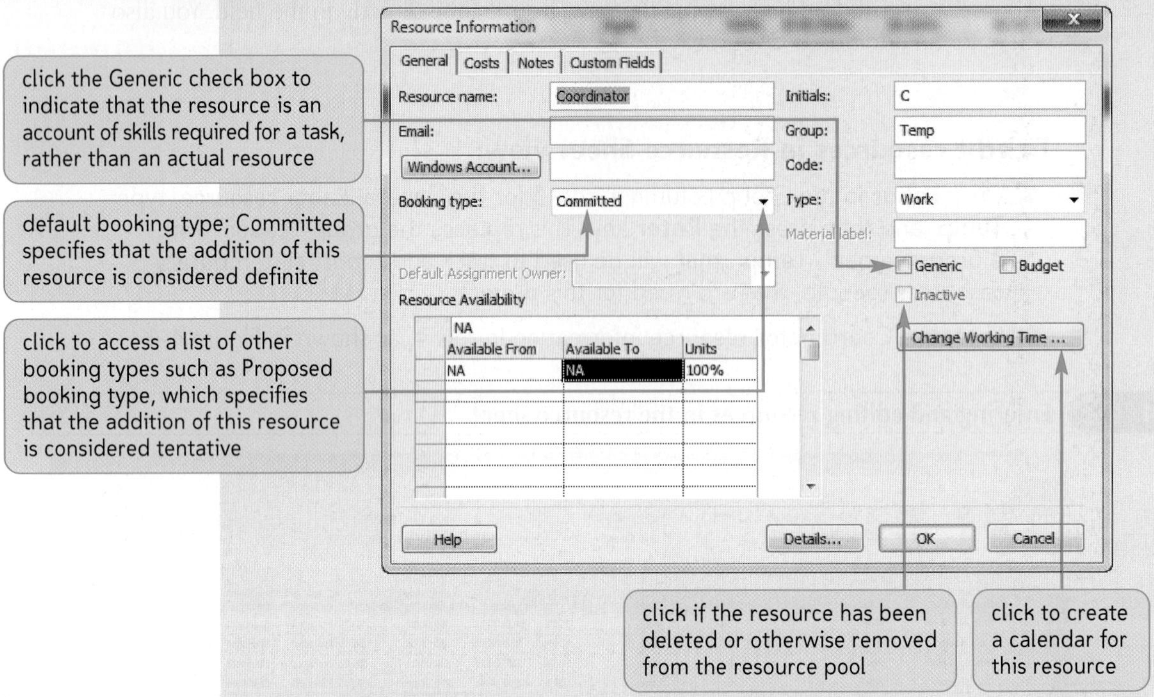
click the Generic check box to indicate that the resource is an account of skills required for a task, rather than an actual resource
default booking type; Committed specifies that the addition of this resource is considered definite
click to access a list of other booking types such as Proposed booking type, which specifies that the addition of this resource is considered tentative
Resource Information
General
Costs
Notes
Custom Fields
Resource name:
Coordinator
Initials:
C
Email:
Group:
Temp
Windows Account...
Code:
Booking type:
Committed
Type:
Work
Material label:
Generic
Budget
Default Assignment Owner:
Inactive
Resource Availability
NA
Available From
Available To
Units
NA
NA
100%
Change Working Time ...
Help
Details...
OK
Cancel
click if the resource has been deleted or otherwise removed from the resource pool
click to create a calendar for this resource

TIP

Select a resource, click the Resource tab, and then click the Information button in the Properties group to open its Resource Information dialog box.

3. In the Resource Information dialog box, click the **Costs** tab, review the fields, click the **Notes** tab, review the fields, click the **Custom Fields** tab, and then click the **General** tab. Each tab provides different information about the selected resource.
4. Click the **Cancel** button to close the Resource Information dialog box for the Coordinator resource.
5. Double-click **Emily Michaels** (resource 1). The Resource Information dialog box opens with the General tab selected. You want to edit her resource information.
6. Click in the **Email** box, and then type **EMich@VPP2014.com**. Emily's email address is entered as part of her resource information.

You have just heard that Emily will be on vacation for a week in September. Next, you will record that Emily will not be working while she is on vacation.

To use the Resource Information dialog box to change working time:

1. Click the **Change Working Time** button to open the Change Working Time dialog box. You can use this dialog box to specify the working time for each resource. The Change Working Time dialog box for a resource works in a similar manner to the Change Working Time dialog box for a task. You can base the working time for a resource on the Standard calendar or any other calendar in the Project file.
2. Scroll the calendar to display **September 2014**.
3. Click the **Exceptions** tab if it is not selected, click in the top **Name** box, type **Vacation**, and then press the **Tab** key.
4. Click the **Start** box in the first row, click the **arrow** that appears, click **September 15, 2014** on the calendar, and then click in the **Finish** box. Now you need to set this vacation time as five days of nonworking time.

5. Click the **Details** button to open the Details for 'Vacation' dialog box.

6. Verify that the **Nonworking** option button is selected, click the **End by** option button, click the **date** arrow to display the calendar, click **19** to select **September 19, 2014** on the calendar, and then click the **OK** button to close the Details for 'Vacation' dialog box. You see the week of September 15–19 is high-lighted in blue, showing that this week is an exception defined on the Exceptions tab. See Figure 4-6.

| Figure 4-6 | Change Working Time dialog box for Emily Michaels |

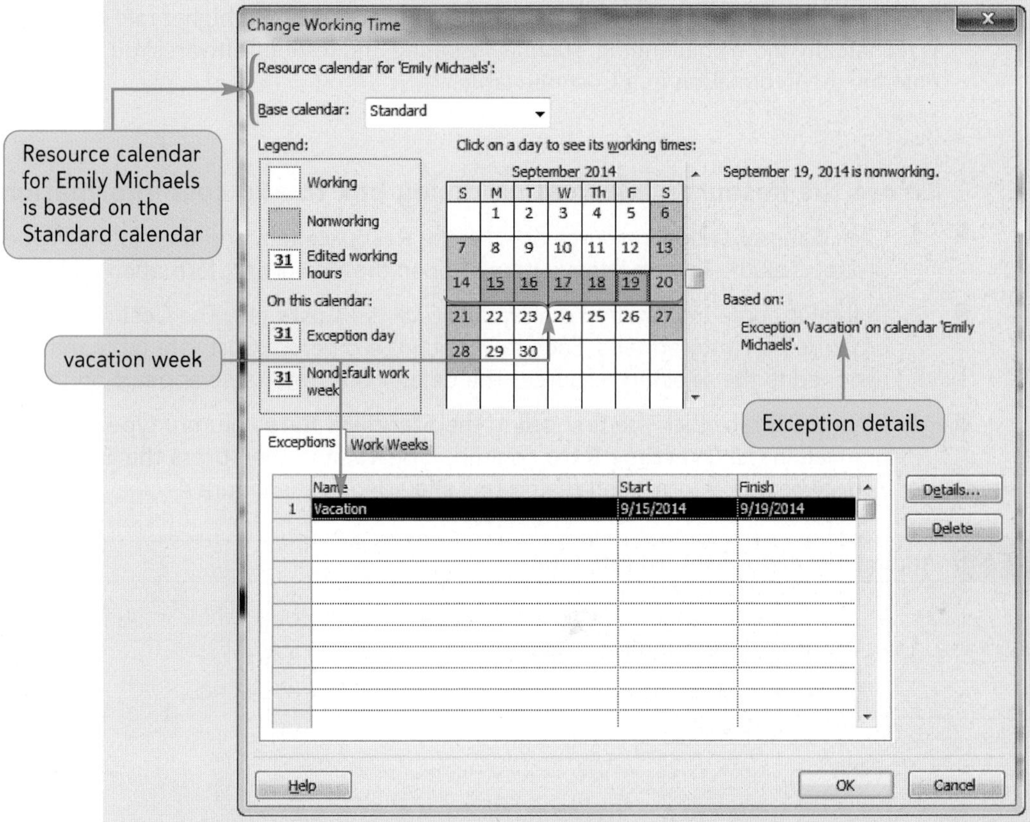

7. Click the **OK** button to close the Change Working Time dialog box. The Resource Information dialog box for Emily Michaels is on your screen. You also want to be able to reach Emily when she's out of the office, so you store her cell phone number along with the other resource information.

8. In the Resource Information dialog box, click the **Notes** tab, click in the **Notes** box, type **Emily's cell phone: 917-555-7373**, and then click the **OK** button. The Resource Information dialog box closes.

Sometimes one resource is responsible for tasks that have different costs associated with them. In this situation, you can also assign different costs to a single resource using the Resource Information dialog box. You can account for discrepancies in the cost levels by using a Cost rate table. A **Cost rate table** is a grid of different hourly and per-use costs that can be stored for a single resource. Project 2010 provides five rate tables (Table A–Table E) for each resource to support varying pay scales and rates. For example, if you were build-ing or renovating a house, you might hire a contractor to help with the finish work. This contractor would be a single resource. However, the contractor might send less expensive labor to clear out the debris from a demolition. That same contractor might then send more skilled labor to trim the rooms. You know that skilled labor is more costly, so you can assign different costs for the same contractor depending on the task being done for the project. Or, if a programmer charges $150/hour for complex programming, $120/hour for standard programming, and $100/hour for meeting time, you can apply three rate tables to the programmer resource. By storing these different rates in the project, you can apply the same resource to many different tasks, but the costs associated with that resource will be calculated according to the chosen rate.

General Labor is a resource that will be contracted from HelpMeRita, an agency that provides temporary employees. The agency has different cost rates that apply depending on the nature of the work. You have already entered the standard rate of $20 per hour with an overtime rate of $30 per hour. You need to enter a higher rate for work that is technically more challenging, such as installing and testing software. You do this by entering the information in a Cost rate table.

To use the Resource Information dialog box to add cost information:

▶ **1.** Click **General Labor** (resource 3), click the **Resource** tab, and then in the Properties group, click the **Information** button to open the Resource Information dialog box.

▶ **2.** In the Resource Information dialog box, click the **Costs** tab. The Cost rate tables are organized on lettered tabs. Each tab contains a different Cost rate table that can be assigned to the selected resource. The default Cost rate table appears on the A tab.

▶ **3.** Click the **B** tab, click the first cell in the **Standard Rate** column, type **30**, click the first cell in the **Overtime Rate** column, type **45**, and then press the **Enter** key. Your Resource Information dialog box should look like Figure 4-7.

| **Figure 4-7** | **Adding new rates in a Cost rate table** |

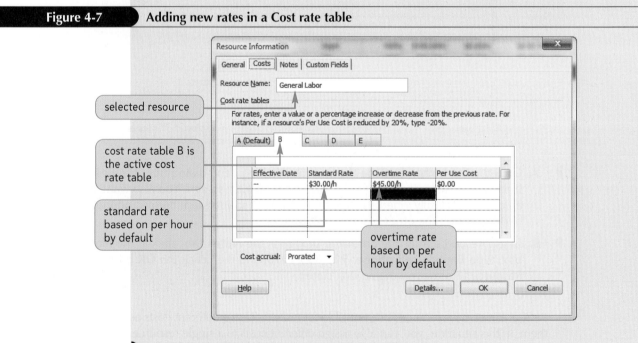

▶ **4.** Click the **OK** button to close the dialog box.

Using the Resource Sheet View to Group Resource Information

A Group By feature is available in Resource Sheet view. You use the Group By feature to get a logical view of the project resources based on groups. Grouping options include No Group, Assignments Keeping Outline Structure, Complete and Incomplete Resources, Resource Group, Resource Type, and Standard Rate. If you click the More Groups option, the More Groups dialog box opens and offers the following additional group: Work vs. Material Resources. Emily has asked you to use the grouping feature to view the resources by group.

To group resources using the Resource Group By command:

1. Click the **View** tab. Notice in the Data group that [No Group] is selected by default.

2. Click the **Group By** arrow. The list of grouping options opens. You can select one of the built-in groups or you can create a custom group.

3. Click **Resource Group**. The resources are organized in the Resource Sheet view based on the Group type that you specified. See Figure 4-8.

Figure 4-8   Grouping resources based on group type

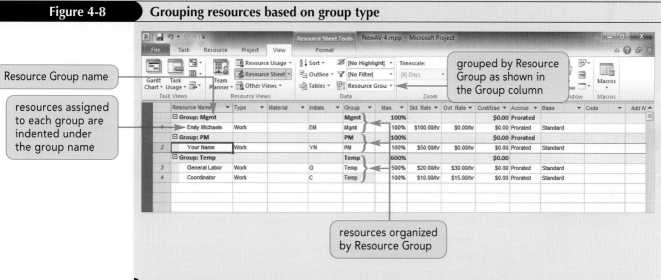

4. In the Data group on the View tab, click the **Group By** arrow, and then click **[No Group]**. Resource Sheet view is ungrouped.

Resource Availability

As a project progresses, you might find that you have to make a change to a resource's availability midway through the project. For example, a resource might be available only part time or for specific dates.

ViewPoint Partners is involved in a local charity that inspects and repairs furnaces for senior citizens. Sidney has asked you to spend 50 percent of your time overseeing this charitable project during the month of October. When you are working for this charity you cannot be working on the AV Presentation Rooms Installation project, so time needs to be blocked off regarding your availability. You change your work availability for the AV Presentation Rooms Installation project using the Resource Information dialog box.

TIP

Many Project 2010 dialog boxes have an Entry bar where you can enter or edit data.

To change the resource's availability:

1. Double-click **your name** (the resource in row 2), and then click the **General** tab in the Resource Information dialog box.

   The Resource Availability table is at the bottom of the General tab. The box at the top of the table is the Entry bar. You use the Available From and Available To cells in the table to enter the Resource availability. If NA is entered in the Available From cell, the resource is available beginning with the project start date. If NA is entered in the Available To cell, the resource is available until the project Finish date. Any exceptions are entered in subsequent rows. By default, the Available From and Available To cells are set to NA.

2. In the first row of the Resource Availability table, click the **Available To** cell, click the **arrow** that appears, scroll to display **September 2014**, and then click **30** on the September 2014 calendar.

3. In the second row of the table, click the **Available From** cell, click in the **Entry bar**, type **10/1/2014**, click the **Available To** cell in the same row, and then type **11/1/2014** in the Entry bar.

4. Click the **Enter** button on the Entry bar, click the **Units** cell in the second row, type **50**, and then press the **Enter** key. By entering 50% units, you specify a part-time availability from 10/1/14 to 11/1/14.

5. Click the third **Available From cell**, type **11/2/2014**, click the **Available To** cell in the same row, type **NA**, click the **Units** cell in the third row, type **100**, and then press the **Enter** key.

   You are available at 100 percent again beginning 11/2/14. See Figure 4-9.

Figure 4-9   **Changing resource availability**

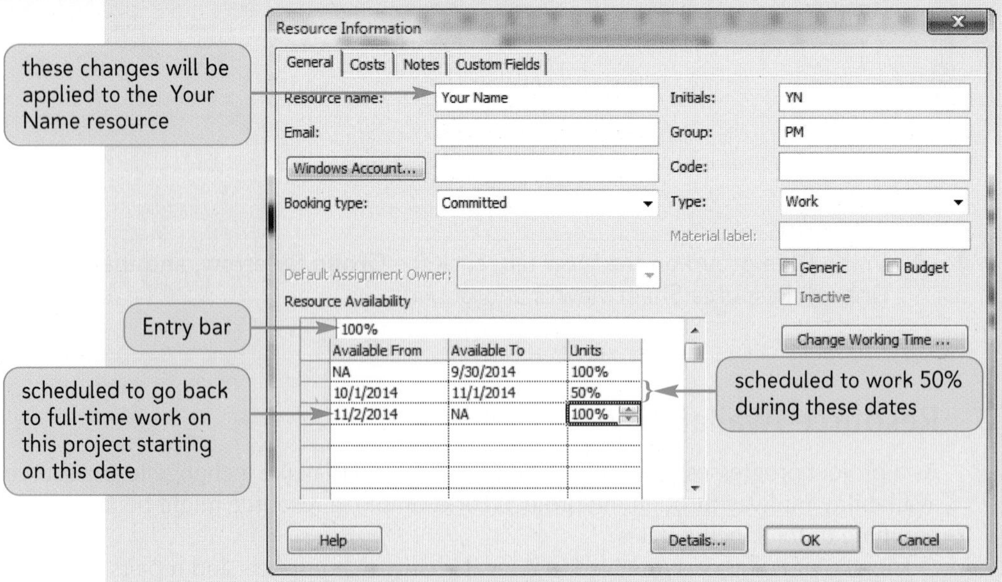

TIP

Tutorial 6 teaches how to pass and share resource information among projects.

You have also learned that as of January 1, 2015, you will be assigned a new rate for all projects and will be scheduled for overtime hours at a higher hourly rate. You decide to record that information in this project.

To change the resource's cost rate:

▶ 1. Click the **Costs** tab. The rate you entered in the resource sheet appears in cost table A.

▶ 2. Click in the **row 2 Effective Date** column, type **1/1/2015** in the Entry bar, click in the **row 2 Standard Rate** column, and then type **60**. Next, you enter the overtime rate, which is the same as the standard rate.

▶ 3. Click in the **row 2 Overtime Rate** column, type **60**, and then press the **Enter** key. Your Resource Information dialog box should look similar to Figure 4-10.

| Figure 4-10 | Entering the new rate |

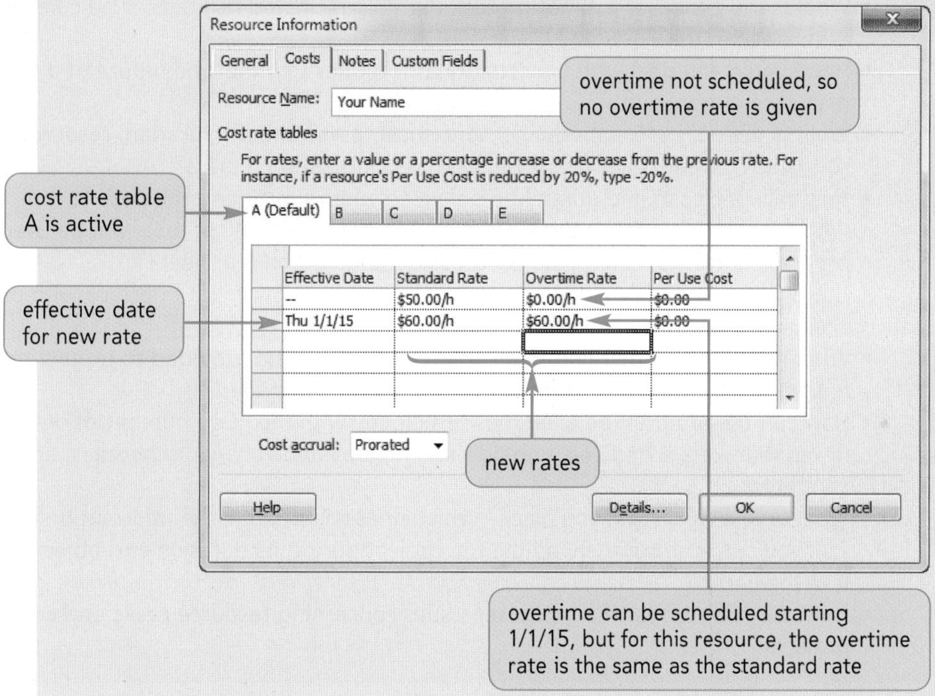

▶ 4. Click the **OK** button, and then click the **Save** button 🖫 on the Quick Access toolbar to save your changes to the file. The new rate will be applied to any project using this Cost rate table starting on January 1, 2015.

Entering resource information into a project takes considerable effort. Remember, the more time you put into these initial entry points, the more accurate the entire project will be. As you have seen, you can track many fields of information about each resource. Fortunately, the most commonly used fields are presented in the Entry table of the resource sheet. The others, such as Email, Resource Availability, Cost rate tables, and Notes, are found by opening the Resource Information dialog box. After the resource data has been entered, you can start assigning resources to specific tasks. Project 2010 automatically calculates task costs by multiplying task durations by the cost information supplied for each resource.

PROSKILLS

Teamwork: Working Together for Successful Project Management

Obviously, there is more to successful project management than mastering the features of a software management tool. It requires organizational support such as a reasonable budget, access to appropriate resources, and a supportive corporate infrastructure that might involve extensive computer networks. Also, the personal characteristics of the project manager are very important. These characteristics include an overall understanding and commitment to the project, attention to detail, self-discipline, and an ability to manage many competing forces.

You will want to work closely with your team as you consider many general project management issues that arise during a project. Some of these determine how you will use and document the project details in project management software. These decisions also have a large impact on the project's success. Project management issues that you might want to explore with your team further include the following:

- To what level of detail should tasks be consolidated or separated in the project?
- What factors are used to determine a summary task?
- What is the policy for estimating task durations? Should risk factors be considered in the calculation of the duration?
- How should you deal with uncertainty as it relates to either the nature of a task or the resources assigned to it?
- What is the policy for scheduling noncritical tasks? Should duration, resources, predecessors, slack, or any other factor be used to prioritize such tasks?
- How will risk, cost, and quality be balanced when shortening the path?
- Who is responsible for updating progress on a project? What tools will be used to gather progress data? How often will progress be updated on a project?
- How will the work breakdown structure be set up? How will it interface with other accounting systems in your business?
- What reports and other communication tools should be provided to project members and management? How often should these reports be provided?
- How can the program be used most efficiently with the huge number of details involved in variable work schedules, unpaid time, holiday and vacation schedules, and union contracts?
- What actual values will you track? Which ones will provide the information needed so that you can appropriately adjust the project during its duration and objectively evaluate it at the end?
- How will you address the multiuser issues concerning resource pools and consolidated projects?

Assigning Resources to Tasks

Now that you have created a general list of resources in your project file, it is time to assign them to specific tasks. The initial resource assignment is critical because in effort-driven tasks the duration won't change if you assign all the resources at the same time. You can always add resources to a task, but, as you add resources, the duration will change unless you remove the check mark from the Effort driven check box. Project 2010 is designed to give you great flexibility in the way that you enter data. Many methods are available to assign resources to specific tasks. Using the Assign Resources button on the Resource tab in the Assignments group is probably the fastest method. Using a resource form in the bottom pane in split screen view is another. Seasoned project managers often prefer this approach because it provides resource information at a glance, such as the actual hours of work assigned to each task. You'll use both techniques to assign resources to tasks.

REFERENCE

Assigning Resources to Tasks Using the Assign Resources Button

- Open the project in Gantt Chart view (or any view in which tasks are displayed in the Entry table).
- Click the Resource tab, and then in the Level group, click the Leveling Options button.
- In the Resource Leveling dialog box, set the Leveling calculations to automatic if you want Project to automatically level resources or to manual if you do not want Project to manually level resources.
- Click the task to which you want to assign a resource.
- Click the Resource tab, and then, in the Assignments group, click the Assign Resources button to open the Assign Resources dialog box.
- Click the resource that you want to assign in the Assign Resources dialog box, and then click the Assign button (or drag the resource selector button to the task in the Entry table to which it should be assigned).
- Click the Close button.

You can use the Assign Resources dialog box to assign resources to a task or to enter new resources. Double-clicking a resource in the Assign Resources dialog box opens the Resource Information dialog box, which you use to edit existing resources. As you assign tasks to resources, the cost information is presented in the Cost column to help you budget for the task and project. You can use the Resource list options button in the Assign Resources dialog box to show or hide filtered information.

INSIGHT

Getting the Most Out of the Assign Resources Dialog Box

When assigning resources, particularly in large projects with many resources, the Assign Resources dialog box offers several tools that can help you with the task. The filter options allow you to better assign resources if you want the resources to meet specific criteria for a task. Click the Resource list options button to filter by various criteria, including when a resource is available to work. The R/D column is used to specify whether a resource is a Request or a Demand. When preparing projects for resource substitution, use this column to specify whether the selected resource must do the task or whether any resource with the required skills can do the task.

To assign resources using the Assign Resources dialog box:

1. Click the **Resource** tab, and then, in the Level group, click the **Leveling Options** button. The Resource Leveling dialog box opens.

2. In the Leveling calculations section, click the **Manual** option button so that Project will not level calculations automatically, and then click the **OK** button to close the Resource Leveling dialog box.

3. Click the **View** tab, and then, in the Task Views group, click the **Gantt Chart** button.

4. Click the **Resource** tab, and then, in the Assignments group, click the **Assign Resources** button to open the Assign Resources dialog box, as shown in Figure 4-11.

Figure 4-11   **Using the Assign Resources dialog box**

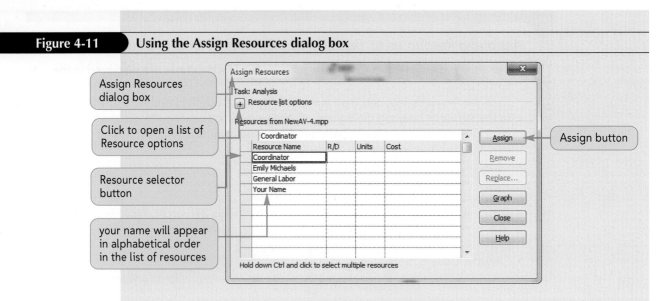

Assign Resources dialog box

Click to open a list of Resource options

Resource selector button

your name will appear in alphabetical order in the list of resources

Assign button

5. In the Entry table, click **Detail current status** (task 2).

6. In the Assign Resources dialog box, click **your name**, and then click the **Assign** button. This assigns you as a resource to task 2. The resources in the Assign Resources dialog box have been rearranged so the resource assigned to task 2 is listed first. A check mark appears in the Resource selector button to indicate you have been assigned to the task. The cost column tells you the cost for that task. In the Gantt chart, your name appears next to the task 2 bar.

7. In the Entry table, click **Conduct needs analysis** (task 3), in the Assign Resources dialog box, click **your name** (if it is not already selected), and then click the **Assign** button. This assigns you as a resource to task 3. You can assign more than one resource to a task at the same time.

8. In the Entry table, click **Build Request for Proposal** (task 6), in the Assign Resources dialog box click **Emily Michaels**, press and hold the **Ctrl** key, click **your name**, release the **Ctrl** key, and then click the **Assign** button.

Your screen should look like Figure 4-12. You have been assigned to task 2 and task 3, and both you and Emily have been assigned to task 6. Resource names appear to the right of the task bar in the Gantt chart.

Trouble? If the duration on your screen for task 6 does not match the duration in the figure, you assigned resources one at a time rather than both resources at the same time. Click the Undo button to remove the assignments and redo step 8.

TIP

The Gantt chart displays resource names to the right of the task bar (by default). You can change this formatting choice by using the Bar Styles dialog box.

Be sure both resources are selected before clicking the Assign button to ensure they are assigned as the initial resources.

Figure 4-12   Resources assigned

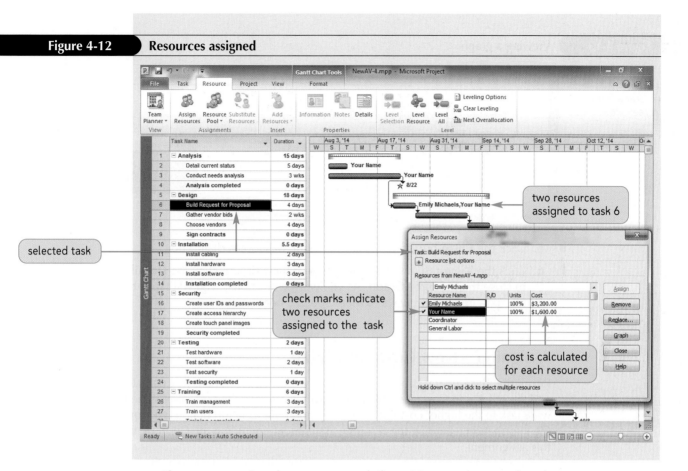

selected task

check marks indicate two resources assigned to the task

two resources assigned to task 6

cost is calculated for each resource

If you want to view the resource work (hours) in a graph, you select the resources you want to graph, and then click the Graph button in the Assign Resources dialog box.

To change units using the Assign Resources dialog box and display a graph:

1. In the Entry table, click **Install software** (task 13), and then, in the Assign Resources dialog box, click the **Units** cell for General Labor.

2. In the Units cell, type **200**, and then click the **Assign** button. The maximum unit of a resource is 100%, but some resources consist of more than one unit that can be applied to a task. You have five General Labor units available for assignment to various tasks in this project. Two general labor workers have been assigned full-time to the Install software task.

3. In the Assign Resources dialog box, click the **Graph** button. The Resource Graph pane opens below the Gantt Chart view.

4. Drag the **Assign Resources** dialog box off the graph, and then scroll the graph to display the week of September 14. The General Labor resource graph for the selected task appears, as shown in Figure 4-13.

TIP

If the Assign Resources dialog box is on top of the task you want to view in the Entry table, drag it out of the way.

TIP

You can also click the Details box in the Split View group on the View tab, click the Details arrow, and then select Resource Graph to open the Resource Graph Form.

Figure 4-13   **Viewing a graph**

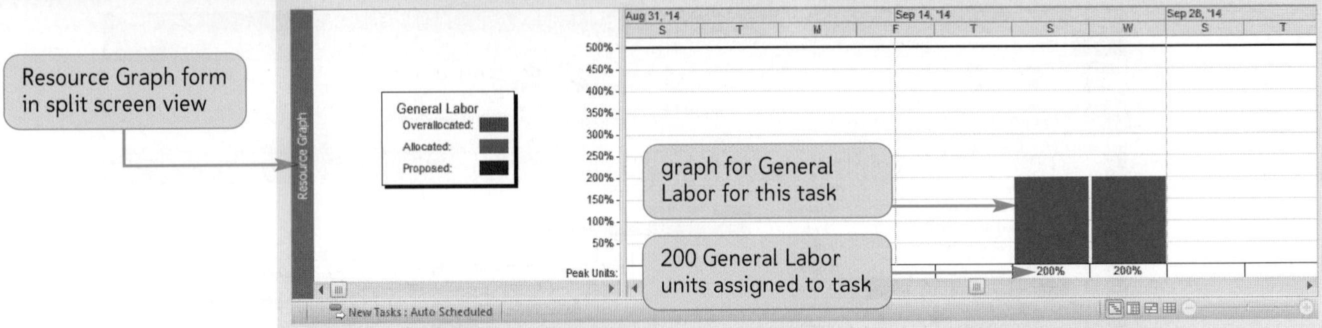

Resource Graph form
in split screen view

graph for General
Labor for this task

200 General Labor
units assigned to task

5. Click the **Close** button to close the Assign Resources dialog box.

6. Click the **View** tab, and then, in the Split View group, click the **Details** check box to close the Resource Graph. As you work with Project you will learn how to view the data in different ways to meet specific needs.

Assigning a New Cost Rate Table

Recall that the General Labor resource has two cost rates. One is in Cost rate table A, and the other is in Cost rate table B. You want to change the cost rate for the Install software task to the higher cost rate. The Assignment Information dialog box contains all of the information regarding the resource assignment, including the Cost rate table used for this assignment.

Based on a review of the resources, you know that you have to pay the General Labor resources at a higher rate for the Install software task. You have to change the Cost rate table for the General Labor resource to Cost rate table B.

To change the Cost rate table for a task using Task Usage view:

TIP

The Task Usage button is also on the status bar.

1. In the Task Views group on the View tab, click the **Task Usage** button to open Task Usage view. Notice that the resources you assigned appear below their tasks in the Entry table in the left pane of Task Usage view, and the number of hours needed for each resource is shown in a day-by-day format in the right pane. Also, if a red indicator appears in the Indicators column, you know that at least one resource assigned to this task is overallocated. You will learn more about overallocations later in the tutorial.

2. In the Usage table, click **General Labor** (the resource assigned to task 13), click the **Task** tab, and then, in the Editing group, click the **Scroll to Task** button. The usage details for task 13 scroll into view in the table on the right, as shown in Figure 4-14.

Figure 4-14 Task Usage view

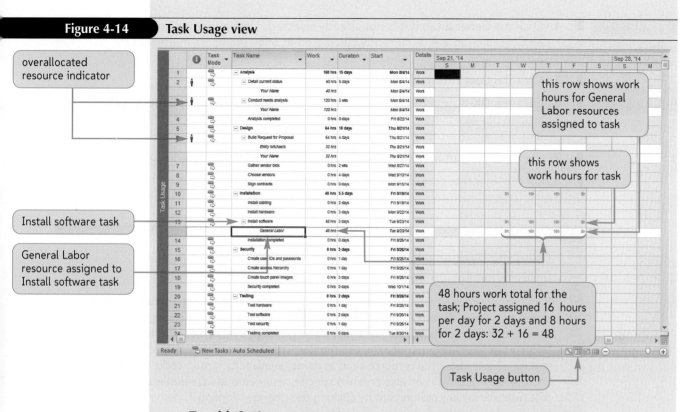

overallocated resource indicator

this row shows work hours for General Labor resources assigned to task

this row shows work hours for task

Install software task

General Labor resource assigned to Install software task

48 hours work total for the task; Project assigned 16 hours per day for 2 days and 8 hours for 2 days: 32 + 16 = 48

Task Usage button

Trouble? If your screen does not match the figure, you might need to drag the split bar left or right.

3. Double-click **General Labor**. The Assignment Information dialog box opens. See Figure 4-15.

Figure 4-15 Assignment Information dialog box

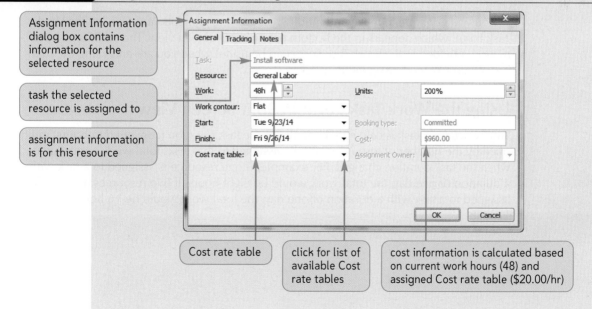

Assignment Information dialog box contains information for the selected resource

task the selected resource is assigned to

assignment information is for this resource

Cost rate table

click for list of available Cost rate tables

cost information is calculated based on current work hours (48) and assigned Cost rate table ($20.00/hr)

TIP

The information in dimmed boxes cannot be changed in the Assignment Information dialog box.

▶ **4.** Click the **General** tab if it is not already selected. Notice that the cost, based on Cost rate table A, is currently calculated at $960 (48 hours multiplied by $20 per hour).

▶ **5.** Click the **Cost rate table** arrow, and then click **B**.

▶ **6.** Click the **OK** button to apply the change, and then double-click **General Labor** to reopen the Assignment Information dialog box. Cost rate table B is now assigned, and the resource cost is calculated at $1440 (48 hours at $30 per hour).

▶ **7.** Click the **OK** button to close the Assignment Information dialog box.

▶ **8.** On the View tab, click the **Gantt Chart** button, and then save your changes.

INSIGHT

Using the Assignment Information Dialog Box vs. the Resource Information Dialog Box

If you double-click a resource name in a Task Usage sheet, the Assignment Information dialog box opens. If you double-click a resource name in a resource sheet, the Resource Information dialog box opens. You could also right-click a resource and then click Information in either situation. You use the Resource Information dialog box to enter specific details about the resource such as name, availability, group code, initials, and booking type. You can also create a specific resource calendar that will apply to that resource for any assignment by clicking the Change Working Time button in the Resource Information dialog box and entering any working time exceptions. The information in the Resource Information dialog box is applied every time you assign that resource to any task. You use the Assignment Information dialog box to make specific changes for the active resource, including number of units; work assigned, completed, or remaining; and which cost rate table is applied. The Notes tab is helpful to enter any notes you might have for this resource.

You will continue to make and modify resource assignments. You will use the Work Task Form, which appears in the bottom pane in split screen view. The additional information provided in the Work Task Form can be useful when you are analyzing the number of hours of work assigned to a task.

Using the Work Task Form in Split Screen View

Total work for a task is calculated initially as the task duration (converted to hours) multiplied by the number of resources initially assigned to that task. Total work is recalculated when the task duration changes. For example, if one resource is assigned to a task with a duration of one day, the total work would be eight hours. If two resources are initially assigned to a task with a duration of one day, the total work would be 16 hours.

REFERENCE

Assigning Resources to Tasks Using Split Screen View

- Open the project in Gantt Chart view or any view in which the task Entry table is displayed.
- Click the View tab, and then, in the Split View group, click the Details check box.
- In the bottom pane, right-click the form, and then click Work to open the Work Task Form.
- In the Entry table in the top pane, click the task that you want to work with so that its resource information is displayed in the Work Task Form in the bottom pane.
- In the Work Task Form, click the next available row in the Resource Name column, and then type a resource or select one from the list.
- In the Work Task Form, assign resource units and modify work for the resource you added.
- When you are finished modifying the resources for an individual task, click the OK button in the Work Task Form.

Emily asks you to assign resources to the tasks in order to see the changes to the work and duration fields. You will use the Work Task Form to accomplish this task.

To use the Work Task Form to make resource assignments:

1. In the Entry table, click **Conduct needs analysis** (task 3), and then, in the Split View group on the View tab, click the **Details** check box. Gantt Chart view is in the top pane, and a form appears in the bottom pane.

2. Right-click the form, and then click **Work**. The Work Task Form opens, as shown in Figure 4-16.

Figure 4-16   **Work Task Form displayed in a split view**

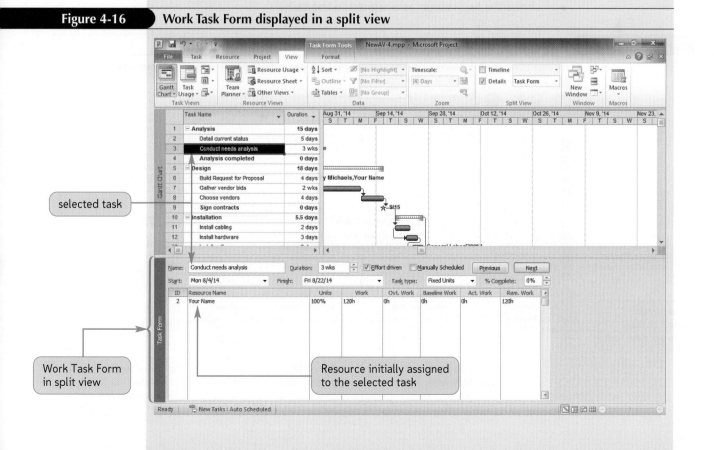

selected task

Work Task Form in split view

Resource initially assigned to the selected task

TIP

You can't see the outline of a cell in a form until you click in the cell.

3. In the Entry table, click **Gather vendor bids** (task 7).

4. In the Work Task Form, click the **first cell** in the Resource Name column, click the **arrow** that appears, and then click **your name**.

5. Click the **OK** button in the Work Task Form. In a form view, the resource assignment isn't finished until you click the OK button in the form. Notice that the duration for this task is two weeks. The work field is calculated at 80 hours, which equals one person working eight hours per day for two weeks.

6. In the Work Task Form, click the **Next** button to select **Choose vendors (task 8)**. You want to be involved in this task, so you assign yourself as the initial resource for this task.

7. In the Work Task Form, click the **first cell** in the Resource Name column, click the **arrow** that appears, click **your name**, and then press the **Enter** key. The information for the rest of the fields in the row is filled in. Pressing the Enter key is the same as pressing the OK button. You are now the initial assignment for this task. You want to add Emily as a second resource.

8. Click the **second cell** in the Resource Name column, click the **arrow**, click **Emily Michaels**, and then click the **OK** button. You and Emily are now assigned as resources to task 8. The initial assignment for this task was you. You were assigned 32 hours of work (4 days) to complete the assignment. Because you pressed the Enter key, any resources you add to the task become an additional resource and Project does not consider them part of the initial assignment. Notice that adding Emily cut the duration in half to 2 days, and each resource will work 16 hours (16 × 2 = 32 = 4 days).

9. Click the **Gantt chart**, click the **Zoom** button, click **Zoom** to open the Zoom dialog box, click the **Entire Project** option button, and then click the **OK** button.

10. Drag the **split bar** so Duration is the last column in the Entry table. Figure 4-17 shows the two resources assigned to the task.

Figure 4-17 | **Using the Work Task Form to assign two resources to a task**

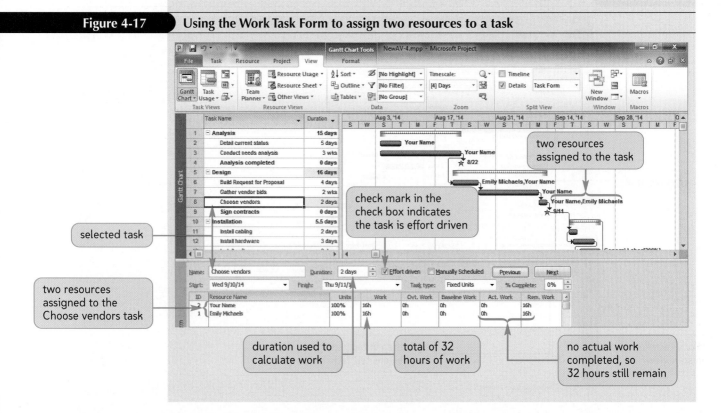

Each resource is assigned 16 hours (the task duration is two working days, which when converted to hours using the Standard calendar is 16 hours). The total work for the Choose vendors task is 32 hours (16 hours multiplied by the two resources). When you start tracking progress and enter values in the Act. Work (Actual Work) column of the Resource Work Task Form, you'll see the value in the Rem. Work (Remaining Work) column automatically recalculated.

You decide to preview the report. You cannot print form views, so the form doesn't appear in the preview screen when you preview the Gantt chart from a split view. However, you can use Task Usage view to preview and print column and row totals.

To print the Task Usage view:

1. Click anywhere in the Entry table, and then, in the Task Views group on the View tab, click the **Task Usage** button. Task Usage view appears above the form.

2. Click anywhere in the Entry table, click the **File** tab, and then, in Backstage view, click **Print**. Notice the Preview pane shows the Task Usage table but not the Work Task Form.

3. In the Print pane, click the **Page Setup** link, and then in the Page Setup – Task Usage dialog box, click the **View** tab.

4. Click the **Print row totals for values within print date range** check box to select it, click the **Print column totals** check box to select it, and then click the **OK** button. The totals are added to the bottom row of the chart on each page.

5. Save your changes to the file.

6. Submit the project file in electronic or printed form, as requested, and then close the project file.

The project planning process is progressing. The tasks and durations are clearly defined, and now you have begun to assign resources to project tasks. In the next session, you'll continue making resource assignments and learn more about the relationship among work, duration, and resource units.

REVIEW

Session 4.1 Quick Check

1. Which view and which table are most commonly used to enter resources?
2. List two ways to assign resources to tasks by using the Resource Assignment dialog box.
3. Explain how you might use the Group field in the resource sheet.
4. Explain how you can use the Max field to record availability information for more than one resource or less than 100 percent availability of a resource.
5. What is the benefit of assigning resources by using the Work Task Form versus the Resource Assignment dialog box?

SESSION 4.2 VISUAL OVERVIEW

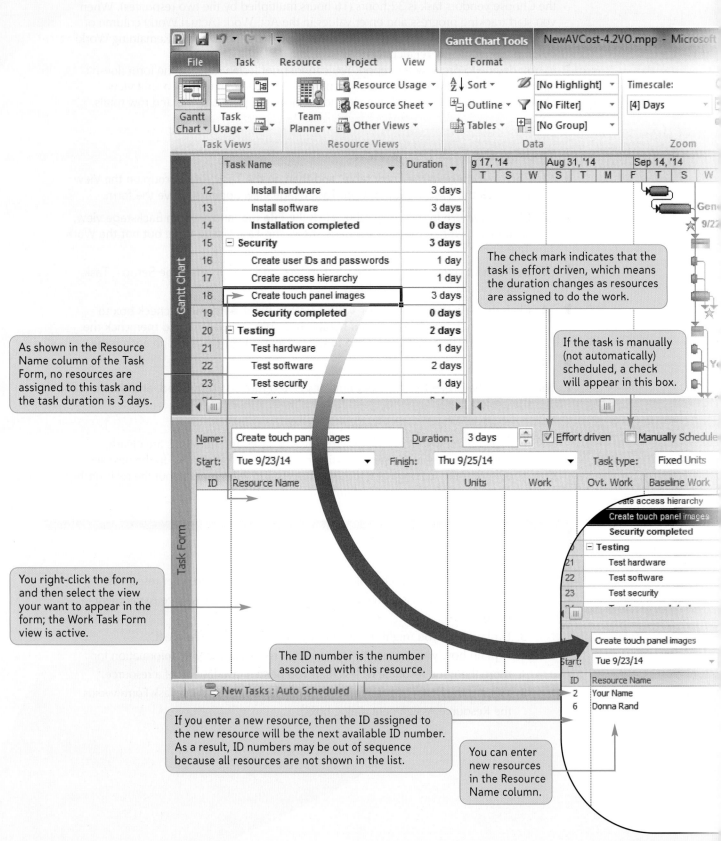

As shown in the Resource Name column of the Task Form, no resources are assigned to this task and the task duration is 3 days.

The check mark indicates that the task is effort driven, which means the duration changes as resources are assigned to do the work.

If the task is manually (not automatically) scheduled, a check will appear in this box.

You right-click the form, and then select the view your want to appear in the form; the Work Task Form view is active.

The ID number is the number associated with this resource.

If you enter a new resource, then the ID assigned to the new resource will be the next available ID number. As a result, ID numbers may be out of sequence because all resources are not shown in the list.

You can enter new resources in the Resource Name column.

HOW WORK AFFECTS DURATION

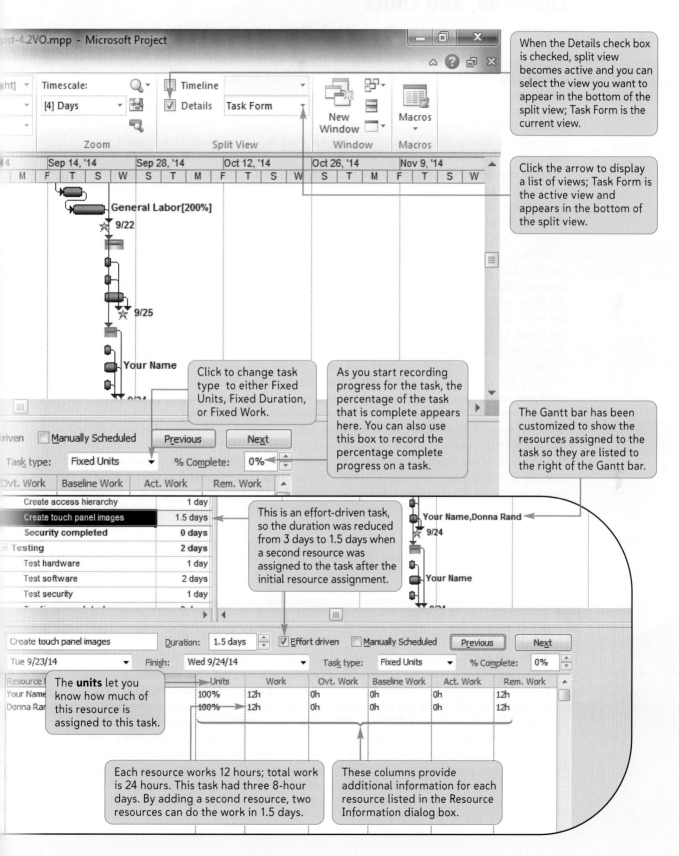

When the Details check box is checked, split view becomes active and you can select the view you want to appear in the bottom of the split view; Task Form is the current view.

Click the arrow to display a list of views; Task Form is the active view and appears in the bottom of the split view.

Click to change task type to either Fixed Units, Fixed Duration, or Fixed Work.

As you start recording progress for the task, the percentage of the task that is complete appears here. You can also use this box to record the percentage complete progress on a task.

The Gantt bar has been customized to show the resources assigned to the task so they are listed to the right of the Gantt bar.

This is an effort-driven task, so the duration was reduced from 3 days to 1.5 days when a second resource was assigned to the task after the initial resource assignment.

The **units** let you know how much of this resource is assigned to this task.

Each resource works 12 hours; total work is 24 hours. This task had three 8-hour days. By adding a second resource, two resources can do the work in 1.5 days.

These columns provide additional information for each resource listed in the Resource Information dialog box.

Understanding the Relationship Among Work, Duration, and Units

Recall that total work for a task is calculated initially as the task duration (converted to hours) multiplied by the number of resources assigned to that task. If you change the duration or the number of resources, it follows that total work is recalculated. Your understanding of the relationship among the total work for the task, the task duration, and the number of resource units assigned to a task is very important in order to manage task schedules and costs. By default, work is calculated in hours and follows this formula: Work = Duration * Units (W=D*U), where the term units refers to resources. You can also rewrite this equation as Duration = Work / Units (D=W/U) to solve for the Duration, rather than calculating for Work.

Some interesting exceptions to this formula exist. First, consider a task that does not yet have a resource assignment. In this situation, the work is calculated as zero hours because zero is substituted for U in the formula. When you complete the formula W=D*U, by substituting the values for D and U, no matter what the value is for D, the result will always be zero because D*0 = 0.

Second, consider the task that has *already* been given an initial resource assignment. For example, you might have a task such as Conduct needs analysis with one resource assigned. When you add a second resource, you double the units. So what happens to the Work = Duration * Units formula in this situation? There are two possibilities. Either the Work value will double or the Duration value will halve so that the equation stays balanced. Usually, the more people assigned to a task, the shorter the task duration should be. When you add additional resource units *after* the initial resource assignment, Project 2010 assumes that the work will remain constant—this forces the duration to change. This assumption is called **effort-driven scheduling**. Work (effort) remains constant and determines (drives) the way that the W = D*U formula will be calculated.

Third, consider the task in which two resources are applied but are not assigned to work the same number of hours on the task—for example, if a task has a duration of one day (eight hours) but you know, based on past experience, that it will require 12 hours to complete. In this situation, you need to assign two resources to the task: one person to work on the task for eight hours (100%) and another person to work on the task for four hours (50%). If you substitute the values into the formula, you get 12 = 8*1.5, where 12 is the work in hours, 8 is the duration in hours, and 1.5 is the units of resources (one at 100% and one at 50%).

Emily reviewed the file and she made some minor changes, such as reassigning resources and changing durations. You will continue to work with the resources in the Project file.

INSIGHT

Assigning Multiple Resources with Effort-Driven Scheduling

When you plan your project, you need to think about each task and the number of resources you need assigned to each task to meet the schedule. For example, you might estimate that the task of painting a house requires 80 hours of total work, so you might assign one person to the job for two weeks. Do you need that job done in one day? Could 10 people complete 80 hours total work in one day? Do you have enough brushes? Will the paint dry in time for a second coat? The answers to these questions vary, but most likely you cannot squeeze an 80-hour job into one day. However, you might be able to assign two people to the job to finish it in one week. You also need to consider the skill level of each resource. For the house painting task, your resources might include skilled painters who work efficiently and quickly as well as novice painters who might take longer and need supervision.

To change the name of a resource:

1. Open the project file **AVCost-4** located in the **Project4\Tutorial** folder included with your Data Files, and then save it as **NewAVCost-4** to the same folder. The project opens in split view, with Gantt Chart view in the top pane and the Work Task Form in the bottom pane. "Your Name" appears as a resource assigned to tasks in the Gantt chart. You will replace Your Name with your own name so that you are listed as an assigned resource.

2. Click the **Resource Sheet** button on the View tab to open Resource Sheet view.

3. In the Resource Name column, click **Your Name**, type your name, press the **Enter** key, click **YN**, type your initials, and then click the **Gantt Chart** button to return to Gantt Chart view. All of the tasks are now updated so that you are listed as a resource.

Sidney Simone has been reviewing the work you and Emily have been doing. In addition to making minor changes to the file, she asks you to see the effect on the task durations if you assign more resources to certain tasks. She wants you to notice that the work hours remain constant but are distributed among the existing and new resources and that the duration is adjusted to reflect the redistribution of hours *after* the initial resource assignment.

To add a resource to a task to see the default relationship among work, duration, and units:

1. In the Entry table, click **Conduct needs analysis** (task 3). Notice that this task has a duration of two weeks (80 hours of work) and that you are the only assigned resource.

2. In the Work Task Form, click the **second cell** in the Resource Name column, click the **arrow**, click **Coordinator**, and then click the **OK** button in the Work Task Form.

   Trouble? If you are not sure if the Work task form is active, right-click the form and verify that the selected form name is Work.

   As shown in Figure 4-18, the 80 hours of work were redistributed evenly between the two resources, you and the Coordinator, and the duration of the task changed from two weeks to one week.

Figure 4-18   **Task with a second resource assignment**

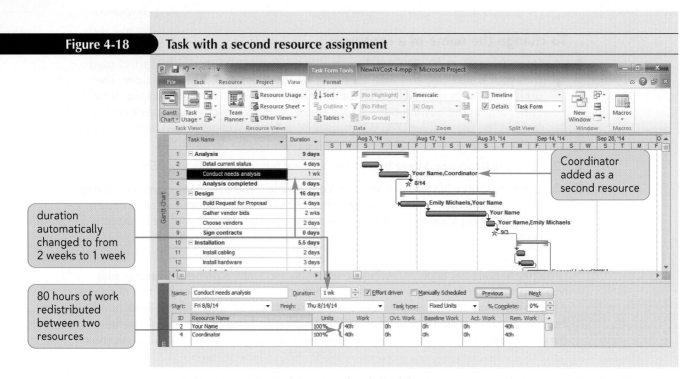

duration automatically changed to from 2 weeks to 1 week

80 hours of work redistributed between two resources

Coordinator added as a second resource

Project 2010 can't determine the skill of the two resources that were just assigned or whether the workload can actually be distributed evenly between them. The assumption that Project 2010 makes when adding new work resources is that the resources have equivalent capabilities to perform the task. Because of this assumption, you'll find it particularly helpful to have the Work Task Form view open so that you can watch the work and duration values change as additional resources are added to a task. Effort-driven scheduling means that adding resources redistributes the work and changes the duration.

You realize that it's not correct to assume that the work could remain a constant 80 hours and be redistributed between the two resources. The task should have a fixed duration of two weeks, and each resource should work 80 hours on the task. You can override this by reentering the correct duration; this will recalculate the work for both resources. You make the changes in the Work Task Form. Also, the Detail current status task (task 2) has a duration of four days, but no resources have been assigned to the task. You will assign resources to that task.

To add a resource and change work for a resource to see the default relationship among work, duration, and units:

▶ **1.** In the Work Task Form, click the **Duration** up arrow to change it from 1w to **2w**, and then, in the form, click the **OK** button.

When you change the duration of an existing task, the work hours automatically adjust for each resource based on the duration of the task. Because the duration for the task is two weeks and each unit (resource) is assigned at 100%, 80 hours are assigned to each resource.

Now you want to assign resources to Detail current status (task 2). You will make an initial assignment of two resources to this task. When your *initial* task assignment includes two resources, Project 2010 assumes that *both* resources are needed to complete the task and that both resources need the same amount of hours to complete the task—so both resources are assigned work (hours) based on the initial duration.

Be sure you do not click the OK button or press the Enter key before completing step 3 to avoid assigning only one resource as the initial resource.

2. In the Entry table, click **Detail current status** (task 2), in the form click the **Resource Name** column first cell, click the **arrow**, and then click your name. Now you need to assign Emily to this task as well.

Trouble? If you clicked the OK button or pressed the Enter key, click the Undo button on the Quick Access toolbar and repeat step 2.

3. Click the **Resource Name** column second cell, click the **arrow**, click **Emily Michaels**, and then, in the form, click the **OK** button. Your screen should look like Figure 4-19. Notice how the duration didn't change from 4 days because both resources were assigned at the same time as the initial assignment.

Figure 4-19   Initial resource assignment with two resources

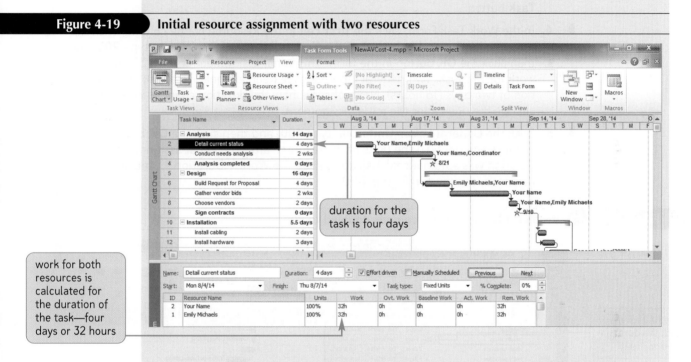

work for both resources is calculated for the duration of the task—four days or 32 hours

Both resources are assigned work hours based on the initial duration (four days, which is 32 hours). If more than one resource is assigned to a task, but both tasks should not be given the same amount of work, you can manually adjust the number of work hours in the Work Task Form.

4. In the Work Task Form, click the **Work** cell for Emily Michaels, type **8h**, and then, in the form, click the **OK** button. In this case, changing the work for Emily to eight hours did not shorten the task duration because the overall task duration is still driven by the resource with the most work hours, who, in this example, is you.

Next, you want to explore the relationship among work, duration, and units when only one resource (General Labor with multiple units) is involved. In this case, the Work = Duration * Units formula can be used without any special considerations for multiple resources. Dates will change, so you drag the split bar to keep an eye on task Start and Finish dates as you change the resource assignments.

To explore the relationship among work, duration, and units when only one resource is assigned to a task and units are changed:

▶ 1. Drag the **split bar** to the right so that the Finish column is the last column in the Entry table.

▶ 2. In the Work Task Form, click the **Next** button, review the form, then click the **Next** button as many times as necessary to select **Install cabling** (task 11), reviewing information about each task when it appears in the Work Task Form.

▶ 3. Scroll the Entry table so that the **Installation** summary task is the first row visible in the table, click the **Task** tab, and then, in the Editing group, click the **Scroll to Task** button.

▶ 4. In the Work Task Form, click the **first cell** in the Resource Name column, click the **arrow**, click **General Labor**, click the **first cell** in the Units column, type **200**, and then click the **OK** button in the form. This initial assignment creates 32 hours of work for this task. Two general laborers have been assigned to a task with a duration of two days (16 hours). Next, observe how the duration changes when you change the units after the initial assignment.

▶ 5. Click the **General Labor Units** cell, type **400**, and then click the **OK** button. Because you doubled the units of the resource after the initial assignment, the duration was automatically halved to keep the Work = Duration * Units formula balanced, as shown in Figure 4-20.

| Figure 4-20 | Install cabling task resource units doubled to 400% |

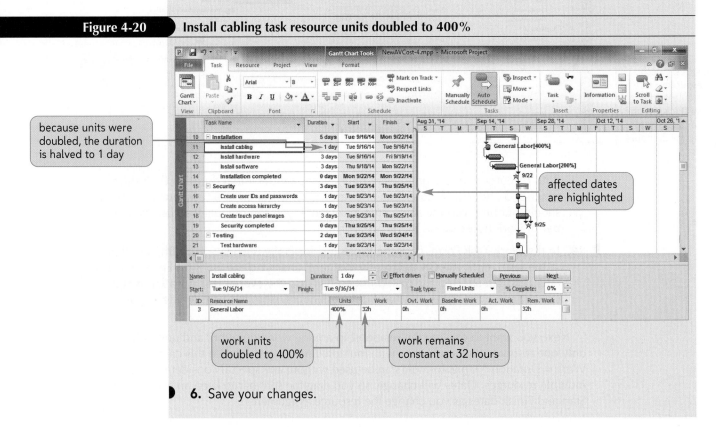

▶ 6. Save your changes.

Figure 4-21 explains how the W=D*U formula works after the initial resource assignment is made and an additional resource is added to a task.

Figure 4-21	What changes in the Work = Duration * Units

After the initial resource assignment, if you:	This item changes to balance the Work = Duration * Units formula:
add a new resource	Duration
modify the units on existing resource	Duration
modify the work	Duration
modify the duration	Work

Creating a Fixed-Duration Task

How the relationship among work, duration, and units is balanced is a function of both *effort-driven scheduling* and the *task type*. **Task type** is a task field that refers to what will remain constant when additional resources are added to a task. The task types you can choose from in Project 2010 are Fixed Units, Fixed Duration, or Fixed Work; by default, the task type is Fixed Units. Task type can be set in the Task Information dialog box on the Advanced tab. As you have seen, tasks are, by default, **effort driven**; that is, when a new resource is added to a task with an existing resource assignment, total work (effort) remains constant and the duration is adjusted (shortened) to accommodate the redistribution of work across multiple resources. For example, review what happened when you added an additional work resource (two more General Labor units) to the Install cabling task that already had an existing resource assignment (two General Labor units): Work was redistributed among the four General Labor units to shorten the duration.

As you might suspect, when effort-driven scheduling is turned *off* and a new resource is added to a task with an existing resource assignment, the work (effort) no longer drives the assignment. With a **fixed-duration task**, the *duration* of the task remains constant. If an additional resource is added to a fixed-duration task and effort-driven scheduling is turned off, then the work (effort) is decreased for each resource. This means that a task's work, rather than the duration, changes when a new resource is assigned. Fixed-duration tasks are usually not effort driven, but it is possible to have an effort-driven, fixed-duration task. Figure 4-22 shows how the same task (with an initial duration of four days and one resource assignment) responds to the assignment of an additional resource when different task types are used and effort-driven task scheduling is both on and off. The figure explains what happens to the relationship among work, duration, and units based on each task assignment.

In summary, the task type (fixed units, fixed duration, and fixed work) affects how a schedule changes if you revise the existing assignment, as shown in Figure 4-22.

Figure 4-22   Effort-driven scheduling and task type relationships

Scenario	Resource Assignment Activity	Task type	Effort Driven?	Duration	Work	Description
1	Janice is the initial resource assignment.	Fixed Units	yes	4 days	32 hours	Initial work is calculated for an effort-driven task.
2	Janice was initially assigned. Ruth is added as a new resource assignment.	Fixed Units	yes	2 days	32 hours	Work remains constant due to effort-driven scheduling but is redistributed between Ruth and Janice. The duration is decreased to balance the W=D*U formula.
3	Janice was initially assigned. Ruth is added as a new resource assignment.	Fixed Duration	yes	4 days	32 hours	Work remains constant due to effort-driven scheduling. The duration remains constant due to a fixed-duration task type. Units are reduced to 50% to balance the W=D*U formula.
4	Janice was initially assigned. Ruth is added as a new resource assignment.	Fixed Work	yes	2 days	32 hours	Work remains constant but is redistributed between Ruth and Janice. The duration is decreased. Fixed-work task types react the same way as fixed-units task types if the fixed-units task type is also effort driven. *Note*: You cannot remove effort-driven scheduling from fixed-work tasks. Fixed-work tasks do not have flexible work values, and are therefore always effort driven.
5	Janice is the initial resource assignment.	Fixed Units	no	4 days	32 hours	Initial work is calculated for a task that is not effort driven. The initial work calculation is the same for a task that is effort driven.
6	Janice was initially assigned. Ruth is added as a new resource assignment.	Fixed Units	no	4 days	64 hours	The task is not effort driven, so the duration rather than work remains constant. Adding Ruth to the task doubles the amount of work to balance the W=D*U formula. This is a fixed-units task.
7	Janice was initially assigned. Ruth is added as a new resource assignment.	Fixed Duration	no	4 days	64 hours	The task is not effort driven, so the duration rather than work remains constant. Adding Ruth to the task doubles the amount of work. If a task is not effort driven, fixed-units and fixed-duration task types react the same way.

Some tasks, such as meetings and seminars, should have fixed durations because no matter how many people attend, the length of the meeting or seminar does not change. To change a task so it is not effort driven you have to clear the Effort driven check box on the Advanced tab of the Task Information dialog box or in the Work Task Form.

REFERENCE

Creating a Fixed-Duration Task That is Not Effort Driven

- In the Entry table, select the task you need to specify as fixed duration.
- Open the Task information dialog box, click the Advanced tab, and then click the Effort driven check box to clear the box.
- Click the Task type arrow, and then click Fixed Duration.

or

- In the Entry table, select the task you need to specify as fixed duration.
- Click the View tab, and then, in the Split View group, click the Details check box.
- In the form in the bottom pane, right-click, and then click Work.
- In the Work Task Form, click the Effort driven check box to clear the box.
- Click the Task type arrow, and then click Fixed Duration.

The task Test software has a duration of two days. If one person is assigned to the task, it will take that person 16 hours. You think that testing will take longer than 16 hours, but you want the duration to remain a fixed two days; therefore, you must change the task type to fixed duration and assign more resources to the task. Sidney has approved the hiring of two more resources, Eli Shalev and Donna Rand, so you add them as resources as you continue to work with the file.

To create a fixed-duration task that is not effort driven:

▶ 1. Scroll down the Entry table, click **Test software** (task 22), click the **Task** tab, and then, in the Editing group on the Task tab, click the **Scroll to Task** button to position the Gantt chart on that task. Notice that on the Work Task Form, the Effort driven check box is checked.

▶ 2. In the Work Task Form, click the **Effort driven** check box to clear the box. Clearing the Effort driven check box means effort-driven scheduling is not active.

▶ 3. Click the **Task type** arrow, and then click **Fixed Duration**. The task is now a fixed-duration task. Now you will add resources to the task to see how the Test software task responds to the assignment of new resources.

▶ 4. In the Work Task Form, click the **first cell** in the Resource Name column, click the **arrow**, click your name, and then in the Work Task Form click the **OK** button. You are the initial resource assignment. Because the initial duration is two days, the initial work calculation is 16 hours.

▶ 5. Click the **second cell** in the Resource Name column, type **Eli Shalev**, and then click the **OK** button. Eli is added as a new resource to a fixed-duration task. Notice that when a new resource is assigned, it is given the next available ID number. As a result, ID numbers may be out of sequence because all resources are not shown in the list. The result is shown in Figure 4-23.

| Figure 4-23 | Adding a new resource for a fixed-duration task |

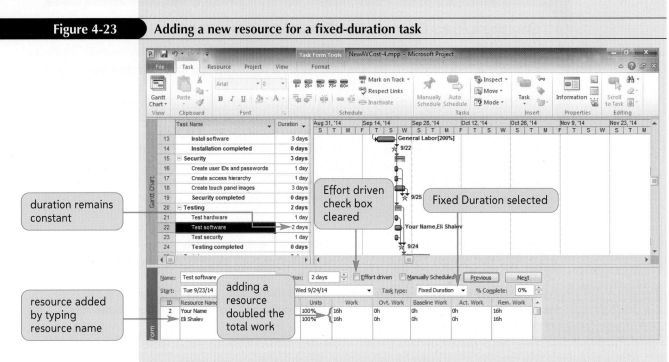

duration remains constant

Effort driven check box cleared

Fixed Duration selected

resource added by typing resource name

adding a resource doubled the total work

Effort-driven scheduling is turned off, so work was *not* held constant. Rather, the duration was held constant (2 days). Adding Eli Shalev doubled the total work because he was also assigned 16 hours of work. The task will take 32 hours of work, but will still be completed in two days.

6. Click the **third cell** in the Resource Name column, type **Donna Rand**, and then click the **OK** button. Once again, the duration was held constant (2 days) and the work was increased, this time from 32 hours to 48 hours (3 resources * 16 hours = 48 hours) because the effort-driven scheduling field is not active and it is a fixed–duration task.

7. Save your work.

Project 2010 uses the next available resource ID when you add new resources. In this case, Eli was added as resource number 5, and Donna was added as resource number 6. Note that the Work Task Form does not provide a field to enter their hourly costs. You can use the resource sheet to assign the costs and complete the other fields.

Task costs are calculated by multiplying the work for an assigned resource by its hourly rate plus any cost per use for the task. The cost associated with a task is zero until a resource with cost information completed is assigned to the task. You will enter task costs next in the tutorial.

To assign costs to a resource:

▶ 1. Click the **View** tab, and then, in the Split View group, click the **Details** arrow.

▶ 2. On the list, click **Resource Sheet**. Resource Sheet view opens in the bottom pane, replacing the Work Task Form. Displaying the Gantt chart in the top pane and Resource Sheet view in the bottom pane is handy because you view only those resources in the resource sheet that are assigned to the currently selected task. From this view, you can enter hourly costs for Eli and Donna and complete their Group and Initials information.

TIP

Your name is highlighted in red text in the resource sheet because you are currently overallocated. You will correct for this in the next session.

▶ 3. Verify that the selected task is **Test software** (task 22).

▶ 4. In Eli's row in the resource sheet, click the **Initials** cell, type **ES**, click the **Group** cell, type **PM**, click the **Std. Rate** cell, type **40**, press the **Tab** key, type **40** in the Ovt. Rate cell, and then press the **Enter** key. Eli's Initials and Group are complete, and the rate of $40.00 per hour is entered for both the standard and the overtime rate fields. If he works overtime, he will be paid the same rate as if he worked regular hours. Overtime hours have to be charged at some rate when entered so even if it is the same rate, you have to enter the amount in the resource sheet.

▶ 5. In Donna's row in the resource sheet, click the **Initials** cell, type **DR**, click the **Group** cell, type **PM**, click the **Std. Rate** cell, type **40**, press the **Tab** key, type **40**, and then press the **Enter** key. Donna's Initials and Group are complete, and the rate of $40.00 per hour is entered for both the standard and the overtime rate fields. Your screen should look similar to Figure 4-24.

| Figure 4-24 | Viewing the Gantt chart and Resource sheet |

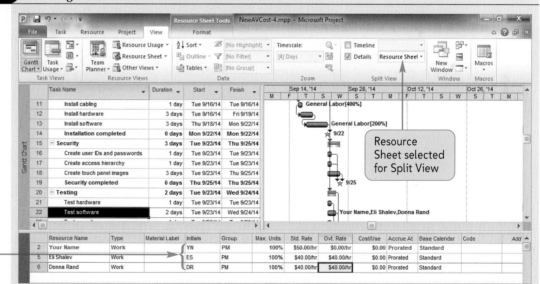

resource information added

▶ **6.** Click any cell in the **Entry table**, press the **Ctrl+Home** keys to navigate to the first task, click the **Zoom** button [🔍▾], click **Zoom** to open the Zoom dialog box, click the **Entire project** option button and then click **OK** to close the Zoom dialog box.

▶ **7.** Press the **down arrow** key to view each of the tasks in your project. As you move from task to task, the resource sheet in the bottom pane changes to display the resources that are assigned to each task. You want to save the file with the resource sheet displayed in the bottom pane.

▶ **8.** Save your changes.

▶ **9.** Submit the project file in electronic or printed form, as requested, and then close the file.

PROSKILLS

Teamwork: Knowing the Workers and the Players

Teamwork is essential for successful project completion. As a project manager, your job will include finding ways to shorten the critical path with techniques such as shortening the durations of tasks on the critical path, removing unnecessary task date constraints, entering negative lag time, and allowing tasks with Finish-to-Start relationships to overlap. You also can shorten the critical path by manipulating resources. For example, if you assign additional resources to a critical task that is effort driven, the additional assignment will shorten the task's duration. If the task is a critical task, adding the additional resource shortens the critical path. Another way to shorten the critical path by manipulating resource data is to assign overtime, which expands the number of working hours in a day and results in the task being completed earlier.

As a manager, you have to know the people you work with and how they might respond to working overtime or to working in groups rather than individually. Just because the critical path shortens on paper, doesn't mean the decision is the correct one if the teams cannot work together.

REVIEW

Session 4.2 Quick Check

1. How is total work calculated?
2. What is the general formula used to calculate work for a task?
3. What is the value of work calculated for a task that does not yet have a resource assignment?
4. How is the duration of a task scheduled when two resources are assigned and they are given different work values?
5. With effort-driven scheduling, what is held constant and what is decreased in the $W=D*U$ formula when an additional resource is added?
6. With fixed-duration scheduling, what is held constant and what is increased in the $W=D*U$ formula when an additional resource is added?
7. What is the default task type?

SESSION 4.3 VISUAL OVERVIEW

The Leveling Gantt Chart view is helpful when reviewing the affects of leveling on tasks.

The word **edays** means elapsed time and usually a delay in schedule.

		Task Name	Leveling Delay
17		Create access hierarch	0 edays
18		Create touch panel imag	0 edays
19		Security completed	0 edays
20		**Testing**	**0 edays**
21		Test hardware	0 edays
22		Test software	0 edays
23		Test security	0 edays
24		Testing completed	0 edays
25		**Training**	**0 edays**
26		Train management	0 edays
27		Train users	8 edays
28		Training completed	0 edays

This task has been **split** and it has been rescheduled.

Name: Detail current status   **Duration:** 3 days   ☑ **Effort driven**   ☐ Manua

Start: Mon 8/4/14   **Finish:** Wed 8/6/14   Task type: Fi

ID	Resource Name	Units	Work	Ovt. Work	Bas
2	Your Name	100%	32h	8h	0h
1	Emily Michaels	100%	8h	8h	0h

Eight hours of overtime have been assigned to each resource for this task. Overtime, not reflected in the Work column, will be calculated in Actual Work as progress is reported.

New Tasks : Auto Scheduled

LEVELING RESOURCES

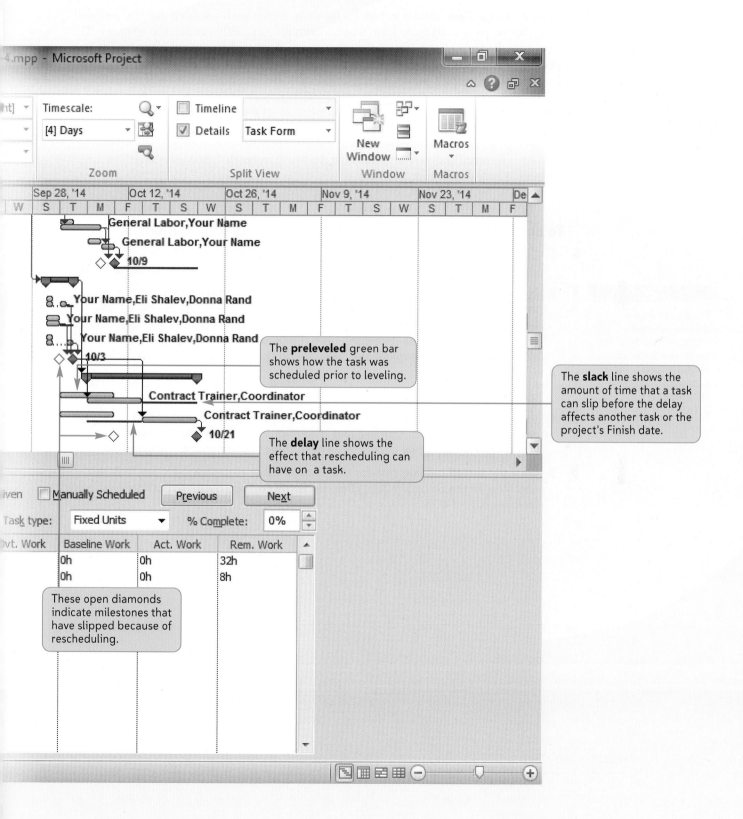

The **preleveled** green bar shows how the task was scheduled prior to leveling.

The **slack** line shows the amount of time that a task can slip before the delay affects another task or the project's Finish date.

The **delay** line shows the effect that rescheduling can have on a task.

These open diamonds indicate milestones that have slipped because of rescheduling.

Using Resource Usage View to Examine Resource Information

Resource Usage view, similar to Task Usage view, shows each resource that has assigned tasks. The left pane is an Entry table that contains resource information. The resource ID appears in the first column. The Indicators column displays the relevant icons for any special conditions for each resource, such as notes or overallocations. Resources appear in the Resource Name column, and assigned tasks are indented below each resource. A Work column displays the total hours assigned for each resource and the number of hours for each assigned task. The right pane displays the number of hours that each resource is assigned to each task in a day-by-day format. After meeting with Sidney to discuss the project, Emily added another resource, a Contract Trainer, and she made additional resource assignments, adjusting durations as needed. Then she saved the Project file as AVLvl-4.mpp.

TIP

You can expand and collapse individual resources in the Resource Usage view just as you can expand and collapse summary tasks in a task Entry table.

To use Resource Usage view to display resource information:

1. Open the **AVLvl-4** project file, which is located in the **Project4\Tutorial** folder included with your Data Files, and then save it as **NewAVLvl-4** in the same folder.

2. In the Resource Views group on the View tab, click the **Resource Usage** button. The Resource Usage sheet opens. Notice how all the resources have tasks assigned. Also notice that the first row resource is "Unassigned." The tasks listed under "Unassigned" are milestone tasks. Because you do not assign resources to milestone tasks, all the milestone tasks are grouped together as "Unassigned."

3. In the Resource Name column, click the **Unassigned (first row resource) Collapse** button ⊟.

4. In the Resource Name column, click the **Emily Michaels (resource ID number 1) Collapse** button ⊟, and then click the **Your Name (resource ID number 2) Collapse** button ⊟. These three resources are collapsed.

5. Click the **Install cabling** task for the General Labor resource, click the **Task** tab, and then, in the Editing group, click the **Scroll to Task** button. Your screen should look like Figure 4-25.

Figure 4-25   **Resource Usage view**

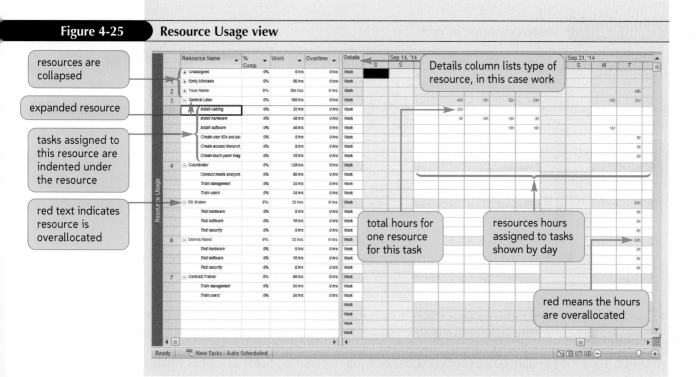

resources are collapsed

expanded resource

tasks assigned to this resource are indented under the resource

red text indicates resource is overallocated

Details column lists type of resource, in this case work

total hours for one resource for this task

resources hours assigned to tasks shown by day

red means the hours are overallocated

TIP

If at any time you want to increase the size of the font for the text in any Entry table, click the Select All button, and then click the Task tab. In the Font group, click the Font Size arrow and select a larger font.

Notice that Your Name, Eli's, and Donna's names are in red. This indicates that these resources are overallocated. Overallocated resources are resources that (assuming the Standard calendar) are assigned more than eight hours of work for a given day or days. You'll address this issue shortly.

Sorting Tasks for Resource Information

The sorting capabilities of Project 2010 highlight specific resource information. You use sorting to reorder the resources in ascending or descending sort order based on the values in the resource fields.

To sort a project for resource information:

1. On the Resource Usage Work table, to the left of the Resource Name column heading, click the **Select All** button (the blank top left cell) to select the Resource Usage sheet.

2. Click the **View** tab, and then, in the Data group, click the **Outline** button.

3. On the menu, click **Hide Subtasks**. All the tasks within each resource are collapsed.

4. In the Data group, click the **Sort** button, click **by Cost**, and then click the first resource listed in the sheet. The resources are now listed from highest cost (Your Name) to lowest cost (Contract Trainer). The Unassigned resources remain at the top of the list, as shown in Figure 4-26. You are the most costly resource in the project.

Figure 4-26 Resources sorted by cost

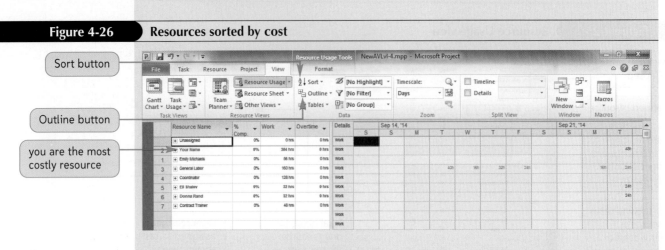

5. In the Data group, click the **Sort** button, and then click **by Name**. Now the resources are listed in alphabetical order by Name.

You sort resource sheets in the same way you sort task sheets, except that the Sort by fields differ. You can sort resource sheets by Cost, by Name, and by ID. You can also open the Sort dialog box. In the Data group, click the Sort button, and then click Sort By. The Sort dialog box lets you specify up to three sort fields as well as whether the fields are to be sorted in ascending or descending order.

Filtering Tasks for Resource Information

You can use Resource Usage view to filter resources to show a subset of resources that meet certain criteria. For example, soon you will need to focus on the overallocated resources (those that have more than eight hours of work assigned for a given day or days).

To filter a project for resource information:

1. In the Data group, click the **Filter** arrow (currently displaying [No Filter] in the Filter box), and then click **Overallocated Resources**. Only those resources that are overallocated are now showing on the resource sheet. The numbers in red in the day-by-day grid in the right pane show the overallocations.

2. Click the **Eli Shalev Expand** button ➕, click the **Task** tab, and then, in the Editing group, click the **Scroll to Task** button.

3. Drag the **split bar** so Work is the last column in the Resource Usage Entry table. You can now see which three tasks create the overallocation for Eli on Tuesday, September 23, 2014, as shown in Figure 4-27. He is scheduled on that day to spend eight hours testing software, eight hours testing hardware, and eight hours testing security, for a total of 24 hours of work on that one day. A resource cannot work 24 hours in one day, so you will have to reallocate the hours. You will do this later in the tutorial.

Figure 4-27	Filtering and examining a specific overallocation

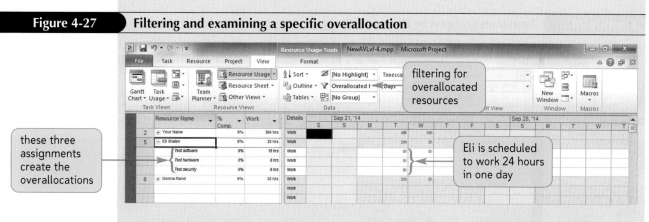

these three
assignments
create the
overallocations

filtering for
overallocated
resources

Eli is scheduled
to work 24 hours
in one day

> **4.** In the Resource Name column in the Entry table, click the **Eli Shalev Collapse**
>   button ⊟.
> **5.** Click the **View** tab, and then, in the Data group, click the **Filter** arrow.
> **6.** On the menu, click **[No Filter]** to view all resources.

Creating Custom Groups for Resource Information

In Project 2010, you group resources in order to understand your resource allocations.
In addition to sorting groups using options available in the Group By list, you can also
create custom groups. To create a custom group, you have to open the Group Definition
dialog box. Sidney wants to view resources grouped by assignments in order to get a
better picture of what's going on with the project. You create this custom group using the
New Group By option.

To group resources for information:

> **1.** In the Data group, click the **Group By** arrow (currently displaying [No Group]),
>   and then click **Resource Group**. The resources are grouped according to the
>   Group names you entered in the resource sheet. See Figure 4-28. Recall that mile-
>   stones are not assigned resources, and so, in Resource Usage view, milestones are
>   grouped as Unassigned. Because no resources have been assigned to milestone
>   tasks, they have no value.

Figure 4-28   Resources grouped by Resource Group

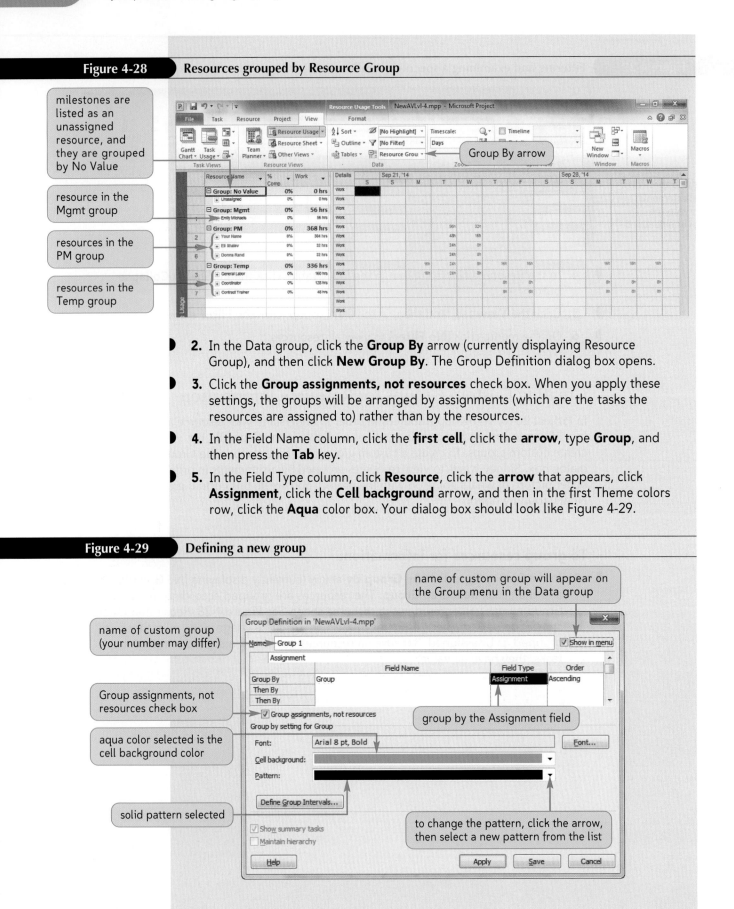

milestones are listed as an unassigned resource, and they are grouped by No Value

resource in the Mgmt group

resources in the PM group

resources in the Temp group

Group By arrow

2. In the Data group, click the **Group By** arrow (currently displaying Resource Group), and then click **New Group By**. The Group Definition dialog box opens.

3. Click the **Group assignments, not resources** check box. When you apply these settings, the groups will be arranged by assignments (which are the tasks the resources are assigned to) rather than by the resources.

4. In the Field Name column, click the **first cell**, click the **arrow**, type **Group**, and then press the **Tab** key.

5. In the Field Type column, click **Resource**, click the **arrow** that appears, click **Assignment**, click the **Cell background** arrow, and then in the first Theme colors row, click the **Aqua** color box. Your dialog box should look like Figure 4-29.

Figure 4-29   Defining a new group

name of custom group will appear on the Group menu in the Data group

name of custom group (your number may differ)

Group assignments, not resources check box

aqua color selected is the cell background color

solid pattern selected

group by the Assignment field

to change the pattern, click the arrow, then select a new pattern from the list

▶ 6. Click the **Apply** button to close the Group Definition dialog box and view the Entry table in the Resource Usage view. The Group By box in the Data group displays the newly defined Group, which is named Group 1. This is a default name; you could change it if you wanted or leave it as is. You see how the sheet groups by assignments and the group cells are a teal color.

▶ 7. In the Data group, click the **Group By** arrow, and then click **[No Group]**.

▶ 8. Double-click **Your Name** to open the Resource Information dialog box for the Your Name resource, change the name to your name, click **YN**, type your initials, and then close the dialog box.

▶ 9. Save your changes.

▶ 10. Submit the project file in electronic or printed form, as requested, and then close the project file.

You can see how filtering, sorting, and grouping in Resource Sheet view help you to determine how your resources are allocated and help you to highlight significant information about your project. Filtering quickly shows you those resources that meet the criteria you select and presents an uncluttered view of the resources by eliminating extraneous information. In addition to the many other filters available, you can quickly see which resources are overbudget, overallocated, or fall within a specific date range. Sorting can identify the most costly resource or develop an alphabetical list of your resources. Grouping quickly shows you how your resources are organized and can present a view to identify shortcomings or strengths in your project planning.

Leveling Overallocations

A resource is **overallocated** if it is assigned more work in a given time period than it has working hours. Usually this means that a resource has been assigned more than eight hours of work in a day. But overallocations can also occur when resources are scheduled to do more than 60 minutes of work in a given hour of a day. If an overallocation exists for a resource that is assigned fewer than eight hours of work in a day, it is probably due to an hour having more than 60 minutes of work. To check if this is the case, change the timescale to hours instead of days in Task Usage or Resource Usage view in order to find the overallocation.

Leveling means to correct overallocations so that no resource is assigned more work than is available in the given time period. There are many ways to level resources using Project 2010. Figure 4-30 identifies some of the methods.

| Figure 4-30 | Methods You Can Use to Level Overallocations |

Method	Description	Pros	Cons
Delay a task	Delay the task and reschedule its Start and Finish dates to a period of time in which the assigned resource is free.	Project 2010 can automatically delay and reschedule tasks. This method is very fast and easy to implement.	The length of the project may be increased.
Split a task	Split a task so as to reschedule remaining work in a period of time in which the assigned resource is free.	Project 2010 can automatically split a task and reschedule the remaining tasks based on changes resulting from the split. This method is very fast and easy to implement.	The length of the project may be increased. The nature of the task might not accommodate splitting.
Assign a different resource	Replace the overallocated resource with a free resource.	This method does not increase the project's length.	Finding a free equivalent resource to assign can be difficult or impossible.
Assign overtime	Assign hours of work to the overallocated resource outside of the regular working day.	This method does not increase the project's length.	This method usually increases the project cost because of overtime labor rates. Overtime might not be an effective way to accomplish some tasks or use some resources.
Assign additional resources	Assign additional resources so the work will be redistributed among all of the resources.	This method does not increase the project's length.	Finding a free equivalent resource to assign to the task can be difficult or impossible. This method will increase the project cost.
Shorten the task duration or the hours of work assigned to a task	Shorten the duration or work hours of the task so that fewer hours of work are required.	If you shorten a task duration, you might also shorten the project's length. Directly decreasing the duration or work hours for an overallocated resource is an effective way to level it.	This method is appropriate only for tasks whose durations or work hours were overestimated initially.

Manually Leveling Overallocations

When leveling resources, it is best to examine the overallocated resources yourself first and use the leveling techniques that do not extend the project's length: reassign work, assign overtime, add additional resources, and shorten task duration. If more leveling is needed after using these techniques, you can use the Project 2010 leveling tools, which delay and split tasks to reassign work to free periods. While this is a fast and effective way to deal with overallocations, it might also extend the duration of the overall project, which might not be acceptable.

REFERENCE

Examining and Adjusting Overallocations

- On the View tab, click the Filter arrow, and then click Overallocated Resources to view only those resources that are overallocated.
- In the Resource Views group, click the Resource Usage arrow, click More Views, click Resource Allocation, then click Apply to open the Leveling Gantt chart in the lower pane and the Resource Usage view in the upper pane.
- Click each resource and task to find and examine overallocations.
- Enter any changes to work assignments that you deem necessary and appropriate at this time.

You decide to use the Project 2010 Resource Management tools available to help you deal with the overallocations. After a project management meeting, Sidney and Emily made some additional changes to the project file. You will use Resource Allocation view to find and examine the overallocations. Resource Allocation view opens with a split screen, with Resource Usage view in the top pane and Leveling Gantt Chart view in the bottom pane. When a resource is selected in the Entry table of the Resource Usage sheet (top pane), the tasks assigned to that resource are displayed in the Entry table in the bottom pane. A Gantt chart showing the tasks appears to the right of the Entry table.

To view overallocations:

1. Open the **AVFin-4** project file located in the **Project4\Tutorial** folder included with your Data Files, and then save the file as **NewAVFin-4** in the same folder. The project file opens in Gantt Chart view.

2. In the Resource Views group on the View tab, click the **Resource Usage** button.

3. In the Data group, click the **Filter** arrow, and then click **Overallocated Resources** to view only those resources that are overallocated.

4. In the Resource Views group, click the **Resource Usage button** arrow, click **More Views**, click **Resource Allocation**, and then click **Apply** to open the Leveling Gantt chart in the bottom pane. The Resource Usage view remains open in the top pane. The bottom pane shows the tasks for which the selected resource in the top pane is overallocated.

5. Point to the **Warning indicator** icon next to Your Name, and then read the ScreenTip. The ScreenTip confirms you need to level the overallocations.

6. Click the **Eli Shalev** Resource Name cell to view the tasks assigned to him in the Leveling Gantt Chart. Eli is overallocated on three tasks: Test hardware, Test software, and Test security.

7. In the Leveling Gantt chart, drag the **split bar** to the right to display the full column name for the Leveling Delay column, right-click the **Test hardware** Task Name cell, review the options on the shortcut menu, and then click **Scroll to task**. The upper pane displays the allocations beginning Wednesday, October 1. The Leveling Gantt chart shows each assignment for tasks on October 1. You see the work assignments, as shown in Figure 4-31.

Figure 4-31	Resource Allocation view

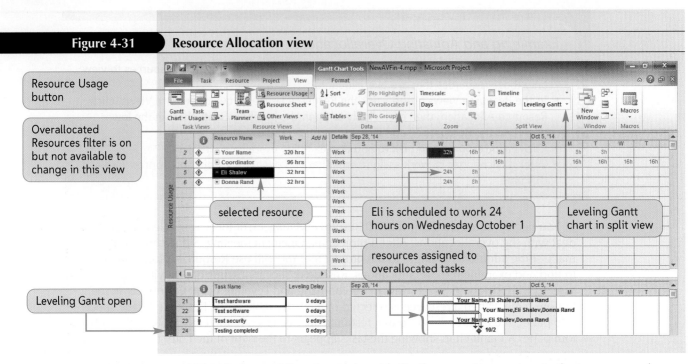

Using Resource Allocation view, with the Resource Usage view in the top pane and the indicators column in Leveling Gantt chart in the bottom pane, you see that Eli is scheduled to work on three tasks for a total of 24 hours on Wednesday, October 1. This impossibility is what is creating the overallocation. In addition, he is scheduled to work a full 8-hour day on Thursday, October 2. So, if you had wanted to move some of the hours from October 1 to October 2, you would create another overallocation. In order to fix this overallocation using your own reassignments, you need to set the manual option in the Resource Leveling dialog box.

To set resource leveling options:

1. Click the **Resource** tab, and then, in the Level group, click the **Leveling Options** button. The Resource Leveling dialog box opens. You need to set the project to calculate leveling manually since you want to see the results for each resource as you reassign work day by day.

2. Click the **Manual** option button if it is not already selected, and then click the **OK** button.

You want to see what happens if Eli spends only four hours of work on the Test software task and two hours each on the Test hardware and Test security tasks on that day.

To level overallocations manually by reducing work:

1. In the Resource Name column, click the **Eli Shalev Collapse/Expand** toggle button as needed to display the list of tasks Eli is assigned to, click the **Wednesday, 10/1/14** cell for the Test software task, type **4h**, and then press the **Enter** key.

   Trouble? If you are unsure of the date, place the mouse pointer over the day column heading in the timescale to display a ScreenTip for the column date.

2. In the **Wednesday, 10/1/14** cell for the Test hardware task, type **2h**, and then press the **Enter** key. The work for Eli is reduced to 14h for that day.

3. With the **Wednesday, 10/1/14** cell for the Test security task as the active cell, type **2h** and then press the **Enter** key. You have reduced the work for Eli to 8h for that day (Wednesday October 1), which means he is no longer overallocated for those tasks. See Figure 4-32.

Figure 4-32 **Changing work entries in Resource Allocation view**

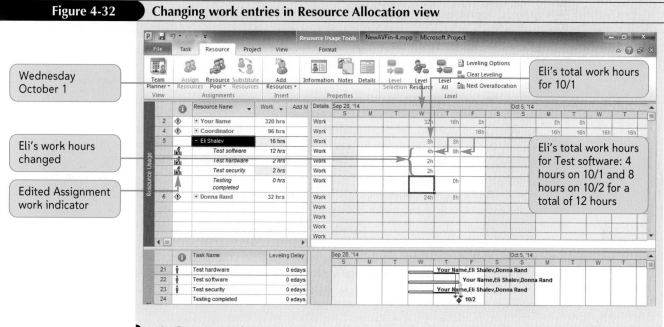

Wednesday October 1

Eli's work hours changed

Edited Assignment work indicator

Eli's total work hours for 10/1

Eli's total work hours for Test software: 4 hours on 10/1 and 8 hours on 10/2 for a total of 12 hours

4. Save your changes.

You immediately notice a few changes to the Resource Usage Entry table. Indicator icons showing that the assignments have been edited appear in the Indicators column to the left of the three tasks you edited. You can see that Eli Shalev is no longer overallocated; his total work for 10/1/14 is recalculated to eight hours, his information is displayed in black, and the Warning indicator no longer appears in the Indicators column next to his name. Notice that Overallocation indicators still appear next to the task names in the Leveling Gantt pane because these tasks are still overallocated even though Eli's overallocation for these tasks has been corrected.

This direct approach to lowering the number of work hours assigned to a resource on a given day is an efficient way to level an overallocation. Manually leveling overallocations by lowering work hours in Resource Allocation view, however, is not appropriate if the number of work hours cannot realistically be reduced. Keep in mind that all the tasks in this project file have the fixed-units task type, except for the summary tasks, which are fixed duration. If you have a fixed-units task and change the units, duration is recalculated; if you change duration, work is recalculated; and if you change the work, duration is recalculated.

Another way to manually level an overallocation is to redistribute the work to other resources. You can redistribute the work by assigning the work to a different resource or by assigning overtime.

REFERENCE

Adjusting Overallocations by Assigning More Resources to Tasks

- Click the Gantt Chart button in the Task Views group on the View tab, then remove any splits.
- Click the Resource tab, and then, in the Level group, click Leveling Options to open the Resource Leveling dialog box.
- Verify that leveling is set to Manual, and then close the Resource Leveling dialog box.
- Right-click the Select All button, then click Entry if it is not the active table.
- Click the Resource tab, and then, in the Level group, click the Go To Next Overallocation button to view each overallocated resource.
- Click the View tab, click the Details check box in the Split View group, and then verify that the Task Form opens in the bottom pane.
- Right-click the form and then click Schedule.
- Redistribute work as needed by adding resources in the Resource Schedule form.
- Click the View tab, click the Resource Sheet button arrow, click More Views, click Resource Allocation, click Apply, and then expand each resource to view the assigned task.
- In the Entry table, double-click any resource to open the Resource Information dialog box to view details and make additional adjustments.

You are already familiar with Task Entry view because you used it to make initial resource assignments. Resource Usage view is helpful to reallocate resources. The Leveling Gantt chart helps you see how task schedules change based on reallocation of resources.

To view overallocations in different views:

1. Click the **Gantt Chart** button 📄 on the status bar to display the Task Entry table with the Gantt chart in the top pane and the Leveling Gantt chart in the bottom pane.

2. Right-click the **Task Name** column in the Task Entry table in the top pane, click **Insert Column**, type **Ind**, press the **Enter** key to insert the Indicators column, double-click the **column divider** between the Indicators column and the Task Name column to adjust the column width, and then drag the **split bar** as needed so that the Duration column is the last column that is visible in the Task Entry table.

3. In the Task Name column in the top pane, click **Detail current status**, click the **View** tab, and then, in the Resource Views group, click the **Resource Usage** button. Resource Usage view helps you identify each task for each resource. The Overallocated Resources filter is still active in this view.

4. Click the **Resource** tab, and then, in the Level group, click the **Next Overallocation** button. The Overallocated 32h cell for Wednesday, October 1, 2014 is selected. See Figure 4-33.

| Figure 4-33 | Using Resource Usage view to view overallocations |

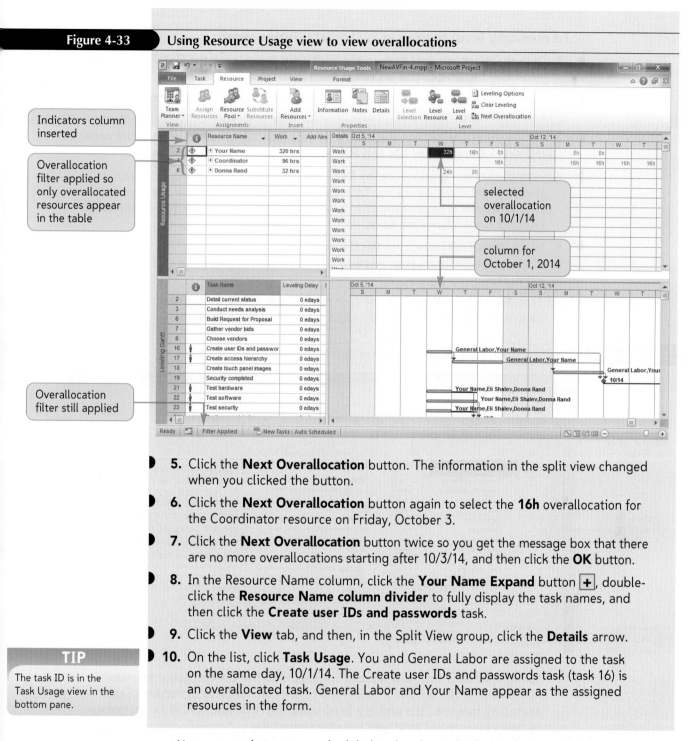

Indicators column inserted

Overallocation filter applied so only overallocated resources appear in the table

Overallocation filter still applied

▶ **5.** Click the **Next Overallocation** button. The information in the split view changed when you clicked the button.

▶ **6.** Click the **Next Overallocation** button again to select the **16h** overallocation for the Coordinator resource on Friday, October 3.

▶ **7.** Click the **Next Overallocation** button twice so you get the message box that there are no more overallocations starting after 10/3/14, and then click the **OK** button.

▶ **8.** In the Resource Name column, click the **Your Name Expand** button ⊞, double-click the **Resource Name column divider** to fully display the task names, and then click the **Create user IDs and passwords** task.

▶ **9.** Click the **View** tab, and then, in the Split View group, click the **Details** arrow.

TIP

The task ID is in the Task Usage view in the bottom pane.

▶ **10.** On the list, click **Task Usage**. You and General Labor are assigned to the task on the same day, 10/1/14. The Create user IDs and passwords task (task 16) is an overallocated task. General Labor and Your Name appear as the assigned resources in the form.

You can see that you are scheduled to do other tasks during the same day that you are scheduled to create user IDs and passwords. This creates the overallocations. You decide to increase the hours for the General Labor resource (you will add more temporary workers to accommodate the additional hours) so that you are no longer scheduled for eight hours of work for that task. You want to use a view that shows the Task Entry table with the accompanying Gantt chart in the top pane and the Schedule Task Form in the bottom pane. You can right-click the active form to select the Work Task Form or a number of other forms. The Work Task Form is the view that you will usually use to redistribute work when you need to level an overallocation.

To manually level resources by redistributing work:

1. Click the **View** tab, and then, in the Split View group, click the **Details** check box to remove the check mark and clear the bottom pane.

2. In the Task Views group on the View tab, click the **Gantt Chart button** to open Gantt Chart view.

3. Scroll so that Create User IDs and Passwords (task 16) is near the top of the pane, right-click **Create User IDs and Passwords,** and then click **Scroll to Task**.

4. In the Split View group, click the **Details** check box to display the Task Form in the lower pane, right-click the **Task Form**, and then, in the menu that opens, click **Work** if it is not already selected. The Create user IDs and passwords task is selected in the Work Task Form.

5. In the Work Task Form, click the **General Labor Work cell (8h)**. The value for Work for the General Labor resource is selected for the Create user IDs and passwords task.

6. Type **16**, click the **Work** cell for Your Name, type **0**, press the **Enter** key, and then click the **OK** button. Your screen should look like Figure 4-34.

| Figure 4-34 | Redistributing work to new resources to eliminate an overallocation |

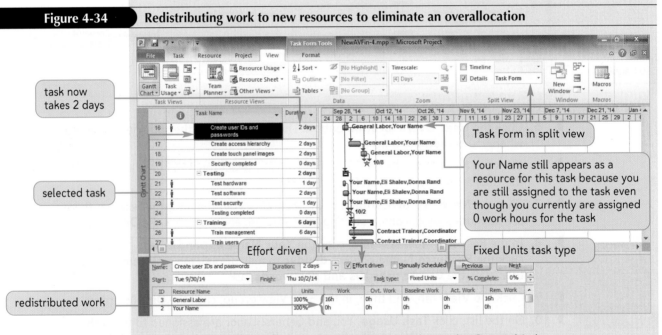

You took 8 hours from yourself and assigned it to the General Labor resource. Redistributing the work to a new resource is a common way to handle an over-allocation. However, the task is a fixed-units, effort-driven task, so by assigning 16 hours to General Labor, you added a second day.

7. In the Resource Name column in the Work Task Form, double-click **General Labor** to open its Resource Information dialog box, and then click the General tab if it is not already selected. You have up to five General Labor resources that you can assign to that task. Currently, one General Labor resource is assigned. You will assign another to bring the task back to one day.

8. Click the **OK** button to close the Resource Information dialog box.

▶ **9.** In the Task Form, click the **General Labor Units** cell, type **200**, and then click the **OK** button. The Create user IDs and passwords (task 16) again has a duration of 1 day.

▶ **10.** Save your work.

Overtime hours

Adding **overtime hours**, work hours outside of those specified by the calendar, is another way to handle overallocations, which can also shorten the critical path. Sidney has agreed to let you assign overtime in order to bring the project in sooner. The Detail current status task is currently scheduled for four days. You checked the Resource Usage sheet and the Task Form Schedule and see that you are currently scheduled to work 32 hours on this task, eight hours over four days (8/4-8/7), and Emily is scheduled to work eight hours on this task on 8/4. The actual work (Act. Work field) for this task will be 40 hours. Emily is willing to work an extra day and overtime to get this task finished faster. She will work her regularly scheduled eight hours on the task, pick up four hours of OT on that day, and then add another 12-hour day, again working four hours of overtime on the task. So, if you assign Emily to work a second day (8 hours) and eight hours of overtime (four hours per day for two days), this task can be completed in two days.

REFERENCE

Assigning Overtime

- Set up a split view with the task Entry table in the top pane in Gantt Chart view and with the Work Task Form in the bottom pane.
- In the Entry table, scroll and then click the task to which you want to assign overtime.
- In the Task Form, click the resource Ovt. Work cell, type the total hours of overtime you want to assign to that resource for that task, and then press the Enter key.
- Enter any additional overtime to resources assigned to that task.
- Click the OK button.

To add overtime hours:

▶ **1.** In the Entry table, scroll to and then click **Detail current status** (task 2). You want to add a second day and the eight hours of overtime to Emily's work time.

▶ **2.** In the Work Task Form, double-click **Emily Michaels** to open the Resource Information dialog box, click the **Costs** tab, verify her Overtime Rate is **$100/hr**, and then click the **Cancel** button. Even though her Standard and Overtime rate is the same, you had to be sure that there was a value in the Overtime rate cell so her time would be charged.

▶ **3.** In the Work Task Form, click the **Your Name Work** cell, and then type **16**. You are now scheduled to work two 8-hour days on this task.

▶ **4.** Click the **Emily Michaels Work** cell, type **16**, click the **Emily Michaels Ovt. Work** cell, type **8**, and then click the **OK** button. Emily is now scheduled to work two 8-hour days and eight hours of overtime (four hours each day). There is 32 hours of work scheduled and 8 hours of overtime for a total of 40 actual hours of work.

Your screen should look similar to Figure 4-35. Notice the duration for the Detail current status task is reduced to two days.

Figure 4-35   **Assigning overtime**

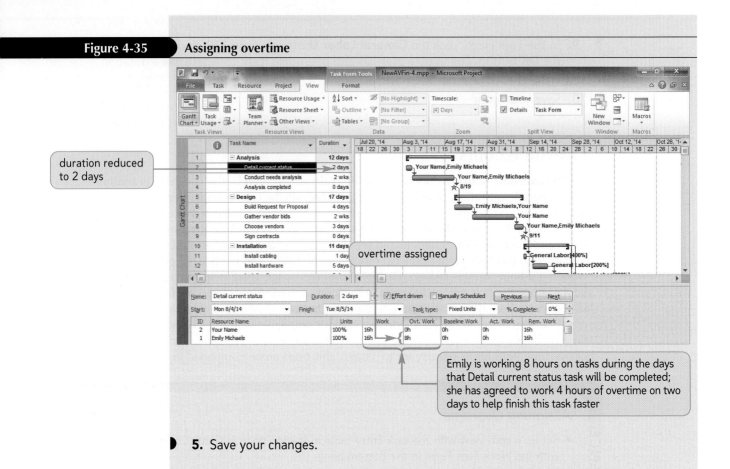

duration reduced
to 2 days

overtime assigned

Emily is working 8 hours on tasks during the days
that Detail current status task will be completed;
she has agreed to work 4 hours of overtime on two
days to help finish this task faster

▶ **5.** Save your changes.

It is important to note that when you just add overtime to a task, the Work field value
does not decrease. The Work field represents *total* work rather than work completed during working hours. Regardless of whether the work is completed during the normal eight-
hour day or during overtime, the Work field remains constant.

Examining Overallocations

Sometimes, you need help figuring out why a task appears to be overallocated. In this
situation, you can examine the Resource Information or Task Information dialog box.

To examine resource allocations:

▶ **1.** In the Gantt Chart, scroll down the Entry table until you can see tasks 25 through
28 in the Training section, right-click **Train management**, and then click **Scroll to
Task** on the shortcut menu. The resources for the Train management task appear
in the Work Task Form.

▶ **2.** Click the **Next** button in the Work Task Form so that **Train users** (task 27) is
selected in the Entry table in the top pane and its corresponding resources are
shown in the Work Task Form in the bottom pane. Notice the resources for task 27
are also Contract Trainer and Coordinator.

These two tasks are scheduled on the same days, so resources are overallocated.

▶ **3.** In the Resource Views group on the View tab, click the **Resource Usage** button.
Contract Trainer does not appear in the Resource Usage form as an overallocated
resource.

4. Click the **Resource Name** column in the top pane, and then, in the Data group, click the **Filter arrow.**

5. In the list, click **[No Filter]**, and then scroll down the Entry table until you see Contract Trainer in black (not red) and with no warning indicator.

6. In the Resource Name column, click the **Contract Trainer Expand** button ⊞ if it is not already expanded. Notice that none of the allocated hours for this resource are red, which is the indicator for overallocation. See Figure 4-36.

Figure 4-36   **Examining the Contract Trainer resource**

7. In the Task Views group, click the **Task Usage** button, scroll down until Train management (task 26) is near the top of your screen, right-click **Train management**, and then click **Scroll to Task**. Train management and Train users do show as overallocated. Yet the assigned resources are not overallocations. How can that be? You will find out why shortly.

You expect the tasks assigned to the Contract Trainer resource to show as overallocated. This resource is scheduled for eight hours of work for two tasks (Train users and Train management) on the same span of days. Any time that a resource, task, relationship, or assignment is not responding as expected, double-click it to open the corresponding Resource Information dialog box and examine its characteristics.

To make changes to resources using the Resource Information dialog box:

1. In the Resource Name column in the Work Task Form, double-click **Contract Trainer** to open its Resource Information dialog box, and then click the **General** tab if it is not already selected. See Figure 4-37.

Figure 4-37   Resource Information dialog box for the Contract Trainer resource

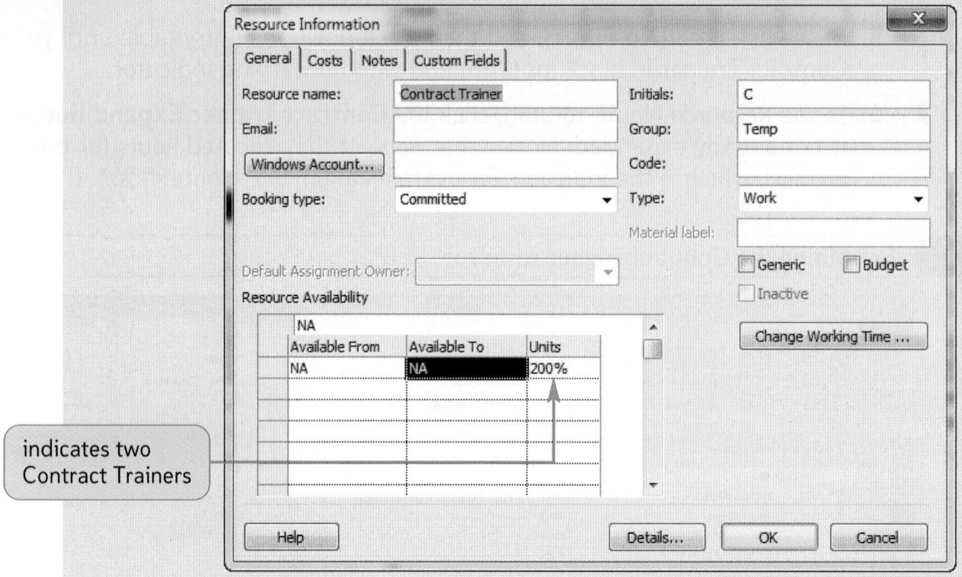

indicates two
Contract Trainers

Information available on the General tab explains why this resource is not over-allocated. Resource allocation is listed at 200% units. When Emily assigned this resource, she had hired two contract trainers, and so she doubled the working hours (8*2 or 16 hours of working time) allocated to this resource on a single day. You can check the Assignment Information dialog box to confirm this.

2. Click **Cancel** to close the Resource Information dialog box, and then, in the Task Usage Entry table in the top pane, double-click **Contract Trainer** for the Train management task. The Assignment Information dialog box tells you that 100%, or one unit, is assigned to the Train management task.

3. Click the **Cancel** button, and then, in the Task Usage Entry table in the top pane, double-click **Contract Trainer** for the Train users task. The Assignment Information dialog box tells you that 100%, or one unit, is assigned to the Train users task. The resource Contract Trainer has two units. Project assumes one unit is working on the Train Management task while the other unit is working on the Train Users task. As a result, Project does not see these tasks as overallocated.

4. Click the **Cancel** button. The Assignment Information dialog box closes.

5. In the Task Views group, click the **Gantt Chart** button arrow.

6. On the menu, click **Gantt Chart**, and then, in the Split View group, click the **Details** check box to remove the split.

7. Press **Ctrl+Home** to move to the first task of the Entry table, right-click **Analysis**, click **Scroll to Task**, and then save your changes to the project.

After examining the project, you have a good idea of where the overallocations are located. You can use the Project 2010 leveling tool to help you with the rest.

PROSKILLS

Decision Making: Project Management Certifications

As a project manager, you want to pursue becoming certified by the industry. As a certified project manager, more jobs and opportunities for career advancement are available to you. The Project Management Institute offers five certification programs. The Project Management Institute Web site, *www.pmi.org*, provides excellent information and resources supporting these credentials.

- Project Management Professional (PMP)
- Program Management Professional (PgMP)®
- Certified Associate in Project Management (CAPM™)
- PMI Scheduling Professional (PMI-SP)®
- PMI Risk Management Professional (PMI-RMP)®

The Project Management Professional (PMP) certification is a professional credential somewhat analogous to the Certified Public Accountant credential for an accountant. It requires rigorous education, experience, and examinations. It also involves agreement and adherence to a code of ethics. The Program Management Professional (PgMP)® certification recognizes the advanced experience and skill of program managers who have shown a proven ability to manage complex, multiple projects and their resources. It is accepted internationally. The Certified Associate in Project Management (CAPM™) certification is intended for those practitioners who provide project management services but are relatively new to the profession. It is a valuable entry-level certification for project practitioners as it demonstrates your understanding of the fundamental knowledge, terminology, and processes of effective project management. The PMI Scheduling Professional (PMI-SP)® certification is for project management professionals who are looking for a specialist role in project scheduling. The PMI Risk Management Professional (PMI-RMP)® certification is for project management professionals looking for a specialist role in project risk management.

Using the Leveling Tools

Project 2010 provides powerful leveling tools that level resources for you based on some assumptions. The tools level work resources but not material resources. They do not adjust task durations, work entries, or resource assignments. The tools level overallocations by delaying and splitting tasks so that the work can be completed by the assigned resource during the available working time. When Project 2010 splits a task, it interrupts the work so that the work starts and then stops, which means that there is a period of time when no work is being done on the task, and then work begins on that task again. As a result, splitting a task usually adds a delay, which is the amount of time between the scheduled start for a task and the time when work actually begins on the task, to a project. Remember, however, that some tasks realistically cannot be split, so be careful when using this option. The leveling tools generally extend the project's length as they move tasks into time periods when a resource is available.

You can level an entire project, you can level by selecting a specific task or a group of tasks, or you can level specific resources. If you use leveling tools and you don't think the solution is a viable one because it extends the project too far or moves a task out too far, you can clear leveling and start over. Leveling is often a trial-and-error process until you find the right combination of assigned resources, assigned work, and assigned dates to the tasks to make the project work for you.

REFERENCE

Leveling Overallocations Using the Leveling Tools

- Display the Gantt Chart view, and then click the Resource tab.
- Filter for overallocated tasks, or display the Indicators column to view overallocated tasks.
- To level all resources and tasks in the project: In the Level group on the Resource tab, click the Level All button.
- To clear leveling: In the Level group on the Resource tab, click the Clear Leveling button.
- To level one overallocated task: In the Indicators column, right-click the overallocated task, then click Reschedule to Available date.
- To level several overallocated tasks: Press and hold the Ctrl key, click to select the tasks to level, and then, in the Level group on the Resource tab, click the Level Selection button.
- To level one or more resources assigned to a task: Select the task or tasks, and then, in the Level group, click the Level Resource button to open the Level Resources dialog box. Click the resources, and then click the Level Now button.

Using Commands in the Level Group to Level Overallocations

Reviewing the project, you see that there are several overallocated tasks and resources. You decide to see what the leveling tools can do to help the situation.

To use the leveling tools to level resources for tasks:

1. In the Zoom group, click the **Zoom Entire Project** button 📇.

2. Scroll down so Test hardware is visible on the screen, in the Task Name column right-click **Test hardware**, click **Scroll to Task** on the shortcut menu, and then click the **Resource** tab. You see the Indicators column has the red indicators telling you there are still overallocated tasks. You decide to see what happens when you level one overallocated task.

TIP

To level several over-allocated tasks: Press and hold Ctrl, click to select the tasks to level, and then, in the Level group, click the Level Selection button.

3. In the Indicators column, right-click the **Test hardware** (task 21) overallocated task icon, and then click **Reschedule to Available date** on the shortcut menu. The task was split, but an overallocation still remains. See Figure 4-38.

Figure 4-38   **Task is split**

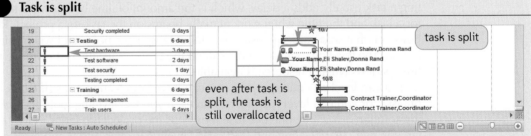

4. Place the mouse pointer on the **split task** and read the ScreenTip.

5. Right-click the **split task**. You see that options include Rescheduling to Available Date, fixing it in the Task Inspector, or ignoring the problem. You decide to try other methods. First, you clear the current leveling.

6. In the Level group in the Resource tab, click the **Clear Leveling** button, and then, in the Clear Leveling dialog box with the **Entire project** button selected, click the **OK** button. The leveling you applied is removed. Next, you decide to level one or more resources assigned to the Test hardware task.

7. In the Level group, click the **Level Resource** button to open the Level Resources dialog box. See Figure 4-39. Your Name, Donna Rand, and Eli Shalev are the resources assigned to the selected Test hardware task. These resources are selected in the dialog box.

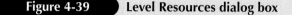

Figure 4-39   Level Resources dialog box

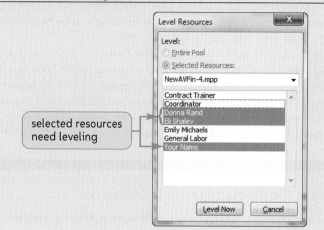

selected resources need leveling

8. Click the **Level Now** button. Several tasks were split, a few dates moved out, and the project Finish date has been delayed by several days. You still have some over-allocated tasks. These are tasks that did not have the selected resources assigned to them. You decide to see how Project might level the entire project at one time. First you clear this leveling.

9. In the Level group, click the **Clear Leveling** button, in the Clear Leveling dialog box, click the **Entire project** option button if it is not already selected, and then click the **OK** button. The overallocations appear again for several tasks.

10. In the Level group, click the **Level All** button. All overallocations are removed because Project leveled all tasks.

11. Click the **Project** tab, in the Properties group, click the **Project Information** button. Leveling has added many days to the project. When you started with this file, the Finish date was 10/10/14; the new Finish date is 10/20/14. You continue to use Leveling tools to see what can be done with the project.

12. Click **Cancel** to close the Project Information dialog box, click the **Resource** tab, and then, in the Level group, click the **Clear Leveling** button.

13. In the Clear Leveling dialog box, click the **Entire project** option button, and then click the **OK** button.

Using the Resource Leveling Dialog Box to Level Overallocations

After you have reviewed all of the overallocations and made adjustments to durations, resource assignments, and work entries where possible to alleviate the overallocations, you can let Project 2010 level the remaining overallocations. The options in the Resource Leveling dialog box can be used to modify the way that leveling is processed.

The most important decision you need to make in the Resource Leveling dialog box is the choice for Leveling calculations, which offers two alternatives: Automatic or Manual. Automatic leveling levels your project *as you enter and adjust the schedule*, while manual leveling levels the project only after you click the Level All button in the Resource Leveling dialog box. If you choose Automatic leveling and you do not want Project to keep reinventing the wheel and relevel tasks and resources that you have already approved, be sure to clear the Clear leveling values before leveling check box so Project levels only new and unleveled assignments.

When you click the Level All button in the Resource Leveling dialog box, you have the choice of either leveling the Entire pool of resources or Selected resources. If you select the Entire pool, all overallocated work resources will be leveled. If you select Selected resources, only those resources you identified before clicking the Level All button will be leveled. Those tasks that cannot be resolved will generate a dialog box in which you have the option to skip those resources or cancel the leveling process.

REFERENCE

Working in the Resource Leveling Dialog Box

- In the Level group, click the Leveling Options button to open the Resource Leveling dialog box.
- In the Leveling calculations section, make sure the desired Manual or Automatic option button is selected.
- In the Leveling range for project section, choose the Level entire project option or choose the Level option, and then set the date range.
- In the Resolving overallocations section, select the check boxes next to the appropriate options.
- Click the Level All button, and then click the OK button.

Using the Leveling Gantt to View Overallocations

You can apply the Leveling Gantt to more clearly show leveling information for the entire project. After the leveling process is complete, the Entry table in Leveling Gantt view will have a new column titled Leveling Delay.

To level the entire project and apply the Leveling Gantt chart to view leveling:

▶ 1. In the Level group, click the **Leveling Options** button to open the Resource Leveling dialog box, click the **Automatic** option button, and then click the **Level All** button.

▶ 2. Click the **View** tab, click the **Gantt Chart** button arrow, click **More Views**, click **Leveling Gantt** in the More Views dialog box, and then click **Apply**.

▶ 3. Drag the **split bar** to the left so Task Name is the last column visible.

▶ 4. In the Zoom group on the View tab, click the **Zoom Entire Project** button ⊞.

5. Scroll down if necessary to see the last task. Figure 4-40 shows Leveling Gantt view for this project after the project has been leveled, which added 10 days to the schedule.

Figure 4-40   Leveling the project

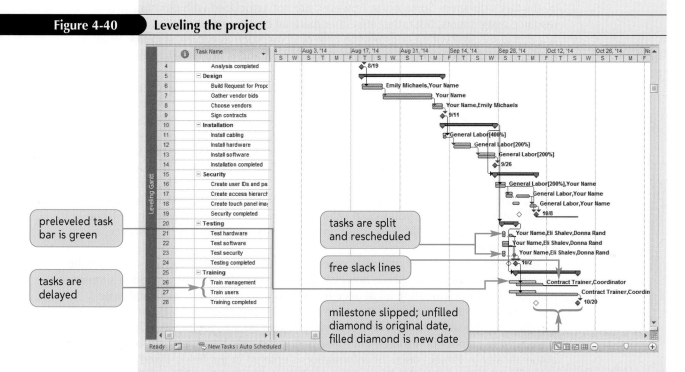

preleveled task bar is green

tasks are delayed

tasks are split and rescheduled

free slack lines

milestone slipped; unfilled diamond is original date, filled diamond is new date

6. Place the mouse pointer on the bars for each of the tasks and read each ScreenTip. Notice that the milestones for Security completed (task 19), Testing completed (task 24), and Training completed (task 28) all slipped as a result of the leveling.

7. Save your work.

Understanding the Leveling Gantt Chart View

INSIGHT

The Leveling Delay column shows the delay in completing each task created by the resource leveling tool as edays, which indicates elapsed time. The Gantt chart uses green bars to represent the schedule for the preleveled task and blue bars to represent the new schedule for the leveled task. When a task is split, you see blue dashed lines between the blue task bars.

These different color bars highlight the effects of leveling on the schedule. The line following a task represents free slack. Recall from Tutorial 3 that free slack is the amount of time that a task can be delayed without the delay affecting subsequent tasks. Delaying a task can cause a slipped milestone, which is identified by an open diamond symbol.

If you do not want the schedule to be lengthened, you can use the Resource Leveling dialog box and change the leveling options. If you click the Clear Leveling button in the Resource Leveling dialog box and then click the OK button, you clear the leveling for the entire project. The Leveling Delay column will display zeros for all of the tasks, and the green leveling bars will be the same lengths as the blue bars. To clear leveling, you use Leveling Gantt view, which shows the leveling before attempting to clear it. The default leveling options might not be best for your project, so be careful in using this feature.

Entering Costs

The cost for a task varies based on the resource type, the hourly cost, and the number of resource units assigned to the task. When you assign a resource to a task, Project 2010 automatically calculates **work costs** for the task—multiplying the resource's hourly rate by the task's duration. Some costs, however, are not associated with per hour (work) resource assignments, but rather are either material costs or fixed costs. A **material cost** is a cost associated with a consumable item or items, such as cables, supplies, or computers. A **fixed cost** is a cost inherent to the task itself and is not driven by the number of resource assignments made, such as a room charge.

The Resource Type field on a resource sheet has three possible values: Cost, Work, and Material. The **Work** value (the default) causes the resource cost to be driven by the duration of the task multiplied by the hourly cost of the resource, plus the cost-per-use charges if applicable. The **Material** value causes the resource cost to be driven by the number of resource units that have been assigned to the task multiplied by the unit cost of the resource (entered in the Std. Rate field). The **Cost** value is used to assign multiple arbitrary costs (not based on work time) to each task. You can use the Material Label field to enter a label to identify the units if necessary. For example, if you are paying for cabling by the linear foot, you would enter the standard rate and then enter the label Foot. The Cost per Use field is for those one-time costs associated with a resource, such as a delivery fee.

You enter both work and material costs by using the resource sheet. You could use the Resource Information dialog box; however, the Resource Sheet view provides a simpler path to enter this information all at once for several resources. Both work and material costs are assigned to tasks in the same way. Work and material costs are considered variable costs because the cost for a task varies based on the resource type, the hourly cost, and the number of resource units assigned to the task. Variable costs are calculated automatically by Project once the information is entered in the fields. Fixed costs are entered in the Fixed Cost field of a task sheet Entry table. The Fixed Cost field contains a single value for each task and does not vary based on the task's duration or resource assignments.

Emily has asked to you to identify project resources as either work costs or material costs. You identify the cost type for a resource by entering the resource name in the Entry table in Resource Sheet view, and then selecting Work or Material in the Type field.

REFERENCE

Identifying a Resource as a Material or Work Cost

- Be sure you are not in a split window view, and then on the View tab, click the Resource Sheet button.
- Enter the resource name, and then change the Type to Material or leave it as Work (the default).
- Enter the other fields for the new resource, including Std. Rate or Cost per Use for one unit of the resource.

The work resource costs are all entered, and now Emily has asked you to enter the material resource costs. You enter these as material resource costs, such as cabling, computers, printers, the file server, and microphones. Then, you associate the resources with their corresponding tasks in the AV presentation rooms installation project so that the total cost of these tasks also includes the costs of the equipment and materials. You enter the resources, identify them as Material costs, and then add additional information as needed, such as Std Rate, Cost/Use, and Accrue.

To enter resources as material costs:

▶ **1.** In the Resource Views group, click the **Resource Sheet** button, and then hide the **Indicators column**. The Entry table in Resource Sheet view lists the seven work resources that you have been working with for the AV presentation rooms installation project.

▶ **2.** In the Entry table, click the **row 8 Resource Name** cell, type **Cabling**, click the **Type** cell, click the **arrow** that appears, click **Material**, press the **Tab** key, type **Ft**, press the **Tab** key, and then type **Cable** in the Initials cell. Next you need to note that you will pay for cabling at the end of the project.

▶ **3.** Click the **Cabling Std. Rate** cell, type **.5**, click the **row 8 Accrue At** cell, click the **arrow** that appears, and then click **End**.

▶ **4.** In rows 9–16, enter the other material resources and their associated costs as shown in Figure 4-41. Be sure to change the Type from Work to Material, enter the initials for each resource shown, enter the Std. Rate or Cost/Use, and change the Accrue cell as indicated in the figure. Note that you don't have to type the $ sign in the Std Rate and Cost/Use fields.

Figure 4-41	Material resources

ID	Resource Name	Type	Material Label	Initials	Group	Max. Units	Std. Rate	Ovt. Rate	Cost/Use	Accrue At
8	Cabling	Material	Ft	Cable			$0.50		$0.00	End
9	Computers	Material		Computer			$1,200.00		$0.00	End
10	Network printer	Material		Printer			$1,000.00		$0.00	End
11	LCD HD 42" display panels	Material		Displays			$1,200.00		$0.00	End
12	Touch panels	Material		TP			$1,000.00		$0.00	End
13	Control system	Material		Control			$20,000.00		$0.00	End
14	Microphones	Material		Mic			$50.00		$0.00	Prorated
15	Speakers	Material		Spkr			$250.00		$0.00	Prorated
16	Digital video recorders	Material		DVR			$800.00		$0.00	Prorated

▶ **5.** Double-click the **column header** dividers to adjust the column widths to view all of the text in each column, and then save your changes.

You have arranged to pay for the cabling, the computer, the printer, the display panels, the touch panels, and the control system at the end of the project, and you will prorate the cost of the microphones, speakers, and digital video recorders. After you have entered the resources into the Entry table in Resource Sheet view and identified them as Material costs, you can assign them to their tasks by using the Resource Assignment dialog box or by using a split screen with the Resource Schedule form open in the bottom pane, just as you did when assigning work resources to a task.

REFERENCE

Assigning Material Resources to Tasks

- In Gantt Chart view, click the View tab, and then click the Details check box to display the Task Form in a split window.
- In the Task Form in the bottom pane, right-click, and then click Work to open the Work Task Form or click Cost to open the Cost Task Form.
- In the Entry table in Gantt Chart view, select a task.
- In the Work or Cost Task Form, click a Resource Name cell, select the desired resource from the list that opens, click the Units cell for that resource, and then assign a number of units.
- In the Work or Cost Task Form, click the Next button to select the next task in the Entry table in Gantt Chart view, and then continue to assign material resources to the tasks.

The Cost Task Form shows total costs for a task as the number of units changes. The Cost Task Form is often used to enter and assign resources, regardless of whether they are work or material resources, so you can view the costs associated with a task.

To assign material resources to a task:

TIP

You can review and change the cost information for a resource by opening its Resource Information dialog box.

1. In the Task Views group, click the **Gantt Chart** button arrow, and then, on the menu, click **Gantt Chart**.

2. In the Split View group, click the **Details** check box to open the Task Form in the bottom pane.

3. Right-click anywhere in the Task Form, and then click **Cost** on the shortcut menu.

4. In the Entry table in the top pane, click **Install cabling** (task 11).

5. In the Cost Task Form, click the **second cell** in the Resource Name column, click the **arrow**, and then click **Cabling**. The Cabling resource is now assigned to the Install Cabling task. Next, you need to identify the number of units so that Project can automatically calculate the cost.

6. Click the **Units** cell for the Cabling resource, type **1000**, and then click the **OK** button in the form. One thousand feet of cabling at $.50 per linear foot totals $500, which is the material cost assigned to this task. The Gantt bar reflects the assignment.

   Trouble? If you cannot see the Gantt bar for the Install cabling task, right-click the task name in the Task Name cell, and then click Scroll to Task.

7. In the Cost Task Form, click the **Next** button to select **Install hardware** (task 12). Currently, the only assigned resource is General Labor.

8. Refer to Figure 4-42 and use the Cost Task Form to assign the resources. Enter the Resource Name by clicking the next available cell in the Resource Name column, clicking the arrow that appears, and then selecting the Resource Name from the list. Enter the Units by clicking in the corresponding Units cell, and then typing the value. Be sure to click the OK button *only* after you enter all the Resources and Units for the Install Hardware task, as shown in Figure 4-42.

   Trouble? Do not type the Resource Name. You will have to scroll through the resources in the Resource Name list to assign some of the material resources that were added at the end of the resource sheet.

| Figure 4-42 | Assigning material resources to a task |

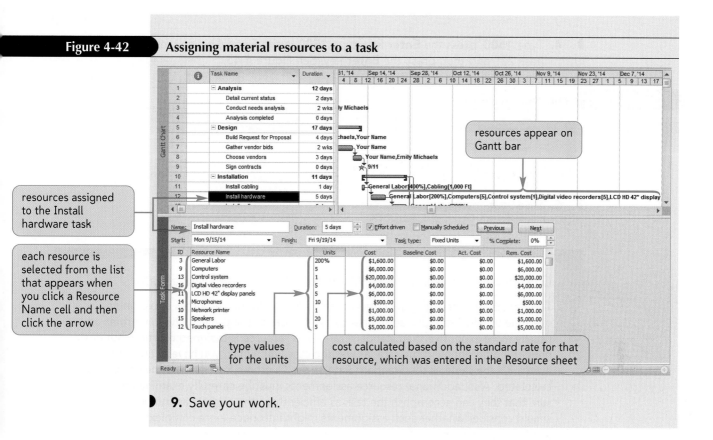

resources assigned to the Install hardware task

each resource is selected from the list that appears when you click a Resource Name cell and then click the arrow

type values for the units

cost calculated based on the standard rate for that resource, which was entered in the Resource sheet

resources appear on Gantt bar

▶ **9.** Save your work.

Fixed Costs

You enter fixed costs into the Fixed Cost field for a task. The Fixed Cost field is the second column in a task sheet when the Cost table is applied to the task sheet.

REFERENCE

Entering Fixed Costs

- Apply a view that includes the task Entry table, such as Gantt Chart view.
- In the Entry table, right-click the Select All button, and then click Cost to apply the Cost table fields.
- Click the Fixed Cost cell for a task, and then enter the fixed cost for that task.

Sidney suggests you rent additional space to facilitate training. You need to enter this cost in the project file. You assign a fixed cost of $1500.00 to Train management (task 26) and Train users (task 27). This amount reflects the cost of renting a lecture room.

To enter a fixed cost:

▶ **1.** On View tab, click the **Details** check box to remove the split.

▶ **2.** In the Entry table, right-click the **Select All** button, and then click **Cost**.

▶ **3.** Scroll down the Entry table, and then click the **Fixed Cost** cell for Train management (task 26).

▶ **4.** Type **1500**, press the **Enter** key, type **1500** in the Fixed Cost cell for Train users (task 27), and then press the **Enter** key. See Figure 4-43.

Figure 4-43	Entering a fixed cost

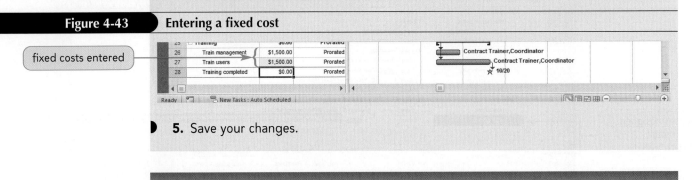

fixed costs entered

▶ **5.** Save your changes.

INSIGHT

Considering Costs and Risks When You Shorten the Critical Path

Techniques for shortening the critical path by manipulating resources or assigning overtime usually introduce additional costs and risks to the project. Overtime rates are usually more expensive than standard rates. If a resource is assigned overtime but does not get a different overtime rate, as was the case with Emily, you have to enter the rate, even if it's the same as the Standard Rate, in the Overtime Rate field so the costs can be calculated. Also, additional resource assignments must be carefully examined to make sure that they can accomplish the task as efficiently as the original assignment. You should consider whether such assignments might introduce extra complexity or create productivity issues by splitting the work among several resources.

Understanding the Relationship Between the Critical Path, Free Slack, and Total Slack

Now that you have entered all of your project's tasks, durations, relationships, resources, and fixed-cost assignments, it's important to take a closer look at the critical path. Recall that the critical path is made up of the tasks that must be completed by the given scheduled dates in order for the project to be completed by the scheduled Finish date. While this understanding of the critical path is accurate in a general sense, it is important to understand the way that Project 2010 determines whether a task is critical. With this information, you'll understand why Project 2010 sometimes calculates the critical path differently than you might expect. In order to be considered critical, a task must meet one or more of the conditions described in Figure 4-44.

Figure 4-44	Conditions under which a task becomes critical

The task becomes critical if the task has...:

0 slack.

a Must Start On or Must Finish On date constraint.

an As Late As Possible constraint in a project scheduled from a Start date.

an As Soon As Possible constraint in a project scheduled from a Finish date.

a scheduled Finish date that is the same as or beyond its deadline date. A deadline date doesn't constrain a task, but it does provide a visual indicator if a scheduled Finish date slips beyond the deadline date.

When project managers discuss slack, they are usually referring to total slack. Remember that total slack is the amount of time that a task can be delayed without delaying the project's Finish date, and free slack is the amount of time that a task can be delayed without delaying any successor tasks. Total and free slack are extremely valuable pieces of information. You can view both by applying the Schedule table to any Entry table.

Next, you need to apply the Schedule table to the Entry table to examine scheduling dates and slack values.

To explore critical tasks and total and free slack:

▶ **1.** In the Entry table, right-click the **Select All** button, and then click **Schedule**. The Entry table changes to the Schedule table.

▶ **2.** Drag the **split bar** to the right so that the Total Slack column is visible, as shown in Figure 4-45.

▶ **3.** Save your work.

| Figure 4-45 | Schedule table applied to the Entry table |

shows total slack is the same as free slack

shows total slack is NOT the same as free slack

The Schedule table displays information to help you manage schedule dates and slack. The Start and Finish date fields are the currently scheduled Start and Finish dates for the dates as calculated by Project 2010. The Late Start and Late Finish date fields are calculated as the latest Start date and latest Finish date that the task could start or finish without affecting the project's Finish date. The Free Slack field is the number of days that the task could be delayed without affecting its successor task. When the Total Slack field is zero, the task is critical and the Start/Late Start and Finish/Late Finish dates are the same. For tasks on the critical path, Free Slack equals Total Slack.

Any positive value in the Total Slack field makes a task noncritical. For example, the Total Slack value for Create access hierarchy (task 17) is calculated as eight days. The eight-day value was calculated by finding the total number of hours that the task could slide (64 hours) and dividing that total by 8 (the number of hours in a regular workday). If a task has free slack of zero, it means that no slack exists between the task and its successor task. Yet the task can have several days of total slack, perhaps 4; that is, it could be delayed up to four days without affecting the project Finish date.

In summary, whenever you are working with a project that appears to calculate the critical path incorrectly, apply the Schedule table to the task Entry table and check the total slack to see if it is positive. Also examine the task constraint and deadline dates.

Communicating Custom Reports

Emily has been talking with you about the report capabilities of Project 2010. You will make a customized report for the AV presentation rooms installation project. Emily has asked you to create a custom report so the information is in a format that meets ViewPoint Partners' specific requirements. Custom reports can have unique colors, fonts, headers, and fields of information.

REFERENCE

Creating a Custom Report

- Click the Project tab, and then, in the Reports group, click the Reports button to open the Reports dialog box.
- Click Custom in the Reports dialog box, click Select, select the specific report that you want to preview, and then click Edit.
- Make any changes, and then click the OK button.
- With the custom report selected, click Select, and then, in Backstage view, print the report or make additional changes.
- If not printing the report at this time, click the Close button to close the Custom Reports dialog box, and then click the Close button to close the Reports dialog box.

With the Project Custom report feature, you can customize the information for your project team.

To create a custom report:

▸ **1.** Click the Project tab, and then, in the Reports group, click the Reports button to open the Reports dialog box.

▸ **2.** In the Reports dialog box, click the **Custom** button, and then click the **Select** button. The Custom Reports dialog box opens. See Figure 4-46.

Figure 4-46 | **Custom Reports dialog box**

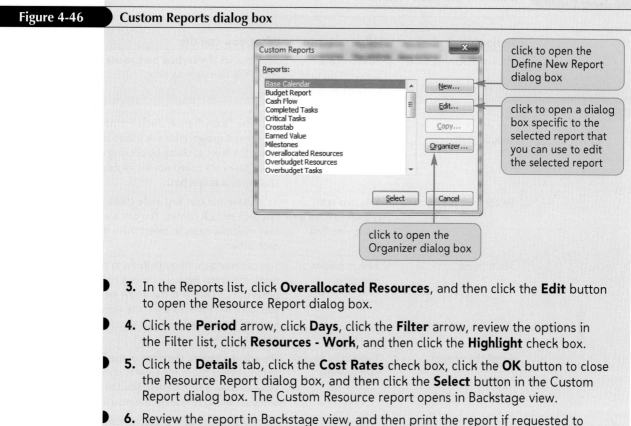

3. In the Reports list, click **Overallocated Resources**, and then click the **Edit** button to open the Resource Report dialog box.

4. Click the **Period** arrow, click **Days**, click the **Filter** arrow, review the options in the Filter list, click **Resources - Work**, and then click the **Highlight** check box.

5. Click the **Details** tab, click the **Cost Rates** check box, click the **OK** button to close the Resource Report dialog box, and then click the **Select** button in the Custom Report dialog box. The Custom Resource report opens in Backstage view.

6. Review the report in Backstage view, and then print the report if requested to print by your instructor.

7. Click the **Project** tab, and then save your changes.

Using the Team Planner

As a project manager, you may want to be able to see an overview of what your team is doing at any given point in the project schedule. The **Team Planner** is a new feature in Project 2010 that does just that. In the Team Planner, Resource names appear in the first column on the left. Each resource in the project is assigned a row. All tasks associated with a resource appear on the same row on the right. Tasks associated with a resource that don't have a Start date or Finish date also appear on the left next to the resource name. Tasks that are not associated with any resource appear at the bottom. Like all Project views, the Team Planner can be used to make changes to the Project file. Refer to Figure 4-47 for actions you can take in the Team Planner.

Figure 4-47 | Actions in the Team Planner

Action	What you see	What you can do
View nonworking time	A resource's nonworking time appears as gray vertical bars	Double-click the vertical bars to see more details about the nonworking time.
See less or more detail about a task	A higher level of detail about task and project information	Click the Team Planner Tools Format tab. In the Format group, click the Rollup button, and then select the level of detail by clicking an outline level. When tasks are rolled up, the highest-level task will appear as a single bar.
Select multiple items	Selected tasks or resources have an orange outline	Hold down the Ctrl key while clicking multiple resource or task names. You can also drag the mouse over multiple items to select them if they are next to each other.
Move items	Task moved to a new time	You can navigate through items in the Team Planner using the arrow keys. To move a highlighted task, press the Ctrl key and the arrow key in the direction you want to move. To scroll the view, press the Alt key and the arrow key. Click to select a task, then drag the task.
Scroll the project	Tasks outside current window	Dragging a task to the edge of the Team Planner will automatically cause the view to scroll. In this way, you can drag a task further into the future (or past) without having to release the mouse button.
Get quick information about tasks	A ScreenTip with information	Place the mouse over a task to read important information about how it is being scheduled.

Sidney wants a clear picture of how the resources are assigned to each task. You use the Team Planner to present this information to her.

To use the Team Planner:

TIP

The Team Planner feature is available only with Project Professional.

1. Click the **View** tab, and then, in the Resource Views group, click the **Team Planner** button. The Team Planner view opens.

2. Double-click **Your Name** to open the Your Name Resource Information dialog box, change **Your Name** to your name, change **YN** to your initials, and then close the dialog box.

3. Right-click **your name**, and then click **Scroll to Task**. The Team Planner shows the resources in the first column and a graphic display of each task assigned to a resource across the timeline.

4. Click the **Resource Name column** arrow. The menu that opens offers options for grouping, sorting or filtering the resources. In a large project with many resources, this can be very helpful. You can use defined filters or create custom filters.

5. Click **Sort A to Z**.

6. Click the **Team Planner Tools Format** tab. The Team Planner should look similar to Figure 4-48.

Figure 4-48   **The Team Planner**

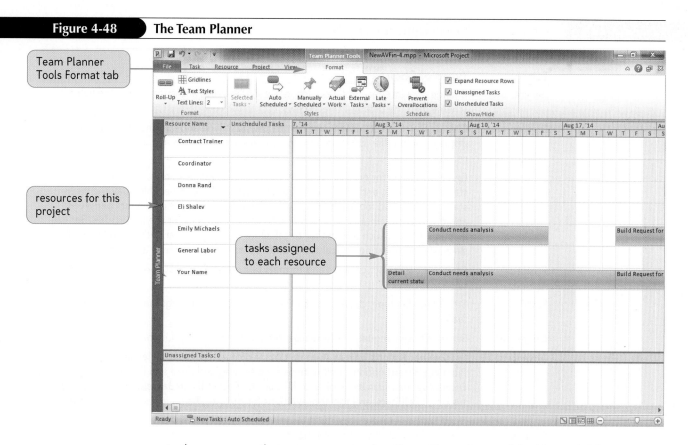

In the same way that you can customize Gantt Chart view and the Network Diagram view, you can also customize Team Planner view. For example, you can show and hide columns, change the color and design of the Team Planner bars, expand row height, and change the appearance of nonworking time. As with any view, you can see more or less detail by dragging the Zoom Slider on the status bar.

Project Options

The Project Options dialog box provides a way to review a number of important default setting choices, which are summarized in Figure 4-49. To open the Project Options dialog box, click the File tab, and then click Options. Project Options are discussed in more detail in the next tutorial. However, it is important to review the options if you want to make any changes to your settings. Sidney asks for a review of the main tabs in the Project Options dialog box.

Figure 4-49   Options in the Project Options dialog box

Tab	Types of Choices
General	Change user interface options such as ScreenTip styles and information, the color scheme, and the default Project views.
Display	Change how Project content such as the calendar type and currency options are displayed in the file. Use to determine if there are indicators and options buttons for certain features. Use to display the Entry bar in the Gantt Chart view.
Schedule	Change defaults for duration and work units, start and end times, effort-driven status, task types, and estimated duration settings. Determine which day the week starts on and what month the fiscal year starts. Set hours per day, hours per week, and days per month. Use to determine calculation options for the project file. Set calculation defaults such as whether to calculate multiple critical paths, how to handle slack when calculating critical tasks, and how to update resource and project status.
Proofing	Change how Project corrects and formats text, set AutoCorrect options, specify dictionary options.
Save	Set default file type, default file and template location settings, and Auto Save features.
Language	Set the Office Language Preferences, such as for display and help.
Advanced	Set General options such as Autofilter on or off for new projects, levels of Undo, Planning Wizard options, Edit options such as drag and drop and in-cell editing, Display options such as number of files on the Recent list in Backstage view, the status bar, scroll bars, and the abbreviations for minutes, hours, days, weeks, months, and years.
Customize Ribbon	Use to change buttons on the Ribbon.
Quick Access Toolbar	Use to change buttons on the Quick Access Toolbar.
Add-ins	View and manage Microsoft Office Add-in programs.
Trust Center	Specify privacy settings for saving personal information with Project files and macro security settings.

Project Summary Information

After you have added all of the work and material resources to your project, it is a good idea to review the project's summary information, especially as it relates to costs. Two ways to show summary information for a project include reviewing the project's properties in the Properties dialog box and adding a project summary bar by clicking the Project Summary Task check box in the Show/Hide group on the Gantt Chart Tools tab.

Reviewing Project Properties

A project **property** is a characteristic of the entire project. After you have entered the initial tasks, durations, relationships, resource assignments, and fixed costs, you'll likely find that reviewing the project properties is valuable because they summarize cost and date statistics for the entire project.

REFERENCE

Reviewing Project Properties

- Click the File tab, and then click Info.
- Click Project Information in the right pane, then click Advanced Properties.
- Click the General, Summary, Statistics, Contents, or Custom tabs to review properties in each category for the project.
- Edit or review project property information, and then click the OK button.

Emily has asked you to review the project properties for the ViewPoint Partners AV presentation rooms installation project. You review the project properties using the Properties dialog box. The information entered automatically in the Summary tab depends on how Project 2010 was initially installed on the computer. The Title field corresponds with the task name in task 0, the project summary task. Changing the task name for the project summary task either on the task Entry table or in the Properties dialog box automatically changes it in the other location.

To review or edit project properties:

1. Click the **File** tab, and then, in Backstage view, click **Info** if it is not already selected.

2. In the right pane, click **Project Information**, and then click **Advanced Properties**. The project's Properties dialog box opens. The project file name precedes the word "Properties" in the title bar of the Properties dialog box.

3. Click the **Contents** tab if it is not already selected. See Figure 4-50. The Contents tab summarizes the project by displaying information about the project's Scheduled Start date, Scheduled Finish date, Scheduled Duration, Work, Cost, and percentage completion statistics. You see that you are close to your budget of $100,000.

Figure 4-50   **Project Properties dialog box with Contents tab active**

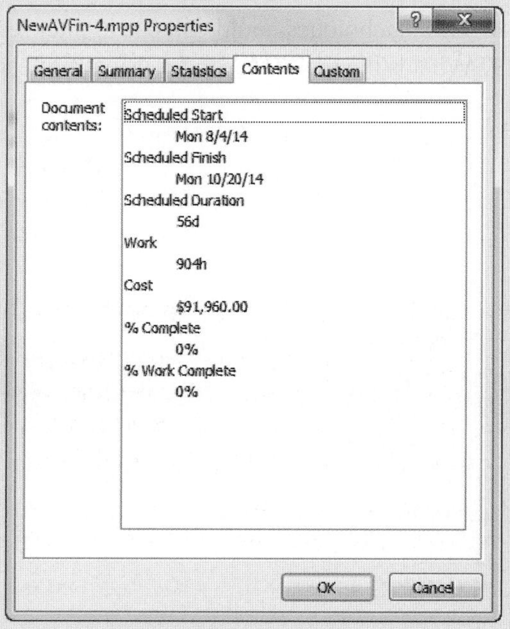

NewAVFin-4.mpp Properties

General | Summary | Statistics | Contents | Custom

Document contents:

Scheduled Start
    Mon 8/4/14
Scheduled Finish
    Mon 10/20/14
Scheduled Duration
    56d
Work
    904h
Cost
    $91,960.00
% Complete
    0%
% Work Complete
    0%

OK   Cancel

▶ **4.** Click the **Summary** tab, and then type your name in the Title text box. The Summary tab contains information you can modify to make searching for and organizing files easier.

▶ **5.** Click the **General** tab. The General tab displays information about the project file, including its location, size, and creation and modification dates.

▶ **6.** Click the **Statistics** tab. The Statistics tab displays additional date information as well as the number of revisions and total file-editing time.

▶ **7.** Click the **Custom** tab. The Custom tab contains information about custom fields that can be added to the project.

▶ **8.** Click the **OK** button to accept the change you made in the Properties dialog box.

▶ **9.** Save your changes, submit the project file in electronic or printed form, as requested, and then close the file.

Working with Project, you learned that you have to be diligent in assigning resources and costs to a project. By doing so, you see how each assignment affects the project dates and task durations. As you assign resources and costs, you can use Project features to keep a watchful eye on the big picture so you can have a successful project plan.

REVIEW

Session 4.3 Quick Check

1. What effect do filtering, sorting, and grouping have on a view of a project?
2. How does Resource Usage view differ from Task Usage view?
3. What is leveling?
4. What are two techniques that you can use to level overallocations? What are two techniques that Project 2010 uses to level overallocations?
5. Which view would you use to see Gantt bars for preleveled and leveled tasks?
6. Differentiate between material and fixed costs.
7. What conditions make a task critical according to Project 2010?
8. What techniques could you use to alter resources to shorten the critical path?
9. What is the major reason for using the Team Planner?

Practice the skills you learned in the tutorial using the same case scenario.

PRACTICE

Review Assignments

Data File needed for the Review Assignments: Train-4.mpp

Part of the ViewPoint Partners AV Presentation Rooms Installation project involves training the people who will use the rooms. You set up training so that the users will be trained and ready to go when the presentation rooms are installed. In this assignment, you will open a partially completed project file that documents training tasks. You will enter resources in the resource sheet, assign them to tasks, handle overallocations, shorten the critical path by using resource information, use the Team Planner, and then view various cost and allocation reports. Complete the following:

1. Open the **Train-4** file located in the **Project4\Review** folder included with your Data Files, and then save the file as **VPTrain-4** in the same folder.
2. Open the Resource Leveling dialog box and be sure Leveling calculations is set to Manual.
3. Switch to Resource Sheet view, and then enter the resources listed in Figure 4-51.

Figure 4-51   **Resources for the VPTrain-4 project**

Resource Name	Type	Material Label	Initials	Group	Max. Units	Std. Rate	Ovt. Rate	Cost/ Use	Accrue At	Base Calendar
Hans Hawke	Work		HH	TR2	100%	$100.00/hr	$120.00/hr	$0.00	Prorated	Standard
George Booth	Work		GB	TR2	100%	$75.00/hr	$100.00/hr	$0.00	Prorated	Standard
Manuals	Material		Man			$30.00			Prorated	
Your Name	Work		YN		100%	$100.00/hr	$120.00/hr	$0.00	Prorated	Standard

4. Save your work.
5. Switch to Gantt Chart view, and then open the Assign Resources dialog box.
6. Make an initial assignment of the resource Hans Hawke to tasks 2, 3, 4, 5, 7, and 8. Make an initial assignment of both Hans Hawke and George Booth to tasks 9 and 11. Close the Assign Resources dialog box.
7. Open the Project Information dialog box, click the Statistics button, and make a note of the Current Cost. Close the dialog box.
8. Switch to Resource Usage view, and then apply a filter to show only overallocated resources. Expand to view the tasks for the overallocated resources. Print the view or write down those tasks that are overallocated. (*Note*: If you don't see any overallocated resources, open the Leveling Options dialog box, click Manual, then click the OK button.)
9. Click the first task for the first overallocated resource, and then scroll to the task.
10. On the Resource tab, click the Next Overallocation button to review the overallocated tasks in Resource Usage view. On your printout or notes, use a highlighter to identify which days contain overallocations and the tasks within each overallocation. (*Hint*: You are using the Standard calendar, so overallocations will occur when work exceeds eight hours per day.)
11. Switch to Task Usage view, split the window, and then open the Work Task Form in the Task Form pane. Select the Identify existing skills task; it is the first overallocation.

12. Resolve the overallocation to the Identify existing skills task by using the Work Task Form to add and then assign a new employee, Helene Park, to the task, and then changing Hans Hawke's units to 0%. Be careful not to change the duration or the work. Click the OK button to accept the changes. (*Hint*: When you assign a new resource, you can simply add the resource name and then click the OK button to fill in the rest of the information associated with the resource.)

13. Open the Resource Sheet view in the top pane, and then change Helene Park's information so that the Std. Rate is **50**, the Ovt. Rate is **60**, and her initials are **HP**.

14. Click the Task Usage button to return to the Task Usage sheet in the top pane.

15. Go to the next overallocation, Distribute training manuals. Open the Project Information dialog box. Record the project's scheduled Finish date on a sheet of paper, and then close the Project Information dialog box.

16. Use the Resource Leveling dialog box to level the entire project. (*Hint*: Click the Leveling Options button.) Make sure the Leveling calculations setting is set to Manual. Open the Project Information dialog box again, and then record the project's scheduled Finish date. Close the Project Information dialog box.

17. Remove the split view and view the Leveling Gantt chart. (*Hint*: You may need to use the Scroll to Task button or Zoom buttons to see the Leveling Gantt Chart.) Preview the Leveling Gantt Chart, and then print it so your name is left-aligned in the header.

18. Split the view, with the Work Task Form in the bottom pane. Switch to Gantt Chart view in the top pane, select the Identify needed skills task (task 3), and then assign Helene Park to task 3 in addition to Hans Hawke. Helene will be paid to observe Hans during this task, so this task is not effort driven. Make sure that after the assignment is made, the duration is still three days and that each resource is assigned to work 24 hours. Notice that tasks 2 and 3 are now overallocated. You will address this later.

19. Select Distribute training manuals (task 5), and then assign 10 units of the Manuals resource to it. Note that even though the task is effort driven and a resource was added, the duration (two hours) did not change. On your paper, explain why.

20. Assign Helene Park to the Hire trainers task (task 9). On your paper, explain what happened to the duration and why. Open the Task Information dialog box, click the Resources tab, and then delete the assignment.

21. Clear the effort-driven check box for the Hire trainers task (task 9), and then assign Helene Park to the task again. Note that this time, the duration stays at four days. On your paper, explain why.

22. View the Resource Sheet, resize the columns so that all information is still visible, and then verify that the sheet will print on one page in landscape orientation. Print the sheet, if requested.

23. Switch to Gantt Chart view, apply the Cost table to the Gantt Chart Entry table, and then enter $1000 in the Fixed Cost cell for the Secure lab space task (task 11). This cost pays for the lab space.

24. Open the Project Statistics dialog box, and record the current total cost for the project on your paper.

25. Select the Develop training documentation task (task 4), and make a note of the cost for Hans working on that task. (*Hint*: Refer to the Total Cost column in the Entry table.)

26. Verify the Work Task Form is open in the bottom pane. Hans Hawke has decided to work two hours of overtime for four days on the Develop training documentation task (task 4) to help the project finish sooner. Enter 8 in the Ovt. Work cell for Hans Hawke for task 4, and then accept the changes in the form. Notice how total work doesn't change when you enter the overtime hours.

27. Refer to the Cost form in Gantt Chart view. What is the total cost for Hans for the Develop training documentation task (task 4)? Record your answer on your paper.

28. View the Project Options dialog box via the File tab, and review the information associated with each category. Using the Advanced category information, write down the current setting for levels of Undo. Using the Schedule category information, write down the current default start time, end time, hours per day, hours per week, and days per month. Close the Project Options dialog box.

29. Assign yourself as a resource to the Schedule classes (task 8) task. Close split view if you still have it open. Preview the Gantt chart (it should fit on one sheet of paper). Print this, if requested.

30. Create a Custom report based on the Base Calendar report. Use the Edit button to change the report text font to bold, 12-point Times New Roman. Add your name left-aligned in the header. Print the report, if requested.

31. View the Team Planner for this project file. Print the view, if requested.

32. Level the entire project, and then note the new Project Finish date on your paper. Review Project statistics. What is the final cost?

33. Save the project, submit the project in electronic or printed form, as requested, and then close the project file.

Apply your skills to complete a project for building a new home.

APPLY

Case Problem 1

Data File needed for this Case Problem: Home-4.mpp

River Dell Development, Inc. You have a part-time job working for River Dell Development, Inc., a general contracting company that manages residential construction projects. The project manager has asked you to use Project 2010 to track resource information and make sure that unplanned overallocations do not occur. You'll also track fixed costs and print reports. Complete the following:

1. Open the **Home-4** file located in the **Project4\Case1** folder included with your Data Files.

2. Save the project file as **NewHome-4** in the same folder.

3. Enter the resources shown in Figure 4-52 in Resource Sheet view. Substitute your name and initials as the first resource. Accept the default entries for columns not listed in Figure 4-52.

Figure 4-52 **Resources for the NewHome-4 project**

Resource Name	Type	Material Label	Initials	Group	Max. Units	Std. Rate	Ovt. Rate
Your Name	Work		YN		100%	$50.00/hr	$75.00/hr
General Contractor	Work		GC	Mgmt	100%	$50.00/hr	$75.00/hr
General Labor	Work		GL	Labor	500%	$30.00/hr	$45.00/hr

4. Return to Gantt Chart view, open a split view, and then use the Work Task Form to assign yourself and the General Contractor as the initial assignment to tasks 2 and 3. Notice that these tasks are now overallocated. You will address this later.

5. Remove the split view to return to Gantt Chart view, and then open the Assign Resources dialog box to assign General Labor (100% units) to tasks 6–11 and 13–17. (*Hint:* Use the Shift and Ctrl key to select the tasks, then click Assign.)

6. Format the critical task bars to show the resource names on the right side.

7. Open the Project Information dialog box and record the project finish date.

8. Split the window, and then display the Work Task Form in the bottom pane. Select the Dig foundation task (task 6), and change the units of the General Labor resource to 300% so that the duration changes to one day. (*Hint*: Be sure to click the OK button to make the change.)

9. Click the Next button to navigate to the Pour cement task (task 7), and then change the units of the General Labor resource to 300% so that the duration changes to one day. (*Hint*: Be sure to click the OK button to make the change.)

10. Add a one-day lag to the link between the Pour cement task (task 7) and the Frame house task (task 8) to give the cement time to dry.

11. Select the Frame house task (task 8), and then change the units of the General Labor resource to 500% so that the duration changes to less than three days.

12. Select the Brick exterior task (task 11), and then change the units of the General Labor resource to 500% so that the duration changes to two days.

13. Open the Project Information dialog box and record the new scheduled Finish date for the project. Open the Statistics dialog box and record the current project cost.

14. Use the More Views dialog box to switch to Resource Allocation view. In the top pane, in the Usage Entry table, select the first resource, and then click the Go To Next Overallocation button to find any overallocations. Write a brief explanation as to why this number of hours causes an overallocation for these resources. (*Hint*: Move the split bars as needed to view the Gantt Chart bars.)

15. Use the Resource Leveling dialog box to level the entire project. Be sure the Leveling calculations are set to Manual.

16. Close the split view, and then switch to Leveling Gantt view. Scroll to the first task in the Gantt chart to view the bars, and then zoom to see the entire project. If requested by your instructor, print the Leveling Gantt Chart. On the printout, and identify which tasks were rescheduled by the leveling tool.

17. Apply the Schedule table to the Entry table, and then review the tasks for Free Slack and Total Slack. On the printout, identify which tasks have the most free and total slack. Write a brief explanation describing what this means.

18. Apply the Cost table to the task Entry table, and then enter the following fixed costs: Planning (task 1): **$50,000**; Exterior (task 5): **$25,000**; Interior (task 12): **$30,000**.

19. Switch to Resource Sheet view and double-click the General Labor resource to open the Resource Information dialog box. Click the Costs tab, and then add a new **$40** standard rate and a **$50** overtime rate for the General Labor resource, effective 9/15/2014. Close the dialog box.

20. Enter the materials and material costs in Resource Sheet view. Refer to Figure 4-53. The delivery charge will be a one-time cost per use for each task to which it is assigned. Accept the default entries for columns not listed in Figure 4-53.

Figure 4-53   **Materials and material costs for the NewHome-4 project**

Resource Name	Type	Material Label	Initials	Std. Rate	Cost/Use	Accrue At
Cement	Material		Cement	$1000.00	$0.00	Prorated
Lumber	Material		Lumber	$8000.00	$0.00	Prorated
Shingles	Material		Shingles	$1500.00	$0.00	Prorated
Insulation	Material		Insulation	$1200.00	$0.00	Prorated
Bricks	Material	brick	Bricks	$0.25	$0.00	Prorated
Delivery	Material		Delivery	$0.00	$1000.00	Prorated

21. View the Gantt chart, split the Window, apply the Cost form to the lower pane, and then assign the following:
    - Delivery cost to Exterior (task 5)
    - One unit of the Cement resource to Pour cement (task 7)
    - One unit of the Lumber resource to Frame house (task 8)
    - One unit of the Shingles to Roof house (task 9)
    - One unit of the Insulation to Install insulation (task 10)
    - 20,000 bricks to Brick exterior (task 11)
    - Delivery cost to Interior (task 12), and then remove the split window

⊕ EXPLORE 22. Save the file, then create the Cash Flow report (in the Costs category). Print the Cash Flow report, if requested, with your name left-aligned in the header.

⊕ EXPLORE 23. View the Properties for the project, add your name to the title field, add your home town to the Subject field, and then close the Properties dialog box.

24. Save the file, submit the files to your instructor in printed or electronic form, as requested, and then close the file.

Apply your skills to organize a job search for recent IT graduates.

Case Problem 2

Data File needed for this Case Problem: Jobs-4.mpp

CommunityWorks   As a counselor at CommunityWorks, a career counseling firm, you continue working on a project to help new college graduates with technical degrees find employment. You use Project 2010 to help you manage the project. The job-training counselors Stephanie Sanchez and Oren Amani are both going to help you with some of the tasks. Many tasks overlap, so you use Project 2010 and its leveling tools to gain a more realistic picture of the time that it will take to find a job. Complete the following:

1. Open the **Jobs-4** file in the **Project4\Case2** folder included with your Data Files.

2. Save the file as **MyJobs-4** in the same folder.

3. Add yourself as the first resource in the Resource Sheet. Use your initials in the Initials column. Use ME in the Group column. There are no labor costs associated with this resource. Do not enter any cost values, and accept the other default values.

⊕ EXPLORE 4. Return to Gantt Chart view, click the Gantt Chart Tools Format tab, remove the check mark from the Summary Tasks check box, and then assign yourself as a resource to all the tasks that are currently displayed in the Entry table.

5. View the Resource Sheet, and add two more resources: **Stephanie Sanchez**, initials **SS**, and **Oren Amani**, initials **OA**. Place them in the **CW** group. These two additional resources get $25/hour and don't get overtime pay.

6. Assign Oren as a second resource to task 2, but make sure the duration for Design a business card stays at four hours. (*Hint*: If the duration changes, click the Undo button on the Quick Access toolbar, and then make a change that will keep the duration from changing when you assign Oren as a second resource.)

7. Assign Stephanie and Oren as additional resources to tasks 3, 4, 5, 7, 8, and 9. Let their assignments reduce the duration of each of the tasks.

8. View the Project Information dialog box, record the currently scheduled project Finish date on a sheet of paper, open the Statistics dialog box and record the current costs, and then label the project information you recorded as Project Finish Date before leveling.

9. Switch to Resource Allocation view, in the top pane, select the task Design a business card, scroll to position the calendar on the first task, and then scroll as needed to view each overallocation for all the resources. For each overallocation, review the day and number of hours of assigned work in that day.

10. Remove the split window, open the Resource Usage view, expand your name to view your hours for Thursday May 1, 2014. Change your hours for the three tasks on that day to 2 hours for Design a business card, 2 hours for Create resume, and 4 hours for the Set appointment task.

11. Change Stephanie's working hours for Thursday May 1, 2014 to 4 hours for each of the two tasks she's scheduled to work on that day to remove the overallocation.

12. Select your name, and then click the Level Resource button on the Resource tab. Use the Level Resources dialog box to level the resource. (When you receive a warning message, click Skip All.)

13. Select Stephanie Sanchez, and then click the Level Resource button. Use the Level Resources dialog box to level the resource.

14. Select Oren Amani, and then click the Level Resource button. Use the Level Resources dialog box to level the resource. Write down the change to the Stephanie Sanchez resource. Write down what happened to the your name resource.

15. View the project properties. On the paper that you have been keeping, record the currently scheduled project Finish date. Label the date Project Finish date after leveling.

16. You and Stephanie are still overallocated. Use the Level All button to level the entire project. View the project properties. Record the currently scheduled project Finish date. Label the date Project Finish date after leveling. Notice that you are still overallocated.

17. Close the split view if it is open, and then apply the Leveling Gantt Chart. Select and then scroll to the first task. Be sure you can see the Leveling Delay column and the Gantt bars with the slack lines, and then scroll through each task to see the delays. You see that some tasks will need to be delayed. This is not acceptable, so you decide to ask a friend to help with some of the tasks.

18. Write down which tasks have been split. Write down which tasks have been delayed.

✦ EXPLORE

19. Double-click the Edit resume task to open the Task Information dialog box, click the Resources tab, and then add the name of one of your friends as a fourth resource for the Edit resume task. Switch to the Resource Sheet, add your friend to the ME group, and add your friend's initials. Click the Gantt Chart button to switch back to the Leveling Gantt Chart view.

20. Assign your friend to the Develop contact database task, and then assign four hours of overtime for your friend.

21. Assign your friend to both call references tasks. Remove the split window if you used it to assign resources to tasks.

22. Open the Resource Leveling dialog box. Clear the leveling for the entire project.

23. Click the View tab, and then, in the Data group, use the Group By command to group the tasks by duration. Print the view, if requested.

24. Click the Resource Usage view button to change to Resource Usage view, and change Stephanie's hours for the tasks on Friday May 2 so she is working 1 hour on the Create resume task, 1 hour on the Meet with counselor task, and 2 hours for the these tasks: Edit resume, Develop contact database, and Research newspaper ads. The Set appointment with recruiter task should remain blank. (*Hint*: After changing the time for the Create resume task, change the times for tasks that already have hours associated with them. If a warning dialog box opens, accept the default setting.)

25. Return to the Gantt Chart view. View the Properties, record the currently scheduled project Finish date, labeling this date as Project Finish date after adding a resource. How many days did the additional resource help you shave from your project?

26. Return to the Gantt Chart view, apply the Cost table, and then enter a fixed cost of $300 for the cost of the cell phone in task 11.

✦ EXPLORE 27. Create the Who Does What When report in the Assignments category, with your name left-aligned in the header. Print the report if requested.

✦ EXPLORE 28. Create the To-do List report in the Assignments category for your friend. Add your name left-aligned in the header. (*Hint*: Be sure to use the arrow to select your friend's name when prompted to Show tasks using.) Print the report if requested.

29. Preview and then print the Leveling Gantt Chart with your name left-aligned in the header. On your Leveling Gantt Chart printout, identify which task has the longest total slack and which task was delayed the longest from the original schedule.

30. Save the file, submit the file to your instructor in printed or electronic form if requested, and then close the project file.

Expand your skills by working on a project for a reunion.

CHALLENGE

Case Problem 3

Data File needed for this Case Problem: Reunion-4.mpp

Western College Reunion As a proud graduate of Western College, you have been asked to help organize the 20th reunion for the graduating class of 1994. You'll use Project 2010 to enter and track the resources (you and two consultants) that will be assigned to each task. Because the reunion *must* occur March 7, 8, and 9 of the year 2014, you scheduled the project from a Finish date and let Project 2010 determine the project Start date. Complete the following:

1. Start Project, and then open **Reunion-4** in the **Project4\Case3** folder included with your Data Files.
2. Save the file as **WReunion-4** in the same folder.
3. Enter the resources shown in Figure 4-54 in Resource Sheet view.

Figure 4-54 Resources for the WReunion-4 project

Resource Name	Type	Material Label	Initials	Group	Max. Units	Std. Rate	Ovt. Rate	Cost/Use	Accrue At
Joe Heller	Work		JH	Consultant	100%	$75.00/hr	$100.00/hr	$0.00	Prorated
Ruth Heller	Work		RH	Consultant	100%	$75.00/hr	$100.00/hr	$0.00	Prorated
Your Name	Work		YN		100%	$30.00/hr	$45.00/hr	$0.00	Prorated

4. Return to Gantt Chart view, and then assign yourself to tasks 2 through 6.
5. Assign yourself and Joe Heller to Survey clients (task 1).
6. Assign yourself and Ruth Heller to tasks 7 and 8.

✦ EXPLORE 7. Assigning yourself as the initial assignment for the Set agenda (task 6) task was incorrect, it should be Ruth Heller. Change this assignment.

✦ EXPLORE 8. Show the Project Summary Task bar. (*Hint*: you have to show Summary Tasks to see the bar.) Change the name of the project summary task 0 to **Western College Reunion**, and then add the Cost text to the right side of the bar. Make a note of the current costs.

9. Apply the Cost table to the Entry table in Gantt Chart view, and then enter fixed costs for the following tasks: Survey clients: **$5000**; Book entertainment: **$25,000**; Determine menu: **$20,000**; Develop promotional brochure: **$1000**; Mail brochure: **$750**. On a sheet of paper, record the initial cost for the project.

10. Because you are using Joe and Ruth Heller as consultants, you will not need to spend as many hours on the tasks that include them as resources. Split the window, and then change the work for you on the Survey clients task (task 1) to 10 hours. On your paper, explain why the duration for the task didn't change from five days when work was lowered.

11. Change your work for tasks 7 and 8 to four hours, and then remove the split window. What affect did this change have on the cost of the project? Record your answer.

12. Switch to Resource Allocation view, and then see which resources are overallocated and when.

13. Apply a filter to show only overallocated resources, expand the resources that are overallocated so that you can see the tasks within each resource, and then pre-view Resource Allocation view. Add your name left-aligned in the header, and then print this view. On the printout, highlight the days and tasks affected by the overallocations.

14. Add the name of one of your friends as a resource to this project file. Your friend will make the same standard and overtime rates as you.

⊕ EXPLORE   15. Switch to Task Usage view. Joe Heller is going to take care of the Determine menu task (task 8) instead of Ruth Heller. Use the Assign Resources dialog box to assign Joe to this task instead of Ruth. You remain assigned to the task.

16. Assign your friend to the following tasks as an additional resource: Determine reunion goals, Determine number of attendees, and Set agenda.

17. Use the Level All button to level the entire pool of resources.

18. Remove the split, and then apply the Leveling Gantt Chart. Adjust the columns and calendar as necessary to see the tasks, and then preview and print the Leveling Gantt Chart.

19. On the Leveling Gantt Chart printout, identify which task has the longest total slack and which task was delayed the longest from the original schedule.

20. View the Team Planner. What does it tell you about unassigned tasks?

21. Preview and print the Gantt Chart. What are the final costs?

22. Save the file, submit the file to your instructor in printed or electronic form as requested, and then close the project file.

Expand your skills by working on a fundraising project.

CHALLENGE

Case Problem 4

Data File needed for this Case Problem: Grant-4.mpp

NatureSpace   NatureSpace is a company that specializes in creating play structures for communities. It can also help in securing grants for the project. You are the project manager assigned to manage the fundraising and building of the new play structure at a local neighborhood park. You are spearheading the fundraising effort to purchase new playground equipment. The equipment must be ready by September 6, 2014, so you scheduled the project from a Finish date and let Project 2010 establish the project Start date. Now you need to enter the resources, costs, and assignments to finish planning the project, and then print some key reports to share with the school administrators. Complete the following:

1. Open the **Grant-4** file in the **Project4\Case4** folder included with your Data Files.

2. Save the file as **MyGrant-4** in the same folder.

3. In the Gantt chart, add a Project Summary Task bar, and then change the task name for task 0 to **Playground Project**.

4. Add the Cost field to the right side of the project summary task bar, and then make a note of the current project cost.

5. Use the Resource Sheet to add the following six resources: **Your Name**, **Mayor**, **General Labor** (500% units), **General Contractor**, **Sponsor**, and **Sunset room**. Add initials as you see fit. The costs for General Labor are $35 Standard rate and $40 Overtime. The other work resources have no costs. Sunset room is a material resource with a $30 per-use cost. The General Contractor and General Labor resources should be assigned to the Labor group.

6. Use the Assign Resources dialog box to make the following initial assignments:
   - Establish committee (task 2), Identify park sponsor (task 3), Enlist volunteers (task 4), and Assign duties (task 5): Your name and Mayor
   - Town meeting (task 6): Your Name, Sponsor, and Mayor
   - Plant sale (task 8), Car wash (task 9), and Coupon book sales (task 10): Sponsor, Volunteers (500%). Volunteers are a new resource that you must add to the project file. You want to enlist five volunteers on the project. You can split the view to see the Task Form. Remove the effort-driven check mark when you enter these resources so that the duration does not change from two weeks for each of the fundraising events as you assign resources. (*Hint*: Assign the Sponsor first, then add the Volunteers and change the units for Volunteers.)
   - Compare prices (task 13) and Get requisition (task 14): Your Name, Sponsor, and Mayor
   - Tasks 16, 17, 18, 20, and 21: General Contractor and General Labor (500 units)
   - Assign the Sunset room resource to task 6 and task 8.
   - Open the Resource Sheet and increase the units of Volunteers to 500%.

7. Use the Resource Information dialog box for the Sunset room to add a per-use cost of $50 to Cost rate table B. The town meeting happens at night, so it costs extra to use the Sunset room. You enter this cost in Cost rate table B.

8. Switch to Task Usage view, double-click Sunset room to open the Assignment Information dialog box for the resource for the Town meeting task, and assign Cost rate table B.

9. What is the current project cost? Write your answer on a sheet of paper.

⊕ **EXPLORE** 10. Change the duration for Town meeting (task 6) to one day. Use the Smart Tag to accept the default option that work has increased and it will take more time.

⊕ **EXPLORE** 11. Switch to Resource Sheet view, and then change the calendar for the General Contractor resource to Night Shift.

12. Resize the columns in Resource Sheet view to fit content, then preview the Resource Sheet and be sure it fits on one page in landscape orientation. Print Resource Sheet view if requested to do so by your instructor.

13. Set the Leveling Options in the Resource Leveling dialog box to Automatic, and then Level All. View the Leveling Gantt chart and explain any delay or split tasks.

14. View the Gantt Chart and insert the Cost text to the right of the Planning, Fundraising, and Building summary task bars.

15. Create the Who Does What When report in the Assignments category. Print the report if requested to print by your instructor.

16. Format the critical task bars in Gantt Chart view by showing resource names inside the bars.

⊕ **EXPLORE** 17. Add your name as the Manager in the Properties dialog box.

18. Preview and then print the Gantt chart with your name in the left section of the header.

19. Use the Team Planner to review all the tasks. Verify that there are no more overallocations. Close the Team Planner.

20. Save the file, submit the files to your instructor in printed or electronic form, as requested, and then close the file.

ENDING DATA FILES

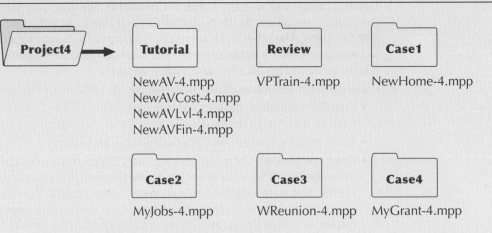

Project4 →

Tutorial

NewAV-4.mpp
NewAVCost-4.mpp
NewAVLvl-4.mpp
NewAVFin-4.mpp

Review

VPTrain-4.mpp

Case1

NewHome-4.mpp

Case2

MyJobs-4.mpp

Case3

WReunion-4.mpp

Case4

MyGrant-4.mpp

PROJECT

OBJECTIVES

Session 5.1
- Set a baseline and create an interim plan
- Review baseline, interim, actual, and scheduled dates
- Work with the Variance and Tracking tables
- Update tasks
- Track costs

Session 5.2
- Create a custom view, a custom table, and a custom report
- Analyze variance, slack, and slippage
- Use the Detail and Tracking Gantt Chart views to track progress
- Add progress lines
- Close a project

Tracking Progress and Closing the Project

Implementing the AV Presentation Rooms Installation Project

Case | *ViewPoint Partners*

The ViewPoint Partners' project file contains the tasks, durations, dependencies, resources, costs, and assignments necessary to install AV presentation rooms. Sidney Simone evaluated the project file, added a few more resources, made minor changes to the tasks, and leveled the overallocations. She approved the currently scheduled project Finish date and total project cost. The project file meets your goals of completing the installation project in three months with the project costs just under $100,000. Now that the planning phase is finished and management approvals are obtained, it is time to start the project and track actual progress. So far your goals of quality, budget, and time are perfect. However, the project has not even started yet.

STARTING DATA FILES

Project5 →

| Tutorial | Review | Case1 | Case2 | Case3 | Case4 |

AV-5.mpp   Train-5.mpp   Home-5.mpp   Jobs-5.mpp   Reunion-5.mpp   Grant-5.mpp
AVFin-5.mpp

SESSION 5.1 VISUAL OVERVIEW

You can use the percent complete buttons to mark tasks 0%, 25%, 50%, 75%, or 100% finished as of the Status date.

The **Tracking table** displays the "actual" fields that show the dates that tasks actually began, and information based on progress information that you enter.

Dates in the Act. Start and Act. Finish columns are entered by you or determined when you update progress as of a Status date based on the percent of a project completed. Actual Finish data is entered by Project when a task is 100% complete.

You can use the **Split Task button** to split a task into two separate parts, or you can position the pointer on the task and then drag the bar to split the task.

The % **Comp.** column tells you the status of a task based on the percentage of the duration completed, which is calculated as (Actual Duration/Duration)*100.

You can use the **Mark on Track** button to mark the task progress based on the Status date, or you click this button and select Update Tasks to open the Update Tasks dialog box, which you use to further control how a task is updated.

If no work has been done on a task, the percent complete, actual duration, actual work, and actual cost values are zero. The remaining duration is the same as the duration field.

NewAV-5.mpp - Microsof

Gantt Chart Tools

File Task Resource Project View Format

Arial 8

0% 25% 50% 75% 100%

B I U

Mark on Track
Respect Links
Inactivate

Gantt Chart Paste View Clipboard Schedule

Gantt Chart

	Task Name	Act. Start	Act. Finish	% Comp.	Phys. % Comp.	Act Du
1	⊟ Analysis	Mon 8/4/14	Wed 8/13/14	100%	0%	
2	Detail c	Mon 8/4/14	Wed 8/6/14	100%	0%	
3	Conduct needs analysis	Thu 8/7/14	Wed 8/13/14	100%	0%	
4	Analysis completed	Wed 8/13/14	Wed 8/13/14	100%	0%	
5	⊟ Design	Tue 8/12/14	Fri 9/5/14	100%	0%	1
6	Build Request for Proposal	Tue 8/12/14	Fri 8/15/14	100%	0%	
7	Gather vendor bids			100%	0%	
8	Choose vendors			100%	0%	
9	Sign contracts			100%	0%	
10	⊟ Installation			96%	0%	9.1
11	Install cabling	Mon 9/8/14	NA	50%	0%	0
12	Install hardware			0%	0%	6.2
13	Install software			0%	0%	
14	Installation completed			0%	0%	
15	⊟ Security			0%	0%	5.8
16	Create user IDs and passwords			0%	0%	
17	Create access hierarchy	Wed 10/8/14	Fri 10/10/14	100%	0%	
18	Create touch panel images	Fri 10/10/14	NA	75%	0%	1
19	Security completed	NA	NA	0%	0%	
20	⊟ Testing	Mon 10/6/14	NA	46%	0%	4.6
21	Test hardware	Mon 10/6/14	Mon 10/6/14	100%	0%	
22	Test software	Tue 10/7/14	NA	50%	0%	
23	Test security	NA	NA	0%	0%	
24	Testing completed	NA	NA	0%	0%	
25	⊟ Training	NA	NA	0%	0%	
26	Train management	NA	NA	0%	0%	
27	Train users	NA	NA	0%	0%	

Ready New Tasks : Auto Scheduled

TRACKING TABLE IN GANTT CHART VIEW

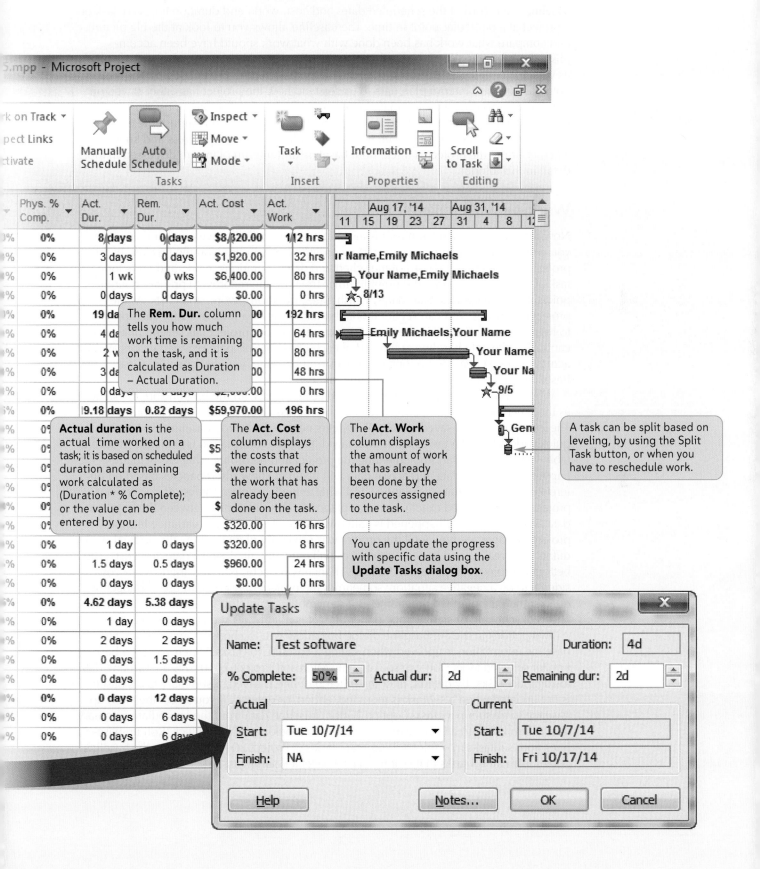

The **Rem. Dur.** column tells you how much work time is remaining on the task, and it is calculated as Duration – Actual Duration.

Actual duration is the actual time worked on a task; it is based on scheduled duration and remaining work calculated as (Duration * % Complete); or the value can be entered by you.

The **Act. Cost** column displays the costs that were incurred for the work that has already been done on the task.

The **Act. Work** column displays the amount of work that has already been done by the resources assigned to the task.

A task can be split based on leveling, by using the Split Task button, or when you have to reschedule work.

You can update the progress with specific data using the **Update Tasks dialog box**.

Understanding Baseline and Interim Plans

Project 2010 allows you to create both a baseline and a series of interim plans. A **baseline** is a record of the scheduled dates and cost, work, and duration for every task of a project at a particular point in time. The baseline allows you to look at the big picture and compare what work has been done with what work should have been accomplished. An **interim plan** is a set of Start and Finish dates that you can save periodically as your project progresses. You save the interim plan after the project begins. You use both baseline and interim plan data to understand how the project has either stayed on or fallen off schedule. Baseline data focuses on scheduled dates, durations, work, and costs, whereas interim plans record only Start and Finish data. You can use the data from the interim plan to compare it with the baseline plan to monitor progress and know whether or not the project is track. Both baseline and interim plans are discussed in more detail in this tutorial.

Working with a Baseline

Now that the AV presentation rooms installation project file is developed and approved, you will set a baseline before you start recording actual progress on the first task of the project. A baseline is a record of the scheduled dates, durations, work, and costs for each task of a project at a particular point in time. The baseline records 20 primary reference points in five categories: Start dates, Finish dates, durations, work, and costs. As the project progresses, you can set additional baselines (up to a total of 11 for each project) to help measure changes in the plan. For example, if your project has several phases, you can save a separate baseline at the end of each phase to compare planned values against actual values. When you no longer need a saved baseline, you can open the Clear Baseline dialog box and select a baseline to clear.

When a baseline is first set, the dates and costs saved with the baseline are the same as the scheduled dates and costs because no progress or costs have been recorded. The information "last saved on (date)" appears next to the word "Baseline" so you can quickly identify when the baseline was saved. Baseline information is available in several table views. As you start implementing the project and recording what has actually happened, baseline data and actual data will begin to show discrepancies based on differences between what was planned and what actually resulted (unless of course your project is implemented *exactly* as it was planned). This difference between the baseline data and what actually happened is called **variance**. Analyzing the variance lets the project manager see how well the project was originally planned, how the original plan differs from reality, and how any variances will affect the final Finish date and costs. The better the project was planned, the less variance will occur. Not all variances are considered to be a negative situation; sometimes the project may come in under budget or quicker than the planned timeframe. But remember, completing a project substantially ahead of schedule or significantly under budget is not always seen as a positive.

Two options in the Set Baseline dialog box allow you to choose how summary task baseline information is updated when saving a baseline for tasks. When you set a baseline for selected tasks, you can specify how Microsoft Project 2010 rolls up baseline data to summary tasks. By default, after the initial baseline is saved, a summary task's baseline is not updated when a subtask is modified, added, or deleted. If you select the "Roll up baseline to all summary tasks" option button, baseline data from the immediate summary task will roll up into all summary tasks to which it belongs. If you select "Roll up baselines from subtasks into selected summary task(s)," Project 2010 will roll up the baseline details from all subtasks that belong to each selected summary task.

REFERENCE

Setting a Baseline

- Click the Project tab, and then, in the Schedule group, click the Set Baseline button.
- On the menu, click Set Baseline to open the Set Baseline dialog box.
- With the Set baseline option button selected, choose the Entire project or Selected tasks option button, as desired, to set a baseline for the entire project or selected tasks.
- Click the OK button.

Now that you are ready to start tracking progress for the ViewPoint Partners AV presentation rooms installation project, you know you have to set a baseline in the project file.

To set a baseline and check statistics:

1. Open the **AV-5** project file located in the **Project5\Tutorial** folder included with your Data Files, and then save it as **NewAV-5** in the same folder. The project file opens in Gantt Chart view.

2. Click the **View** tab, and then, in the Resource Views group, click the **Resource Sheet** button.

3. In the Resource sheet, change the Your Name resource to your name and initials, and then switch back to Gantt Chart view.

4. Click the **Project** tab, and then, in the Properties group, click the **Project Information** button. Note that the currently scheduled Start date is 8/4/14 and the currently scheduled Finish date is 10/23/14. You can find more overall project information in the Projects Statistics dialog box, which is accessible through the Project Information dialog box.

TIP

You can check statistics to get an overview of the project at any point, even before you track progress.

5. In the Project Information dialog box, click the **Statistics** button. Note that the current project cost is $99,870.00, the current work is calculated as 912 hours, and the current duration is calculated as 59 days. Because you have not saved this project with a baseline, all baseline data is either NA or zero. See Figure 5-1.

Figure 5-1   Project Statistics dialog box

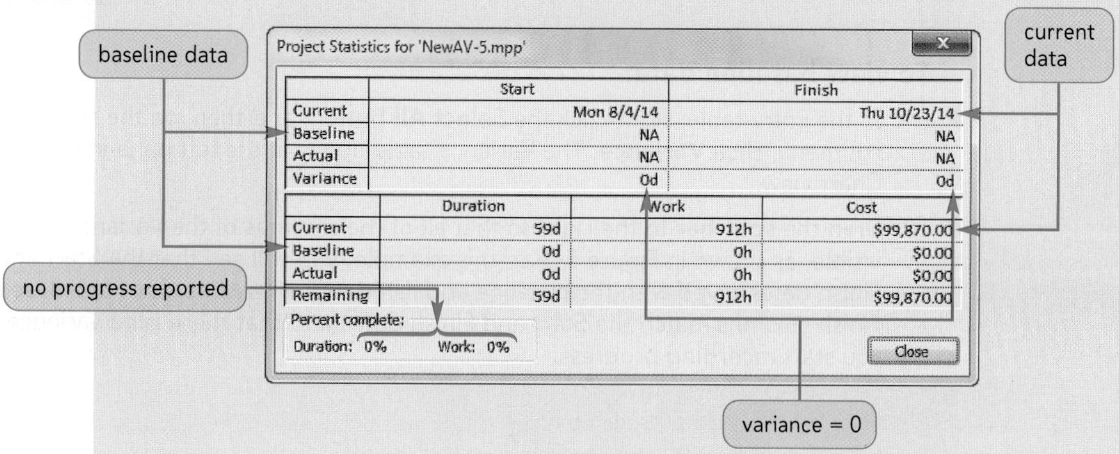

6. In the Project Statistics dialog box, click the **Close** button. Satisfied with the overall statistics for this project and knowing you have approval for these costs and dates, you want to set a baseline.

7. In the Schedule group, click the **Set Baseline** button, and then, on the menu, click **Set Baseline**. The Set Baseline dialog box opens, as shown in Figure 5-2. In this dialog box, you can set a baseline for the entire project or for selected tasks. By default, baselines are set for the entire project.

Figure 5-2 Set Baseline dialog box

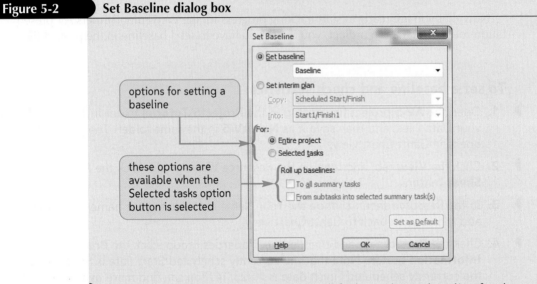

8. Click the **OK** button to accept the defaults and set a baseline for the entire project.

After setting a baseline for the project, you can look at the baseline data, which is displayed in various tables. Remember that you can open different tables in the task sheet by right-clicking the Select All button in the upper-left corner of the task sheet, and then, on the list, clicking the table of your choice. To view the baseline dates for individual tasks, you will apply the Variance table to the Entry table.

To view baseline data:

1. In the Entry table, right-click the **Select All** button, and then, on the shortcut menu, click **Variance**. The Variance table opens in the left pane in Gantt Chart view.

2. Drag the **split bar** to the right so that all of the columns of the Variance table are visible, as shown in Figure 5-3. In this example, you will see that the Start and Finish dates saved with the baseline and listed in the Baseline Start and Baseline Finish columns match the Start and Finish dates and that there is no variance until you start recording progress.

Figure 5-3 — **Variance table**

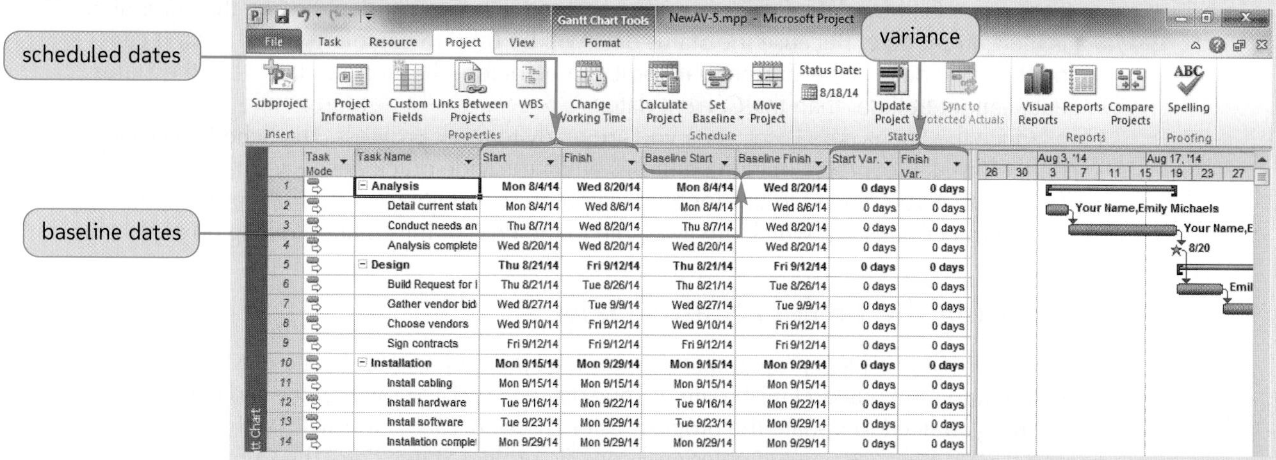

Trouble? If you see pound signs (######) in columns it means the data is too wide to fit. Double-click the right edge of the column heading to widen the column so all the information in the column is displayed.

While you can track progress on a project without a baseline, you will not get variance information without a baseline. Baseline dates and costs are used to calculate the variance. In order to get the most accurate information, it is important that you set a baseline at the point in time at which the project is completely planned but has not yet been started.

INSIGHT

Using Baselines for Future Planning

Regularly monitoring variance and comparing actual data with the baseline data is good project management practice. This information can be used to determine the quality of your planning and can be useful for future projects. Baseline information that consistently differs from current data may indicate that your original plan is no longer accurate, possibly because the scope needs review due to scope creep or because the nature of the project has changed. Other possible reasons for changes in the original plan include weather-related delays, labor issues, or personal problems such as missed time with specific resources. If you plan a new or similar project in the future, this information will serve as a guide so you can better estimate costs and dates.

Now that the baseline is created, you can start tracking actual progress and view variance information. At this point, because actual work on the project has not yet started, the scheduled Start and Finish dates and the baseline Start and Finish dates for each task are the same—and the variance is zero.

Getting Ready to Track Progress

Once a project is underway, project managers update a project with actual information for start dates, hours worked, and costs. This information is recorded in Actual fields, such as the Actual Start Date field. Project managers update the project with actual information in a variety of ways. Many set aside a specific day each week, called the **Status date,** to record all of the actual progress data based on the progress documentation that they received from the previous week. It is important that you identify the Status date before updating entries so that actual data versus planned data is accurate. The Status date is the same as the Current date unless you specify a different Status date. If you do not enter a Current date, Project assumes that today's date, as identified by the computer, is the Current date. Because the Status date will be used to calculate actual data, it can be the same date as the Current date or it can be before the Current date—but the Status date cannot be later than the Current date.

Once the Status date is set, then you are ready to track progress. The Schedule group on the Task tab contains Tracking buttons, which provide quick access to many of the features that you'll need to use for tracking progress. Another way to track progress is using project statistics, which are available in the Project Information dialog box.

Entering the Project Status Date

The ViewPoint Partners project that you are working on has a Start date of Monday, 8/4/14 and a scheduled Finish date of Thursday, 10/23/14. Now that the project has begun, you need to update the progress as of Friday, 8/15/14. You will set the Status date as 8/15/14. Because you are entering a specific project Status date, the Current date field won't be used in any tracking calculations.

To fully understand the implications of tracking a project and to have your screens match the figures in this book, you must start this tutorial as though the Current date is Monday, 8/18/14. This will put your project in the same time frame as when the ViewPoint Partners AV presentation rooms installation project is occurring, which will allow you to update actual progress on the project. Throughout this tutorial, you will be changing the Current date and the Status date to reflect the passage of time needed to show progress.

REFERENCE

Entering a Project Status Date

- Click the Project tab, and then, in the Properties group, click the Project Information button to open the Project Information dialog box.
- In the Status date box, enter the project Status date, or click the arrow and choose a date from the calendar.
- Click the OK button.

or

- To change the Status date without reviewing the information in the Project Information dialog box, click the Project tab, and then, in the Status group, click the Status Date button to open the Status Date dialog box.
- Enter a date in the Select Date box, or click the Date arrow and then click a date from the calendar.
- Click the OK button.

To enter the project Status date:

▶ **1.** In the Properties group on the Project tab, click the **Project Information** button to open the Project Information dialog box.

▶ **2.** In the Status date box, click **NA**, and then type **8/15/14**. You are updating the project's status as of Friday 8/15/14.

▶ **3.** Click the **Current date** arrow to display the calendar, click the **right** or **left arrow** as many times as necessary to display **August, 2014**, and then click **18** to specify that the Current date is Monday 8/18/14, as shown in Figure 5-4.

| **Figure 5-4** | Setting the Status date and the Current date |

enter the Current date here

enter the Status date here

Project Information for 'NewAV-5.mpp'

Start date:	Mon 8/4/14	Current date:	Mon 8/18/14
Finish date:	Thu 10/23/14	Status date:	Fri 8/15/14
Schedule from:	Project Start Date	Calendar:	Standard

All tasks begin as soon as possible.

Priority: 500

Enterprise Custom Fields

Department:

Custom Field Name | Value

Help | Statistics... | OK | Cancel

▶ **4.** In the Project Information dialog box, click the **OK** button. The Status date, 8/15/14, appears in the Status date box on the Project tab in the Status group. If you want to update the Status date without reviewing the Project Information, you can click the Project tab, and then, in the Status group, click the Status Date button to open the Status Date dialog box and enter a date.

The Current and Status dates are updated in the Project Information dialog box. The Status date will be used the next time you update the project by entering task progress information.

Understanding Project Dates and Task Dates

In addition to the Status date and the Current date, you work with a variety of other dates in Project. Understanding the implications that various dates (both project dates and task dates) have on a project is essential to successfully tracking progress. Figure 5-5 outlines the different types of project and task dates that you'll use in this tutorial.

Figure 5-5   Summary of project and task dates

Date	Description	Special Considerations	Best Way to View These Dates
Project Start date	The date on which the entire project starts	If a Start date is entered, Project 2010 schedules all tasks as soon as possible and retains control over the project Finish date.	Project Information dialog box
Project Finish date	The date on which the entire project ends	If a Finish date is entered, Project 2010 schedules all tasks as late as possible and retains control over the project Start date.	Project Information dialog box
Project Current date	Today's date or the date that you want Project to consider as today's date	This date determines the Current date line on the Gantt chart and the default date from which new tasks are scheduled.	Project Information dialog box
Project Status date	The date used to measure project progress	This date helps determine how tasks are updated and rescheduled.	Project tab, Status group, Status dialog box
Task Start and Finish dates	The dates on which the individual task is scheduled to start and finish	If the New Task mode is set to Auto Scheduled, the task's Start and Finish dates are calculated by Project 2010. These dates are constantly changed and recalculated as you assign resources, create dependencies, and level overallocations. Note that if you manually enter a task Start or Finish date, you might create a constraint on that task, such as a "Start No Earlier Than" or "Finish No Earlier Than" constraint that restricts Project 2010's ability to reschedule that task.	Apply the Entry table to the task sheet. The Start and Finish fields represent the scheduled Start and Finish dates for individual tasks.
Task Baseline Start and Baseline Finish dates	The dates on which the individual task was scheduled to start and finish when the baseline was saved	These dates are copied from the currently scheduled task Start and Finish dates, which can be found in the Task Information dialog box, at the point in time at which the baseline is saved. Save a baseline using the Set Baseline dialog box. You can establish up to 11 different baseline plans for a project.	Apply the Variance table to the task sheet.
Task Actual Start and Actual Finish dates	The dates on which the individual task actually started and actually finished	These dates are entered either manually or automatically by using the buttons on the Tracking toolbar. In either case, these dates are based on actual progress information periodically collected by the project manager throughout the life of the project.	Apply the Tracking table to the task sheet.
Task Interim Start and Interim Finish dates	The dates on which the individual task was scheduled to start and finish when the interim plan was saved	These dates are copied from the currently scheduled task Start and Finish dates at the point in time when the interim plan was saved. They do not change. You can establish up to 10 different interim plans for a project.	Create a custom table, and insert the interim Start and Finish fields (Start1 through Start10 and Finish1 through Finish10).

Reviewing the Tracking Buttons

Now that you've established the project Status date, you are ready to track progress. You use the buttons on the Task tab in the Schedule group and in the Tasks group to access some of the tracking features that Project 2010 provides to update and monitor progress in a project. The buttons are described in Figure 5-6. You will learn to work with these commands in the remaining sections of this tutorial.

Figure 5-6	Buttons for updating and rescheduling tasks

Button	Name	Description
	Mark on Track	Marks the selected tasks as updated on schedule according to the schedule based on the Status date.
	Mark on Track button arrow	Opens a menu: Click Update Tasks to open the Update Tasks dialog box, where you can make changes specific to the selected task's progress; click Mark on Track to update the tasks on schedule based on the Status date.
	Respect Links	Moves the selected tasks so their dates are determined by their task dependencies.
	Inactivate/Activate	Marks the selected task as inactive so the task no longer affects the project schedule. Tasks are still in the project but do not affect scheduling of other tasks or resources.
	Split Task	Splits a task into two separate parts.
	Move Task	Moves the task forward or back in the project schedule if the resources are available to work.
	0% Complete	Marks the selected tasks as 0% complete as of the Status date, and actual date, work, and duration data is updated.
	25% Complete	Marks the selected tasks as 25% complete as of the Status date, and actual date, work, and duration data is updated.
	50% Complete	Marks the selected tasks as 50% complete as of the Status date, and actual date, work, and duration data is updated.
	75% Complete	Marks the selected tasks as 75% complete as of the Status date, and actual date, work, and duration data is updated.
	100% Complete	Marks the selected tasks as 100% complete as of the Status date, and actual date, work, and duration data is updated.

INSIGHT

Using the Project Summary Task Bar as You Track Progress

You might find that the Project Summary task bar is helpful when tracking a project. Because the Project Summary task bar reflects overall project information, it's a good way to monitor project statistics while viewing the Gantt chart. For example, you can format it to display the Finish date as well as the current project cost. This way, as you update your project, these valuable statistics are easily viewed on the Gantt Chart.

Using Project Statistics to Monitor Progress

The Project Statistics dialog box provides an overall summary of the date, duration, work, and cost information for a project in progress as of the Status date. This summary is a snapshot of the information at that point in time. You had a brief look at it earlier, but now that you have saved a baseline, you want to reexamine it.

To display project statistics:

▶ **1.** In the Properties group on the Project tab, click the **Project Information** button.

▶ **2.** In the Project Information dialog box, click the **Statistics** button. The Project Statistics for 'NewAV-5.mpp' dialog box opens, as shown in Figure 5-7. The Project Statistics dialog box has been updated to include baseline data. Because no actual progress has been recorded for this project, the variance between the current (scheduled) dates and the dates saved with the baseline is zero.

| Figure 5-7 | Project Statistics dialog box with Baseline data |

Baseline Start and Finish dates

Baseline Duration, Work, and Cost data

▶ **3.** Click the **Close** button in the Project Statistics dialog box.

Understanding and Tracking Variance

TIP

Variance numbers greater than zero indicate tasks are behind schedule; numbers less than zero mean tasks are ahead of schedule.

Variance is defined broadly as the difference between two values. You can calculate variances in dates, hours, or costs. In Project 2010, you want to see the difference between what you planned for and what actually happened. You can view variance values in the Variance table. Because Emily Michaels, the technology specialist, scheduled the AV presentation rooms installation project from a Start date, Project retains control of the project's scheduled Finish date. Project 2010 will recalculate the project's Finish date and calculate variance after you enter actual start and finish dates for individual tasks. The formula for calculating variance is Variance = Currently scheduled (date/work/cost) – Baseline (date). This formula indicates that projects ahead of schedule have a *negative* variance, and projects behind schedule have a *positive* variance. To help you can understand how Project 2010 calculates variance, Figure 5-8 shows the relationship between the Finish and Baseline Finish dates for the same task using three hypothetical cases. In the first case (task 1a), the task is on schedule, so the Finish date and Baseline Finish date are the same and variance is zero. In the second case (task 1b), the task is ahead of schedule. You can see this because the currently scheduled Finish date is earlier than the Baseline Finish date. The fact that the task is ahead of schedule is shown as a negative variance; the difference in the dates mathematically creates a negative number. In the third case (task 1c), the task is behind schedule. You can see this because the currently scheduled Finish date is later than the Baseline Finish date. The fact that the task is behind schedule is shown as a positive variance because the calculated difference in the dates is a positive number.

Figure 5-8	Examining variance

Task	Start	Finish	Baseline Start	Baseline Finish	Start Variance	Finish Variance	Notes
Task 1a	Wednesday May 3	Thursday May 4	Wednesday May 3	Thursday May 4	0 days	0 days	on schedule — no variance
Task 1b	Wednesday May 3	Wednesday May 3	Wednesday May 3	Thursday May 4	0 days	-1 days	ahead of schedule — negative variance
Task 1c	Wednesday May 3	Friday May 5	Wednesday May 3	Thursday May 4	0 days	1 day	behind schedule — positive variance

For the ViewPoint Partners project, the current Start date is the same as the originally scheduled Start date because no actual progress has been tracked. In addition, the Start Var. and Finish Var. fields are zero because no actual progress has been tracked. The project is neither ahead of nor behind schedule. As you update tasks with actual data, the currently scheduled Start date and the Variance data could change. As you work with a project file, you will want to update the status of the tasks. As you update tasks, you will find that some tasks are on schedule, some are behind schedule, and some are ahead of schedule. You can update an individual task or a group of tasks. You can update tasks using several methods, including adding data to the Tracking table, clicking buttons in the Schedule group on the Gantt Chart Tools Format tab, or updating the Task Information dialog box.

Updating Tasks and Using the Tracking Table

To enter actual progress data into a project, you can use sheet, form, or graphical views. You record project progress by entering data, including actual dates, actual durations, actual costs, and actual work. Most project managers enter actual Start and Finish dates for individual tasks and allow Project 2010 to automatically update the data for actual duration, cost, and work fields based on default formulas. Others prefer to enter actual work hours while leaving the cost and date calculations to Project 2010.

When you enter actual Start and Finish dates for a task, many other actual fields of information are updated. For example, the actual Start and Finish dates of a task determine the actual duration (actual Finish date – actual Start date), which in turn determines the actual work (Work = Duration * Units). The actual work value is used to calculate the actual cost (Cost = Work Hours * Cost/Hr/Resource). To enter the actual Start and Finish dates and observe the effect on other actual fields, you use the Tracking table because it provides all of the actual fields (actual date, actual duration, actual work, and actual cost) in a single sheet view. If you see an error in the scheduled duration, you can change the duration in the Tracking table.

To apply the Tracking table to the task sheet:

1. In the Variance table, right-click the **Select All** button, click **Tracking**, widen the columns to fit content, and then drag the **split bar** so that the Act. Work column is the last column visible. Currently, the value of the Rem. Dur. (remaining duration) field for all tasks equals the Duration value as seen in the Entry table because no progress has yet been applied to this project.

2. Click the **Detail current status (task 2) Act. Dur.** cell, type **2d**, and then press the **Enter** key. The Tracking table should look like Figure 5-9. The remaining duration for the task is calculated as 1 day. The actual and remaining duration fields for the Analysis summary task have been updated. A progress bar appears on the task bar. Cost data has also been calculated.

| Figure 5-9 | Tracking table with duration data entered |

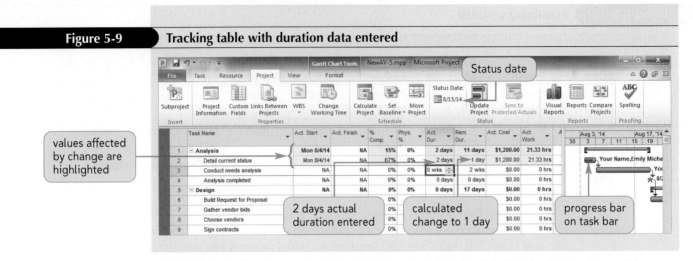

Even though you can type actual values directly into each field in the Tracking table, you will want to use the buttons on the Task tab in the Schedule group whenever possible. When you use these buttons, several actual fields (dates, duration, work, and costs) are updated simultaneously and automatically. The **progress bar** within each task bar in the Gantt chart represents the percentage of the task that has been completed. You can update a task to show percentage complete as of the project Status date, or you can update the task to show complete as scheduled.

INSIGHT

Understanding Which Tasks to Update

The tasks that you update are driven by the progress information that you have collected, perhaps via updates by your team or by visual inspection. In a small project, you might simply *know* what tasks need to be updated because you are involved in the completion of each task in the project. In larger projects, you'll want to establish a regular status reporting system with others so that the status information is collected in a timely manner and entered accurately. Establishing regular status meetings and reporting requirements are essential for good management and successful project completion. You can use this program information to know which tasks to update.

Updating Tasks that are on Schedule

If your project is being completed according to schedule, you can quickly report its progress. Use the Mark on Track button in the Schedule group to update the scheduling information for selected tasks to indicate if actual dates, costs, and work match the scheduled dates, costs, and work.

The ViewPoint Partners AV presentation rooms installation project is progressing smoothly. You need to update those tasks that are on schedule as of the Status date.

To update the task that is on schedule as of the Status date:

1. Click **Detail current status** (task 2), click the **Task** tab, and then, in the Schedule group, click the **Mark on Track** button. This task was completed in 3 days and has no remaining work.

2. Adjust column width as needed to fit content, drag the **split bar** to see the Act. Work column, and then compare your screen to Figure 5-10.

Figure 5-10   Updating a task that is on schedule

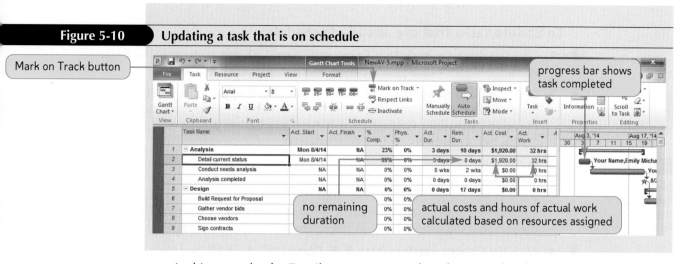

In this example, the Detail current status task (task 2) is updated as scheduled, which means the scheduled Start date (8/4/14) is automatically entered in the Act. Start (actual start) date field. Project 2010 uses this date and the value in the Rem. Dur. (remaining duration) field to calculate the actual Finish date. In turn, the Act. Dur. (actual duration), Act. Cost (actual cost), and Act. Work (actual work) fields also are updated. The project is going well, and you continue to update tasks.

To update multiple tasks that are on schedule as of the Status date:

▶ **1.** Click **Conduct needs analysis** (task 3), press and hold the **Shift** key, click **Build Request for Proposal** (task 6), and then release the **Shift** key.

▶ **2.** In the Schedule group on the Task tab, click the **Mark on Track** button to update these tasks.

▶ **3.** Save your work.

When you update a project, only actual data for tasks scheduled *before* the Status date are updated. You can't update actual values for a task "as scheduled" that is scheduled in the future. The Conduct needs analysis task is only 70% complete as of the Status date, so the milestone task (Analysis completed) is not updated. Tasks in the Design phase, such as Build Request for Proposal, do not update because the scheduled Start and Finish dates for these tasks are after the Status date for which you are updating progress. When you updated the progress, these tasks could not be updated as of the Status date using the Mark on Track button.

Updating Tasks that are Ahead of Schedule

If a task is being completed ahead of schedule, you can use the Percent Complete buttons on the Task tab in the Schedule group to indicate progress even if the task is scheduled for the future. Alternatively, you can enter the specific progress dates, duration, cost, or work data directly into the Tracking table. As you enter task progress, Project continues to calculate variance if it exists.

You got a jump on things and completed all the work in the Analysis phase and some of the work for the Design phase tasks ahead of schedule, and you want to enter this information for the project.

To update tasks that are ahead of schedule:

1. Click the **Analysis (task 1) % Comp.** cell, type **100**, and then press the **Enter** key. All subtasks in the Analysis phase are marked as 100% completed.

2. Click the **Build Request for Proposal (task 6) % Comp.** cell, type **60**, and then press the **Enter** key. Data is updated for the Design summary task as well as for the Build Request for Proposal (task 6) task. The Gather vendor bids (task 7) % Comp. cell is selected.

3. In the Schedule group, click the **25% Complete** button ⊟. This action updates the Gather vendor bids task to be 25% complete in the areas of duration, cost, and work. It also copies the scheduled Start date from the Task Information dialog box into the Act. Start field. Project 2010 enters the scheduled Start date as the actual date (even if the actual date is in the future) unless you manually change the date.

4. Click the **Choose vendors (task 8) % Comp.** cell, type **10**, and then press the **Enter** key. The Tracking table should look like Figure 5-11. Even though these three tasks (6, 7, and 8) are not scheduled to start until after the Status date, you are able to enter data that shows what percentage of work has been completed.

TIP

The date entered in the Act. Start column alerts you to the fact that these tasks are ahead of schedule.

| Figure 5-11 | Updating tasks that are ahead of schedule |

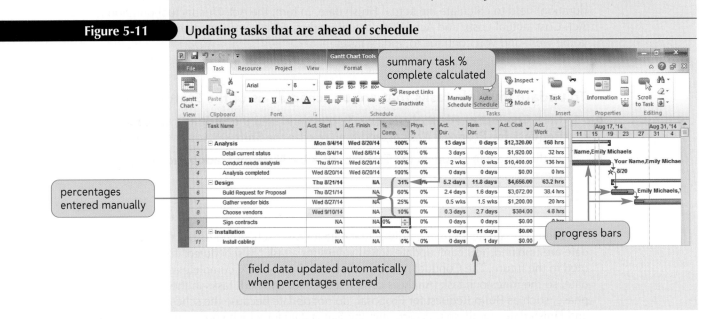

You know that many tasks will need updating, and you want to take advantage of Project features to make your job easier. You can use the fill handle to enter the same data down a column just as you used the fill handle to copy durations to multiple tasks in earlier tutorials. The fill handle is the small black box that appears in the lower-right corner of a selected cell.

To use the fill handle to enter data:

▶ 1. Click the **Build Request for Proposal (task 6) % Comp.** cell. This task is 60% complete. You can copy values from one cell to other cells below it by dragging the fill handle.

▶ 2. Place the Fill pointer + on the **Build Request for Proposal (task 6) % Comp.** cell fill handle, and then drag the **fill handle** for that cell down to the **Gather vendor bids (task 7) % Comp.** cell. As a result of the fill, the Design summary task is updated to 51% complete.

▶ 3. Save your work.

You can enter any percentage in the % Comp. field for any subtask or summary task. As you update tasks using either the Percent Complete buttons or % Comp. field, the currently scheduled Start date will be copied into the Act. Start date field. The currently scheduled Finish date will be copied into the Act. Finish date field.

Projects often have many tasks that start or finish on the same date. You can quickly update actual start and finish dates for more than one task that has the same date or that has the same percentage completed. Press and hold the Ctrl or Shift key to select each task that you want to update, and then, on the Project tab, in the Status group, click Update Project to open the Update Project dialog box. Click Update work as complete through, type or select a date, and then click the selected tasks option button and complete the dialog box. You will use this dialog box later in the tutorial.

You can also enter actual dates. Entering an actual start or finish date for a task changes the task's scheduled dates. Baseline dates, however, are not affected by changes that you make to the actual or scheduled dates. If you enter an actual finish date for a task, Project calculates it to be 100% complete. If you are updating one task at a time, you use the Update Tasks dialog box. The Update Tasks dialog box is available by clicking the Task tab, in the Schedule group, clicking the Mark on Track button arrow, and then clicking Update Tasks on the menu.

REFERENCE

Updating Progress Using the Update Tasks Dialog Box

- Select the task to be updated.
- On the Task tab, in the Schedule group, click the Mark on Track button arrow, and then click Update Tasks to open the Update Tasks dialog box.
- Enter the actual dates, durations, or percent complete information as appropriate for that task.
- Click the OK button.

To enter the Actual Start date:

▶ 1. Click **Build Request for Proposal** (task 6), and then, in the Schedule group on the Task tab, click the **Mark on Track** button arrow.

▶ 2. On the list, click **Update Tasks**. The Update Tasks dialog box opens.

▶ 3. In the Actual section, click the **Start** arrow to open the calendar.

▶ 4. Scroll as needed to August 2014, and then click **15** to select August 15, 2014. See Figure 5-12.

Figure 5-12   Update tasks dialog box for Build Request for Proposal task

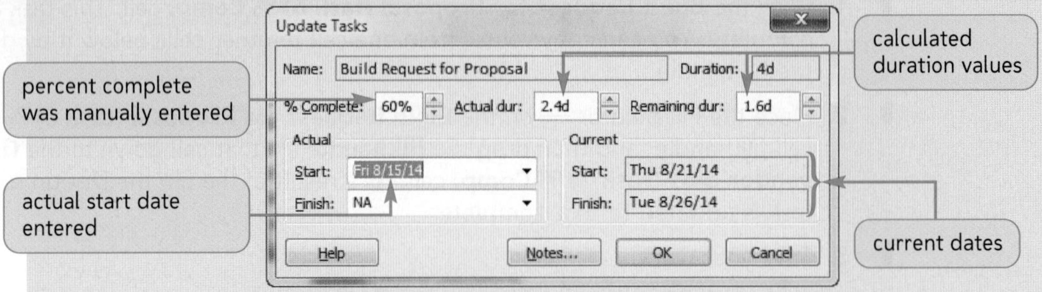

percent complete was manually entered

actual start date entered

calculated duration values

current dates

> **5.** Click the **OK** button to close the Update Tasks dialog box. The Gather vendor bids task has also started on 8/15.

> **6.** Click **Gather vendor bids** (task 7), and then, in the Schedule group on the Task tab, click the **Mark on Track** button arrow.

> **7.** On the list, click **Update Tasks**. The Update Tasks dialog box opens.

> **8.** In the Actual section, click the **Start** arrow to open the calendar, and then click **15** to select August 15, 2014.

> **9.** Click the **OK** button to close the Update Tasks dialog box.

> **10.** Save your work.

This project is moving along and time is passing. In order to see the effects of a project progressing, you have to update the Current and Status dates to indicate that time has passed. You will set a new Current date (Monday 8/25/14) as well as a new Status date (Friday 8/22/14). After entering the new dates, you will continue to update the project file.

To update the Current date and the Status date:

> **1.** Click the **Project** tab, and then, in the Properties group, click the **Project Information** button.

> **2.** In the Project Information dialog box, click the **Current date** arrow, and then click **25** in the August 2014 calendar to specify Mon 8/25/14 as the new Current date.

> **3.** Click the **Status date** arrow, and then click **22** to specify Fri 8/22/14 as the new Status date.

> **4.** Click the **OK** button. The Status date is updated; you see the change in the Status group on the Project tab.

INSIGHT

Updating Tasks When Using Microsoft Project Server

Project 2010 provides a Web-based communication system called Microsoft Project Server that allows many people working in various locations and times to view and update the project. A **workgroup** is a subset of resources that exchanges status information about parts of a project through a network. You might want to exchange part of a project because perhaps not all members of the project should see all parts of the project plan, based on confidentiality or relevance.

In projects where the data is collected through Microsoft Project Server and tasks are updated through a network, the options allow project managers to accept or reject task and calendar updates. These options are available only if you have set up Microsoft Project 2010 Professional to run with Microsoft Project Server.

Creating an Interim Plan

While you hope that your initial baseline plan remains a realistic yardstick throughout a project, this is often not the case. To help project managers clearly see how a project varies from its initial baseline, project managers commonly save an interim plan at various stages in the project (such as after each major phase or at the beginning of each month). An interim plan is a set of Start and Finish dates that you can save periodically as your project progresses. The set of dates might be for selected tasks or for the entire project. Project managers can then compare interim dates to the initial baseline dates. Unlike a baseline, the interim plan does not save duration, work, or cost values; instead, an interim plan saves only Start and Finish dates. You can save up to ten interim plans for a project.

An interim plan helps project managers more clearly determine which phases or time periods were realistically scheduled and which were not. Because default tables, views, or reports do not provide information based on the interim plan, you can define custom tables and views that contain the interim plan fields so that you can quickly view and report on this information.

REFERENCE

Saving an Interim Plan

- Select the tasks for which you want to create the interim plan, or select no tasks if you want to save an interim plan for the entire project.
- Click the Project tab, and then, in the Schedule group, click the Set Baseline button.
- On the menu, click Set Baseline to open the Set Baseline dialog box.
- Click the Set interim plan option button to make the boxes under that option button active.
- If needed, click the Copy arrow, click the interim Start/Finish date field, click the Into arrow, and then click the appropriate Start/Finish date field.
- Click the Entire project or Selected tasks option button, and then click the OK button.

You decide to save an interim plan after completing each major phase of the ViewPoint Partners project. You will use this information to compare the interim plans to the baseline, which will help you more easily determine how accurate the initial planning was for each phase. With the Analysis phase complete and the Design phase just over half done, this is a good time to save an interim plan.

To save an interim plan for selected tasks:

▶ **1.** Drag to select from **Analysis** (task 1) through **Analysis completed** (task 4). Tasks 1 through 4 are selected.

▶ **2.** In the Schedule group on the Project tab, click the **Set Baseline** button.

▶ **3.** On the menu, click **Set Baseline**. The Set Baseline dialog box opens.

▶ **4.** Click the **Set interim plan** option button, and then, in the For section, click the **Selected tasks** option button.

   Trouble? Be sure to select the Selected tasks option button to avoid setting an interim plan for all tasks in the project.

▶ **5.** Click the **OK** button. The currently scheduled dates in the Start and Finish fields for the selected tasks are copied into the Start1 and Finish1 fields. The Start1 and Finish1 fields are not yet visible in the Tracking table but will be added in the next section.

The interim date values will be useful as more progress is reported for the project. However, for the example in this tutorial, the interim plan you saved will be used to learn how to view interim dates. To view the interim dates, you must add them by inserting the Start1 and Finish1 columns in the Tracking table.

Inserting Interim Plan Columns in the Variance Table

When you are tracking progress, it is difficult to get all of the information that you want to see at one time on the screen because you are working with several sets of Start and Finish dates for each task (scheduled, baseline, actual, and potentially interim dates). By default, the baseline dates are shown in the Variance table and the Actual dates are shown in the Tracking table. The scheduled Start and Finish dates are shown in several tables (and are labeled Start and Finish). It's important that you know how to create a table with the columns of information that you want to see. You can easily insert or hide a column in any table.

You might want to display more columns, such as the columns that show the actual dates, scheduled dates, and baseline dates, on one table. For example, the second and third columns in the Variance table show the scheduled Start and Finish dates for each task. You might want to insert the Act. Start and Act. Finish and the Start1 and Finish1 columns in this table so that you can compare the interim plan dates (Start1 and Finish1) with the dates in these other columns. When you insert a new column, a Field name list opens and includes all of the fields of data that are available in the project file.

To insert columns in the Variance table:

▶ **1.** In the Tracking table, right-click the **Select All** button, click **Variance** to apply the Variance table, and then drag the **split bar** to the right as needed so that all of the columns of the Variance table are visible. The rightmost column is Finish Var. You see that some tasks in the Design phase show a negative variance. This negative is because you entered tasks that were ahead of schedule.

▶ **2.** Right-click the **Start** column heading, and then click **Insert Column**. The new Column is inserted and the list of available field names opens.

▶ **3.** Press the **A** key to quickly scroll to the field names that start with the letter A. The Actual Start field is about midway in the list. See Figure 5-13.

Figure 5-13 · **Inserting a column in the Variance table**

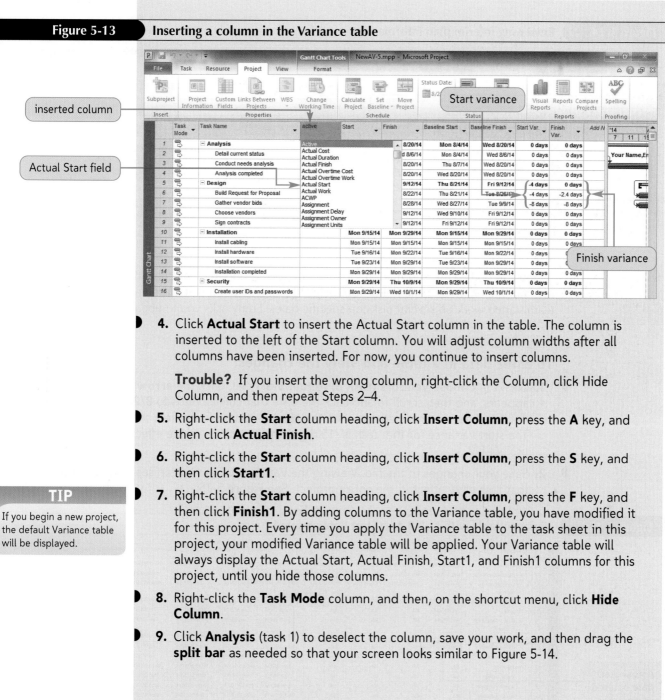

4. Click **Actual Start** to insert the Actual Start column in the table. The column is inserted to the left of the Start column. You will adjust column widths after all columns have been inserted. For now, you continue to insert columns.

   Trouble? If you insert the wrong column, right-click the Column, click Hide Column, and then repeat Steps 2–4.

5. Right-click the **Start** column heading, click **Insert Column**, press the **A** key, and then click **Actual Finish**.

6. Right-click the **Start** column heading, click **Insert Column**, press the **S** key, and then click **Start1**.

TIP

If you begin a new project, the default Variance table will be displayed.

7. Right-click the **Start** column heading, click **Insert Column**, press the **F** key, and then click **Finish1**. By adding columns to the Variance table, you have modified it for this project. Every time you apply the Variance table to the task sheet in this project, your modified Variance table will be applied. Your Variance table will always display the Actual Start, Actual Finish, Start1, and Finish1 columns for this project, until you hide those columns.

8. Right-click the **Task Mode** column, and then, on the shortcut menu, click **Hide Column**.

9. Click **Analysis** (task 1) to deselect the column, save your work, and then drag the **split bar** as needed so that your screen looks similar to Figure 5-14.

Figure 5-14   **Reviewing interim plan information**

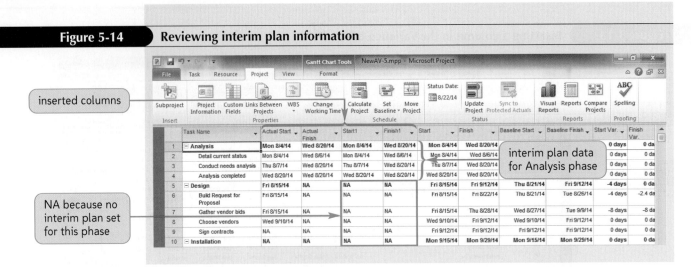

You can update the information for any field, such as the Act. Start date field, by entering information in the table fields. You review the notes from the Status meeting. The team started work on several tasks on specific dates. Emily asks you to update the file.

To enter data in a table and view the changes:

1. Click the **Choose vendors (task 8) Actual Start** cell, click the **arrow** that appears, and then scroll to and click the date that corresponds to **8/20/14**. The Act. Start date is changed and the Start date is updated to reflect that change. The start variance for that task is -15 days. This created a ripple effect through the project file.

2. Save your changes to the file. Viewing the Variance table you can see how starting that task early affected the entire project. See Figure 5-15.

Figure 5-15   **Variance table with task 8 Act. Start date updated**

	Task Name	Actual Start	Actual Finish	Start1	Finish1	Start	Finish	Baseline Start	Baseline Finish	Start Var.	Finish Var.
1	⊟ Analysis	Mon 8/4/14	Wed 8/20/14	Mon 8/4/14	Wed 8/20/14	Mon 8/4/14	Wed 8/20/14	Mon 8/4/14	Wed 8/20/14	0 days	0 days
2	Detail current status	Mon 8/4/14	Wed 8/6/14	Mon 8/4/14			8/6/14	Mon 8/4/14	Wed 8/6/14	0 days	0 days
3	Conduct needs analysis	Thu 8/7/14	Wed 8/20/14	Thu 8/7/14			20/14	Thu 8/7/14	Wed 8/20/14	0 days	0 days
4	Analysis completed	Wed 8/20/14	Wed 8/20/14	Wed 8/20/1			20/14	Wed 8/20/14	Wed 8/20/14	0 days	0 days
5	⊟ Design	Fri 8/15/14	NA	NA	NA	Fri 9/2/14	Tue 9/12/14	Thu 8/21/14	Fri 9/12/14	-4 days	-8.3 days
6	Build Request for Proposal	Fri 8/15/14	NA	NA	NA	Fri 8/15/14	Fri 8/22/14	Thu 8/21/14	Tue 8/26/14	-4 days	-2.4 days
7	Gather vendor bids	Fri 8/15/14	NA	NA	NA	Fri 8/15/14	Thu 8/28/14	Wed 8/27/14	Tue 9/9/14	-8 days	-8 days
8	Choose vendors	Wed 8/20/14	NA	NA	NA	Wed 8/20/14	Tue 9/2/14	Wed 9/10/14	Fri 9/12/14	-15 days	-8.3 days
9	Sign contracts	NA	NA	NA	NA	Tue 9/2/14	Tue 9/2/14	Fri 9/12/14	Fri 9/12/14	-8.3 days	-8.3 days
10	⊟ Installation	NA	NA	NA	NA	Tue 9/2/14	Wed 9/17/14	Mon 9/15/14	Mon 9/29/14	-8.3 days	-8.3 days
11	Install cabling	NA	NA	NA	NA	Tue 9/2/14	Wed 9/3/14	Mon 9/15/14	Mon 9/15/14	-8.3 days	-8.3 days
12	Install hardware	NA	NA	NA	NA	Wed 9/3/14	Wed 9/10/14	Tue 9/16/14	Mon 9/22/14	-8.3 days	-8.3 days
13	Install software	NA	NA	NA	NA	Wed 9/17/14	Wed 9/17/14	Tue 9/23/14	Mon 9/29/14	-8.3 days	-8.3 days
14	Installation completed	NA	NA	NA	NA	Wed 9/17/14	Wed 9/17/14	Mon 9/29/14	Mon 9/29/14	-8.3 days	-8.3 days
15	⊟ Security	NA	NA	NA	NA	Wed 9/17/14	Mon 9/29/14	Mon 9/29/14	Thu 10/9/14	-8.3 days	-8.3 days
16	Create user IDs and passwords	NA	NA	NA	NA	Wed 9/17/1			Wed 10/1/14	-8.3 days	-8.3 days
17	Create access hierarchy	NA	NA	NA	NA	Fri 9/19/1			Tue 10/7/14	-8.3 days	-8.3 days
18	Create touch panel images	NA	NA	NA	NA	Thu 9/25/14	Mon 9/29/14	Wed 10/8/14	Thu 10/9/14	-8.3 days	-8.3 days
19	Security completed	NA	NA	NA	NA	Mon 9/29/14	Mon 9/29/14	Thu 10/9/14	Thu 10/9/14	-8.3 days	-8.3 days
20	⊟ Testing	NA	NA	NA	NA	Wed 9/17/14	Thu 9/25/14	Tue 9/30/14	Tue 10/7/14	-8.3 days	-8.3 days
21	Test hardware	NA	NA	NA	NA	Wed 9/17/14	Thu 9/18/14	Tue 9/30/14	Wed 10/1/14	-8.3 days	-8.3 days
22	Test software	NA	NA	NA	NA	Thu 9/18/14	Wed 9/24/14	Wed 10/1/14	Mon 10/6/14	-8.3 days	-8.3 days
23	Test security	NA	NA	NA	NA	Thu 9/18/14	Thu 9/25/14	Wed 10/1/14	Tue 10/7/14	-8.3 days	-8.3 days
24	Testing completed	NA	NA	NA	NA	Thu 9/25/14	Thu 9/25/14	Tue 10/7/14	Tue 10/7/14	-8.3 days	-8.3 days

Ready   New Tasks : Auto Scheduled

Because you redefined the columns for the Variance table, it will always display the Act. Start, Act. Finish, Start1, and Finish1 columns for this project file. If you want to keep your default Variance table and the modified Variance table so that both are available in this project, you can create a custom table based on the modified Variance table. You will learn how to create a custom table in Session 5.2.

Time is passing and this project continues to move along. In order to see the effects of a project progressing, you have to update the Current and Status dates. To do this, you set a new Current date (Monday 9/1/14) as well as a new Status date (Friday 8/29/14), and then you continue to update the project file.

To update the Current date and the Status date:

▶ **1.** In the Properties group on the Project tab, click the **Project Information** button.

▶ **2.** In the Project Information dialog box, click the **Current date** arrow, and then set **Mon 9/1/14** as the new Current date.

▶ **3.** Click the **Status date** arrow, and then set **Fri 8/29/14** as the new Status date.

▶ **4.** Click the **OK** button.

The Current and Status dates are updated in the Project Information dialog box. These dates will be used the next time you update the project by entering task information, either manually or using the Mark on Track button.

Understanding Conflicts and Updating the Project

The installation and design teams have been making tremendous progress and have begun the task of running some cable. The currently scheduled Start date for the Install cabling task is 9/8/14. Your notes state that it started on 8/25/14. As you have learned, you can update tasks ahead of schedule. Now you will update tasks ahead of schedule by entering the actual date that they started.

To enter the Actual Start date:

▶ **1.** In the Variance table, right-click the **Select All** button, and then click **Tracking** to apply the Tracking table. The default Tracking table includes the Act. Start and Act. Finish columns. These were columns you had to add to the default Variance table. The default Tracking table does not include the columns associated with the interim plan (Start1 and Finish1). If you wanted to view those columns in the default Tracking table, you would have to insert them.

▶ **2.** Click the **Install cabling (task 11) Act. Start** cell, type **8/25/14**, and then press the **Enter** key.

Project 2010 allows you to enter actual work for a task even though it is scheduled for the future and has a Finish-to-Start relationship with a predecessor task (Sign contracts) that has not yet been completed. Emily corrects your notes and says that the contractor did not start on 8/25, although she is unsure of the exact date, and that one hour of work has been completed on the task. Next, you decide to reset the actual Start date to NA and then to enter one hour of work on this task to reflect what has been done and let Project 2010 calculate the other numbers.

TIP

The Actual Work cell is the rightmost cell in the Tracking table.

To enter work to calculate the Start date:

1. On the Quick Access Toolbar, click the **Undo** button 🔄 to set the actual start date for Install cabling (task 11) back to NA.

2. Drag the **split bar** as needed to the right until you can see the Act. Work column, and then click the **Install cabling (task 11) Act. Work** cell.

3. Type **1**, and then press the **Enter** key. Notice how the scheduled Start date of Tuesday 9/2/14 was entered as the Act. Start date for the Install cabling task and the task is calculated at 3% complete. Project 2010 does not warn you when you enter work to show progress on a date that comes after the Status date. Notice that costs have been calculated for the work done. See Figure 5-16.

Figure 5-16   **Work entered for task 11**

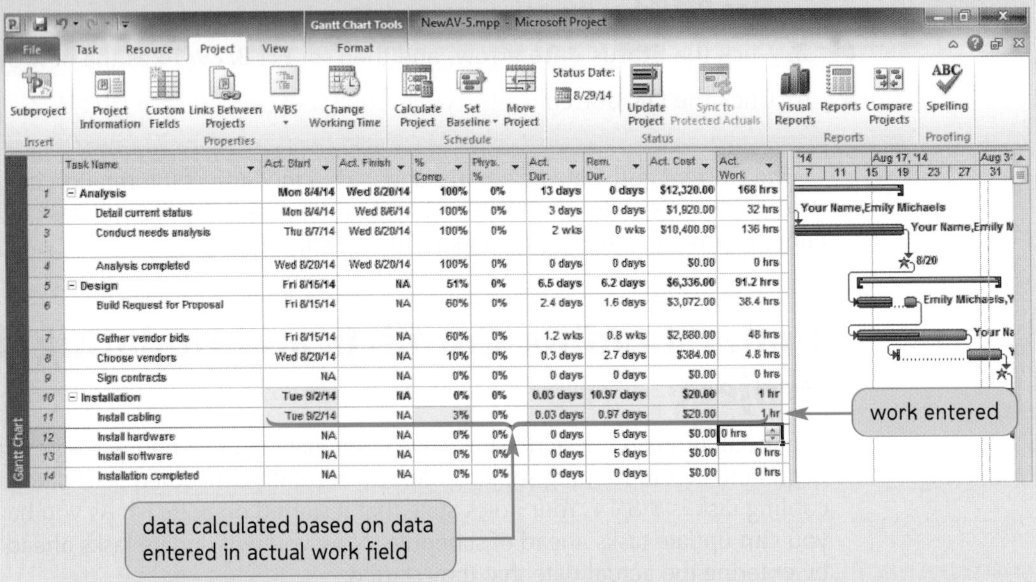

4. Right-click **Install cabling** (task 11), and then, on the shortcut menu, click **Scroll to Task**.

5. On the Quick Access toolbar, click the **Save** button 💾 to save the file.

Recall the formula Work = Duration * Units. Four General Labor work resources are assigned to the Install cabling task. You entered one hour in the Act. Work cell. Project 2010 calculated the actual duration (Act. Dur.) as 3/100 of a day. The remaining duration (Rem. Dur.) is the difference between the current duration (one day for this task) and the actual duration (0.03) and is, therefore, calculated as 0.97 days.

INSIGHT

Overriding Conflicts and the Planning Wizard

You may find that when you enter actual Start dates, you create a conflict. The Planning Wizard provides assistance in these cases. For example, the Planning Wizard warns if an action will cause a scheduling conflict because you have indicated work has started on a successor task that has a Finish-to-Start relationship with a predecessor task that hasn't been finished yet. You can cancel the action or allow the scheduling conflict. Project 2010 allows actual entries to override logic, but Project 2010 does not retain this information or track logic errors. If you override the Planning Wizard warning, you will not be reminded of this conflict in logic again.

Updating Tasks that are Behind Schedule

Time is moving quickly. Three more weeks have passed and the ViewPoint Partners project is progressing. Some tasks are now complete. A few other tasks are running behind schedule. If a task is behind schedule, you can use the Percent complete buttons on the Task tab in the Schedule group to indicate progress, just as you did for tasks that are ahead of schedule. Or, you can enter the specific progress dates or duration, cost, or work data directly into the Tracking table. For example, after dropping off the cabling and beginning the task, the installers ran into problems with the existing walls and the task was delayed. They have completed only 50% of the work for the Install cabling task by 9/12/14, even though that task was scheduled to be finished on 9/15/14.

You need to set a new Current date as well as a new Status date, and then continue to update the project file.

INSIGHT

Rescheduling Work

Project can help you with rescheduling tasks that are behind schedule. Right-click any task in the Tracking table and click Reschedule to Available Date. This feature schedules the remaining duration for a task that is behind schedule so that it will continue from the Status date. Work that is behind schedule is rescheduled based on options you specify on the Calculation tab of the Options dialog box.

To update tasks that are behind schedule:

1. In the Properties group on the Project tab, click the **Project Information** button.

2. In the Project Information dialog box, click the **Current date** arrow, set **9/15/14** as the new Current date, enter **9/12/14** as the new Status date, and then click the **OK** button.

3. Click **Choose vendors** (task 8), click the **Task** tab, and then, in the Schedule group, click the **75% Complete** button 📷.

4. Click **Install cabling** (task 11), and then, in the Schedule group, click the **50% Complete** button 📷. See Figure 5-17.

Figure 5-17   Updating a task that is behind schedule

50% Complete button

actual cost as of the Status date

remaining duration as of the Status date

50% completed as of the Status date

actual work completed as of the Status date

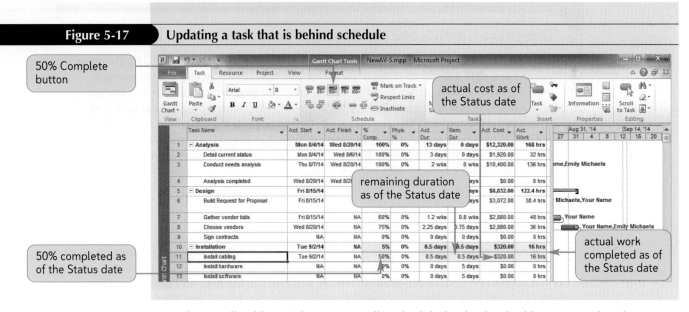

The Install cabling task was originally scheduled to be finished by 9/15/14, but the progress reports indicate that only 50% of the work was completed by the Status date 9/12/14. Notice that 50% of the duration (.5 days) is automatically entered in the Act. Dur. cell and 50% of the duration is displayed (.5 days) in the Rem. Dur. cell. The Act. Work cell is calculated at 16 hours because 1/2 day of actual duration is equal to four hours of work for each resource that is assigned to this task, and four resources are assigned to the task. The Act. Cost field ($320) is calculated by multiplying the Act. Work hours by the resource's hourly rate (16 hours * $20/hr).

You just got the good news that the some of the work of installing the hardware has started. You continue to update the tasks.

To compare baseline and variance information and update task information:

1. Apply the **Variance** table, and then compare the Baseline Start date with the Start date for Install hardware (task 12). Note that the Baseline Start date for Install hardware (task 12) is 9/16/14, which is 13 days after the originally sched-uled Start date of 9/3/14. *Note*: The dates for this project have been greatly exaggerated to help illustrate the concepts in this book. A project this far behind schedule at this point in the plan would be considered poorly managed.

2. Apply the **Tracking** table, click **Build Request for Proposal** (task 6), press and hold the **Shift** key, click **Sign contracts** (task 9), and then, in the Schedule group on the Task tab, click the **100% Complete** button 🔲.

3. Click **Install hardware** (task 12), and then, in the Schedule group, click the **25% Complete** button 🔲.

4. Save your work.

Rescheduling Tasks that are behind Schedule

To determine whether a task is on schedule, ahead of schedule, or behind schedule, Project 2010 has several options that allow you to use the Status date to determine on what date actual data is applied to a task and when the remaining work for that task is scheduled.

To view calculation options:

1. Click the **File** tab, click **Options**, click **Schedule** in the left pane, and then scroll to the bottom of the Project Options window. The default calculation options are shown in Figure 5-18.

Figure 5-18   **Calculation options**

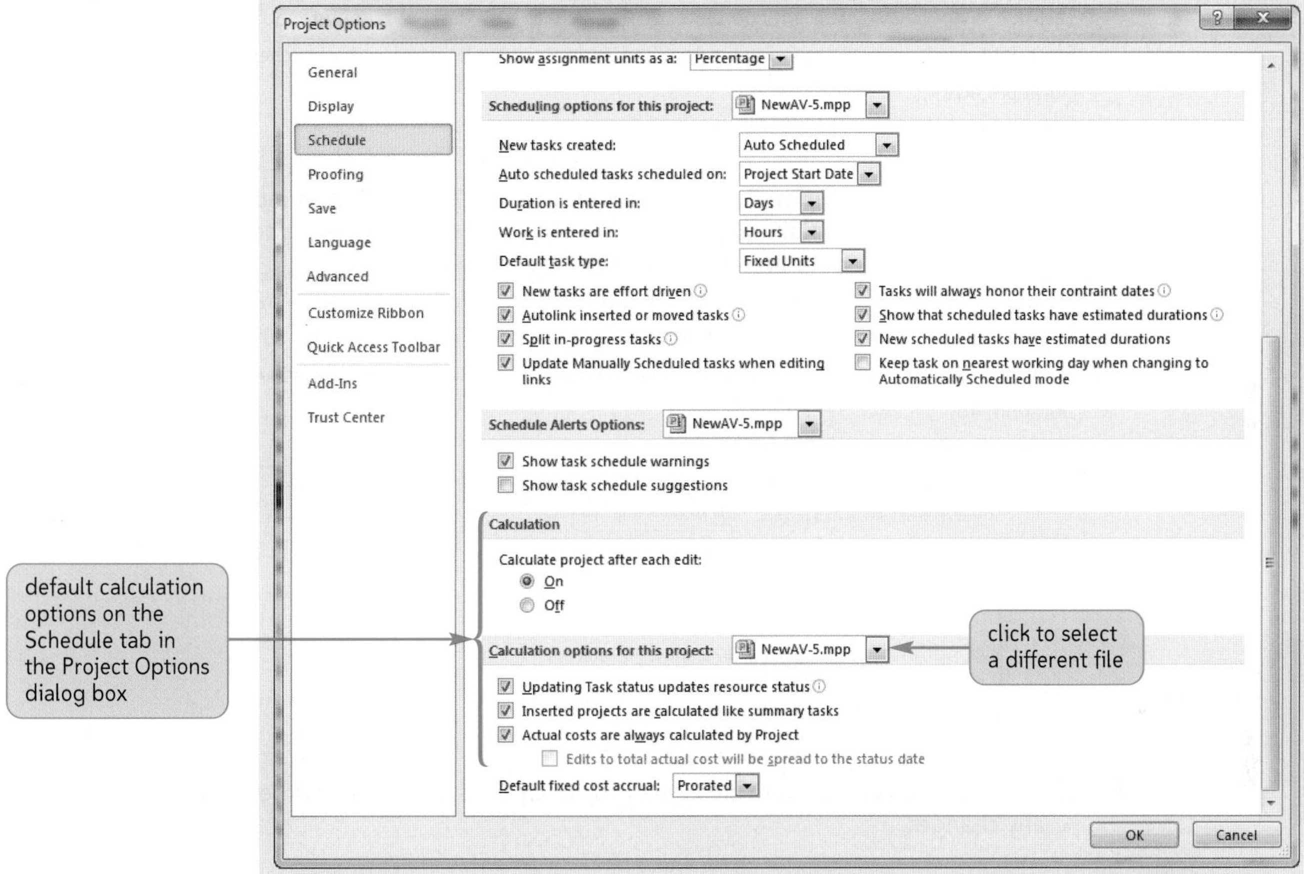

default calculation options on the Schedule tab in the Project Options dialog box

click to select a different file

2. In the Project Options dialog box, click **Advanced** in the left pane, and then scroll down to the bottom of the dialog box. The options on the Advanced tab determine Earned Value options as well as options for rescheduling work. Understanding how these settings affect work will be helpful as you update the project. For now, none of these check boxes is selected.

As you can see from the options in this dialog box, you have tasks that are in progress but behind schedule. You have three choices. If you select the "Move end of completed parts after status date back to status date" check box, you also have the option of selecting the "And move start of remaining parts back to status date" check box. These options are discussed in more detail in Figure 5-19 as Option 1 and Option 1a. If you select the "Move start of remaining parts before status date forward to status date" check box, you have the option of selecting "And move end of completed parts forward to status date" check box. These options are discussed in more detail in Figure 5-19 as Option 2 and Option 2a. As you learned earlier, if a Status date is not set, then the Current date is used. Constraints on tasks are ignored if any of these options are selected; an actual start date always overrides a constraint. These options are applied only when you enter values for actual work, actual duration, and % complete for a task. The options are not applied when actual data are entered for a summary task.

Figure 5-19	Comparing calculation options

	Option 1: Move end of completed parts after status date back to status date	Option 1a: And move start of remaining parts back to status date
Status date 5/9	Task start: moved to 5/7	Task start: moved to 5/7
Task 1:	Percent complete: 50%	Percent complete: 50%
Start date: 5/14	Remaining work: scheduled to start 5/16	Remaining work: scheduled to start 5/9
Duration: 4d		
Actual start: 5/7	Task is split	

	Option 2: Move start of remaining parts before status date forward to status date	Option 2a: And move end of completed parts forward to status date
Status date 5/9	Task actual start: remains at 5/1	Task actual start: moved to 5/7
Task 2:	Percent complete: 50%	Percent complete: 50%
Start date: 5/1	Remaining work: scheduled to start on 5/9	Remaining work: scheduled to start on 5/9
Duration: 4d		
Actual start: 5/1	Task is split	

Calculation options for this project: NewAV-5.mpp

- ☐ Move end of completed parts after status date back to status date
  - ☐ And move start of remaining parts back to status date
- ☐ Move start of remaining parts before status date forward to status date
  - ☐ And move end of completed parts forward to status date
- ☐ Edits to total task % complete will be spread to the status date ⓘ
- ☐ Calculate multiple critical paths ⓘ
- Tasks are critical if slack is less than or equal to   0   days

▶ **3.** Click the **Cancel** button to close the Project Options dialog box without making any changes.

Rescheduling Work

Once a project has slipped behind schedule, you need a quick way to reschedule those tasks that should have been finished but are not completed. Project 2010 provides such a tool with the reschedule uncompleted work option. You can use the Update Project dialog box, which opens when you click the Update Project button in the Status group on the Project tab, to quickly update the task information needed to reschedule the task. Unless you have changed the default calculation options shown in Figure 5-18 and discussed in Figure 5-19, you can reschedule tasks that are behind schedule to start on the project's Status date using the Update Project dialog box.

Another week has passed. The Status date is Friday 9/19/14 and the Current date is Monday 9/22/14. One task that is behind schedule is Install hardware (task 12). This task needs to be rescheduled because it has only had 25 percent of the work completed by the Status date of 9/19/14.

To update Project Information and check on the Finish date:

▶ **1.** Click the **Project** tab, and then, in the Properties group, click the **Project Information** button.

▶ **2.** In the Project Information dialog box, set the Current date to **9/22/14**, set the Status date to **9/19/14**, and then click the **OK** button.

▶ **3.** Double-click **Install hardware** (task 12) to open the Task Information dialog box, click the **General** tab if it is not already selected, and then observe the currently scheduled Finish date for the task (Monday 9/10/14).

▶ **4.** Click the **OK** button in the Task Information dialog box.

You want to use the Gantt chart to help you understand the scheduling issues for the project. You'll reorganize the screen so that the Gantt chart is visible. The progress bar within each task bar in the Gantt chart indicates how much of that task has been completed. Tasks that are behind schedule are not automatically rescheduled. You must specifically indicate when a task that is behind schedule should be rescheduled.

To reschedule tasks that are behind schedule using the Gantt chart:

▶ **1.** In the Tracking table, right-click the **Select All** button, click **Entry** to apply the Entry table, and then drag the **split bar** to the left so that the Task Name column is the last column visible in the Entry table. Check marks in the Indicators column confirm that the tasks in the Analysis and Design phases are 100% complete.

▶ **2.** Right-click **Install hardware** (task 12), and then click **Scroll to Task**, so that the Gantt chart looks like Figure 5-20.

Figure 5-20	Viewing progress on the Gantt chart

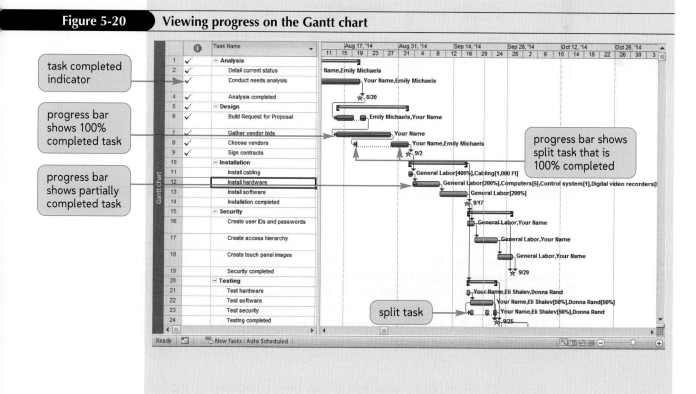

3. Place the pointer over the **Install hardware** (task 12) progress bar, read the ScreenTip, place the pointer over the **Choose vendors** (task 8) progress bar, read the ScreenTip, and then place the pointer over the **Install cabling** (task 11) progress bar and read the ScreenTip. The task Install hardware is 25% completed, so the black progress bar fills 1/4 of the blue task bar. The task Choose vendors (task 8) is 100% complete, so the black progress bar fills the blue task bar. Install cabling (task 11) is 50% complete, so the black progress bar fills half the task bar.

4. With the **Install hardware task** (task 12) selected, click the **Task** tab, and then, in the Tasks group, click the **Move** button to open the menu. The options to move a task are divided into three sections: Move Task Forward, Move Task Back, and Reschedule Task.

5. In the Move Task Forward section of the menu, click **Incomplete Parts to Status Date**. Your screen should look similar to Figure 5-21.

Figure 5-21	Incomplete part of split task rescheduled

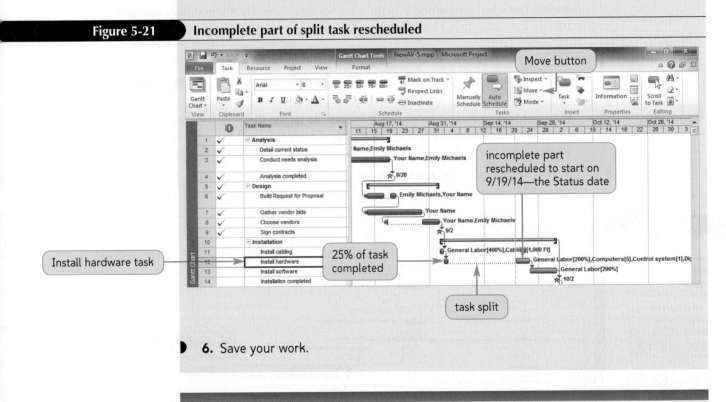

6. Save your work.

Splitting a Task, Though Easy to Do, Is Not Always an Option

INSIGHT

Not all tasks lend themselves to being split. Although Project makes it easy to split a task using several tools, this might not always be logically possible. As a project manager, you need to understand the nature of the task before simply applying the split. If a task lends itself to splitting, you can use the Move button in the Tasks group or the Split Task button in the Schedule group. To manually split a task, select the task, click the Split Task button in the Schedule group, click the bar for the task, and then drag the bar to the new Start date for the second part, using the ScreenTip as a guide.

Because 25 percent of the work had already been completed on the Install hardware task, it was split and the remaining 75 percent of the work was rescheduled as of the Status date (9/19/14). The Install hardware task has a Finish-to-Start relationship with

Install software (and several successor tasks), so several other tasks were rescheduled as well. If any tasks had partial work already completed, they would have been split and rescheduled, as indicated by their relationships with other tasks.

If you want to specify a split date other than the Status date, click the task to select it, and then on the Task tab, in the Schedule group, click the Split Task button. You will be prompted to enter the specific information needed to split the task.

INSIGHT

When Should a Project Be Updated?

Usually, you wouldn't wait an entire month before updating a project's progress. The needs of your business and the availability of the progress information determine how often you update progress. Some executives want the project manager to enter and report progress information daily, whereas others require weekly or monthly reports. The preference is really up to you or management. However, once you determine an update schedule, it is a good idea to keep to the schedule and update the project accordingly.

Updating Progress by Using the Update Tasks Dialog Box

Some project managers prefer using the Gantt chart rather than the Tracking table to update progress. You can update progress on a task using either the Gantt chart or the Update Tasks dialog box.

More time has passed, and you need to update progress so you have a better understanding of the work that has been done and still needs to be done on the ViewPoint Partners project.

Many project managers like to use the Update Tasks dialog box to update progress because it also shows the currently scheduled task Start and Finish dates (the default Tracking table does not show the scheduled Start and Finish dates). You decide to use this feature to continue to update progress for several tasks.

To update tasks using the Update Tasks dialog box:

▶ 1. Click the **Project** tab, and then, in the Properties group, click the **Project Information** button.

▶ 2. In the Project Information dialog box, set **Mon 10/13/14** as the Current date, set **Fri 10/10/14** as the Status date, and then click the **OK** button. Install cabling is 100% complete and the Install hardware task was completed on September 26, so you need to update the project file.

▶ 3. Click **Install cabling** (task 11), click the **Task** tab, and then, in the Schedule group, click the **100% Complete** button [100%]. The task is marked completed; a check mark Completed indicator appears in the Indicators column for the task.

▶ 4. Click **Install hardware** (task 12) if it is not already selected.

▶ 5. In the Schedule group on the Task tab, click the **Mark on Track** button arrow.

▶ 6. On the menu, click **Update Tasks**. The Update Tasks dialog box opens. You can enter actual dates, durations, and percentages completed in the Update Tasks dialog box.

   Trouble? If you clicked the Mark on Track button, rather than the Mark on Track button arrow, the task will be updated to the currently scheduled Finish date of 9/25/14. Click Undo and then repeat Steps 3 and 4 to open the Update Tasks dialog box.

▶ 7. Click **NA** in the Finish box, and then type **9/26/14**. See Figure 5-22.

Figure 5-22   **Update Tasks dialog box for the Install hardware task**

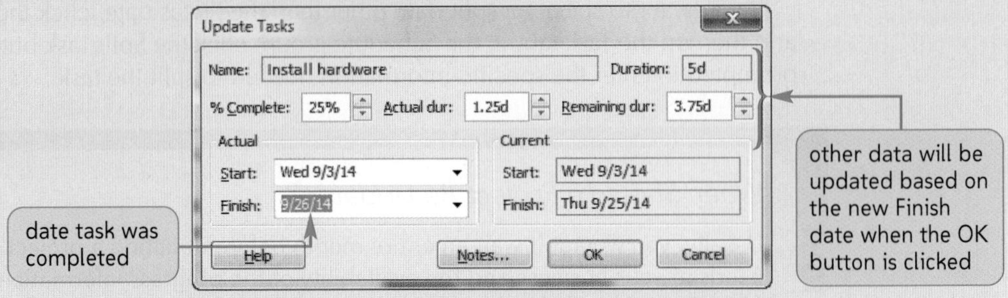

8. Click the **OK** button. A progress bar is added to the task bar that shows the task is completed, and a Completed indicator appears in the Indicators column for the task.

9. Click **Install software** (task 13), press and hold the **Ctrl** key, click **Create user IDs and passwords** (task 16), and then, in the Schedule group, click the **Mark on Track** button arrow.

10. On the menu, click **Update Tasks** to open the Update Tasks dialog box. The fields are not filled in because more than one task is selected. However, you can still enter update information which will be applied to the selected tasks.

11. In the % Complete box, type **100**, and then click the **OK** button. The task bars for the Install software task and the Create user IDs and passwords task are each updated with a progress bar to show that the tasks are completed, and a Completed indicator appears in the Indicators column for each task.

Projects are fluid, and so, even though you plan for certain resources and costs, situations and scope can change during a project. You can always make changes to a project plan, even during the project. You got late word from the team that more General Labor resources can be assigned to the security work in order to get the project back on track. Emily spoke with the team and it is possible for them to work on creating the access hierarchy and the touch panel images at the same time. Also, you will not have to work on the touch panel images. You change the resources and dependencies for both tasks.

To change resources and dependencies:

1. Click **Create access hierarchy** (task 17), click the **View** tab, and then, in the Split View group, click the **Details** check box to open the Task Form.

2. In the Task Form, click the **General Labor Units** cell, type **200**, click the **OK** button, click the **Next** button to move to the Create touch panel images task (which is the next task), click the **General Labor Units** cell, type **200**, and then click the **OK** button. Both these tasks now have twice as many General Labor resources assigned to the task. Now you have to change the dependency between the tasks.

3. Right-click the **Task Form**, and then, on the shortcut menu, click **Resources and Predecessors**.

4. In the Type cell for the Create access hierarchy task, click **FS**, click the **Type arrow**, and then click **SS**.

5. Click in the **Units** cell for your name, type **0**, and then click the **OK** button. You are not working on the touch panels. You now have two General Labor resources working on each of these tasks at the same time. See Figure 5-23.

Figure 5-23 | **Assigning resources and changing dependencies**

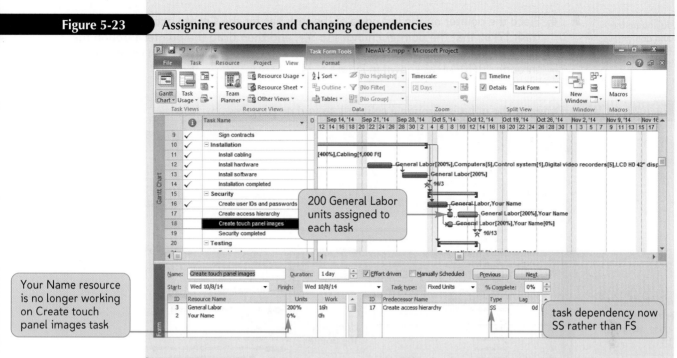

Your Name resource is no longer working on Create touch panel images task

200 General Labor units assigned to each task

task dependency now SS rather than FS

▶ **6.** In the Split View group, click the **Details** check box to remove the split screen view and close the Task Form.

▶ **7.** Save your work.

You need to continue to update project progress, but you will use the Gantt chart to do so rather than the Update Tasks dialog box.

Updating Progress by Using the Gantt Chart

Another way to update actual progress on a project is by using the Gantt chart itself. You can drag the pointer through a task bar to show increased progress. If a task is split, you can drag right through the split to update progress.

You continue to update the progress of the tasks in the ViewPoint AV presentation rooms installation using the Gantt chart.

To update progress using the Gantt chart:

▶ **1.** Right-click **Create user IDs and passwords** (task 16), and then, on the shortcut menu, click **Scroll to Task**.

TIP

In the Gantt chart, several different mouse pointers are available depending on where you point on the bar. Each pointer is used for one specific task, such as to move a task to a new date, extend the duration of the task, or update progress.

▶ **2.** In the Gantt chart, point to either edge of the task bar for **Create user IDs and passwords** (task 16). A Progress ScreenTip appears, which indicates the progress of the task and gives its Actual Start and Complete Through dates. ScreenTips on the Gantt chart provide useful information as progress is recorded.

▶ **3.** Point to either edge of the bar for **Create access hierarchy** (task 17). A ScreenTip appears indicating the Start and Finish dates for that task. If progress had been recorded for the task, the ScreenTip would also display actual Start and Complete Through dates.

> Be sure you update the progress and don't move the task; the ScreenTip must say Complete Through.

4. Place the pointer on the left edge of the task bar for the **Create access hierarchy** (task 17) so that the pointer changes to %▸, and then drag the pointer through the split to the right until the ScreenTip indicates that progress has been completed through 10/10/14, as shown in Figure 5-24.

Figure 5-24 | **Dragging the pointer through a split task to update progress**

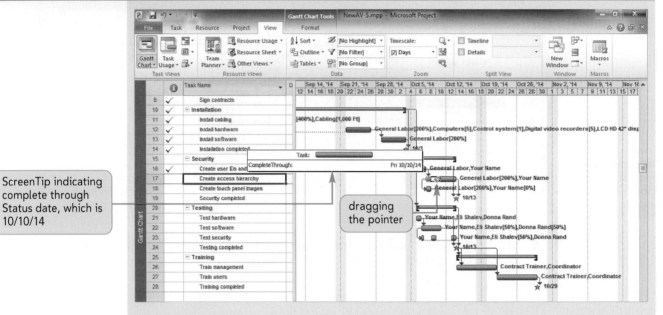

ScreenTip indicating complete through Status date, which is 10/10/14

5. Click the **Task** tab, click the **Installation completed** task (task 14), and then, in the Schedule group, click the **100% Complete** button.

6. Save your work.

Updating the Project by Using the Update Project Dialog Box

The Update Project dialog box is useful when you want to track and update groups of tasks but don't need the detail that you applied to the tasks when using the Update Tasks dialog box or the Gantt chart. You can update progress information for some or all of the tasks in a project as of a specific date, or you can reschedule uncompleted work to start after a specific date. You specify the Status date, which is the date you use to update the schedule. Project 2010 calculates the percent complete dates for each task by setting the schedule dates as actual dates for the selected tasks. When you use the options in the Update Project dialog box, if the scheduled Start date is after the Status date, that task is set to 0% complete because no work has been done. If the scheduled Finish date is before the Status date, the task is updated as 100% complete. If the scheduled Start date is before the Status date and the scheduled Finish date is after that date, the task is in progress and Project 2010 will calculate the percentage based on the dates and enter it as a value in the percent complete field for that task.

REFERENCE

Updating the Project Using the Update Project Dialog Box

- Click the Project tab, and then, in the Status group, click the Update Project button.
- In the Update Project dialog box, click the Entire project or Selected tasks option button.
- To update tasks based on work completed and the specified date, click the Update work as complete through option button, specify the Set as 0% – 100% complete or Set 0% or 100% complete only option button, click the arrow in the top box, and then click the Status date on the calendar.
- To reschedule uncompleted work, click the Reschedule uncompleted work to start after option button, click the arrow in the bottom box, and then specify the date for the uncompleted work to start after in the calendar.
- Click the OK button.

If you want Project 2010 to automatically split the in-progress tasks (for example, because resources are overscheduled and you need to spread out the tasks to accommodate the resources available or because you have to wait for a predecessor task to be completed before you can finish a task that has an FS relationship), you have to open Backstage view and click the Split in-progress check box on the Schedule tab of the Options dialog box.

The ViewPoint AV installation room project is completed through the Security phase. The team is working on the Testing phase tasks.

To update progress for completed tasks using the Update Project dialog box:

1. Scroll and zoom out on the project to see the tasks and the task bars for the Security, Testing, and Training phases in the Gantt Chart.

2. Click **Test hardware** (task 21) to select the task, and then place the pointer over the task bar to read the ScreenTip. The task was scheduled to finish on 10/6/14.

3. Click **Create access hierarchy** (task 17), press and hold the **Ctrl** key, click **Create touch panel images** (task 18), click **Test hardware** (task 21), and then release the **Ctrl** key. You use the Update Project dialog box to update these three selected tasks.

4. Click the **Project** tab, and then, in the Status group, click the **Update Project** button. The Update Project dialog box has two main options.

5. Verify that the **Update work as complete through** option button is selected, verify that the **Set 0% - 100% complete** option button is selected, and then click the **Selected tasks** option button. See Figure 5-25.

Figure 5-25	Update Project dialog box

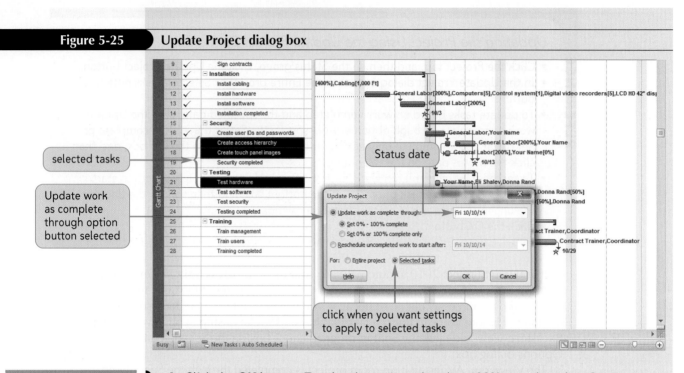

TIP

Remember, you can switch tables to quickly view information not shown in the current table, such as switching to the Tracking table to view the % complete information.

▶ **6.** Click the **OK** button. Test hardware is updated as 100% complete, but Create touch panel images (task 18) is only 99% complete and Create access hierarchy is updated to 67% complete.

If you attempt to update a task that has not started yet, Project 2010 applies a Start No Earlier Than constraint to the task. Next, you look at the Test Software (task 22) task. Because the Test Software task had not started by its scheduled Start date, the task has slipped. Project 2010 can take care of rescheduling the incomplete work.

To update progress for partially completed tasks using the Update Project dialog box:

▶ **1.** Click **Test software** (task 22) to select the task, click the **Task** tab, and then, in the Schedule group, click the **50% Complete** button 🔳. The Test software task is partially completed because the touch panels are not quite ready.

▶ **2.** Click the **Project** tab, and then, in the Status group, click the **Update Project** button.

▶ **3.** In the Update Project dialog box, click the **Reschedule uncompleted work to start after** option button, click the **active calendar** box, click the **arrow** to open the calendar, select **10/15/14**, and then click the **Selected tasks** option button, as shown in Figure 5-26.

| Figure 5-26 | Rescheduling work using the Update Project dialog box |

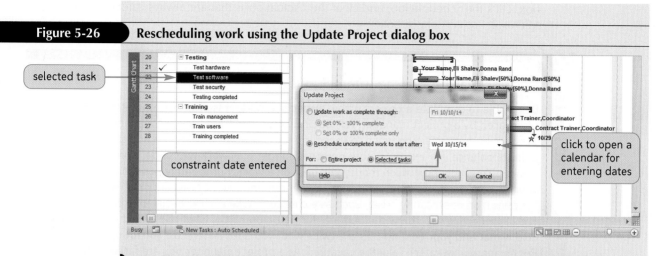

4. Click the **OK** button. The task is split and work is rescheduled. See Figure 5-27.

| Figure 5-27 | Test software task is split and rescheduled |

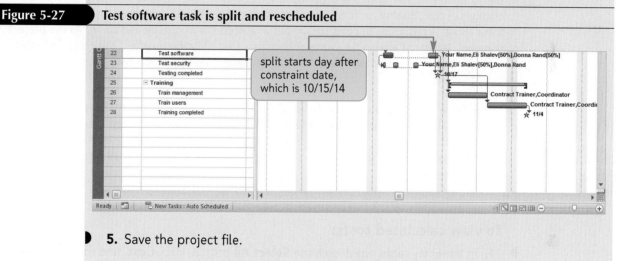

5. Save the project file.

The Test software task is behind schedule, but some progress has been made on the task as evidenced by the progress bar.

Sidney has asked you to take a look at the project costs. You know that Project can track costs. You review the costs as you continue to work on the file.

Tracking Costs

Cost tracking is how you determine whether the project is staying close to budget or not. Project 2010 tracks costs for project tasks, resources, and assignments. As you update the progress of the tasks, actual costs are automatically calculated by multiplying the actual duration by the cost/hour for each resource assigned to the task. **Total costs** are the calculated cost of a project, task, resource, or assignment for the duration of the project. Total costs include actual fixed costs. As you learned in Tutorial 4, fixed costs are costs associated with the task that are neither specific nor driven by any particular resource. They are costs inherent to the task itself. You enter fixed costs into a task's Fixed Cost field. **Timephased costs** are task, resource, or assignment costs that are distributed over time. You can specify the time period for which you need to monitor the costs in the Task or Resource Usage views. Baseline, remaining, and scheduled costs are available in these views. Cost variances are calculated by Project 2010. By default, Project automatically calculates actual cost values as you update progress. If you do not want Project 2010 to calculate actual costs, you can open the Project Options dialog box, click the Schedule tab, and clear the "Actual costs that are always calculated by Microsoft Project" check box.

Decision Making: Staying within Budget

Being able to complete a project within a specified budget is often one of the most difficult tasks faced by a project manager. As you probably know from trying to manage your own personal budget, deciding when to spend money and when to pull back and say "no" is a delicate balance. For example, your personal budget may work well under normal circumstances. You know how much money you earn on a weekly or monthly basis, and you plan your housing, food, clothing, education, and entertainment costs accordingly. However, what happens if an opportunity arises, such as a chance to take a very special unexpected trip with a friend? Do you "blow the budget" for that month? Or, what happens if there is a very cold winter and your heating bills are twice what you anticipated? Do you lower the heat? Put on another sweater? Take the vacation? As a project manager you are faced with these types of decisions during a project. If a phase in the project is taking longer, do you spend the additional money to hire another contractor? If decisions need to be made regarding changes in cost, quality, or time, a project manager must consider what to prioritize among these three. A reduction in costs may result in a decrease in quality and so on. As the project manager, you must always be aware of decisions that will directly affect the cost of a project and how decisions you make related to cost will affect the rest of the project.

PROSKILLS

You have been given some of the costs for the ViewPoint Partners AV presentation rooms installation project. Sidney tells you that the attorney will charge two thousand dollars as the fixed fee to read and review the contracts. Sidney also asks you to use the Project filtering feature to see which resources and tasks are overbudget. You continue to work on the file.

To view calculated costs:

1. In the Entry table, right-click the **Select All** button, click **Cost**, and then drag the **split bar** to display all columns to view all the data.

2. Click the **Sign contracts (task 9) Fixed Cost** cell, type **2000**, and then press the **Enter** key.

3. Click the **View** tab, and then, in the Task Views group, click the **Task Usage** button to open Task Usage view.

4. In the Usage table, right-click the **Select All** button, click **Cost**, drag the **split bar** all the way to the right to view all the columns up to the Remaining column, and then, double-click each **column heading divider** as needed to display all the data in that column. The Cost table in Task Usage view shows you Fixed, Baseline, Variance, and Actual costs for each task. See Figure 5-28. The AutoFilter is active so you can filter for specific amounts.

TIP

Project does not save baseline information for the Fixed Cost field, so you cannot track variance in the Fixed Cost field over time.

Figure 5-28   **Cost table applied to Task Usage View**

AutoFilter is available for all fields

fixed cost for Sign contracts task

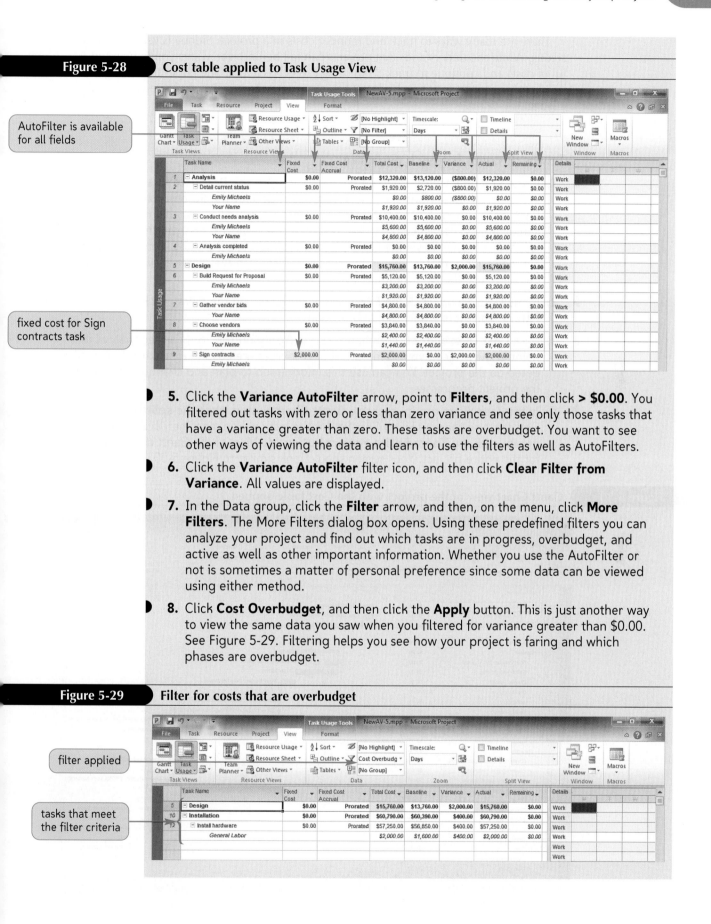

5. Click the **Variance AutoFilter** arrow, point to **Filters**, and then click **> $0.00**. You filtered out tasks with zero or less than zero variance and see only those tasks that have a variance greater than zero. These tasks are overbudget. You want to see other ways of viewing the data and learn to use the filters as well as AutoFilters.

6. Click the **Variance AutoFilter** filter icon, and then click **Clear Filter from Variance**. All values are displayed.

7. In the Data group, click the **Filter** arrow, and then, on the menu, click **More Filters**. The More Filters dialog box opens. Using these predefined filters you can analyze your project and find out which tasks are in progress, overbudget, and active as well as other important information. Whether you use the AutoFilter or not is sometimes a matter of personal preference since some data can be viewed using either method.

8. Click **Cost Overbudget**, and then click the **Apply** button. This is just another way to view the same data you saw when you filtered for variance greater than $0.00. See Figure 5-29. Filtering helps you see how your project is faring and which phases are overbudget.

Figure 5-29   **Filter for costs that are overbudget**

filter applied

tasks that meet the filter criteria

There are many ways to track and monitor costs in a project. Sidney is very cost conscious. While she understands that projects can fall behind, she wants you to be mindful of costs and continue to track them using Project as a tool. She hopes that doing this will keep project costs within budget. She asks you to see how much the resources are costing.

To check costs for each resource:

1. In the Resource Views group on the View tab, click the **Resource Usage** button, in the Usage table right-click the **Select All** button for the Resource sheet, click **Cost**, and then drag the **split bar** to the right to display all the columns with Remaining as the last column. The Resource Usage view shows you the following for each resource: Resource Name, Cost, Baseline Cost, Variance, Actual Cost, and Remaining (that is, the remaining cost). Although AutoFilter is available, you decide to use the Filter feature.

2. In the Data group, click the **Filter** arrow, and then, on the menu, click **More Filters**. The More Filters dialog box opens.

3. Click **Cost Overbudget**, and then click the **Apply** button. You can see that, at this point in the project, your General Labor resources are costing more than budgeted on the project. You can use this information to plan and change strategy as the project progresses.

4. In the Task Views group, click the **Gantt Chart** button, drag the **split bar** in the Cost table so that the Fixed Cost field is the last column, and then in the Zoom group, click the **Zoom Entire Project** button. Most of the Gantt chart is visible for the entire project. Your screen should look similar to Figure 5-30.

| Figure 5-30 | Gantt Chart view of the project with the Cost table applied |

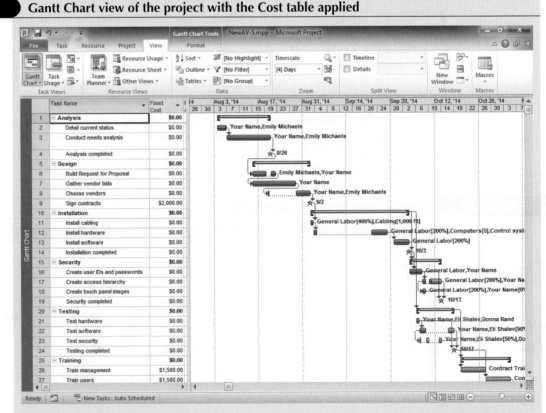

The project still has incomplete tasks. These tasks will be updated as the tasks progress and then are completed by the team.

▶ **5.** Click the **File** tab, and then, in Backstage view, click **Print**.

▶ **6.** Click the **Page Setup** link, add your name left-aligned in the header, and then print the Gantt chart if directed by your instructor.

▶ **7.** Save your changes, and then close the file.

Updating progress on a project is not difficult, but understanding how the many dates and actual data fields interact can be a challenge. This session was organized to show you that it is possible to update tasks that are on schedule, ahead of schedule, in conflict with the schedule, and behind schedule. In addition, it showed you how to reschedule work that was behind schedule and how to mark progress using the Update Tasks dialog box and the Gantt chart.

In a real project, however, you would most likely use some sort of tracking form that recorded each resource's actual progress for each task in the project. If you had planned your project so well that tasks were actually completed exactly as they were scheduled, you could use the buttons on the Task tab in the Schedule group to mark tasks as "Updated as Scheduled" or a "Percentage Complete" as of the Status date. In reality, however, you would probably enter actual values (such as the Actual Start, Actual Finish, and Actual Work) on a regular (perhaps a weekly) basis and let Project 2010 take care of determining whether those actual values put your schedule ahead of or behind schedule.

REVIEW

Session 5.1 Quick Check

1. What are baseline dates based on?
2. What is variance, and how is it calculated?
3. What do positive and negative variance indicate?
4. What table do you apply to the task sheet to see baseline dates? What table do you apply to see actual dates? What table do you apply to enter actual fixed costs?
5. Identify three methods that you can use to track and update progress on a task.
6. When you update tasks that are on schedule or reschedule tasks that are behind schedule, what date is used to determine which tasks should be updated or rescheduled?

SESSION 5.2 VISUAL OVERVIEW

You can open the More Tables dialog box to apply a table to the current view or to create a new table.

You can create or apply a task table or a resource table; a **task table** has fields specific to tasks and a **resource table** has tasks specific to resources.

The **More Tables dialog box** displays a list of available task or resource tables, depending on which option button is selected. The tables in your list depend on tables stored in the Global.MPT file.

CompareDates is a user-created table; it is not one of the default options but it is available in the More Tables dialog box for this project file.

The **Organizer** provides a way for you to manage tables, views, and reports across Project files.

The Edit button opens the selected table so that you can make changes to an existing table.

The Copy button opens the selected table so that you can create a new table based on the selected table; the new table will be available in the More Tables dialog box.

P | File | Task | Resource

Resource Usage ▾ | Sort ▾ | [No Hi...] ▾ | Timescal

[N... ▾ | [4] Days

[No Group] ▾

Gantt Chart ▾ | Usa...

More Tables

Tables: ⦿ Task | ○ Resource

- Baseline
- **CompareDates**
- Constraint Dates
- Cost
- Delay
- Earned Value
- Earned Value Cost Indicators
- Earned Value Schedule Indicators
- Entry
- Entry and Fixed Cost
- Export

New...

Edit...

Copy...

Organizer...

Apply | Cancel

'14 | Aug 3, '14
S | W | S | T | M | F

0 days

1	
2	
3	
4	
5	
6	
7	
8	
9	Sign contracts
10	**Installation**
11	Install cabling	Mon 9/15/14
12	Install hardware	Tue 9/16/14
13	Install software	N
14	Installation completed	N
15	**Security**	N
16	Create user IDs and passwords	NA
17	Create access hierarchy	NA
18	Create touch panel images	NA
19	Security completed	NA
20	**Testing**	**NA**
21	Test hardware	NA
22	Test software	NA
23	Test security	NA
24	Testing completed	NA

Detail Gantt

Ready | New Tasks : Auto Scheduled

CREATE A CUSTOM TABLE

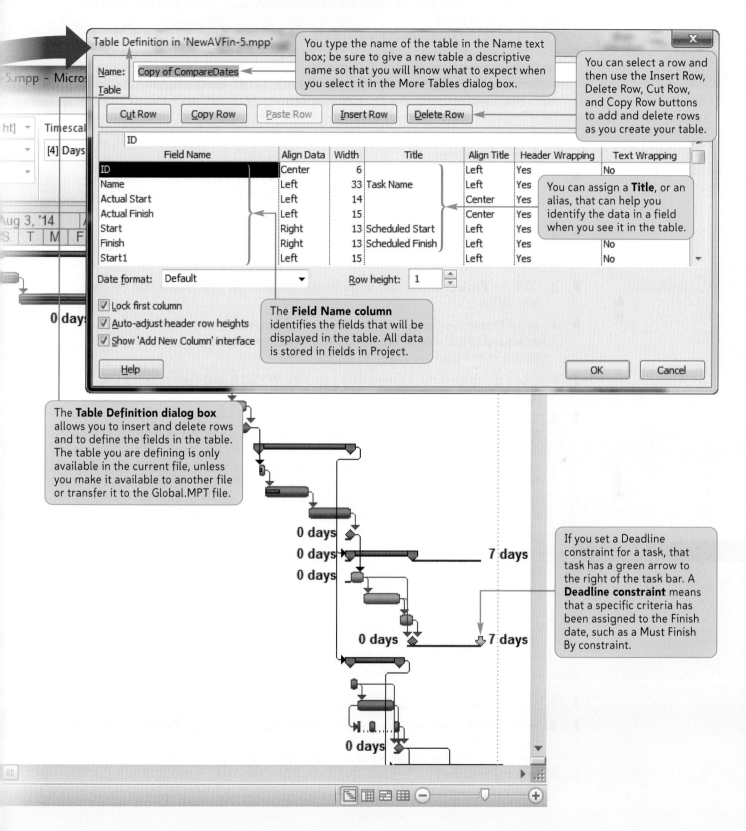

You type the name of the table in the Name text box; be sure to give a new table a descriptive name so that you will know what to expect when you select it in the More Tables dialog box.

You can select a row and then use the Insert Row, Delete Row, Cut Row, and Copy Row buttons to add and delete rows as you create your table.

Table Definition in 'NewAVFin-5.mpp'

Name: Copy of CompareDates

Table

| Cut Row | Copy Row | Paste Row | Insert Row | Delete Row |

ID

Field Name	Align Data	Width	Title	Align Title	Header Wrapping	Text Wrapping
ID	Center	6		Left	Yes	No
Name	Left	33	Task Name	Left	Yes	
Actual Start	Left	14		Center	Yes	
Actual Finish	Left	15		Center	Yes	
Start	Right	13	Scheduled Start	Left	Yes	
Finish	Right	13	Scheduled Finish	Left	Yes	No
Start1	Left	15		Left	Yes	No

You can assign a **Title**, or an alias, that can help you identify the data in a field when you see it in the table.

Date format: Default

Row height: 1

☑ Lock first column
☑ Auto-adjust header row heights
☑ Show 'Add New Column' interface

The **Field Name column** identifies the fields that will be displayed in the table. All data is stored in fields in Project.

Help   OK   Cancel

The **Table Definition dialog box** allows you to insert and delete rows and to define the fields in the table. The table you are defining is only available in the current file, unless you make it available to another file or transfer it to the Global.MPT file.

0 days

0 days

0 days

0 days

7 days

0 days

7 days

If you set a Deadline constraint for a task, that task has a green arrow to the right of the task bar. A **Deadline constraint** means that a specific criteria has been assigned to the Finish date, such as a Must Finish By constraint.

0 days

Working with Baselines

Project 2010 can save up to 11 baselines for each file. At some point, you may want to clear one or all of them.

Sidney reviewed your project file and made a few modifications. To illustrate the concepts in this session, she has asked you to go back in time from the last session and to enter a new current date of Monday September 15, 2014. This is after the Analysis phase was complete and before any other subsequent project tasks were completed. You set the new Current date, and then you clear the baseline.

To clear a baseline:

1. Open the **AVFin-5** project file located in the **Project5\Tutorial** folder included with your Data Files, and then save the file as **NewAVFin-5** in the same folder. The project file opens in Gantt Chart view.

2. In the Resource Views group on the **View** tab, click the **Resource Sheet** button, change the Your Name resource to your name and initials, and then switch back to Gantt Chart view.

3. Click the **Project** tab. Notice in the Status group under Status date that the date is 9/12/14.

4. In the Properties group, click the **Project Information** button. The currently scheduled Finish date is Tue 10/23/14. In order for your screens to match the figures in this book, you need to set the Current date.

5. Select the **date** in the Current date box, type **9/15/14**, and then click the **OK** button.

6. In the Schedule group, click the **Set Baseline** button, and then, on the menu, click **Clear Baseline**. The Clear Baseline dialog box opens, as shown in Figure 5-31. You can see the date that the last baseline was saved in this file. You want to clear this baseline and then set a baseline as of the current date you just set. Clearing baseline or interim information is useful when you want to share a project plan with somebody but do not want them to see your plan's baseline or interim information. You also want to keep an eye on variance, which is based on baseline data.

| Figure 5-31 | Clear Baseline dialog box |

7. Click the **OK** button to clear the baseline plan.

8. In the Schedule group, click the **Set Baseline** button, click **Set Baseline**, and then click the **OK** button to set a baseline for the entire project based on the Current date—9/15/14. The baseline is a snapshot of your schedule at the time that you save the baseline.

Creating a Custom Table

In the last session, you inserted and hid columns in a table to view the fields as needed. When you inserted columns into a table, such as the Cost or Variance table, that table was redefined. For some projects, you may want to create a table that can be viewed at any time without changing the Project 2010 default table settings.

You can create a custom table containing the fields that you want and then give the new table a descriptive name. In this way, you can preserve the default tables that Project 2010 provides, while developing unique tables to communicate key information during the project. You can create either task or resource tables. Task tables can be applied only to sheets that list tasks, and resource tables can be applied only to resource sheets.

Sidney has asked to see how the project schedule is affected by minor delays that have occurred in the ViewPoint Partners AV presentation rooms installation project. You decide to create a new table called CompareDates that contains the actual, scheduled, and baseline Start and Finish dates. This new customized table will be based on the modified Variance table that you used in Session 5.1.

The More Tables dialog box lists the default task tables included in Project 2010. If you click the Task option button, you see a list of the default task tables. If you click the Resource option button, you see a list of the default resource tables. You can use the More Tables dialog box to create a new table, edit any of the existing tables, or create a copy of an existing table.

The column name is often the same as the field name, but sometimes the column name needs to be more descriptive. You use the Table Definition dialog box to give columns more descriptive names. For example, the Start and Finish fields can be some-what confusing as column names unless you understand that these field names represent the currently scheduled Start and Finish dates for a task. If you want to provide a more descriptive name for a column, you type the new name in the Title field.

REFERENCE

Creating a New Table

- In any current table, right-click the Select All button.
- On the shortcut menu, click More Tables to open the More Tables dialog box.
- Click New to create a new table, or click an existing table that most closely represents the table you want to create, and then click Copy to create a copy of that table.
- In the Table Definition dialog box that opens, type a descriptive name for the new table.
- In the Field Name list, click any fields that you don't want to include in the new table, and then click the Delete Row button.
- To add a field, click a field name in the Field Name list, click the Insert Row button, click the arrow that appears in the blank cell in the Field Name list, select a field name or type a new field name, and then specify the other characteristics of the new column, including alignment, width, and title.
- Click the OK button.

For your work on this project, you need to create a new custom table to display certain fields that don't exist in any of the default tables. However, because the Variance table already contains many of the fields that you want to display, you'll build your custom table based on a copy of the Variance table. In addition, you will give the new table a descriptive name so that you can identify it in the shortcut menu. Because you are creating a task table, you need to be in a task view, such as Gantt Chart view.

To create the new table:

▶ **1.** Verify you are in Gantt Chart view. You plan to create a task table, so you need to be in a view, such as Gantt Chart view, that has a task sheet.

▶ **2.** In the Entry table, right-click the **Select All** button, and then click **More Tables**. The More Tables dialog box opens.

TIP

The tables are listed in alphabetical order.

▶ **3.** With the **Task** option button selected, scroll the Tables list, and then click **Variance**. See Figure 5-32. You'll base the new table on the Variance table.

Figure 5-32 **More Tables dialog box**

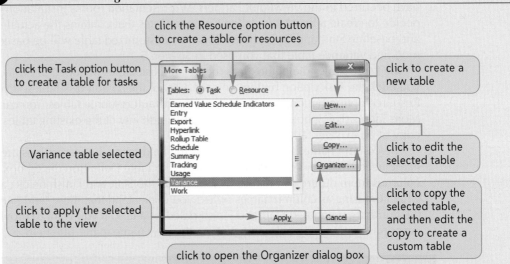

click the Resource option button to create a table for resources

click the Task option button to create a table for tasks

click to create a new table

Variance table selected

click to edit the selected table

click to apply the selected table to the view

click to copy the selected table, and then edit the copy to create a custom table

click to open the Organizer dialog box

▶ **4.** Click the **Copy** button. The Table Definition in 'NewAVFin-5' dialog box opens. When you create and save a new table, it is added to the Tables list in the More Tables dialog box.

▶ **5.** With the text in the Name box selected, type **CompareDates**, and then click the **Show in menu** check box so that this table appears on the shortcut menu when you right-click the Select All button for a table. See Figure 5-33. Each column of the table is identified by its field name, which is listed in the Field Name column in the Table Definition dialog box. The characteristics of each column are included in the same row as its field name. The order of the rows in the dialog box is the order from left to right that the columns will appear in the table. You need to add two more fields, Actual Start and Actual Finish, to the table.

Figure 5-33   Table Definition dialog box

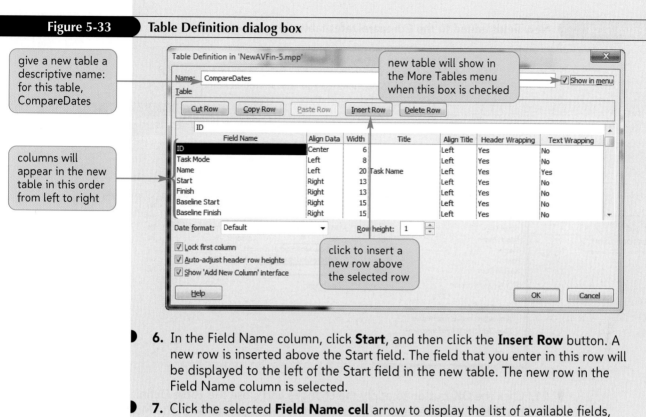

give a new table a descriptive name: for this table, CompareDates

new table will show in the More Tables menu when this box is checked

columns will appear in the new table in this order from left to right

click to insert a new row above the selected row

6. In the Field Name column, click **Start**, and then click the **Insert Row** button. A new row is inserted above the Start field. The field that you enter in this row will be displayed to the left of the Start field in the new table. The new row in the Field Name column is selected.

7. Click the selected **Field Name cell** arrow to display the list of available fields, click **Actual Start**, and then press the **down arrow** key. The new field is inserted with default settings for alignment and width, and the Start field is selected.

8. Click the **Insert Row** button to add another blank row. The new blank row is between the Actual Start field name and the Start field name.

9. Click the selected **Field Name cell** arrow, click **Actual Finish**, and then press the **Down Arrow** key. Your Table Definition dialog box has two new fields.

10. Click the **Title** cell for the Start field, type **Scheduled Start**, press the **Enter** key to move to the **Title** cell for the Finish field, type **Scheduled Finish**, and then press the **Enter** key. Your dialog box should look like Figure 5-34.

TIP

If you press the Delete key or use the Cut command within the Table Definition dialog box, you will delete or cut the entire row, not the individual cell within the current row.

Figure 5-34   New fields added to the CompareDates table

> text entered in the Title cells are displayed as column headings for their corresponding fields; if no text is entered, then the Field Name is used as the column heading

Table Definition in 'NewAVFin-5.mpp'   [X]

Name: CompareDates   ☑ Show in menu
Table

[Cut Row] [Copy Row] [Paste Row] [Insert Row] [Delete Row]

Field Name	Align Data	Width	Title	Align Title	Header Wrapping	Text Wrapping
Task Mode	Left	8		Left	Yes	No
Name	Left	20	Task Name	Left	Yes	Yes
Actual Start	Left	10		Center	Yes	No
Actual Finish	Left	10		Center	Yes	No
Start	Right	13	Scheduled Start	Left	Yes	No
Finish	Right	13	Scheduled Finish	Left	Yes	No
Baseline Start	Right	15		Left	Yes	No

> two new fields inserted before Start

Date format: Default   Row height: 1

☑ Lock first column
☑ Auto-adjust header row heights
☑ Show 'Add New Column' interface

[Help]   [OK]   [Cancel]

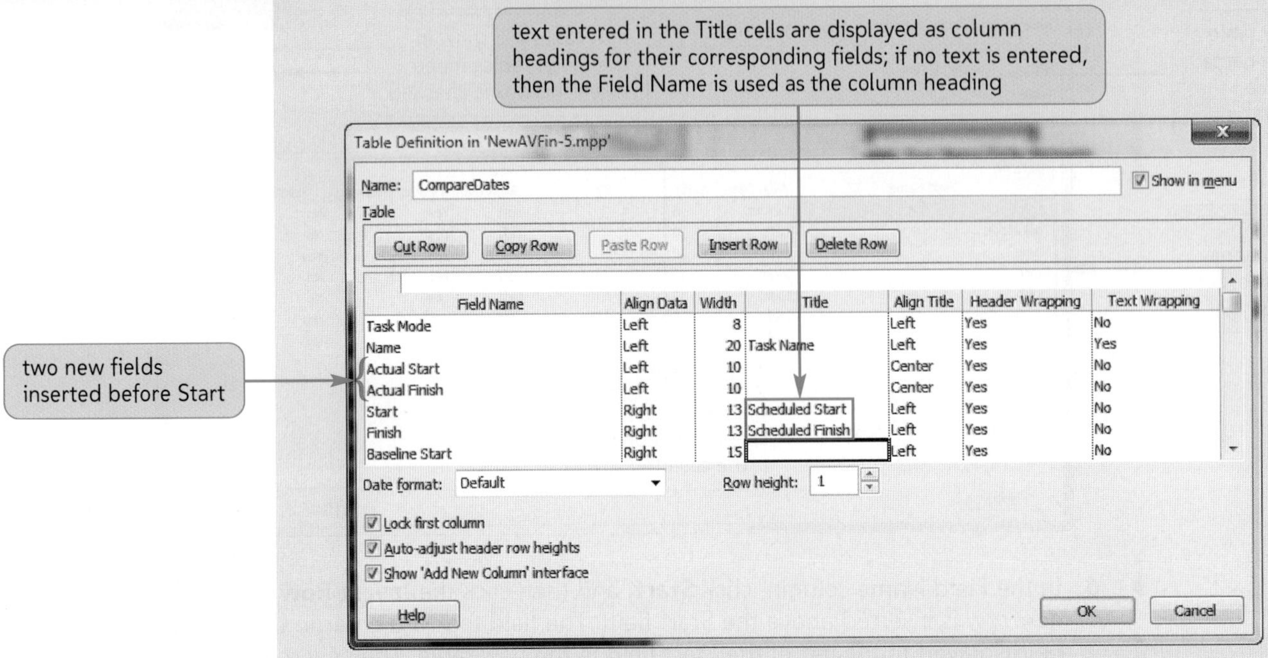

▶ **11.** Click the **OK** button to apply the changes and close the Table Definition dialog box. The CompareDates table is added to the list of tables in the More Tables dialog box and is the currently selected table.

Trouble? If a warning message appears stating that the CompareDates table already exists in "Global.MPT" and asking if you want to replace the table, click the Yes button. Someone may have completed this tutorial using this installation of Project before you.

▶ **12.** In the More Tables dialog box, click the **Apply** button to apply the selected CompareDates table.

▶ **13.** Drag the **split bar** to the right so the last column is Finish Var., and then resize columns as needed to fit column content. Your screen should look like Figure 5-35.

Figure 5-35   CompareDates table

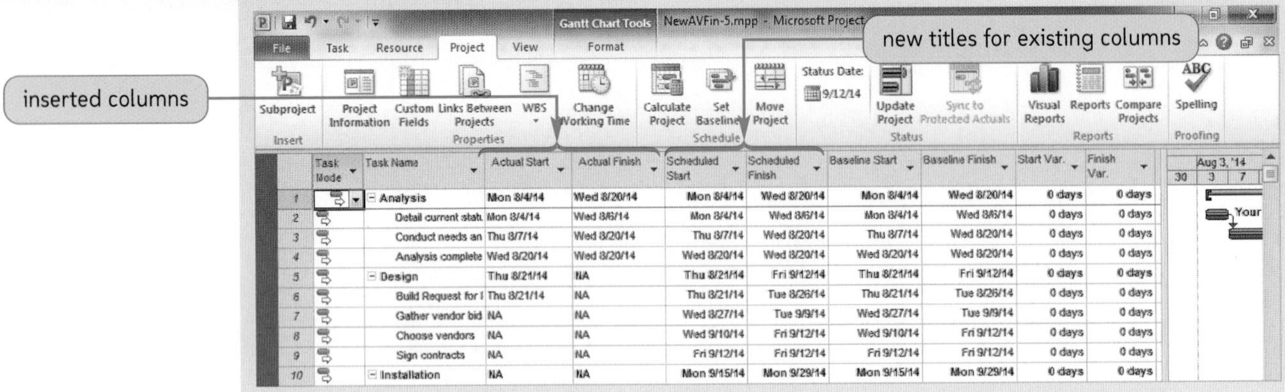

> new titles for existing columns

> inserted columns

	Task Mode	Task Name	Actual Start	Actual Finish	Scheduled Start	Scheduled Finish	Baseline Start	Baseline Finish	Start Var.	Finish Var.
1		⊟ Analysis	Mon 8/4/14	Wed 8/20/14	Mon 8/4/14	Wed 8/20/14	Mon 8/4/14	Wed 8/20/14	0 days	0 days
2		Detail current statu	Mon 8/4/14	Wed 8/6/14	Mon 8/4/14	Wed 8/6/14	Mon 8/4/14	Wed 8/6/14	0 days	0 days
3		Conduct needs an	Thu 8/7/14	Wed 8/20/14	Thu 8/7/14	Wed 8/20/14	Thu 8/7/14	Wed 8/20/14	0 days	0 days
4		Analysis complete	Wed 8/20/14	Wed 8/20/14	Wed 8/20/14	Wed 8/20/14	Wed 8/20/14	Wed 8/20/14	0 days	0 days
5		⊟ Design	Thu 8/21/14	NA	Thu 8/21/14	Fri 9/12/14	Thu 8/21/14	Fri 9/12/14	0 days	0 days
6		Build Request for I	Thu 8/21/14	NA	Thu 8/21/14	Tue 8/26/14	Thu 8/21/14	Tue 8/26/14	0 days	0 days
7		Gather vendor bid	NA	NA	Wed 8/27/14	Tue 9/9/14	Wed 8/27/14	Tue 9/9/14	0 days	0 days
8		Choose vendors	NA	NA	Wed 9/10/14	Fri 9/12/14	Wed 9/10/14	Fri 9/12/14	0 days	0 days
9		Sign contracts	NA	NA	Fri 9/12/14	Fri 9/12/14	Fri 9/12/14	Fri 9/12/14	0 days	0 days
10		⊟ Installation	NA	NA	Mon 9/15/14	Mon 9/29/14	Mon 9/15/14	Mon 9/29/14	0 days	0 days

You can put any combination of task fields together to create a unique task table or any combination of resource fields together to create a resource table. You can also title any field so it is more descriptive or helpful to you. Project 2010 provides approximately 200 different fields of information for each task and resource. You can use this information to manage the schedule and resources for your projects. With all this information at your fingertips, you'll want flexibility when creating your own tables of information.

Creating a Custom View

After you have used Project 2010 for a while, you'll develop your own favorite techniques for viewing, entering, updating, and analyzing data. Just as you created, named, and saved a custom table, you can create, name, and save a custom view. A **custom view** is any view that is saved with a name and differs from the Project 2010 default views.

REFERENCE

Creating a Custom View

- In the View group on the Task tab, click the Gantt Chart button arrow, and then click More Views to open the More Views dialog box.
- Click New to create a new view, or click an existing view that most closely represents the custom view that you want to create, and then click Copy.
- In the View Definition dialog box that opens, type a descriptive name for the view in the Name box.
- Click the Table arrow, and then select a table to appear as the default.
- If desired, click the Group arrow, and then click a group.
- If desired, click the Filter arrow, click a filter, and then, if you want to highlight the filtered tasks instead of hiding the other tasks, click the Highlight filter check box to select it.
- Keep the Show in menu check box selected to display the new view in the View menu.
- Click the OK button.

Custom views can contain a set of fields in a particular view (sheet/table, form, graphical, or a combination of these), a grouping (tasks sorted and outlined together that meet a common criteria), and/or a filter.

PROSKILLS

Problem Solving: Using the Web to Find Project Solutions

As you continue to work with Microsoft Project 2010, you may find you are faced with a problem on how to use the program to best manage your project. In addition to the Help system, you can access the Project Help Web page by clicking the Help button on the Ribbon, and then clicking the "Visit Office.com" link to access Project Help and How-to including articles and videos on many topics. If you cannot find a solution using the Project Help system, you should consider using resources on the Web.

A wealth of information about Project 2010 exists on the Web; you can find the information provided by Microsoft through several links. Office on the Web offers a direct link to the most up-to-date information about Project 2010. To access this site directly, go to *www. microsoft.com/office/products*, and then click the link for Project to open the Project page. The Microsoft Office Project page includes important information for Project, resources for project managers, and a link for software updates to Project 2010. The site offers resources for users of previous versions of Project, pricing and ordering information, case studies, training solutions, discussion groups, extensive FAQs, and support documentation. Consider visiting this site periodically as you work with Project and manage your projects. Helpful discussion groups can be found if you search through Google Groups and Facebook.

A great source of information is the MSDN Community. At the Microsoft Developer Network site you have access to a vast array of community support pages, including forums, blogs, newsgroups, events and Web casts for your project. You might consider the following sites as resources:

- Microsoft Project Users Group: *www.mpug.com*
- Microsoft Office Project Developer Center: *http://msdn.microsoft.com/office/program/project/*
- Microsoft Office Project TechNet: *http://technet.microsoft.com/en-us/office*
- 4PM: *www.4pm.com*
- PMForum: *www.pmforum.org*

Time has passed and it is now the beginning of October. A progress report with updates regarding tasks has just come in, and you see that more tasks have made progress. You update the Current and Status dates and these tasks in the file. Please remember that many of the dates and values used in this book are exaggerated to help make a point when teaching these concepts.

To update tasks:

1. Open the **Project Information** dialog box, set the Current date to **Mon 10/6/14**, set the Status date to **Fri 10/3/14**, and then click the **OK** button.

2. In the CompareDates table, click **Gather vendor bids** (task 7), click the **Task** tab, and then, in the Schedule group, click the **50% Complete** button 🔲. The task is updated as 50% completed.

3. Click **Choose vendors** (task 8), and then, in the Schedule group, click the **25% Complete** button 🔲.

4. Click the **Build Request for Proposal (task 6) Actual Finish** cell, type **9/30/14**, and then press the **Enter** key. You immediately see how this task has a positive finish variance of 25 days because this task finished after its scheduled finish date. The variance ripples down through the tasks in the project.

5. Save your work.

During your last meeting with Sidney, she asked if there was a way to view the project that would quickly show actual, scheduled, and baseline date information for critical tasks. To satisfy this request, you will develop a custom view based on Gantt Chart view. When you create a custom view, you include these characteristics: screen, which identifies the current view; table, which identifies the table serving as the basis for the custom table; grouping, which identifies how you want the tasks or resources grouped; and filter, which identifies how you want to filter the tasks or resources. You'll call the view Critical Dates.

To create and apply a custom view:

1. Drag the **split bar** so that the last visible column is the Scheduled Finish column.
2. Click the **View** tab, and then, in the Data group, click the **Filter** arrow.
3. On the menu, click **Completed Tasks**. You select this filter because you want to see quickly which tasks are done.
4. Right-click **Detail current status** (task 2), and then, on the shortcut menu, click **Scroll to Task**. Place the pointer on each task bar and read the ScreenTip that appears. The Actual Finish column confirms that tasks 2, 3, 4, and 6 are complete. The progress bars confirm that these tasks have been marked 100% complete. The Design summary task appears in the list because the subtask Build Request for Proposal task is complete. Task 4 is a milestone.
5. Click the **Task** tab, and then, in the View group, click the **Gantt Chart** button arrow.
6. On the menu, click **More Views**. The More Views dialog box opens. Gantt Chart view is the view that most closely resembles the custom view that you need to create.
7. In the Views list, with **Gantt Chart** already selected, click the **Copy** button. The View Definition in 'NewAVFin-5' dialog box opens, as shown in Figure 5-36. The View Definition dialog box indicates that the table applied to the task sheet is CompareDates, there is no group assigned, and the filter is set to Completed Tasks. The current name, by default, is "Copy of &Gantt Chart."

Figure 5-36 Creating a custom view

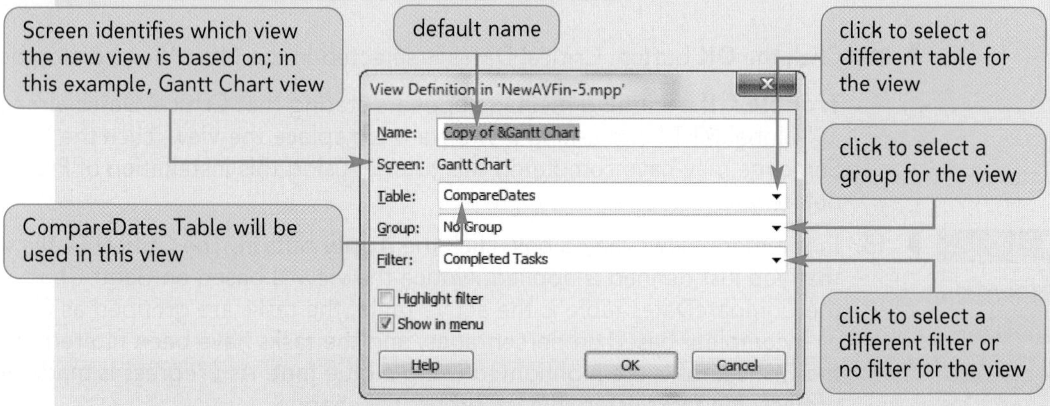

When you create and save a custom view, it is added to the list of views in the More Views dialog box. It is good practice to use a descriptive name for each custom view because this will help you to identify the view in the More Views dialog box. Views are listed in alphabetical order.

▶ **8.** In the Name box, type **Critical Dates**. The name you typed is more descriptive than the default name. You want this view to group the tasks in Complete and Incomplete groups.

▶ **9.** Click the **Group** arrow, and then click **Complete and Incomplete Tasks**. The tasks will be grouped as complete or incomplete. The groups range from 0% Complete to 100% complete. Next, you want to filter this view for Critical tasks. When you copy a view, if you have set a filter, it will appear in this dialog box if you use the view as a base for your custom view. The filter is currently set for Completed Tasks, the filter you applied in Gantt Chart view before you copied the view.

▶ **10.** Click the **Filter** arrow, and then click **Critical**. Usually when this filter is applied, only Critical tasks will appear. However, if you filter for Critical tasks and check the Highlight filter check box, then all tasks will appear and the Critical tasks will be highlighted. You decide it is important to see all tasks and to highlight the Critical tasks so they stand out.

▶ **11.** Click the **Highlight filter** check box. When the Highlight filter check box is checked, Project will display all the tasks and highlight the tasks that meet the filter criteria, in this case, the Critical tasks. Project highlights the tasks by using a different font color. The View Definition dialog box should look like Figure 5-37.

Figure 5-37	View Definition dialog box completed

▶ **12.** Click the **OK** button. Critical Dates is selected in the More Views dialog box.

Trouble? If a warning message appears stating that Critical Dates already exists in "Global.MPT" and asking if you want to replace the view, click the Yes button. Someone may have completed this tutorial using this installation of Project before you.

TIP

Custom views are saved in each project.

▶ **13.** In the More Views dialog box, click the **Apply** button. The Critical Dates view that you just defined is applied. Notice the view is based on Gantt Chart view, the CompareDates table is the active table, the tasks are grouped as Complete or Incomplete based on percentages, and the tasks have been filtered so that the Critical tasks are highlighted using a blue font. As progress is made on the project, the tasks listed in each group will change.

▶ **14.** Press the **Ctrl+Home** keys, adjust column width to fit content as needed, drag the **split bar** all the way to the right to display the Finish Var. column, and then click the **View** tab. Your screen should look like Figure 5-38.

Figure 5-38   Custom Critical Dates view applied

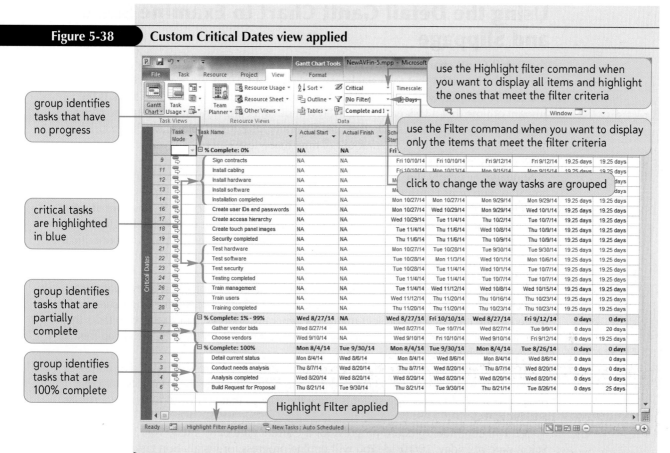

group identifies tasks that have no progress

use the Highlight filter command when you want to display all items and highlight the ones that meet the filter criteria

use the Filter command when you want to display only the items that meet the filter criteria

critical tasks are highlighted in blue

click to change the way tasks are grouped

group identifies tasks that are partially complete

group identifies tasks that are 100% complete

Highlight Filter applied

15. In the Task Views group, click the **Gantt Chart** button arrow, and then notice that your new custom view Critical Dates appears on the menu.

16. On the menu, click **Gantt Chart**, in the Data Group click the **Filter** arrow, and then click **[No Filter]**. The familiar Gantt Chart view appears in the project window.

17. Save your work.

You can edit or copy a custom view just as you edit or copy a built-in view.

Using the Organizer

INSIGHT

You can use the Organizer dialog box to delete a custom view, copy a view from one project to another project, or make a view available for every project. To open the Organizer dialog box, click the File tab to open Backstage view, click Info, and then click the Organizer button. To delete a custom view, click the view name in the list of views within the current project (in the list on the right), and then click the Delete button. You can also copy custom views that you create from the current project in the list on the right, and then click the Copy button. In the next tutorial, you'll learn how to work with the other features of the Organizer dialog box, including the global template.

Using the Detail Gantt Chart to Examine Slack and Slippage

The **Detail Gantt chart** is a Gantt chart with extra bars that show total slack and slippage. Recall from Tutorial 4 that total slack (also called total float) is the amount of time that a task can be delayed without the delay affecting the entire project, and free slack is the amount of time that a task can be delayed without affecting any successor tasks. When project managers speak of slack, they are generally referring to total slack. If the task has no successors, free slack is the amount of time that a task can be delayed without delaying the entire project's Finish date.

Slippage, or simply **slip**, is the difference between a task's scheduled Start and baseline Start date or its Finish date and baseline Finish date. A noncritical task can slip without affecting the project Finish date. If a noncritical task slips too much, however, it can become a critical task, which affects the critical path and might extend the length of the project. So you need to track slippage on all tasks to see whether the project's noncritical tasks were planned properly as well as to anticipate and deal with potential changes in the critical path.

As a project progresses, project managers use the Detail Gantt chart to evaluate total slack and slippage to determine where to focus their efforts. After addressing issues related to the critical path, project managers generally address issues related to tasks that have the least amount of slippage as the next highest priority, if they hope to keep their projects on schedule.

To see how this works, you have to record some more progress on tasks. For purposes of this book, you will enter exaggerated dates to better illustrate the concepts. In a real project, you would make adjustments along the way so that you would see actual results and progress.

You will continue to record progress for a Current date of Monday, 10/13/14 and a Status date of Friday, 10/10/14. You will update progress for Installation tasks that have been delayed by several days using the custom Critical Dates view you created.

To update record progress:

1. Open the **Project Information** dialog box, set the Current date to **10/13/14**, and then set the Status date to **10/10/14**. You are updating the project's status as of Friday 10/10/14.

2. Click the **OK** button.

3. Click the **View** Tab, and then, in the Task Views group, click the **Gantt Chart** button arrow.

4. On the menu, click **Critical Dates**.

5. In the CompareDates table, click **Install cabling** (task 11), click the **Task** tab, and then, in the Scheduling group, click the **75% Complete** button 🔲.

6. Click **Install hardware** (task 12), and then, in the Scheduling group, click the **50% Complete** button 🔲.

7. Click the **Gantt Chart** button arrow, and then click **Critical Dates** to refresh the table and see the Install cabling (task 11) and Install hardware (task 12) tasks move to the new group.

8. Save your work.

Next, you decide to use the Detail Gantt chart to continue updating the project and observing the effects of the updates. You use Detail Gantt Chart view because you want to track slack and slippage, which appear as clearly defined bars.

To use the Detail Gantt chart:

▶ 1. In the View group on the Task tab, click the **Gantt Chart button** arrow, and then click **More Views**.

▶ 2. In the More Views dialog box, click **Detail Gantt**, and then click the **Apply** button. The Detailed Gantt chart is applied. The font seems a little small, so you change the font size to make the text easier to read.

▶ 3. Click the **Select All** button, and then, in the Font group on the Task tab, click the **Font Size** arrow.

▶ 4. On the menu, click **10**. The font in the table changes to 10 point.

▶ 5. Click **Analysis** (task 1) to deselect the table, and then drag the **split bar** so the Task Name column is the rightmost column.

▶ 6. Right-click **Installation** (task 10), and then, on the shortcut menu, click **Scroll to Task**.

▶ 7. Click the **View** tab, and then click the **Zoom Entire Project** button so the Detail Gantt Chart appears as shown in Figure 5-39.

Figure 5-39   Detail Gantt Chart

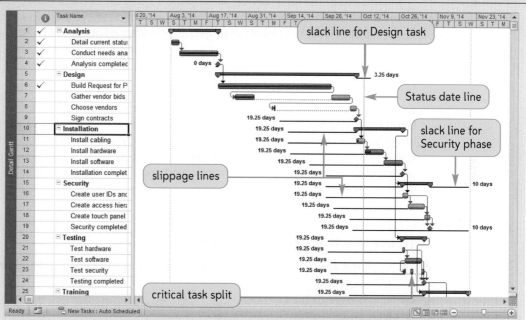

▶ 8. Point to the **slack line** after the Security (task 15) bar in the Gantt chart. The Slack ScreenTip displays information about the line.

▶ 9. Point to the **Create user IDs and passwords (task 16)** slippage line to the left of the bar. The ScreenTip displays information about the Slippage line.

▶ 10. Drag the **split bar** to show the Leveling Delay column, and then scroll down to view the Train users task (task 27). The Train users (task 27) task has 8 edays in that column.

On the Detail Gantt chart, the task bars for the critical tasks are formatted in red and the task bars for the noncritical tasks are blue. Slack lines are to the right of a task bar. The Leveling Delay column shows the delay in completing each task, which is shown as edays and indicates elapsed time. For this project, the Train users (task 27) task has a leveling delay of 8 edays.

The slack line represents total slack, the amount of time a task can be delayed without the delay affecting the Finish date for the entire project. The task bars in the Security phase are not critical; they are in blue. The Security Slack ScreenTip indicates that the task is currently scheduled to finish on 11/6/14. The Free Slack date is 11/20/14, which means the task will still be on schedule as long as it finishes by 11/20/14. The Detail Gantt chart shows the total number of days of free slack after the slack bar. Again, these delayed dates are exaggerated to help explain the concepts by creating enhanced lines.

INSIGHT

Understanding Slippage

If a project has slippage, that is, falls behind schedule, several factors may be responsible. You may have overestimated a realistic Start date, you may not have applied sufficient resources, or you may have encountered unforeseen problems during the project. You can view slippage lines in Detail Gantt Chart view. Lines appear to the left of the task bar. As with all bars, they can be formatted to stand out on the chart. A ScreenTip informs you of the total number of slippage days to the left of the slippage bar. If you see that a task has slipped, you will need to keep a close eye on the task to be sure that the slippage does not cause the project to end after its projected Finish date.

Using the Tracking Gantt Chart

Another valuable Gantt chart is the Tracking Gantt chart. For each task, the **Tracking Gantt chart** displays two task bars. The bars are placed so one is above the other. The lower bar shows baseline Start and Finish dates, and the upper bar shows actual Start and Finish dates. This view allows you to compare the baseline and actual dates so that you can see the difference between your plan and the how the project is progressing on its current schedule.

To use the Tracking Gantt Chart:

1. Click the **Task** tab, and then, in the View group, click the **Gantt Chart** button arrow.

2. In the Built-in group on the menu, click **Tracking Gantt**. The Tracking Gantt chart is applied.

3. Click the **Select All** button, and then, in the Font group on the Task tab, click the **Font Size** arrow.

4. On the menu, click **10**, and then click **Analysis** (task 1) to deselect the table.

5. Resize the column widths to fit content, drag the **split bar** so that the Task Name column is the last column in the table, press the **Ctrl+Home** keys, click the **View** tab, and then, in the Zoom group, click the **Zoom Entire Project** button so that the Tracking Gantt chart appears as shown in Figure 5-40. Baseline bars are gray, progress bars for noncritical bars are blue, and progress bars for critical tasks are red. The percent complete appears to the right of progress bars.

Figure 5-40   **Tracking Gantt Chart view**

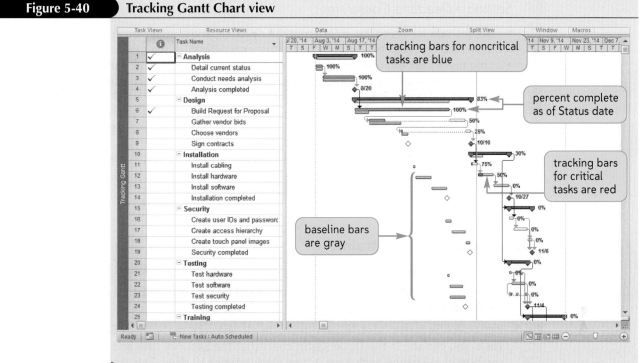

▶ **6.** Point to the **Create touch panel images (task 18) baseline bar**. The Baseline ScreenTip displays Baseline Start and Finish dates as well as the duration.

INSIGHT

Formatting Progress Bars

In the same way that you can format the different bar styles in Gantt Chart view—using colors and patterns to help identify summary tasks, critical tasks, milestones, and so forth—you can format progress bars. By default these bars are black; however, they can be any color or pattern. To format a progress bar, open the Format Bar Styles dialog box and then change the style to meet your specific design needs for the project.

Working with Slack and Deadline Dates

As the AV presentation rooms installation project currently stands, the Security phase has 10 days of total slack, but this value might be misleading. For example, you might not want to explicitly create a Finish-to-Start relationship between the Security tasks and any other tasks in the project, and yet you certainly don't want to wait until the very end of the project to have the security completed. You could apply any of a variety of constraints to the task, such as "Finish No Later Than" or "Must Finish On," to ensure that the task is done in a timely manner.

One constraint that is a bit different from the others is the **deadline constraint**. The deadline constraint is a **flexible constraint**. It is flexible in that it does not dictate the scheduled Start and Finish dates of a task, which an inflexible constraint, such as the "Must Start On" or "Must Finish On" constraint, does dictate. Therefore, it is used more as a guideline than as a fact that your project must obey. The deadline constraint works well when you are trying to realistically display total slack values and yet maintain task-scheduling flexibility.

REFERENCE

Setting a Deadline Constraint

- Click the task for which you want to set the deadline, and then, in the Properties group on the Task tab, click the Information button; or double-click the task.
- In the task's Task Information dialog box, click the Advanced tab, and then, in the Deadline box, enter the deadline constraint date; or click the Deadline arrow and select the constraint date in the calendar.
- Click the OK button.

After a brief consultation with Sidney and the team, Emily asks you to set a deadline constraint for the Security completed task to be sure the task is completed in a timely manner and to help pull the project in on time.

To set a deadline constraint:

▶ 1. Click the **Task** tab, and then, in the View group, click the **Gantt Chart** button arrow.

▶ 2. In the Built-In section on the menu, click **Detail Gantt**. You switched the view to the Detail Gantt chart.

▶ 3. Right-click **Security** (task 15), and then, on the shortcut menu, click **Scroll to Task**. You can see in the Detail Gantt chart that the Security task and the Security completed milestone each have a total slack time of 10 days. This number is unrealistic because the project is running very late already, so you need to set a deadline constraint for the task, Security completed (task 19), that is allowing the Security phase this amount of slack.

▶ 4. Double-click **Security completed** (task 19) to open the Task Information dialog box.

▶ 5. Click the **General** tab if it is not already selected to view the currently scheduled Finish date, which is 11/6/14.

▶ 6. Click the **Advanced** tab, click in the Deadline box to select **NA**, type **11/11/14**, and then click the **OK** button. The Detail Gantt chart with the deadline date applied to the Security completed task is shown in Figure 5-41. In all Gantt charts, a deadline constraint is identified as a green arrow that points to the right edge of a slack line. The new slack value for the Security completed task is 3.75 days, which is more realistic than the previous 10-day calculation.

Figure 5-41 | **Detailed Gantt Chart view with a deadline constraint**

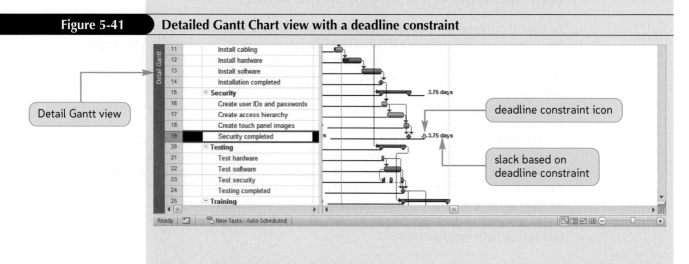

▷ **7.** Click the **File** tab, preview the Detail Gantt chart, click the **Page Setup** link, add your name left-aligned in the header, print as directed by your instructor, and then save your changes.

Adding Progress Lines

In addition to the slack, slippage, and various bars that appear in Gantt Chart view, you can add progress lines to help evaluate how the project is progressing. **Progress lines** give you a visual representation of all tasks that are in progress. The lines connect the tasks to create a line chart that gives you a quick visual of those tasks that are on schedule, behind schedule, and complete. The lines are drawn based on the percentage completion value for each task. The peaks that point to the left indicate work that is behind schedule. Peaks that point to the right indicate work that is ahead of schedule. The distance of the peak to the vertical line is a visual representation of the degree that the task is either ahead (peaks to the right) or behind (peaks to the left) schedule. The line is drawn based on the Status date.

You use the Progress Lines dialog box to set preferences for the progress lines. You can set the appearance for the dates, intervals, and the styles for the progress lines. If you have progress lines from a previous Status date, you can set the new lines so they are formatted differently than the previous progress lines to make it easy to compare progress through the project.

REFERENCE

Displaying Progress Lines

- Display the Gantt Chart.
- Click the Gantt Chart Tools Format Tab, and then, in the Format group, click the Gridlines button.
- On the Gridlines menu, click Progress Lines.
- Click the Line Styles tab to change the style of the progress lines, including the line type, shape, color, and pattern; to add progress points to mark where the line connects to the task bars; and to display dates for each progress line.
- If you have progress lines from a previous status date, set the new lines using different settings so you can compare the two sets of progress lines.
- Click the Dates and Intervals tab to set the time intervals and date options for the progress lines.
- Click the OK button, and then view the Gantt chart to see the lines.

You decide that you want to use progress lines to see how the ViewPoint Partners AV presentation rooms installation project is moving along. These lines will better help you compare the scheduled dates to the actual dates with a visual graph.

To display progress lines:

▷ **1.** Right-click the **Select All** button, and then, on the menu, click **CompareDates**.

▷ **2.** In the CompareDates table, click **Analysis (task 1)** to deselect the table, and then drag the **split bar** to the left so that Actual Start is the last column displayed.

▷ **3.** Click the **Gantt Chart Tools Format** tab, and then, in the Format group, click the **Gridlines** button.

▶ **4.** On the menu, click **Progress Lines**. The Progress Lines dialog box opens with the Dates and Intervals tab on top.

▶ **5.** In the Current progress line section, click the **Display** check box, and then verify that the **At project status date** option button is selected. Refer to Figure 5-42.

Figure 5-42   **Progress Lines dialog box**

progress lines can display at the Status date or Current date

progress lines can display in relation to the actual or baseline plan

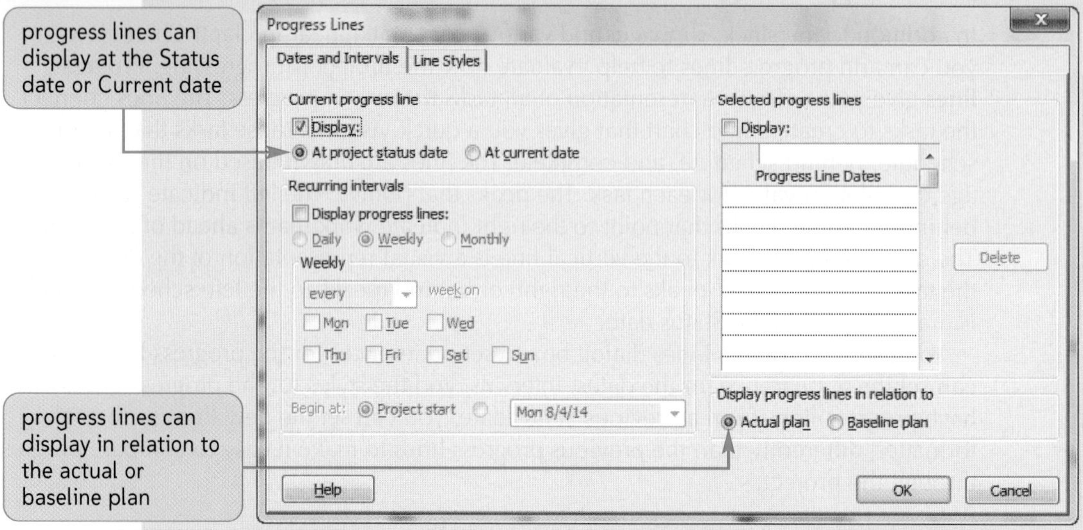

▶ **6.** Click the **OK** button. A red progress line appears on the Gantt chart. The default is to display the progress line based on the project Status date. You can also display a project line based on the Current date.

▶ **7.** Right-click **Design (task 5)**, and then, on the shortcut menu, click **Scroll to Task**.

▶ **8.** Click the **View** tab, and then, in the Zoom group, click the **Zoom Entire Project** button 🖳. You view the progress line. See Figure 5-43.

Figure 5-43   **Progress lines on Gantt chart**

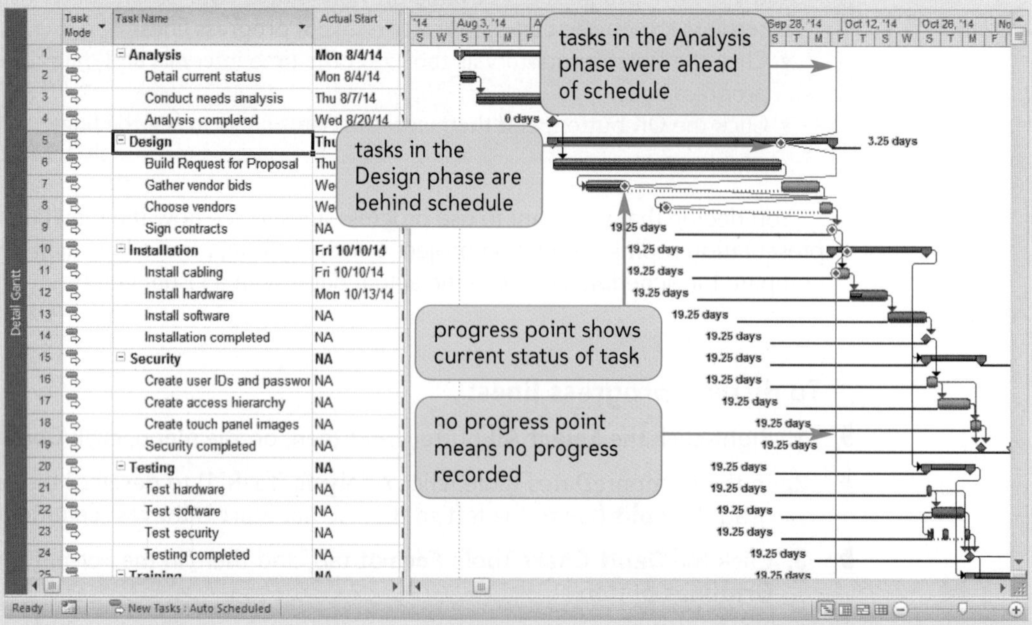

tasks in the Analysis phase were ahead of schedule

tasks in the Design phase are behind schedule

progress point shows current status of task

no progress point means no progress recorded

TIP

To remove or change a progress line, double-click the progress line to open the Progress Lines dialog box.

> **9.** Save your work. The progress line helps you to visualize which tasks are ahead of schedule, behind schedule, and on schedule. Circles with red dots are the progress points, indicating where the task is as of the Status date.

Using Project Progress Reports

Recall that in addition to the many sheet and graphical views that you can print at any time, Project 2010 also provides reports that summarize information and focus on various areas of your project. Reports used during the progression of the project help you to manage and prioritize work in progress to best meet the goals of finishing the project on time and within budget. For example, the Current reports focus on current project date progress, and the Costs reports focus on current project costs. Remember that certain reports are only relevant to certain viewers, and these reports can be made extremely specific by customizing them to your needs.

You can edit each report to show and summarize the specific fields of information about which you want to report. In addition, you can use the Custom category to create a completely new report or to copy any existing report and modify it to meet your individual needs. If you have saved custom tables, filters, or views, you can use those definitions to create custom reports as well.

Current Activity and Cost Reports

The reports in the Current Activities category help you to analyze progress on your project. You can use these reports to highlight various types of progress on the AV presentation rooms installation project.

To view a Current Activity report:

> **1.** Click the **Project** tab, and then, in the Reports group, click the **Reports** button. The Reports dialog box opens with six large icons that show each of the six report categories.

> **2.** Click the **Current** icon, and then click the **Select** button. The Current Activity Reports dialog box provides access to six reports that summarize task progress.

> **3.** Click the **Should Have Started Tasks** icon, and then click the **Select** button. The Should Start By dialog box opens, and you are prompted for a date. The date you enter determines which tasks are displayed in the report. You want to see the list of tasks that should have already started by the Status date.

TIP

You can click the arrow to display a calendar and click the desired date.

> **4.** Click in the **Start by** box in the dialog box, type **10/10/14**, and then click the **OK** button. The Should Have Started Tasks report appears in the Print preview pane in Backstage view.

> **5.** On the status bar, click the **Actual Size** button 🖼 and scroll to view all pages. The data is not distributed well across the pages.

> **6.** Click the **Page Setup** link, click the **Page** tab if it is not selected, click the **Landscape** option button if it is not already selected, click the **Adjust to** down arrow as needed to display **95%**, and then click the **OK** button. The report now fits neatly on one page. You see the tasks that should have started already.

> **7.** Change Your Name to your name center-aligned in the header, and then submit the report to your instructor, either in printed or electronic form as requested.

Task costs are a concern for Sidney. You preview and then print as requested a Cost report.

To view a Cost report:

▶ 1. Click the **Project** tab, and then, in the Reports group, click the **Reports** button.

▶ 2. Click the **Costs** icon, click **Select**, click the **Cash Flow** icon, and then click the **Select** button. The Cash Flow report appears in Backstage view. The Cash Flow report gives you a detailed analysis of how money is being spent by task for each week of the project.

▶ 3. Click the **Page Setup** link, on the Page tab click the **Adjust to** down arrow as needed to display **80%**, and then change Your Name to your name so it is center-aligned in the header.

▶ 4. Print the report as requested.

▶ 5. Click the **Task** tab to return to the Gantt Chart view, and then save your work.

If you want to see a report by day or by month, you can create a custom report and select the time period that best meets your needs.

Developing a Custom Report Based on a Custom Table

Sometimes you will want either to customize an existing report or to create an entirely new report based on the custom tables, filters, and views that you have developed. Project 2010 allows you to edit any of its reports or to create an entirely new report by using the Custom report category.

REFERENCE

Editing an Existing Report

• On the Project tab, in the Reports group, click the Reports button.
• Double-click the report category that meets your reporting needs, click a report that most closely matches the report that you want to edit, and then click Edit to edit the existing report.
• Make the appropriate changes within the Reports dialog box, name the new report, and then click the OK button.

In working with Sidney, some specific reporting requirements have been developed. You can meet these needs by editing one of the Current reports and adding the required additional fields.

To create a new report based on a custom table:

▶ 1. Click the **Project** tab, and then, in the Reports group, click the **Reports** button. The Reports dialog box opens.

▶ 2. Double-click the **Current** icon.

TIP

Be careful how many elements you add to a report; a cluttered report is difficult to understand.

▶ 3. Click the **Tasks Starting Soon** icon, and then click the **Edit** button to open the Task Report dialog box with the **Definition** tab selected. You can use this dialog box to edit many different elements of a report.

4. Click the **Table** arrow, and then click **CompareDates**. The CompareDates table has the fields that you need for this custom report.

5. Click the **Filter** arrow, on the list of criteria click **Slipping Tasks**, and then click the **Highlight** check box. The Definition tab is shown in Figure 5-44.

Figure 5-44   **Definition tab in the Task Report dialog box**

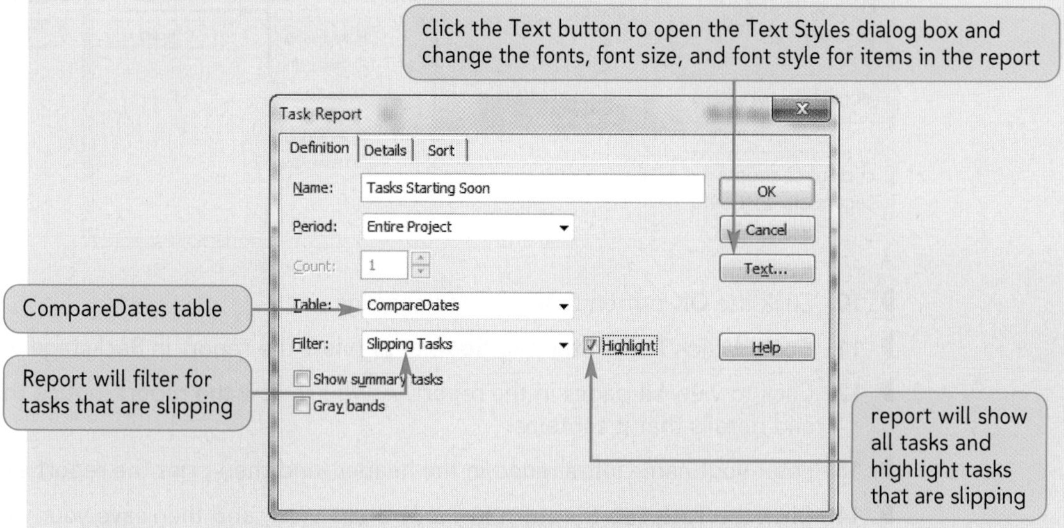

click the Text button to open the Text Styles dialog box and change the fonts, font size, and font style for items in the report

CompareDates table

Report will filter for tasks that are slipping

report will show all tasks and highlight tasks that are slipping

6. Click the **Details** tab. You can customize the details that appear for each task. For this report, you want Task notes and the Assignment schedule, which should already be selected. Additional formatting options such as borders, gridlines, and totals are also available.

7. Click the **Border around details** check box, and then click the **Gridlines between details** check box. This adds a border and gridlines to make the report more attractive and easier to read.

8. Click the **Sort** tab. You can sort by three fields and determine either ascending or descending order for each field.

9. Click the **Sort by** arrow, press the **S** key, scroll down the list, and then click **Start**. You set the Start field as the primary sort field. You accept the default sorting option that makes the ID field as the secondary sort field. Both sort orders are ascending. See Figure 5-45.

| Figure 5-45 | Sort tab in the Task Report dialog box |

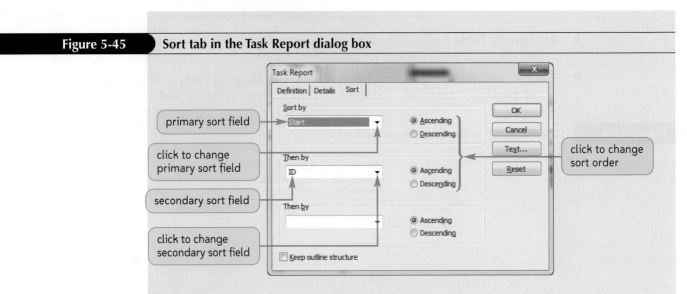

▶ **10.** Click the **OK** button to accept the settings.

▶ **11.** Double-click **Tasks Starting Soon** to preview the report in Backstage view.

▶ **12.** Click to view all pages in the report. As you review the report, notice the fields and details that it contains.

▶ **13.** Enter your name left-aligned in the header, and then print the report as requested.

▶ **14.** Click the **Task tab** to return to Gantt Chart view, and then save your work.

Reports provide an excellent communication tool for the staff and management at ViewPoint Partners.

Creating a New Report

The problem with editing existing reports is that your editing changes override the report choices originally provided by Project 2010 for this project. If your changes are extensive, you might want to create an entirely new report to preserve the default settings for the Project 2010 reports. Once you have created a new report, you can copy new report definitions to other projects using the Organizer dialog box, which you will learn more about in the next tutorial.

You decide that for some reporting, rather than copying any of these reports and modifying them, you'll create an entirely new report. You can choose from four different types of custom reports: Task, Resource, Monthly Calendar, and Crosstab.

A **crosstab report** summarizes a numeric field for a resource or task over time. The numeric field is usually work or cost. The unit of time is usually days or weeks, although other options such as quarters, half years, or thirds of months are available. The structure of the report is that the row headings are the resources (or tasks if you select Tasks) and the column headings are units of time. The numeric field for a resource (or task) is summarized in the intersection of the column and row for that resource (or task).

A monthly calendar report provides you with an overview of the project plan formatted similar to the Calendar for a month. When you set up the report, you select the calendar, such as Standard, Night Shift, or any custom calendar upon which to base the report. You specify the time period, filter, and different highlighting. When working as a project manager, this report will help you plan resources in advance for the upcoming tasks.

In order to help organize other office activities around the installation project, Sidney asks you to create a custom report to show the team the tasks that are in progress as a monthly calendar. You'll create a Monthly Calendar report to meet this need.

To create a new report:

1. Click the **View** tab, and then, in the Task Views group, click the **Calendar** button 🔳.

2. Click the **Project** tab, and then, in the Reports group, click the **Reports** button.

3. Double-click the **Custom** icon in the Reports dialog box. The Custom Reports dialog box opens, containing an alphabetical list of all available reports.

4. Click the **New** button in the Custom Reports dialog box. The Define New Report dialog box opens. You want to see information in a calendar format, so you'll choose a Monthly Calendar.

5. Click **Monthly Calendar**, and then click the **OK** button. The Monthly Calendar Report Definition dialog box opens. You must name the new report as well as determine the base calendar and which tasks will appear in the report.

TIP

You can create a Monthly Calendar report on any calendar, such as Night Shift or special calendars you created in the project.

6. In the Name box, type **ViewPoint Partners In Progress Tasks** as the descriptive title for the report.

7. Click the **Filter** arrow, review the options, and then click **Incomplete Tasks**. By creating a calendar of incomplete tasks, the staff can know what to expect in the office. The Calendar will be based on the Standard Calendar. See Figure 5-46.

| Figure 5-46 | Monthly Calendar Report Definition dialog box |

8. Click the **OK** button. The **ViewPoint Partners In Progress Tasks** report is added to the Reports list in the Custom Reports dialog box.

9. With **ViewPoint Partners In Progress Tasks** selected in the Custom Reports dialog box, click the **Select** button to display the new custom report.

10. Review the report, zooming as necessary.

11. Add your name left-aligned in the header, and then print the report as requested.

12. Close all open dialog boxes, save the changes, and then close the file.

The report provides the information that you need to present to ViewPoint Partners. As you update and continue to track the progress of the AV presentation rooms installation project, you can access this report at any time from the Custom Reports dialog box.

Closing a Project

Closing a project (as opposed to saving and closing a project file) means finalizing the data that is stored in the project file. "Closing a project" is not a feature of Project 2010, but rather a point in time or announcement that you, as the project manager, declare in order to clarify that the project is finished and the reports are final. In other words, it can be seen as a milestone.

Once all tasks have been completed and no additional progress information will be reported on the ViewPoint Partners AV presentation rooms installation project, you will establish a date on which the project is officially "closed," and you'll schedule a meeting with Sidney to review final cost and variance reports. Figure 5-47 summarizes several reports provided by Project 2010 that are used after the project is closed to analyze its overall success. Many of these reports can be used to evaluate progress during the project as well. When a project has had all tasks completed, the check marks in each row of the Indicators column show that you, the project manager, have updated the actual dates for each task and that each task has been completed. Actual project closure may take place by getting a signed document from the client stating the project has been officially accepted.

Figure 5-47	Project 2010 reports used to analyze a closed project

Type of Information	Report Category	Report Name	Report Description
Summary	Overview	Project Summary	A summary of the project information, including date, duration, work, and cost values for the scheduled versus baseline values
Summary	Overview	Top-Level Tasks	A summary of the major phases showing Start, Finish, cost, and work values for each phase
Summary	Overview	Milestones	A summary of the milestones showing Start, Finish, cost, and work values for each milestone
Task Information	Current	Completed Tasks	Shows duration, Start, Finish, cost, and work values for each completed task
Cost	Costs	Budget	Shows fixed costs, total costs, baseline costs, variance costs, actual costs, and remaining costs for all tasks
Work	Workload	Task Usage	Crosstab report of summarized work; tasks and their assigned resources are displayed in the row area, and the columns are organized by weeks
Work	Workload	Resource Usage	Crosstab report of summarized work; resources and their assigned tasks are displayed in the row area, and the columns are organized by weeks

Session 5.2 Quick Check

REVIEW

1. What four characteristics do you specify when creating a new custom view?
2. Why is the Detail Gantt chart such a valuable tool for a project manager during the progression of the project?
3. What is the purpose of an Interim plan?
4. Why would you apply a highlight filter to a view?
5. What is the purpose of the title field in the Table Definition dialog box?

Practice the skills you learned in the tutorial using the same case scenario.

PRACTICE

Review Assignments

Data File needed for the Review Assignments: Train-5.mpp

Part of the AV presentation rooms installation project involves training so that the users will be ready to go when the presentation rooms are installed. In this assignment, you will open the Training project file with the final project plan. You are now in the middle of this project and need to update its progress. You also need to save a baseline, track progress, analyze variance, and print several reports that highlight important progress and variance information. Complete the following:

1. Open the **Train-5.mpp** project file located in the **Project5\Review** folder included with your Data Files, and then save the file as **VPTrain-5**.
2. Open the Project Information dialog box. The current Finish date is 11/18/14. Enter **10/17/14** as the Current date. Notice that the Status date is already set to **10/17/14**, and then close the Project Information dialog box.
3. Change Your Name in the Project Summary task to your name.
4. Clear the baseline for the entire project and then save a baseline for the entire project.
5. Apply the Tracking table, drag the split bar to display the % Comp. column.
6. Mark as on track the tasks Identify existing skills (task 2) and Identify needed skills (task 3).
7. Update the Develop training documentation (task 4) as 20% complete.
8. Use the Develop training documentation (task 4) Task Information dialog box to review the scheduled Start and Finish dates.
9. Zoom in on the Develop training documentation task, click the Split Task button in the Schedule group, and then drag the bar to reschedule the remaining work for the Develop training documentation (task 4) so that the task is split and the remaining work is moved to begin as of the Status date (10/17/14).
10. Read the ScreenTips available for the progress, split, and task lines for task 2, task 3, and task 4 in the Gantt chart.
11. Update the Hire trainers task (task 9) as 25% complete.
12. Check the project statistics. The Current Finish date should now be 11/28/14, and the Finish Variance is 8 days.
13. Based on the values in the Project Statistics dialog box, determine which two values were used in the calculation of the Finish Variance. Write the formula (with the specific values labeled appropriately) on a piece of paper, and then close the Project Statistics dialog box.
14. Drag the split bar to the right to view all of the columns in the Tracking table, and resize the columns so that all the data can be viewed.
15. Change the Current date to **11/7/14** and the Status date to **11/7/14**.
16. The contract development went better than expected. For the Develop contract task (task 7), enter an Actual Start date of **11/5/14** and an Actual Finish date of **11/7/14**.
17. Print the Tracking table (if requested) with your name left-aligned in the header, and then circle the values for the Develop training documentation task (task 4).
18. Mark the Develop training documentation task (task 4) as 90% complete. Record the new values on the printout or any paper. Explain how the entry affects the values.
19. Mark the Secure lab space task (task 11) as 100% complete, and note the 32 hours of Actual Work for this task. Save your changes.
20. Apply the Variance table to the task sheet, and then insert the Actual Start and Actual Finish columns between the Task Name and the Start columns.

21. Adjust the columns so that all data is visible, hide the Task Mode column, drag the split bar as far to the right as possible so that none of the Gantt chart is visible, and then print the Variance table (as requested) with your name left-aligned in the header. (It should print on one page without the Gantt chart.) On the printout or any paper, identify how the Start Var. and Finish Var. fields are calculated. Also identify which sets of dates are calculated once automatically, which are recalculated constantly as project progress is entered, and which you enter directly as tasks are completed.

22. Apply the Cost table to the task sheet, resize the columns as needed to fit content, drag the split bar to the far right as necessary so that none of the Gantt chart is visible, and then enter **$2000** as a fixed cost for the Hire Trainers task (task 9).

23. Select tasks 4 through 11, use the Update Project dialog box to update the schedule for these selected tasks as 0%–100% complete, and then view the Tracking table.

24. Drag the split bar to the left, and then open the Progress Lines dialog box to add a progress line.

25. Change the Current date to **11/14/14** and the Status date to **11/14/14**. Select the Schedule classes task (task 8) through the Hire trainers task (task 9), and then use the Mark on Track button to update these tasks.

26. Check the project statistics and determine how you are doing on the budget for the project. Write the answer on your paper.

27. In the Cost table, move the split bar as far right as possible, adjust column widths as needed to fit content, add your name left-aligned in the header, and then print the Cost table (if requested). On your printout or any paper, identify which tasks compare the values in the Cost, Baseline, and Variance columns. On your printout or any paper, identify the tasks that are overbudget or under budget, and give at least two reasons why a task might have cost variance.

28. Change the Current date to **11/21/14** and the Status date to **11/21/14**.

29. Apply the Tracking table to the task sheet, and then enter an Actual Finish date for Hire trainers (task 9) and Sign lab contract (task 12) as **11/20/14**.

30. Create a new table called **VPVariance** based on a copy of the Variance table with the following fields in this order: ID**,** Name, Start, Finish, Start Variance, Finish Variance, Duration Variance**,** Work Variance, and Cost Variance. Click the Delete Row button to remove unwanted fields, if any, from the original. Accept all of the default formatting.

31. Apply the new table to the task sheet, drag the split bar to the far right to hide the Gantt chart, resize all columns to view all data, and then preview the Variance table with your name left-aligned in the header and **FINAL VARIANCE DATA** in the center of the header. Print as requested.

32. View the Task Usage report in the Workload category, and then print the report (as requested) with your name left-aligned in the header. On the printout or paper, highlight which week had the most hours of work assigned.

33. Open the Task Usage report in the Workload category for editing, and then change the Work field to **Cost**. Preview and print the report (as requested) with your name in the left section of the header. On the printout or paper, highlight which week had the highest cost.

34. Apply the Detail Gantt chart view. Hide the Task Mode column. Zoom the Gantt chart so you can see the entire chart. Drag the split bar so the Duration column is the last column visible. Preview and then print the Detail Gantt (as requested) with your name left-aligned in the header. On the printout or paper, identify the longest slippage line or lines. Write the definition for total slack and slippage on your paper.

35. Save the project file, submit the file in electronic or printed form as requested, and then close the file.

Apply your skills to a project for building a new home.

APPLY

Case Problem 1

Data File needed for this Case Problem: Home-5.mpp

River Dell Development, Inc.   You have a part-time job working for River Dell Development, Inc., a general contracting company that manages residential construction projects. You are using Project 2010 to track progress on a project. The house is finally under construction. In this assignment, you will open a project file that Karen Reynolds, the manager, has been working on to create the final project file. You'll save a baseline, track progress, and print various reports to highlight progress and final project information. Complete the following:

1. Open the **Home-5** file located in the **Project5\Case1** folder included with your Data Files. Save the project file as **NewHome-5** in the same folder.

⊕ EXPLORE

2. Click the File tab, click Project Information, and then click Advanced Properties. Enter your name in the Title field on the Summary tab in the Properties dialog box.

3. In Resource Sheet view, change the resource "Your Name" to your name and your initials, and then switch back to Gantt Chart view.

4. This project is currently scheduled to start on 8/1/14 and finish on 10/17/14. For the purposes of this exercise, change the Current date to **8/1/14** in the Project Information dialog box. Notice that the Status date is set at 8/1/14.

5. Save a baseline for the entire project.

6. A few weeks have passed, and work on this project is progressing. You need to update its progress. You update the project on a Monday with the status as of the previous Friday. Change the Current date to **8/18/14** and the Status date to **8/15/14**.

7. View the Tracking table and update the Secure financing (task 2) and the Purchase lot (task 3) tasks as on track.

8. The project is a little ahead of schedule; mark the tasks Planning (task1), Dig foundation (task 6), and Pour cement (task 7) as 100% complete. On a sheet of paper, write down what happens to subtasks when a summary task is marked 100% complete.

9. Save an interim plan for tasks 1 through 4. Be sure the interim plan is for selected tasks and not the entire project. Accept the other default settings.

10. Another two weeks have passed, and you continue to update progress. Change the Current date to **9/1/14** and the Status date to **8/29/14**.

11. Enter **8/22/14** as the Act. Start date for Frame house (task 8) and **8/26/14** as the Act. Finish date.

12. Enter **8/27/14** as the Act. Start date for Roof house (task 9) and **8/30/14** as the Act. Finish date.

13. Apply the Detail Gantt Chart view and Zoom to view the entire project. On paper, note the task name and number of days for any tasks that have slack. Also note which tasks have slipped and by how many days.

14. Enter **9/12/14** as the deadline date for Brick exterior (task 11).

15. Preview and print the Detail Gantt chart (as requested) with your name left-aligned in the header. On your paper, identify the longest slack line(s).

16. Preview and print the Tracking Gantt chart (as requested) with your name left-aligned in the header. On the printout or paper, identify the actual and baseline bars.

17. Another few weeks have passed, and you continue to update progress. The house is finished, the General Contractor was able to push his crew and completed the job before the scheduled 10/27/14 Finish date. Change the Current date to **10/20/14** and the Status date to **10/17/14**.

18. Apply the Tracking table.

19. Use the Mark on Track button to update task 10 and task 11 as scheduled.

⊕ EXPLORE 20. It took only two days to install the plumbing and only three days to install the electric. They started work on 9/12/14. Use the Update Tasks dialog box to enter the Actual Start and Finish dates and mark these tasks as 100% complete. Be sure to enter remaining duration as 0.

21. Select task 15, task 16, and task 17, and then open the Update Project dialog box to update work on these tasks as complete through the Current date, using the Set 0%–100% complete option.

22. Mark the summary tasks as all 100% complete.

23. Apply the Variance table, display all the columns, and then preview and print the Variance sheet (as requested) with your name left-aligned in the header. On the printout or paper, indicate what the variance means for tasks 7 through 9.

24. View the Network diagram. What changes have been made to the boxes to tell you that the tasks are complete?

25. Return to Gantt Chart view, apply the Work table to the task sheet, and then insert the Fixed Cost and Cost fields to the left of the Work field.

26. Create a new view named **Cost and Work** based on the Task Sheet. The view should show the Work table, be set to No group, and filter for completed tasks. Be sure the view will appear on the shortcut menu.

27. Apply the Cost and Work view, and then preview the view in landscape orientation. Add your name right-aligned in the header. Print the view as requested.

28. View the Resource Usage report in the Workload category, remove the &[ProjectTitle] and the &[Manager] codes from the center of the header, and then add your name left-aligned in the header. Print the Resource Usage report as requested.

29. Open the Resource Usage report in the Workload category for editing. Change the Weeks column heading to Days and the Work field to Cost. Preview the report, and then print the last two pages of the revised report (as requested) with your name left-aligned in the header as requested. Save the project.

⊕ EXPLORE 30. Click the Project tab, and then click the Visual Reports button. View the Cash Flow report on the All tab. (*Note:* You need Microsoft Excel installed to view this report.) Print the first page of this report (as requested). Save the report as **HomeVis-5.xlsx**. Close the worksheet file.

31. Save your changes, submit the project in printed or electronic form as requested, and then close the project file.

Apply your skills to complete a project for a job search.

APPLY

Case Problem 2

Data File needed for this Case Problem: Jobs-3.mpp

CommunityWorks As a counselor at CommunityWorks, a career counseling firm, you continue working on a project to help new college graduates with technical degrees find employment. You used Project 2010 to help manage the project. After reviewing your task list, Oren Armani, the manager, has made a few changes to the project file so it will work for a job search. In this assignment, you will open a project file with the final project plan. You'll save a baseline, track progress, and print various reports to highlight progress and track the project information. Complete the following:

1. Open the **Jobs-5** file located in the **Project5\Case2** folder included with your Data Files, and then save the file as **MyJobs-5** in the same folder.

2. Click the File tab, click Project Information, and then click Advanced Properties. Enter your name in the Title field on the Summary tab in the Properties dialog box. This project is currently scheduled to start on 5/1/14 and finish on 5/23/14. For purposes of this exercise, change the Current date to **5/1/14**.

3. Save a baseline for the entire project.

4. In Resource Sheet view, change the "Your Name" resource to your name and initials and the "Your Friend" resource to the name and initials of one of your friends.

5. Now you are in the middle of this project and need to update its progress. Change the Current and Status dates to **5/8/14**.

6. In Gantt Chart view, select Design a business card (task 2), and then scroll to the task in the Gantt chart.

7. Apply the Tracking table. Select Design a business card (task 2), Create resume (task 3), and Meet with counselor (task 4), and then click the Mark on Track button to simultaneously update these tasks as on track as scheduled.

8. Mark Finalize resume (task 5) as 35% complete.

⊕ EXPLORE

9. Use the Move button to reschedule the remaining work (Incomplete parts) for Finalize resume (task 5) to the Status date, to reschedule work for that task.

10. Apply Detail Gantt Chart view, and print the Detail Gantt chart (as requested) with your name left-aligned in the header. On your printout or paper, identify the total slack for the tasks in the Existing Contacts (task 12) and Establish new contacts (task 15) phases.

11. Change the Constraint type for the Call references task (task 13) to As Late As Possible. On your printout or paper, explain what happened to the total slack value for Existing contacts.

⊕ EXPLORE

12. Create a new custom Crosstab Report type report. Name the report **Weekly Job Hunt**, and then for the column change Weeks to **Days**. Click the Details tab to set the report to Show Row totals and Column totals, and then click the OK button. Select the report to preview the Weekly Job Hunt report, add your name left-aligned in the header, and then print as requested.

13. Apply the Tracking table. Select tasks 7 through 9 (Set appointment with recruiter, Develop contact database, and Research newspaper ads) and then set an interim plan for these tasks.

14. Add the Start1 and Finish1 columns to the Detail Gantt chart where you think this data will be most useful.

15. Set the Status and Current dates to **6/5/14**. Then use the Update Project dialog box to update all the tasks as complete through 0%–100%.

16. View the final Variance table. Hide the Task Mode column and view the Entire project for the Gantt chart.

17. Save the file, submit the project in printed or electronic form as requested, and then close the project file.

Expand your skills to work on a project for the reunion.

CHALLENGE

Case Problem 3

Data File needed for this Case Problem: Reunion-5.mpp

Western College Reunion   As a proud graduate of Western College, you continue to help organize the 20th reunion for the graduating class of 1994. Part of the job is encouraging donations, so you want the project to be presented in a professional way. The reunion will take place on March 7, 8, and 9, 2014. Time is getting close, and your team has been busy getting ready for the event. In this assignment, you will open a project file with the final project plan. You'll save a baseline, track progress, and print various reports to highlight progress and final project information. Complete the following:

1. Open **Reunion-5** located in the **Project5\Case3** folder included with your Data Files.

2. Save the file as **WReunion-5** in the same folder.

3. In Resource Sheet view, change the Your Name resource to your name and initials, change the "Your Friend" resource to the name and initials of one of your friends, and then return to Gantt Chart view.

4. This project is currently scheduled to start on 1/31/14 and finish on 3/7/14. (Remember, it is scheduled from the project Finish date.) Change the Current and Status dates to **2/1/14**.

5. The project planning is complete; set a baseline for the entire project.

6. Time has passed, and you need to update progress. Enter **2/14/14** as the Current and Status dates.

7. Apply the Tracking table. Mark the Survey clients task (task 1) as on track as scheduled.

8. Mark the Determine reunion goals task (task 2) as 50% complete. Mark Determine number of attendees (task 3) as 50% complete.

9. Zoom the Gantt chart as needed to make the chart fit on one page, and then preview and print the chart (as requested) with your name left-aligned in the header. On the printout or paper, write an explanation for the automatic split for the Determine number of attendees task. (*Hint*: Remember that this project is scheduled from a project Finish date. What default constraint is placed on tasks in this situation? What would that mean if part of a task was finished ahead of schedule?)

10. More time has passed. Enter **2/21/14** as the Current and Status dates.

11. Mark the Determine reunion goals task (task 2) as 100% complete.

12. Using the Tracking table, enter **2/16/14** as the actual start date for the Set budget task (task 4). (*Note*: This is two days later than it is currently scheduled.) When the Planning Wizard opens, allow the scheduling conflict.

13. Open split screen view, and then open the Resource Work form in the bottom half of the screen. Add Joe Heller as a resource for Set budget (task 4). This should redistribute half of the work (16 hours) to Joe Heller, which should change the duration of the task from four days to two day. Adding Joe makes up for starting the task late.

14. Remove the split screen view, and then scroll to view the changes to task 4 in the Gantt chart.

15. More time has passed. It's a week before the reunion. Enter **2/28/14** as the Current and Status dates.

16. Mark the Determine number of attendees (task 3) as on track as scheduled.

17. Mark the Set budget task (task 4) as 100% complete.

⊕ EXPLORE 18. Change the actual duration of Set agenda (task 6) to five days.

19. Move the split bar right until you are able to view the Rem. Dur. column for the last two tasks. Write down on a sheet of paper the Rem. Dur. for both tasks.

20. Update the tasks Book entertainment (task 7) and Determine menu (task 8) to 50%.

21. Update Develop promotional brochure (task 9) to indicate that the task has an actual duration of two days and a remaining duration of zero days.

22. Update Mail brochure (task 10) to 100%, but set it with an actual duration of 2 days. What assumptions does Project 2010 make when you enter an actual duration value that is less than the remaining duration? Write the answer on your paper.

    Set the remaining duration for Mail brochure (task 10) to 0 days.

23. More time has passed. It's the reunion. Enter **3/7/14** as the Current and Status dates.

24. Update the project using the Update Project dialog box, use the Set 0% or 100% complete only option for work completed through March 7, 2014.

⊕ EXPLORE 25. Click the File tab, click Project Information, and then click Advanced Properties. Enter your name on the Summary tab in the Title box of the Properties dialog box.

26. View the Project Summary report in the Overview category. Print the report as requested.

27. Save the file, submit the project in printed or electronic form as requested, and then close the project file.

Use your skills to work on a project for a playground.

CREATE

Case Problem 4

Data File needed for this Case Problem: Grant-5.mpp

NatureSpace   As a project manager at NatureSpace, a company that specializes in creating play structures for communities, you continue to work on a project to purchase and install new playground equipment. The equipment must be ready by September 6, 2014, so you scheduled the project from a Finish date and let Project 2010 establish the project Start date. In this assignment, you will open a project file with the final project plan. You'll save a baseline, track progress, save an interim plan, create a custom view, and print various reports to highlight progress and final project information. Complete the following:

1. Open the file **Grant-5** located in the **Project5\Case4** folder included with your Data Files, and then save the file as **MyGrant-5** in the same folder.

2. In Resource Sheet view, change the Your Name resource to your name and initials.

3. Return to Gantt Chart view. (*Hint*: As you work in various views, move the split bar so only the Task Name column is visible, and zoom as needed to see the chart.)

⊕ **EXPLORE**

4. Use the Internet to research how long other communities have taken to build playgrounds. Read meeting minutes and newspaper articles to find out if any component took longer than expected. Examine the durations in the project file and adjust any that seem unrealistic. Add any tasks or resources that are missing.

5. This project is currently scheduled to start on 6/16/14 and finish on 9/6/14. It is scheduled from a project Finish date. The project planning has been moving along nicely. Change the Current date and the Status date to **7/1/14** in the Project Information dialog box.

6. Use the Set Baseline dialog box to set a baseline for the entire project.

7. Open the Project Information dialog box. A few weeks have passed, and you are in the middle of this project and need to update its progress. Enter **7/18/14** as the Current date and as the Status date.

8. Apply the Tracking table to the task sheet, and then mark Planning (task 1) as 100% complete.

9. Mark Plant sale (task 8) as 50% complete.

10. Drag the split bar to the right so that you can view the Act. Work column if it is not already showing. Add 3 days of actual duration for the task Car wash (task 9).

11. Apply the Cost table to the sheet, enter a fixed cost of **$100** for supplies needed for the car wash to the Car wash task (task 9), and enter **$125** for fixed cost in Coupon book sales task (task 10).

12. Switch back to the Tracking table, update the Coupon book sales task (task 10) as 25% complete. Print the Tracking table as requested. Be sure to fit to one page, add your name left-aligned in the header, and add the filename left-aligned in the header.

13. A few weeks have passed, and you are in the middle of this project and need to update its progress. Enter **8/15/14** as the Current date and as the Status date.

14. Update the Building summary task (task 12) to 50% complete.

15. Determine why the Purchase Equipment task (task 13) was marked as 78% complete, the Compare prices task was marked 100% complete, and the Get requisition task was marked 63% complete when the Building task (task 12) was marked 50% complete. Note this on the printout or paper. (*Hint*: Look at the total duration for all of the tasks as determined by the Act. Dur. and Rem. Dur. fields for this phase. Total the duration for all three tasks, and then calculate 50% of that total duration.)

16. Select all the subtasks in the Building phase, and then set an interim plan for the selected tasks.

EXPLORE 17. Save a second baseline for this project. Open the Set Baseline dialog box, click the Set baseline arrow, click Baseline 1, and then click the OK button.

18. Open the Project Information dialog box. More time has passed. You are finished with this project and need to update progress. Change the Current and Status dates to **9/9/14**.

19. Insert the Indicators column into the Tracking table to the left of the Task Name column. Resize the column to fit the indicators.

EXPLORE 20. Try to use the Update Tasks dialog box to update the Fundraising task (task 7). Why can't you update the task using the Update Tasks dialog box?

21. Close the Update Tasks dialog box without making any changes, and then use the 100% Complete button to mark Fundraising (task 7) and Set Budget (task 11) as 100% complete.

22. Use the 100% Complete button to mark the major phase Building complete. Notice how all subtasks are updated.

23. Apply the Cost table to the task sheet to record the following fixed cost. Enter **3000** in the Fixed Cost cell for the Building (task 12) to cover the costs of inspections, contracts, and construction insurance.

EXPLORE 24. Apply the Variance table and insert the Baseline 1 Duration column, Baseline Cost, Baseline1 Fixed Cost and Baseline1 Cost. What are the differences between the cost columns?

25. Create the Resource Usage report in the Workload category, and then print the report as requested. Be sure to add your name left-aligned in the header.

EXPLORE 26. Apply the Multiple Baselines Gantt view. (*Hint*: Use the More Views dialog box.) Zoom and scroll the Gantt chart as needed to see all of the chart. Use the ScreenTips to help you view and understand the multiple baselines. Preview the chart, add your name left-aligned in the header, and then print the multiple baselines chart as requested.

27. Return to Gantt chart view, apply the Entry table, save your changes, submit the files in electronic or printed form as requested, and then close the file.

ENDING DATA FILES

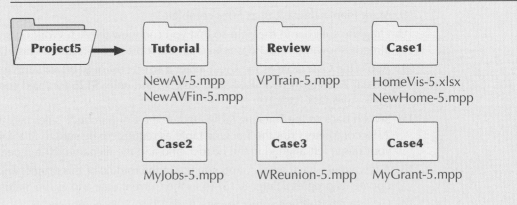

Project5 →	Tutorial	Review	Case1
	NewAV-5.mpp	VPTrain-5.mpp	HomeVis-5.xlsx
	NewAVFin-5.mpp		NewHome-5.mpp

	Case2	Case3	Case4
	MyJobs-5.mpp	WReunion-5.mpp	MyGrant-5.mpp

Sharing Project Information

Making Project Information Available to Others

Case | *ViewPoint Partners*

First you successfully created a Project 2010 file that was used to plan the installation of five presentation rooms with AV capabilities at ViewPoint Partners. Then you used the file to successfully manage the actual project. So far you have worked independently in the project, other than sharing project reports with others. One of the best features of Microsoft Project is the ability to share information and develop projects with others simultaneously.

Now, Sidney Simone and others at ViewPoint Partners want you to integrate segments of the project data with other software tools. You will use the completed AV Installation project file and the Training Lab project file to share and analyze information in various ways. You'll also learn about some of the advanced features of Project 2010 so that the next time you manage a project, you'll be able to use it even more effectively.

OBJECTIVES

Session 6.1
- Copy or export Project 2010 data to other Microsoft Office programs
- Copy or import data from Microsoft Office programs to Project 2010
- Create a link between Project 2010 information and Microsoft Excel
- Embed data in Project 2010
- Use the Drawing tool

Session 6.2
- Use and create Project 2010 templates
- Use the Project 2010 global template and Organizer
- Create and share a resource pool
- Use master projects
- Create a hyperlink between a Project 2010 file and a Microsoft Word document
- Create a custom field

STARTING DATA FILES

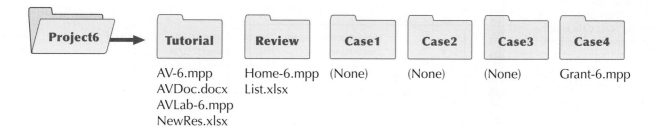

Project6 →	Tutorial	Review	Case1	Case2	Case3	Case4
	AV-6.mpp	Home-6.mpp	(None)	(None)	(None)	Grant-6.mpp
	AVDoc.docx	List.xlsx				
	AVLab-6.mpp					
	NewRes.xlsx					
	Software.mpp					

SESSION 6.1 VISUAL OVERVIEW

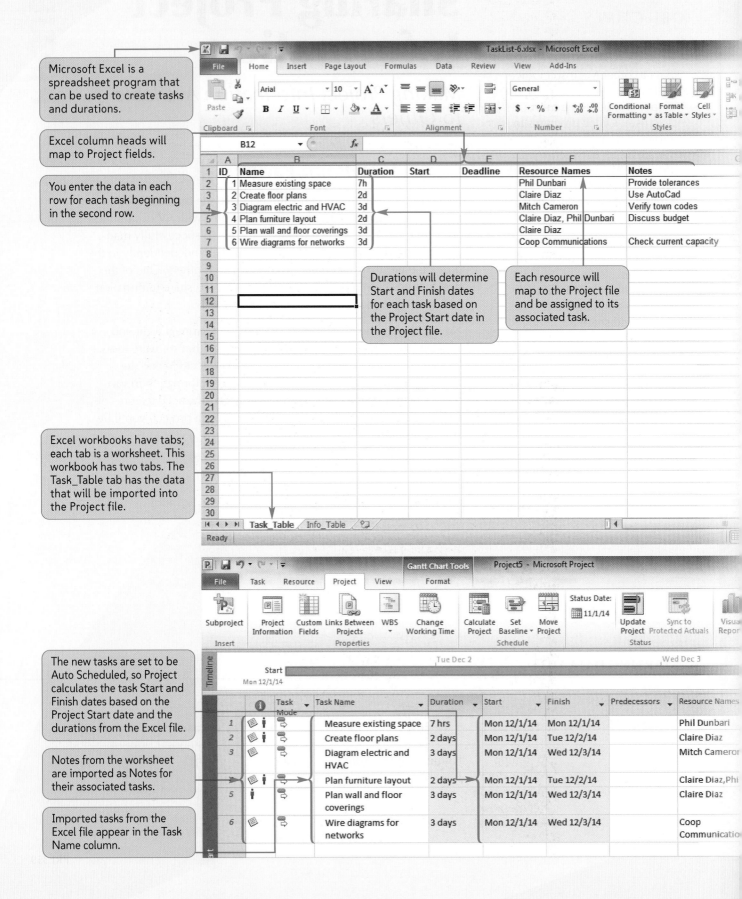

Microsoft Excel is a spreadsheet program that can be used to create tasks and durations.

Excel column heads will map to Project fields.

You enter the data in each row for each task beginning in the second row.

Durations will determine Start and Finish dates for each task based on the Project Start date in the Project file.

Each resource will map to the Project file and be assigned to its associated task.

Excel workbooks have tabs; each tab is a worksheet. This workbook has two tabs. The Task_Table tab has the data that will be imported into the Project file.

The new tasks are set to be Auto Scheduled, so Project calculates the task Start and Finish dates based on the Project Start date and the durations from the Excel file.

Notes from the worksheet are imported as Notes for their associated tasks.

Imported tasks from the Excel file appear in the Task Name column.

IMPORTING TASKS FROM EXCEL

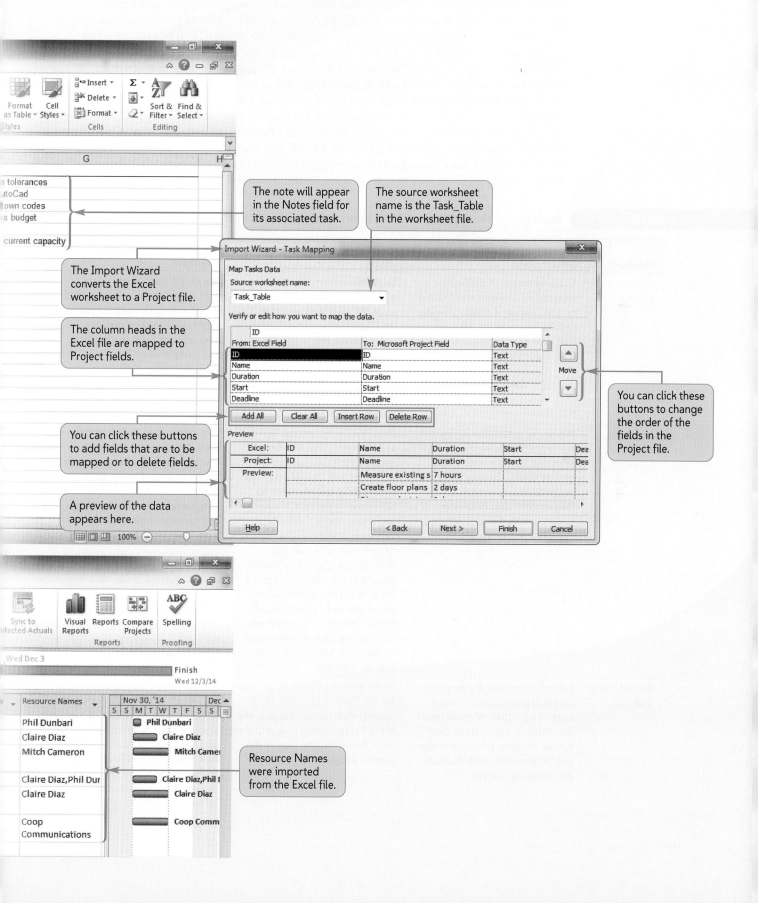

The note will appear in the Notes field for its associated task.

The source worksheet name is the Task_Table in the worksheet file.

The Import Wizard converts the Excel worksheet to a Project file.

The column heads in the Excel file are mapped to Project fields.

You can click these buttons to add fields that are to be mapped or to delete fields.

A preview of the data appears here.

You can click these buttons to change the order of the fields in the Project file.

Resource Names were imported from the Excel file.

Sharing Project Data with Other Programs

Project 2010 provides many features that allow you to manage, analyze, and report project information. Because it is part of the Microsoft Office suite of programs, you can share project information with people who don't use Project 2010 but do use other programs in Microsoft Office, such as Word and Excel. For example, an Excel user might want to copy some of the cost data from your Project 2010 file into an Excel worksheet to incorporate into a budget or graph. If you export the Project file to Excel, the **Project map** feature will create an Excel file with all the data from the project file. Alternatively, a manager might develop a task list in Outlook that you want to import into Project to add to the project plan. Project also integrates with Access using **Open Database Connectivity (ODBC)** standards. ODBC provides a standard software interface for accessing database management systems (DBMS). You can exchange data between Project 2010 and other files in several ways, as described in Figure 6-1.

Figure 6-1	Methods for sharing Project 2010 information with other programs

Method	Description	Steps	Example
Copy and paste	Copying means to duplicate selected information and place it on the Clipboard. Pasting means to take a copy of the information that is on the Clipboard and insert it at a specified location.	Select the information that you want to copy (cells within a sheet view, for example), and then click the Copy button in the Clipboard group on the Home tab. Open the destination file, click where you want the information to be pasted, and then click the Paste button in the Clipboard group on the Home tab.	You might want to copy data from a Cost sheet in Project 2010 to an Excel worksheet. Or you might want to copy resource data from an Excel worksheet and paste it into a Resource sheet in Project 2010.
Import or export	Importing and exporting involve the process of converting data from one file format to another. Import means to bring in, and export means to send out. Project 2010 uses data maps to define how the data will be imported and exported.	Import data by clicking Open in Backstage view, and then choosing the file that you want to import into Project 2010. To export data, use the Save As command in Backstage view, and then choose the file type you want to export. The Import/Export Wizard guides you through the steps. The Import Wizard starts when you open a file that Project 2010 does not recognize as a Project file. The Export Wizard is launched when you use the Save As command to save a Project file as a non-Project file type.	You might want to import information such as resource data into a project file that is already stored in other Project 2010 databases, ODBC-compliant databases, or Excel worksheets. You can also import task lists from Outlook into a Project file.

You might want to export Project 2010 data to other project databases, to ODBC-compliant databases such as Microsoft SQL Server, to an HTML file, to a text file, to Excel for special numeric analysis, or to Excel as a pivot table. |
| Earned value analysis | Earned value data allows you to measure project performance against a budget. When earned value data is exported to Excel for further analysis, project managers call the resulting worksheet an earned value analysis. | Right-click the Select All button for the Task Sheet, click More Tables, click Earned Value in the More Tables dialog box, and then click Apply. Finally, export the data to Excel. | Earned value analysis indicates how much of the budget should have been spent in view of the amount of work completed, and the baseline cost for the task, assignment, or resource. Earned value is also referred to as budgeted cost of work performed (BCWP). |

| Figure 6-1 | Methods for sharing Project 2010 information with other programs *(continued)* |

Method	Description	Steps	Example
Linking	Linking means to copy data from one file (source) to another (destination) so that only one physical copy of the data exists in the original source file. In addition, changes to the data made in either the source file or the destination file dynamically update the data in the linked file as long as both files are open.	Select the information that you want to link (cells within a sheet view, for example), and then click the Copy button. Open the destination file, click where you want the information to be linked, click the Paste Special button arrow in the Clipboard group on the Home tab, and then click Paste Link option button.	You might want to link an entire Microsoft Excel file into your Project file so that changes made to the original Excel data are dynamically updated in Project.
Embedding	Embedding is a way to copy or insert data from one application file into a different application file. The difference between embedding data and importing data is that embedded data can be edited using the features of the data's native application even though it is physically stored in another application file, but imported data can be edited using only Project features. Changes made to the embedded data are not automatically made to the original file. Embedding is preferred when you wish to use all the features or functionality of the original application.	Select the information that you want to embed (a graph within Excel, for example) from the source file, and then click the Copy button in the Clipboard group on the Home tab. Open the destination file, click where you want the information to be embedded, click the Paste Special button arrow, and then click the Paste option button.	You can embed an Excel graph in a Project file so that you can store the actual graph in the Project 2010 file.

Using Microsoft Office Excel to Analyze Numeric Data

Project 2010 is part of the Microsoft Office 2010 suite of programs, which also includes Microsoft Word, Microsoft PowerPoint, Microsoft Access, and Microsoft Outlook. Data can be integrated and shared seamlessly among those programs. For example, Excel is an excellent tool for analyzing and graphing numbers. People use Excel to track expenses and budgetary information. When you work with cost information in Project, you might find that the tools in Excel are better for some types of analysis. You can also copy Project information and paste it into an Excel worksheet to satisfy the requests that Excel users might have for Project 2010 data.

Copying Sheet Data from Project 2010 to Excel

ViewPoint Partners is a market research firm, and its partners use Excel extensively for their accounting and budget management requirements. Excel is also very useful when organizing numerical data and using formulas. Sidney wants you to use Excel to analyze the cost of a Training Lab project. The project was created by the Training team and is in a Project file called AVLab-6. To do so, you copy data from Project into Excel. When you work in Excel, the **cell address** is the column letter and row number for the intersection of the column and row for that cell. A group of cells in Excel is called a **range**. To select a range, click the first cell in the proposed range and then drag the pointer to the last cell in the range. Each cell is identified by a unique cell address. Ranges are defined by the first cell address in the upper-left corner of the block or group of cells and the last cell address in the lower-right corner of the range; for example, A2:G3 defines the range of cells from A2 through G3.

REFERENCE

Copying Data from Project 2010 into an Excel Worksheet

- View the project in a sheet view containing the data that you want to copy.
- Select the rows and columns that you want to copy.
- On the Task tab, in the Clipboard group, click the Copy button.
- Start Excel, and then click the cell where you want to paste the copied data.
- In Excel, click the Home tab, and then, in the Clipboard group, click the Paste button.

The Training Lab project is already completed, and you have been asked to analyze what it cost. Excel can help highlight and analyze the cost data. While you can copy any level of detail from Project to Excel, Sidney wants you to analyze the summary tasks.

To copy Project 2010 data into an Excel worksheet:

1. Open the **AVLab-6** project file located in the **Project6\Tutorial** folder included with your Data Files, and then save the file as **NewAVLab-6** in the same folder. The project file for the Training Lab project opens in Gantt Chart view.

2. Replace Your Name with your name as the Project Summary task.

3. In the Entry table, right-click the **Select All** button, and then click **Cost**. The Cost table is applied. The Cost table displays several fields that contain cost information including actual, baseline, and total costs.

4. Drag the **split bar** to the far right side of the screen so that the Remaining column is the last visible column in the Cost table.

   Trouble? If you cannot see all information in the Cost table, resize the columns so that all of the data is visible.

TIP

To select only certain rows, columns, or cells, drag through just the specific items that you want to copy.

5. Click the **View** tab, and then, in the Data group, click the **Outline** button.

6. On the menu, click **Outline Level 1** to show only the summary tasks. Tasks 0, 1, 6, and 10 are visible in the Cost table.

7. Click the **Task** tab, and then, in the Cost table, click the **Select All** button. The entire Cost table is selected.

8. In the Clipboard group on the Task tab, click the **Copy** button 🗎. When you click the Copy button, the data you've selected is copied to the Clipboard.

9. On the Microsoft Windows taskbar, click the **Start** button 🔘, point to **All Programs**, click **Microsoft Office**, and then click **Microsoft Excel 2010**. A new blank worksheet opens in a Microsoft Excel window. The title bar displays Book1-Microsoft Excel, and cell A1 (column A, row 1) is selected.

   Trouble? If Microsoft Excel 2010 is not installed on the computer that you are using, you might be able to use other spreadsheet software available on your computer. However, your screens will not match the figures in these steps and you might need to click different buttons and commands.

10. Maximize the Excel window if it does not fill the screen, and then, in the Clipboard group on the Home tab, click the **Paste** button. The tasks and the costs are copied into the rows and columns in the Excel worksheet.

    Trouble? If a menu opens when you click the Paste button you clicked the Paste button arrow instead of the button. Click cell A1, and then click the Paste button.

▸ **11.** Double-click the right edge of each lettered **column header** to adjust the column widths to fit the content, and then click cell **A1**. Each of the four rows from the Cost table is now a row in the worksheet. Each of the eight columns from the Cost table is now a column in the worksheet. See Figure 6-2.

Figure 6-2   **Project data copied into the Excel worksheet**

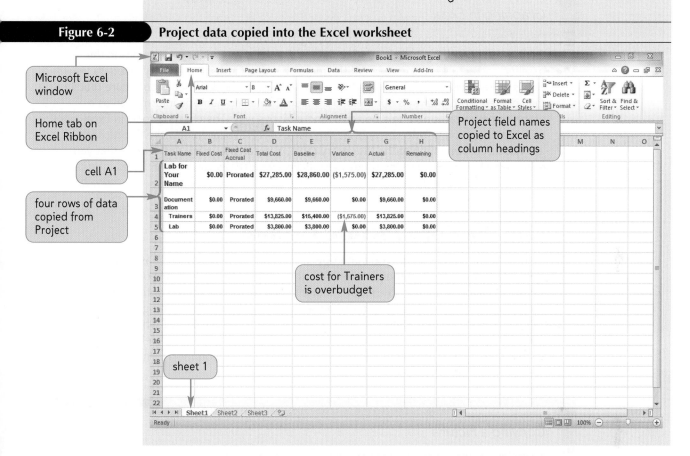

Sidney asks you to print the worksheet. She will hand out these pages to the staff at the status meeting.

To print and save the Excel workbook:

▸ **1.** Click the **File** tab, and then click **Print**. The worksheet appears in Backstage view in the Preview pane.

▸ **2.** Click the **Page Setup** link to open the Page Setup dialog box with the Page tab the active tab, click the **Landscape** option button, and then click the **OK** button. The Page Setup dialog box closes and the Preview pane shows the page in landscape orientation.

▸ **3.** Verify the print settings in Backstage view, and then, if requested to print the file, click the **Print** button in the center Print pane. The printout highlights the information you need to convey; that is, the cost for the Trainers is overbudget.

▸ **4.** Click the **File** tab if it is not the active tab, click **Save As**, navigate to the **Project6\Tutorial** folder, and then save the worksheet with the filename **NewAVLab-6.xlsx**. You return to the Project window.

Trouble? If you don't see the Project window on your screen, then, on the Windows taskbar click the NewAVLab-6 Project button.

Now that data is copied into Excel, you could use some of its powerful features, such as graphing, to analyze the data. You can offer these options to others at ViewPoint Partners, including staff in the accounting department, who often use Excel to manage budgets.

INSIGHT

Graphing in Excel

One of the most common reasons for copying numeric data to Excel is to be able to use the powerful graphing and charting tools. For example, you might want to graph the baseline and actual costs for each of the major summary tasks. Presenting cost data visually as a graph conveys the information in a manner that can be understood more readily than presenting the data as numbers in a sheet. Displaying numeric information as a graph communicates data in a powerful and effective way. The charting tools in Excel can create a graph to help you analyze the data. This is similar to how the Gantt chart is a visual representation of the task entry table. You can use many of the skills that you mastered when working in the sheet views in Project 2010 as you work in Excel.

Using the Copy Picture Feature

With the Copy Picture feature, you can copy almost any view of a project as a picture. Once copied, you can paste the picture in another Office file, such as a Word document or a PowerPoint presentation. The Copy Picture dialog box allows three options. The For screen option copies the information on the screen with all color formatting intact. The For printer option copies the view as it would be printed on a black-and-white printer. The To GIF image file option allows you to create a GIF file (for use in a Web page or other programs). A **GIF (graphics interchange format)** file is a common form of graphical image, often used for Web pages.

REFERENCE

Copying a Picture

- Display the view that you want to copy as a picture.
- In the Clipboard group on the Task tab, click the Copy button arrow, and then click Copy Picture.
- Select the For screen option to copy the information on the screen with all color formatting intact; select the For printer option to copy the view as it would be printed using a black-and-white printer; or select the To GIF image file option to create a GIF file (for use in a Web page or other programs), and then specify the filename and location for the GIF file.
- Open the file (such as a Word document or PowerPoint presentation) in which you want to paste the image, and then if you copied it using the For screen or For printer option, use the Paste command in that program to paste the image. If you saved the view as a GIF image, insert the image into the new document using the Picture button in the Illustrations group on the Insert tab.

Copy the Gantt Chart as a Picture

You find the Copy Picture feature useful for sharing information about the ViewPoint Partners AV presentation rooms installation project. You decide to paste an image of the project into a Word document to send to the managers.

To copy a picture of the Gantt chart and paste it in a Word document:

▶ **1.** In the Cost table, click **Lab for Your Name** (task 0), right-click **Lab for Your Name** (task 0), and then click **Scroll to Task**.

▶ **2.** Click the **View** tab, and then, in the Data group, click the **Outline** button.

▶ **3.** On the menu, click **All Subtasks**, widen the Task Name column as needed to fit the content, and then collapse the Write progress reports task.

▶ **4.** Drag the **split bar** toward the left edge as needed so that only the Task Name column is visible on the sheet, and then, in the Zoom group, click the **Zoom Entire Project button** . The task bars begin at 10/1/14. See Figure 6-3.

| **Figure 6-3** | **Gantt Chart view** |

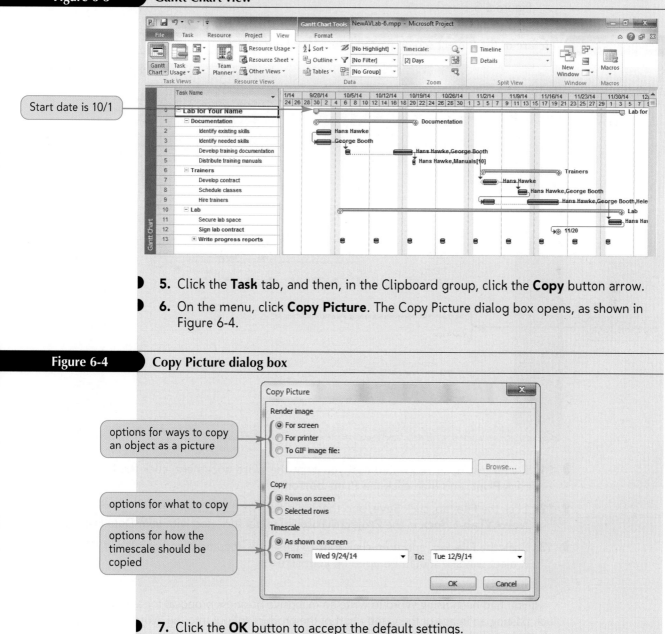

Start date is 10/1

▶ **5.** Click the **Task** tab, and then, in the Clipboard group, click the **Copy** button arrow.

▶ **6.** On the menu, click **Copy Picture**. The Copy Picture dialog box opens, as shown in Figure 6-4.

| **Figure 6-4** | **Copy Picture dialog box** |

options for ways to copy an object as a picture

options for what to copy

options for how the timescale should be copied

▶ **7.** Click the **OK** button to accept the default settings.

8. On the Windows taskbar, click the **Start** button 🔘, point to **All Programs**, click **Microsoft Office**, and then click **Microsoft Word 2010**.

   Trouble? If Microsoft Word 2010 is not installed on your system, you can use a previous version of Microsoft Word or another word processor such as WordPad to complete this exercise. WordPad is located in the Accessories submenu of the All Programs menu.

9. In the Clipboard group on the Home tab, click the **Paste** button. The image of the Gantt Chart view is pasted in the Word document using the settings you specified in the Copy Picture dialog box.

10. Press the **Enter** key twice, type **This Gantt chart represents actual progress on a finished project.**, press the **Enter** key, and then type your name, as shown in Figure 6-5.

Figure 6-5	Picture of the Project screen pasted into a Word document

Home tab on the Word Ribbon

type this text

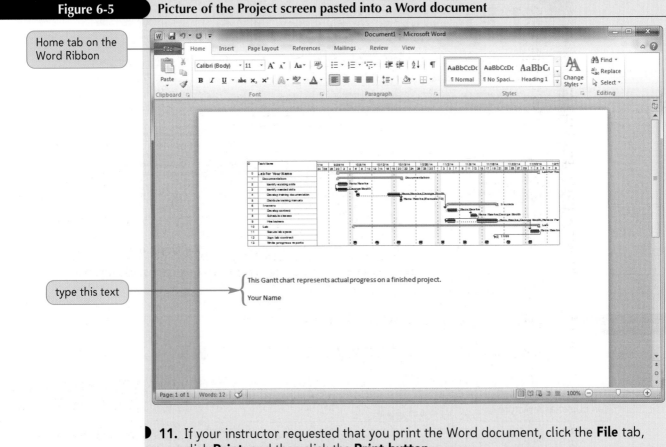

11. If your instructor requested that you print the Word document, click the **File** tab, click **Print**, and then click the **Print button**.

12. Click the **File** tab, click **Save**, and then save the Word document as **NewAVLab-6.docx** in the **Project6\Tutorial** folder included with your Data Files.

13. Click the **File** tab, and then click **Exit** to close the document and exit Word. The Project window should be open on your screen.

If you had been using Word to write an extensive business proposal for a new product, pasting an image of the Gantt chart of the product rollout into the Word document would have helped illustrate the phases, milestones, and time span of the project.

Copying the Gantt Chart as a GIF

Sidney also wants you to save a copy of the Gantt chart as a GIF file so she can use it on the ViewPoint Partners Web site. When you specify the GIF file option in the Copy Picture dialog box, you also must identify a filename and location for the file.

To copy Gantt Chart view as a GIF file:

▶ 1. In the Clipboard group on the Task tab, click the **Copy** button arrow, and then click **Copy Picture**. The Copy Picture dialog box opens.

▶ 2. Click the **To GIF image file** option button, click the **Browse** button, navigate to the **Project6\Tutorial** folder included with your Data Files if this is not already the active folder, and then verify the default text in the File name box is NewAVLab-6 and the Save as type is GIF Image Files.

▶ 3. Click the **OK** button in the Browse dialog box, and then, in the Copy Picture dialog box, click the **OK** button. The Gantt chart is saved as a GIF file in the Project6\Tutorial folder.

You can view GIF files in many different graphics programs. At ViewPoint Partners, employees use Internet Explorer to browse Web pages on the Internet, and the computers have the Windows Paint program installed as well as the Microsoft Office Picture Manager. The program used to open GIF files depends on which software program is associated with the GIF file type on your computer. On Windows machines, this can be Internet Explorer, Microsoft Office Picture Manager, as well as other programs.

To view a GIF file:

▶ 1. On the Windows taskbar, right-click the **Start** button 🪟, and then click **Open Windows Explorer** to open a Windows Explorer window.

▶ 2. Navigate to the **Project6\Tutorial** folder, and then double-click the **NewAVLab-6** GIF file. Because the GIF format is typically used for Web pages, Emily assigned Internet Explorer as the default program that opens GIF files on the ViewPoint Partner computers. The GIF file opens in the program associated with GIF files on your computer, similar to Figure 6-6.

Figure 6-6   Final NewAVLab-6 Gantt chart being viewed as a GIF file

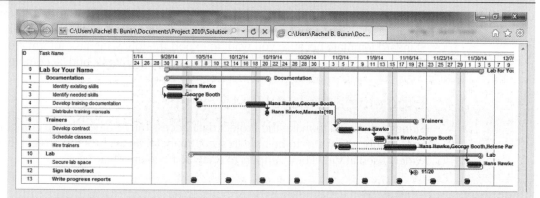

▶ **3.** In the program window that is currently displaying the GIF image, click the **Close** button ☒ to close the program.

Trouble? If a message window opens asking if you want to close all tabs or the current tab, click the current tab option to close the tab with the GIF image.

▶ **4.** On the Windows taskbar, click the **NewAVLab-6 Project** button.

You see the benefit of capturing the Gantt Chart as a GIF image. Image files can be inserted in documents, on Web pages, and in e-mail messages to help communicate information about a project to team members.

PROSKILLS

Written Communication: Business Web Pages and Intranets

An **intranet** is a private network designed for a specific group of people. It looks and functions like the Internet, but the content is not available to anyone outside the private intranet. In an organization, the intranet is the system you log into as an employee. Intranets are useful for publishing information specific to the group that uses it. For example, a company might post company news, holiday schedules, or special announcements. Intranets can also be useful if you are working on a project and want to post project information to a specific group of people who have access to the intranet. Or, as a student, you may need to access a school intranet to view your grades and submit assignments.

You can use GIF files to help illustrate ideas and enhance the intranet pages. Once you have saved an image from a Project file as a GIF file, you can insert it on an intranet page by using a Web page development program such as Microsoft Sharepoint Designer, Adobe Dreamweaver, or any other program that creates **HTML (Hypertext Markup Language)** codes, the language used to create Web and intranet pages.

Exporting Project Data to Excel

The fields of a project revolve around three major categories: tasks, resources, and assignments. When you export a project to a new format, the fields in the Project file must map to the corresponding fields in the new program. A map defines how fields in Project 2010 are translated to fields for display in another file format such as HTML, Excel, or Access. When you begin the export process, the Export Wizard dialog box opens. By using the Export Wizard, you can quickly export all of the fields for a given category to the new format. Project has a list of predefined maps for most standard export tasks. Each map is designed with a special purpose in mind. You will use the Standard template because you want to export the following task information: ID, name, durations, resources, start and finish dates, unit assignments, and % complete.

Exporting a Project File to Excel

Sidney asked you to make the Project data accessible to others in the company. Specifically, she wants to be able to see a financial analysis of the project. Excel is widely used at ViewPoint Partners to analyze financial data.

REFERENCE

Exporting a Project 2010 File to Excel

- Click the File tab to open Backstage view, and then click Save & Send.
- In the File Types section, click Save Project as File.
- In the Other File Types section, click Microsoft Excel Workbook, click the Save As button, and then click Save.
- In the Export Wizard dialog box, click the Next button, click the Project Excel Template option button as the format of the data you want to export, and then click the Finish button.
- Open a Windows Explorer window, navigate to the location where you saved the Project file as an Excel file, and then double-click the Excel file to view the information exported from the Project 2010 file into an Excel file.

You decide to export the Project file data to an Excel file so that it can be used by other departments, such as the accounting department.

To export a Project 2010 file to Excel:

▶ **1.** Click the **File** tab to open Backstage view, and then click **Save & Send**.

▶ **2.** In the File Types section, click **Save Project as File**.

▶ **3.** In the Other File Types section, click **Microsoft Excel Workbook**, and then click the **Save As** button.

▶ **4.** In the File name box, type **NewAVLabExp-6,** and then click **Save**. The Export Wizard dialog box opens.

▶ **5.** Click the **Next** button to move to the second screen in the wizard. You want to export using the Project Excel template format.

▶ **6.** Click the **Project Excel Template** option button, and then click the **Finish** button.

Now that the Project file has been exported to Excel, you can open the file in Excel and view the data.

To view the Excel file:

▶ **1.** On the Windows taskbar, click the **Windows Explorer window** button for the **Project6\Tutorial** folder, and then double-click the **NewAVLabExp-6** Microsoft Excel Workbook file. The exported Project 2010 file opens in Excel. The worksheet has three worksheet tabs: Task_Table, Resource_Table, and Assignment_Table. Excel organizes each table in the Project 2010 file as its own sheet.

▶ **2.** Double-click the border between the column headings as needed to view all the column data on the Task_Table worksheet. The first sheet in Excel contains the data from the task Entry table. Field names, which are the column headings in Project 2010, are entered in row 1 in Excel. Each row contains a task and its associated information. All fields are complete for the task Entry table. See Figure 6-7.

Figure 6-7 Exported Project file in Excel: active worksheet Task_Table

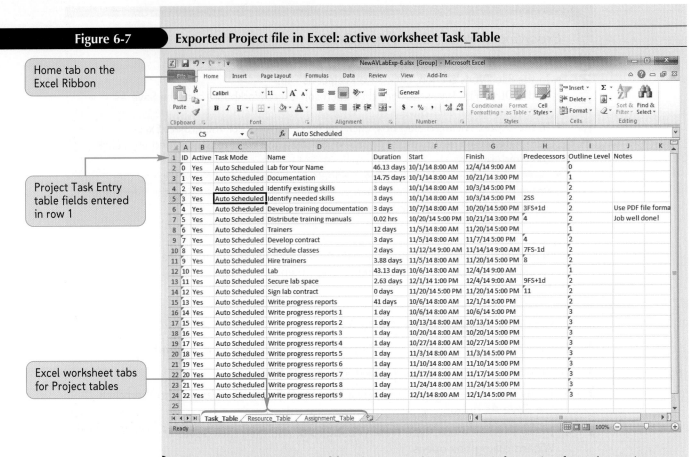

Home tab on the Excel Ribbon

Project Task Entry table fields entered in row 1

Excel worksheet tabs for Project tables

3. Click the **Resource_Table** tab to view the resource information from the project file, and then adjust the columns as needed to see all the data. See Figure 6-8.

Figure 6-8 Exported Project file in Excel: active worksheet Resource_Table

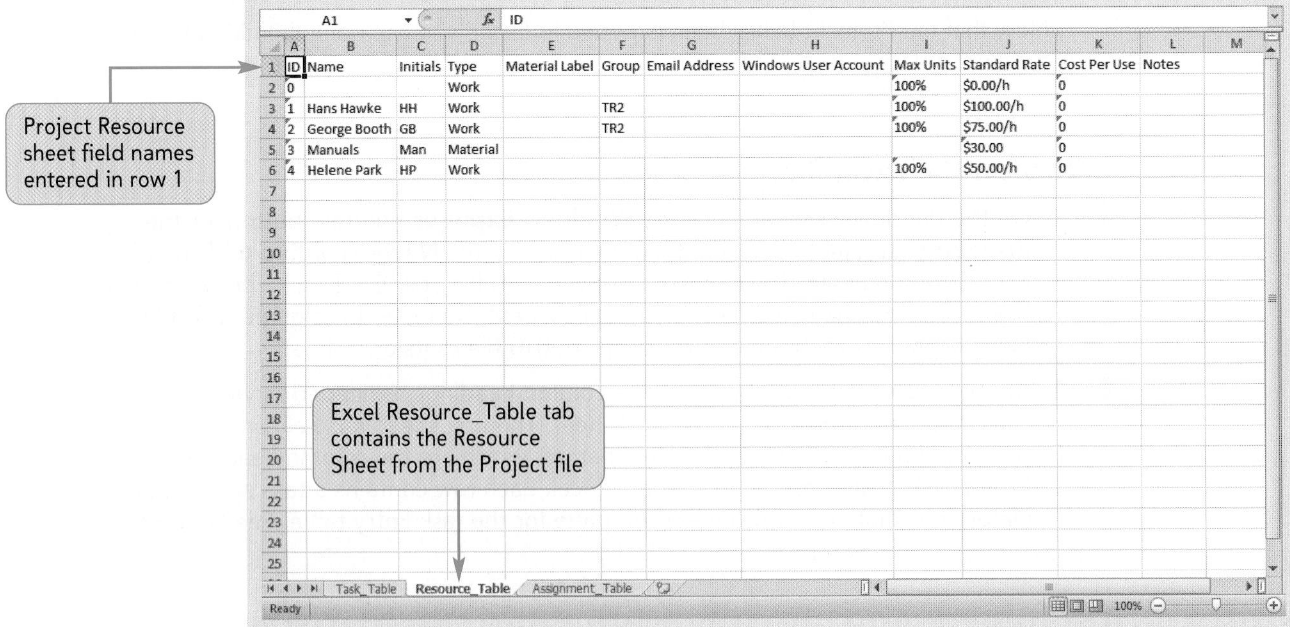

Project Resource sheet field names entered in row 1

Excel Resource_Table tab contains the Resource Sheet from the Project file

4. Click the **Assignment_Table** tab to view the assignment information from the project file, and then adjust the columns as needed to view the information. See Figure 6-9.

Figure 6-9   **Exported Project file in Excel: active worksheet Assignment_Table**

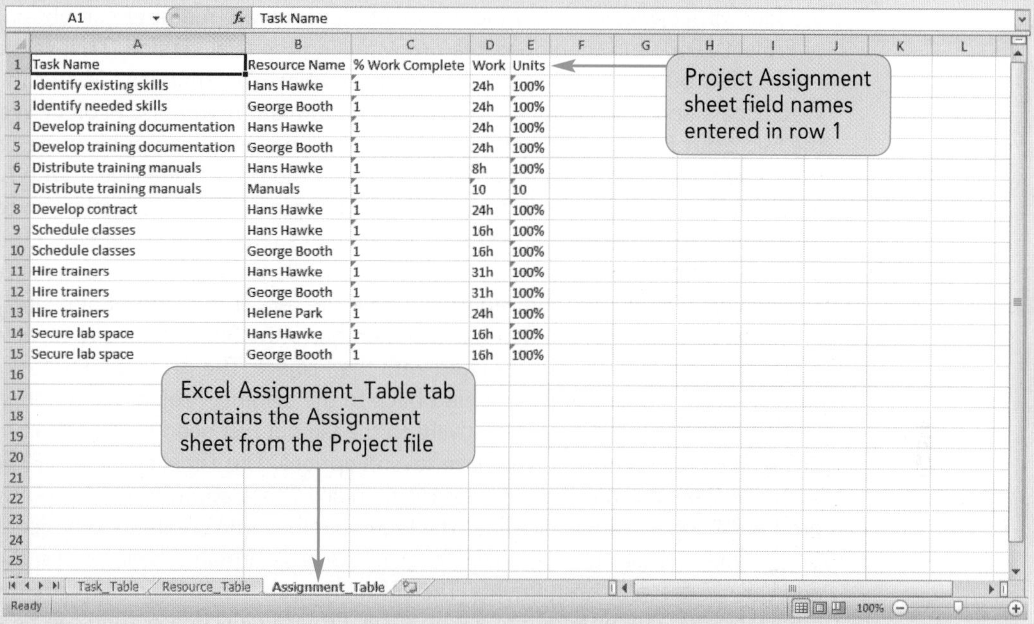

Project Assignment sheet field names entered in row 1

Excel Assignment_Table tab contains the Assignment sheet from the Project file

	Task Name	Resource Name	% Work Complete	Work	Units
1	Task Name	Resource Name	% Work Complete	Work	Units
2	Identify existing skills	Hans Hawke	1	24h	100%
3	Identify needed skills	George Booth	1	24h	100%
4	Develop training documentation	Hans Hawke	1	24h	100%
5	Develop training documentation	George Booth	1	24h	100%
6	Distribute training manuals	Hans Hawke	1	8h	100%
7	Distribute training manuals	Manuals	1	10	10
8	Develop contract	Hans Hawke	1	24h	100%
9	Schedule classes	Hans Hawke	1	16h	100%
10	Schedule classes	George Booth	1	16h	100%
11	Hire trainers	Hans Hawke	1	31h	100%
12	Hire trainers	George Booth	1	31h	100%
13	Hire trainers	Helene Park	1	24h	100%
14	Secure lab space	Hans Hawke	1	16h	100%
15	Secure lab space	George Booth	1	16h	100%

Task_Table / Resource_Table / **Assignment_Table**

Be sure to click the Close button for the file, not for the program. Do not exit Excel.

5. On the Excel Ribbon, click the **File** tab, click **Close** to close the Excel file (but not the Excel program), and then click the **Save** button to save the changes when prompted.

PROSKILLS

*Team Work: Communicating with Team Members Who Don't Have
Project 2010 Installed*

Microsoft Office suite is available in several configurations. As a result, a team member
may not have Project 2010 as part of his or her Microsoft Office suite installation. If this is
the case and you need to share Project information with these colleagues, you can consider
the following options for viewing a project plan. A team member can obtain a trial version
of Project 2010, and then open the project using the trial version. Trial versions typically
expire after 60 days, so this is a short-term solution. Alternatively, Microsoft provides
Web access and storage for sharing files among team members. **Project Web Access** is
the Microsoft Project Web application. A project manager can publish the project and
then give those on the team permission to view the project in Project Web App. Another
option is Microsoft Sharepoint, designed for people who work together on teams. Using
SharePoint 2010, people can set up Web sites to share information with others, manage
documents from start to finish, and publish reports to help everyone make better decisions.
The person who created the report can save the report to a SharePoint site, without using
Project Web App. A team member can then go to the SharePoint site to view and edit task
and resource information associated with the Project. The project information that is edited
on the SharePoint site will be copied back to the original Project file automatically.

If you aren't working collaboratively on the file but just need to show team members what's
going on with your project, you have several options. The Timeline view in Project 2010 can be
copied and pasted in an e-mail message or in any Office application for a quick view of Project
progress along a graphic timeline. The team member who created the project can use the
Copy Picture feature to copy a GIF image of the project plan showing tasks, durations, start
and finish dates, and assignments. The GIF image can then be sent to team members in an
e-mail, printed out, or added to a Web page. Project 2010 information can be also be copied
and pasted into the common Office application documents. The person who created the project can copy the information from Project 2010 and paste it into applications like Word, Excel,
PowerPoint, or Outlook while retaining formatting and column heading information. You can
then view project information in those Office applications. The Visual Reports feature in Project
is another option for importing into and then viewing files in either Excel or Visio. As you can
see, there are many ways to work on a team with Project 2010 files.

Apply Earned Value Data to a Task Sheet and Export It to Excel

Many people use Excel to analyze financial data, so Project provides a way to show project
costs as a budget and then to compare expected progress with actual progress. This process,
which is called **earned value analysis (EVA)**, uses budget values for each task to calculate
useful variance values. These budget values can be easily exported to Excel to show useful ratios. When you perform an EVA, you must use a Project file that was used during the
actual project, that is, one that has actual and baseline values. The project can have data
recorded from several tasks, a phase, or the entire project in which you recorded actual
versus baseline data so as to examine earned value analysis.

Sidney has asked you to further analyze the costs within the NewAVLab project file.
First, you need to apply the Earned Value table to the project.

To apply the Earned Value table to a task sheet:

1. On the Windows taskbar, click the **NewAVLab-6** Project button to display the Project window.

2. In the Cost table, right-click the **Select All** button, click **More Tables** to open the More Tables dialog box, click **Earned Value**, and then click the **Apply** button.

3. Drag the **split bar** all the way to the right, and then resize the columns so that as much data as possible is visible, as shown in Figure 6-10.

| Figure 6-10 | Earned value table in Project |

The fields of the Earned Value table are described in Figure 6-11. The variance values (SV, CV, VAC) can be either negative or positive. A negative variance indicates that you're overbudget; a positive variance indicates that you're under budget.

| Figure 6-11 | Fields of the Earned Value table |

Field	Name	Description
Planned Value (PV)	Budgeted cost of work scheduled (BCWS)	The planned cost of a task between the task's Start date and the project Status date
Earned Value (EV)	Budgeted cost of work performed (BCWP)	The value based on the percentage of the budget that should have been spent for a given percentage of work performed on a task
AC	Actual cost of work performed (ACWP)	The total actual cost incurred while performing work on a task during a given time period
SV	Scheduled variance (SV)	The cost difference between the work performed and the work scheduled to be performed: SV = BCWP − BCWS
CV	Cost variance (CV)	The cost difference between a task's budgeted cost and its actual cost: CV = BCWP − ACWP
EAC	Cost (EAC: estimate at completion)	Total scheduled cost for a field
BAC	Baseline Cost (BAC: budget at completion)	Total baseline cost for a field
VAC	Variance at completion (VAC)	Difference between the baseline and scheduled cost for a field: VAC = BAC − EAC

When you apply the Earned Value table in the middle of a project, you get an idea of where you might be able to reallocate money and resources (from those with positive variances to those with negative variances) in order to keep the project within budget.

INSIGHT

Exporting Earned Value Data to Excel

To do further analysis on the earned value data, you can export the data contained in the Project Earned Value table to Excel. Exporting data is usually faster than creating a sheet view with the specific fields that you need and then copying and pasting them into an Excel spreadsheet, although the results of both actions are essentially equivalent. For example, it is common to want to calculate the cost performance index (CPI = BCWP/ACWP) or schedule performance index (SPI = BCWP/BCWS). Both of these values are calculated by creating a ratio from two other earned value indicator fields, so the formula creation capabilities in Excel are the perfect tool to create these valuable ratios. A CPI value that's greater than 1 indicates that you're under budget. A value that's less than 1 indicates that you're overbudget.

Each time you apply the Earned Value table, the values are updated to reflect the current Status date. When you apply it after the project has been completed, the CV (Completion Variance) value for the project summary task shows if the project is over-budget or under budget.

REFERENCE

Exporting Earned Value Data to Excel

- In the table in Gantt Chart view, right-click the Select All button, click More Tables, click Earned Value in the More Tables dialog box, and then click the Apply button.
- Click the File tab, click Save As, navigate to the location where you want to save the Excel file, enter an appropriate filename in the File name box, click the Save as type arrow, click Microsoft Excel Workbook, and then click the Save button.
- The Export Wizard dialog box opens, click the Next button to continue.
- Click the Selected Data option button, click the Next button, click the Use existing map option button, and then click the Next button.
- Click the Earned value information Template option as the format of the data you want to export, and then click the Finish button.
- Open a Windows Explorer window, navigate to the location where you saved the Excel file, and then double-click the Excel file to view the earned value data in Excel.

Sidney asks you to export the earned value data to Excel so the accounting department can access the data.

To export earned value data to Excel:

▸ 1. Click the **File** tab, and then click **Save As**. The Save As dialog box opens. The files in the Project6\Tutorial folder are displayed in the Save As dialog box.

▸ 2. Click to the right of the filename in the File name box, and then type **-EV**. The exported file will be named NewAVLab-6-EV.

▸ 3. Click the **Save as type** arrow, and then scroll to and click **Excel Workbook**.

▸ 4. Click the **Save** button. The first screen in the Export Wizard dialog box opens.

5. Click the **Next** button, verify that the **Selected Data** option button is selected, click the **Next** button, and then click the **Use existing map** option button. You can read the options for using a new or existing map in the Wizard dialog box.

6. Click the **Next** button, and then click **Earned value information** in the Export Wizard - Map Selection dialog box. See Figure 6-12. The Export Wizard dialog box determines exactly which fields of data to export based on the selected mapping option. For the Earned value information mapping option, the Tasks (rather than the Resources or the Assignments) will be exported as well as the column headers.

Figure 6-12	Export Wizard - Map Selection dialog box

7. Click the **Next** button. The Task data will be exported and the Excel data will include column headers.

8. Click the **Next** button to view the Task mapping and preview the results, click the **Next** button again to view the Export Wizard - End of Map Definition dialog box, and then click the **Finish** button. The earned value data is now saved as an Excel spreadsheet on your computer.

9. On the taskbar, click the **Microsoft Excel** button to open the Excel window, click the **File** tab, click **Open**, navigate to the **Project6\Tutorial folder**, and then double-click **NewAVLab-6-EV.xlsx**. The file opens in Excel.

10. Click the **File** tab, and then click **Close**. The Excel worksheet closes but the Excel program remains open.

You can use Excel to develop formulas for further analysis of the data and to create charts to display the data. Not only is exporting data often faster than copying and pasting it, but the export process also preserves the field names and enters them in row 1. This is a benefit over the copy and paste method.

INSIGHT

Using Microsoft Office PowerPoint as a Presentation Tool

PowerPoint is the presentation graphics program in Microsoft Office. You use it to create professional slide show presentations. PowerPoint slides are an excellent way to illustrate and present your ideas, using slides, outlines, speaker's notes, and audience handouts. A presentation can include text, drawn graphics, clip art, photographs, tables, and charts. Presentations can also include features such as Flash animation files, animated clip art, links to Web sites, sounds, and movie clips. PowerPoint can include snapshots of your project, reports, or most other visual features included in the Project file. For example, you could use earned value data to create slides that update management in the middle of a project. These slides could include charts, tables, and bullet points to help identify how money and resources might be allocated based on earned value data in order to stay within budget.

PowerPoint presentations are viewed using a computer and monitor, or for an audience, on a screen using a projector. You can also publish a presentation on the Internet, giving others access to your presentation at their convenience. As a project manager, PowerPoint provides an excellent way to present information about an ongoing project.

Starting a Project Plan by Using the Excel Task List Template

Excel works seamlessly to integrate data with Project 2010. A user who is more familiar with Excel than Project might choose to use an Excel template to start a new project. The data in this Excel file can then be imported into Project to create a Project file.

To open the Excel task list template:

1. On the Windows taskbar, click the **Microsoft Excel** button to display the Excel window if it is not open on your computer, click the **File** tab, and then click **New**. The Excel Backstage view opens with the New tab active.

2. In the Available Templates pane, click **Sample templates**, scroll the list in the middle pane, click the **Microsoft Project Task List Import Template** icon, and then click the **Create** button. A new workbook named Microsoft Project Task List Import Template1 appears in the window.

3. Click the **Task_Table worksheet** tab. See Figure 6-13.

Figure 6-13   New Excel worksheet based on Microsoft Project Task List Import Template

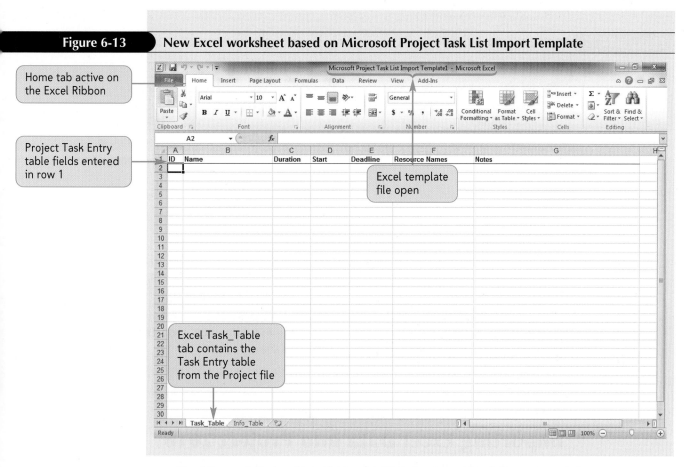

Home tab active on the Excel Ribbon

Project Task Entry table fields entered in row 1

Excel template file open

Excel Task_Table tab contains the Task Entry table from the Project file

The Microsoft Project Task List Import Template1 workbook has two worksheets, one named Task_Table that contains task information, and one named Info_Table, which has information that should not be modified because it provides the rules for the table. The Task_Table default fields are displayed as the column headings ID, Name, Duration, Start, Deadline, Resource Names, and Notes. The fields in this Excel template match the fields in the Entry table in Project. So, when you have to import this data to Project, there is no need to map data fields. If you edit the template, Project will attempt to map any additional fields automatically; if it can't map the fields automatically, you can map them manually.

InteriorDesigns, the architects who helped design the new office and AV presentation rooms at ViewPoint Partners, provided a list of tasks that describes the building and redesign process, including durations and notes. You will reconstruct the task list using an Excel spreadsheet. Entering data into an Excel worksheet is not much different than entering data into the Entry table in Project 2010. You will use your skills to create a task list in Excel.

To create a task list using the Excel task list template:

1. Enter the IDs, tasks, durations, resources, and notes exactly as shown in Figure 6-14 into your Excel worksheet, beginning in cell A2.

Figure 6-14   Task list for new tasks

ID	Name	Duration	Start	Deadline	Resource Names	Notes
1	Measure existing space	7h			Phil Dunbari	Provide tolerances
2	Create floor plans	2d			Claire Diaz	Use AutoCad
3	Diagram electric and HVAC	3d			Mitch Cameron	Verify town codes
4	Plan furniture layout	2d			Claire Diaz, Phil Dunbari	Discuss budget
5	Plan wall and floor coverings	3d			Claire Diaz	
6	Wire diagrams for networks	3d			CoopCommunications	Check current capacity

   2. Click the **File** tab, click **Save** to open the Save As dialog box, navigate to the **Project6\Tutorial** folder, select the text in the File name box, type **TaskList-6**, and then click the **Save** button in the Save As dialog box.

   3. Click the **File** tab, and then click **Close**. The file closes, but Excel is still running.

Importing Excel Data into Project 2010

Importing data into a Project file means to convert it from a non-Project file format into a Project file format. Copying data from a non-Project file format to a Project file, rather than importing data, can accomplish the same results under certain conditions. For example, if the information that you want to import is in an Excel file and the structure of the spreadsheet columns matches the structure of the sheet fields within Project, you can copy the data from the Excel spreadsheet and directly paste it into a Project sheet. However, the import process is more powerful and flexible and allows for data that doesn't exactly match. For example, when you import data, you can map how the columns of the Excel spreadsheet will match the fields in the Project file. The Import/Export Wizard is as helpful in importing files as it is in exporting files. If you can let the Import/Export Wizard import the data based on default settings, Project attempts to automatically map the fields in the non-Project file to fields in the Project files. During the import process, you can also choose to work through the mapping screens and manually map the fields.

REFERENCE

Importing Excel Data into a Project 2010 File

- Create a new project or open the Project 2010 file into which you want to import the data.
- Click the File tab, and then click Open.
- Navigate to the location where the Excel file containing the data to import is stored, click the Files of type arrow, click Microsoft Excel Workbook, click the Excel file that contains the data, and then click the Open button.
- In the Import Wizard dialog box, click the Next button, and then do one of the following:
- If you created the file from the Excel Tasks List Template, click the Project Excel Template option button, click the option to import the file as a new project, append the data to the active project or merge the data into the active project, and then click the Finish button.

or

- If you are importing from a file in which you know that the fields map to a Project file, click the Use existing map option button, select the map for your data from the Map Selection list, and then click the Finish button; or click the Next button, specify if you want to import the file as a new project, append the data to the active project or merge the data into the active project, click the Next button, select the types of data to import, and then click the Finish button.

or

- If you are importing from a file that was created in Excel but that does not map to an existing sheet in Project, click the New Map option button to import the file as a new project, append the data to the active project or merge the data into the active project, specify the data and Excel options, click the Next button, click the Next button, and then click the Finish button.

or

- If you are importing the Excel data into a Project file when using a custom data map, click the New Map option button, click the Next button, click the As a new project or append data to the active project option button that most closely resembles the custom data map that you want to create, click the Edit button, click "Enter a new data map name" (if you want to reuse this data map later), click the check boxes for the data items that you want to import, define how each Project field maps to each Excel Worksheet Field (column), and then click the Finish button.

You want to incorporate the new tasks and resources you just entered in Excel into the Project file. You use the Import/Export Wizard to import the tasks list file that you just created and saved in Excel.

To import task data from Excel into Project 2010:

1. On the Windows taskbar, click the **Microsoft Project** button. The Project window opens.

2. Click the **File** tab, click **New**, click **Blank project**, and then click the **Create** button.

3. Click the **Task** tab if it is not the active tab, and then, in the Tasks group, click the **Mode** button.

4. On the menu, click **Auto Schedule**. Any new tasks will be scheduled automatically.

5. Click the **Project** tab, and then, in the Properties group, click the **Project Information** button.

▶ **6.** In the **Start date** box in the Project Information dialog box, type **12/01/14** as the Start date, click in the **Current date** box, type **11/01/14** as the Current date, and then click the **OK** button. You want Project to calculate dates based on the durations you entered in the Excel worksheet and the project Start date. Next, you'll import the Excel tasks list file that you just created and saved.

▶ **7.** Click the **File** tab, click **Open** to open the Open dialog box, navigate to the **Project6\Tutorial** folder if it is not the active folder, click the **Files of type** arrow, scroll to and click **Excel Workbook (*.xlsx)**, click **TaskList-6** in the file list, and then click the **Open** button. The Import Wizard starts.

▶ **8.** Click the **Next** button, click the **New map** option button if it is not already selected, and then click the **Next** button. In this screen in the wizard, you have several options: You can create a new project, append the data to the active project, or merge the data into the active project. Because you already have a new project open, you will append the data to the active project.

▶ **9.** Click the **Append the data to the active project** option button, and then click **Next**. You want to import the tasks as well as the column headers.

▶ **10.** Click the **Tasks** check box, then click **Next**. The Import Wizard – Task Mapping dialog box shows you how the fields from the Task_Table worksheet in the TaskList-6.xlsx workbook will be mapped to the Project file. See Figure 6-15.

Figure 6-15   Import Wizard Task Mapping dialog box

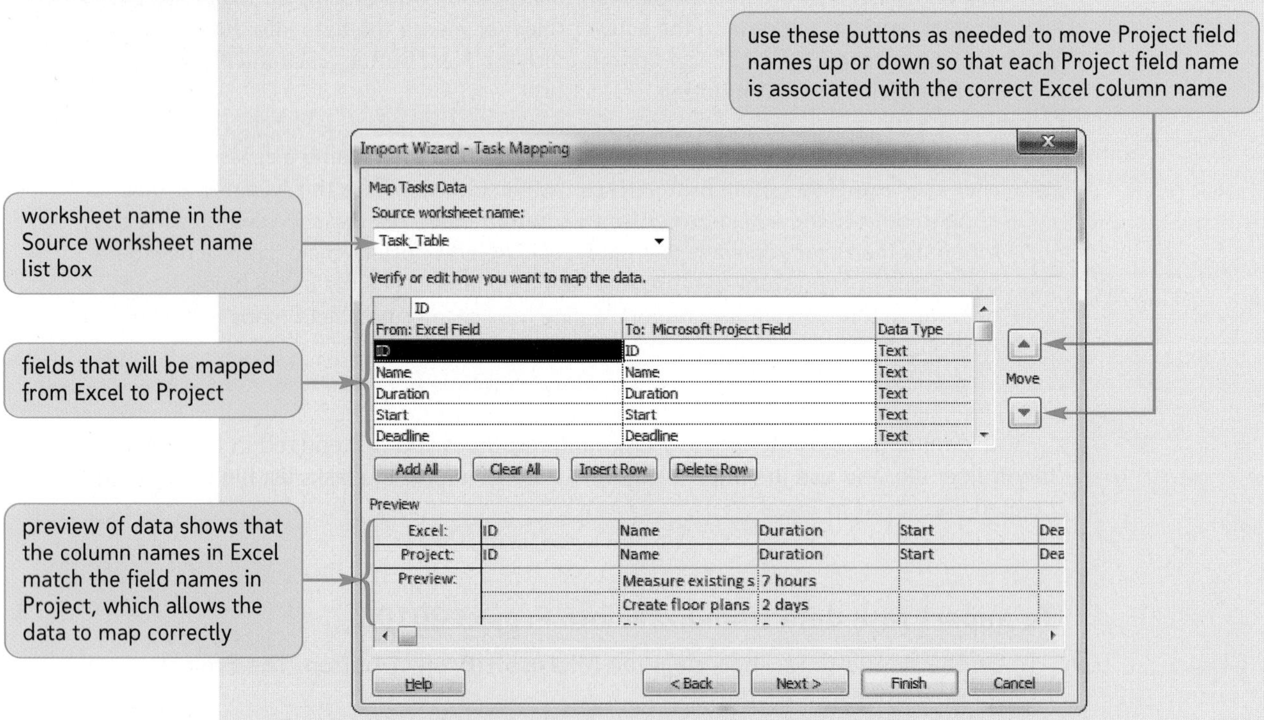

▶ **11.** Click the **Finish** button. The TaskList-6.xlsx file is imported as a Project 2010 file. The tasks, durations, and resources are entered into the Entry table. Start and Finish dates are calculated automatically.

12. Drag the **split bar** to the right to display the Resource Names column. You see how the other columns were automatically mapped. The Duration field in the Excel spreadsheet was imported to the Duration field in the Project file.

Project used the Current date 11/01/14 and the Start date 12/1/14 that you entered to determine the Start and Finish dates for the tasks based on the duration data you entered in the Excel file and imported into the file. If you had not changed the Current date in the Project Information dialog box, then the Start and Finish dates would be based on the date determined by the computer clock. Resources are assigned to their tasks. Notice that the notes were also imported and a notes icon is added next to each task in the Indicators column. See Figure 6-16.

Figure 6-16   **Task list imported into the Entry table from Excel**

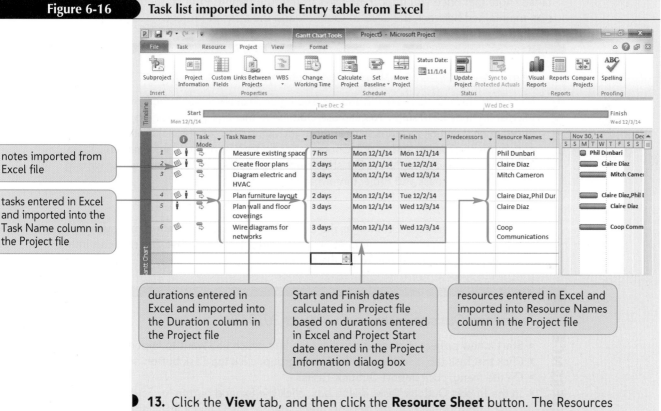

notes imported from Excel file

tasks entered in Excel and imported into the Task Name column in the Project file

durations entered in Excel and imported into the Duration column in the Project file

Start and Finish dates calculated in Project file based on durations entered in Excel and Project Start date entered in the Project Information dialog box

resources entered in Excel and imported into Resource Names column in the Project file

13. Click the **View** tab, and then click the **Resource Sheet** button. The Resources were entered at 100%. If you continued to work with this project file, you would add additional information about the resources such as their standard and overtime rates.

14. On the Quick Access toolbar, click the **Save** button to open the Save As dialog box, navigate to the **Project6\Tutorial** folder included with your Data Files if it is not the active folder, and then, in the File name box, type **TaskList-6**.

15. Click the **Save as type** arrow, click **Project (*.mpp)**, and then click the **Save** button. The dialog box closes and the project file is saved.

Importing Outlook Tasks into a Project File

If you use Outlook for contact management and use the Tasks folder to create, assign, and manage your to-do list, you can import all or selected tasks into Project. When you import tasks, the Import Outlook Tasks dialog box opens and displays all the Task folders from the local Outlook file; it will not pull tasks from Public folders (those folders shared by all users on the network). The tasks are grouped by Folder name and then Category name. You determine which tasks to import by clicking the check box to the left of the task name. Multiple tasks can be selected by holding down the Ctrl or Shift key while selecting the tasks or by clicking the check box next to the category name to choose a group of tasks. After you identify which tasks you want to import, click the OK button. The Outlook tasks are appended into the currently open Project file. Task dates, as defined in Microsoft Outlook, are ignored when imported into Project. You have to schedule the tasks and assign Start and Finish dates using Project 2010. It is also important to note that once you import the tasks from Outlook into Project, there is no connection maintained between the tasks in Outlook and the tasks in Project.

INSIGHT

Using Microsoft Outlook as a Personal Information Manager

Microsoft Office Outlook 2010 is the messaging and collaboration program in the Microsoft Office 2010 suite. You can use Outlook to manage your business and personal information. Outlook includes several tools, including Mail (for e-mail), Calendar (for appointments, events, and so on), Contacts (for address and phone information), Tasks (for keeping a to-do list), Notes (for short reminders and such), and Journal (for writing and tracking business and Project information).

ViewPoint Partners uses Outlook as the company personal information management system for e-mail, contact management, and scheduling. The fact that Outlook can integrate with Project is a great feature for the company.

REFERENCE

Importing Outlook Tasks into a Project 2010 File

- Start a new project or open the Project file into which you want to import the data.
- Click the Task tab, and then, in the Insert group, click the Task button arrow.
- On the menu, click Import Outlook Tasks.
- In the Import Outlook Tasks dialog box, click the Expand button for Folder: Tasks in order to display tasks in the appropriate folder for the Outlook installation on the computer you are using.
- Click the check box next to each task you want to import, or click Select All to select all the tasks.
- Click the OK button.

The leasing agent for the building that houses the ViewPoint Partners offices developed a task list for tasks that must be completed in the coming months. You want to enter the tasks in Outlook, and then import the task list into Project and append it as part of the TaskList-6 Project file.

To import Outlook tasks into a Project 2010 file:

▶ **1.** On the View tab, click the **Gantt Chart** button.

▶ **2.** On the Windows taskbar, click the **Start** button 🪟, point to **All Programs**, click **Microsoft Office**, click **Microsoft Outlook 2010** to start Microsoft Outlook, and then maximize the Outlook program window, if necessary.

Trouble? If you don't have Microsoft Outlook installed on your computer, read but do not complete the steps.

▶ **3.** In the Navigation pane on the left, click the **Tasks** button. The Tasks window opens. See Figure 6-17.

| Figure 6-17 | Outlook Tasks Window |

Home tab active on the Outlook Ribbon

tasks on your task list will differ

click check box to select the task for any action

▶ **4.** In the New group on the Home tab, click the **New Task** button to open the Untitled - Task window.

▶ **5.** In the Subject box, type **Review lease agreement**, select the text in the **Due date** box, type **12/15/2014**, click in the **Notes** window, and then type **Call Mr. Griffin for sublease clause**. See Figure 6-18.

Figure 6-18   New Outlook task

subject

Due date entered

note entered in
Notes area

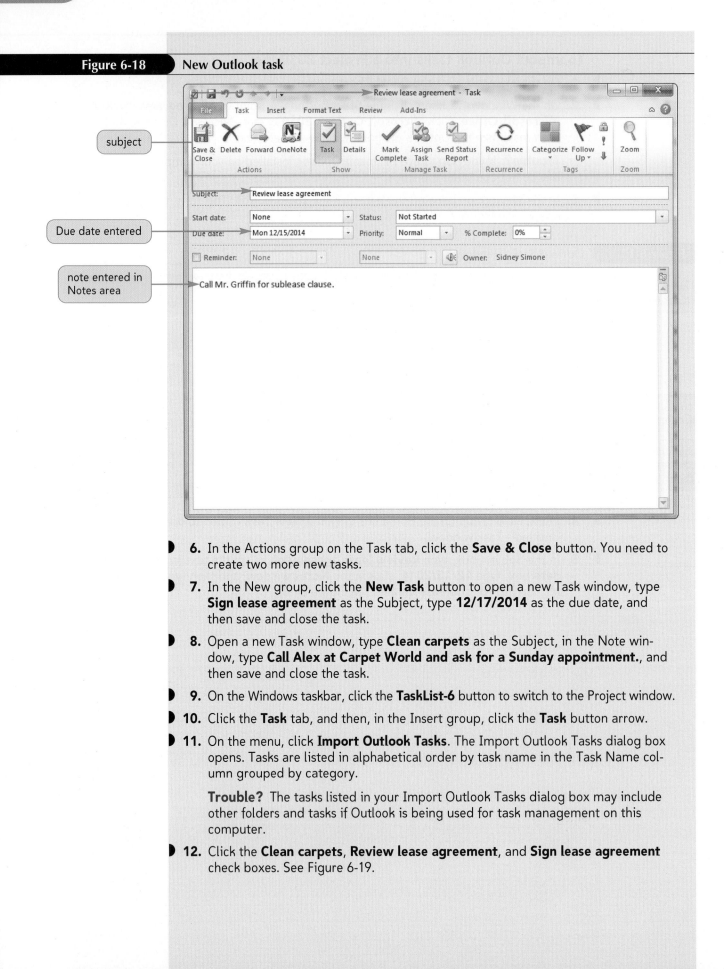

▶ **6.** In the Actions group on the Task tab, click the **Save & Close** button. You need to create two more new tasks.

▶ **7.** In the New group, click the **New Task** button to open a new Task window, type **Sign lease agreement** as the Subject, type **12/17/2014** as the due date, and then save and close the task.

▶ **8.** Open a new Task window, type **Clean carpets** as the Subject, in the Note window, type **Call Alex at Carpet World and ask for a Sunday appointment.**, and then save and close the task.

▶ **9.** On the Windows taskbar, click the **TaskList-6** button to switch to the Project window.

▶ **10.** Click the **Task** tab, and then, in the Insert group, click the **Task** button arrow.

▶ **11.** On the menu, click **Import Outlook Tasks**. The Import Outlook Tasks dialog box opens. Tasks are listed in alphabetical order by task name in the Task Name column grouped by category.

Trouble? The tasks listed in your Import Outlook Tasks dialog box may include other folders and tasks if Outlook is being used for task management on this computer.

▶ **12.** Click the **Clean carpets**, **Review lease agreement**, and **Sign lease agreement** check boxes. See Figure 6-19.

Figure 6-19   Selected Outlook tasks to be imported into the Project file

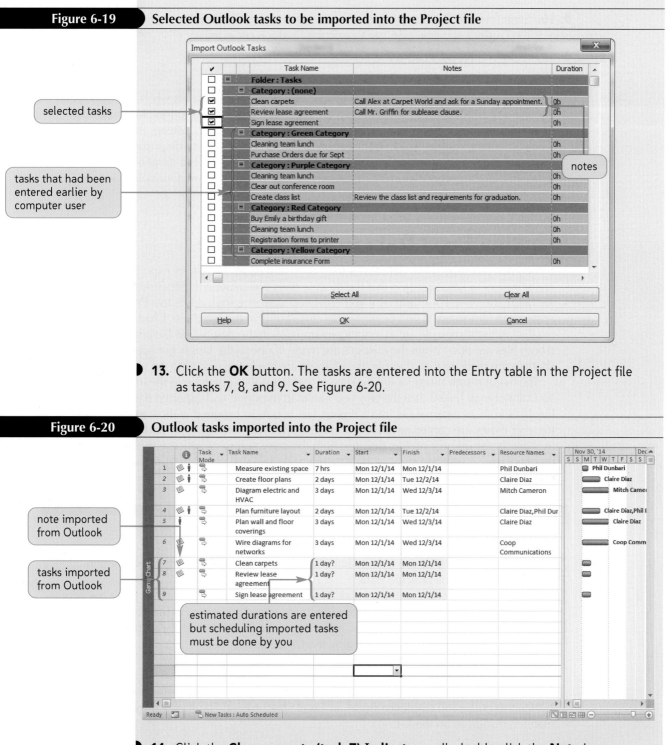

selected tasks

tasks that had been
entered earlier by
computer user

notes

▶ **13.** Click the **OK** button. The tasks are entered into the Entry table in the Project file
as tasks 7, 8, and 9. See Figure 6-20.

Figure 6-20   Outlook tasks imported into the Project file

note imported
from Outlook

tasks imported
from Outlook

estimated durations are entered
but scheduling imported tasks
must be done by you

▶ **14.** Click the **Clean carpets (task 7) Indicators** cell, double-click the **Note** icon,
and then click the **Notes** tab in the Task Information dialog box that opens. The
note you entered in Outlook was transferred as a note to Project 2010. Durations
are estimated; you can change that later when you create the schedule for the
imported tasks.

▶ **15.** Click the **OK** button to close the Task Information dialog box, and then save your
changes to the TaskList-6 project file.

▶ **16.** Switch to the Outlook program window, and then click the **Close** button [X] on the Outlook window title bar to exit the Outlook program.

▶ **17.** Close the **NewAVLab-6** Project file.

A date associated with an Outlook task does not stay with the task when it is imported into Project 2010. You can see that the Due dates you entered in Outlook for these tasks didn't import when you imported these tasks into the Project file. Instead, the Current date you entered in the Project Information dialog box was used to determine the task Start date. After importing tasks from Outlook, you have to enter the durations, the Start dates if different from the Current date, and the Finish dates for any Outlook tasks you import into Project.

Linking Excel Data to a Project File

Sometimes you should link data rather than copy and paste, import, or export data. The major benefit of linking data is that the process does not create a duplicate copy of data in the destination file. For example, if you link Excel data (the source file) to a Project file (the destination file), the data will be physically stored only in the Excel file. Changes made to the data in the source file are automatically updated in the destination file and vice versa if both files are open when the changes are made. If one of the files is not open when changes are made to the other file, the changes are made the next time the file is opened.

The major disadvantage of linking data is that it is not as powerful as the import process. You cannot map linked data the way you can map imported and exported data. Also, if you link data from an external file into a Project file, you must ensure that the two files travel together if they are copied or moved; otherwise, you will "break a link" and get an error message in the destination file. Because both the copy and paste process and the import process create a separate copy of the data in the Project file, you don't have to worry about "breaking a link" to the source file if the Project file is moved or copied.

REFERENCE

Linking Excel Data to a Project 2010 File

- Select the data that you want to link in Excel, and then use the Copy command in Excel to copy the selected data.
- Open the Project file, and then click a cell in the table where you want to paste the data.
- Click the Task tab, and then, in the Clipboard group, click the Paste button.
- On the menu, click Paste Special, and then, in the Paste Special dialog box, click the Paste Link option button followed by the OK button.

ViewPoint partners is growing. Sidney has hired four new staff members and she has decided to create the employee list as an Excel spreadsheet. She has also included some material resources on the list.

To link resource data from Excel into a Project 2010 file:

▶ **1.** On the Windows taskbar, click the **Windows Explorer window** button to display the Project6\Tutorial folder.

2. Double-click the **NewRes.xlsx** Excel file in the folder to open it in Excel. The New Resources in the Excel file are shown in Figure 6-21. The column headings and the arrangement of the columns in the Excel file help you identify the field names and the arrangement of the fields in the Project Resource Sheet Entry table. The column heading names do not have to be an exact match because you are not importing the headings, you are only using the file as a reference for the pool.

Figure 6-21	New Resources in the Excel file

3. Click cell **A2**, and then drag down and to the right to cell **J7**. The range of cells A2 through J7 is selected.

4. In the Clipboard group on the Home tab, click the **Copy** button 📋, and then click the Project button on the Windows taskbar to switch to the **TaskList-6** Project file.

5. Click the **View** tab, and then click the **Resource Sheet** button in the Resource Views group to switch to Resource Sheet view. You want to link the resources from the Excel worksheet to the Project 2010 file.

6. Click the **row 5** row selector. The entire row is selected.

7. Right-click the **selected row**, and then click **Paste Special** on the shortcut menu. The Paste Special dialog box opens.

8. Click the **Paste Link** option button, and then click the **OK** button. The dialog box closes and the data from Excel is linked to the resource sheet. As shown in Figure 6-22, data linked from an outside source is indicated by the link symbol in the lower right-hand corner of a cell.

Figure 6-22   **Linking resources to the Excel file**

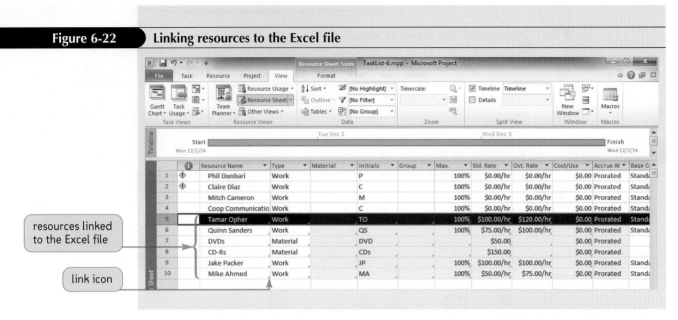

You just found out that the rate for Tamar Opher was entered incorrectly. You have to update the files.

To update linked resource data from Excel into a Project 2010 file:

▶ **1.** Click the **NewRes.xlsx** button on the taskbar to switch to the Excel window containing the NewRes.xlsx workbook, and then click cell **H2**. This cell contains the Std. Rate cell for Tamar.

▶ **2.** Type **120**, and then press the **Enter** key.

▶ **3.** Click the **TaskList-6** button on the taskbar to switch back to the Project window. The Std. Rate for Tamar in the Project 2010 file is updated to $120/hr because the information is linked to the Excel file where you just made that change.

▶ **4.** Save the **TaskList-6** project file.

▶ **5.** Switch back to the Excel window, save the NewRes.xlsx workbook file, and then exit Excel.

▶ **6.** Close the open Windows Explorer window.

Linked files make it possible for you to know that the data is always current in all relevant files. You know that both the Excel and Project files are up-to-date for the resource information.

INSIGHT

Embedding Information in Project 2010

Embedding differs from linking in that the destination file contains a separate copy of the data, so changes to the data in either the source or destination file are not automatically updated in the other location. Embedded data differs from copied and pasted data in that it retains the ability to be modified with the tools from its native application. For example, if you embed an Excel graph in a Project file, you will retain the ability to modify the graph using Excel tools even though the graph is physically stored in the Project file.

Embedding also refers to the ability of a program such as Project to insert data created by shared Office programs. When you insert embedded data directly into the Project file (instead of copying it from an external source), any changes to the data exist only within the Project file. There is no link between the files. You use the Paste Special command to embed data.

Using the Drawing Tool

The Drawing tool allows you to add drawn shapes, lines, and boxes to a Gantt chart. It is commonly used to annotate or draw attention to key information. Adding graphical effects to the Gantt chart helps you to communicate information. If you have previous experience with drawing objects in other applications, you will find the buttons and functions to be similar in Project.

You want to convey as much information as possible to management. You decide to use the Drawing tools to annotate the Gantt chart. You also know that you can work with an object after you draw it. Once the drawn object is on the Gantt chart, you can move, resize, or format it.

To use the Drawing tool to annotate the Gantt chart:

1. Switch to the **TaskList-6** project file if it is not already in the active window, and then switch to Gantt Chart view.

2. Right-click the **Timeline**, and then click **Show Timeline** to close the Timeline.

3. Drag to select all of the task names from **Measure existing space** (task 1) to **Sign lease agreement** (task 9), click the **Task** tab, and then, in the Schedule group, click the **Link Tasks** button ⊜. Tasks 1 through 9 are now linked. Start and Finish dates have been updated to reflect the dependencies among the tasks.

4. Drag the **split bar** to the right of the Start column, and then click any empty cell in the Entry table.

5. Click the **Gantt Chart Tools Format** tab, and then, in the Drawings group, click the **Drawing** button. The Drawing tools menu appears.

6. On the Drawing menu, click **Text Box**, and then move the pointer to a blank area to the left of the blue bars. The pointer changes to +.

7. Drag the + pointer to draw a two-inch wide box within the white area in the Gantt chart to the left of the blue bars from the Project Start date line, from about task 6 to about task 8. A text box appears in the Gantt chart with a blinking insertion point. Sizing handles—the small white rectangles—appear around the edges of the selected text box. An object must be selected in order to be moved, resized, or formatted.

8. In the text box, type **Need to ask Claire to work the weekend to save time.**, as shown in Figure 6-23.

Figure 6-23   Adding text to the Gantt chart

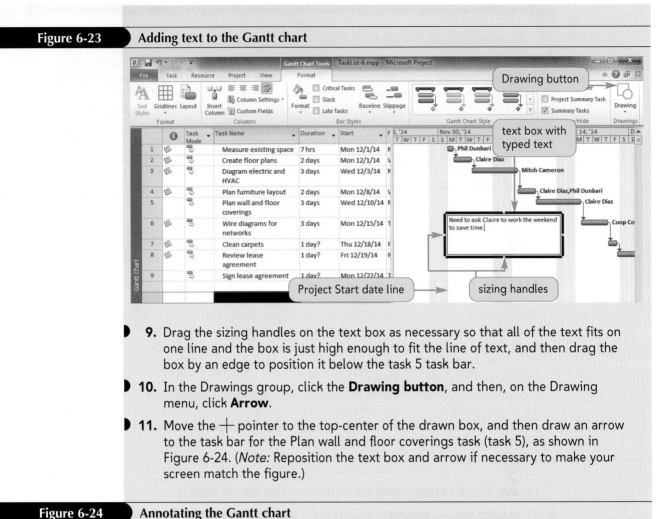

9. Drag the sizing handles on the text box as necessary so that all of the text fits on one line and the box is just high enough to fit the line of text, and then drag the box by an edge to position it below the task 5 task bar.

10. In the Drawings group, click the **Drawing button**, and then, on the Drawing menu, click **Arrow**.

11. Move the $+$ pointer to the top-center of the drawn box, and then draw an arrow to the task bar for the Plan wall and floor coverings task (task 5), as shown in Figure 6-24. (*Note:* Reposition the text box and arrow if necessary to make your screen match the figure.)

Figure 6-24   Annotating the Gantt chart

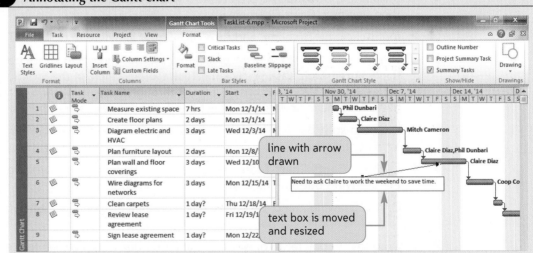

12. Click the **File** tab, click **Print**, add your name left-aligned in the header, and then print the Gantt chart if requested.

13. Save your changes, and then close the **TaskList-6** project file.

You can embed boxes, shapes, arrows, and lines from the Drawing toolbar into a Gantt Chart. These graphical objects are very useful for pointing out trends, important dates, and significant events.

REVIEW

Session 6.1 Quick Check

1. Give an example of the type of data that you would copy from Project 2010 and paste into Excel.
2. What tab and command do you use to export Project 2010 data?
3. What is the purpose of data mapping when you import data from one program to another?
4. What is the main advantage of linked data?
5. What tools are available on the Drawing menu, and when might you use them?

SESSION 6.2 VISUAL OVERVIEW

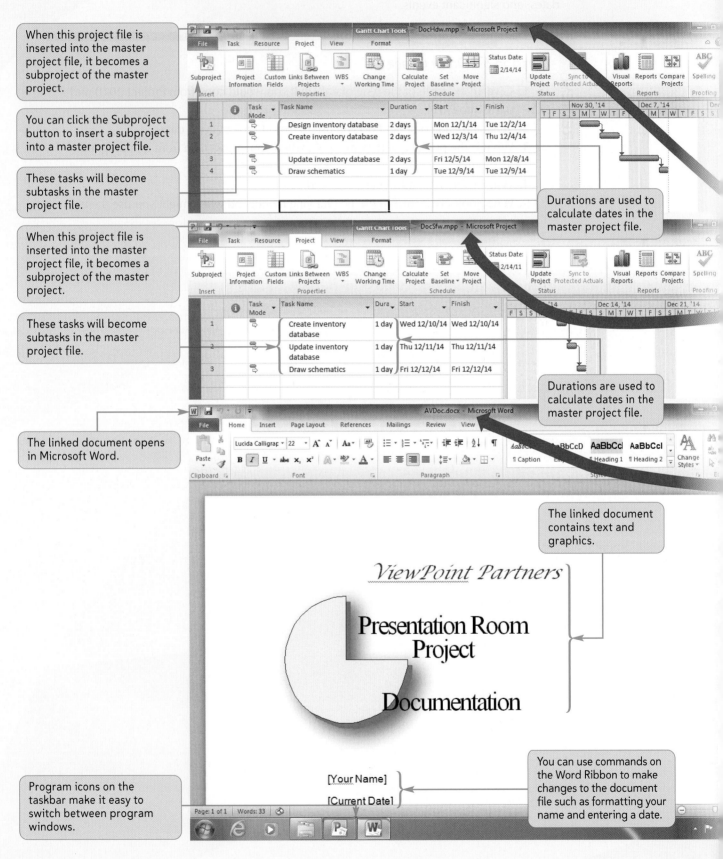

When this project file is inserted into the master project file, it becomes a subproject of the master project.

You can click the Subproject button to insert a subproject into a master project file.

These tasks will become subtasks in the master project file.

When this project file is inserted into the master project file, it becomes a subproject of the master project.

These tasks will become subtasks in the master project file.

The linked document opens in Microsoft Word.

Program icons on the taskbar make it easy to switch between program windows.

Durations are used to calculate dates in the master project file.

Durations are used to calculate dates in the master project file.

The linked document contains text and graphics.

You can use commands on the Word Ribbon to make changes to the document file such as formatting your name and entering a date.

MASTER PROJECT AND ITS SUBPROJECTS

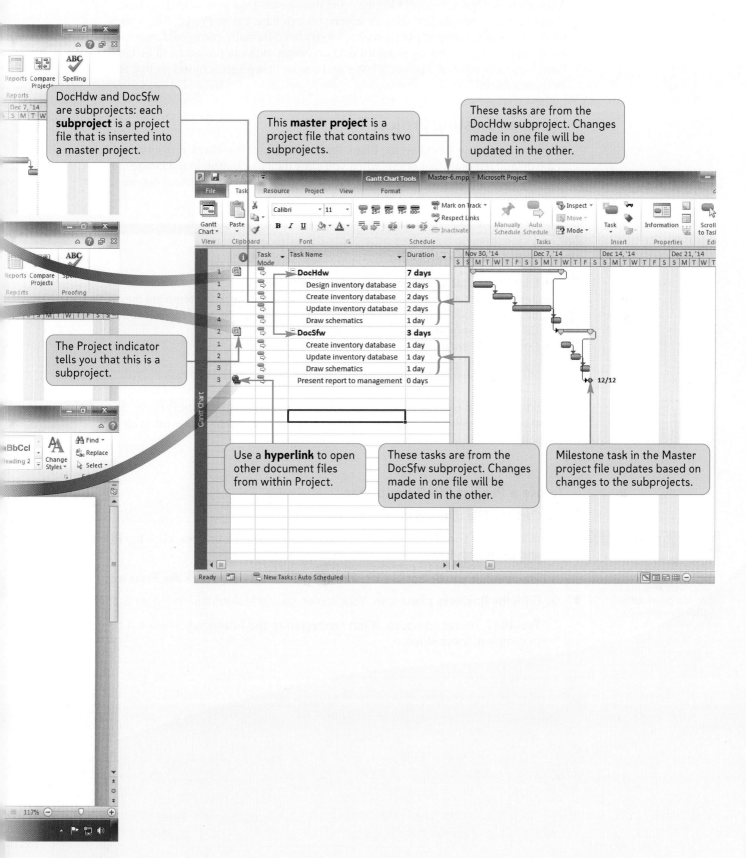

DocHdw and DocSfw are subprojects: each **subproject** is a project file that is inserted into a master project.

This **master project** is a project file that contains two subprojects.

These tasks are from the DocHdw subproject. Changes made in one file will be updated in the other.

The Project indicator tells you that this is a subproject.

Use a **hyperlink** to open other document files from within Project.

These tasks are from the DocSfw subproject. Changes made in one file will be updated in the other.

Milestone task in the Master project file updates based on changes to the subprojects.

Working with Project Templates

A **template** is a special Project file that contains sample information such as task, resource, cost, and baseline data on which you can base a new Project file. A template is basically a project plan sample that has been partially completed. A template is a powerful tool for storing standard data on which multiple projects will be based. Templates help you build projects faster and ensure that projects based on that template are standardized.

Using an Existing Project Template

All new projects are based on the Blank Project template. The Blank Project template is the default template that opens when you click the New button in Backstage view. In addition to the Blank Project template, Project provides many templates you can use to build Project 2010 files.

REFERENCE

Using a Project Template

- Click the File tab on the Ribbon, and then click New.
- In the Available Templates section in the center pane, click the template option that best meets your needs. If you are connected to the Internet, you can select from Office.com templates.
- Double-click the template that you want to use.

Sidney wants to expand the types of Project files used at ViewPoint Partners. She asks you to explore the Project Templates to see if any are relevant to your work with the company.

TIP

To find additional templates, search the Office.com Web site to find and download templates from Microsoft.

To use a Project 2010 template:

1. Click the **File** tab, and then click **New**.

2. In the Office.com Templates section under Available Templates, click the **Plans and proposals** icon.

   Trouble? If you do not see the Plans and proposals icon, click the Plans icon.

3. Click the **Business plans** icon. Your screen should look similar to Figure 6-25.

   Trouble? If your computer is not connected to the Internet, you will not be able to complete these steps.

Figure 6-25   **Project templates**

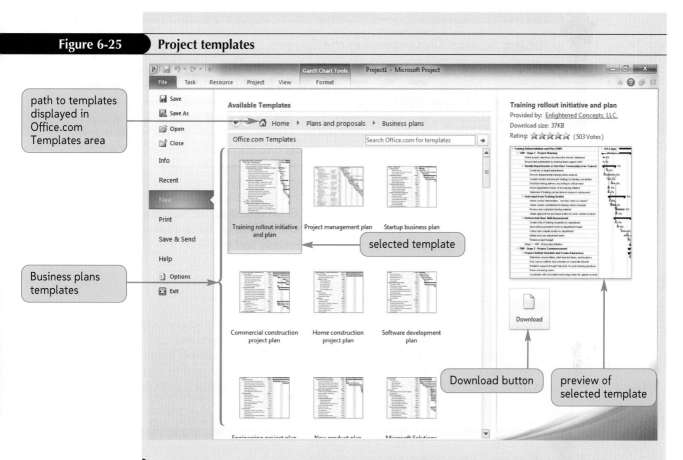

path to templates displayed in Office.com Templates area

Business plans templates

selected template

Download button

preview of selected template

4. Scroll to review the available plans, and then click the **New product plan** icon. A thumbnail of the template appears in the right pane.

Trouble? If you are not authorized to download files from the Internet on the computer you are using for this book, read but do not complete the next steps.

5. Click the **Download** button to download and open the template. A New Product Plan project file opens with many tasks organized into phases. Each task has durations, and the tasks are linked with appropriate dependencies. Sample resources are also entered.

6. Click the **View** tab, and then, in the Resource Views group, click the **Resource Sheet** button to switch to Resource Sheet view. The sheet includes 11 resources entered as samples. If you continued to work with this template, you would enter the resources, units, and rates for resources specific to your project, and then save the file with a unique filename.

7. Click the **File** tab, click **Close**, and then click the **No** button to close the project file without saving any changes.

The purpose of basing a project file on a template file is to give you a fast start in developing a new project and to help you organize and remember the many details of a project.

PROSKILLS

Problem Solving: Understanding the Systems Development Life Cycle

Whether you work as a project manager in a small company or in a large company, project managers often discuss major projects using terms from the traditional **systems development life cycle (SDLC) model**. This model is commonly used to manage the development of a new information system, but it can be modified and applied to almost any project. The methodology typically consists of five to seven phases. The model that is commonly used has six stages within a project: definition, evaluation, design, installation, implementation, and maintenance.

SDLC models have been studied and implemented in corporations throughout the world. When building a project file, a project manager can use these SDLC categories as the phases or summary tasks in a project. Using the SDLC model as the foundation for a project should result in a high-quality project that meets or exceeds customer expectations, comes in on time and within the budget, and works effectively and efficiently.

Creating a Custom Template

In addition to using the default templates provided with Project, you can create your own templates. If you manage many projects that are very similar and each project you build contains the same basic tasks, then you should create a custom template so that you don't need to remember and reenter the common tasks for each new project that uses these tasks. Each project you build using the custom template can then be adjusted to suit the specific needs of that project.

REFERENCE

Creating a Project Template

- Enter the tasks and other data that you want to store in the template.
- Click the File tab, and then click Save As to open the Save As dialog box.
- In the File name box, type a name for the template.
- Click the Save as type arrow, and then click Project Template.
- Click the Save button.

Sidney suggests you use the systems development life cycle (SDLC) model phases to create a template. The SDLC phases will be entered as summary tasks. Once it is created, you can use the template to build other projects and you won't have to reenter these summary tasks. Next, you create a custom template.

To create a Project template:

1. Click the **File** tab, click **New**, then double-click the **Blank project** button to open a new blank Project in the open window. The first step is to enter the tasks and other data that you want to store in the template.

2. On the status bar, click **New Tasks: Manually Scheduled**, and then click **Auto Scheduled-Task dates are calculated by Microsoft Project**. You want auto scheduling to be in effect for any tasks entered in the template.

3. Click the **View** tab, and then, in the Split View group, click the **Timeline** check box to remove the mark and close the Timeline.

TIP

Template files have the .mpt filename extension, while project files have the .mpp filename extension.

4. Enter the six phases of the SDLC model, as shown in Figure 6-26.

Figure 6-26   Six phases of the SDLC model

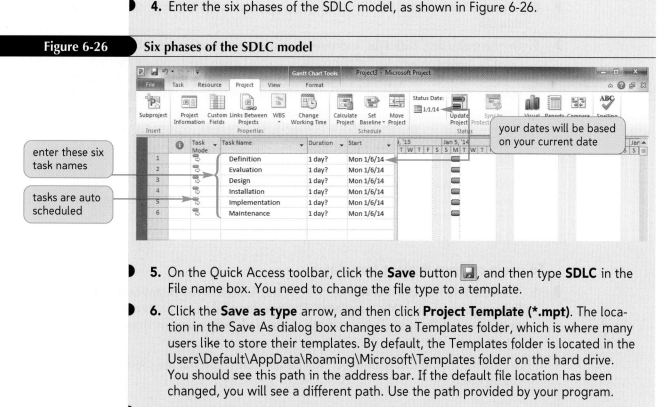

5. On the Quick Access toolbar, click the **Save** button 🖫, and then type **SDLC** in the File name box. You need to change the file type to a template.

6. Click the **Save as type** arrow, and then click **Project Template (*.mpt)**. The location in the Save As dialog box changes to a Templates folder, which is where many users like to store their templates. By default, the Templates folder is located in the Users\Default\AppData\Roaming\Microsoft\Templates folder on the hard drive. You should see this path in the address bar. If the default file location has been changed, you will see a different path. Use the path provided by your program.

7. Click the **Save** button. The Save As Template dialog box opens, prompting you to check the type of data that you do *not* want saved in the template. See Figure 6-27.

Figure 6-27   Save As Template dialog box

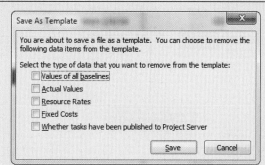

You have not entered any baseline, actual, resource, or fixed cost values into this file, so you do not need to worry about these check boxes for this template. However, if you decided to save a finished project as a template, it would be important to ask yourself whether you really wanted to save baseline and actual costs in the template or whether you wanted to delete this data from the template. Also, if a project file has sensitive data, such as personal information about resources or confidential cost information, you might not want that data saved with the template. You can use this dialog box to omit data you do not want saved in the template. If you elect to keep sensitive data in a template or if you do not want everyone to have access to your template, you can save the template to the location of your choice rather than the default location. If you save to a unique location, you will have to navigate to open the template because it will not be available in the My templates section.

▶ **8.** Click the **Save** button. Now that the template is saved, SDLC.mpt appears in the title bar.

▶ **9.** On the menu bar, click **File**, and then click **Close** to close the template. If you need to make changes to the template, you must open the template by clicking the File tab, clicking Open, navigating to the location where the template is stored, clicking the template, and then clicking the Open button. If you want to open a new Project file based on this template, you must click the File tab, click New, click My templates, click the template file you want to use, and then click the OK button.

It is always a good idea to make sure that a template you create is working properly. Next, you'll open a new Project file based on the template you created, and then you will enter data in the new file.

To use a custom Project template:

▶ **1.** Click the **File** tab, click **New**, and then, in the Available Templates section of Backstage view, click **My templates**. The new template that you created should appear on the Personal Templates tab in the New dialog box, as shown in Figure 6-28.

Trouble? If others have created Project templates, you will see them in this dialog box.

| **Figure 6-28** | **Personal templates in the New dialog box** |

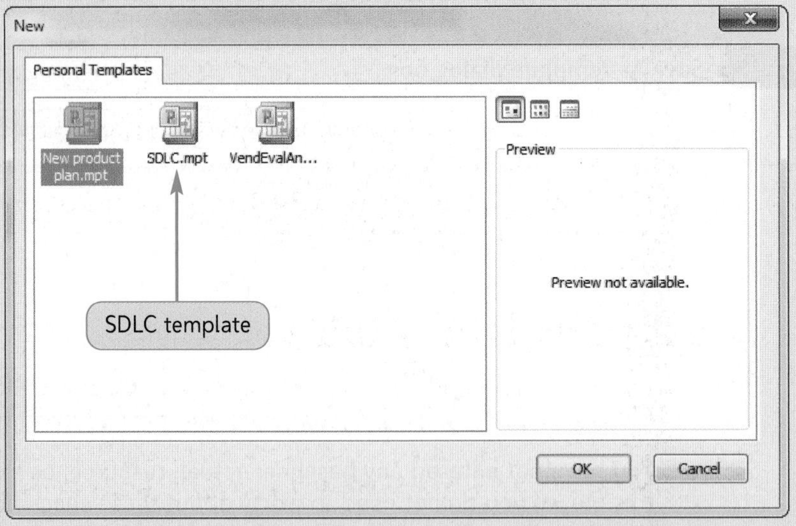

▶ **2.** On the Personal Templates tab in the New dialog box, click the **SDLC.mpt** file, and then click the **OK** button. A new project file is created based on the template you created.

▶ **3.** Click the **Project** tab, and then, in the Properties group, click the **Project Information** button. The Project Information dialog box opens. You will create this project in real time starting from today's date.

▶ **4.** Click the **OK** button. You'll add a unique task for this project to one of the summary tasks in the file.

TIP

If your computer is not set to display file extensions, you will see SDLC in the dialog box.

▶ **5.** Click **Evaluation** (task 2), click the **Task** tab, and then, in the Insert group, click the **Task** button.

▶ **6.** In the Task Name <New Task> cell, type **Schedule kickoff meeting**, and then press the **Enter** key.

▶ **7.** Click **Schedule kickoff meeting** (task 2), and then, in the Schedule group, click the **Indent Task** button ⬛. The task is indented as a subtask under task 1.

▶ **8.** Switch to **Gantt Chart** view if it is not the active view, preview Gantt Chart view in Backstage view, add your name left-aligned in the header, and then print Gantt Chart view if requested.

▶ **9.** In Backstage view, click **Save As**. The Save As dialog box opens. Note that although you opened a template file, the file type in the Save as type box is Project (*.mpp). When you create a project based on a template, the file opens as a Project file. You need to save it with a meaningful filename.

▶ **10.** Navigate to the **Project6\Tutorial** folder included with your Data Files, and then click the **Save** button.

▶ **11.** Close the file.

Deleting the Custom Template

Sometimes you might want to remove a custom template from your computer. You will now delete this template.

To delete the Project 2010 template:

▶ **1.** Click the **File** tab, click **New**, and then click **Recent templates**. The SDLC template appears in the Recent templates section.

▶ **2.** Right-click the **SDLC template** icon, and then, on the shortcut menu, click **Remove template**.

▶ **3.** Click the **Task tab** on the Ribbon to return to Project.

Working with Data Templates

In addition to Project templates, which are used to build project files, you can create a special type of template called a **data template**, also called a **box template**. Each data template defines how a box type associated with that data template is formatted in Network Diagram view. Once a data template is created, you can share it with other projects. The default data template is called Standard.

The default formatting for the **Standard data template** includes scheduled Start and Finish dates as well as the letter X on tasks that are complete. You can change the default formatting by creating a new data template and applying it to a box type. For example, you can create a data template that displays baseline and actual costs instead of scheduled Start and scheduled Finish dates, and then apply that data type to the noncritical summary box type. You can also specify new borders, shapes, and colors for the boxes in data templates you create.

Creating and Applying a Data Template

ViewPoint Partners is going to use Project files in several presentations. You want to create a custom format for the network diagram that shows baseline and actual costs in the box. You also want to be able to copy this data template to another project file.

REFERENCE

Creating and Applying a Data Template

- Click the Network Diagram button on the View tab, and then click the box type (summary, subtask, milestone) in the network diagram for which you want to create a new data template.
- Click the Network Diagram Tools Format tab, and then, in the Format group, click the Box Styles button to open the Box Styles dialog box.
- Click the More Templates button, and then click the New or Copy button to create a new data template.
- Make the appropriate choices for the new data template in the Data Template Definition dialog box, click the OK button, and then click the Close button to close the Data Template Definition and Data Templates dialog boxes.
- To apply the new data template, click the Data template arrow in the Box Styles dialog box, click the name of the new data template that you just created, and then click the OK button in the Box Styles dialog box to apply the selected template.

To create a new data template:

1. Click the **File** tab, click **Open**, navigate to the **Project6\Tutorial** folder included with your Data Files, and then double-click the **AV-6** file.

2. Save the file as **NewAV-6** in the same folder.

3. Click the **View** tab, and then click the **Network Diagram** button 🖼. The Analysis box is selected. See Figure 6-29.

Figure 6-29 ⟩ **Network Diagram view**

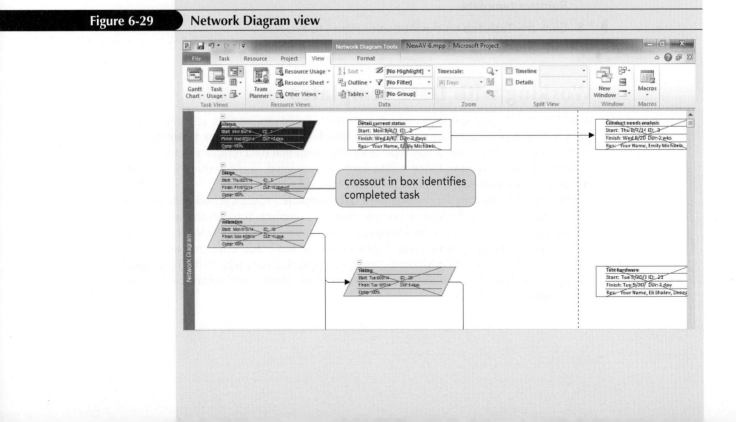

crossout in box identifies completed task

4. Click the **Network Diagram Tools Format** tab, and then, in the Format group, click the **Box Styles** button. The Box Styles dialog box opens. Notice that Noncritical Summary is selected in the Style settings for list. This is because the box type you selected in the network diagram is a noncritical summary task.

5. Click the **More Templates** button to open the Data Templates dialog box.

6. In the Templates in "Network Diagram" list box, click **Standard**, and then click the **Copy** button. The Data Template Definition dialog box opens. Using this dialog box, you rename the template and define the box by identifying the cells, formatting, and font. The default template name is "Copy of Standard."

7. In the Template name box, type **Cost Information**, click **Start** in the Choose cell(s) section, click the **arrow**, press the **B** key, and then click **Baseline Cost**.

8. Click **Finish** in the Choose cell(s) section, click the **arrow**, press the **A** key, and then click **Actual Cost**. See Figure 6-30. The Data Template Definition dialog box shows you the placement of the data fields you selected to appear in the Network diagram box. You can also change other features such as the font and alignment.

Figure 6-30	Data Template Definition dialog box

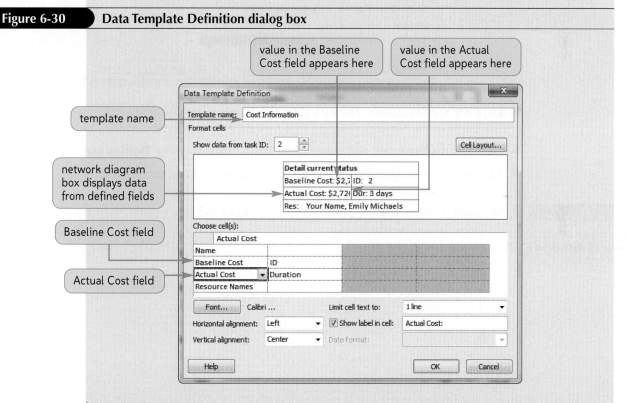

9. Click the **OK** button, and then, in the Data Templates dialog box, click the **Close** button.

10. In the Box Styles dialog box, click the **Data template** arrow, and then click **Cost Information**. The Box Styles dialog box looks like Figure 6-31. The Cost Information data template is applied to the preview of the Noncritical Summary box.

Figure 6-31   **Box Styles dialog box**

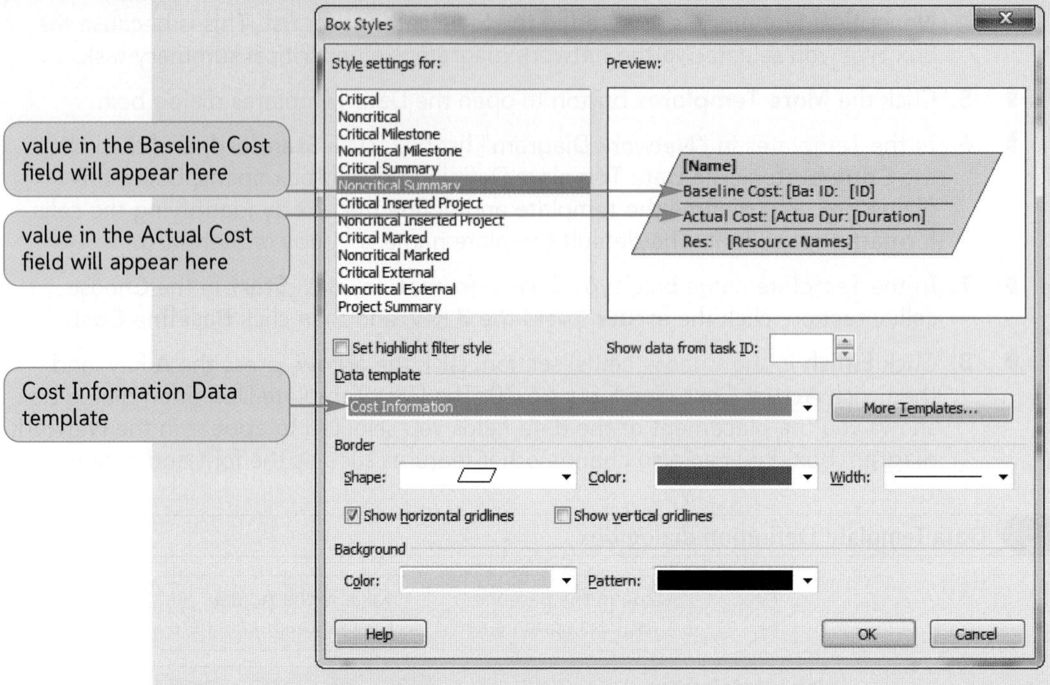

value in the Baseline Cost field will appear here

value in the Actual Cost field will appear here

Cost Information Data template

11. Click the **OK** button. The new Cost Information data template is applied to the boxes in the network diagram that contain the noncritical summary tasks.

12. Click the **View** tab, and then, in the Data group, click the **Outline** button

13. On the menu, click **Outline Level 1**. All summary tasks should display baseline and actual costs.

14. Zoom in to review the data as shown in Figure 6-32.

TIP

You also can view detail information by placing the pointer on each box.

Figure 6-32   **Cost Information template applied to the network diagram**

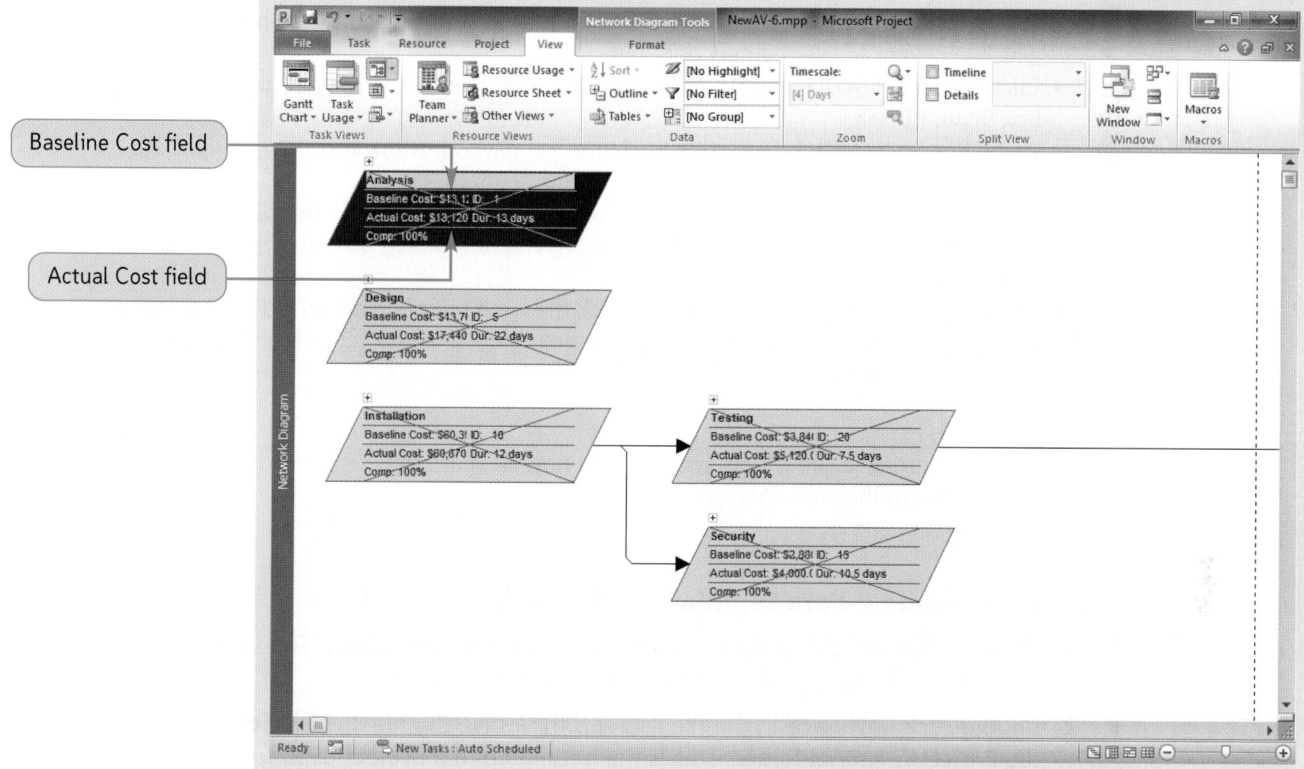

▶ **15.** Save your work.

▶ **16.** Preview the network diagram, add your name left-aligned in the header, print the first page of the network diagram if requested, and then save your changes.

Sharing Data Templates

You can use the new data template you created with other projects. If you are working at a company and want to present a standard format for all network diagrams across all projects, using data templates is a good way to guarantee that all printouts have the same format.

REFERENCE

Sharing a Data Template

- On the View tab, click the Network Diagram button, and then click the box type for which you want to use the new data template.
- Click the Network Diagram Tools Format tab, and then, in the Format group, click the Box Styles button.
- In the Box Styles dialog box, click the More Templates button, and then, in the Data Templates dialog box, click the Import button.
- Make the appropriate project and template choices in the Import Template dialog box, click the OK button to close the Import Template dialog box, and then close the Data Templates dialog box.
- To apply the imported data template, click the Data template arrow in the Box Styles dialog box, click the name of the new data template, and then click the OK button in the Box Styles dialog box.

Next, you'll create a sample project to learn how to share the custom Cost Information data template from the NewAV-6 project.

To share the new data template with another project:

1. Click the **File** tab if it is not the active tab, and then click **Open**. The Open dialog box should display the files in the Project6\Tutorial folder.

2. Double-click **Software** in the file list, and then save the file as **NewSoftware** in the Project6\Tutorial folder. This is the beginning of a project used to manage a new software installation. Currently, the project has two summary tasks and a few resource assignments. A baseline has been saved, but no progress has been recorded on the project, so the baseline and scheduled costs are the same.

3. Click the **View** tab, and then, in the Task Views group, click the **Network Diagram** button to view the default network diagram, as shown in Figure 6-33. The critical summary tasks display scheduled Start and scheduled Finish dates in the box. You'll apply the Cost Information data template to the summary tasks in this file.

| Figure 6-33 | Default Network Diagram view for the NewSoftware project |

4. Be sure the **Analysis** box is selected, click the **Network Diagram Tools Format** tab, and then, in the Format group, click the **Box Styles** button to open the Box Styles dialog box.

5. In the Box Styles dialog box, click the **More Templates** button, and then, in the Data Templates dialog box, click the **Import** button. The Import Template dialog box opens. Currently, the Cost Information data template is only in the NewAV-6 file. You need to import it into this file.

6. In the Import Template dialog box, click the **Project** arrow, click **NewAV-6.mpp**, click the **Template** arrow, and then click **Cost Information**. See Figure 6-34.

Figure 6-34　　Importing a Data Template

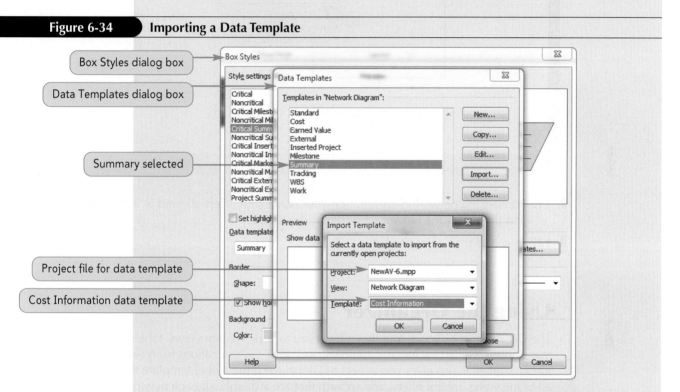

Box Styles dialog box

Data Templates dialog box

Summary selected

Project file for data template

Cost Information data template

---

7. Click the **OK** button. The Cost Information data template is imported into the NewSoftware file. The Preview section in the Data Templates dialog box shows you the information that the selected Cost Information data template will display.

8. Click the **Close** button. Now that the data template has been imported into this project, you need to select it for the network diagram.

9. Verify that **Critical Summary** is selected in the Style settings for list.

10. In the Box Styles dialog box, click the **Data template** arrow, click **Cost Information**, and then click the **OK** button. The Cost Information data template is applied. The final network diagram is shown in Figure 6-35. You can see that Baseline Cost and Actual Cost are displayed in the critical summary task boxes.

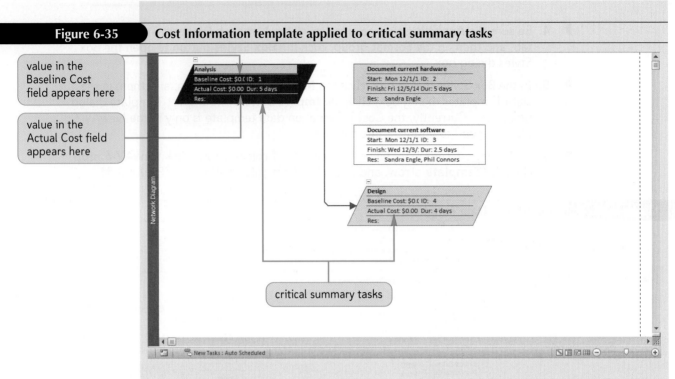

11. Preview the network diagram, add your name so it is left-aligned in the header, and then print the network diagram if requested.

12. Save and then close the file.

Using the Organizer

The **Organizer** is a special tool that allows you to copy custom views, tables, filters, data maps, forms, calendars, macros, toolbars, and other customizations from one project file to another. It also gives you access to Global.MPT, the global template that stores all of the views, tables, filters, and so forth that are available for each new project. Each new file that you create (regardless of the template that you use) has access to all of the items in the Global.MPT template as well. Therefore, if you have created a custom view, calendar, or report and want it to be available to every project, you should copy it to the Global.MPT template using the Organizer.

REFERENCE

Using the Organizer to Change the Global.MPT File

- Click the File tab, click Info, and then click Organizer to open the Organizer dialog box.
- Click the desired tab.
- Click the element that you want to copy from the Global.MPT file to the project file or vice versa, and then click the Copy button.
- Click the Close button in the dialog box.

Emily asked you to create a custom table that contains the Entry table fields plus the Fixed Cost field. ViewPoint Partners wants this table for future projects. After you create it, the new table will exist only in the NewAV-6 project, but you can use the Organizer to copy it to the Global.MPT template so that you can use it in any project.

To create the new table and use the Organizer:

1. In the NewAV-6 file, switch to **Gantt Chart** view.

2. In the Entry table, right-click the **Select All** button, click **More Tables**, click **Entry** in the Tables list if it is not already selected, and then click the **Copy** button. The Table Definition dialog box opens, allowing you to name the table as well as edit the fields in the table.

3. Type **Entry and Fixed Cost** in the Name box.

4. In the Field Name column, click **Duration**, and then click the **Insert Row** button.

5. In the new cell in the Field Name column, click the **arrow**, type **fix** to quickly scroll to the Fixed Cost field, and then click **Fixed Cost**. The Table Definition dialog box should look like Figure 6-36.

Figure 6-36	Table Definition dialog box

table named Entry and Fixed Cost

new Fixed Cost field added to table

6. Click the **OK** button, click the **Apply** button to apply the Entry and Fixed Cost table, drag the split bar to the right to view the fields, and then adjust column widths as needed to fit content.

7. Click the **File** tab, click **Info**, and then click the **Organizer** button. The Organizer dialog box opens.

8. Click the **Tables** tab, click **Entry and Fixed Cost** in the 'NewAV-6.mpp' list, and then click the **Copy** button. The new table is copied to the Global.MPT template, as shown in Figure 6-37.

Figure 6-37   Organizer dialog box

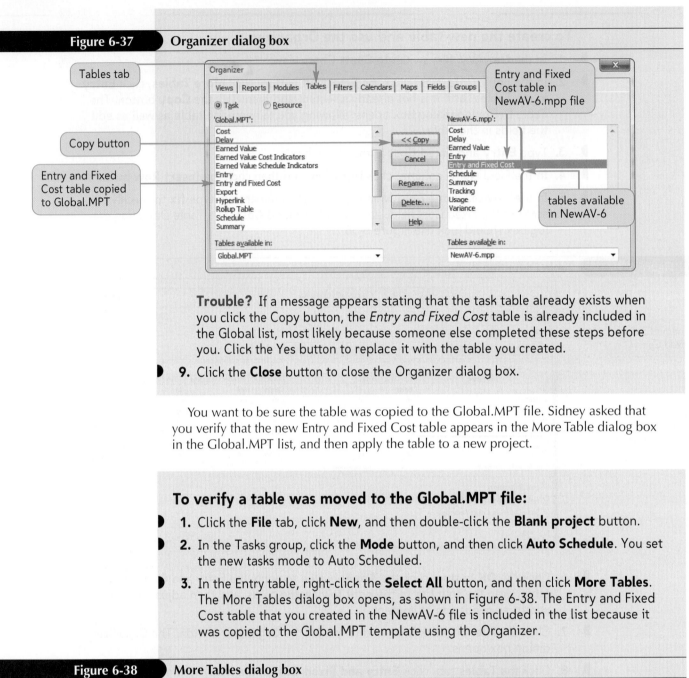

Trouble? If a message appears stating that the task table already exists when you click the Copy button, the *Entry and Fixed Cost* table is already included in the Global list, most likely because someone else completed these steps before you. Click the Yes button to replace it with the table you created.

▶ **9.** Click the **Close** button to close the Organizer dialog box.

You want to be sure the table was copied to the Global.MPT file. Sidney asked that you verify that the new Entry and Fixed Cost table appears in the More Table dialog box in the Global.MPT list, and then apply the table to a new project.

To verify a table was moved to the Global.MPT file:

▶ **1.** Click the **File** tab, click **New**, and then double-click the **Blank project** button.

▶ **2.** In the Tasks group, click the **Mode** button, and then click **Auto Schedule**. You set the new tasks mode to Auto Scheduled.

▶ **3.** In the Entry table, right-click the **Select All** button, and then click **More Tables**. The More Tables dialog box opens, as shown in Figure 6-38. The Entry and Fixed Cost table that you created in the NewAV-6 file is included in the list because it was copied to the Global.MPT template using the Organizer.

Figure 6-38   More Tables dialog box

▶ **4.** Click the **Entry and Fixed Cost** table in the list, and then click the **Apply** button.

▶ **5.** Drag the **split bar** to the right as needed to make sure that the Fixed Cost field has been applied to the task sheet.

▶ **6.** Click the **File** tab, click **Close** to close the new project, and then click the **No** button when prompted to save the changes.

▶ **7.** Save your changes to the **NewAV-6** file, and then close the file.

Because others might have access to Project 2010 on the computer you are using, you need to delete the table you saved to the Global.MPT template.

To delete the table:

▶ **1.** Create a new blank project file.

▶ **2.** Click the **File** tab, click **Info**, click **Organizer** to open the Organizer dialog box, and then click the **Tables** tab.

▶ **3.** Click **Entry and Fixed Cost** in the 'Global.MPT' list box, click the **Delete** button, and then click the **Yes** button to confirm the deletion.

▶ **4.** Click the **Close** button to close the Organizer dialog box.

Another way to access the Organizer dialog box is by clicking the Organizer button in other dialog boxes that define custom elements, such as the More Tables, the More Views, and the Custom Reports dialog boxes. You can also access the Organizer dialog box by clicking the File tab, clicking Info if it is not the active tab, and then clicking the Organizer button.

Using Resource Pools

A **resource pool** is a project file that usually contains only data associated with resources, such as resource name, costs, units, and calendar information. A resource pool file is linked to other Project files in a way that allows you to share the resources in the pool. The benefits of using a resource pool include the ability to do the following:

• Enter shared resources only once.
• Schedule resources while taking into consideration resource allocations made in other projects.
• Identify conflicts among assignments in different projects.
• Manage resource units, costs, and calendars in only one place.

Creating a Resource Pool File

ViewPoint Partners needs to be able to expand the pool of resources that they use for upcoming projects. Sidney has suggested you create a resource pool file that can be used to maintain resources used in all ViewPoint Partners projects. You will create a resource pool file for the AV projection rooms installation project.

To create the resource pool file:

▶ **1.** Create a new blank project file, close the **Timeline**, set the new tasks mode to **Auto Scheduled**, open the **Project Information** dialog box, enter **12/01/14** as the Start date for the new project, and then click the **OK** button.

▶ **2.** Click the **View** tab, and then, in the Resource Views group, click the **Resource Sheet** button.

▶ **3.** Enter the information for four new resources shown in Figure 6-39.

| Figure 6-39 | New resources typed into resource sheet |

▶ **4.** Save the file as **Pool** in the **Project6\Tutorial** folder included with your Data Files.

The four resources you want to include in the shared resource pool are now entered in the Pool project file. When you want to manage resource information among multiple files, you should create a resource pool file that can be shared with all project files. When you create a resource pool file, it is good practice to include the world "pool" in the filename. This will help you recognize the file as a pool resource file.

Sharing Existing Resources between Project Files

If you already have resources in another project that you want to add to the resource pool, you can share that project's resource information with the resource pool. Once the resources are added to the resource pool, other projects can also use them. When you share resources, you need to determine which file should take precedence if conflicts between the two files arise. **Precedence** determines which file's resources and resource information will be used if conflicts arise when they are merged (for example, if two resources with the same name have different cost values). The "Pool takes precedence" option means that the resource pool file will overwrite conflicting information from the sharing file. The "Sharer takes precedence" option allows the sharing file to overwrite information in the resource pool and other sharing files. You can shift and share resources from as many project files to the resource pool file as you want.

REFERENCE

Sharing Existing Resources with a Resource Pool File

- Open the resource pool file.
- Open the file that contains resources that you want to share with the resource pool.
- In the project that contains resources that you want to share with the resource pool, click the Resource tab, and then, in the Assignments group, click the Resource Pool button.
- On the list, click Share Resources to open the Share Resources dialog box.
- Select the Use resources option button, click the From arrow, and then click the filename of the file that contains the resource pool.
- In the On conflict with calendar or resource information section, click an option button to determine whether the pool or sharer will take precedence, and then click the OK button.

ViewPoint Partner resources are in both the Pool file and the NewAV-6 file. The list of resources is different in each file. You want to share the resources available in both files between the two files in order to get the maximum use out of the available personnel. Next, you will share the resources between the two files.

To share the existing resources between two files:

1. Click the **File** tab, click **Open**, navigate to the **Project6\Tutorial** folder if it is not the active folder, and then double-click **NewAV-6**.

2. In the Resource Views group on the View tab, click the **Resource Sheet** button to view the 18 resources that are currently available in the project file.

3. Double-click the **Your Name** resource to open the Resource Information dialog box, type your name in the Resource name box, double-click **YN**, type your initials, and then click the **OK** button. You want to share these resources with the existing resource pool so that they can be available for other projects. The NewAV-6 file will become a shared file; it is the project that contains resources that you want to share with the resource pool file. Once a file becomes a shared file, it is a linked file. Each time you open the shared file, you will receive a message asking if you also want to open the linked file.

4. Click the **Resource** tab, and then, in the Assignments group, click the **Resource Pool** button.

5. On the menu, click **Share Resources**. The Share Resources dialog box opens. You set the preferences for sharing the resources with the resource pool.

6. Click the **Use resources** option button if it is not selected. This option directs Project to share the resources in the active file, NewAV-6.

7. Click the **From** arrow, click **Pool** if it is not already selected, and then verify that the **Pool takes precedence** option button is selected, as shown in Figure 6-40. This option directs Project to use Pool as the resource pool file, and if conflicts exist between the NewAV-6 and Pool files to use the data in the pool file to resolve them.

> **TIP**
>
> If you plan to make changes in the shared file that you want reflected in the linked file, then you need to be sure both files are open at the same time.

| Figure 6-40 | Share Resources dialog box |

click the Resource Pool button to open the Share Resources dialog box

NewAV-6 resources

name of file that is going to share resources

name of file that will be used as the pool file

when selected, resource information in the file used as the Pool file (in this case, Pool.mpp) takes precedence over resource information in the sharer file (in this case, NewAV-6.mpp) if there is a conflict

when selected, resource information in the file used as the Sharer file (in this case, NewAV-6.mpp) takes precedence over resource information in the Pool file (in this case, Pool.mpp) if there is a conflict

While resources are shared between the two files, the way the files are listed in the Share Resources dialog box determines which file is the sharer file and which file is the pool file. The **Sharer file** is the active file and the one to which you assign the Use resources option button; it is the first file listed in the Share Resources dialog box. The "Sharer takes precedence" option refers to the active file (the one listed near the top of the dialog box after the phrase "Resources for." The **Pool file** is the file you select using the From list. The "Pool takes precedence" option refers to the file listed in the From box. When sharing files, it is important that the Sharer file is the active file and the Pool file is listed in the From box in the Share Resources dialog box.

▶ **8.** Click the **OK** button. The four resources from the Pool file are now shared with the NewAV-6 file and are added to its resource sheet, and the 18 resources from the NewAV-6 file are shared with the Pool file and added to its resource sheet.

▶ **9.** Click the **Project** button on the taskbar, and then click the **Pool Project file** thumbnail. All 18 resources from the NewAV-6 file are now available in the Pool file, as shown in Figure 6-41.

| Figure 6-41 | Resources are shared |

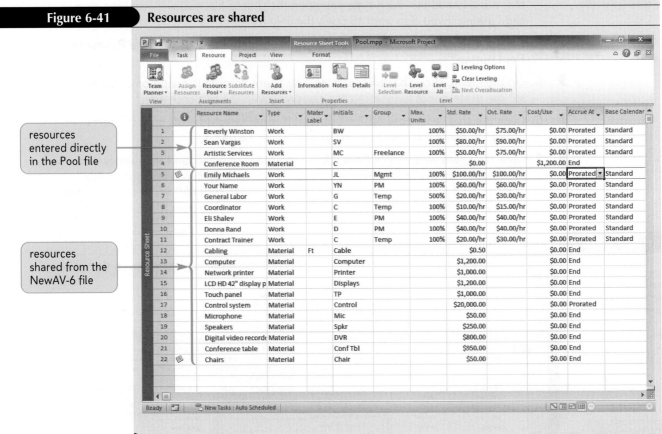

▶ **10.** Save your work.

Updating and Refreshing the Pool

When both the sharing and resource pool files are open on your computer, as resource information is entered in one file, the other file will be updated automatically. If many different users need access to the resource pool file, however, the situation becomes a little more complex. Only one person can have read-write access at a time to the resource pool file. **Read-write access** is the ability to both open the file (read it) and edit the file (write to it). When one person is using the file with read-write access, all others using the file at the same time have only read access.

If you are working with a resource pool file and do not have read-write access to it (or if the resource pool file is not currently open on your computer), you can still update the resource pool manually with changes made in your project. To do so, click the Resource Pool button, and then click Update Resource Pool. To make sure that the resource pool is updated with changes made to other projects that share the pool, click the Resource Pool button, and then click Refresh Resource Pool. When you have read-write access to both the sharing and resource pool files, both the Update Resource Pool and Refresh Resource Pool menu options are dimmed because resources are automatically updated and these menu options are not needed.

To update a resource pool (with read-write access to the pool file):

▶ **1.** Be sure **Pool** is the active project, click the **row 2 Std. Rate** cell (Sean Vargas), type **95**, click the **row 2 Ovt Rate** (Sean Vargas), type **120**, and then press the **Enter** key.

▶ **2.** Click in the blank **Resource Name** cell for row 23, type **Printer supplies**, press the **Tab** key, type **M** to select **Material**, click the **Cost/Use** cell for row 23, type **200**, and then press the **Enter** key. The resource changes are entered in the shared Pool file.

▶ **3.** Click the **Project** button on the taskbar, and then click the **NewAV-6 Project file** thumbnail. The new resource in row 23, as well as the rate changes for Sean Vargas in row 2, have been automatically updated in this sharing file, as shown in Figure 6-42.

Figure 6-42	Resources updated in NewAV-6 file based on information entered in Pool file

NewAV-6 Project file

rates updated based on information entered in the Pool file

new resource added to NewAV-6 file based on information entered in the Pool file

		Resource Name	Type	Material Label	Initials	Grou	Max.	Std. Rate	Ovt. Rate	Cost/Use	Accrue	Base	Code	Ad
1		Beverly Winston	Work		BW		100%	$50.00/hr	$75.00/hr	$0.00	Prorated	Standard		
2		Sean Vargas	Work		SV		100%	$95.00/hr	$120.00/hr	$0.00	Prorated	Standard		
3		Artistic Services	Work		MC	Freelanc	100%	$50.00/hr	$75.00/hr	$0.00	Prorated	Standard		
4		Conference Room	Material		C			$0.00		$1,200.00	End			
5		Emily Michaels	Work		JL	Mgmt	100%	$100.00/hr	$100.00/hr	$0.00	Prorated	Standard		
6		Your Name	Work		YN	PM	100%	$60.00/hr	$60.00/hr	$0.00	Prorated	Standard		
7		General Labor	Work		G	Temp	500%	$20.00/hr	$30.00/hr	$0.00	Prorated	Standard		
8		Coordinator	Work		C	Temp	100%	$10.00/hr	$15.00/hr	$0.00	Prorated	Standard		
9		Eli Shalev	Work		E	PM	100%	$40.00/hr	$40.00/hr	$0.00	Prorated	Standard		
10		Donna Rand	Work		D	PM	100%	$40.00/hr	$40.00/hr	$0.00	Prorated	Standard		
11		Contract Trainer	Work		C	Temp	100%	$20.00/hr	$30.00/hr	$0.00	Prorated	Standard		
12		Cabling	Material	Ft	Cable			$0.50		$0.00	End			
13		Computer	Material		Computer			$1,200.00		$0.00	End			
14		Network printer	Material		Printer			$1,000.00		$0.00	End			
15		LCD HD 42" display panel	Material		Displays			$1,200.00		$0.00	End			
16		Touch panel	Material		TP			$1,000.00		$0.00	End			
17		Control system	Material		Control			$20,000.00		$0.00	Prorated			
18		Microphone	Material		Mic			$50.00		$0.00	End			
19		Speakers	Material		Spkr			$250.00		$0.00	End			
20		Digital video recorder	Material		DVR			$800.00		$0.00	End			
21		Conference table	Material		Conf Tbl			$950.00		$0.00	End			
22		Chairs	Material		Chair			$50.00		$0.00	End			
23		Printer supplies	Material		P			$0.00		$200.00	Prorated			

> **4.** Open **Backstage** view to preview the resource sheet for the NewAV-6 file, open the **Page Setup** dialog box, and then click the **Page** tab if it is not already selected.

> **5.** Click the **Landscape** option button, and then click the **Fit to** option button. Now the resource sheet will print in landscape mode on one page.

> **6.** Click the **Header** tab, click the **Center** tab, and then change Your Name to your name so that it is center-aligned in the header.

> **7.** Print the resource sheet if requested, save your changes, and then close the NewAV-6 file.

> **8.** Save your changes to the Pool file, and then close the file.

You can see the power of a shared resource pool. It helps ensure that changes are accurately reflected across all projects that share resources.

Using a Master Project

A master project, also called a consolidated project, is a project file that contains subprojects. A **subproject** is a project file that is inserted into a master project. Just as a project summary includes summary tasks, which can include individual tasks, a master project can include subprojects. A Project file is not inherently multiuser—that is, by default, only one person can have read-write access to a Project file at any time. However, using the master project-subproject organization allows more than one person to enter, edit, and update tasks simultaneously by working in separate subproject files that are linked to a master project. The master project and its subprojects must be stored on a server that all users have access to in order to allow multiuser access. Viewing or printing the master project displays or prints the latest updates in any of its subprojects.

Creating a Master Project and Its Subprojects

A master file can contain master-level tasks, it can serve as a container into which subprojects are linked, or it can contain both master-level tasks and linked subprojects. The scope of an entire project can be viewed from the master project.

REFERENCE

Creating a Master Project

- Create a new project, or open an existing project file that you want to use as the master project.
- Create subproject files.
- In a sheet view, click the row where you want the subproject to be linked.
- Click the Project tab, and then, in the Insert group, click the Subproject button to open the Insert Project dialog box.
- Navigate to the folder that contains the subproject file, and then double-click the filename to insert it as a subproject into the master project.

Sidney at ViewPoint partners has asked you to explore working with a master project and its subprojects. For this example, the master file will be a container for two sub-projects and it will also contain one master-level task. The master-level task will be added after the subprojects are added to the master project.

TIP

When you create master projects and subprojects, be sure to use filenames that will help you easily identify the files that you are working with.

To create a master project:

1. Create a new blank project file, and then set the new tasks mode to **Auto Scheduled**.

2. Open the **Project Information** dialog box, change the Start date to **12/1/14** and the Current date to **11/1/14**, and then close the Project Information dialog box.

3. Save the file as **Master-6** to the Project6\Tutorial folder included with your Data Files.

Next, you'll create the two subprojects that will be linked to the master project. One subproject will contain the tasks for documenting the hardware at ViewPoint Partners; the other subproject will contain the tasks for documenting the software.

To create the two subprojects:

1. Create a new blank project file, set the new tasks mode to **Auto Scheduled**, and then open the **Project Information** dialog box.

2. Change the Start date to **12/1/14** and the Current date to **11/1/14**, close the Project Information dialog box, and then save the file as **DocHdw** to the Project6\Tutorial folder included with your Data Files. This new project is the first of the two subprojects.

3. Close the Timeline, and then enter the following three tasks: **Create inventory database, 2 days; Update inventory database, 2 days;** and **Draw schematics, 1 day**.

4. Select the three tasks, click the **Task** tab, and then, in the Schedule group, click the **Link Tasks** button ⬡ to create the relationships. Your screen should look like Figure 6-43.

| Figure 6-43 | Document Hardware project |

tasks are Auto Scheduled

three new tasks typed directly in the DocHdw file

DocHdw.mpp Project file

tasks are linked

5. Save the file.

6. Create a new blank project file, set the new tasks mode to **Auto Scheduled**, and then open the **Project Information** dialog box.

▶ **7.** Change the Start date to **12/1/14** and the Current date to **11/1/14**, close the Project Information dialog box, and then save the file as **DocSfw** to the Project6\Tutorial folder included with your Data Files. This new project is the second of the two subprojects. Note that both new projects use the same Start date and Current date.

▶ **8.** Close the Timeline, and then enter the same three tasks that you entered in the Document Hardware file: **Create inventory database**, **Update inventory database**, and **Draw schematics**. Set the duration as one day for each task, and then link the three tasks. The project, the durations, and relationships are shown in Figure 6-44.

Figure 6-44	Document Software project

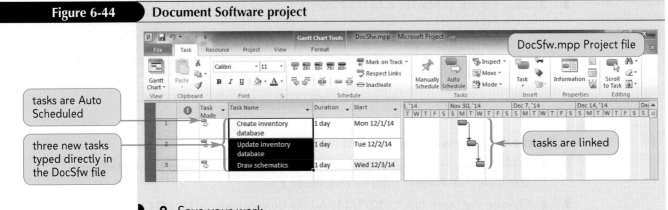

▶ **9.** Save your work.

You now have the three project files that you need to create a master project file with two subproject files. When you insert a project file in a master file as a subproject, you can choose to insert it as a file with read-write access or as a file with read-only access. The default is to insert the file with read-write access. If you want to select the read-only option, then, in the Insert Project dialog box, click the Insert button arrow and select the option Insert Read-only. To change a read-only file to allow for read-write access, click the Insert button arrow in the Insert Project dialog box, and then select the Insert option. You work with these three open files to set up the subprojects in the master project.

To insert the subprojects into the master project:

▶ **1.** Click the **View** tab, and then, in the Window group, click the **Switch Windows button** ⊞▾. The three open files are listed on the menu. See Figure 6-45.

Figure 6-45	Switch Windows options

2. Click **Master-6**, and then close the Timeline. The blank master project file is now the active window and should fill your screen. Now you'll insert the first subproject in the first blank row of the project.

3. Click the **row 1 Task Name cell**, click the **Project** tab, and then, in the Insert group, click the **Subproject** button. The Insert Project dialog box opens. It resembles the Open and Save dialog boxes. The files in the Project6\Tutorial folder should be listed in the dialog box.

4. Click **DocHdw.mpp**, and then click the **Insert** button. The Document Hardware project file is inserted as the first task in the master project file. The Project 2010 icon appears in the Indicators column.

5. Point to the **Project 2010 Indicator** in row 1. The ScreenTip that appears tells you that this is an inserted project and displays its path. See Figure 6-46. Next, you'll insert the second subproject in the second blank row of the project.

| Figure 6-46 | DocHdw project inserted as subproject in master project file |

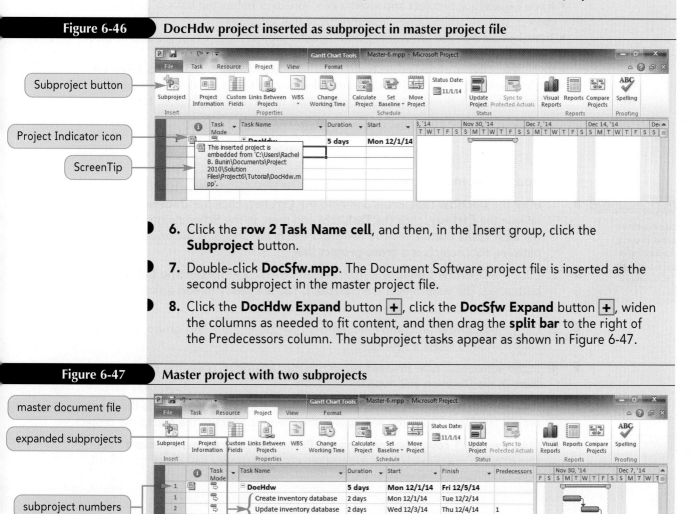

6. Click the **row 2 Task Name cell**, and then, in the Insert group, click the **Subproject** button.

7. Double-click **DocSfw.mpp**. The Document Software project file is inserted as the second subproject in the master project file.

8. Click the **DocHdw Expand** button ⊞, click the **DocSfw Expand** button ⊞, widen the columns as needed to fit content, and then drag the **split bar** to the right of the Predecessors column. The subproject tasks appear as shown in Figure 6-47.

| Figure 6-47 | Master project with two subprojects |

Notice that each subproject is labeled with a number and the tasks within each project are numbered 1, 2, and 3. Project 2010 sequentially numbers the subprojects in a master project but not the tasks in each subproject. The tasks in each subproject have their own row numbering system that starts with 1.

Updating a Master Project

Updating a master project is very similar to updating any other project. For example, you can add tasks, resources, and relationships at the master project level. You can set a baseline and can record actual progress in the master project. As you work with master project files and subproject files, it is important to know the following:

- Any changes to subprojects are automatically updated in the master project and vice versa if all files are open and the user has read-write access to all files.
- You can add tasks to both the subprojects and the master project from within the master project file.
- If you expand a subproject and insert a new row in or below the tasks of that subproject, you are adding a new row directly to that subproject.
- To make sure that you are working at the master project level (when you add or move master-level tasks, for example), collapse all of the inserted subprojects.
- If you select the "Inserted projects are calculated like summary tasks" check box on the Schedule tab of the Project Options dialog box (which is the default), then all subproject calculations in the master project file are treated as summary tasks.

Next, you want to add a final task to the master project.

To modify the master project:

TIP

You can also create an external cross-project link for a task using the Predecessor tab of the Task Information dialog box.

1. Click the **DocHdw** task, press and hold the **Ctrl** key, click the **DocSfw** task, release the **Ctrl** key, click the **Task** tab, and then, in the Schedule group, click the **Link Tasks** button. The two subprojects are linked. A dependency created between subprojects is a **cross-project link**.

2. Click the **DocHdw Collapse** button, and then click the **DocSfw Collapse** button. The subprojects are collapsed. You are ready to add a task at the master level.

3. Click the **DocHdw** task, and then, on the Task tab in the Insert group, click the **Task** button to insert a new task.

4. In the active cell, type **Present report to management**, press the **Tab** key, and then, in the Duration cell, type **0**.

5. Press the **Enter** key. This task is a milestone and is entered directly into the master project file. Next, move the new task in the master project to the end of the project.

6. Click the **row 1 row selector**, drag the **Present report to management** milestone task in row 1 below row 3, and then click any empty cell. See Figure 6-48.

Figure 6-48   Milestone task entered

Figure 6-48   Milestone task entered

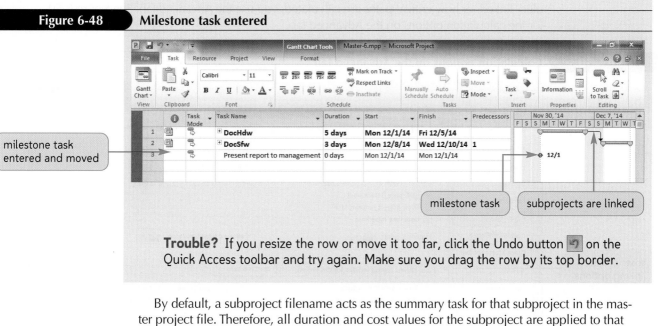

milestone task entered and moved

milestone task

subprojects are linked

Trouble? If you resize the row or move it too far, click the Undo button ↺ on the Quick Access toolbar and try again. Make sure you drag the row by its top border.

By default, a subproject filename acts as the summary task for that subproject in the master project file. Therefore, all duration and cost values for the subproject are applied to that subproject's task name in the master project. You can change the way that the master file calculates the subproject by changing the Calculation options in the Options dialog box, using either the Schedule tab or the Advanced tab depending on the type of changes you want to make. If you need to make changes to calculation options related to scheduling, you use the Schedule tab. See Figure 6-49 for the calculation options on the Schedule tab.

Figure 6-49   Calculation options on the Schedule tab

calculation options

Show assignment units as a:	Percentage ▾

Scheduling options for this project: 📑 Master-6.mpp ▾

New tasks created: Auto Scheduled ▾
Auto scheduled tasks scheduled on: Project Start Date ▾
Duration is entered in: Days ▾
Work is entered in: Hours ▾
Default task type: Fixed Units ▾

☐ New tasks are effort driven ⓘ
☐ Autolink inserted or moved tasks ⓘ
☑ Split in-progress tasks ⓘ
☑ Update Manually Scheduled tasks when editing links

☑ Tasks will always honor their contraint dates ⓘ
☑ Show that scheduled tasks have estimated durations ⓘ
☑ New scheduled tasks have estimated durations
☐ Keep task on nearest working day when changing to Automatically Scheduled mode

Schedule Alerts Options: 📑 Master-6.mpp ▾

☑ Show task schedule warnings
☐ Show task schedule suggestions

Calculation

Calculate project after each edit:
◉ On
○ Off

Calculation options for this project: 📑 Master-6.mpp ▾

☑ Updating Task status updates resource status ⓘ
☑ Inserted projects are calculated like summary tasks
☑ Actual costs are always calculated by Project
    ☐ Edits to total actual cost will be spread to the status date
Default fixed cost accrual: Prorated ▾

OK   Cancel

If you need to make changes to calculations options related to how tasks are rescheduled, linked, or how critical paths are calculated, you use the Advanced tab. See Figure 6-50 for the calculation options on the Advanced tab.

Figure 6-50   **Calculation options on the Advanced tab**

cross project linking options

calculation options

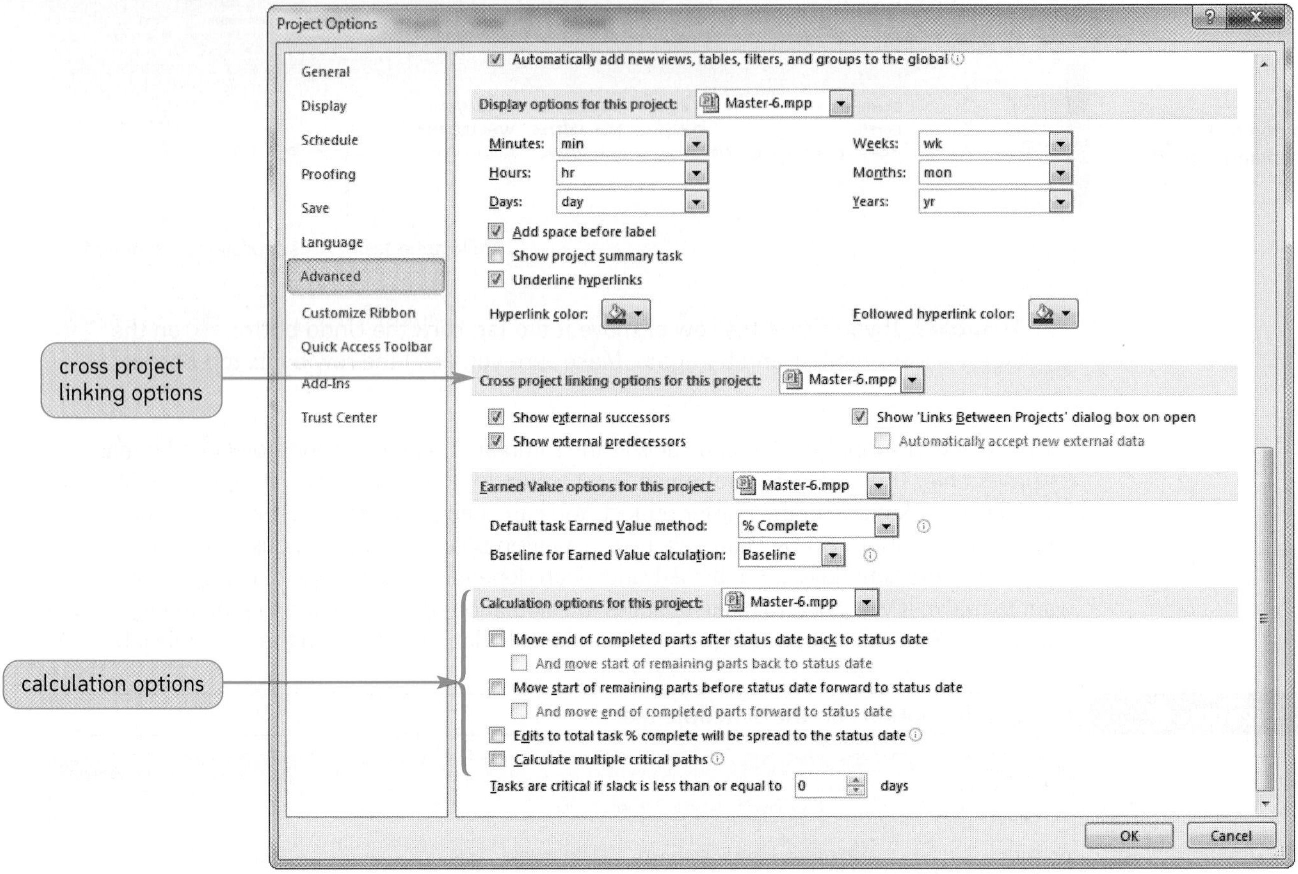

Project 2010 allows you to create dependencies between subprojects as well as between subprojects and master-level tasks in the master project. You decide to link the milestone to the second subproject so it will be updated when the task is complete.

To link the subproject task to the master-level task:

1. Click the **DocSfw** task, press and hold the **Ctrl** key, click the **Present report to management** task, release the **Ctrl** key, and then, in the Schedule group on the Task tab, click the **Link Tasks** button 🔗.

2. Click the **DocHdw Expand** button ➕, and then click the **DocSfw Expand** button ➕ to view the expanded master project.

Emily points out that there is a task missing from the DocHdw. Next, you will add the missing task to the subproject from within the master project file.

To add the task to the subproject from within the master project:

1. In the list of tasks for the DocHdw subproject, click the **Create inventory database**, and then, on the Task tab in the Insert group, click the **Task** button to insert a new task.

▶ **2.** In the active cell, type **Design inventory database**, press the **right arrow** key, type **2** in the Duration cell, and then press the **Enter** key. The new task for the subproject is added to the master project as well as to the DocHdw subproject. You will verify this after you link the task in a Finish-to-Start relationship to another task in the subproject.

▶ **3.** Drag to select **Design inventory database** and **Create inventory database** (tasks 1 and 2 in the DocHdw subproject), and then, in the Schedule group on the Task tab, click the **Link Tasks** button.

▶ **4.** Drag the **split bar** so the Duration column is the last column showing. Your master project looks like Figure 6-51.

| Figure 6-51 | Updated master project |

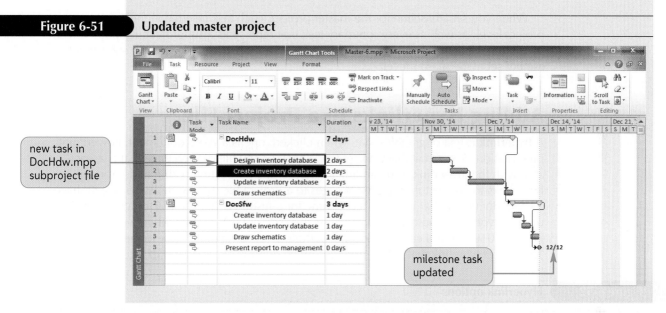

new task in DocHdw.mpp subproject file

milestone task updated

Next, you will review the DocHdw subproject file to see how the change made in the master project file affected the subproject file.

To review the subproject file:

▶ **1.** Click the **View** tab, and then, in the Window group, click the **Switch Windows button**.

▶ **2.** On the menu, click **DocHdw**, and then confirm that it now contains four tasks instead of three.

▶ **3.** In the Window group, click the **Switch Windows button**, and then, on the menu. click **Master-6** to make it the active window.

▶ **4.** On the Quick Access toolbar, click the **Save** button. A dialog box opens asking if you want to save changes to the DocSfw file. You will be able to save all the subprojects with one click.

▶ **5.** Click the **Yes to All** button to save changes to the subprojects.

▶ **6.** Preview the **Master-6** Gantt Chart view, add your name left-aligned in the header, and then print the Gantt Chart view if requested.

▶ **7.** Save your changes.

When you are finished creating your master project and before work begins on any of the tasks, you should set a baseline so that you can track actual progress against your initial plan.

To set the baseline for the master project:

▶ **1.** Click the **Project** tab, and then, in the Schedule group, click the **Set Baseline** button.

▶ **2.** On the menu, click **Set Baseline**.

▶ **3.** In the Set Baseline dialog box, click the **OK** button to set the baseline for the entire project.

When you set a baseline for the master project, each task inserted at the master project level, as well as every summary task that represents a subproject, is updated with baseline field values. However, baseline values for individual tasks in each subproject are not set at the master level.

Adding Hyperlinks to a Project File

A **hyperlink** is text or graphics that, when clicked, opens a Word document, PowerPoint presentation, Access database, Excel worksheet, or any file or Web page that is associated with that hyperlink. You can link to another file or location within a file. You use hyperlinks to connect files and Web pages to a Project file. For example, you might have a Word document that includes the resume for a resource that is hired for a project. By using a hyperlink, you can quickly access this external information while working in the Project 2010 file. You can also use a hyperlink to link to another view in the Project file. The Insert Hyperlink dialog box provides many options, summarized in Figure 6-52.

Figure 6-52	Hyperlink options

Link to Option	Suboption	Creates a Hyperlink to	What Appears in the Box
Existing File or Web Page	Text to display as the hyperlink; Current Folder	A file	Files and folders in the current folder; you can select from the list or enter the path in the address box.
	Text to display as the hyperlink; Browsed Pages	A Web page	Paths to Web pages you have browsed recently using the default browser on the computer; you can select from the list or enter the path in the address box.
	Text to display as the hyperlink; Recent Files	An existing file on your computer	Paths to files you have used recently; you can select from the list or enter the path in the address box.
Place in This Document	Text to display as the hyperlink; Views	One of the Project views	A list of the available views in Project.
Create New Document	Text to display as the hyperlink; Name of new document box; When to edit: now or later	A new file you create	A box where you can type the name of a new file of any type that your computer supports; browse to the directory where you want the file stored.
E-mail Address	Text to display as the hyperlink; E-mail address; Subject; Recently used e-mail addresses	An e-mail address	The e-mail address you want to use; the subject of the e-mail. You can enter an e-mail address or choose from a list of e-mail addresses that you have recently used.

REFERENCE

Adding a Hyperlink

- In a sheet view, right-click a task or resource to which you want to add the hyperlink.
- Click Hyperlink on the shortcut menu.
- In the Insert Hyperlink dialog box, click the appropriate button in the Link to list, click the appropriate button in the middle pane, navigate to the file or location for the hyperlink, and then select it.
- Click the OK button.

You have started a Word document that will summarize the documentation information you have collected for the ViewPoint Partners AV installation project. Sidney suggests that you add a hyperlink to the last task of your master project to link to this document.

To add the hyperlink:

▶ **1.** Right-click the **Present report to management** task in the Master-6 file, and then, on the shortcut menu, click **Hyperlink**. The Insert Hyperlink dialog box opens. The default Existing File or Web Page button is selected in the Link to list on the left, and the Current Folder button is selected in the Look in pane in the middle of the dialog box. You want to browse for an existing Word file, AVDoc.doc, which is located in the Project6\Tutorial folder.

▶ **2.** Navigate to the **Project6\Tutorial** folder included with your Data Files, and then click **AVDoc.docx**. See Figure 6-53.

Figure 6-53	Insert Hyperlink dialog box

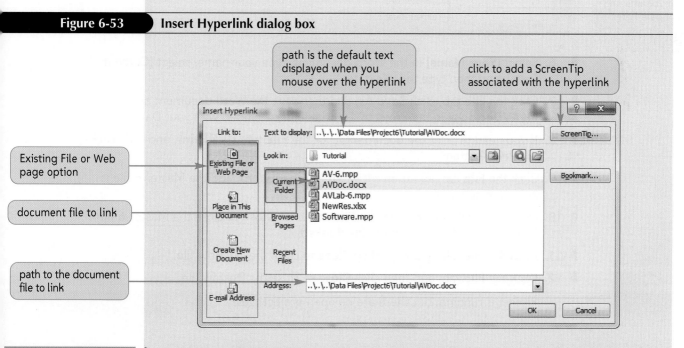

You can change the Text to display text and create a helpful message for any hyperlink.

▶ **3.** Click the **OK** button to select the address location and close the Insert Hyperlink dialog box, and then in the Indicators column for the "Present report to management" task, position the pointer on top of the **hyperlink** indicator. The ScreenTip appears with the linked filename.

▶ **4.** Right-click the **hyperlink** indicator, point to **Hyperlink**, and then click **Open in New Window** on the shortcut menu.

> **5.** Click the **Yes** button to continue and accept this document from a trusted source. The AVDoc Word file opens, as shown in Figure 6-54.

| Figure 6-54 | AVDoc Word document |

document is in a Word window

type your name and current date here

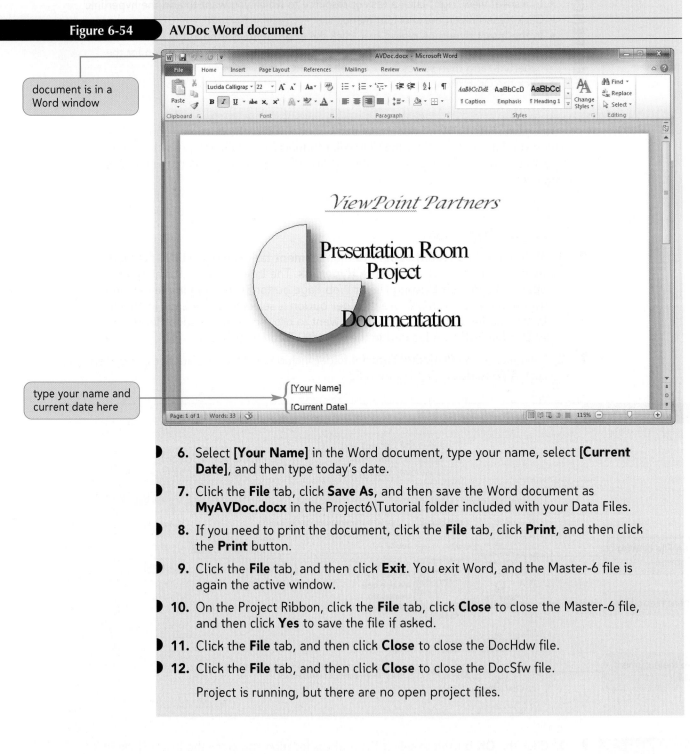

> **6.** Select **[Your Name]** in the Word document, type your name, select **[Current Date]**, and then type today's date.

> **7.** Click the **File** tab, click **Save As**, and then save the Word document as **MyAVDoc.docx** in the Project6\Tutorial folder included with your Data Files.

> **8.** If you need to print the document, click the **File** tab, click **Print**, and then click the **Print** button.

> **9.** Click the **File** tab, and then click **Exit**. You exit Word, and the Master-6 file is again the active window.

> **10.** On the Project Ribbon, click the **File** tab, click **Close** to close the Master-6 file, and then click **Yes** to save the file if asked.

> **11.** Click the **File** tab, and then click **Close** to close the DocHdw file.

> **12.** Click the **File** tab, and then click **Close** to close the DocSfw file.

> Project is running, but there are no open project files.

INSIGHT

Working with Multiple Critical Paths

As you recall, each project has only one critical path that determines the project's Finish date. If you are working with multiple projects, you need to have created a master project in order to show the critical path across all the projects.

In the case of a master project, you can view the critical paths for the master project as well as for the subprojects. Although there is only one critical path for the entire master project, each subproject has a separate critical path. Project allows you to show those critical paths by changing a default setting in the Options dialog box. Refer back to Figure 6-50.

Working with Custom Fields

A **custom field** is a field that is defined by a user for a specific purpose. It can be used with either tasks or resources. A custom field can simply be an existing field that is renamed, such as changing Flag1 (an existing field and field name) to Requires outside vendor. For more elaborate requirements, a custom field can contain a value list to provide specific values for a field when you want to limit input. By defining a custom field as a lookup table, you can control the data that is entered in the field. Custom fields can be defined using the Customized Fields dialog box. Custom fields are project-specific, but they can be copied from project to project using the Organizer.

Renaming a Field to Create a Custom Field

A **flag field** is a field you can use to indicate whether a task, resource, or assignment needs further attention or some additional action. Task fields can only be set to one of two states: Yes or No. There are 20 flag fields (Flag1 through Flag20) provided for each task, resource, and assignment. By default, all flag fields are set to No, but they can be set to Yes to mark an item for special identification, such as to mark the field as a priority or as needing special attention for some other reason. For example, you might want to use the resource Flag1 field to identify resources that are being used for the first time (subcontractors, consultants, other outsourced resources, and so on). By filtering for the resource Flag1 field set to Yes, you can find the new resources and more easily examine their performances. In this way, you can use flag fields to create any type of custom grouping of resources or tasks that you desire.

REFERENCE

Using a Flag Field on a Sheet View

- Right-click the Select All button, and then apply the table to which you want to add the flag field.
- Right-click the column heading where you want to insert the flag field, and then click Insert Column.
- Type F to display the flag fields in the list.
- Choose a flag field from the Field name list, enter a descriptive title or other changes if desired, and then click the OK button.

Although this project has finished and all tasks are complete, you want to discuss several of the tasks with Sidney. You will rename the task Flag1 field, insert a column to display the new custom field, and then set the flag to indicate which tasks require further action.

To create the custom field based on the flag field and use it in sheet view:

▶ **1.** Open the project file **NewAVLab-6**, which is located in the **Project6\Tutorial** folder included with your Data Files. You created this project file in Session 6.1.

▶ **2.** In the table, right-click the **Select All** button, click **Entry** if it is not already selected, and then drag the **split bar** so that the Duration field is the last one visible in the table.

▶ **3.** Right-click the **Duration** column heading, click **Insert Column** on the shortcut menu, press the **F** key and the **L** key in rapid succession to quickly scroll to the flag fields, and then click **Flag1**. The Flag1 field is inserted to the right of the Task Name column.

▶ **4.** In the Properties group on the Project tab, click the **Custom Fields** button. The Custom Fields dialog box opens. See Figure 6-55.

TIP

You can manually adjust the header row width or specify that the header text wraps within the specified width. The height of the header row will increase as you wrap text within it.

Figure 6-55	Custom Fields dialog box

Task fields are shown

Flag1 field selected

field options

▶ **5.** Click the **Rename** button, and then, in the New name for 'Flag1' box, type **Review with Sidney**. You can name the field anything to identify its purpose in the file.

▶ **6.** Click the **OK** button, and then click the **OK** button to close the Custom Fields dialog box. The new Review with Sidney column appears to the right of the Task Name column. By default, all values in a flag field are set to No. The only other option for a flag field is Yes.

▶ **7.** Click the **Develop training documentation (task 4) Review with Sidney** cell, click the **arrow** that appears, and then click **Yes**. The cell now contains Yes as the value.

8. Click the **Hire trainers (task 9) Review with Sidney** cell, click the **arrow** that appears, click **Yes**, and then press the **Enter** key. Your screen should look similar to Figure 6-56.

| Figure 6-56 | Customized flag field |

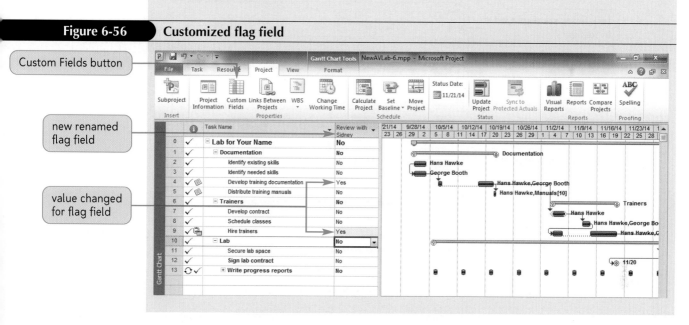

Custom Fields button

new renamed flag field

value changed for flag field

Creating a Custom Field Based on the Cost1 Field

You create a custom field when you want to define your own fields and specify the type of values that the field can contain. When you create a customized field, you determine if it is a cost or resource field. The types of fields available are Cost, Date, Duration, Finish, Flag, Number, Start, and Text. The default names are Cost1 through Cost10 for Cost, Date1 through Date10 for Date, and so forth. You can rename the field so it is easily identified as you enter data in Project. You can also set a value list that is a predetermined finite number of possible values for the field from which you can chose. You can set graphical indicators that will appear if the field meets criteria you specify when defining the field.

Sidney has asked the partners to make contributions to help cover the costs of some of the tasks associated with the Training Lab. These costs must be entered and tracked. There are three levels for the contributions: $50, $100, and $150. You will add the Partner Cost custom field to the NewAVLab-6 file. These levels indicate the amount of the contribution needed for its associated task.

To create the customized field and use it in sheet view:

1. Right-click the **Review with Sidney** column heading, and then, on the shortcut menu, click **Custom Fields** to open the Custom Fields dialog box. The Review with Sidney field is selected. The Task option button is also already selected.

2. Click the **Type** arrow, and then click **Cost**. The Cost1 Field is selected.

3. Click the **Rename** button. The Rename Field dialog box opens.

4. Type **Partner Cost**. See Figure 6-57.

Figure 6-57 Creating a custom field

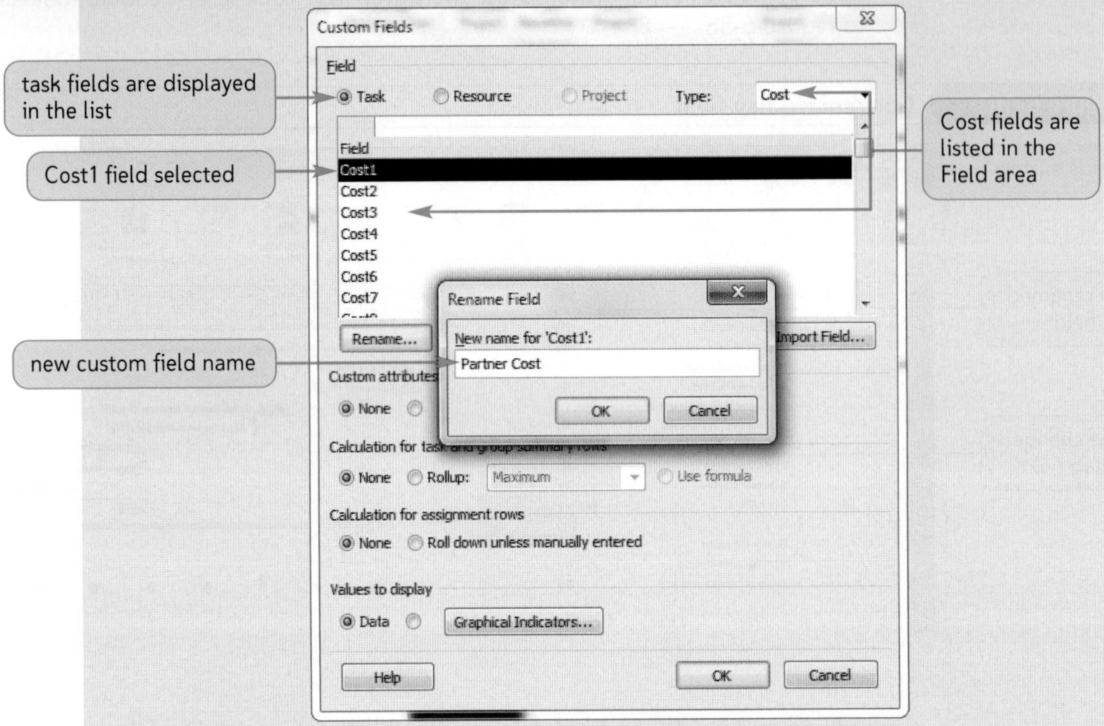

5. In the Rename Field dialog box, click the **OK** button. The Rename Field dialog box closes.

TIP

Because it's a cost field, you don't have to enter values with dollar signs and cents; the numbers are formatted as currency automatically.

6. In the Custom attributes section of the Customize Fields dialog box, click the **Lookup** button to open the Edit Lookup Table for Partner Cost dialog box, click the **Row 1 Value** cell, type **50**, press the **Enter** key, type **100**, press the **Enter** key, type **150**, and then press the **Enter** key. See Figure 6-58.

Figure 6-58 Edit Lookup Table for Partner Cost field

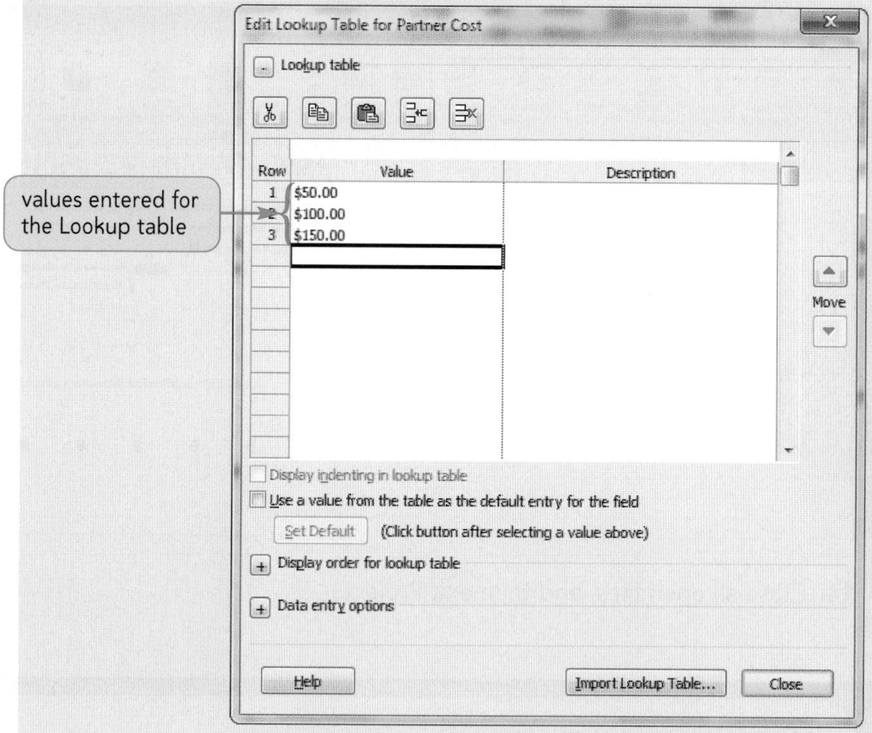

values entered for the Lookup table

7. Click the **Close** button to close the Edit Lookup Table for Partner Cost dialog box, and then click the **OK** button to close the Custom Fields dialog box.

8. Right-click the **Review with Sidney** column heading, click **Insert Column** on the shortcut menu, press the **P** key to scroll the Field name list, and then click **Partner Cost (Cost1)**. The field is inserted in the sheet.

9. Drag the **split bar** and adjust the columns so you can see all data in the Partner Cost and Review with Sidney fields.

10. Click the **Develop Contract** (**task 7**) **Partner Cost** cell, and then click the **arrow**. The values you entered in the Edit Lookup Table for Partner Cost dialog box appear in the list.

11. Click **$50.00** from the list. $50.00 appears in the cell.

12. Click the **Schedule classes** (**task 8**) **Partner Cost** cell, click the **arrow**, click **$150.00**, click the **Secure lab space** (**task 11**) **Partner Cost** cell, click the **arrow**, click **$100.00**, and then press the **Enter** key.

13. Save the project file. Compare your screen to Figure 6-59.

| Figure 6-59 | Custom Partner Cost field |

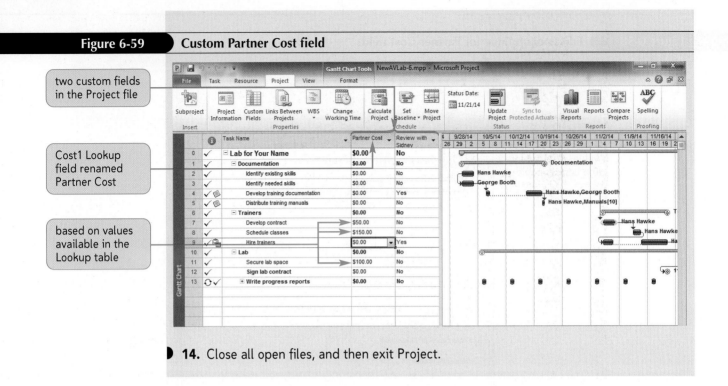

two custom fields
in the Project file

Cost1 Lookup
field renamed
Partner Cost

based on values
available in the
Lookup table

▶ **14.** Close all open files, and then exit Project.

REVIEW

Session 6.2 Quick Check

1. What is the purpose of a data template?
2. What is the purpose of the Organizer? What types of items do you copy and manage with the Organizer tool? Where are these items stored?
3. What are the benefits of using a resource pool?
4. What does resource precedence mean?
5. Why would you create a master file with subprojects?
6. What is the purpose of a hyperlink in a Project 2010 file?
7. What are the possible values that can be entered in a flag field?

Practice the skills you learned in the tutorial using a familiar scenario.

PRACTICE

Review Assignments

Data Files needed for the Review Assignments: Home-6.mpp, List.xlsx

The house-building project is completed, but you want to use this project to help with planning in future home-building projects. In this assignment, you will open a project file that documents the tasks that were completed. You will use Project 2010's powerful data-sharing capabilities to share data with Excel and Word files. You'll explore templates, the Organizer, resource pools, and master files. Complete the following:

1. Open the **Home-6** project file located in the Project6\Review folder included with your Data Files, and then save the project as **NewHome-6** to the same folder.

2. In Resource Sheet view, change Your Name to your name and the initials YN to your initials.

3. Switch to Gantt Chart view, view the Project Summary Task bar, and change the task name to your name.

4. Apply the Cost table to the task sheet, and then drag the split bar to the far right to see the columns of the cost table.

5. Show only the Outline Level 1 tasks.

6. Drag to select all the cells that contain data in the Cost table, and then copy the data to the Clipboard.

7. Start Excel, open a new blank worksheet, and then paste the cost table data into the range of cells A2:H6. Resize the columns so that all of the data is displayed clearly. Save the workbook as **NewHome-6.xlsx** to the Project6\Review folder included with your Data Files.

8. Enter "Actual" in cell D1 and "Baseline" in cell E1, save the file, and then exit Excel.

9. With Microsoft Project NewHome-6 as the active window, apply the Earned Value table to the task sheet.

10. Drag the split bar to the far right, hide the SV column, and then resize the columns so that all of the data in each field is visible.

11. Expand all the tasks. Preview the Earned Value table, add your name left-aligned in the header, and then print it if requested.

12. Create a new blank project file, set the new task mode to Auto Scheduled, and then set the Start date to 11/1/14 and the Current date to 10/25/14. Hide the first two columns so the first column is Task Name and the second is Duration. Close the Timeline.

13. Import the Excel workbook, **List.xlsx**, located in the Project6\Review folder included with your Data Files. (*Hint*: In the Open dialog box, navigate to the location where the Excel file containing the data that you want to import is stored, click the Files of type arrow, click Excel Workbook (*.xlsx), click the List.xlsx Excel file that contains the data, and then click the Open button.) This workbook lists four tasks and corresponding durations for another phase of the NewHome-6 project. You need to create a new map for this data.

14. In the Import Wizard, click the New map option button if it is not already selected. Choose the option to append the data to the active project, click the Tasks check box as the type of data to map, and be sure to import the headers. Choose Sheet1 as the source worksheet. Look at the mapping fields to determine whether the Task Name and Duration fields were mapped correctly. (*Hint*: Fields that are in the Excel spreadsheet will appear in black.) The Duration field is mapped, but the Task Name field is not. Click the (not mapped) cell, click the arrow, press the "N" key, and then click Name to map the Task Name field. Finally, click the Finish button.

15. Save the new project file with the filename **List-6.mpp** in the Project6\Review folder.

16. Link the four tasks in the **List-6.mpp** file with finish-to-start relationships. Save your changes.

17. Switch to the **NewHome-6** Project file.

18. In the first blank row (task 18), insert the subproject **List-6.mpp**. Outdent the subproject to the same summary task level as Planning, Exterior, and Interior.

19. Expand the List-6 task, and then link Install carpeting (task 17) and Molding (task 1) in the subproject list with a finish-to-start relationship.

20. Start Outlook and create two tasks: **Install wallpaper** and **Install banisters**. *(Note: If you do not have Outlook installed on your computer, skip to Step 23.)*

21. Switch back to the **NewHome-6** Project file, and then import the two tasks you created in Outlook below the Install appliances task to create task 6 and task 7 as subtasks of the List-6 task.

22. Link the two new imported tasks with the other tasks in the phase in an FS relationship, and then change the duration for the Install wallpaper task to **3** days, the Install banisters task to **2** days, and the duration for the Molding task to **4** days.

23. Rename the Molding task as **Install molding**.

24. Switch to the List-6.mpp Project file, view the imported tasks, view the changed task name, and then set a baseline for the project as of today's date.

25. Switch back to the **NewHome-6** Project file, and then save your changes to the master and subproject files.

26. Set a second baseline using the Baseline 1 field. (*Hint*: Click the Set baseline arrow, then click Baseline 1.)

27. For both open project files, preview Gantt Chart view, add your name left-aligned in the header, and then print them if requested.

28. Switch to Gantt Chart view for the NewHome-6.mpp file, apply the Tracking table, click task 0, scroll to the task if its task bars are not clearly visible, and then zoom the Gantt Chart as necessary so that all of the bars are clearly visible with the Act. Work column as the last column. Copy the picture as a GIF image file and save it to the Project6\Review folder as **NewHome-6.gif**.

29. With NewHome-6 as the active file, switch to Task Usage view, go to the first task, and then scroll down to view the List-6 task (the subproject). Preview the Task Usage printout, add your name left-aligned in the header, and then print the first two pages of Task Usage view. On the printout, identify the List-6 summary task and its subtasks.

30. Create a new table by copying the Usage table. In the new table, insert the Cost field before the Start field. Name the table **Usage Facts**. Apply the Usage Facts table to the task sheet. Adjust the split bar and columns so that all of the data in the Task Name, Work, Duration, and Cost fields are visible, and then, if requested, print the first page of the project showing the custom table. Save your changes.

31. Copy the Usage Facts table to the Global.MPT template. If you get a message that the table already exists, replace it with your table.

32. Save and close both open project files, and then create a new project based on the Home Construction template from Office.com. (*Hint*: Review templates in the Plans and then the Business plans categories to find the Home Construction template.)

33. Switch to Task Usage view, apply the Usage Facts table, resize columns as needed, and then move the split bar so that the Task Name, Work, Duration, and Cost fields are clearly visible.

34. Note that the cost value is $0.00 for each resource assignment. Why? Switch to Resource Sheet view, and then enter **100** in the Std. Rate cell for the Concrete Contractor and the Electric Contactor. Change the Owner resource to your name.

35. Switch back to Task Usage view. Note the changes. Insert a new column that is based on the Flag1 field to the left of the Work column. Rename the field **Permit needed?**.

36. In the field Permit needed?, change the value from No to Yes for three of the tasks.

37. Save the project file as **ResHome.mpp**. Preview the Task Usage view, add your name to the left header, and then print the first page if requested.

38. Delete the Usage Facts table from the Global.MPT file.

39. Close and save any open files, close any open windows, exit Excel and Outlook, and then exit Project 2010.

Use your skills to create a new project file and a presentation file for a firm.

APPLY

Case Problem 1

There are no Data Files needed for this Case Problem.

New Paltz Ventures   You have been hired at New Paltz Ventures, a project management consulting firm. New Paltz Ventures contracts for projects ranging from traditional construction projects, to information systems installations, to new product deployments. The templates that come with Project 2010 represent some of the most common types of project categories, so you'll explore these templates further to see if they can be applied to the jobs that you'll be working on at the firm. You are also responsible for presenting new ideas for projects; you will create a PowerPoint presentation file with new product deployment ideas. To complete this case, you will need Internet access.

1. Complete the following: Create a new Project file based on the Startup business plan template. Click the File tab, click New, and then navigate to and download the Startup business plan template, which is part of the Office.com online Plans and proposals/Business plans collection. Adjust column widths to fit content, and zoom the Gantt chart as needed. Scroll down and notice that there are over 100 tasks in the template. Save the Project file as **SBPlan.mpp** in the Project6\Case1 folder included with your Data Files. Display various Outline levels to get a feel for the phases and lengths of the sample tasks in this project. Scroll through the tasks. When you are done examining the project, make sure you display all the subtasks again.

2. Switch to Resource Usage view, replace Manager (ID 5) with your name, and change the Project Start date to 2/1/14.

3. Return to the Gantt Chart view, drag the split bar to display the Task Name column and the Duration column, and then scroll the Gantt chart to task 1.

4. Use the Copy Picture feature to create a GIF file of the screen. Save the GIF image as **SBPlan.gif**.

5. Switch to Task Usage view, and then set up the columns to show Task Name, Work, and Duration. Hide the Indicators and Task Mode columns, scroll to the first task, and then use the Copy Picture feature to create a GIF file of the screen.

6. Save the GIF image as **SBPlan-TU.gif**.

⊕ EXPLORE

7. Start PowerPoint and create a new blank presentation. On slide 1, type: **Templates for New Paltz Ventures** as the title and your name as the subtitle. In the Slides group, click the New Slide button to insert a blank slide 2, click the Insert Picture from File icon, and then insert the **SBPlan.gif** file you created. Title the slide **Small Business Plan Template**.

8. Use any PowerPoint skills you may have to enhance the slide.

9. Click the Home tab, and then, in the Slides group, click the New Slide button to insert a blank slide 3 using the Title and Content slide style. Title the slide **Small Business Plan Template Task Usage view**.

10. Click the Insert Picture from File icon to insert the **SBPlan-TU.gif** GIF file you created. Enhance the slide in any way.

11. Insert a fourth new slide, give the slide the title **Project Template Facts**, then click under the title and type three or four bullet points providing reasons why you might use this template. Save the file as **SBPlan.pptx**.

12. Switch to Project, show Outline Level 1 in Gantt Chart view, copy the four Project phase task names and durations, switch back to PowerPoint, and then copy them into a new Slide 5 using Paste Options-Picture. Title slide 5 as **Copy as Picture**.

13. Close the Project file, saving your changes.

14. Create a new project file based on another template of your choice. Explore the template to get a feel for its content and purpose. Change one resource to your name. Create a view that shows your name on the screen. Zoom the entire project. Use the Copy Picture feature to create a GIF file of the screen. Save the GIF image as **Template2.gif**.

15. Return to PowerPoint. Insert a new slide 6, and then paste the picture. Change the title to reflect the second template you explored. Save the file.

16. Add a concluding slide to your PowerPoint presentation. This slide might state the broad benefits of using templates. Save and then close the presentation.

17. Return to Project, and close the Project file without saving changes.

Apply your skills to integrate data for a career consulting firm.

CREATE

Case Problem 2

There are no Data Files needed for this Case Problem.

Delaware21   As the office manager for Delaware21, an environmental watch organization in New Castle County, Delaware, you help the firm provide outreach and educational services for businesses that have to attain compliance with the new laws regulating the environmental impact of business in the community. Delaware21 has a large training department that gets people up to speed on the software they use to provide services to their clients. You are currently using Project 2010 to manage the upgrade to the latest version of Microsoft Office for the business. You'll use the Infrastructure Deployment template to quickly create a project file to manage this large effort. Then you'll use this file to explore various ways to share the Project 2010 information with other Office 2010 applications. To complete this case, you will need Word and Excel installed on your computer. You will also need Internet access. Complete the following:

1. Open Backstage view in Project, and click the New tab. In the Search Office.com for templates box, type **Infrastructure Deployment**, and then press Enter.

2. Create a new project based on the Infrastructure deployment plan template.

3. Change the project Start date to **1/15/15** in the Project Information dialog box, and then save the project file as **OffDep-6.mpp** to the Project6\Case2 folder included with your Data Files.

4. Adjust column width to fit the content, and then zoom as needed to see the entire Gantt chart.

5. In the Entry table, replace Template in the task name in row 1 with your name.

6. In the Resource Sheet, add your name as the last resource, enter **$50** per hour as the standard rate for the first resource, and then use the Fill Handle to enter a standard rate of $50 per hour for the remaining resources.

7. In Gantt Chart view, show Outline Level 2, and then zoom out on the Gantt chart to see the Entire Project.

8. Drag the split bar so that you can see the Duration and Start columns, and then scroll the Gantt chart so that you can see the summary bars.

9. Copy the Gantt Chart view as a GIF file, and then it to the Project6\Case2 folder with the filename **OffDep-6.GIF**.

10. Start your browser and go to *www.microsoft.com/office*. Research five interesting facts about Microsoft Office 2010. You will use this information to help motivate the employees as they make the transition to Office 2010. Find facts that are relevant for a new user who is learning how to use Office 2010, especially Word, Excel, and Outlook.

11. Start Word, and in a new blank document, type the results of your research on the new products in Microsoft Office 2010. Then add a new paragraph: **Project planning for the Office deployment detailed above is almost complete. The following figure shows the major phases of the project. I will continue to provide information regarding the status of deployment as the project progresses.** Press the Enter key two times, and then type your name.

12. Press the Enter key, click the Insert tab, and then, in the Illustrations group, click the Picture button.

13. Navigate to the Project6\Case2 folder, and then double-click the **OffDep-6.GIF** file.

14. Proofread, preview, and then print the Word document as requested. Save the Word document as **OffDep-6.docx** in the Project6\Case2 folder, and then exit Word.

15. In the **OffDep-6.mpp** Project file, insert a hyperlink for the Infrastructure Deployment Your Name task (task 1). Link the hyperlink to the **OffDep-6.docx** file in the Project6\Case2 folder.

16. Show all subtasks.

17. Apply the Entry table if it is not the active table, and then drag the split bar so that the Duration field is the last field visible in the Entry table.

EXPLORE 18. Insert a flag field to the left of the Duration column. Right-click the Flag1 field, and then click Field Settings. Change the title to **Manager Approval**, and then right-align the title using the Field Settings dialog box.

19. Change the Review Current Infrastructure task (task 9) Manager approval cell to Yes, and then do the same for the Design task (task 36).

20. Show Outline Level 2, and then display the Finish column.

21. Switch to Resource Sheet view, and then enter the following changes to the hourly costs in the Ovt Rate cell for these four resources:
    - Your name $80/hour
    - Project management $75/hour
    - Deployment resources $50/hour
    - Management $100/hour

22. Switch to Gantt Chart view, and then insert the Cost field to the right of the Duration column.

EXPLORE 23. Select the task name Scope (task 2) through the task name Post Implementation Review (task 95), press and hold the Ctrl key, click the Scope (task 2) Cost cell, drag through the Post Implementation Review (task 95) Cost cell, release the Ctrl key, right-click, and then click Copy Cell to copy the selected data.

24. Start Excel, and then paste the task names and costs for the summary tasks into the first two columns. Widen each column as needed so that you can see all of the cost data in the workbook.

EXPLORE 25. Create chart of your choosing that makes sense for the data based on all of the pasted data. Create a title, and format the legend. Use Formatting and Layout tools available to enhance the chart so it looks attractive.

26. Enter your name in an empty cell in the worksheet. Preview the chart, and then print it if requested.

27. Save the workbook as **Costs.xlsx** in the Project6\Case2 folder.

28. Exit Excel, close the browser window, and then close the Project file, saving changes if prompted.

Use your skills to create a new project for an animal shelter.

CREATE

Case Problem 3

There are no Data Files needed for this Case Problem.

Brooklyn Fur&Paws Shelter   You have recently been hired by the animal shelter Brooklyn Fur&Paws Shelter. Your experience using Project 2010 to plan projects will be very useful as you help them expand the shelter's services and organize resources by using project management software. You will create a master project that contains two subprojects for the shelter. Complete the following:

1. Create a new blank project file, and then set the new tasks mode to Auto Scheduled.
2. Open the Project Information dialog box. Change the Start date to **10/1/14** and the Current date to **9/1/14**, and then close the Project Information dialog box. Close the Timeline.
3. Save the file as **BFMaster** in the Project6\Case3 folder included with your Data Files.
4. Create a new blank project file, set the new tasks mode to Auto Scheduled, close the Timeline, and then open the Project Information dialog box.
5. In the Project Information dialog box, change the Start date to **10/1/14** and the Current date to **9/1/14**, and then save it as **Cats-6** in the Project6\Case3 folder. This new project is the first of the two subprojects.
6. Enter the following three tasks: **Organize spaying clinic**, **2 days**; **Sign up volunteers**, **2 days**; and **Determine food supplier**, **1 day**.
7. Select the three tasks, then link them as Finish-to-Start dependencies to create the relationships.
8. Create a new blank project file, set the new tasks mode to **Auto Scheduled**, close the Timeline, and then open the Project Information dialog box. Change the Start date to **10/1/14** and the Current date to **9/1/14**, and then save it as **Dogs-6** in the Project6\Case3 folder. This new project is the second of the two subprojects. Note that both new projects use the same Start date and Current date.
9. Enter the same three tasks that you entered in the Cats file: **Organize spaying clinic**, **Sign up volunteers**, and **Determine food supplier.** Set the duration as 1 day for each task, and then link the three tasks. You now have the three project files that you need: a master project file and two subproject files.
10. Switch to the BFMaster-6.mpp file. Click the row 1 Task Name cell, and then open the Insert Project dialog box. The files in the Project6\Case3 folder should be listed in the dialog box.
11. Click **Cats-6.mpp**, and then click the Insert button. The Cats project file is inserted as the first task in the master project file. The Project 2010 icon appears in the Indicators column.
12. Point to the Project 2010 Indicator in row 1. The ScreenTip that appears tells you that this is an inserted project and displays its path.
13. Insert the file **Dogs-6.mpp** as the second subproject in the second row of the BFMaster.mpp project file.
14. Expand all the tasks and widen the columns as needed to fit content, and then drag the split bar to the right of the Predecessors column.
15. Link the **Cats-6** task to the **Dogs-6** task.
16. Collapse the subprojects so you see only the summary task bars for the two subprojects.
17. Add a task at the master level. Use the Insert Milestone button to insert the new task **Budget approvals** milestone task above the Cats-6 summary task, and then move the milestone task below row 3. Click any empty cell to deselect the milestone task.
18. Link the **Dogs-6** task to the Budget approvals task.

19. Show all subtasks to view the expanded master project.

20. Insert a new task above the Organize spaying clinic task in the Cats-6 subproject. Type **Organize rabies clinic** as the Task Name. The task has a duration of 2 days.

21. Switch to the Cats-6.mpp file and verify that the new task was entered into that file.

22. Switch back to the master project file. Drag the split bar so the Duration column is the last column showing.

23. Set a baseline in the master project for the entire project.

⊕ **EXPLORE** 24. You can create hyperlinks in a Project file to a Web page. Find a Web page for an animal shelter in your area. Create a hyperlink from the Budget approvals task in the BFMaster file to the local shelter Web site.

25. Test the hyperlink.

⊕ **EXPLORE** 26. In the BFMaster file, view the Network Diagram, open a copy of the Standard data template, and rename the data template **MyBFTemplate**. Make some changes to the template (such as the font used for field names, the alignment of fields, and which fields are displayed), and then close the dialog box.

27. Add your name to the left section of the headers for all three Gantt charts. Print the Gantt Chart views if requested.

28. Save your changes to all the files, and close all the files.

Expand your skills to work on a fundraising project.

CHALLENGE

Case Problem 4

Data File needed for this Case Problem: Grant-6.mpp

NatureSpace Your job at NatureSpace has been rewarding. The project is complete and it was a success. The playground is built, and the kids and adults are thrilled with the outcome. Other towns in the state are looking to build similar playgrounds. A departing employee asked that you review a file she created to serve as a model. The project had three main phases: Planning, Fundraising, and Building. The Building Committee wants to be able to manage any new building by having the Building phase in a separate Project 2010 file. You'll break the Building phase tasks into their own project file and link that file back to the **Grant-6** master project file as a subproject. Complete the following:

1. Open the file **Grant-6** located in the Project6\Case4 folder included with your Data Files, and then save the project as **MyGrant-6** in the same folder.

2. Change the Your Name resource to your name and the initials YN to your initials.

3. In Gantt Chart view, select rows 9 through 11 (Choose contractor through Build playground), use the Cut command to cut the tasks, and then click **Yes** in the warning box that opens.

4. Create a new blank project, change the task mode to Auto Scheduled tasks, close the Timeline, schedule the project from the Finish date, and then change the Finish date to **9/6/14**.

⊕ **EXPLORE** 5. Paste the tasks you cut into the first three rows in the new project.

6. Save the new project with the name **Bldg-6** in the Project6\Case4 folder.

7. Switch to the MyGrant-6 project file, delete Building task 8, and then click **Yes** in the warning box that opens.

8. Insert the Bldg-6 project as a subproject in row 8, so that it appears at the same level as the Planning and Fundraising summary tasks.

9. Link the Fundraising summary task and the Bldg-6 summary task, and then expand the Bldg-6 Summary task to view the subtasks.

10. Preview Gantt Chart view, add your name left-aligned in the header, and then print the first page if requested.

11. Save the changes to all the files.

EXPLORE 12. Create a new resource pool file with the name of two of your friends. Add any information you want for these two new resources. Name the file **ParkPool.mpp**.

13. Switch to MyGrant-6, and share resources between the MyGrant-6 and ParkPool files. Be sure precedence goes to pool, and then review the resource sheet to confirm the two resources from the PoolPark file were added.

14. Switch to the ParkPool file, and then verify resources have been added to the file.

15. Switch to MyGrant-6, display Gantt Chart view, add the task **Playground complete** as a milestone task, and then move it to be the last task in the master project.

16. Save and close all open files.

ENDING DATA FILES

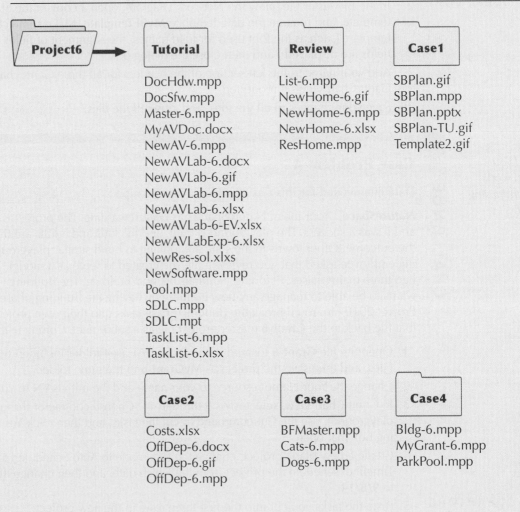

Project6 →

Tutorial
DocHdw.mpp
DocSfw.mpp
Master-6.mpp
MyAVDoc.docx
NewAV-6.mpp
NewAVLab-6.docx
NewAVLab-6.gif
NewAVLab-6.mpp
NewAVLab-6.xlsx
NewAVLab-6-EV.xlsx
NewAVLabExp-6.xlsx
NewRes-sol.xlxs
NewSoftware.mpp
Pool.mpp
SDLC.mpp
SDLC.mpt
TaskList-6.mpp
TaskList-6.xlsx

Review
List-6.mpp
NewHome-6.gif
NewHome-6.mpp
NewHome-6.xlsx
ResHome.mpp

Case1
SBPlan.gif
SBPlan.mpp
SBPlan.pptx
SBPlan-TU.gif
Template2.gif

Case2
Costs.xlsx
OffDep-6.docx
OffDep-6.gif
OffDep-6.mpp

Case3
BFMaster.mpp
Cats-6.mpp
Dogs-6.mpp

Case4
Bldg-6.mpp
MyGrant-6.mpp
ParkPool.mpp

Teamwork

Working with a Team to Create a Project File

Teamwork is a collaborative process that requires managers and nonmanagers to work together to achieve a common goal or outcome. It usually involves setting aside individual prominence for the greater good of the team's collective work. Teamwork may involve collaboration among internal members of an organization, or it may cut across company boundaries to include customers, suppliers, or other organizations.

Teamwork is a critical skill because, with few exceptions, most organizations rely heavily on teams to complete tasks. Learning the different roles team members play, how they complement each other for efficient task completion, and how to lead and motivate a team toward goal achievement can mean the difference between professional success and failure. Whether the teams are ad hoc and short-lived or ongoing and strategic, the ability to work effectively on a team is a professional skill everyone needs to develop. Developing strong teamwork skills may lead to team leadership positions and eventually to career progression into larger managerial roles.

What Is a Team?

Growing up you may have participated in group sports or academic activities such as the debate team or glee club. In a work environment or in school, you may have been assigned a group project and worked with others as part of a team. But what exactly is a team?

The American Heritage Dictionary describes a **team** as a "group organized to work together." Teams are more than just people in a group. In fact, teams consist of individuals who have skills, talents, and abilities that complement each other. When joined in a team, members produce **synergy**—which is the working together of two or more people to produce results that are greater than the results a single individual could achieve. It is this sense of shared mission and responsibility for results that makes a team successful in its efforts to reach organizational goals.

Types of Teams

Organizations support various types of teams. Some are formal, while others are more informal. Some meet in person; others have members who have never met face-to-face. Depending on the work you do, the type of teams you participate in will vary. Knowing a little bit about each type of team can help make you a more valued member of any team. **Formal teams** are organized within the company as part of its official structure. A **virtual team** is one whose members rarely, if ever, meet in person to work on team tasks. Instead, technology makes it possible for members to be geographically distant yet work as if everyone was in the same room. When team members are across country borders and span the globe, they are often referred to as **global teams**. Global teams are usually virtual teams as well, but virtual teams do not have to be global teams. **Informal teams or groups** sometimes arise in the workplace when the members themselves join forces to solve a problem, work on a task, or simply meet to talk over lunch. Since they are not appointed by management and their duties are not specifically outlined in job descriptions, there is little or no direct accountability or reporting of results to the organization.

ProSkills

Characteristics of Teams

Have you ever heard someone say he is a "team player?" Members on a team should get to know how the other team members work, so that each person's contribution to the mission will have the most value. On a football team, not everyone plays the role of quarterback; the team needs other players working with the quarterback if touchdowns are to be scored. However, before the first play is ever made, the members bring their skills to the group and spend time learning each others' moves so they can catch the pass, block, or run toward the goal line. They learn how to work together toward their common goal of winning the game. The best teams have members whose background, skills, and abilities complement each other. The following are tips for successfully working on teams:

- Remember that everyone brings something of value to the team.
- Respect and support each other as you work toward the common goal.
- Try to see criticism or questions from the other person's perspective before taking offense or jumping to conclusions.
- Seek ways to encourage or support a team member who needs assistance so the team's work is not affected.
- Decide early which communication technologies the team will use to keep the flow of information moving smoothly.
- Deal with negative or unproductive attitudes immediately so they don't damage the team's energy and attitude.
- Get outside assistance if team members can't move beyond the obstacle facing them.
- Provide periodic positive encouragement or rewards for contributions.

PROSKILLS

Create a Project File for a Residential Move

Most people have changed their place of residence at least once by the time they become adults. More often than not, moving from one home to another happens several times during a person's life. Moving can be simple, for example, a college student moving from one dorm room to another. A move can be slightly more involved, such as a couple moving from one apartment to another in the same city. Or, it can be quite complex, such as a family selling a home in one state, purchasing a home in another state, packing, and moving. No matter how large or small the move, tasks and teams are involved. Moving demands teamwork from the people who prepare for the move, the people who plan and organize the move, the people who do the actual work of the move, and the people settle those who have moved. A move involves such broad phases as finding a new location, signing a lease, or buying and closing on a new home, and contacting utility companies. Tasks include specific actions such as sorting, disposing of unwanted items, packing, cleaning, and possibly painting before the move. Some tasks, such as unpacking, storing, and disposing of packing containers occur after the move. Fortunately, Microsoft Project can help organize and track the tasks, resources, and costs of a move as well as help with the planning and management.

ProSkills

In this ProSkills exercise, you'll use Project to create a project file that will contain information of your choice, using the Project skills and features presented in Tutorials 1–6. As you develop the Project file, think about the team you will have to assemble to reach your goal of a cost-effective and efficient residential move.

Note: Please be sure *not* to include any personal information of a sensitive nature in the project file you create because the file for this exercise is intended to be submitted to your instructor. Later on, you can update the project file with such information for your personal use.

1. Think about a future move in your life. Alternatively, you can refer to a recent move and use information from that experience to build this project.

2. Identify your team members, that is who will work with you to successfully make this move. Meet with your team to discuss the plan and who is responsible for each aspect of the project.

3. Start Project and begin a new file. If you are planning a future move, plan the project using the date you have to move into the new residence as the project Finish date; otherwise, use today's date and plan it from a Start date.

4. Enter the task names and durations for all of the tasks. Be sure to create a project file with at least 20 tasks. You can add tasks as you work on this file. Organize the tasks into summary tasks and subtasks. Enter milestone tasks. Enter any recurring tasks that might be part of the move.

5. Link the tasks. Think about the relationships between the tasks and enter any lag or lead time.

6. Enter deadlines or special constraints for any of the tasks.

7. Create a task calendar that accounts for at least one nonworking holiday during the move. For example, consider the team members who may observe personal or religious holidays during the length of this project. Assign the calendar to a task.

8. View the network diagram and review the critical tasks. Make some adjustments to shorten the critical path.

9. Think about the resources you need for the move. Assign at least three different group designations to the resources. Add the resources and any costs to the resource sheet. Add material resources, such as boxes, tape, and bubble-wrap to the project file in addition to the work resources.

10. Assign resources to the tasks. Check for overallocations and level any overallocations. Be mindful of the schedule.

11. Change the working hours for one of the resources. For example, maybe the movers can work over a weekend or after 5 pm on a weekday.

12. Add any fixed costs associated with the project, such as a permit fee.

13. Create a resource pool file with at least two new resources that you can use for other projects. Use fictitious names if necessary. Share the pool resources with the moving project file. Be sure the pool file is identified as the "Pool takes precedence" file when the resources are shared. Assign the two shared resources to some of the tasks in the moving project file.

14. Format the network diagram so that it is pleasant to view and provides any additional information you might need in each box.

15. Format Gantt Chart view to show milestones and summary tasks with special formatting. Add text to the bars.

16. Create a custom view that includes a view of the grouped resources based on the By group filter.

17. Create one new table in the file, and then use the Copy Picture feature to create a GIF file of the table. Import the GIF file into Word or PowerPoint and then point out what makes your table a custom table. Insert a hyperlink from the Project file to the Word or PowerPoint document.

18. Set a baseline, and then save the file.

19. Print at least two reports for the Project file, and then print Gantt Chart and Network Diagram views.

20. Imagine that time is passing and you are updating the project. Work with the file to see what happens if you fall behind schedule or if tasks occur ahead of schedule. Use the Tracking and Variance tables. Print each view for each new status date as you update the file.

21. Create and save a custom view. Create and save a custom table.

22. Link cost data to an Excel spreadsheet file. Use the Excel charting tool to create a graph of the cost data.

23. Print the Gantt chart, the network diagram, and the calendar for the project.

24. Close the file and then exit Project 2010.

GLOSSARY/INDEX

sharing
> data templates, PRJ 405–408
> resources between project files, PRJ 412–414

Sheet view A spreadsheet-like representation of data in which each task is displayed as a row and each piece of information (field) about the task is represented by a column. PRJ 32, PRJ 33

shortening a critical path
> by changing calendars and task constraints, PRJ 186–189
> by changing task information, PRJ 179–185
> costs and risk, PRJ 266

slack The amount of time that a task may be delayed from its scheduled start date without delaying the entire project. PRJ 38, PRJ 138, PRJ 239
> critical path, free slack, and total slack related, PRJ 266–268
> defining critical path using, PRJ 138–139

slack bar A bar on the Gantt chart used to represent slack. PRJ 149

slip. *See* slippage

slippage The difference between a task's scheduled Start or Finish date and its baseline Start or Finish date when the project falls behind schedule. Also called slip. PRJ 338–340

Smart Tag A button that appears when you delete a task or resource, change resource assignments, or change Start or Finish dates, work, units, or durations and that displays options to help you complete the action. PRJ 81, PRJ 82

SNET. *See* Start No Earlier Than constraint

SNLT. *See* Start No Later Than constraint

software, project management, benefits, PRJ 9–13

sort To reorder the resources or tasks in a sheet in an ascending or descending order based on the values of a field. PRJ 241–242

source file The file from which an object is linked, copied, or embedded. PRJ 362, PRJ 363, PRJ 388

split a task To interrupt the work on a task so that there is a period of time when no work is being done on the task, and then work begins on that task again; splitting a task adds a delay to a project. PRJ 246, PRJ 286, PRJ 314
> tasks lending themselves to, PRJ 314

split bar The vertical bar that divides the table and the Gantt chart in Gantt chart view. PRJ 3

split screen view, work task form, PRJ 220–223

Split Task button, PRJ 295

split window A view in which the screen is split into two parts (two views); the top view is often Gantt Chart view, and the bottom view is often a form view. PRJ 39–41

SS. *See* Start-to-Start

Standard calendar A calendar used to schedule tasks within the project that specifies Monday through Friday as working days with eight hours of work completed each day and Saturday and Sunday as nonworking days. PRJ 60, PRJ 68–77
> changing, PRJ 68–73

Standard data template The template that provides default formatting for the Project file. PRJ 401

Start column, PRJ 28

Start date The day on which the project will start. PRJ 7
> enter work to calculate, PRJ 308
> entering, PRJ 307

Start No Earlier Than (SNET) constraint, PRJ 187

Start No Later Than (SNLT) constraint, PRJ 187

Start-to-Finish (SF) A dependency type that specifies that the first task must start before the second task can finish. PRJ 100, PRJ 108

Start-to-Start (SS) A dependency type that specifies that the first task must start before the second task can start. PRJ 99, PRJ 100, PRJ 108

statistics, monitoring progress, PRJ 295–296

status bar, PRJ 2

Status date A date for which you enter the progress information for a given project; helps determine how project progress is measured when tasks are updated and rescheduled. PRJ 291–292
> entering, PRJ 292–293

Std. Rate field, Resource Sheet view, PRJ 205

subproject A project file that is inserted as tasks into a master project. PRJ 395, PRJ 416
> creating, PRJ 417–418
> inserting into master project, PRJ 418–419

subtask, PRJ 98

successor task A task that cannot be completed until after a given task has completed; the second task described in a dependency. PRJ 7, PRJ 100

summary bar, PRJ 135

Summary Table view, PRJ 33

summary task A grouping of tasks that logically belong together. Summary tasks are listed in bold text in the Task Entry table. Each display a Collapse/Expand button to its left so that showing or hiding the task can easily be done within that phase. Also called phase. PRJ 98, PRJ 99, PRJ 114–122
> creating, PRJ 115–118
> expanding and collapsing, PRJ 120–122
> nesting, PRJ 120

summary task bar A bar representing a summary task in the Gantt chart. PRJ 99, PRJ 116

synergy The working together of two or more people to produce results that are greater than those results a single individual could achieve. PRJ 441

systems development lifecycle (SDLC) model A model commonly used to manage the development of a new information system that has between five and seven stages that roughly equate to the phases within a project: project definition, evaluation of current process, design, construction, installation, and evaluation; it can be modified and applied to almost any project. PRJ 398

T

table A format applied to a sheet to display different fields. PRJ 32
> custom. *See* custom table
> navigating, PRJ 78

Table Definition dialog box, PRJ 327, PRJ 330–331, PRJ 409

Table view, PRJ 32, PRJ 33

task A specific action that needs to be completed within the project. PRJ 7
> assigning costs, PRJ 235–236
> assigning material resources, PRJ 264–265
> assigning resources, PRJ 214–223, PRJ 227–231
> calendars. *See* task calendar
> critical, PRJ 102

TASK REFERENCE

TASK	PAGE #	RECOMMENDED METHOD
Action, undo	PRJ 83	Click
Action, redo	PRJ 83	Click
AutoFilter, use	PRJ 144	*See* Reference box: Using the AutoFilter
AutoFilter, use Custom dialog box	PRJ 146	Click View tab, click Filter arrow, click Display AutoFilter, click AutoFilter arrow on a column in the Entry table, point to Filters, click Custom, complete Custom AutoFilter dialog box
Backstage View, open	PRJ 25	Click File tab
Bar, format	PRJ 155	*See* Reference box: Formatting Individual Items in the Entry Table and Bars in the Gantt Chart
Bar Styles, format	PRJ 148	*See* Reference box: Applying Format Changes to Bars for a Task Category in a Gantt Chart; or Click Gantt Chart Tools Format tab, click Format button, click Bar Styles, complete dialog box
Baseline and Variance information, compare	PRJ 290	Right-click Select All button for a task table, click Variance
Baseline, clear	PRJ 328	Click Project tab, click Set Baseline button, click Clear Baseline, click OK
Baseline, set	PRJ 289	Click Project tab, click Set Baseline button, click Set Baseline, click OK
Calculation options, view	PRJ 311	Click File tab, click Options, click Advanced; or Click File tab, click Options, click Schedule
Calendar, view	PRJ 33	Click View tab, in Task Views group, click Calendar button
Calendar view, change	PRJ 90	Click View tab, in Task Views group click Calendar button, then use tools on the Calendar Tools Format tab and in Month pane to customize Calendar view
Column, hide in table	PRJ 63	Right-click column heading, click Hide Column
Column, insert in table	PRJ 123	Right-click column heading, click Insert Column, type field name, press Enter key; or In Entry table, drag split bar to reveal Add New Column column, click Add New Column arrow, scroll list, click desired field name, click OK
Cost rate table, change for a task	PRJ 218	Click View tab, click Task Usage button, double-click the resource for the task, in Assignment Information dialog box click General tab, click Cost rate table arrow, make changes as needed, click OK
Costs, enter fixed	PRJ 265	*See* Reference box: Entering Fixed Costs
Critical path, techniques to shorten	PRJ 179	*See* bullet list on page
Critical path, shorten by changing task durations	PRJ 180	Click Duration cell for a critical task, enter a reasonable smaller number
Critical path, shorten by changing constraints	PRJ 188	*See* Reference box: Changing the Constraints to Shorten the Critical Path
Critical path, shorten by changing dependencies	PRJ 182	*See* Reference box: Changing Dependencies to Shorten the Critical Path
Critical path, shorten by changing lag time	PRJ 183	*See* Reference box: Adding Negative Lag to Shorten the Critical Path

TASK	PAGE #	RECOMMENDED METHOD
Critical path, shorten by changing the calendar	PRJ 186	*See* Reference box: Applying a Calendar to a Task to Shorten the Critical Path
Critical path, shorten by changing type of dependency	PRJ 184	*See* Reference box: Changing the Type of Dependency to Shorten the Critical Path
Custom field, create	PRJ 428–430	Right-click column heading that is to the right where you want new column, click Custom Fields, click field, in Custom Fields dialog box specify all attributes, click OK; or Select a column, click Project tab, click the Custom Fields button, click Field, specify the attributes, click OK
Custom cost field, create as lookup table	PRJ 431–432	Define Cost field and insert into table, click Project tab, click the Custom Fields button, in the Custom Fields dialog box click Rename button, name the field, click OK, in the Custom attributes section of Custom Fields dialog box, click the Lookup button to open the Edit Lookup Table dialog box, enter values in each row, press Enter key, click Close, click OK
Custom table, create	PRJ 329	*See* Reference box: Creating a New Table
Custom view, create	PRJ 333	*See* Reference box: Creating a Custom View
Data template, create	PRJ 402	*See* Reference box: Creating and Applying a Data Template
Data template, share	PRJ 406	*See* Reference box: Sharing a Data Template
Date range, filter	PRJ 142	Click View tab, click Filter arrow, click Date Range, click in Date Range dialog box, type date after which you want to filter or click arrow and select date on calendar, click OK, click in Date Range dialog box, type date before which you want to filter or click arrow and select date on calendar, click OK
Deadline constraint, set	PRJ 342	*See* Reference box: Setting a Deadline Constraint
Dependencies, create	PRJ 101	*See* Reference box: Linking Tasks with an FS Dependency in Gantt Chart View; or Select tasks to link, click 🔗
Dependencies, delete	PRJ 105	Double-click link line in chart, click Delete; or In the Entry table, click and drag to select tasks, click Task tab, click Unlink Tasks button 🔗 in the Schedule group
Detail Gantt chart, view	PRJ 339	Click View tab, click the Gantt Chart button arrow, click More Views, click Detail Gantt in the More Views dialog box, click Apply
Duration, change in calendar	PRJ 91	Drag end of task bar in calendar
Duration, change in entry table	PRJ 88	Select number in Duration cell, type new number; or Click Duration cell up or down arrow for duration you want to change
Duration, change in Gantt chart	PRJ 89	Drag end of task bar in Gantt chart
Duration, change in network diagram	PRJ 90	Click task box in network diagram, click Duration cell, type new duration value
Duration, change in split view	PRJ 40	Click Duration cell, type a number; or Click Duration cell up or down arrow for the duration you want to change
Earned Value Data, export to Excel	PRJ 376	*See* Reference box: Exporting Earned Value Data to Excel
Earned Value Data, view	PRJ 375	Right-click Select All button of any task table, click More Tables, click Earned Value in More Tables dialog box, click Apply

TASK	PAGE #	RECOMMENDED METHOD
Entry bar, show or hide	PRJ 167	*See* Insight box: A Familiar Interface: the Entry Bar; or Click File tab, click Options, click Display tab, click Entry bar check box
Entry table, format individual items	PRJ 155	*See* Reference box: Formatting Individual Items in the Entry Table and Bars in the Gantt Chart
Entry table, format task category	PRJ 152	*See* Reference box: Applying Formatting to Text for a Task Category in an Entry Table
Excel data, import into Project file	PRJ 381	*See* Reference box: Importing Excel Data into a Project 2010 File
Excel data, link to Project file	PRJ 388	*See* Reference box: Linking Excel Data to a Project 2010 File
Excel task list template, use	PRJ 378	In Excel, click File tab, click New, click Sample templates, click Microsoft Project Task List Import Template icon, click Create
Finish date, enter	PRJ 21–22	Click Project tab, click Project Information button, click Schedule from arrow, click Project Finish Date, enter Finish date, click OK
Fixed costs, enter	PRJ 265	*See* Reference box: Entering Fixed Costs
Fixed-duration task, create	PRJ 233	*See* Reference box: Creating a Fixed-Duration Task That Is Not Effort Driven
Flag field, add	PRJ 430	*See* Reference box: Using a Flag Field on a Sheet View
Gantt chart, annotate	PRJ 391	Click Gantt Chart Tools Format tab, click Drawing button, click Text Box tool, draw a box, type text
Gantt chart, change print settings	PRJ 47	Click File tab, click Print, specify options in Backstage view, click Page Setup link, set options in Page Setup dialog, click OK
Gantt chart, copy as a GIF	PRJ 369	Click Task tab, click Copy button arrow 📋 ▾, click Copy Picture, click To GIF image file option button in Copy Picture dialog box, click Browse, navigate to desired folder, click OK, click OK
Gantt chart, copy as a picture	PRJ 366	*See* Reference box: Copying a Picture
Gantt chart, format	PRJ 148	*See* Reference box: Applying Format Changes to Bars for a Task Category in a Gantt Chart
Gantt chart, print preview	PRJ 47	Click File tab, click Print
Gridlines, format	PRJ 158	Click Gantt Chart Tools Format tab, click Gridlines button, click Gridlines, click line type in Line to change list, click Type arrow and click style, click Color arrow and click color box, click At interval option button, set other options to meet your needs, click OK
Help, access help system	PRJ 52	See Proskills box: Problem-Solving: Getting Help; or Click 🔵
Hyperlink, insert	PRJ 425	*See* Reference box: Adding a Hyperlink
Interim plan	PRJ 303	*See* Reference box: Saving an Interim Plan
Lag and Lead Times, enter	PRJ 110	*See* Reference box: Entering Lag Time
Leveling tools, use	PRJ 258	*See* Reference box: Leveling Overallocations Using the Leveling Tools
Link lines, format	PRJ 159	Click Gantt Chart Tools Format tab, click Layout button, set desired options, click OK
Master Project, create	PRJ 416	*See* Reference box: Creating a Master Project
Material resources, assign to tasks	PRJ 262	*See* Reference box: Identifying a Resource as a Material or Work Cost

TASK	PAGE #	RECOMMENDED METHOD
Material resources, enter	PRJ 265	Click View tab, click Resource Sheet button, click a Resource Name cell and type name of the resource, click the Type cell for that resource and click Material, press Tab key, continue to enter information about resource
Milestone, insert	PRJ 94	Click Task tab, click the Task Name cell in the table where you want to insert Milestone, click Insert Milestone button in the Insert group, enter task name
Multiple Level Undo, change default options	PRJ 83	Click File tab, click Options, click Advanced tab, change number in Undo levels box, click OK
Network Diagram view, change to	PRJ 35	Click View tab, click the Network Diagram button
Network Diagram, format individual tasks	PRJ 176	*See* Reference box: Formatting an Individual Task in Network Diagram View
Network Diagram, format tasks of one type	PRJ 175	*See* Reference box: Formatting All Tasks of One Type in Network Diagram View
Note, enter for resource	PRJ 209	Double-click resource, click Notes tab in Resource Information dialog box, click Notes box, type note, click OK
Note, enter for task	PRJ 35–36	Double-click task, click Notes tab in Task Information dialog box, click Notes box, type note, click OK
Organizer, display	PRJ 409	Click File tab, click Info, click Organizer
Organizer, use to change Global.MPT file	PRJ 408	*See* Reference box: Using the Organizer to Change the Global.MPT File
Outlook tasks, import into Project file	PRJ 384	*See* Reference box: Importing Outlook Tasks into a Project 2010 File; or Click Task tab, click Task button arrow, click Import Outlook Tasks
Overallocations, level	PRJ 247	*See* Reference box: Examining and Adjusting Overallocations
Overallocations, level using Task Entry form	PRJ 250	*See* Reference box: Adjusting Overallocations by Assigning More Resources to Tasks
Print codes, enter	PRJ 50–51	Click File tab, click Print, click Page Setup link, click Header or Footer tab, click in Alignment box, click buttons or type codes, click OK
Progress lines, add	PRJ 343	*See* Reference box: Displaying Progress Lines; or Click Gantt Chart Tools Format tab, click Gridlines button, click Progress Lines, complete dialog box
Progress, update	PRJ 298–303	*See* Reference box: Updating Progress Using the Update Tasks Dialog Box; or Updating tasks using the Update Tasks dialog box: Click the task to update, click Task tab, click Mark on Track button arrow in the Schedule group, click Update Tasks, select settings in Update Tasks dialog box, click OK; or Using the Tracking buttons in the Schedule group and Tasks group on Task tab: Click task you want to update, click button in the Schedule group or Task group; or Drag 📊▸ on the Gantt Chart bar
Project, save first time	PRJ 25	*See* Reference box: Saving a Project for the First Time
Project, update	PRJ 319	*See* Reference box: Updating the Project Using the Update Project Dialog Box
Project 2010 file, export to Excel	PRJ 371	*See* Reference box: Exporting a Project 2010 File to Excel

TASK	PAGE #	RECOMMENDED METHOD
Project calendar, create an exception	PRJ 68	*See* Reference box: Creating an Exception to the Project Calendar
Project file, exit	PRJ 51	Click the File tab, click Exit
Project file, open an existing	PRJ 30	*See* Reference box: Opening an Existing Project
Project file, save with new name	PRJ 31	*See* Reference box: Saving a Project with a New Name
Project Information, view	PRJ 21–22	Click Project tab, in the Properties group, click Project Information
Project Properties, view and edit	PRJ 273	*See* Reference box: Reviewing Project Properties
Project statistics, display	PRJ 289	Click File tab, click Info, click Project Information arrow, click Project Statistics; or Click Project tab, click Project Information button, click Statistics button
Project status date, enter	PRJ 292	*See* Reference box: Entering a Project Status Date
Project summary task bar, create	PRJ 119	Click Gantt Chart Tools Format tab, click Project Summary Task check box
Recurring task, enter	PRJ 92	*See* Reference box: Entering Recurring Tasks
Relationship diagram, view	PRJ 37	Select task, click Task tab, click Gantt Chart button arrow, click More Views, double-click Relationship Diagram in More Views dialog box
Report, create custom	PRJ 268	*See* Reference box: Creating a Custom Report
Report, display custom	PRJ 268	*See* Reference box: Creating a Custom Report
Report, edit	PRJ 268	*See* Reference box: Creating a Custom Report
Report, view	PRJ 136	Click Project tab, click Reports button, click report category icon, click Select, click report, click Select
Resource Information, enter and edit	PRJ 204	*See* Reference box: Entering and Editing Resources
Resource Pool, use	PRJ 412	*See* Reference box: Sharing Existing Resources with a Resource Pool File
Resource Usage view, use	PRJ 240	Click View tab, click Resource Usage button
Resource, change units using Assign Resources dialog box	PRJ 217	Select task, click Assign Resources button, in Assign Resources dialog box click Units cell, type units, click Assign, click Close
Resources & Predecessors form, show	PRJ 40	Click View tab, click Details check box to open split screen view, right-click form in the bottom pane, click Resources & Predecessors
Resources, assign to tasks using Assign Resources dialog box	PRJ 215	*See* Reference box: Assigning Resources to Tasks Using the Assign Resources Button
Resources, assign to tasks using Resource Work Form	PRJ 221	*See* Reference box: Assigning Resources to Tasks Using Split Screen View
Resources, change working time	PRJ 208–209	Double-click resource to open Resource Information dialog box, click General tab, click Change Working Time button, complete Change Working Time dialog box options, click OK
Resources, collapse	PRJ 240	Click ▬
Resources, create custom group	PRJ 243–244	Click View tab, click Group By arrow, click New Group By, set options in Group Definition dialog box, click Apply
Resources, edit	PRJ 204	*See* Reference box: Entering and Editing Resources
Resources, enter	PRJ 204	*See* Reference box: Entering and Editing Resources
Resources, enter cost information	PRJ 208	Open Resource Information dialog box, click the Costs tab, click a cost rate table tab, enter information for standard and overtime rates

TASK	PAGE #	RECOMMENDED METHOD
Resource, expand	PRJ 240	Click ⊞
Resources, filter	PRJ 242–243	Click View tab, click Resource Usage button, click Filter button arrow, click criteria
Resources, group in Resource Sheet view	PRJ 211	Click the View tab, click Resource Sheet button, click Group By arrow in the Data group, click group
Resources, group in Resource Usage view	PRJ 243	Click the View tab, click Resource Usage button, click Group By arrow in the Data group, click desired group
Resources, sort	PRJ 241–242	Click desired Resource view, click Sort arrow in the Data group, click desired sort criteria
Schedule date options, change	PRJ 62	*See* Reference box: Changing Default Project Scheduling Options
Schedule task options, change	PRJ 62	*See* Insight box: The Difference Between Manually Scheduled and Auto Scheduled Tasks
Scheduling constraint, add	PRJ 188	Open Task Information dialog box , click Advanced tab, click Constraint type arrow, click constraint, click OK
Sheet Data, Copy from Project 2010 to Excel	PRJ 364	*See* Reference box: Copying Data from Project 2010 into an Excel Worksheet
Start date, enter	PRJ 21–22	Click Project tab, click Project Information button, verify Schedule from is set to Project Start Date, enter Start date, click OK
Start date, schedule from	PRJ 21–22	Click Project tab, click Project Information button, click Schedule from arrow, click Project Start Date, click OK
Subprojects, insert into a master project	PRJ 418–419	View Entry table in Gantt Chart view, click Task Name cell above which you want to insert subtask, click Project tab, click Subproject button, in the Insert Project dialog box navigate to drive and folder containing subproject file, select file, click Insert
Summary task, create	PRJ 115	*See* Reference box: Creating a Summary Task
Table, apply a new table	PRJ 38	Right-click Select All button, click desired table
Task, collapse or expand in the network diagram	PRJ 170	Click ⊟ or Click ⊞
Task, copy	PRJ 84	*See* Reference box: Cutting or Copying and Moving Tasks
Task, create in Network Diagram view	PRJ 165	Place pointer in blank area below where you want new task, drag to draw a box
Task, delete	PRJ 82	*See* Reference box: Deleting a Task or the Contents of a Cell in the Entry Table
Task, enter	PRJ 23–24	Click Task Name cell, type task name; or Click Task tab, click Task arrow, click Task
Task, enter in Network Diagram view	PRJ 164	*See* Reference box: Entering Tasks Using Network Diagram View
Task, filter in Network Diagram view	PRJ 174	In the Data group on the View tab, click Filter arrow, select filter as needed
Task, mark on track as scheduled	PRJ 298	Select task, click Task tab, click Mark on Track button
Task, move	PRJ 84	*See* Reference box: Cutting or Copying and Moving Tasks
Task, move in Network Diagram view	PRJ 171	*See* Reference box: Moving Tasks in Network Diagram View

TASK	PAGE #	RECOMMENDED METHOD
Task, outdent and indent	PRJ 115–116	Click ⬅ and ➡
Tasks, sort	PRJ 241	Click View tab, click Sort, click desired sort criteria
Task, update ahead of scheduled	PRJ 300	Apply Tracking table, enter % complete or actual dates in table; or Click Task tab, select tasks to be updated, click Mark on Track button arrow, click Update Tasks, enter % complete
Task calendar, create	PRJ 73	*See* Reference box: Creating a Task Calendar
Task cell, delete contents	PRJ 82	*See* Reference box: Deleting a Task or the Contents of a Cell in the Entry table
Task dependencies, create	PRJ 100–104 PRJ 106–108	Click task bar or box in Gantt chart view, then drag to task to link to; or In a table, select tasks to link, click 🔗; or In a split view, select task in a table or chart, right-click form, click Predecessors & Successors, enter tasks in the Predecessors or Successors fields in form, click OK
Task dependencies, delete	PRJ 105	Select the tasks, click ⬚
Task dependencies, edit	PRJ 108	*See* Reference box: *Editing Task Dependencies*; or Double-click link line, make changes in Task Dependency dialog box, click OK
Task entry mode, change	PRJ 21	Click Task tab, click Mode button, click Auto Schedule or Manually Schedule; or Click New Tasks button on status bar, click task mode; or Open Task Information dialog box, click General tab, click Task mode option button, click OK
Task group, show	PRJ 121	Click View tab, click Outline, click Outline level you want to show
Task information, change general information	PRJ 33–34	Double-click the task, click General tab in the Task Information dialog box, make changes as needed, click OK
Task Inspector, open or close	PRJ 181	Click Task tab, click Inspect button in the Tasks group
Template, create	PRJ 398	*See* Reference box: Creating a Project Template
Template, delete from Organizer	PRJ 410	Click File tab, click Info, click Organizer, click desired tab in Organizer dialog box, click template in the 'Global.MPT' box, click Delete, click Yes, click Close
Template, use	PRJ 396	*See* Reference box: Using a Project Template
Text, format	PRJ 152 PRJ 155	*See* Reference box: Applying Formatting to Text for a Task Category in an Entry Table and *See* Reference box: Formatting Individual Items in the Entry Table and Bars in the Gantt Chart
Timeline, hide	PRJ 18	Click the View tab, click Timeline check box; or Right-click Timeline, click Show Timeline
Timeline, show	PRJ 18	Click the View tab, click Timeline check box; or Right-click the view area (such as the Gantt chart area), click Show Timeline
Timescale, change the major and minor timescale	PRJ 45–46	Double-click Timescale, complete dialog box; or Click Zoom buttons on the Status bar; or Click the View tab, click Zoom buttons in Zoom group
Timescale, format	PRJ 156	Click the View tab, click the Timescale arrow in the Zoom group, click Timescale to open Timescale dialog box, click Non-working time tab, select formatting options as needed, click OK
Timescale, set scale	PRJ 157	Double-click Timescale, click appropriate Tier tab, click Units arrow, click number, click Label arrow, click label, select other options as needed, click OK

TASK	PAGE #	RECOMMENDED METHOD
Tracking Gantt chart, view	PRJ 340	Click View tab, click Gantt Chart button, click More Views, click Tracking Gantt, click Apply
Tracking table, apply	PRJ 297	Right-click Select All button, click Tracking
View Bar, turn off	PRJ 15	Right-click View bar, click View Bar
View Bar, turn on	PRJ 14	Right-click far left side of the Project window, click View Bar
View, print	PRJ 46–47	Click File tab, click Print, click Page Setup link, set options, click OK
View, split window, close	PRJ 41	On View tab, click Details check box; or Double-click horizontal split bar
View, split window, open	PRJ 39	On View tab, click Details check box
View, switch	PRJ 32–34	Click View tab, select a view; or Click a button on status bar
View, zoom	PRJ 43–44	Click Zoom In button or Zoom Out button on status bar; or Click the Zoom button on View tab, select desired zoom level
WBS code, define and display	PRJ 122	*See* Reference box: Defining and Displaying WBS Codes in Entry Table
Window, split to form and sheet view	PRJ 39	Click View tab, click Details check box
Working times, change for project	PRJ 69	Click Project tab, click Change Working Time button, modify all project, task, and resource calendars in Change Working Time dialog box
Working times, change for resource	PRJ 208–209	Double-click resource, click Change Working Time, select calendar, make changes as needed, click OK